Reading and Writing
Teaching for the Connections

Reading and Writing
Teaching for the Connections

Second Edition

Bill Harp
University of Massachusetts Lowell

Jo Ann Brewer
Salem State College

Harcourt Brace College Publishers

Fort Worth   Philadelphia   San Diego   New York   Orlando   Austin   San Antonio
Toronto   Montreal   London   Sydney   Tokyo

Publisher	Ted Buchholz
Editor in Chief	Christopher P. Klein
Senior Acquisitions Editor	Jo-Anne Weaver
Developmental Editor	Tracy Napper
Project Editor	Christopher Nelson
Production Manager	Cynthia Young
Senior Art Director	David A. Day
Photo Researcher	Steven Lunetta/Page to Page

ISBN: 0-15-500958-3

Library of Congress Catalog Card Number: 93-81046

Address for Editorial Correspondence:
Harcourt Brace College Publishers, 301 Commerce Street, Suite 3700,
Fort Worth, TX 76102.

Address for Orders:
Harcourt Brace & Company, 6277 Sea Harbor Drive, Orlando, FL 32887-6777.
1-800-782-4479, or 1-800-433-0001 (in Florida).

To
Cassi, Hillary, and Nathan — that they may learn
to love reading and writing.

And in memory of
Melanie, whose short life gave us
great joy.

About the Authors

Bill Harp's elementary school teaching experience ranges from Head Start through sixth grade. After completing his doctorate at the University of Oregon, he taught at the University of Delaware and Oregon State University. He left OSU to be an elementary school principal and coordinator of programs for the gifted. He later returned to OSU to coordinate the elementary education program. He is currently professor of Language Arts and Literacy and Graduate Coordinator in the College of Education, University of Massachusetts Lowell. In 1994, he was the recipient of the Exemplary Teaching Award for his work in the master's program. Dr. Harp has published several books in the area of whole language. He has been active in the International Reading Association, holding offices in local council and state organizations, and is a frequent IRA conference and workshop speaker.

Jo Ann Brewer has many years of teaching experience in kindergarten and primary classrooms, and has been an Assistant Superintendent for Instruction. Her experience includes teaching in culturally diverse settings and in open schools. She earned a doctorate in early childhood education at Texas Tech University, and currently teaches reading and children's literature courses at Salem State College in Massachusetts. She makes frequent conference and workshop presentations in the areas of language development and children's literature. Dr. Brewer is active in the National Association for the Education of Young Children and the International Reading Association.

Preface

We are delighted to present the second edition of *Reading and Writing: Teaching for the Connections*. Since writing the first edition we have continued to research, study, and learn from our students and many, many teachers. Our friend Jan Duncan of New Zealand says that there are only two kinds of teachers in the world: green and growing, or ripe and rotting. We have worked hard to stay green and growing. We believe that the improvements made in this edition reflect our ever-growing understanding of bringing children to literacy.

Chapter 1 discusses the characteristics, systems, theories, and principles of language development, especially how these principles fit in with an interactionist view of development. The importance of context and the part oral language plays in the development of literacy also ground this foundational chapter.

In examining the development of language and implications for teaching reading and writing, we have added the important work of Brian Cambourne to Chapter 2. Cambourne's conditions for literacy learning are presented as the hallmarks of the classroom environment we hope our students will create for learners. We have also significantly added to the discussion of the cueing systems and the importance of children's learning to use the strategies of reading as well as the skills.

Our treatment of the writing process in Chapter 3 has been significantly changed to present writing as a recursive process that begins with forming intentions of audience and purpose, researching and organizing information, selecting appropriate forms, and then rough drafting. This is followed by a discussion of response, revision, and publication—all presented as a recursive rather than linear process. We have come to a deeper understanding of how we as writers really use the process, and we hope that teachers and children will benefit from this understanding. Writers move back and forth between the various aspects of the writing process, sometimes even changing form, audience, or purpose as the piece develops.

Chapter 4 is an important new addition to the text. We combined the contents of the original chapter on language experience with the latest research on emergent literacy. This chapter examines the critical considerations in the early stages of literacy and, when used with the first three chapters, builds a solid foundation for the rest of the book.

While we still believe that the teacher as decision maker is an important concept, we have replaced the decision-making and program support chapters with a new Chapter 5 on assessment and evaluation. Making this change allowed expanded coverage of areas that have become increasingly important to teachers. The new edition has expanded treatment of miscue analysis and portfolio assessment and evaluation.

Chapter 6 is also new to this edition. We believe that all children are special, but today's regular classroom teachers are being asked to teach students with special needs, including children with learning disabilities, children who are gifted and talented, and children with limited English proficiency. This chapter examines the regular education initiative and the literacy adaptations to be made for children with special needs.

Chapter 7 examines the reader's use of the cueing systems: graphophonic, semantic, syntactic, and schematic. This chapter focuses on helping readers use the cueing systems in the creation of meaning. Here the nature of skills instruction is examined and important questions about phonics instruction are addressed. Readers are encouraged to teach skills at the point at which children need the instruction, within the context of real, communicative reading and writing activities.

We have strengthened Chapter 8, which deals with creating meaning with connected text. The Guided Metacomprehension Strategy, introduced in the first edition, is refined here and greater emphasis has been placed on schema theory and helping children monitor their own creation of meaning. The previous sections on comprehension taxonomies have been replaced with a consideration of Raphael's important work on the relationships among questions, text, and answers.

Chapter 9, which deals with basal readers, is still viewed as a bridging chapter—one that will help the teacher bridge between the basal and innovative classroom practice. The recent improvements in basals are recognized and readers are encouraged to think of ways to use the basal in child-centered, communication-focused instruction.

Chapter 10, which deals with using literature in the reading/writing program, has been refocused to spotlight organizational strategies for literature-based reading programs. Essential considerations are examined through four classroom scenarios.

Chapter 11, which deals with content area reading, has been revised to focus on the strategies readers use in making meaning with expository texts.

Chapter 12 highlights the applications of these strategies to reading in the sciences, social studies, the arts, and math.

Cathy Gunn, a nationally known expert on technology in the elementary school, has contributed an excellent Chapter 13 that deals with the use of technology in the reading/writing program. We are grateful to her for her work.

We want our readers to know that the teaching strategies we advocate and the classroom vision we share are working for real, practicing teachers. Four such talented teachers wrote pieces for the Epilogue, in which we are invited into their classrooms to see how they plan meaningful, integrated curriculum activities for their learners.

All of the improvements we made to the second edition have one goal: to create classrooms where children learn to love reading and writing. In a nation where many adults do not read books at all and where *TV Guide* is the best-selling weekly periodical, instructional changes are imperative. Teaching children *how* to read and write is not enough; we must create an environment that invites them to *want* to read and write—for real, communicative purposes.

Our dreams for the second edition of this book would not have come true without the assistance of some very talented people. The reviewers were Mary Jo Campbell, Edinboro University; Sheila Cohen, SUNY Cortland; Doris Fitzgerald, Lander University; Michael Ford, University of Wisconsin at Oshkosh; Steve Hansell, Wright State University; Sharon Lee, University of South Dakota; Bob Rickelman, University of North Carolina at Charlotte; and Karen Robinson, Otterbein College. We appreciate their careful and thoughtful review of the manuscript and thank them for their helpful suggestions throughout the revision process. We are also grateful to Tracy Napper at Harcourt Brace for her assistance and endless patience. Our thanks are extended as well to Pam Hatley, who was a tremendous help in securing permissions and dealing with countless details, and to a great many others at Harcourt Brace.

The journey to successful teaching is long. We sincerely hope that the students who study this book become the very best teachers they can be.

Contents

Chapter 3

The Writing Process   69

Chapter 4

Emergent Literacy   114

Chapter 5

Assessing Children's Reading and Writing Progress   163

Chapter 6

Working with Children with Special Needs   190

Chapter 7

Using the Cueing Systems   227

Chapter 8

Creating Meaning with Text   267

Chapter 9

Basal Readers in the Reading/Writing Program   302

Chapter 10

Literature in the Reading/Writing Program   326

Chapter 11

Assisting Children with Content-Area Reading   366

Chapter 12

Planning for Literacy Instruction Throughout the Day   408

Chapter 13

Reading, Writing, and Technology: *Making the Connection*   443

EPILOGUE: *Putting It All Together*   489

Chapter 1
The Development of Language

Chapter Overview

▼ Language is a system of communication on which members of social groups agree. Reading and writing are language-based processes. All languages have universal characteristics: They are arbitrary, rule governed, and continually evolving.

▼ Language systems—phonology, morphology, semantics, syntax, and pragmatics—help describe language and its uses in a given context.

▼ Learning language is a complex process. Children learn meaning, form, and functions of language all at once, and it is impossible to describe any of the processes accurately in isolation.

▼ Learning to use oral language and learning to read and write are closely related processes.

▼ Classroom teachers can help children increase their competence in the use of language.

Language and Literacy

In the author's note at the beginning of her book *Flossie and the Fox*, Patricia McKissack (1986) observes that long before she was a writer, she was a listener. She listened to family stories and to the language used around her. McKissack is not alone. Each reader and writer is also a listener and a participant in the language around him or her. Each person who comes to be literate learns about language in its oral and written forms by becoming a part of his or her speaking, reading, and writing community.

This book is about literacy, the ability to read and write our language. It is about helping children achieve literacy so they can manage easily the functional uses of written language—such as applying for a job, filling out forms, getting a driver's license—and so they can also appreciate the power and beauty of words and take pleasure in the human ability to share thoughts and ideas through the medium of written language.

Literacy is best conceptualized as a continuum on which anyone's degree of skill could be plotted but on which there is no point labeled "enough literacy." A child of 3 might be using sentences that are several words in length, scribbling with the expectation that others could "read" the scribbles, know it is the print in books that one reads, and many of the reasons one might read. A child in the upper elementary grades might be able to read many books independently, to compose a persuasive essay, and to use language to explain complex concepts (such as how to program the VCR). An adult who is a college graduate can read many different kinds of print, choose the appropriate form for meeting his or her goals in writing, such as poetry, essay, reports, personal communications, and use all the forms effectively, and use language to debate complex political issues with colleagues. But even the most well-read person you know becomes more literate in the course of reading new material or employing a new structure in writing. For example, a person familiar with several types of writing structures might read Eastern poetry for the first time or write an article for the newspaper. The beginning point of the continuum is the development of the ability to use oral language. Once past infancy children are engaged in learning about oral language and printed language at the same time. For example, a child may be using two- or three-word sentences, writing in scribbles, and beginning to recognize the difference between the Cheerios and the Froot Loops boxes. As individuals move along the continuum, they are able to use speaking, writing, and reading to meet their changing needs.

Because language learning is integral to the process of becoming literate, we begin by discussing language, what we know about children learning language, and how that knowledge will help us aid children as they become more literate.

What Is Language?

Almost everyone uses language and uses it so effortlessly, that it is easy to forget what a complicated phenomenon it is. We can hear the exact same words in different contexts and know the meanings are not even close. If your brother grabs you, gives you a big hug, and says, "You're such a nut!" it may mean he loves you and enjoys your humor. If you fail to turn in a paper and your professor said, "You're such a nut!" you would probably not think it was a compliment. Some simple words such as *play* have multiple meanings, yet we usually are able to understand what someone is trying to tell us when he or she uses the word. Some words are acceptable in our families, but not in school; some words bring us comfort when we hurt; others hurt us deeply. Identifying some of its characteristics will help us discuss this complicated system we call language.

Characteristics of Language

Language can be defined rather narrowly to include only spoken or sign language or much more broadly to include any system of communication used by a social community. For our purposes, **language** is defined as a system of

Children recognize the role language plays in their daily lives.

© 1994 George White

communication used by human beings that is produced either orally or by signs. Because this is a book about reading and writing, we also focus on language that can be extended to its written form.

Language has some defining characteristics. First, it is rule governed. For example, all languages have rules that determine how words are ordered in sentences. These rules are learned intuitively by native speakers of the language, and only those speakers who make a scientific study of the language are likely to be able to verbalize the rules. To illustrate such rules, hold up four new yellow pencils and ask a group to describe what you have in your hand. If they say "pencils," ask for more detail. They might say "long pencils." If asked again, they might say "long yellow pencils." Finally, they would say "four long yellow pencils." The placement of number words in the series of modifiers is governed by a rule. Native English speakers would never say "yellow four pencils."

A second characteristic of language is that it is arbitrary. There are no logical connections between the sounds we use to label a certain object and the object itself. It is merely by common social agreement that we use a particular combination of sounds to represent that object. For example, there is nothing in the sounds of the word *table* that is connected to the object. Only a very few words—such as *buzz* and *hiss*—have any concrete connection with their referents, the objects or ideas they represent.

Third, language is dynamic, always changing. New words are constantly entering our lexicon and others are being discarded. Meanings are also changing. With a little thought, you can probably list 30 or 40 words that have been added within the last five years and 10 or so that have changed meanings. *Program, virus,* and *debug* are terms that communicate meanings to the computer generation that are different from their former meanings.

Systems of Language

Language is composed of several systems: phonology, morphology, syntax, semantics, and pragmatics.

The broadest of the language systems is **pragmatics,** the use of language to express intentions and to get things done. Social uses of language include pragmatics and the rules of politeness. For example, some cultures have rules about younger people initiating conversations with older people, and all have rules for appropriate language for use in houses of worship, on the playground, and at mealtime. A speaker of any language would not be considered competent in that language before mastering the basic rules for language use in various social contexts. Hymes (1974) described the ability to use language and to use it correctly in various interactions as "communicative competence." For example, one could know many words in a language, but not be able to use them correctly in communicating a given idea, or one could know words and how to use them in sentences, but not know the social rules for using them. Children learning language must internalize the rules for using language in social interactions and achieving their communicative goals in various situations.

Berko-Gleason (1985) believes all language use has three aspects: the intent of the speaker to obtain some goal (inform, request, persuade, promise); the actual form of the utterance (syntax, semantics, and phonology); and the response of the listener. She provides the following examples of sentences:

1. "Excuse me, sir, do you have any matches?"

2. "Dear, give me a light."

3. "I see matches. Give me those matches. All you have, right now!" (p. 344)

Even though the intent of all the sentences is the same (to get matches), the form is certainly different. One can assume the first sentence was spoken to an unknown male. If the third sentence, which was probably spoken to a child for whom the adult was responsible, had been spoken to a male stranger, the response would probably have been quite different than to the first sentence.

A child who understands the pragmatic applications of language will be able to draw on that knowledge as an aid in comprehension. Just as oral language differs in different situations, print will vary in form depending on the intended audience of the piece and the social relationship between the writer and reader. For example, you might write a personal letter to one of your siblings in which the language would be quite informal and much of the meaning would be available to the reader through shared home experiences rather than through the actual print. When children read, they expect certain language rules to apply. If they understand the purpose, form, and intent of a text, it will certainly aid their attempts to comprehend the material.

The **syntactical** system of a language contains the rules for combining words into phrases and sentences and for transforming sentences into other sentences. The syntactical system provides us with information about word meanings because of their place in a sentence. For example, if you heard,

The cribbet zooked the lattle.

you would know the event took place in the past and that *zooked* was something done to the *lattle*. Different languages have different syntactical rules. For example, in English we usually place the adjective before the noun (white house); in Spanish the adjective usually follows the noun (*casa blanca*).

Children mastering the syntactical system learn how to construct negatives, questions, compound sentences, passives, imperatives, and eventually complex sentences that employ embedded forms. Children in school may still be confused by such sentence patterns as "Before you sharpen your pencil, please put your books on your desk." Young children will often embed a clause but not in the mature form. They might say, "The chair, what I sitting on, is yellow." A common language research question is to provide a doll whose eyes are blindfolded and ask if the doll is easy to see. Young children often misinterpret this question and answer no. As they master the syntactical system, they are not confused by embedded forms or forms in which the action is delayed.

As children read, they often rely on syntactical cues when attempting to decipher an unknown word. In a sentence such as "He will fix the chairs" a child might read "He will fix the cheap" and then correct his error because "cheap" will not fit the syntactical pattern of the sentence.

The **semantic** system governs meaning at the word, sentence, and text level. Learning semantics means acquiring vocabulary and meanings associated with words. Children commonly use words that are part of adult language,

Language is developed through interaction with peers.

© Joel Gordon

but assign their own meanings. A very young child may use a word such as *horsie* to stand for all large four-legged animals. As the semantic system is refined, horsie is replaced by cow, mule, elk, and so on. Children learning to read and write use the semantic system in order to obtain meaning from sentences and passages. There is not a one-to-one correspondence between a word and its referent. For example, when readers encounter *cat* in print, each may picture a different cat according to individual experience, but they also share enough meaning to understand the author's use of the term.

Vygotsky (1954/1986) emphasizes the interaction between the child and adults in building the child's semantic knowledge. He writes,

> The language of the environment, with its stable, permanent meanings, points the way that the child's generalizations will take. The adult cannot pass on to the child his mode of thinking. He merely supplies the ready-made meaning of a word, around which the child forms a complex [concept or idea cluster]. . . . The lines

along which a complex develops are predetermined by the meaning a given word already has in the language of adults. . . . Verbal intercourse with adults thus becomes a powerful factor in the development of the child's concepts (pp. 67, 69).

When an adult tells the child he or she is turning on the light, the child begins to form a concept of light that may grow in sophistication to include the light of day, a feeling of lightness, and metaphorical meanings of light. The child needs to talk with adults to continue building concepts and gaining the language with which to label them.

In thinking about semantics, think about some words that are learned by association, by having the word and the object presented together such as *bottle, ball, blanket.* Other words are learned as children develop ideas to fit words presented to them by adults. For example, love is a complex concept and children cannot be presented with "love." So when a 3-year-old says, "I love you," it may represent a beginning concept of the abstract love, but is certainly not a mature understanding of the meaning.

At the sentence level, the meanings of words are influenced by the surrounding words. We could never comprehend common words such as *play* and *run* without a context. In the sentence about fixing the chairs, "cheap" does not fit syntactically, but it also does not fit semantically. Maybe "cheap" can be fixed, but not usually. At the text level, think about the differences in the meanings of "cat" in the nursery rhyme about the gingham dog and the calico cat, in a newspaper report about a cat burglar, in a veterinarian's report on diseases in cats, or in Tennessee Williams' play, *Cat on a Hot Tin Roof.*

The **morphological** system of language deals in the smallest units of meaning—morphemes—in a language. Some words are morphemes; some are combinations of morphemes. *Cow* is an example of a word that is a morpheme. Cows is a combination of the free morpheme *cow* and the bound morpheme *s.* The *s* is bound because it signals meaning but cannot stand alone. Other morphemes signal changes of tense, person, or number rather than changing the meaning of the word such as the *-ed* in walked or the *-ing* of singing. Mastering English morphology includes learning how to form possessives, plurals, and verb tenses. Children learning to read and write have to attend to meaning as conveyed by various morphological forms. When children read, they must learn to recognize the various forms of pluralizing a word, such as adding an *-s,* an *-es,* or changing the spelling in such words as *teeth* or *mice.* Children may also use morphological knowledge when trying to unlock words with prefixes and suffixes (like *un* lock).

Phonology is the sound system. It includes the sounds that we use to make words, rules for combining the sounds, and patterns of stress and intonation. Different languages use different sounds and allow different combinations of sounds in words. Some languages, for example, make use of clicks that are absent from English. In some, like Chinese, differences in pitch indicate different meanings for the same combination of sounds. The task of the child is to learn to distinguish differences in phonemes—the smallest units of sound in a language—and intonational patterns that signal different meanings.

About 150 sounds are used in human languages. Babies babbling produce all these sounds, but quickly drop the sounds not needed in their native language. Research indicates that babies use only the sounds of their home language by the age of 6 months (Grieser & Kuhl, 1989). Not all sounds are mastered by all children before school age. Some sounds such as *r*, *th*, *l*, *s*, and *z* are not mastered by 100% of children until age 7 or 8. After that age, children who cannot produce the sounds are usually provided with speech therapy to help them.

Theories of Language Development

As teachers of reading and writing, we all operate with theories of how language and reading and writing develop. These theories are important because they influence our choice of materials, strategies, and evaluation systems. For instance, teachers who believe language learning occurs in small logical steps, shaped by a system of rewards and punishments, favor a reading program that emphasizes mastery of small steps such as learning all the letters of the alphabet before working on reading tasks. Those who believe language (and therefore reading and writing) is learned more holistically see the learning of reading as a process best supported by experiences that emphasize the wholeness of language. It is important, then, to become aware of the theoretical explanations for the process of learning language and to begin to consider ways of putting your beliefs into practice in the classroom.

Theorists of language development fall into three basic groups: the behaviorists, the linguistic theorists, and the interactionists. All of them attempt to answer the questions of (1) the role of other speakers, (2) the influence of the environment, and (3) the importance of individual response in developing language. The following section presents rather simplified explanations of these very complex theories.

Behaviorist View

The behaviorist view of learning describes the learning of language just as it describes other learning: the acquiring of knowledge as the result of repeated interactions with the environment. The consequences of the interactions—reward or punishment—determine whether the interaction is repeated. Behaviorism is based on the learning theories of Edward Thorndike and B. F. Skinner (Hill, 1977). Behaviorists rely on stimulus-response and operant conditioning to shape the learning of an individual. However, in learning language, the behaviorists do not believe the production of every single word must be rewarded; the child's success in communicating with a listener is intrinsically rewarding, so the attempts at language are continued.

In the view of behaviorists, language behavior, like other behavior, can be shaped by operant conditioning. A learner is rewarded for the production of given language behaviors and a reinforcement schedule is adopted to maintain the learning. For example, if a teacher wanted a child to learn to raise his hand before speaking in a group, he would be rewarded for raising his hand at every incidence for a few days, then at every two incidences, and then at every four until the rewards were no longer needed to maintain the behavior. By the same token, a child would be ignored if she spoke without raising her hand in order to extinguish that behavior.

The behaviorist view is that a child accumulates knowledge through repeated exposures to stimuli and the learning process is directed by the adult who controls the sequence of stimuli and the reward system. Therefore, the most effective teaching presents a carefully selected stimulus and then controls the rewards or punishments connected with the child's responses to the stimulus.

Behaviorists note that children often parrot words or phrases they have heard, but they do not have good explanations for regressions in children's language and resistance of children's language to modification (Berko-Gleason, 1985). Children often exhibit more mature forms of language such as using "went" as the past tense of go, then regress to "goed," and then learn to use "went" again. Berko-Gleason relates the story of her son who was trying to tell her about the baby rabbits at school that day. He said, "We holded the baby rabbits." She replied, "You held the baby rabbits." This exchange was repeated about eight times until the mother finally said, "Did you hold the baby rabbits tightly?" and he replied, "No, we holded them loosely." You might have tried to correct a child's utterance with just as much success. Behaviorists focus primarily on reinforcement, rewards or punishments, rather than on the intent of the child or the child's knowledge of language rules.

A reading program that reflects the behaviorist view of language development consists of practicing the elements of reading and combining the elements in a predetermined sequence. For example, children might learn to respond to a presentation of the letter *m* by saying "mmmm." Teachers would control the reward system, perhaps passing out tokens for correct responses and withholding them for incorrect ones. Children would practice such skills as dividing words into syllables by using the consonant-vowel-consonant pattern or circling all the pictures of objects that begin with /t/ on worksheets and getting stars or stickers if their work was correct.

Linguistic View

Some theorists look at language acquisition from a linguistic point of view. They explain the rapid acquisition of language in young children by concluding that language is basically inherent in the human brain and only needs social triggering to begin its rapid development. Chomsky (1965) described a Language Acquisition Device, or LAD (a structure in the brain), that is vital in acquiring language. This device allows the child to process language input and generate language that reflects a knowledge of language structures. More recently, Crystal (1987) proposed that the LAD provides children with "general procedures for discovering how language is to be learned" (p. 234). Proponents of the linguistic view believe the child's linguistic environment does not suffice to explain how the child discovers adult grammar. Arguments in support of the linguistic view are that only humans have the biological equipment for producing speech, it is almost impossible to suppress language in humans, and the sequence for language learning is basically the same for all human beings. Arguments against the linguistic model include the fact that learning language is much more than learning the grammar of the language and that the environment is often not sufficient to encourage language development, even though it exposes children to language. For example, children whose only exposure to language is television develop very little speech (Bohannon & Warren-Leubecker, 1989, p. 199).

Those who believe language is an innate human characteristic do not believe reading and writing are innate; obviously, many people do not learn to write or read. In the 1950s and 1960s, some reading programs were developed that relied on the linguistic patterns in words for selecting the order of word presentation to beginning readers. For example, the easiest pattern was supposed to be a consonant-vowel-consonant pattern such as in *cat*. The next pattern was consonant-vowel-consonant-silent *e* such as *cake*. A few remnants of the word pattern system remain in current reading programs, but a linguistic pattern is not the major focus of any modern reading program.

Interactionist View

Interactionists are theorists who believe language is learned through interaction. Interactionists "assume that many factors (e.g., social, linguistic, maturational/biological, and cognitive) affect the course of development and that these factors are mutually dependent upon, interact with, and modify one another" (Berko-Gleason, 1985, p. 188). The cognitive interactionists rely heavily on the work of Piaget (1959) and Vygotsky (1954/1986) in explaining language acquisition. To the interactionists, children's language reflects cognitive development, and language learning is governed by the same basic processes that underlie other learning.

The interactionists believe that children are intrinsically motivated to learn, they explore their physical and social environments, and knowledge is not just an accumulation of facts, but reflects actual changes in the way a child views the world or solves a problem. In Piaget's work, the stages of cognitive development are marked by changes in the way children think, not in the amount of knowledge they possess. To an interactionist, the child is the principal agent of his or her own learning. Learning, therefore, involves active

Learning to use a telephone directory is a meaningful reason for reading.

© Michael Hagan

participation in the process and reflection on what one sees and does. Learning language, then, involves the child in actively trying to participate in the process of communication and in reflecting on the effects of the language on those with whom he or she is trying to communicate.

Social interactionists recognize that human beings possess the specialized physiological equipment for producing speech and that cognitive development is tied to language development, but they focus on the use of language as a tool for interaction. Vygotsky (1954/1986), in particular, believed children's speech required stimulation by adults and that this stimulation was most effective in what he called the zone of proximal development. This zone is defined as the area between where the child can function independently and where he or she could function with adult assistance. Vygotsky believed cognitive growth was enhanced by language as well as interactions with objects in the environment. He thought many of the concepts of the mature thinker would not be developed without an adult supplying the language and stimulating the child to learn more.

Interactionists regard intentionality (what the child intended to communicate) as critical in language development and stress the importance of the linguistic environment for the child learning language. Children are constantly producing hypotheses and testing them in social situations. The social interactionists point to the early learning of social words such as *mama*, *dada*, and *bye-bye* as evidence of the importance of social interactions in the learning of language. Interactionists also point to the errors children make (such as "goed" and "runned") as reflecting the generalizations that children have made about language. They theorize that children generalize the "rule" that in order to form a past tense of a verb, one adds -*ed*. Children then have to learn the exceptions to that rule. They explain regressions in language in terms of the child's application of new knowledge or interactions in new social situations. In our example of first using "went" correctly, then using "goed" as the past tense form of *go*, the interactionists would explain that the first use of *went* was probably from hearing adults use it, but without much understanding, and the later use of "goed" reflected learning the rule. Therefore, an interactionist would see the error of "goed" as an indication of language growth.

One might question the interactionists about how children analyze language at such a young age and can learn the grammar of their language from this analysis. One might also question the importance of dialogue with others in learning language. No one argues that a social environment where language is used is not necessary for learning language, but environments differ so drastically that no one can pinpoint exactly what is critical in the environment. Heath (1983), for example, found that in some communities, the adults tended to talk to other adults while holding the baby facing out on their laps. In other words, there was not much interaction with the babies until they learned to produce words of their own.

Teachers who believe children are the principal agents in their own language development allow students to choose much of their own reading material and provide instruction when an individual displays a need for it, rather than on a predetermined schedule. These teachers focus on meaning and communication as purposes for reading, not on decoding letters as the key to reading. The reward system is primarily intrinsic: A feeling of success at each step in reading and writing spurs the child on to the next achievement.

The activities and examples recommended in this book reflect an interactionist point of view regarding how children learn oral language and how the principles that make learning language so universal for humans can be applied to helping children become more literate.

Principles of Language Development

Most of us have little experience, if any, with children who have not learned to communicate through either oral or sign language. We sometimes forget that the process is not a magical one; children do have to learn to use language, and it does take time and effort. Observers of young children learning language have derived some principles of language development: Language learning is self-generated, informal, active, holistic, and variable (Butler &

Turbill, 1984; Halliday, 1982; Jaggar, 1985). These principles represent an interactionist point of view in explaining language development.

Language Learning Is Self-Generated

To say language learning is a self-generated, creative process is to say the learning is controlled by the learner and does not require external motivation. Most parents think they reward their children for language production, and in fact they do, at least for the first few words. But consider the typical weekday morning at home, when Daniel can't find his lunch money, Sarah can't find her shoes, the washing machine is running over, the dog is chewing up Mom's new contract, the telephone is ringing, and the toast is burning. Baby, sitting in the high chair and studiously experimenting with the effects of gravity on oatmeal, says "down" for the first time. Who attends to and rewards that language?

This illustration does not imply that language learning does not require other people. To learn language does require social contact; no child learns language in a vacuum. It just means that children in situations of language usage learn to speak without reward for each word learned. Communication with significant others is enough to keep the child learning. The best motivation for gaining literacy is the example of significant others. When teachers and others share the excitement they find in written words, they provide children with a powerful incentive to learn to read and write.

Language Learning Is Informal

Learning of oral language occurs without formal instruction. Parents do not give language lessons to their children. With the exception of such rituals as "peek-a-boo" and "this little piggy," parents rarely teach language directly. They play with children, sing with them, make cookies with them, show them the world, and supply words to label the environment, but they do not focus on teaching the child to speak. Participating with the child in daily living is the focus, and language develops as one result. Language is learned through use in meaningful contexts, not through talking about it or analyzing it.

If you have had any experience with a 3- or 4-year-old child, you will know how many questions they ask in the course of any activity. Listen, for example, as such a child and his father fill the bird feeder. "What is this? Where did you get it? Will it grow? What is the name of those birds? Where do they go when they fly away? How will they know the seed is here? Can they smell the seeds? Will the cat catch a bird? I wish I could fly like a bird," and on and on. As the parent or caregiver answers these questions (and thousands of others each day), the child is learning language. No parent or caregiver would consider planning a language lesson on birdseed and teaching the child all the vocabulary of feeding birds.

We are not suggesting that children learning to read and write never have instruction. Rather, we are saying that instruction should take place in a context meaningful to the learner and the instruction should focus on accomplishing communication rather than on isolating the forms of language.

Language Learning Is Active

Learning the labels we use to name a cat and a dog is a good illustration of the active nature of language learning. Suppose a child is approached by a cat. The child may know the word *cat* and call the animal "cat." The nearest adult will probably respond, "Yes, that is a cat." If the child had said "dog," the adult would probably have answered, "No, that's not a dog. It's a cat." Rarely would anyone point out to the child the salient characteristics that distinguish a cat from a dog (partly because it is almost impossible to do so). The child must take the label *cat* and decide what it is about this particular animal that makes it not a dog.

Children are continually engaging in such active learning processes as they learn to communicate. They need to have opportunities for active involvement in learning to read and write. For example, encourage children who need more materials for an art project to write a list of supplies they need. Some will be able to use only scribbles or symbols at first, but experience will teach them that they must use particular symbols in order to make the message useful. They will apply problem-solving skills by copying the word *glue* from the glue bottle or discovering other strategies that get them what they need. Active learning also occurs when a class has memorized a poem by rote. The teacher displays the words on a chart for the first time and allows the children to try to read the poem on their own before supplying the words for them. The moment of triumphant success brings joy to children and teacher alike.

Language Learning Is Holistic

The process is holistic in that children learn about the forms and functions of language all at once. Phonetics (sounds), semantics (meanings), syntax (word order), and pragmatics (rules for using language) all work together simultaneously. A child attempting to ask for a cookie learns to approximate the phonemes in the word *cookie*, at the same time learns what to expect when the approximation is close enough, and learns it is of no value to ask her infant brother for a cookie. No one would suggest that language be broken into artificial, discrete units to make it easier to learn.

Language development and the development of literacy are closely related. For years, it has been generally accepted that knowledge of language was required before children could extend that knowledge to the written language system. The newer research does not in any way diminish the importance of a child's oral language in the development of literacy, but it looks at literacy as developing along with language. In other words, we used to believe children should not have any experience with reading and writing until they had a firm grasp of the spoken language. As observers of young children now know, children are learning about written language systems before they have mastered the oral language system. Young children in a literate society such as ours begin to explore the written language system at a very early age and concurrently with their growing command of oral language.

One child learned to read "Kraft" at age 2 because she saw it on a tower near her home everyday. At the same time, she was building more complex sentences orally. If we know language is not learned by practicing its components outside the process of using it, then it follows that learning reading and writing must also be a holistic process involving children in actual experiences that require reading and writing. Children learning written language begin to label their scribbles, and then insist their writing says something. The focus of their work in written language is communication. No parent would approach teaching a child to talk by saying, "Today you will practice pronouncing all the nouns on this list. Then tomorrow we will practice some verbs." Yet instruction in reading and writing often requires children to practice some part of the process in isolation from the rest. For example, children might be asked to underline the plurals in sentences that have no meaning for them. Instruction that uses what we know about language learning would have children attend to the plurals found in their stories about the baby chicks that have just hatched or in the books about baby chicks that are on the table near the incubator.

Language Learning Is Variable

Each individual has a unique set of experiences and a personal environment that differs somewhat from that of others. Even though children acquiring language pass through predictable stages and most children in the world acquire speech on a similar schedule, there are individual differences. Nevertheless, nearly all will achieve competence in communicating and will have mastered most of the skills required for clear communication by age 5 or 6.

Children vary in their approach to language. One child may start by learning the names of everything in the immediate environment, whereas another tackles social words such as "hi" and "bye-bye" first. Yet each acquires both kinds of vocabulary, and both become competent speakers of their language. Likewise, children differ in their personal approaches to written language, and all learners in a classroom will certainly not be at the same point in the process of acquiring literacy. Teachers can recognize these differences and help children move forward at their own pace while remaining confident in the children's ability to succeed.

The Sequence of Language Learning

Language development follows a fairly predictable sequence, individual variations notwithstanding. Most children move from differentiated crying (crying

Children whose second language is English learn their new language quickly in a supportive environment.

© Susan Lapides

that varies in sound, depending on stimulus—hunger, wetness, tiredness, and so on) through cooing, babbling, and one-word sentences. Soon they will deliver longer utterances and learn to produce negatives and questions. At the same time, children's comprehension of spoken language is developing rapidly. By the time they begin school, children will have mastered most of the basic forms in their native language. The chart in Figure 1.1 summarizes typical language development for the first four years of life.

Older children continue to offer a challenge to teachers who are interested in language development. Certain changes in language occur as children mature. For example, very young children take every word literally. One soccer coach told his team of 5-year-olds, "We've got to be on our toes for this game." The little players obligingly balanced on their tiptoes. There are thousands of such stories about young children responding in literal terms to expressions that were meant figuratively. By the time most children are age 8 or so, they have begun to understand that many words and phrases have multiple meanings; and by about age 11, they giggle over the double meanings of almost everything they hear. They also begin to participate much more in language play that relies on double meanings for humor. Teachers of older children need to appreciate the growth these stages represent, just as teachers of very young children must recognize the meaning of errors in verb forms.

Even though most children have mastered the basic forms in their native language by the age of 5 or 6, there is still much for the teacher to do in terms of encouraging language development in school. Children need to continue to hear and use complex sentence patterns, such as sentences that employ embedded clauses. Often teachers will help children become aware of the varied sentence patterns employed by successful authors to encourage the children to vary their own sentence patterns. Children encounter many new concepts in school, and the value of their exposure to the subject matter areas depends to a great extent on their understanding of the relevant vocabulary.

Stage	Age Range	Mean Length of Utterance (Average Number of Words per Sentence)	Characteristics	Typical Sentences
I	12–26 months	1.00–2.00	Vocabulary consists mainly of nouns and verbs with a few adjectives and adverbs; word order preserved	Mommy bye-bye. Big doggie. Baby bath.
II	27–30 months	2.00–2.50	Use of inflections; correct use of plurals; use of past tense; use of *be*, definite and nondefinite articles, some prepositions	Dolly in bed. Them pretty. Milk's all gone. Cars go fast.
III	31–34 months	2.50–3.00	Use of yes–no questions, *wh-* questions (who, what, where); use of negatives and imperatives	Daddy come home? Susie no want milk. Put the baby down.
IV	35–40 months	3.00–3.75	Embedding one sentence within another	I think it's red. Know what I saw? That's the truck Mommy buyed me.
V	41–46 months	3.75–4.50	Coordination of simple sentences and propositional relations	I went to Bob's and I had ice cream. I like bunnies 'cause they're cute. Jenny and Cindy are sisters.

Figure 1.1—Stages of Linguistic Development, According to Brown (1973)

Source: From "Recognize Language Development and Delay in Early Childhood" by Joyce Ury Dumtschin, 1988, *Young Children*, 43:3, p. 19. Copyright ©1988 by the National Association for the Education of Young Children. Reprinted by permission.

Halliday (1982) described the process of language development as learning language, learning about language, and learning through language. For older children, the teacher can help the children focus on the origins of interesting words and phrases (learning about language) and help them master the vocabulary of new content areas or topics (learning through language).

Children also need to increase their awareness of social rules for language use and gain more flexibility in their employment of speech registers. (*Register* is the linguistic term for the vocabulary and sentence patterns we use, depending on the situation, such as talking informally with our family, making a speech at a banquet, giving an oral report, talking with friends at the frozen yogurt shop.) For example, children in the classroom are frequently admonished, "Use your inside voice." Some children may have no idea what the teacher means by that phrase. They may need to practice speaking in situations that require the use of various speech registers.

The Context for Language Learning

The report of Pellegrini's (1991) research is just one of the many articles in which the recognition of context for learning and using language and literacy is highlighted. More than 20 years ago, Cazden (1970) believed the situations in which language users are placed determines the form of the language that will be used. Other researchers have looked more specifically at the influence of context on literacy learning (Edwards, 1989; Snow, 1983; Teale, 1984). Of the studies of language and literacy, one of the most powerful is that of Shirley Brice Heath reported in *Ways with Words* (1983). Heath documented the language and literacy experiences of three communities located in the Piedmont region of the Carolinas. She called these communities Trackton, Roadville, and the townspeople. The townspeople represented the usual middle-class orientations toward language learning but Trackton and Roadville represented quite different attitudes and behaviors.

Trackton was a community of mostly black mill workers and Roadville was a community of mostly white mill workers. The two communities were about the same in terms of income and education. Heath discovered vast differences in the ways the children were socialized to use language and literacy. For example, in Trackton, the telling of interesting stories was highly valued. However, these stories were not necessarily factual and certainly were not linear. Male children were taught to participate in verbal teasing, beginning at about age 2 and were taunted if they failed. Children in Trackton did not expect adults to ask them questions and when adults did ask questions, the most typical question was one of analogy (What is that like?).

In Roadville, children were expected to know the names of things and to answer the many questions they were asked. From the time of infancy, questions were addressed to babies and when the children could talk, answers were expected. Roadville parents believed they needed to provide appropriate experiences for their preschoolers to prepare them for school. Although stories in Roadville might have been told for fun, they were usually based on an actual happening. Children in Roadville were taught to tell truthful, linear stories. Children were often admonished to pay attention to how stories go and not to make up things. The most common questions asked of preschoolers in Roadville were questions/statements in which the adult would ask a question such as, "Do you want to take your nap now?" followed by a statement, "I know you're getting sleepy."

In each of these communities, the adults cared about the use of language, but they valued different aspects of it and expected it to be used differently by children. All children learn language within a context and the influence of that context is very significant in terms of what is learned, how it is learned, and how language is performed. Remember that a classroom is a context for learning and what and how children are expected to use language there is very important.

Context describes the social setting and the social interactions within a setting. One aspect of the context for literacy learning was described by Bruner (1983) as scaffolding. *Scaffolding* is defined as the support of the adult for the child's language while the child moves to the next step (much like the scaffolding that workers use while they construct each new floor of a multistory building). Bruner found that when adults read the same book over and over to a child, the language used by the adult in one interaction shows up the child's speech in succeeding interactions. When observed in such behavior as story reading, parents seem to instinctively ask questions to which children can respond easily. At first, a reader may ask such questions as "Where is the dog?" which requires only pointing behavior. In another few weeks, they will ask, "What does the doggie say?" and finally they will ask the child to fill in some of the text as the story is read. As Heath (1983) noted, some parents may ask these questions differently, for example asking, "What is that like?" but they will modify the questions if the child has difficulty answering them.

This concept of scaffolding is important for teachers as they build support systems for children that help them succeed where they are while they move to the next stage. If a child cannot yet read a given piece of material without adult help, then the teacher has to make decisions about what kind of help to offer and for how long.

Pellegrini (1991) found that children from homes generally considered "at risk" also have many literacy experiences except that the contents may be a toy catalog or a newspaper rather than a narrative story. He recommends that teachers not think of these children as at risk, but begin to look at the many forms of language and literacy and view them as different rather than as a deficit to the child. A child who helps his parent clip the cents-off grocery coupons for the products the family buys may not have the same experience as a child who is read stories each day, but it is a literacy experience and the child can use what has been learned from it if the teacher will accept that learning and expect success in language and literacy from that child as from any other child. The point for teachers is not to make the assumption that support for language and literacy happens only in middle-class homes.

From the research on language development and the observations of children coming to be literate are some elements that are common to both endeavors.

Oral Language and the Development of Literacy

None of the theorists who attempt to explain the development of language would deny the importance of the environment in the child's development of oral language. The environment for the development of literacy is also essential. It must be supportive and provide meaningful opportunities for use in order to maximize the child's opportunities for growth.

Supportive Environment

If you asked the parents of a newborn child whether they expected their child would learn to use language, they would certainly say yes, probably also giving you a look that reflected some doubt about your sanity. Parents expect their children to become successful speakers. Mistakes or errors in early speech are treated as normal. Many people go through life with funny nicknames that they acquired from an older brother or sister who could not pronounce their names. Almost everyone knows a few "family words," usually someone's baby talk, that remains in the family's private vocabulary. Nobody's parents worry that their child, playing tennis at age 20, will still be saying, "Ball all gone." We all expect our children's language to mature and in time match the adult model.

Children who have learned to speak in an atmosphere where everyone expects they will be successful may be confronted with an entirely different attitude when they are attempting to learn to read and write. It is not at all uncommon to find instructional programs where teachers regard each error as cause for remediation of some kind, rather than as an indication of the child's current thinking. For example, a child who makes an error in reading may not need remediation in a phonic rule; the child may need more background experience in order to comprehend the material. A young writer may spell unconventionally, but the teacher can focus on intended meaning rather than concentrating on the errors. This sort of teacher attends carefully to information about what children do know about written language and does not look for perfection in form before allowing participation in the process.

Just as children learning language need people in their environment who are interested in them and anxious to communicate with them, so they also need support for their developing literacy. Supportive parents allow children to "write" with safe writing implements as soon as they can hold the instrument and show interest in writing. Parents may also supply written language for the child at early ages. Many parents of even tiny babies read to them so they can begin to enjoy the rhythm and sound of written language. They also supply the babies with books especially made for them. After a number of experiences with such books, children begin to associate reading experiences with positive feelings and to make hypotheses about the workings of the written language system. In her classic study of early readers, Durkin (1966) found that many parents of "natural readers" (children who teach themselves to read without direct instruction) were unaware of the help they were giving their children in learning to read. The child would come to the parent and ask what a word said, get a response, and go off to figure out the relationships between the squiggles on the page and what they meant. The nurturance of literacy demands the same conditions that learning language requires: time, support, and an expectation of success.

Meaningful Opportunities

The learning of language is most easily accomplished by those children who have meaningful interactions with others who support and value their efforts. Supportive adults respond to a child's intent, not to the form of his or her utterances. For example, when a very young child makes sounds accompanied by gestures that indicate the cookie jar, the adult is likely to respond to the intent of the child rather than to the speech actually produced. Most parents tend to correct the content rather than the form of their children's language. For example, if the child comes racing into the house and shouts, "Power Rangers camed on TV on Tuesday," the parent is likely to respond, "No, Power Rangers will be on on Thursday." The logical extension of this knowledge about language development is that the teaching of reading and writing must always focus on the meaning rather than on the surface structure of the child's responses.

Goodman (1986, p. 8) has summarized these principles of a supportive environment and meaningful interaction succinctly:

What makes language very easy or very hard to learn?

It's easy when:	It's hard when:
It's real and natural.	It's artificial.
It's whole.	It's broken into bits and pieces.
It's sensible.	It's nonsense.
It's interesting.	It's dull and uninteresting.

What makes language very easy or very hard to learn?

It's relevant.	It's irrelevant to the learner.
It belongs to the learner.	It belongs to somebody else.
It's part of a real event.	It's out of context.
It has social utility.	It has no social value.
It has purpose for the learner.	It has no discernible purpose.
The learner chooses to use it.	It's imposed by someone else.
It's accessible to the learner.	It's inaccessible.
The learner has power to use it.	The learner is powerless.

For the development of language and literacy, the implications of Goodman's statements are clear. Children need to talk about, read about, and write about interesting experiences in their lives. They need to have their language accepted and valued. They need to use language, reading, and writing for purposes of real communication. In many classrooms, activities involve children in using language, reading, and writing in these ways. In one kindergarten classroom we observed, children were choosing books to take home from the classroom collection. They had to write the title of the book on the large envelope used for transporting the book. Their writing was not graded or corrected, but the teacher noticed that legibility quickly increased with their desire to perform the task.

In the same classroom, children were learning rhymes. After they had learned the words by rote, the words were placed on a chart and they were allowed to manipulate them (substitute words, move them around) as they read the rhyme and tried to make new versions of it. These children had real reasons for talking, reading, and writing.

Teachers concerned with the development of literacy want to help children make as many connections as possible with language, reading, and writing. They treat speaking, reading, and writing as experiences in communication.

Language in the Classroom

The language environment in a school setting is influenced by the context of the classroom, the language experiences of the learners, and the native languages of the learners. Teachers have a great deal of control over how the classroom is structured for language growth and how learners who speak other than standard English are treated in the classroom.

The Classroom Context

School language is often quite different from home language, and the way children are expected to learn it may differ as well. Zutell (1980) observed, "The predominant modes of learning at home are demonstration and performance; at school, oral instruction and skill practice take their place" (p. 19). In other words, children at home are learning language as they listen to others use it successfully, and they get feedback on their own competence when they achieve their intentions. Wells (1986) observed that the language environment for most children was much richer at home than at school. At school, the teacher may give instructions about language use that are separate from any use of language by the learner. The teacher may then ask children to practice isolated skills such as selecting the correct verb form to complete a sentence, with no feedback other than the grade on the paper.

Just like the home, the classroom offers a particular context for language learning, defined by its own needs and potentials. Teachers plan activities in accordance with their need to meet certain instructional goals. They must also maintain order and set appropriate limits, such as for noise level. These are all areas for application of language skills.

Teachers who want to encourage language growth need to know what children can do with language. How can they use it? Are there some functions of language that are more readily observable than others? Is children's playground language very different from their classroom language? How does a child make needs known, settle arguments, pretend, or discuss? Teachers who are interested in fostering the development of literacy in their classrooms want to become skilled observers of the child's use of language because of the many connections among speaking, listening, reading, and writing.

Dialects and Limited English Speakers

Teachers must be prepared to deal with the needs of children who speak dialects different from their own or whose native language is not English. Teachers can encourage development of literacy by being sensitive to language differences and planning activities that are useful to all children.

Speakers of Dialects

You will be responsible for teaching reading to many children who speak dialects. Many people define *dialect* as speech that differs from their own. The fact is that all of us speak a dialect of some kind. A dialect is rule governed and consistent, and its use does not merely represent errors in grammar or degenerative language. There are regional dialects, social-class dialects, and ethnic dialects. As a teacher you must remember that children who speak dialects are not using undeveloped language and are not less capable as learners than children who speak the so-called standard English of the community. Jaggar (1980) says that our judgments of the correctness of children's speech are social judgments, not linguistic ones.

Dialects differ in vocabulary, syntax, and morphology. Instances of vocabulary difference are such terms as those that denote a milk-and-ice-cream drink, a paper container used for carrying objects home from shopping, and parts of a car. They may also include some verb usages, such as "carry" for "take" ("He will carry you to town"). Syntactical differences often involve the deletion of some words. For example, in some dialects the correct form of "He is working today" is "He be working," which indicates that the subject is working at present. Morphological differences include the dropping of some inflectional endings, such as those of the possessive ("that girl shoes"), and the indication of tense and number by different rules ("He go there yesterday"). The differences in dialect are usually minor.

Teachers of children who speak dialects different from the local majority dialect need to be aware of the dialectical differences and to think about their implications for instruction in the classroom. Differences in pronunciation may affect instruction in spelling and phonics. For example, if a child says "dem," the teacher taking dictation will still record "them." Children who speak one of the Bostonian dialects learn to recognize *car* as the word they pronounce "cah." Children who say "ain't" can learn to read "isn't." If the goal of reading instruction is comprehension rather than absolute accuracy, then the teacher of a child who renders "His mother went to town" as "He mama go to town" will not assume the child cannot read.

The written language of books is quite different from the spoken language of many children, even those who speak a more nearly standard dialect, yet children learn to read it. Being aware of differences and sensitive to them means understanding that children can be successful as readers and writers even when their language does not match standard dialects. Children need many opportunities to use language in a variety of situations that are meaningful, such as storytelling, sharing, dramatic activities, choral readings, story and poetry writing, letter writing, and even writing notes to classmates. "Our job, then, is not to change children's language but to help them expand the language they already have. We must start by accepting the children's dialects and recognizing that, though they are different, they are not deficient. Children can think logically, learn effectively, and talk intelligently in any dialect" (Jaggar, 1980, p. 28). Most of the difficulties in learning to read encountered by children who speak a dialect are in the minds of the instructors.

Bilingual Speakers

Children whose first language is not English also need extra help in reading. Many schools offer special bilingual programs for students who do not speak

English; some provide a tutor whose objective is to help the child learn English; others do nothing at all and expect the classroom teacher to assist the child within the regular classroom context. Even in schools that in theory support bilingual programs, it is often impossible to provide such programs for all the languages that might be represented. Because most teachers work with non-English-speaking children at some time, they need to be aware of some of the research on acquisition of a second language and the classroom implications of that research.

The most successful second-language learning shares some of the same conditions that make learning our mother tongue an easy process. First, the learner needs someone with whom to talk and needs support for attempts at communication. The second-language learner uses the strategies of simplification and overgeneralization that are also common in native-language development. For example, a second-language learner may simplify all verbs to one tense and depend on the context to help communicate the real message: "Go" stands in for "went," and an adverbial phrase such as "last week" takes care of the tense. Finally, second-language learners gradually fine-tune their communications for greater effectiveness. For young children, this process may take only a few months; for older children, it may take longer. As in learning a first language, "For a learner to be free to learn another language, the learner must be able to trust others to respond to the messages communicated and not be laughed at or singled out. In addition, a learner must be active in seeking people to talk with" (Urzua, 1980, p. 38). The best school environment for second-language learning includes support, encouragement, meaningful purposes for communication, and a classroom structure that allows for talking with others who speak the second language.

Piper (1993, pp. 210–211) has developed the following guidelines for helping teachers think about the language development of bilingual speakers:

1. Get as much information as possible about the child's language background. Try to determine if the child is a talker or shy at home. Find out what languages the child's playmates speak.

2. Be careful about the conclusions you draw from the information you gather. Assuming a child who does not speak much does not know much about language can be very dangerous.

3. Compare the child's language only to other similar bilingual children.

4. Understand that second-language learners will make grammatical errors. There are common generalizations made by second-language learners that are not correct.

5. Be aware that second-language learners may lose some of their competence in their first language. For example, a child may move away from the environment in which the first language was used regularly and therefore lose some ability to use that language.

6. Know it is normal for second-language learners to use both languages to communicate. Linguistic borrowing describes what happens when a word from one language is inserted into a sentence of the other language. Code switching is switching back and forth between languages, but not necessarily single words. Both are normal for bilinguals.

7. Learn as much as possible about the cultures represented in the classroom. Make sure this information is both for traditional and contemporary lifestyles. Use this information in order to determine if any test used to evaluate bilingual speakers is biased.

Second-language learners also need as much instruction as possible in their native language, especially in content areas. The research is clear that "the most effective way for bilingual students to develop both academic concepts and English language proficience is through their first language" (Freeman & Freeman, 1993, p. 553). These authors suggest that the environmental print in the classroom reflects the first language of the learners, books and other media materials are available in the first language, children be encouraged to publish books and stories in their first language, these learners read and write in their first language, and first-language videos are used to present academic concepts. Teachers may need to rely on community members and volunteers in order to implement these suggestions, but they are important in thinking about how schools can help second-language learners succeed.

Oral Language Activities

All the children in your classroom—speakers of standard dialect, speakers of other dialects, and children whose first language is not English—need planned activities in language development. Remember that children learn language not to talk or read or write about language, but because they want to talk or read or write about the world (Cazden, 1981). The most successful oral language activities offer children a wide variety of speaking situations that require the use of many different speech registers. Activities should provide practice in both formal and informal uses of language. These are a few suggestions.

Conversation

Children are encouraged to talk to each other in the process of completing projects, while having meals together, and at other times when talking casually is appropriate. Arrange the room so children can work in small groups, conducive to conversation. Invite children to participate in setting the rules of the classroom that determine when the children may talk and when they must be quiet. For example, the teacher might list the daily schedule on the board and ask the children to help determine the level of talking that would be most comfortable for the group during each activity. Having something interesting to talk about also stimulates conversation. Some teachers choose to set up a table to display a collection of novel or thought-provoking items, changing the selection frequently to maintain student interest. Older children might enjoy having oral pen pals who communicate by audiotapes.

Sharing

Sharing time in classrooms—formerly known as "show and tell"—can be productive if the teacher is careful to ensure the child's participation in the language process. In some classrooms, sharing times involve so much teacher direction that very little language is actually practiced by the child. Children can share in small groups rather than with the whole class so the teacher does not have to maintain audience attention for the speaker. Some teachers also help children develop their ability to ask questions during sharing time.

Discussion

Discussions differ from conversations in that generally the talk is confined to a given topic. Teachers can offer opportunities for small-group discussions, such as planning a strategy in problem solving or learning about a given topic. Children can participate in more formal whole-class discussions of current events or responses to a speaker or television program. Unable to hold to one topic for very long, younger children have difficulty maintaining a discussion, but they can practice by discussing how they did their artwork or what happened in a story they have just heard. As children mature, they are able to sustain discussions for longer periods.

Role Playing or Creative Dramatics

Role playing can be encouraged by setting up a dress-up area where costumes or items of apparel are available for children to use. In costume, children assume various roles and adopt language appropriate to the roles. For example, if the children are interested in hospitals (perhaps after a field trip), costumes for nurses and doctors, stethoscopes, and other medical tools might be added to the dress-up center to encourage role playing. Older children might dramatize experiences they have read about, learning both the context for the language and the remarks and responses appropriate to the situation such as an encounter between a rebel and a Tory during the American Revolution.

Responses to Literature

Choral readings, storytelling, acting out stories, puppets, and narrating slide shows or filmstrips are some of the ways to encourage oral language as response to literature. Some children's literature is written in beautiful language, and children can make it their own through these activities. Children can learn the language used by the author and learn to express the same thoughts in their own language as they retell or re-create stories, poems, or plays.

Music

Children can dramatize parts of songs, learn the lyrics, and compose new lyrics to fit new situations. Children can listen to carefully selected pieces of music and discuss the feelings evoked by the music. They can also listen to the music in movies or television programs and talk about its effects or the match between the music and the story.

Reporting

Children should have opportunities to share interesting information with their peers in the more formal register of a report. Spend time first in working out how to prepare such reports, beginning with how to do the necessary research and then how to organize the material for presentation. Teachers may arrange for children to report to small groups at the beginning. Reporting to a small group will help children develop the necessary speaking skills and perhaps reduce the initial stress of speaking to the whole group. Children can be encouraged to report to the whole group when the teacher feels they will be successful.

Practicing the Social Usage of Language

Plan authentic classroom situations that give children the opportunity to learn speech appropriate to such activities as performing introductions, delivering messages, initiating and receiving telephone calls, and requesting information.

From Oral Language to Print

Here are some classroom activities that help children make connections between spoken and written language ("print" refers to anything written, not just to printed and mechanically reproduced writing):

1. The children listen to and tell stories, then have the chance to write a response or to see the words in print.

2. The children use puppets to tell a story, then write the script for the puppets. They might also put together a book of puppet plays that have been written by the class.

3. The children learn fingerplays or other rhymes by rote and then have the print presented on charts. A chart with clear plastic pockets in which the words on cards can be placed and rearranged by the children is particularly useful for presenting fingerplays or rhymes. Children can

be encouraged to match the words or phrases and then to substitute new words in the rhymes.

4. The children learn songs by rote and then have the print presented on charts. Individual song booklets can also be made for each child so they can all read along as they sing.

5. The children have play experiences that involve communication and are accompanied by the appropriate print. For example, children playing they are going on a train ride might want to make signs for the stations and the cars. They might also make tickets and schedules. Children playing shoe store might need sale signs, size signs, books for writing sales slips, and a catalog of shoes.

6. The children take field trips to gain the nonprint information they need to make sense of print. These trips can be followed by a written record of their trips and experiences. For example, children visiting a farm will see animals and buildings they may meet later in print. They could also write or dictate a story about their trip, make a booklet of stories about it, or keep a scrapbook of their experiences that included stories and mementos of each trip.

Classroom Activities for Older Children:

1. Conduct a structured interview. The class may develop questions that each interviewee can be asked. For example, in interviewing community members about their feelings about a proposed park, the information gathered would be more manageable if all persons interviewed answered the same questions.

2. Write and perform a skit, a piece of poetry, or some other creative use of language.

3. Give directions. Some teachers set up a communication game in which two children are separated by a screen of some kind. One child creates a pattern with pattern blocks or cut pieces of paper and then gives directions to the other player so the pattern can be reproduced.

4. Role-play situations in which the children use the language that they believe their character would use. This activity is especially useful if followed by a discussion of the language and the decisions that were made about language use.

5. Organize discussions in which children can express their personal understandings of the topics introduced in class.

6.   Interview a number of adults in the community to learn about the use of oral language in the workplace.

7.   Interview a personnel manager to learn about how he or she expects candidates for a job to use language and the importance of language use in determining who is selected for a job.

In summary, children need an opportunity to use language about something that is meaningful to them. What they will do tomorrow in class, how long they have had their fish, whose dog had puppies, who has a new baby sister, how much their plant has grown, what they will have to eat later—all these activities of daily living are the content of children's talk, reading, and writing. Teachers can make the most of the numerous connections between spoken and written language in order to help children increase their competence in both.

Oral Language Activities for Limited English Speakers

Classroom teachers who want to help non-English-speaking children achieve a command of English give thought to the classroom environment and plan activities that make learning English as much like learning a first language as possible. Take the following suggestions just as a starting point for your own ideas:

1.   Plan activities that require children who speak English and children learning English to work together. For example, students could play a board game or build with blocks or Legos. A game situation is informal enough that most children will converse even though they might not communicate in formal situations.

2.   Encourage bilingual children to share their first language through bulletin boards, classroom labels, signs, and holiday decorations.

3.   Share (or find someone else to share) stories, poetry, or familiar songs in the child's native language and then in English.

4.   Use good-quality trade books (nonspecialized, commercially available books) in the child's language and share their contents with the class in both languages.

5.   Be careful not to segregate non-English-speaking children or to exclude them from activities you fear they will not understand. They learn language by listening and watching and following examples as well as from instruction.

6. Base writing and reading activities on the child's growing vocabulary in English. In the beginning, children can create booklets listing and illustrating the new words they learn. After a few weeks, most children are learning too rapidly to continue this technique.

7. Encourage the child's parents to participate by sharing books, songs, rhymes, and other language traditions with the class.

Major Ideas in This Chapter

▼ Language is a system of communication used by human beings and consists of several elements: The phonological, morphological, semantic, syntactic, and pragmatic components are part of every language.

▼ Children learn all the systems at once, not one at a time. No one theory can explain all there is to know about how language is developed. The behaviorists believe language is learned basically like any other learning—through stimulus and response. The linguists propose that language is innate in human beings because almost every human learns language to some degree and it is learned so quickly the usual learning theories cannot explain how a child masters so much so quickly. The interactionists seem to have the most comprehensive explanation of language learning; they believe language is learned through the interaction of the learners with the speakers in their environments.

▼ Learning language is a very natural process for most children. When surrounded by an environment that expects their success, treats errors as signs of growth, and supports their learning, most children make outstanding gains in language before coming to school.

▼ The context of the school can help children gain skill in language by encouraging children to use language in a variety of ways, by supporting and encouraging language use, and by providing a classroom environment that emulates that of the best home environments as much as possible. Teachers need to respect dialectical differences rather than see them as errors.

▼ Children whose language is not standard or not English need teachers who understand how a first language is learned best and can replicate as many of the first-language learning conditions as possible.

Discussion Questions: Focusing on the Teacher You Are Becoming

1. Your class is reading some of the stories from *The Tales of Uncle Remus: The Adventures of Brer Rabbit* (Lester, 1987). Although Lester has simplified the dialect in the original Harris version, it remains a prominent feature of the stories. A parent who is observing asks how you know that such stories will not have a negative influence on children's use of language. What will you say?

2. You have accepted a teaching position in a district where they have an "oral language" program that consists of having the teacher write one or two sentences on the board each morning. These sentences contain errors in spelling, punctuation, or grammar. Children must write the sentences correctly on their own paper. When another teacher asks you what you think of this program for developing oral language, what do you say?

3. Explain what you believe to be the most critical elements in planning for oral language development. What are some effective classroom activities for helping children gain skill in oral language?

4. Talk with a small group of your classmates about your own dialects. Which elements of dialects might cause difficulty for children learning to read? How can you plan to help those children?

Field-Based Applications

1. Listen to your students talking. Record some examples of their speech in various situations (classroom discussions, playground, lunchroom, unstructured time with other children) and compare their language with that found in the reading textbooks or social studies and science textbooks. Are the topics, sentence lengths, constructions, and level of formality similar to children's speech? Different from children's speech? Should they be similar or different?

2. Be alert for children's language that is particularly poetic or creative and record it to share with others.

3. Set up conversation-stimulating classroom areas such as a dress-up center and for a few days record the types of language used there. Would children have had the same opportunities for language use in other areas of the classroom?

4. Make an exhibit of realia (objects used to relate classroom teaching to real life) you think will increase children's knowledge and use of vocabulary. For example, you might bring in different kinds of plants and leaves and teach children the vocabulary to describe them if they are interested.

5. Record on videotape or audiotape your read-aloud sessions with children. What kinds of language patterns and interactions do you use? For example, you might note the number of questions you ask, the number of questions the children ask, the number of repetitions you use, and perhaps the number of times you encourage children to fill in words as they listen.

6. Record the pattern of language interactions in a classroom discussion. How many are student-student, student-teacher, teacher-student? If you find the interactions are predominantly teacher-student, plan activities encourage more language use among students.

7. Read a story that employs dialect appropriately and talk about dialects with your class. What are some common features of your students' local dialect?

Chapter 2
The Reading Process

Chapter Overview

▼ Children need to use reading and writing in classrooms that are child centered rather than material centered. Teachers must be aware of the factors contributing to success in gaining literacy so they can plan classroom experiences accordingly.

▼ Teachers need to understand the observable developmental stages through which children pass en route to becoming proficient readers.

▼ Reading and writing are developmental processes occurring at differing rates in different children. Learning to read can be facilitated by classroom conditions that match those in place for natural oral language learning.

▼ Reading and writing are inverse processes. The writer transforms ideas into print, and the reader transforms the print into ideas. A transaction occurs between the ideas of the author and the ideas of the reader.

▼ Reading combines the reader's knowledge of how language works with the ability to draw on related prior experience.

It is a foggy fall morning and you are standing in the back of a first-grade classroom. You are observing the children in this class in order to complete an assignment for your current course in reading methods. You watch as the children begin to enter the classroom, take off their jackets, and then go to the attendance board. There they move their name tags to the side of the board marked "At School Today." They proceed to the board where lunch information is recorded. You see some children select a slip of paper with their name on it and insert it in a pocket marked "Milk." Others find their names and insert them into pockets marked "Hot Lunch" or "Lunch from Home." You watch carefully as they then move off to various activities available in the classroom. Some children pick out books and sit on a comfortable sofa to read them. Others find paper and markers and begin making drawings. Some children write or draw in their journals. A few decide to play with the blocks or sand, and several more choose the dramatic play area, where they carry on a complicated dialogue about space travel.

You walk around to observe more closely what each is doing. Some of the children who are drawing have begun to label their drawings, others to write stories about their drawings. Children working in their journals have written stories, made lists of words, or drawn pictures. One of the children on the sofa is reading new material very fluently, and another is reciting the words from memory. You notice that some of the children playing with the blocks are getting paper to make signs for their buildings; the others take no notice. Two who were using the dramatic play area have gone to the library to find information about a particular spacecraft, whereas the rest are content to continue the play without any research. You are impressed by how carefully the teacher is monitoring these activities, aware of what each child is doing. You think, "Will I ever be able to do that?"

What conclusions can you draw about development of literacy from these observations? You notice that these children are at all stages of development in learning to read and write. Some are quite capable readers, some are obviously interested in print and aware of what print does, and some seem indifferent to reading and writing.

You go back to your education class with more questions than answers. What is this process we label *reading?* What do readers do as they read? How did the children, who are all approximately the same age, come to differ so widely in their reading and writing abilities? What are some of the experiences that foster the development of literacy, both in and out of school? What experiences can the teacher provide in school that will help children continue to grow in their ability to read and write? Your search for the answers to these questions begins with thinking about the range of approaches to the teaching of reading.

Reading in the Classroom

The questions and confusion that arose from your classroom observations are indicative of the questions and confusion present in the literacy profession as a whole. Great debate and strong opinions exist about how best to bring children to literacy. Proponents of various views use expert opinion, personal experience, and research data to support their positions. These opposing views distribute along a continuum ranging from bottom-up approaches at one end to top-down approaches at the other. Understanding this continuum will help you understand the debates about teaching children to read and write.

Approaches Continuum

At one end of the continuum are those approaches known as *bottom up.* Advocates of these approaches believe the best way to teach a child to read (or to write) is to break the task down to the smallest possible pieces, teach the hierarchy of pieces, and in the process the child will learn to read or write. Persons subscribing to this view would advocate that children must learn, for example, all of the letters and their corresponding sounds before they can learn to read. These proponents often march under the "Phonics First" banner.

In the center of the continuum are the *balance of approaches* advocates. They believe the best way to teach a child to read is to have the largest possible bag of tricks: some discrete skills, some whole sentences, some whole stories. They try to strike a balance between a focus on sounding out letters and words and understanding sentences. These proponents often march under the "Eclectic" banner. Most basal publishers target this segment of the continuum.

Wepner and Feeley (1992) examined first- and fourth-grade reading materials in seven basal reading series with 1989 copyrights. The researchers questioned the literature selections within basals, the ratio of skill work to "real" reading, the treatment of skill work within the programs, and the emphasis on and guidance in using strategies in reading. The first-grade texts had more basal-created stories than trade book originals. In fourth grade, 80% of the stories came from outside sources. First graders were generally offered 11 pages of skill work for each 7 to 9 pages of literature. Fourth graders were asked to complete an average of 8 pages of skill work for each 8- to 15-page selection. In addition, 72% of the first graders' skill work was unrelated to what was presented in the basal; fourth-grade basals offered 57% of the skills work unrelated to the reading material.

At the far right end of the continuum are the *top-down* advocates. They believe learning to read and write should be as natural as learning to speak. They advocate beginning with whole stories that the teacher reads to the children, then with the children, and finally the children can read them by themselves. They advocate teaching skills in the context of meaningful reading and writing activities at the point at which the child needs the skill instruction. These proponents march under the "Integrated Language Arts" or "Whole-Language" banners.

Bottom-Up Approaches

These approaches are known as the sight approach, the phonic analysis approach, or the linguistics approach. Considering each of these approaches will deepen your understanding of the concept of bottom-up approaches to reading.

The **sight approach** to reading instruction means that students are presented with words to be learned as wholes. They depend on visual memory to recall the word when it is presented in different contexts. The words are studied by configuration (shape of the word) and by repeated presentations. Critics of the sight approach say that children cannot learn to generalize what they know about words to new words and therefore lack skill in decoding

Print is available to learners in many forms in a good reading/writing classroom.

© Michael Newman/PhotoEdit

unfamiliar material. The old Dick and Jane books were based primarily on the sight approach, which explains the constant repetition in the stories: "See Dick. See Dick run. See Dick run and run. See Dick."

The **phonic analysis approach** focuses on learning the letter–sound relationships and practicing those sounds. In some phonics approaches, the words are learned as wholes first, then analyzed in terms of their component sounds, and then repeated as wholes. This process is called an *analytic* approach to phonics. In the *synthetic* approach, the words first are sounded out by using the letter–sound relationships, and then the word is pronounced by blending the sounds. Pronouncing the words is supposed to trigger knowledge of the word from the child's oral vocabulary. Vocabulary in books intended to teach reading is selected on the basis of phonic rules. Sometimes the result of selecting words on such a basis is sentences or stories that are not very meaningful. For example, a story about a coyote was selected for inclusion in one basal reader, a text designed to teach reading. The word *coyote* was changed to *fox* because *fox* followed the phonic rules already learned whereas *coyote* did not. Of course, the change produced an inaccurate story about foxes.

Some phonics approaches drill children on sound–symbol relationships for many hours of lessons before the children ever read a story or other piece of connected text.

The **linguistic approach** groups words together on the basis of their spelling patterns. Several years ago, there were some basal series based on the patterns found in words. Usually the first pattern introduced to beginning readers was the consonant-vowel-consonant (CVC) pattern. Words such as *cat, hat, mat, fat, red,* and *bed* follow the CVC pattern. Next came the consonant-vowel-consonant-silent *e* (CVC*e*) pattern: *like, home, page, ride,* and so on. The stories produced by selecting words on the basis of their patterns were often nonsensical and bore little resemblance to real language. Most basal readers today include some skill exercises that call for noting the CVC or CVC*e* pattern of words and for producing new words by substituting different consonants for the beginning consonant. Children might be asked to change the *m* of *mat* to *b, c, f, h, p, r, s, t,* and *v* and then read the words they have produced.

Top-Down Approaches

These approaches are exemplified by the language experience approach and by the philosophical orientation to literacy instruction referred to as whole language.

The **language experience approach** is founded on the notion that reading is all about creating meaning, and the most meaningful thing a young child can read is his or her own language. It is further based on the belief that all children come to school with experiences about which they can talk, and that what children can say can be written down by them or by a scribe. What they or others can write, can then be read. You will learn much more about language experience in Chapter 4. Some attempts have been made to create language experience curriculum materials, but a language experience curriculum depends on a very knowledgeable teacher who looks first at children and then creates learning activities that meet their needs. The same could be said about whole language.

Whole language is difficult to explain in a brief statement. Many people would classify whole language as an approach to reading. We think whole language is much more than that. We believe it is a philosophical stance about how teaching and learning should look, not just an approach to teaching reading. It is a mind-set toward teaching that empowers both the teacher and the learner. Whole-language teachers draw on research in language and child development, linguistics, psycholinguistics, sociolinguistics, anthropology, and education in creating their curriculum.

Whole-language instruction is based on the premise that when children are learning to read they need to learn from materials written for a variety of purposes rather than materials written for reading instruction. For example, children learn to read poetry, narrative stories, nonfiction reports, and descriptive writings. As they read each type of material they learn the characteristics and constraints that define a given genre and its purpose. The teacher first reads a literary selection to the children, they later read it with him or her, and finally they read it on their own. When children are learning to read using interesting materials, they do not mind revisiting a text. One typical technique is the teacher's modeling of fluent reading; another is to read a Big Book together until the class knows it well and then writing individual stories following the model of the Big Book. (A *Big Book* is a large-size version of a book for whole-class instruction, either commercially published or prepared by the teacher.) Writing is an integral part of reading instruction in the whole-language classroom. Skills are taught in context and as children need them.

Whole-language instruction focuses on such ideas as the author's intent, the intended audience for the piece, the point of view of the author, and the knowledge that the author needed before writing. Children learn to recognize conventions used by professional authors so they can employ those conventions in their own writing. The advocates of whole-language instruction view reading as much more than a collection of discrete skills that can be practiced outside the reading experience.

Proponents of bottom-up approaches and top-down approaches are locked in a very heated and serious debate about how best to teach children to read and write. Along the road to becoming a teacher, you must carefully examine the approaches, their underlying rationales, the philosophical underpinnings, and make an informed decision about what you believe about bringing children to literacy. This is a critical point because what you believe will very dramatically affect the nature of your instruction and the culture of your classroom. We believe that the challenge is not to ascertain the best approach to teaching reading and writing; no one knows for sure what that is. The challenge is to become as knowledgeable about all the approaches as you can, define a solid philosophical base, and then meet the needs of children. Snow, Barnes, Chandler, Goodman, and Hemphill (1991) discovered that many different aspects of school practice had an effect on the literacy achievement of their subjects, but classrooms using a wide variety of materials and activities in literacy instruction produced the most gains in vocabulary and reading comprehension. Consider your emerging beliefs about literacy instruction as you read the following descriptions of a traditional classroom and a whole-language classroom.

Traditional Classrooms

According to the traditional view, reading begins with the child's mastering the names of the letters, then mastering the letter–sound relationships, then learning some easy words in isolation, and finally reading simple stories with highly controlled vocabularies. What is overlooked in this plan is that little children learning to speak do not learn all their sounds *before* they use words, and they do not learn hosts of words *before* they use sentences (Clay, 1991).

We know that children learn to use print in steps that are not nearly so linear. Very young children may recognize whole words in context long before they learn the alphabet and may learn about story structure and reading purposes in conjunction with learning some letters or letter–sound relationships. Traditional programs often separated instruction in language, reading, and writing. A typical day might have included a session in which the children could practice language skills. For example, young children might have been asked to match words that rhyme, and older children might have been asked to make sentences using 10 new vocabulary words. At another time in the day, they might have had a writing lesson. For many young children, such a lesson involved copying a piece of poetry from the chalkboard; older children might have completed a sentence such as, "On my summer vacation I . . . " At yet another time in the same day, children would be expected to read, usually from materials that had a rigorously limited vocabulary. These activities were often unrelated and unconnected. In programs that treat language, reading, and writing as parts of the whole of becoming literate, children use all these processes at once. They become more adept at reading as they read stories and poems they and their classmates have written. They become better readers and writers as they broaden their knowledge of language through exploratory activities and projects that expand their vocabulary and their language usage.

It is hazardous to try to paint the picture of a traditional classroom with a single brush. There are great variations from classroom to classroom. Typically classrooms have been organized around a fixed schedule with time blocks tied to curriculum areas. Following is a typical daily schedule in a traditional classroom:

8:00–8:15	Attendance, lunch count, morning announcements.
8:15–9:15	Reading groups: teacher meets with each of three groups for about 15 to 20 minutes each. The activities of each group are defined by the teacher's guide to the basal reading program in use. When a group is not working with the teacher, they are completing work-book pages accompanying the day's story.
9:15–9:50	Handwriting instruction: the teacher models the formation of certain letter forms on the chalkboard and children practice them in exercises in their hand writing workbook.
9:50–10:20	Recess.
10:20–10:40	Reading aloud to the class by the teacher.
10:40–11:15	Math instruction using textbooks and worksheets.

11:15–11:45   Art instruction, PE instruction, and music instruction on a rotating schedule.

11:45–12:45   Lunch and recess.

12:45–1:30   Language arts instruction: lessons in writing and grammar using a textbook and workbook.

1:30–2:30   Science or social studies instruction on a rotating schedule; science for two weeks followed by social studies for two weeks. Textbook instruction using worksheets, film, and other print materials.

2:30–2:45   Recess.

2:45–3:15   Skill reinforcement time: small-group instruction with the teacher using workbook pages and worksheets to teach or reinforce basic skills in reading, language arts, or math.

3:15   Dismissal.

It is important to notice that in the traditional classroom, curriculum areas are treated as discrete, unconnected subjects and time blocks. Instruction is driven by instructional materials. Whole-language classrooms present a very different view of the teaching/learning process.

Whole-Language Classrooms

Let's begin our consideration of whole-language classrooms with the following scenario:

The teacher is reading an enlarged text of *Greedy Cat* (Cowley, 1988) with a group of first graders. The group has been selected because this text would be too difficult for the children to enjoy in any other way. In shared reading the children have visual access to the text, but they benefit from the voice support of the teacher to accomplish the reading. It is a wonderful New Zealand story about a greedy cat who looks in the shopping bag and eats whatever Mum has brought from the store. The predictable text follows a pattern of "Mum went shopping and bought some - - - -. Along came Greedy Cat. He looked in the shopping bag. Gobble, gobble, gobble, and that was the end of that." After the first episode the children are eagerly reading along with the teacher, usually needing support for only the names of the things Mum buys at the store.

The teacher reads ". . . and that was the end of that!" and asks, "What would you like to do with this story now?" The responses from the children are eagerly offered and extremely varied. One child suggests they could write about Greedy Cat. Some want to make shopping lists for their mother. One child quietly offers the possibility of reading the book to a partner or alone. When several children say that's what they want to do, the teacher poses the question of how they can arrange for everyone who might want to reread the book to get a turn. One child suggests a sign-up sheet and busily finds paper and a paper clip to put the sign-up sheet on the cover of the Big Book. Another child suggests that he and a partner could make up a game about Greedy Cat. One child asks, "Could we just go back to doing what we were doing before we read the story?"

The teacher then allows each child to choose how to respond to Greedy Cat or permits them to return to activities they were engaged in earlier. Most of the children initiate one of the choices of activities suggested by the group. Grant, Eric, and Julie have their heads together on the creation of a game. They make several trips to the game cupboard to get ideas for their game board. Olivia goes to the teacher with a writing problem. She wants to write "Greedy cat is too hungry." But she isn't sure which spelling of "to," "two," or "too" is right. The teacher seizes the moment to help Olivia find the word she wants, add it to her interest list, talk about the three spellings, and get on with her writing.

As the children complete their chosen activities they share with each other and some move on to the library corner, activity centers, or to complete work started earlier. The teacher calls a group of six to the large table to engage in a guided reading activity with small copies of Greedy Cat.

In this classroom, as in other whole-language classrooms, the children are viewed as experimenters, each hypothesizing and testing individual theories. The teacher is the director of the laboratory. The teacher sets the stage for the children to explore, experiment, and grow. The teacher then observes carefully for ways to lead from behind by providing additional experiences that will take the children toward greater literacy. The schedule for the day is highly flexible, and driven, not by instructional materials, but by the needs of the learners. A typical day (it varies from day to day) in a whole-language classroom might look like the following schedule:

8:00–8:10   Whole-class meeting: reading to the children, shared reading, storytelling. Discussion of authors and stories.

8:10–8:25   Independent reading: sustained silent reading by each child.

8:25–8:45   Whole-class activity: activity to introduce day's work; a lesson on modeling a writing skill; a lesson on a convention of writing; focus on writing or reading process.

8:45–9:30	Group activities: independent activities such as free reading, writing peer conferencing, computers, special interests, etc. Compulsory activities such as reading, retellings, notetaking, proofreading, things assigned by the teacher. Teacher-led activities such as small-group lesson, individual teaching, conferencing, monitoring the work of children.
9:30–9:45	Sharing time including a critique of the previous activities, movement, cooperation, sharing books, sharing writing.
9:45–10:00	Recess.
10:00–11:20	Teacher takes guided or shared reading groups while rest of class works on projects drawn from thematic unit or science or social studies units.
11:20–11:30	Teacher carefully monitors children's progress and takes anecdotal notes.
11:30–12:00	Teacher taking running records or conducting a handwriting lesson or other mini-lesson.
12:00–12:45	Lunch and recess.
12:45–1:00	Midday meeting: critique morning's activities and performance. Sharing, small-group accomplishments.
1:00–2:00	Repeat of morning's group activities, time to work in cooperative learning groups, time for meeting individual needs. The content here is often drawn from science and social studies.
2:00–2:15	Recess.
2:15–3:15	Art, music, physical education, science, or social studies on a rotating schedule.

What Is Whole-Language Instruction?

The scenario and schedule just outlined give us some insight into what is meant by whole language. Consider the important features of what happened in this classroom.

▼ Children were exposed to literature that confirmed what they know about how language works. The predictable text of *Greedy Cat* allowed even the emergent readers in the group to join in the reading, feel success, and find a way to respond to the selection.

▼ Whole-language teachers think differently about readers' development and the nature of texts. In traditional classrooms the readability of *Greedy Cat* would have been determined, and only children reading instructionally at that level would have been exposed to the text. Because whole-language teachers think of readers developmentally, the same text can be used with all children, but the expectations for engagement with the text vary. In the scenario the teacher determined that *Greedy Cat* posed enough challenges for the selected group of children that the text was used as a shared reading text. In shared reading the children all have visual access to *Greedy Cat*, and the teacher lent her voice support to the oral reading. With another group the teacher might have decided to use a guided reading approach with the children—segmenting their reading and helping them deal with the challenges of the text as they read silently and discussed the selection and the reading process. For other children, *Greedy Cat* could be easy enough that they could read it by themselves.

▼ Whole-language teachers engage in assessment as an ongoing part of instruction. The teacher in our scenario noticed each child's participation in the shared reading of *Greedy Cat* and decided which children would benefit from a follow-up guided reading activity. The teacher made an instantaneous decision to engage Olivia in a lesson on writing "to," "two," and "too." That objective was not planned in advance, but became important as Olivia exhibited a need for the instruction.

▼ Whole-language teachers empower children to make choices about what they learn and how they demonstrate that learning. Notice that the question at the end of the shared reading was, "What would you like to do with this story now?" This opened the situation to the wide variety of responses the children chose. Whole-language teachers believe that literacy develops naturally through meaningful, functional use of language. The literacy activities the children chose were meaningful and functional to them.

▼ Whole-language teachers value risk taking and see it as an essential part of learning. We learn from our mistakes, from our approximations. Olivia is an example. She took a risk in spelling *too*, and the teacher used that risk taking as a moment for teaching.

▼ Whole-language teachers create learning activities that are language rich, success oriented, and carried out in a noncompetitive environment. In whole-language classrooms the *process* is often of equal importance to the *product*.

▼ Whole-language teachers create environments in which children use print in a variety of forms for a variety of important purposes. We saw this, again, in the scenario, when children responded to *Greedy Cat* in a variety of ways. (Adapted from Harp, 1991)

Whole-language classrooms contain many books, directions, schedules, messages, and other materials for reading. Such classrooms stress functional reasons for writing, such as operating message centers and signing up for activities, and they provide well-stocked writing centers. Materials produced by the children are used in ongoing activities. Teachers make writing a part of typical projects such as hatching eggs so records can be kept, activities checked off, charts produced, and reference material used. Daily classroom routines provide opportunities for functional uses of print, from taking attendance to rotating responsibility for chores. The print is child centered in that most of it is produced by children and reflects their activities and interests.

The experiences of children in whole-language classrooms are different from those of children in conventional classrooms not only in terms of what they do but in terms of how they feel about themselves as readers and how they perceive reading. The way in which Rasinski (1988) has described the experience of his son Mikey in becoming literate clarifies the importance of interest, purpose, and choice in the literacy-gaining process. Mikey was involved in a kindergarten program that allowed him to choose to participate in making books and engage in reading and to decide for himself how to accomplish tasks. As a result, Mikey saw himself as a reader and writer. In first grade, Mikey's teacher employed a reading program that depended on worksheets and stories with controlled vocabulary in order to achieve reading goals. Mikey was suddenly confronted with a change in his perception of the reading process: No longer an activity that furthered his personal goals, reading became a task to be performed for someone else. Clearly, Mikey's second teacher had a different understanding of the conditions for literacy learning.

In fact, the teacher's view of literacy and how it is achieved has a profound effect on the way a child views reading and writing. The U.S. Office of Education First Grade studies of the late 1960s (Stauffer, 1969) established that the teacher is one of the most critical factors in the reading process. This is as true today as it was more than 30 years ago. Teachers who choose to treat learning to read as part of the bigger process of becoming literate provide activities that encourage children to use print to achieve their own goals and to explore how others use it. Your own experience over years of teaching will provide the best answers to some of your questions about the best ways to bring children to literacy. We believe the teaching profession in the United States has typically made learning to read more difficult than it needs to be. We urge you to create the conditions in your classroom that existed for each of us to become oral language learners. These conditions for learning will facilitate learning to read and write just as they supported learning to speak.

The Conditions for Literacy Learning

Cambourne (1988) has helped us understand that the differences between learning oral language and coming to fluency in reading and writing are minimal. The conditions that exist to facilitate oral language learning must exist to promote fluency in literacy. Consider the following eight conditions he identified, and think about what evidence we would look for in a classroom to prove the conditions exist there.

Immersion

As learners of oral language we were constantly immersed in language. Many parents talk to babies while they are in the womb. We assign intentionality to the gurgles and giggles of newborns. Just as these very young children are immersed in oral language, so must emergent readers and writers be immersed in texts of all kinds. Evidence of the existence of this condition would be a classroom in which print is used for a variety of purposes: informing, persuading, directing, controlling. The classroom library would be well stocked, including the publications of class authors.

Demonstration

Each time the oral language learner was immersed in language, the use of language was being demonstrated. Literacy learners need many demonstrations of how texts are constructed and used. It seems that teachers come easily to demonstrating reading. Children need to be read to many times during the day, not just for 15 minutes after lunch. However, teachers seem to have difficulty demonstrating writing. This is probably because we have received so few demonstrations of writing ourselves. By demonstration of writing we mean actually showing children how you think through the process of writing a piece—and then demonstrating that writing.

Engagement

Cambourne (1988) makes the critical point that unless children are engaged with immersion and demonstration, little learning will occur. Engagement implies that learners are convinced they are potential doers or performers of the demonstrations, that learning these things will be beneficial, and that these new learnings can be tried out without fear of harm if the performance is not strictly correct. All teachers have experienced the child who fails to learn despite immersion in texts and many demonstrations of reading. We agree with Cambourne's notion that lack of learning is often the result of limited (or nonexistent) engagement on the part of the learner. We as teachers have failed to help students see themselves as potential "doers" of the activity.

Expectation

Parents of young children fully expect their toddlers to make tremendous leaps toward oral language fluency, and to accomplish the task within a few years. Rarely do parents (barring unfortunate circumstances) worry about their children coming to fluency in oral language. Why, then, do some parents respond so negatively when young children spell a word the best they can at the time or make a mistake when reading orally? As teachers (and we have to help parents achieve this too) we must have high expectations that children will learn to read and write. The higher our expectation, the greater our children's success.

Responsibility

As parents we have often been grateful that we did not have to teach our children to speak. In fact, in coming to fluency in oral language, children take responsibility for their own learning. They appreciate the need for clear, useful communication and modify their language to maximize its use. So children can be responsible for learning to read and write. We need to help children decide what the next learning steps are to be and how they will take them.

Use

As oral language users we practiced our control over language in very real ways—to get things done and to get our needs met. In the reading/writing classroom children need many opportunities daily to practice reading and writing in ways that are real, communicative, and authentic. We suspect that no one reading this text has, as an adult, drawn three rectangles on a piece of paper and then practiced addressing envelopes in the rectangles. Why? This is a truly inauthentic exercise. We address envelopes for the purpose of mailing something. Children need nonartificial ways to use reading and writing.

Approximation

Most families can identify certain words or phrases a youngster approximated that were deemed so charming they have become part of that family's vocabulary. When the 2½-year-old approached with a plate at a 45-degree angle and said, "Mommy cookies all gonded, all gonded," Mommy didn't reply with, "Now, honey, that isn't the way we would say that." Mommy responded to the communication and probably enjoyed the child's approximation of standard speech. We wonder why it is that parents who were so charmed by approximations in oral language are so disturbed by their children's approximations in reading and writing. *Mistakes are a natural, developmental part of all learning.* As knowledgeable teachers we must learn to see the mistakes as road signs that help us better understand the developing reader and writer. And we must be very careful how we respond to these approximations.

Response

Cambourne asserts that learners must receive feedback on their attempts at reading and writing that is relevant, appropriate, timely, readily available, nonthreatening, with no strings attached. We must help children understand that mistakes are a natural part of learning, and the mistakes help them define what they need to learn next. The responses parents and teachers make to the child's efforts in literacy are critical factors in success.

We believe the conditions for literacy learning as Cambourne defined them are critical. In fact, when we are asked to evaluate a school's literacy program, we begin by looking to see if these conditions exist in classrooms. Once you have understood the conditions for literacy learning, you are ready to understand the reading process itself.

Reading: An Interactive Process

As teachers who are continually learning, our views of the reading process have changed dramatically since the late 1970s. In the past we used to think of the reader as a blank slate on which the ideas of the author were to be written, an empty vessel into which the thoughts of the author could be poured.

Now, due to the work of Ken Goodman (1968), Yetta Goodman, Dorothy Watson, and Carolyn Burke (1987), David Rumelhart (1977, 1982), Marie Clay (1985, 1991), and many others, our views of the reading process have changed dramatically. We now understand that reading is an **interactive process.** There is a true interaction between the ideas and language of the author and the ideas and language of the reader. Through this interaction meaning is created, a meaning in many ways unique to the reader. Marie Clay (1979) likened the reading process to the old game Twenty Questions. She says, "Reading is something like that game. The smarter readers ask themselves the most effective questions for reducing uncertainty; the poorer readers try lots of trivial questions and waste their opportunities to reduce their uncertainty" (p. 7). As teachers it is our challenge to help all readers ask the effective questions that help them monitor their creation of meaning.

Definitions of Reading

Clay (1991) recognizes that what the reader brings to the text is critical. Of her definition of reading she says,

I define reading as a message-getting, problem-solving activity which increases in power and flexibility the more it is practiced. My definition states that within the directional constraints of the printer's code, language and visual perception responses are purposefully directed by the reader in some integrated way to the problem of extracting meaning from cues in a text, in sequence, so that the reader brings a maximum of understanding to the author's message." (p. 6)

More simply stated, Clay views the reading process as a problem-solving activity in which the problem is one of getting the author's message by using the cues on the printed page and the reader's background knowledge.

Ken Goodman (1970, p. 5) offered this definition: "Reading is a complex process by which a reader reconstructs, to some degree, a message encoded by a writer in graphic language." Reading and writing are so closely connected that we really need to talk about writing as we talk about reading.

The notion that the reader creates meaning was further explained by Rosenblatt (1978):

The reader brings to the text his past experience and present personality. Under the magnetism of the ordered symbols of the

Teachers help children use the supports found in predictable texts.

© 1994 David J. Sams/Texas Inprint

text, he marshals his resources and crystallizes out from the stuff of memory, thought and feeling a new order, a new experience, which he sees as the poem. This becomes part of the ongoing stream of his life experience, to be reflected on from any angle important to him as a human being. (p. 12)

Rosenblatt so clearly recognized that the reader transacts with the text to create new meaning that she named the "product" of that transaction *the poem*. Her definitions (1978) of the reader, the text, and the poem are interesting.

The *reader* is the person seeking to make meaning by transacting with (actively reading) a text, of whatever kind. The *text* is the collection of word symbols and patterns on the page, the physical object you hold in your hand as you read. The *poem* is the literary work created as the reader transacts with the text.

One of the greatest advances in our thinking about reading is that the meaning *is not in the text itself*. Meaning is created through the transaction between the reader and the text. Reading is a process resulting in meaning created by the blending of the author's ideas and the background knowledge of the reader.

When we look at the activity of the writer we see that the writer begins with ideas, transforms those ideas into language, and then converts the language into written symbols. Now the reader enters the picture. The reader begins with the written symbols, translates them into language, draws on his or her background of experiences to interpret that language, and then transforms the language into ideas. The goal is that the ideas with which the reader ends will match the ideas with which the writer began. They rarely, if ever, match exactly because of differences in the life experiences of the two persons, but if the writing/reading process has worked, the match will be close. Figure 2.1 illustrates the inverse nature of the writing and reading processes.

The figure takes special notice of the reader's background experiences and knowledge of how language works. We are coming to a better understanding of the importance of background experiences. At one time, the interpretive aspect would not have been included in the figure. Now we recognize that our background experiences affect how we interpret the world, both in reality and in print. We are continually building theories (inferences, perceptions, assumptions) about the nature of people, our language, and our world based on our experiences. These cognitive structures are called *schemata* (singular: schema). Schemata are simply organized chunks of knowledge and experience, often accompanied by feelings (Weaver, 1994). Rumelhart (1982) called schemata the building blocks of cognition.

To understand schemata better, think about family holiday celebrations. Your schema for family celebrations on the Fourth of July may include a trip to the river, a picnic, rides on a boat, water skiing, and fireworks. A close friend may have a very different schema for Fourth of July celebrations. It

Figure 2.1—Reciprocity of Writing and Reading

might include watching a parade and listening to patriotic speeches. When you invite your friend to your family's celebration, there will be a real difference in expectations and interpretations. Reading about Fourth of July celebrations would be similarly colored by those differing schemata.

Clearly, the schemata we bring to the printed page very much determine the meaning we give to the print. The reader comes to the printed page with a rich cache of meanings to be given to the ideas (as expressed in the words) of the author. The act of reading is thus a very interactive process between the writer and the reader (May, 1986). The continual interaction between the ideas of the author and the schemata of the reader results in the reader's bringing meaning to the printed page. Clearly the degree to which the reader *reconstructs* (to use Kenneth Goodman's term) the message of the writer depends on the orchestration of a great many factors. The interaction between the ideas of the author and the schemata of the reader have a ripple effect that can change our understandings over time.

Consider your schemata for teaching reading as they existed before reading this chapter. You probably drew on your own experience as a child recalling reading circles with other children, reading in turn as the teacher listened, a basal reader, flash cards, and workbook pages. As you have read this chapter you may have realized that your schemata for teaching reading and ours differ. This may have caused you to change your schemata or to reread our thoughts with a more critical or more open stance. As you rethink your understandings about teaching reading, you then bring changed knowledge to a rereading or rethinking of this text, thus producing the ripple effect over time in this interaction between you and the ideas of the authors.

A closer look at the components of reading not only helps to define reading but provides some terminology you will need in order to talk about the reading process.

Components of the Reading Process

Reading is so complex that it is difficult to break it apart and talk about the components. When we discuss them, we risk creating the impression that a given component is more important than others. Mature readers use all the components selectively as necessary to create meaning, and probably use them in combination so rapidly they don't notice discrete steps at all. Our purpose here is to outline the components so you will have a working knowledge of the terminology used to describe the reading process.

Predicting, Confirming, and Integrating

What is the reader doing during this interaction between the ideas of the author and the ideas of the reader? Many things are happening simultaneously—not in a linear fashion as our discussion might imply. Several concepts are critical to understanding the reading process.

1. The printed page is rich in cues that enable the reader to create meaning. These cues exist in the sounds represented by the letters, the meanings represented by the words, and the meaning signaled by the structure of the sentences and entire text. As we use the reading process we sample the fewest possible of the cues to help us create meaning. It is almost as if the reader hovers above a line of print, dipping down to use only the most minimal cues necessary to create meaning. As long as the process is working smoothly, very few cues are used. When we realize we are in difficulty as a reader we slow down and use more of the cues.

2. When you read, as when you listen to a speaker, you are continually predicting what is going to be said next (Smith, 1978). When you have predicted what the author will say next (sometimes almost unconsciously), you sample from the fewest possible of the cues on the page to *confirm* your prediction. If your prediction is confirmed—what you thought you would read is what you read—you have created meaning

fairly effortlessly. The next step in the process is to *integrate* what you have read with what you already know (Goodman, Y., 1980).

3.   If the prediction you made is not confirmed by what you read, you then must either rethink your prediction and reread or reread to see if you accurately created meaning.

4.   The more challenging the text (complicated language or unfamiliar topic) the more of the cues you use and the slower the process takes place.

Traditionally, it was believed that children would learn to read by acquiring a discrete set of skills (learning letter–sound relations and learning words, learning syllable patterns, and so on) and orchestrating these skills into the act of reading. While such skills are part of the various cueing systems, we now realize that learning to use strategies such as those just described are critical to learning to read. Children learn the skills gradually over time because they learn many different ways of working with print. Children build up a network of strategies that act on stores of knowledge to create meaning from print (Clay, 1991). Clay lists a host of things children learn as they construct this repertoire of strategies:

▼   the aspects of print to which they must attend

▼   the aspects of oral language that can be related to print

▼   the kinds of strategies that maintain fluency

▼   the kinds of strategies that explore detail

▼   the kinds of strategies that increase understanding

▼   the kinds of strategies that detect and correct errors

▼   the feedback control mechanisms that keep their reading and writing productions on track

▼   the feed-forward mechanisms (like anticipation or prediction) that keep their information-processing behaviors efficient

▼   and most important of all how to go beyond the limits of the system and how to learn from relating new information to what is already known. (p. 326)

Encompassed in many of Clay's learnings is the ability to selectively use the many cues that exist on the printed page. Children actively process printed information and construct new learning as they manipulate the cueing systems.

The Cueing Systems

Let's examine the cues on the printed page in greater detail because understanding the cueing systems is fundamental to understanding the reading process. Four cueing systems are in operation when we read.

The Graphophonic Cueing System

Our language is an alphabetic one: Sounds are represented by letters. Linguists don't agree on how many sounds exist in American English, but most suggest there are 44 sounds or phonemes. Of course, we have only 26 letters or graphemes with which to represent these sounds. This lack of phoneme/grapheme correspondence makes the graphophonic cueing system very challenging to use. Nevertheless, the letters on the printed page represent sounds, variation in sounds, or the absence of sound.

The Semantic Cueing System

The words in our language represent meanings. The semantic cueing system consists of the cues provided by the meanings of words in the same or nearby sentences.

The Syntactic Cueing System

Our language is organized by a set of principles that describe how utterances may be created. Word order and sentence structure are very important. The reader's understanding of these principles permits the use of the syntactic cueing system. Here cues are provided by the structure of the sentence. For example, the word *the* tells you to look for a noun.

The Schematic Cueing System

The predictions we make as we read are confirmed in part by using the graphophonic, syntactic, and semantic cues on the printed page. But the comprehension process is greatly facilitated by another cueing system. We said earlier that the ideas you have about people, your language, and the world are called schemata. The cues to understanding provided by your schemata are called the *schematic cueing system*. This cueing system may be the most powerful contributor to *comprehension*. We have defined *comprehension* in a way that recognizes the importance of schematic cues. Comprehension is the interaction of the ideas of the author and the schemata of the reader that leads to understanding. We discuss the comprehension process more fully in Chapter 8.

Our ability to use the cueing systems and our actual use of them develop over time and reading experiences. Aulls (1985) has described the changes that take place in our use of the various cueing systems as we become more mature readers and writers; Figure 2.2 illustrates them. Note that the knowledge sources listed on the left range from simple to complex. The scale on the

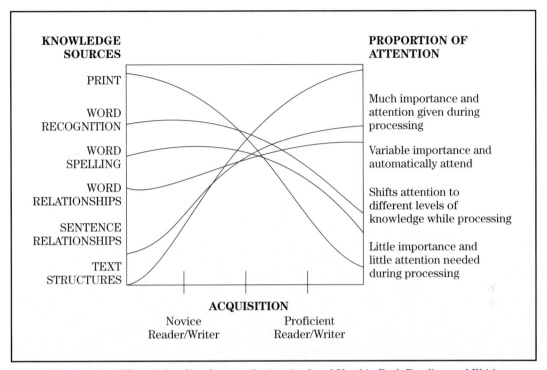

Figure 2.2—Levels of Knowledge Simultaneously Acquired and Used in Both Reading and Writing Acquisition

Source: Mark W. Aulls, "Understanding the Relationship between Reading and Writing," *Educational Horizons 64* (Fall 1985): 39–44.

right moves from greater to smaller amount of attention paid to the sources of knowledge by the reader/writer. As the reader/writer moves across the bottom of the chart from inexperience to proficiency, the amount of attention he or she pays to each knowledge source changes rather dramatically. For example, the beginning reader/writer pays the most attention to the print; the proficient reader/ writer pays the least.

The beginning reader/writer pays little attention to the text structure, but the mature reader pays more attention to the structure (forms of poetry, time sequence, use of flashback, and so on) than to any other aspect of the reading process. If we think about it, we know that when we sit down to read the newspaper we have a clearly defined (although sometimes unconscious) set of expectations for the reading experience. We anticipate that certain kinds of information will be found in certain sections of the paper and that some kinds of information are consistently there, whereas others vary. We know the material to be read will be presented in newspaper style, which means the first paragraph of a news article will cover all the major facts. We can read on if we are interested in more detail or skip to another article if we have all the information we want. It also means a certain vocabulary will be employed and that eloquent prose is not usual.

All our reading experiences as mature readers are colored by our expectations for the structure of the text and by our life experiences. As a textbook reader for at least 12 or 13 years, you hold certain expectations for textbooks. For example, you expect headings and subheadings to help you determine which pieces of information are the most important and mark transitions to new topics. You also expect a certain type of language. If your expectations were not met, you would have to spend additional time on the reading task. You have become very sophisticated in the use of the reading process.

Bearing in mind the components of the reading process, think again about the children whose classroom activities we described at the beginning of the chapter. Let's examine the development of reading ability that leads to such dramatic variations within a group of children.

Sequential Stages in the Reading Process

The changes that take place in the reader's proficiency have been described as stages in the reading process. Although it is potentially deceiving to think of the development of reading ability as a linear process, it is instructive to consider the stages children generally move through as readers.

In describing the general sequence of beginning reading, authors have looked at different aspects of reading behavior. Cochrane, Cochrane, Scalena, and Buchanan (1984) described the following stages that have often been quoted in the literature on teaching reading:

1. Magical stage. Children seek to understand the purpose of books and begin to think books are important. They think books are magical—they contain stories. Looking at books, holding them, and taking favorite books with them are signs of this stage. Parents or teachers must provide models of the importance of reading by reading to themselves, reading to children, and talking about books.

2. Self-conception stage. Children begin to view themselves as readers and begin to engage in reading-like activities. They may pretend to read books, supplying words suggested by the pictures or by previous experiences with the books.

3. Bridging reader stage. Children become more and more aware of the actual print in the reading process. They are able to pick out familiar words and notice words that have personal significance. Those who write stories will be able to read them back and can also begin to read familiar print from poems, songs, or nursery rhymes. Some children believe each word represents a syllable and are confused when they try to match them up. Most children begin to recognize the letters of the alphabet.

4. Take-off reader stage. Children begin to use three cueing systems (graphophonic, semantic, and syntactic) together in a process. They are

The reading/writing program offers children a variety of ways to learn.

© Spencer Grant/Stock Boston

excited about reading and want to read to others. They begin to recognize words even when they are out of context. They become more aware of environmental print and tend to read everything, such as cereal boxes. In this period they may become too attentive to each word or even each letter and overuse the graphic system, seeing reading as the decoding of sounds and words rather than the creation of meaning.

5. Independent reading stage. Children are able to read unfamiliar books by themselves. They construct meanings using not only the print but also their previous knowledge and experience and the author's cues about meaning. Independent readers are able to predict how the author might express meaning through various syntactic or semantic structures. They are most successful with material that is related directly to their experience, but are able to understand the structure and language of familiar story genres or common expository material, such as the record of a science experiment.

6. Skilled reader stage. Children are increasingly able to read material that is further and further removed from their own experiences. They have learned to read and begin reading to learn. They begin to process print that serves specialized purposes, such as in the telephone book or a menu, as well as enjoying stories and poetry. They are able to apply the process of reading to other areas, such as reading music or reading another language.

7. Advanced skilled stage. Children at advanced skilled levels use print to fulfill individual needs. They process material at various speeds and with a level of attention to detail that is consistent with the purpose of the reading. They choose to read on a regular basis.

Why should you be a student of the stages in reading development? Teachers who have a developmental perspective are able to plan instructional activities that are most appropriate for children. The daily activities you plan for students should be selected because of where children are in their development of literacy rather than because they happen to appear next in the textbook and teacher's guide. We hope an overview of the development of the reading process will help you be more comfortable with children as they move through the developmental process, knowing they will continue to grow and develop as readers and writers.

Keys to Success in Learning to Read

Children do not enter school with empty minds; they have had many and varied experiences. Some have been taken to the library, read to frequently, and engaged in conversations about books. They live with adults who read and write and who use words for problem solving, self-education and enrichment, and entertainment. Others live in environments where they have never observed an adult reading or writing. Their homes lack books, magazines, and newspapers, and the world outside their homes has offered them limited experiences that involved language or reading or writing. Huey (1908/1961, p. 19) said, "The home is the natural place for learning to read in connection with the child's introduction to literature through storytelling, picture reading, etc. The child will make much use of reading and writing in his plays using both pictures and words."

Ideally all children will have had such a wonderful beginning in the development of literacy, but for most that ideal is far from reality. The responsibility of the teacher, then, is to help every child learn the language, the functions of print, and the pleasures of the written word that will make the development of literacy possible for each one.

We might well have subtitled the first chapter of this book "The Heart of the Matter," for language is at the very heart of the process of learning to read, write, speak, and think. In addition to receiving strong support in their development of language, children will benefit from several other kinds of experiences in gaining literacy: having opportunities to generate and test hypotheses about print, having opportunities to come to the reading experience with the relevant nonvisual information (and the freedom to use it), and having opportunities to learn the purposes and functions of reading personally. In addition, each child needs to read printed material that is meaningful and predictable and have a teacher or parent who stresses meaning more than mechanics. Understanding these needs will help answer questions about how children have attained such different abilities. Teachers who meet these needs provide the optimal environment for children to learn to read.

Forming Hypotheses

Children need opportunities to generate and test hypotheses about print. Children learning to talk are constantly generating and testing hypotheses about language and how it works. An observer of young children will note that they try out various combinations of sounds when attempting to communicate their needs. The feedback is usually immediate: The child either does or does not get whatever he or she wanted. The child can adjust language, gestures, and other accompanying behaviors accordingly. Children also begin making the same sorts of hypotheses about print in the environment. For instance, the child observes a truck on the highway bearing a familiar logo and remarks, "That says 'Pay Less.' " The adult will usually respond, "Yes, that says 'Pay Less,' " if it does, otherwise making the correction: "No, that says 'Baskin-Robbins.' " Most adults will not say, "Now, Amanda, pay attention. See, that letter is a *B*, not a *P*. Sound out the letters and you will know what it says." Children learn to recognize commonly seen words such as *exit* and *stop*, as well as commercial logos such as McDonald's and Kraft, through repeated exposure to the print embedded in the context and through repeated feedback.

Yetta Goodman (1980, 1986) found that most 3-year-olds could read some environmental print when it was presented in context. Children who could not read the exact name of the item could supply a generic label for it. For example, they might say "toothpaste" when shown Colgate. Such findings indicate that children respond to print in ways that relate to their experience, rather than just randomly. Goodman found that the ability to read environmental print was not related to ethnic, racial, geographic, or linguistic differences. Goodman also examined the child's understanding of print in discourse. She found that this understanding begins early. Most 3-year-olds know how to handle a book, and most 5-year-olds know it is the print that is being read.

Teachers can find ways daily for children to interact meaningfully with print. When teachers transcribe what children say, make charts of song lyrics, and write lists of tasks to be done, they are creating opportunities for children to make their own hypotheses about print and how it works and to test their guesses. A good example of problem solving with print was observed in a local kindergarten. The children were a little upset that not all of them had had a turn to use the new play area. As a group they tried to solve the problem. One child suggested that a list could be made of the children who had had a turn and then all the others would have a turn before those children could play there again.

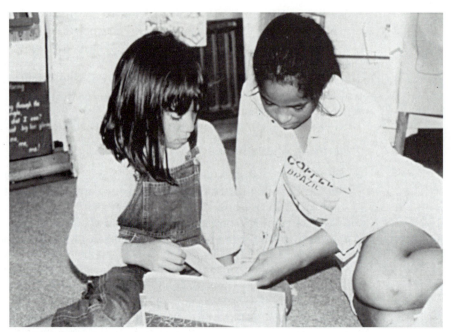

Reading with a partner turns the process into a three-way interaction.

© Michael Hagan

The teacher agreed. The child got a clipboard and some paper and went to the name board to copy down the names of the children to be surveyed. She copied only the geometric shape that was on each child's name card. When she began her survey, she found that the information she had was not enough to be useful, and she was soon back at the board copying the print for each name.

In another class, the children had learned to read a short story about Halloween. The words (and some pictures) had been placed in a pocket chart. Other word cards were available. Some children could read the story only exactly as they had memorized it, but others would substitute words in the sentences and then try to read the new sentences they had made. Freeman and Whitesell (1985, p. 24) recommend that teachers encourage children "to take risks in interpreting all kinds of printed text."

In exploring print, children develop the oral language with which to discuss written language. They begin to learn the concepts and labels of *book*, *page*, *word*, *letter*, and so on. It is important that encounters with the language about print take place in meaningful contexts. In some classrooms, children learn the names of the letters or learn to repeat the letter–sound relationships totally apart from their interactions with print. Therefore, children may believe these activities are unrelated to reading or writing, or they may come to believe that reading is simply "sounding out words." Placing this much importance on sounding out (one aspect of using the graphophonic cueing system) is misguided. Children often are heard to make mistakes, correct them, and learn new words without any sign of "sounding out." Further, some children who learn letter–sound relationships are not able to read more challenging texts. Finally, a sounding-out strategy does not explain how some readers can read a new word with understanding supported by the text but may mispronounce the word aloud (Clay, 1991).

As children develop the vocabulary for discussing written language, they are able to talk about what they are doing when they participate in reading and writing experiences. Yetta Goodman (1986) defines the ability to think about and explain the use of language in some overt way as the development of metalinguistic ability. Of course, the child's explanations may not match those of adults for some time. Goodman's research also revealed that many children's metalinguistic knowledge and their level of performance do not match. For example, some children can read and write in the conventional sense without having the ability to think about their knowledge of written language. Others begin thinking about how the language works before they can perform as readers.

Children often demonstrate their knowledge of language in the classroom. For example, in creating sentences that followed the pattern learned in Hoberman's *A House Is a House for Me* (1982), the group had started with "A doghouse is a house for a dog" and were having great difficulty in coming up with a satisfactory second line that would rhyme with *dog*. Finally one child jumped up with a solution: "The sky is the home for the fog." Since the *A* for the next line was already on the chart, he was asked why it had to be changed to *The*. His reply certainly indicated a knowledge of how language worked when he answered, "Everyone knows there is only *one* [sky]." In addition to admiring his poetic language, we can applaud his understanding of the workings of language. Helping children develop the vocabulary of written language and helping them think about their understanding of how language works furthers the goal of literacy.

We can also tap into a child's understanding of reading as a process by conducting a simple interview. We recommend doing this procedure with all emergent readers early in the year and with all children in later grades who are having problems coming to fluency in reading. The interview could be repeated over time to capture changes in perceptions. We recommend asking four questions and inviting verbal, not written, responses.

1. What is reading?

2. What do you do when you read?

3. When you come to a word you don't know, what do you do?

4. If you were going to help someone become a better reader what would you do?

Responses to these questions can be very helpful in determining the degree to which children view reading as a process. For example, if the answer to the first question is something like "sound out words" instead of "make a story in my head," one would suspect the child does not fully understand that reading is a meaning-making process. For a more complete reading interview see *Reading Miscue Inventory: Alternative Procedures* by Goodman, Watson, and Burke (1987).

Applying Experience

Children need opportunities to come to reading experiences with relevant nonvisual information and have the freedom to use it. Children cannot read material comfortably unless the content is related to their experience. Neither can adults. The following excerpt (Stanley-Samuelson, 1987, p. 105) illustrates the need for background knowledge that relates to the material to be read:

Various eicosanoids appear to be involved in the regulation of a variety of physiological and behavioral areas in representatives of many invertebrate phyla. In some cases (such as mediation of behavioral thermoregulation), the evidence for an eicosanoid function is based on treatment of animals with a single compound and observation of the response. At this level of observation, it remains to be established that eicosanoids are physiologically involved. Given a good base of preliminary observations, important research goals would be to firmly show that, in the case at hand, PGs do mediate thermoregulatory behavior. In still other cases, such as the role of PG in releasing egg-laying behavior in crickets, there is sufficient evidence to accept that certain PGs do release egg-laying, although some details of the physiological mechanism—where in the central nervous system PGs act and how they alter behavior— are not yet understood. Research in this area could usefully be aimed, not at reaffirming the role of the eicosanoid, but at acquiring more details of the action. In study areas where considerable biochemical details are established—as in starfish oocyte maturation—cellular events remain unknown. Again, understanding how eicosanoids act remains a major research goal.

Even if you could pronounce each word correctly, you would find the passage meaningless unless you had enough previous knowledge of biology. For some children, teachers will need to spend instructional time providing experiences that form the background for comprehension. For example, many children have not ridden on an escalator or in an elevator, attended a birthday party or a circus, or seen a farm or zoo. If children meet these concepts in print before they have experience with which to connect them, the print may be meaningless.

Having experience is not enough if the child is not allowed to use it. Some teachers do not wish children to read and write about their experiences because they are not as "pretty" as the teachers would like. For some children, daily life means relationships marked by violence, fathers or mothers who are absent, and homes without enough food. These children must be allowed to relate print to their own worlds before they can relate to reading traditional stories of middle-class children visiting grandparents on the farm.

Discovering Purpose

Children need opportunities to learn the purposes and functions of print personally. In an ideal world, children would grow up observing the functions of print in a personal way. They would get letters from distant friends and relatives and hear thousands of stories that had been carefully crafted with well-chosen words. They would have followed directions for constructing a toy or model and consulted the encyclopedia to learn more about dogs or dinosaurs. They would have written thank you notes to their grandparents, received invitations to parties, held their own tickets to the *Nutcracker* ballet, and organized their collections of favorite books.

In the real world, not all children have had the chance to learn about print in such ways. Teachers can help children use print to send meaningful messages. For example, children in the morning session of kindergarten may want to tell the afternoon group not to destroy a partially completed block structure. Children who are observing the new crab in the aquarium might be provided with books about crabs, paper on which to record their thoughts or observations, and charts to track whose turn it is to care for the crab. Children may need to see the teacher write a note inviting their parents to visit the class. They may, with the teacher's help, need to compose a message to another child, explaining their feelings about being denied a turn on the swing at recess time. They need to have experience in seeing their own words being recorded and hearing them read at a future time. Without coming to an understanding of the power of print, why would any child want to struggle with the hard work of learning to read and write? A real and personal reason for reading and writing makes the effort worthwhile.

Some of the greatest reasons children have for learning to deal with print (both reading it and writing it) are social in nature. The desire to communicate with someone else is a powerful purpose for using print. The desire to know is another powerful purpose. The purpose a reader has for engaging with a text will affect the way that reader reads. The strategies a reader uses will depend on what the reader wants to know and how much the reader already knows about the topic. The answers to these two questions will help the reader coordinate background knowledge and the use of the cueing systems (Vacca, Vacca, & Gove, 1991).

Recognizing Meaning

Children need printed material that is meaningful and predictable. Children learning to read and write need to know the printed material they are given says something. Adults read for information, pleasure, guidance, and other purposes, but certainly not just to practice the process of reading. Given materials that do not relate at all to their experience or do not contain language that is real to them, children find reading to be too much effort. They should not be expected to "read" nonsense words. (Playful language used in some books for children is an exception, of course. Such books create a context in which made-up or pretend words mirror the child's own playful experiences with language.) Some well-intentioned reading theorists have created tightly controlled vocabulary texts to teach children to read. In doing so, the creators of such material have ignored what children know about how language works *before* they entered school. In trying to make the language simple, they have often made it more difficult to read.

Predictable materials include pattern books (books with repetitive language patterns) and materials in which the language is predictable in the sense of sounding like real speech. If children are reading materials that describe feeding a hamster, they will be able to predict the word that is omitted from this sentence:

> The hamster, Speedy, ate some of the food pellets and hid some in
> the corner of his _____.

Contrast the task of reading from material that is sensible with that of reading

> The fan was on the _____.

when the missing word is not *floor* or *table* but *van.*

Emphasizing Message

Children need a teacher or parent who stresses meaning, not mechanics. Children learning language have had numerous experiences with adults who have been concentrating on their meaning rather than on the form in which they were expressed. In fact, adults assign intentionality to even very young babies. We act as if they meant to tell us they want food or a toy they can see or a chance to look out the window long before they can communicate much of that meaning. Children learning to read and write need teachers who respond to their intentions in using written messages, not to the technical precision with which they express themselves.

Young children need to know that teachers will respond to their attempts to read and write with an emphasis on what they mean. Four-year-olds who write random letters expect adults to respond with recognition, not to correct the form. If a child writes "is crem" on the family grocery list, he or she expects to get a treat, not a lesson on spelling. Children who say "Samuel gots three little kittens" when the text reads "Samuel has three little kittens" should receive approval for their ability to understand print rather than correction to achieve an exact match with the text. Even professional readers often make errors when reading aloud. Beginning readers need support for their attempts and a teacher who trusts that some errors in oral reading—those that do not change the meaning—are best ignored in most situations. When we correct children on every oral reading miscue, we are signaling them that word-by-word "perfect" reading is more important than meaning. This is not to say that perfect reading is never important. There are many situations in which perfect reading is necessary, for instance, in reading recipes, solving math problems, following directions to an unfamiliar place, and carrying out instructions for assembling a model. Initially, however, teachers should be sure to stress meaning rather than mechanics.

The Current Status of Reading Instruction

The U.S. government has authorized the testing of fourth graders, eighth graders, and twelfth graders in a number of areas taught in the public schools. This project is known as the *National Assessment of Educational Progress (NAEP)*. The most recent report on progress in reading was released in September 1993. Although some criticize the test, the data yield interesting information about the current status of reading instruction.

According to NAEP data, 59% of fourth graders, 69% of eighth graders, and 75% of twelfth graders reached at least the "basic" level of achievement. Smaller percentages reached the "proficient" level, and 2% to 4% reached the "advanced" level on the NAEP test of reading.

Support for the reading/writing/literature connection was found in the NAEP data. Fourth-grade students whose teachers reported heavy emphasis on literature-based reading instruction had higher average reading proficiency than students who received little or no such emphasis. A similar pattern was found for instructional emphasis on integrating reading and writing.

Teachers reported using a variety of materials in reading instruction. Forty-nine percent reported using a combination of both basal and trade books, 36% reported relying solely on basals, and 15% reported not using basal materials at all. Fifty-one percent of the fourth graders reported using worksheets and workbooks daily. Teachers reported that nearly 3 out of 4 students wrote about what they read on at least a weekly basis ("Analyzing the NAEP Data," 1993/1994).

Some critics take exception to the NAEP data. We suggest that as a teacher of reading you need to pay close attention to the NAEP results. The profession and the public will use these data to make judgments about how you and your colleagues are doing in bringing children to literacy. In a very real sense, judgments will be made about your understanding of the reading process and your ability to teach it, based on the performance of children in your school and school district.

Major Ideas in This Chapter

▼   The conditions that existed to facilitate fluency in oral language use should exist in classrooms to promote fluency in reading and writing. These conditions are immersion and demonstration accompanied by engagement, as well as expectation, responsibility, use, approximation, and response.

▼   Reading is a process in which the reader interacts with the ideas and language of the author in the re-creation of meaning. This creation of meaning is very much affected by the background knowledge and experience of the reader.

▼   The cueing systems are crucial to the creation of meaning. Graphophonic, semantic, syntactic, and schematic cues are used by the reader as the predicting, sampling, and integrating aspects of the reading process are used.

▼   Reading and writing are inverse processes that begin with the author's ideas and end, if successful, with the reader re-creating those ideas as modified by the reader's background experiences. Comprehension is the creation of meaning resulting from this interaction between the ideas of the author and the schemata of the reader.

▼   Children learning to read need to be able to form hypotheses about print, to acquire and use nonvisual information, to read predictable and meaningful texts, to have teachers who respond to their intentions more than their performance, and to learn the purposes and functions of print personally.

▼   Reading develops over time in stages that are observable but not always linear and sequential.

▼   Readers and writers engage in highly similar activities. Classroom activities should be structured to reinforce this similarity in ways that are developmentally appropriate for learners. Teachers should encourage children to use print in ways that have meaning and purpose for them. Teachers in whole-language classrooms create situations in which children use the processes of literacy in authentic ways.

▼   How teachers see the reading/writing processes has a profound effect on how they teach and therefore on how children view these processes.

Discussion Questions: Focusing on the Teacher You Are Becoming

1. A first-grade teacher in the building in which you are observing puts a poem on the board for the children to copy each morning and then hands out a packet of dittoed worksheets called "morning work" for them to do. Discuss the appropriateness of these activities in light of the reading/writing connection and the developmental nature of the reading/writing processes. What might be done instead?

2. Interview three young children (ages 5 to 7), asking them, "What is reading?" and "What do you do when you read?" Interview three older children (ages 8 to 11), asking them the same questions and adding, "What do you do when you are reading and you come to a word you don't know?" and "How would you help someone become a better reader?" Share the results of your interviews with your classmates and discuss these children's views of the reading process.

3. Discuss how your views of the reading process may have changed as a result of studying this chapter. What goals regarding reading instruction do you and your classmates now have for yourselves as teachers?

4. Revisit each of Cambourne's eight conditions for literacy learning and discuss specific evidence you would look for in classrooms to prove the conditions exist there.

Field-Based Applications

1. Plan three ways to include reading and writing in daily classroom routines.

2. Observe three teachers conducting reading lessons. Compare and contrast the lessons in terms of what you can infer about the teachers' views of the reading process.

3. Refer to Figure 2.2. Observe a novice reader/writer at work and see if you can verify the chart's ranking of attention to knowledge sources. Do the same with a proficient reader/writer.

4. Help each child write and read his or her own story about a recent classroom experience (or experience outside school). How fluently

were the children able to read the story? What does this tell you about the value of background experience in reading and writing?

5. Help children keep their own logs of the reading they are doing in a journal or on the computer. As the children mature, they can record much more extensive information about each book.

Chapter 3
The Writing Process

Chapter Overview

▼ Learning to write is very much like learning to speak and to read. It is a developmental process that moves through observable stages. Teachers must have a good understanding of these stages if they are to provide appropriate instruction.

▼ Reading and writing are closely connected. One reinforces the other. It is appropriate for children to write during the instructional time allocated to reading.

▼ Classroom environments may be structured to foster writing development. In such classrooms, use of oral language is encouraged and celebrated, children engage in activities that invite thinking, talking, reading, and writing, and literature is shared frequently. Children value each other's work, and the teachers value the work of children.

▼ Writing is a very complex, recursive process that consists of forming intentions, composing and drafting, correcting and publishing, and producing outcomes. Writers move back and forth across these phases as they produce a piece of writing.

It is a beautiful Tuesday morning. The sun is shining. The kids have been unusually eager to work today. You are feeling really good about the morning. You were even a little surprised when they so eagerly went to work on the books they are writing, but then you know how much they like to write. You have been taking dictation from some children while others were composing on their own. Now you are standing next to the door of the classroom just enjoying the excitement of the activity and feeling good about yourself as a teacher. Your reflections turn to the powerful connections between reading and writing.

1. *Writing and reading are closely connected. Students must experience and understand the connection.* Children need to understand that both reading and writing involve ideas. Just as they write ideas when they compose, they are also reading ideas when they read. Glance back at Figure 2.1 to be reminded of the reciprocal relationship between writing and reading discussed in Chapter 2.

69

2. *Children need practice reading material that is truly interesting to them.* Children are typically egocentric. Material they have written about their own experiences and thoughts is almost always of great interest to them. They truly enjoy reading their own writing. One teacher reported the joy in the children's voices when she returned stories they had dictated and she had typed. When they saw their writing efforts, they exclaimed, "These are *our* words!" When we create classroom libraries of the important books written by our students, we are providing a valuable source of interesting reading material for reading practice.

3. *The act of composing reinforces concepts important to reading comprehension.* The concepts of word, sentence, topic sentence, main idea, supporting details, sequence, and plot are all reinforced when children write. Reinforcement also occurs during writing conferences as child and teacher engage in important instructional dialogue about composing. All these concepts (and more) are central to good reading. In this way writing helps to promote reading comprehension.

4. *The act of writing strengthens reading ability.* Any of us who have encouraged disabled readers to write know that writing helps children improve their reading skills. Almost as if by magic, children who write enjoy increased success in decoding the printed symbol. The more they write, the better they can read. The research on the reading/writing connection supports this powerful link.

The Reading/Writing Connection

Teachers often observe that the words young children use in their own writing stay with them more readily than the words they encounter in reading textbooks. When children write or dictate as part of the reading program, they are constantly asking for words that are important to them. Bennett (1971) concluded that emotionality and meaningfulness account for their superior recall of their own words.

In their book entitled *Key Words to Reading*, Jeannette Veatch, Florence Sawicki, Geraldine Elliott, Eleanor Flake, and Janis Blakey (1979, pp. 38–39) very strongly state the argument in favor of making writing a part of the reading program: "Writing, by its very nature, is an analytical skill or ability. Therefore, the sooner a child can write independently, the sooner he can read independently. Once the writing ability is acquired, the problem of decoding words in reading is simplified." Veatch et al. also argue (p. 47) that the service words (markers such as *this, it, that, saw,* and *there*), often so difficult to absorb, are more readily learned by children who write as part of the reading program.

Perhaps nowhere has the case for writing as a way to learn reading been better presented than in Marie Clay's 1982 edition of *What Did I Write? Beginning Writing Behaviour*. She states, "The theories and experiments . . . suggest many links between early writing activities and the skills needed in learning to read." Some of the skills and concepts that can be learned are these:

▼   How to attend and orient to printed language

▼   How to organize one's exploratory investigation of printed forms

▼   How to tell left from right

▼   How to visually analyze letters and words

▼   What to study in a word so as to be able to reproduce it

▼   How to direct one's behavior in carrying out a sequence of movements needed in writing words and sentences.

Additional research evidence (Stotsky, 1983) shows that when teachers combine writing activities with the reading of student texts (such as social studies or science), both reading comprehension and retention are improved. Bearse (1992) demonstrated that when children were immersed as readers in a particular genre, certain aspects of that genre began appearing in their writing. In *Becoming a Nation of Readers*, Anderson and others (1985) noted that children should spend more time writing because it tends to promote better reading. Gillin (1994) found that essay writing about a topic before reading resulted in greater critical thinking during reading.

The Beginnings of Writing

Since the time that Chomsky (1971) suggested nonreaders should be writing, there has been a flurry of activity as researchers looked at young children and their writing. The resulting information has greatly expanded our view of what writing is and how it develops.

The more traditional view defined writing in terms mostly limited to handwriting. Children were expected to copy letters until they could successfully reproduce a close approximation of the teacher's model. Then they were expected to copy sentences. Copying exercises came from the handwriting text or from a verse or quotation on the board. Children's attempts at writing on their own were basically ignored and certainly not encouraged. Atkins (1984) reports hearing a teacher tell a young child's parents that the child needed to "do something constructive" with her time because she had wasted time writing in the margins of her worksheet. In light of the research

Children respond to authentic reasons for writing.

© 1994 George White

today, writing is generally defined in a much broader sense and includes the child's first efforts at making marks on paper—beginning with scribbles.

Developmental Stages

Parents of young children have known for years that children believe they can write. They have cleaned the results off walls and tables. One $3\frac{1}{2}$-year-old we know wrote all over a hall wall. She tried to convince her parents that her 9-month-old brother had done the writing. What gave her away? The only word spelled correctly was her brother's name! Such interest in writing has typically been ignored or dismissed as scribbling and viewed as unimportant in the scheme of instruction. Goodman and Altwerger (1981) found that when they asked 3-year-old children if they could write, the children would answer, "Of course," and make marks on paper they expected could be interpreted.

These same 3-year-olds claimed not to be able to read because they had not been taught to do so.

We now recognize that children construct their understanding of written language in a developmental sequence that is distinguishable and very similar for every child. As soon as children begin to make marks with writing instruments, they are beginning to learn about written language and how it works. The first stage in the development of writing is scribbling (Figure 3.1). Just as

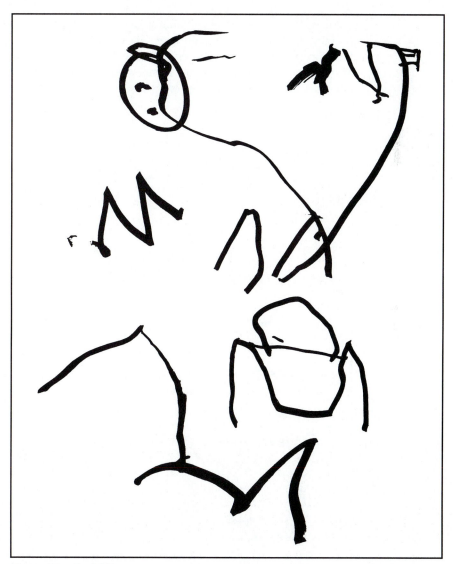

Figure 3.1—Scribbling

children babble before they use words, they scribble all kinds of forms before they learn which of those forms are letters and which are not.

By the linear repetitive stage, children have discovered that writing is usually horizontal and moves in a string across the page (Figure 3.2). Schickedanz (1987) found that children in this stage thought that a word referring to something larger had a longer string of forms than a word referring to something smaller. In other words, children looked for some concrete connection between words and their referents.

Even though there are slight variations in observations, most researchers do agree that the next stage is a random letter stage (Figure 3.3). Children learn which forms are acceptable as letters and use them in some random order to record words or sentences. They may produce a string of letters that have no relation to the sounds of the words they are attempting to record. They may also include some forms that are not recognizable as letters because their repertoire of letters is so limited.

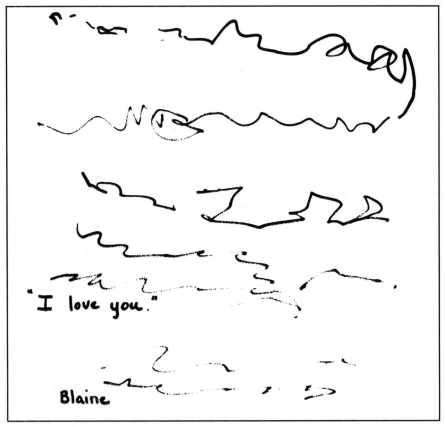

Figure 3.2—Linear Repetitive Writing

Figure 3.3—Random Letter Stage

In the stage of early phonemic writing (Figure 3.4), children begin to make the connection between letters and sounds. The beginning of this stage is often described as letter name writing because children write the letters whose name and sound are the same. This is when they are likely to write the word *you* with the letter "u." In time they begin to represent words with graphemes that reflect exactly what they hear. For example, they may use "hz" for *he's*.

As children gain more experience with the written language system, they begin to learn its conventions and to spell some words in conventional ways even though the spelling is not phonetic. A good example is the word *love*. Being exposed to this word so often, children begin very early to spell it in its conventional form. This stage of writing is called transitional: Children are moving from their phonetic spelling to standard or conventional spelling (Figure 3.5).

Children learning spoken language generalize rules, for example, that adding -*ed* produces the past tense of a verb. Similarly, children learning written language generalize that adding *e* to the end of a word indicates a long vowel sound. The child who drew this picture added the *e* to *boon*, then marked it out, perhaps reasoning that the two *o*'s produced the correct sound without the *e*.

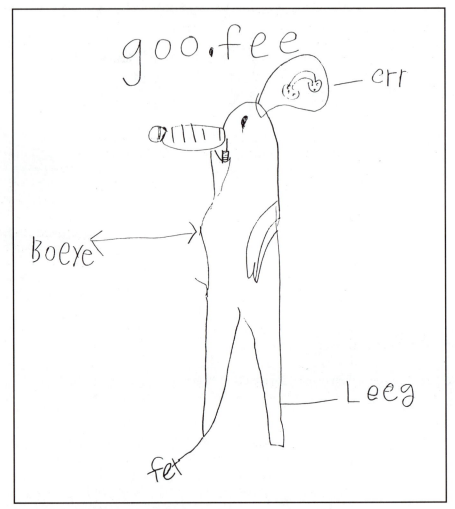

Figure 3.4—Early Phonemic Writing

Finally, children achieve mostly conventional spelling. Just as children move slowly from babbling to adult speech, they need time to adopt the conventions of written language. Children put considerable time and effort into mastering adult speech. Support from sensitive adults aids them in their task. Our hope is that children will have the same support as they proceed from scribbling to mature written language.

Discovery of Governing Principles

Clay (1982) describes several concepts and principles that children discover as they learn about written language. As you observe children's writing, you will recognize these writing behaviors. Children explore the **flexibility principle,** which describes "the limits within which each letter form may be varied and still retain its identity" (Clay, 1982, p. 63). The **inventory principle** refers to the observation that children often take stock of their own learning in a very systematic way, such as making lists of all the letter forms they know or all the words they can write (Figure 3.6). Clay defines the **recurring principle** as "the tendency to repeat an action" that contributes to the child's ability to form letters quickly and habitually. It becomes very helpful when the child realizes that "the same elements can recur in variable patterns" (Clay, 1982, p. 64). For example, a child may write, "I like Tom. I like Pedro. I like Alicia."

Finally, the **generating principle** describes what children do when, knowing some elements and some rules for combining them, they produce new statements—that is, statements which differ in some respect from models they have encountered (Figure 3.7). Such behavior is basic to the development of language because children will not hear someone else speak every

Figure 3.5—Transitional Stage

Figure 3.6—Inventory Principle: Child Displays Entire Repertoire

sentence they want to produce; they just know the elements and the rules for combining them. It is logical that they use this same technique when attempting to master written language systems.

Some concepts basic to written language have no relationship to the sounds of words and thus to spoken language. Among them are directionality, space around words, and the use of abbreviations. As children gain more experience, they must also learn to deal with page and book arrangements.

Directionality is the convention that in English, for example, writing begins on the left and moves to the right. Clay (1982) observes that children may temporarily ignore what they know about directionality when presented with the problem of a word they cannot fit on a line or a page. With experience, they learn to carry words over to the next line or page.

Children learning to leave spaces around words must deal with negative space (what is left out), a difficult concept. Some children attempt to handle the space by placing periods after each word, in an attempt to recognize spaces but to make them positive rather than negative. Abbreviations are understood only by children having clear concepts of letter and word and their interrelationships. The use of abbreviations usually signals a child's comprehension that words are constructed out of letters and that the letters of abbreviations "stand for" words and could be filled out or expanded into full forms (Clay, 1982).

Children do not make these discoveries about written language and its conventions without considerable experience exploring writing, forming hypotheses about how print works, and then getting feedback that verifies

Figure 3.7—Generating Principle: Child Produces New Statements

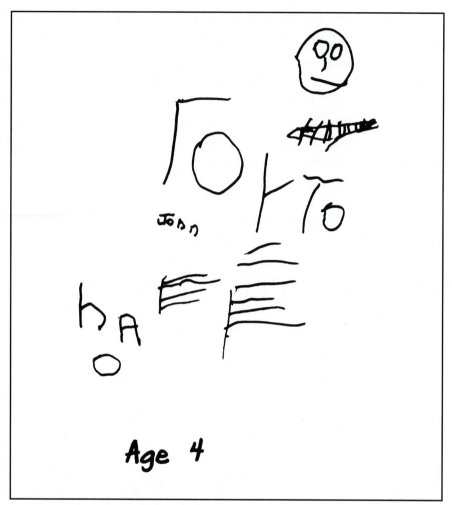

Figure 3.8—Experimentation with the Flexibility Principle

their guesses. A child's exploration of the flexibility principle illustrates this need very well (Figure 3.8). The child writes an *F* and shows it to an adult, who confirms it is an *F*. Now the child adds two more cross strokes and asks if it is an *F*. The answer is no. Perhaps the child then turns it on its side or backward. Eventually the child determines exactly how much variation is allowed in the form while still qualifying as an *F*. To make learning as successful as possible, the child needs to write frequently, with understanding adults nearby who respond to the child's accomplishments and know the ability to write with adult conventions is learned over a period of time. No child should be expected to write perfectly at first, any more than a child is expected to speak perfectly at first.

The Current Status of Writing Achievement

Critics of current American education have consistently pointed out our shortcomings in the teaching of writing. Frankly, we believe today's high school and college students have difficulty in writing because they were not taught how to write in elementary and middle school—and possibly not in high school. Secondary schools cannot be expected to make up the deficit in writing skills caused by a lack of prior instruction.

How serious is the problem? The National Assessment of Educational Progress in Writing reported that even the best students who are able to write informative and narrative pieces have trouble preparing arguments and evidence in persuasive writing ("New NAEP Report," 1994). Fewer than 20% of students can write at an "elaborated" or well-developed and detailed level. The NAEP test measured the performance of 30,000 fourth-, eighth- and twelfth-grade students in persuasive writing, narrative writing, and informative writing. Highlights of the report include the following:

▼ Teachers in top-performing schools report that they often ask students to write about literature and to choose their own topics.

▼ Students in top-performing schools report that they are asked to plan their writing, write more than one draft, and focus on the mechanics of writing.

▼ Effective writing instruction includes an emphasis on the teaching of the writing process; integrating reading, writing, and language; and a focus on quality and coherence in writing.

▼ About half of the eighth graders and one third of the twelfth graders reported rarely ever being given writing assignments of three or more pages.

In 1990 when students were asked to provide a written response to a reading selection, they exhibited great difficulty in composing thoughtful analyses or interpretations. Less than 15% of 9-year-olds and less than one third of 13-year-olds and 17-year-olds were able to construct a satisfactory written response (Valencia, Heibert, & Kapinus, 1992).

A study conducted by the Center for the Study of Writing (1991) reported that most writing assignments in school focus on skill instruction and grammar drills rather than on real composition, that is, determining audience and purpose, organizing information, rough drafting, revising, editing, and publishing.

The limited progress in improving writing ability in America's children might be explained, at least in part, by the struggle American teachers are having in deciding *how* to teach writing. A study (Applebee, 1990b) examined National Assessment of Educational Progress data to address the relationships between student outcomes and instructional practices. The report concluded that in both reading and writing instruction teachers seem to have effected a compromise between educational practices that are treated in the professional literature as incompatible, such as using wonderful children's literature to teach reading and having children do workbook pages from a basal reading series. We believe reading and writing instruction will improve dramatically when teachers have formulated a strong philosophy of instruction that is built on a solid knowledge base. This philosophy of instruction will then guide teaching so such compromises in educational practice will not occur. But change is very slow. Foertsch (1992) reports that despite extensive research suggesting that effective reading instruction includes moving from an emphasis on workbooks to combining reading and writing activities, schools are slow to make the change.

A 1987 report ("Newsnotes," 1987) strongly recommended that teachers should not just correct grammar and punctuation on writing assignments but also focus on a student's ideas and organization. We believe this recommendation is extremely important. It may well be the pivotal point in improving writing skills in today's and tomorrow's students. In fact, we suspect too many teachers have made too few writing assignments and then essentially given students no feedback on their writing. Telling a student that a piece of writing is worth a 75 or a B+ *in no way* helps that student improve his or her writing. Students need frequent writing assignments on which they get constructive feedback that can be used in revising and reworking a writing piece. Writing instruction will improve as teachers learn to evaluate ideas and organization as part of viewing writing as a process. Let's explore the myriad of ways we can encourage writing growth and development in the classroom.

The Act of Writing: Making It Authentic for Children

Before we examine the process of writing, pause and consider the kinds of writing you have done in the last week. Make a list of the *kinds* of writing you have done. Now revisit your list and write beside each kind of writing you noted the *purpose* for which you did that writing. Finally, note the *audience* for whom each type of writing was done.

Our prediction is that you have produced a wide variety of kinds of writing within the past week for known audiences and for authentic purposes. By "authentic purposes" we mean the real purposes for which lifelong writers write—to explain, to persuade, to record events, to command, to amuse, to tell stories, to invent, to find out, to share opinions, and so on.

Now consider the kinds of writing you know that children do in school. Do these school kinds of writing have the authenticity that your writing has? If not, there is something wrong with the kinds of writing children are doing in school. We suspect that no one reading this text has, as an adult, copied someone else's sentences from a letter and circled all the nouns or completed the writing of a story from an opening paragraph someone else wrote. Why? Because that would be a silly thing to do. We would only be concerned about nouns or other parts of speech if we were trying to improve a piece of our own writing. When we write, we write on topics of our choice and within our interests. We don't finish a piece of writing started by others.

The writing we do with children should always be characterized by *a variety of authentic kinds of writing, purposely written for a known audience.* These are the criteria by which we judge classroom activities in writing. These are also the criteria by which we engage children in the writing process.

The Nature of the Writing Process: A Complex, Recursive Process

In the first edition of this text we stated that the writing process consists of six steps: prewriting, composing the rough draft, getting response and making revisions, editing, completing the final draft, and sharing or presenting. We then presented a detailed discussion of each of these steps. Despite our explanation that the process was not linear, the outline of steps appeared much more linear than we liked.

We have been very impressed by the work of Jan Duncan and Ro Griffiths and others with the New Zealand Ministry of Education (1992) who have articulated the writing process in quite a different way than the traditional six steps. The New Zealand curriculum document *Dancing with the Pen: The Learner as a Writer* is available in the United States. The following discussion of the recursive writing process is adapted from it.

Describing the writing process as a set of steps such as prewriting, rough drafting, response, revision, and so on, very much implies the process is linear. One decides what to write, puts words on paper, gets a response to that construction, and then modifies the piece. In fact, writing is recursive. The writer decides, for example, what to write, begins the piece, changes plans for the writing, and decides on another purpose. Then she begins writing again. Long before the piece is finished, words are deleted and thoughts are reexpressed in different language. Sometimes, as the piece unfolds, the purpose, design, or even the audience may change. Therefore pieces of writing may be abandoned along the way and never reach their intended audience.

The New Zealand (NZ) writing model has recognized a wider range of writer behavior than our original six-step model. The first phase of the NZ model is forming intentions.

Forming Intentions

Dancing with the Pen (1992, p. 24) defines forming intentions as follows:

Children can more easily be immersed in writing when the necessary tools are readily available.

© Michael Hagan

During this stage, the writer clarifies the purpose for writing, gathers information, and tests ideas about content and form in relation to the audience proposed. Forming intentions for writing can involve the writer in thinking, talking, drawing, remembering, reflecting, searching for more information and organising all this into rough sections or sequences. This may take place before, during and after the actual drafting.

Forming intentions consists of choosing topics, determining the audience, finding out, selecting and ordering information, and selecting appropriate forms.

Choosing Topics

Children will write well only about what they know. Authors should be free to select a topic drawn from their own unique background of experience. They should be encouraged to think, observe, experience, and talk with you and other students about what they *might* write. Our experience has shown that the more children can talk about what they might write, sharing those ideas in a group, the more diverse and detailed is the writing within that group.

Teachers honor their students as writers when they encourage them to make their own topic decisions and to ask their own research questions. In choosing topics, you may want to engage children in conducting research, brainstorming, and looking at books, films, or drama to help them make a selection and to foster a growing sense of "I know what I want to say" about that topic. We suggest that as you talk with children about what they might write, you engage them in sensory awareness: "How do you think the boy will feel in your story? What words can you use to describe the way the grease felt when the detective touched it? Close your eyes and imagine how the candy shop smelled. What words could you use to help your reader know that smell?" Nurturing a child's sense of command of the subject will build excitement for the writing. McAuliffe (1994), in studying the writing of second graders, found that *intent* was critical in the process of written communication. The greater the students' intent to share meaning, the greater their efforts at writing with clarity.

Determining the Audience

Reexamine the list of kinds of writing you made at the beginning of this discussion. It is likely you knew the audience (even if it was only you) for each kind of writing you listed. Real writers do not write without knowing the audience. Children should never write without the audience in mind. It is very telling to visit a classroom where writing is being done and say to a child, "Who is the audience for this piece?" If the response is "I don't know" or "the teacher," chances are great that not enough consideration has been given to determining audience.

When we are discussing children's purposes for writing we should challenge them to consider their audience. Certainly sometimes audience will be self or the teacher, but children will often write for other known, but perhaps unseen, audiences. Good writers always write with their audience in mind—to respect that audience, to meet that audience's needs. So children as writers must begin to make these considerations. As children define purposes for writing they should also define the audience.

Finding Out, Selecting, and Ordering Information

During this phase of the writing process writers are considering what they know about the topic, what they need to research about the topic, and how they can best organize the information to make it clear to their audience.

Here children are willing to get assistance from classmates, the teacher, the librarian, parents, and others in finding answers to questions and thinking about how to organize the information. Very young writers may draw to help them organize their thoughts; more mature writers may make diagrams or outlines to organize information. As with any aspect of the writing process, it is critical that you *demonstrate* these important skills frequently for your students. Here is where the important study skills so often taught in isolation can be integrated with the reading/writing program. It is as children are collecting information for a writing piece that they should learn and practice such skills as skimming, scanning, note taking, and using glossaries, tables of content, and indexes. Here is where interviewing, observing, questioning, and summarizing come so critically into play.

Selecting Appropriate Forms

Consider the kinds of writing you listed earlier. Commonly students list letters, diary writing, reports, term papers, letters to editors, instructions, explanations, and lists. As a teacher you will need to introduce your students to these many different forms and more. Often this is done through sharing various genres of literature and discussing the form or through mini-lessons. At other times you may demonstrate writing of various forms and encourage students to follow your model. Children must be helped to ask the important question, "Given my purpose and audience, what is the best form for my writing to take?" The ability to answer this question in a variety of ways develops slowly over time in a text-rich environment.

Composing and Drafting

The six-step model of the writing process suggests the rough drafting stage is where words are put on paper and that nothing is done with them during this drafting process. *Dancing with the Pen* (1992, p. 24) describes the composing and drafting phase much more accurately in terms of what real writers do:

> As writers' intentions become represented on paper, they frequently reread the text to establish how their work is developing with regard to the original plan. Departures from the original plan may be made and, during this stage of writing and revising, writers may attend to details such as correcting spelling, punctuation, or grammar. However, concern with changes to surface features at this stage may hinder the composing process, as attention is diverted from the meaning of the writing.
>
> The composing and drafting stage of the writing process covers two apparently conflicting aims. The first is the need to write fluently, speedily, crashing through technical barriers such as handwriting, spelling, and punctuation, and getting things down as best one can from one's plan. Second is the over-riding need to convey ideas successfully, involving playing with words, testing them to their utmost for clarity and inventiveness, wrestling with

them and their meanings to enrich expression and make communication work. (p. 55)

Clearly, in this view of the writing process, the writer is not simply drafting, but is considering the unfolding of the piece as the drafting is going along, and is willing to make changes in this process. Here the author switches back and forth between rehearsal (trying the words out mentally) and composition (writing them down). The writing here is often tentative and exploratory: "How do I want to say that? I'll try it like this. No, I don't like the sound of that. Here, let's try it this way." Good writers shift continuously between rehearsal and composition. You should model this process over and over again on the chalkboard so children see how the shifting works: thinking, writing, crossing out, writing again, thinking, changing. Rough drafts should be double spaced to facilitate changes.

Young authors must learn the difficult lesson (which we have all tried to avoid) that there is no such thing as a "finished" first draft. Rarely, if ever, is a first draft done well enough to be a last draft. Almost any piece of writing can be improved. Knowing the first draft will seldom be the last draft encourages some children to take risks they otherwise would not take. However, we believe children should have the choice of whether or not to take a rough draft any further through the writing process. All of us who have ever tried to write know that sometimes we truly dislike a rough draft and do not want to carry on with it. Young authors have an equal right to abandon work they prefer not to complete.

A second important lesson about rough drafts is that it is appropriate for children to use words they may not know how to spell. Limiting children to words they can spell reduces dramatically the quality of their writing. Children who are encouraged to use the words they choose, even if they have to invent the spelling, will produce much more interesting writing. Their improvisations represent their best judgments about spelling, and frequent application of spelling knowledge while writing encourages spelling competency (Gentry & Gillet, 1993).

Conferring with students who are in the composing and drafting phase can lead to improved writing, a payoff that many feel warrants the investment of time. Drafting conferences can be very short—one to two minutes. They involve a quick reading of the draft and asking a key question or two to help the author think about content or organization. "Kelly, who do you think will want to read this?" "Josh, do you really want to tell your reader this much about the clues before the detective begins to solve the mystery?" "Amy, you have been writing about the party. What is going to happen next?" "Is there anything I can help with?" The focus of the conference during the rough draft stage is to help children get their ideas onto the paper. Graves (1983) offers these four principles for helping children during conferences:

1. Follow the child. Base what you say on what the child last said.

Sharing student-authored texts underscores how much the teacher values the work.
© Michael Hagan

2. Ask questions you think the child can answer. When you ask questions first that you are sure the child can answer, you can then follow with more challenging questions.

3. Help the child to focus. Children often know so much about a topic that they simply have too much to say, and then they get off the track. Questions that help children narrow and focus are important here.

4. Offer a final reflection. Say something to the child that encourages his or her continued effort to get words on paper.

It is imperative that during the composing and drafting phase the focus is on the creation and communication of meaning, not on the mechanics. Once the meaning is clearly conveyed, the mechanics can be repaired. Now content and organization become the focus, with some attention to mechanics. There are many ways to handle this stage. The goals are for the author to respond to his or her own writing and to get feedback from others. To the author, the steps in this phase might look like this:

1. Reread the draft to myself. Does it say what I wanted to say? Make revisions as I see the need for them.

2. Share my draft with a friend and/or the teacher. Then check to see if the reader understands what I meant to say. Make revisions as I see the need for them or as suggested.

3. Go back over my draft to see all the ways I can make it better.

Revision groups are a helpful way for children to get feedback from their peers on the writing.

Revision Groups

Ideally the class is divided into revision groups of six children each who remain together throughout the school year. Every child who is able to function in a group is placed in one, and others are permitted to join (or rejoin) when ready. The stability of the revision group is important so the group may evolve a sense of group identity and develop a high level of trust. The task of the revision group is to look at both content and mechanics. Revision groups can be very effective in giving young authors good feedback on their writing. However, the success of the revision group totally depends on the care you take in preparing them for the task and in monitoring their work on an ongoing basis. We believe children in third grade and above can learn to function effectively in revision groups.

These are the procedures for the group:

1. Each member reads his or her composition aloud to the group.

2. After a piece is read, each member names at least one thing he or she especially liked about the composition and suggests one or more things to the author as an improvement. Children should be encouraged to make comments of this sort: "I like the way you got your reader's attention early in the story. The dialogue sounds just like the way the characters would really speak, I think. I think you gave too many hints about the solution of the mystery too early in the story. Can you tell us more about how the graveyard looked in the dark?"

3. The author records the comments on the back of the last page of the composition or within the composition at appropriate places.

4. The author asks the group if anyone has further comments or suggestions.

5. Two members of the group exchange papers and read very carefully for mechanics.

In practice, the revision group need not operate in the lockstep fashion this list suggests. You and your students can modify the steps to your liking. As the level of trust grows within the group and as the group gains experience in conducting the revision sessions, you will see tremendous improvement in the comments and suggestions and, in turn, in the writing products of the group.

To a very large extent, the success of a revision group depends on the guidance it gets from you in conducting step 2. You must carefully teach writers the kinds of things to listen for and to say. At first, they will need frequent reminders and reinforcement. You can help by hanging a chart on the wall with suggestions of things to look for and to comment on during editing group time. Marjorie Frank (1979, p. 110) has suggested these emphases in editing with young children or new writers:

▼   Substituting stronger words (more colorful, specific)

▼   Rearranging words within a sentence

▼   Expanding sentences

▼   Cutting apart a short paragraph to reshuffle sentences for a different sound or meaning

▼   Making up better titles

▼   Changing endings

▼   Adding one detail to the ad or article or story.

Frank suggests (p. 111) that older children or more experienced writers in revision groups should work toward these aims:

▼   Revising whole pieces

▼   Coordinating ideas within paragraphs

▼   Varying sentence length and structure

▼   Examining word use, using specific and/or vivid words

▼ Eliminating overused words and expressions

▼ Making effective transitions

▼ Appealing to specific audiences

▼ Adapting form and style to a particular purpose

▼ Inventing exciting beginnings and strong conclusions

▼ Creating moods

▼ Incorporating dialogue into the writing

▼ Arranging details in logical order

▼ Supporting statements with specific details

▼ Eliminating unimportant words or phrases.

With the completion of the revision group's work, the author is ready to proceed to the next step in the writing process: correcting and publishing.

Correcting and Publishing

The New Zealand writing model has two aspects to the correcting and publishing section; one is proofreading and the other is publishing.

Proofreading

Here the focus shifts from making the meaning clear to correcting mistakes in the conventions of punctuation and spelling. The writer checks on facts, quotations, references, and diagrams to be sure all are correct. We embrace the New Zealand conception that any writing to be read by others should be correct. This is a serious point of contention among American educators. The steps in proofreading may take a variety of forms:

1. Finish my rough draft.

2. Read my writing to correct the errors I can find. (Here is where a red pen may be helpful. Authors use a red pen to mark the corrections they can make. That makes it easy for you to see their progress.)

3. Find a partner for partner editing.

4. Follow all the steps on the partner editing chart.

5. Make all the corrections I can make.

6. Take my draft to an editing committee.

7. Make final corrections.

Partner Editing

We have found the following procedures work in partner editing:

1. Find a partner.

2. Exchange papers.

3. Read your partner's paper silently.

4. At the bottom or on the back of the paper, write
   a. something you liked about the paper (not handwriting);
   b. something that could be improved (not neatness or crossing t's);
   c. a list of misspelled words spelled correctly.

5. Show punctuation corrections in the margins.

6. After you have done steps 4 and 5, read the paper aloud to the author and then read your a, b, and c. Discuss with the author why you made the comments you did. If the writer and you cannot agree on what needs improvement, then ask a third person. If there is still no agreement, then take it to the teacher.

7. Return the paper to the owner.

8. The author makes the suggested revisions and corrections and then prepares to write the final draft.

The success of a partner editing procedure depends on how well you prepare your students before they try it. It is important to post the list of steps prominently in the classroom. Go over the steps with the whole class several times so everyone understands the meaning and importance of each step. The first few times you may find it helpful to walk the class through the procedure step by step.

Editing Committees

Editing committees are small groups of from three to five students who are charged with a single editing task. The task might be to read rough drafts to

Figure 3.9—Candidate for Membership on the Comma Committee

Source: Reprinted with special permission of King Features Syndicate.

check for complete sentences or to read for proper ending punctuation. Perhaps, thinking of Billy in the cartoon (Figure 3.9), the task would be to check for commas. Billy belongs on the Comma Committee because he is really interested in commas and likes using them. He needs a little fine tuning of his understanding of the use of commas, but we suspect he can learn very quickly to use them properly. You will find other children who are using commas correctly or need only a little reinforcement to do so. These children should be on the Comma Committee.

We suggest the following steps in using editing committees:

1. Select the writing (composition or mechanical) skill or skills you wish to highlight next in your year-long writing plan.

2. Teach a lesson on the selected skill to those children who need the instruction.

3. Check writing samples following the lesson to identify those children who are correctly using the highlighted skill or, with a little attention from you, soon will be.

4. Identify from three to five children who will serve on the editing committee. You might want to have them spend some time sitting at an "editors' table" during part of the writing period. Let them create hats or badges that name their committee, or hang a sign above the table.

5. Instruct children to edit their own work first using a red pen.

6. Ask authors in your class to submit their rough drafts to the editing committee after they have completed self-editing.

Work with partner editing or with a revision group could follow the work of the editing committee. You might have more than one editing committee at work at any given time. Editing committees involve many children in the editing process and elevate the concern for correctness to an appropriate level. During the year, each child should have the opportunity to serve on one or more editing committees.

What to Edit

Learning what to look for in the editing process should be an outgrowth of a series of lessons over the year. Techniques to cover in those lessons include (but are not limited to) capitalization, punctuation, spelling, structural form, sentences, paragraphs, grammar, vocabulary, and composition. At any stage in the editing process, the focus should be on *some* of these points rather than all of them. As writing skill improves, you can add more and more editing checkpoints and expect children to make corrections. Meanwhile, you may have to act as copy editor much of the time. By this we mean that you simply correct some of the errors as you type the final copy—or ask the school secretary or a parent volunteer to provide this service. The table in Figure 3.10 shows some standard editing marks. We suggest that you make a large chart of these to display in your classroom and teach your students the meaning of each mark. You will be amazed at how well students will be able to use them in time. Check your school district's curriculum guide to see which editing marks should be introduced at each grade level.

Frankly, getting editing done with a group of children is a very difficult task. You can easily feel overwhelmed when a dozen children all need your editing attention at one time. To help you in this important task, we offer some suggestions:

1. Stagger the beginning of writing activities so the children are at different stages in the writing process at any one time. Some children may be

Function	Mark	Example
Delete		The bird flew out of the window.
Insert	∧	The weather today is cold and rainy.
Paragraph indent	¶	¶ Dolphins are not fish. They are mammals.
Capitalize	≡	I grew up in bangor, Maine.
Add period	⊙	The child lived in a cottage high in the mountains⊙
Add comma	∧	I have two cats a dog and a parakeet.
Add apostrophe	⋎	My brothers name is Richard.

Figure 3.10—Editing Marks

doing artwork to illustrate their stories while some are researching ideas; some are creating first drafts while others are editing. Not everyone will need your attention so desperately at the same time.

2. Do not plan to do all the editing yourself. We suspect that many experienced teachers would be ashamed to admit how many student drafts piled up on their desks awaiting their editing attention until the author lost interest in (or forgot about!) the piece. You cannot do the whole job yourself. If you are fortunate, you will have volunteers to help. In some schools, arrangements are made for older students to help younger students; some schools have a publishing house where the students can get help. Parents and other community members volunteer time to work in the publishing house, assisting children in editing and bookbinding.

3. Use self-editing and peer editing. Encourage students to read their own writing carefully, looking for errors and strengths. After correcting the errors they find, they have a friend read the work aloud to them. Children will frequently hear mistakes when someone reads their writing aloud that they overlooked when they read it themselves.

Deciding what to correct and what to ignore for the present is certainly one example of the art rather than the science of teaching. Much depends on the child's age and previous experience with writing. Too much editing may discourage the budding writer, and too little may not challenge the writer as learner of conventions. One rule of thumb says for the very youngest writers, do not attempt corrections; for experienced kindergarteners, one correction per project is enough, and so on. For beginning writers, corrections should be made with the child's permission. One might say, "Juan, we usually spell 'there' *t-h-e-r-e*. So that no one will be confused by this word, do you want to change the spelling here in your story?" As children learn about various conventions, they can be marked for correction in their writing. By the time children leave elementary school they should correct spelling, sentence structure, agreement, and paragraphing errors. They should be able to write a final draft that is correct by adult standards.

Publishing

The final stage is the "getting it perfect" stage. Taking into consideration all editorial suggestions, the author prepares the final polished draft. The author makes final decisions about how the work will appear on the page, then carefully copies the work and proofreads the copy. This draft represents the author's very best work.

We strongly recommend that if children are doing the work by hand, they make only one final copy. Permit children to use erasable pens and/or correction fluid, to glue paper over an error, or even to draw a single line through an error. Although we refer to this stage as the "getting it perfect" stage, we all need to recognize that young hands are going to make mistakes. We have too often seen interest in writing destroyed by making children copy a final draft over and over until it is perfect.

Many teachers and students like the ease of doing the final draft using a word processor. In fact, in many classrooms students write the original rough draft on the computer and do all revising and editing using the word processing program.

Having decided to publish a final draft, a child needs ready access to the materials and tools of publication. Many teachers set up a publishing corner in the classroom. More and more schools are creating "publishing houses" staffed by volunteers who assist children in doing bookbinding and preparing other forms of presentation. Figure 3.11 shows how a school's publishing house might look. Made from refrigerator cartons, held together with large pop rivets, the publishing house could be set up in the school library or a classroom. The publishing house contains all the things children need to publish or otherwise present their work; for example, computers and word processing programs, typewriters, art supplies for bookbinding and illustration, pens, pencils, marking pens, scissors, crayons, paper cutter, and spiral binder.

Bookbinding is becoming more and more popular as a way of publishing a child's writing. Instructions for bookbinding are presented in Appendix A.

Children need to write *daily*. Recall that it is only through constructive feedback and revision that a child's writing skill grows. In some classrooms the editing and sharing/presenting processes are so protracted that children

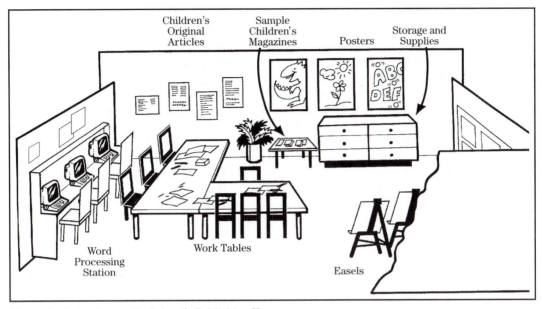

Figure 3.11—Features of a School's Publishing House

publish only two pieces in a school year. Wise teachers are cautious in ensuring that no one publishing effort takes too much time. Graves (1983) warns that publishing two pieces in one year does not constitute a writing program for a child. When we allow a child to write only two pieces in a grading period, we have robbed that child of chances to grow in writing as surely as if we had allowed the child to "fill in the blanks" all the time and called that our writing program!

Writing Portfolios

How is the decision made regarding which of a child's efforts should be published? We believe in making it a collaborative decision between the child and the teacher, weighted in the child's favor. Although it is rare that a child should be permitted to decide *not* to write, it should be commonplace for the child to decide *what* to write—and what to publish. Each child should have a writing portfolio in which to place each rough draft and keep work in progress. The portfolio can be as simple as a manila folder kept in a cardboard box or as fancy as you wish to have children make them. Children should be permitted (taught and encouraged) to select from the rough drafts in the portfolio those that should be taken through the entire writing process.

If writing samples from throughout the year are kept in the portfolio, you will have a record of children's writing development. It is great fun on the last day of school to have children look at the writing they did at the start of the school year. While taking delight in their growth in writing, the children will protest loudly that they didn't write "that baby stuff!" Similar use may be made of a daily log or journal. On a recent school visit, a first grader proudly showed us his journal, rejoicing in the strides he had taken in his writing since the beginning of the year. We took great pleasure in hearing him read two of his most recently published books.

The writing samples in the portfolio can be evaluated against criteria established by the faculty in your school for clarity, content, and mechanics. You could establish the criteria you value (*value* is at the heart of the word *evaluation*) for emergent writers, developing writers, and fluent writers. These criteria, then, could be used to evaluate selected pieces across the year.

Figure 3.12 illustrates the evaluation of one piece of writing by the teacher against criteria established by the faculty for meaning, structure, and conventions of writing. You will see that the teacher evaluated meaning using the criteria of quality of ideas, clarity of ideas, and relevance of the form to the purpose. In terms of structure the teacher looked at organization, unity, and sequence. With regard to conventions, the piece was evaluated for spelling, usage, and punctuation. Evaluation criteria drawn from the curriculum across the year could be used to periodically evaluate a piece of writing from the child's portfolio. The piece and the written evaluation could become a permanent piece of the portfolio, documenting growth over time.

TITLE	**Meaning**	**Structure**	**Conventions**
	ideas	organization	spelling
	clarity	unity	usage
	relevance of form	sequence	punctuation
"MY FAMILY"	*Ideas are clearly expressed and easy to understand, although not well developed.*	*Sequenced from initial idea; all statements tie into initial statement.*	*Simple use of comma; not using apostrophe of possession.*

Figure 3.12—A Teacher's Evaluation of a Piece of Writing from a Child's Portfolio

Source: Adapted from Margaret Hayes, Ministry of Education, Auckland, New Zealand.

A chronology of writing growth is only one of the uses of the writing portfolio. Other uses serve you, the student, and the parents:

1. The portfolio is a diagnostic tool for you. By quickly glancing through the portfolios, you can determine which writing skills to focus on next. You can also determine candidates for small skill groups or editing committees.

2. Children can be guided to examine recent writing samples in the portfolio and set some personal writing goals. The goals can be listed on the inside cover of the portfolio and checked off as they are reached. We recommend a two-column sheet stapled inside the folder cover. One column is headed "Things I Am Doing Well as a Writer"; the second column is headed "What I Need to Work on Next." In Manchester, New Hampshire, the use of portfolios is guided by the belief that readers and writers know more about their own abilities and progress than anyone else. Therefore, they should be the prime evaluators of themselves and their work (Hansen, 1992b).

3. The portfolio is a tool for you to use in parent conferences. Your selection of pieces from the portfolio can demonstrate a child's development in the writing process. Include an explanation of the writing portfolio in your "back to school night" presentation of your writing program to parents. They will see the importance of the portfolio and understand why their children will not be bringing home everything they write.

Outcomes

The final phase of the New Zealand writing model is outcomes—sharing audience response. It is important for young writers to see their writing reach its intended audience and to get feedback from that audience. Here the author seeks the response of readers. Writers learn to accept constructive criticism of their work, and readers learn to respond to the writing of others without offending. The goal here is for writers to look forward to the responses of their readers, to know they will grow as writers, feel good about their writing, and see communication improve.

As we have described it, the writing process is not a simple one. But neither is it so complex as to be beyond the reach of children. Figure 3.13 summarizes the important aspects of the process.

In this chapter we have underscored the need for writing to be a part of the reading program. Further, we have insisted that writing be seen as a process—an ongoing, recursive process—in which children have many opportunities to select what they write and then polish and publish that writing. Children need frequent constructive feedback on their writing from a variety of audiences if their writing is to improve. We sincerely believe the writing program must focus on the *process* rather than on the *product*.

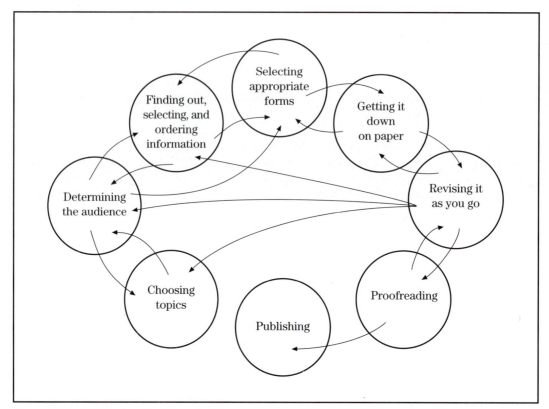

Figure 3.13—Writing Is a Recursive Process

What About Spelling?

Although this is not a textbook on the teaching of the language arts, it seems no discussion of writing can ignore the issue of spelling instruction. The debate centers around whether or not to teach spelling, and to a lesser degree how to teach spelling.

Krashen (1993) reviewed studies of spelling accuracy dating from 1897 that show consistently high levels of spelling competence, and concluded that such competence could not occur from formal instruction alone. Krashen further concluded that even if teaching the rules of spelling worked, they would not be of much use because students do not learn them very well. Some evidence exists that writing improves spelling ability, but no one could learn to spell all of the words fluent writers use from successive approximations in writing. Collins (1980) has shown that the more meaningful reading children do, the better they can spell. The 1992 National Assessment of Education Progress found a mutually beneficial relationship when children engage in both reading and writing activities. Spelling instruction alone, writing activity alone, and reading alone do not account for competence in spelling. However, it is more likely that spelling is acquired in a combination of ways—through reading and writing (Krashen, 1993). This leads us to believe that elementary teachers should take a multifaceted approach to spelling that is tied to the reading and writing children are doing. In fact, teachers play a critical role in the spelling development of children (O'Flahavan & Blassberg, 1992). We recommend the following aspects of spelling instruction:

▼ If working with emergent writers, teachers should identify a list of 20 words that first and second graders should be able to spell by the end of each grade. While no formal spelling instruction should be given on these words, the children should be tested on their ability to spell them four times during the school year. Our experience tells us that these four spelling tests will clearly document the developmental nature of spelling, and will be powerful tools in parent/teacher/student conferences.

▼ Because writing contributes to spelling ability, there should be links between the words children are trying to write and the words they learn to spell. We recommend that each week during a writing conference the teacher and child examine recent writing drafts to identify words which were *almost* spelled correctly. These words that children have wanted to write are going to be the easiest to learn because they are almost correct. Each child would then have a list of three to five words that are uniquely his or hers to learn that week. When the teacher and child find these words correctly spelled in a piece written by the child, they are crossed off the list as mastered.

▼ Teachers at each of the elementary grade levels should decide which of the words most frequently used in writing should be mastered at each grade level. High-frequency word lists have been put into handbook form for use at various grade levels (Sitton, 1990). Give the lists to children and make the expectations clear that these words are to be correctly spelled in their work. In finished writing products these words will be correctly spelled. The teacher and child can cross each word off the list when they have been successfully used in daily writing.

▼ Remember that spelling, like reading and writing, is a developmental process similar to learning to talk (Wilde, 1990). Therefore, it is critical that Cambourne's conditions for literacy learning discussed in Chapter 2 be in place in your classroom. When children are immersed in text production, they are practicing that critical ability of going from sound to symbol—to encode our language. Their successive approximations are as important here as they were in practicing oral language. You will see them take responsibility for the refinement of their approximations as they use their spelling to make their writing more acceptable to their known audience. They benefit from the demonstrations of accurate spelling when they read and when you demonstrate writing for them. Your response to their spelling efforts must indicate your desire to help them become better spellers and that you fully expect them to master spelling.

Bodycott (1993) describes the work of one fourth-grade teacher whose spelling program reflects Cambourne's conditions for literacy learning. The teacher, "Mr. D," has each of his students keep a spelling folder. The front of the folder reflects the teacher's beliefs about spelling in three statements: "Spelling Is for Writing; Learn Those Words You Need to Use; and Standard Spelling Is Important." Two sections make up the spelling folder. One is "Words of Interest." Here students choose words from a variety of sources: approximations discovered in proofreading, interesting words they discover in reading or discussions that they might want to use in writing, or words frequently misspelled in other curriculum areas. Words may be added to this section at school or at home. Each entry is dated and accompanied by a sentence illustrating the meaning of the word.

These "Words of Interest" lists form individual pools of words from which children select words each week (minimum of five) for revision in their writing. They meet with Mr. D on the suitability of the words selected. Following successful revision the words are initialed by the student and then recorded in the folder's second section, "Words to Use."

Words entered into the "Words to Use" section are alphabetically organized and become a cumulative record of the child's spelling success. The thesaurus is used to find synonyms that can be used to extend word meanings in future writings. Spelling instruction in Mr. D's classroom focuses on three main steps: (1) what to do when you are unsure about how to spell a word (try out spelling by sound, by meaning, by articulation, by analogy, asking if it looks right and if it sounds right); (2) what to do when you have found the word; and (3) using the word. Cambourne's conditions are evident in the description of Mr. D's program, and even more clear in the following description of the "Learning to Spell Cycle" found in his classroom. As you think about this approach to spelling, consider the places where children are immersed in text, where they are taking responsibility for their learning, where they are using approximations to learn, and where they are getting immediate feedback. In this strategy children are engaged in the spelling process.

1. Unsure About a Spelling

    ▼   Think about the word carefully.

    ▼   Say it over in your mind.

    ▼   Say it aloud, pronouncing it as clearly as you can.

▼   Try spelling as it sounds.

▼   Think of other words that sound the same.

▼   Try spelling it different ways.

▼   Ask yourself, "Where have I seen or heard the word?"

▼   Check around the room.

▼   Look in a book.

▼   Ask someone else for an opinion.

▼   If you think you're close, check the dictionary.

▼   Ask the teacher.

2.   Found the Word

▼   Write the word in your "interest list."

▼   Test yourself.

▼   Look at the word carefully: its size, shape, and letter combinations.

▼   When you think you can remember it, cover it up and write it down; review to see if you're correct; try again.

▼   Enter the word once reviewed in your "Words to Use."

3.   Use the Word

▼   Use the word in your writing as often as you can.

Fostering Writing in the Classroom

Now that you have a better understanding of the writing process, think about ways to foster writing in your classroom. There are many important things you can do. Here we describe ways to encourage oral language, to create an intriguing environment, to set up writing centers, to use quality literature, to demonstrate writing, and to celebrate the work of your students. All of these strategies will foster writing in your classroom.

Encouraging Oral Language

Writing begins when children have something to say and they *believe* they can put it on paper. Children are naturally curious about their world, and most are excited about sharing their ideas. The teacher's jobs are to promote their natural curiosity, to provide maximum opportunities for children to talk about their view of the world, and then to let them write their ideas however they can. Children will write willingly only when they have something to communicate. We can expand what children have to say when we promote oral communication in classrooms. Classrooms where children are truly learning must of necessity be somewhat noisy places! People learn by sharing their views of the world with each other. When children express something they believe, listeners should respond. Feedback from listeners either confirms or challenges their ideas. Talking about new ideas strengthens both those ideas and the quality of communication itself.

As children have new experiences, they must be allowed—in fact, encouraged—to talk about them so their expanding concepts can be tested, challenged, and reinforced. Children who can discuss new concepts they are learning are acquiring a vocabulary that is meaningful and therefore usable to them as they write. It's simple: The more children know and the more comfortable they are with language, the more they will have to say and the more willing they will be to write. Perhaps Lee and Rubin said it best: "Talk provides the stepping stones between what is thought about and what is written. After a new and interesting experience we 'talk our thoughts' before we write them" (1979, p. 203).

Providing an Intriguing Environment

A classroom that encourages writing must be a place where interesting things are going on that invite children to think, talk, read, and write. The classroom is organized to allow participation in a wide variety of activities, such as going on field trips, interacting with classroom visitors, caring for animals and plants, responding to a wide variety of literature, and conducting scientific research. Children need to have experiences that are novel or, if familiar, at least have a new twist. Children's lively interest in science favors many activities designed to investigate phenomena in the environment.

Children developing new concepts can talk about them, read about them, and write about them. For example, children could participate in an activity such as hatching silkworms, gathering food for the larvae, and observing the metamorphosis of the larvae. They would find that they had to do research about when silkworms can be hatched, what will happen to the silk if the larvae are allowed to mature, and how to preserve some eggs so another generation of silkworms can be grown. Children involved in such activities are constantly talking about their observations, reading from a variety of sources, listening to the teacher read, and writing about their experiences and feelings. Activities that encourage thinking, talking, reading, and writing should be an ongoing part of every school day.

Setting Up Writing Centers

Teachers who value writing will make sure the classroom invites writing by providing an area where a wide variety of papers and writing instruments are available at all times. The writing itself need not take place in the writing center, but the materials necessary for helping children achieve their own writing goals should be readily available to all. Some teachers display objects or pictures in writing centers that may stimulate children to write. However, that stratagem is not necessary if the classroom is alive with interesting activities and children are experimenting and thinking.

If a computer with word processing software is not available for your writing center, we suggest that you at least include one or more primary-level (large print) typewriters. Children enjoy being able to render their final drafts in real print.

Stock a bin in the writing center with scraps of construction paper (and other interesting kinds of paper) from the art center. For some reason, children are highly motivated by the chance to write on a strangely shaped piece of paper. Adding machine tape is a favorite. Sometimes it really does not matter what the writing is done on, as long as the children are writing!

Supplying Quality Literature

Children who write need exposure to competent adult models of writing, just as children learning to speak need models of mature speech. The best models of excellent writing are available to children through high-quality children's literature. Teachers are responsible for selecting the best in children's literature and bringing it into classrooms. Children are not likely to be able to write poetry without having heard and read many examples of good poetry. They are not likely to be able to write good descriptive passages without having experience with the writing of authors who are masters at using descriptive language. Teachers can bring the literary models to the child through reading aloud, telling stories, and providing books that children can read for themselves.

Watch for especially beautiful or apt phrases and help children notice and appreciate those finds. Examples of language that delights, touches, transports, or enlightens can be transcribed onto charts as they are discovered. Children must also learn to observe writing techniques they might be able to use as models. For example, they might see facts presented in ways that are unusually interesting. Tomie dePaola's *The Popcorn Book* (1978), *The Quicksand Book* (1977), and *The Cloud Book* (1975) are good examples. Of course, children need to be encouraged to share writing they find especially well done. Only as children begin to read with conscious attention to the writing will they become better writers.

Smith (1983) believes there is too much to learn about writing for children to learn only from instruction. He says, "Children must read like a writer, in order to learn how to write like a writer" (p. 562). Children who are reading like writers learn to appreciate the conventions and style of the authors and actively seek to learn from them. Calkins (1983, p. 86) shares her experience with 7-year-old Greg as he comes to understand how the writer and the product are related:

> "Before I ever wrote a book [said Greg], I used to think there was a big machine, and they typed a title and then the machine went until the book was done. Now I look at a book and I know a guy wrote it and it's been his project for a long time. After the guy writes it, he probably thinks of questions people will ask him and revises it like I do, and copies it to read to about six editors. Then he fixes it up, like how they say." Greg and I are both learning how reading is made. And we both read differently because we have an insider's view of reading.

Readers do not read like writers every time they read. For example, readers who do not expect to write a newspaper article will read without consciously looking for the elements of style and format that make newspaper writing distinctive. However, readers who do expect to write for a newspaper will read it while observing the writing and structure carefully. Even though we may not always read everything as if we were going to write, literature serves as a storehouse of written language from which we can later draw.

Bill Martin Jr (1975, p. 16) describes how we save what we read for future use:

> Each of us has a linguistic storehouse into which we deposit patterns for stories and poems and sentences and words. These patterns enter through the ear (and the eye) and remain available throughout the course of a lifetime for reading and writing and speaking. The good reader is a person who looks at a page of print and begins triggering patterns that have been stored in his linguistic treasury. These patterns range all the way from the plot structure an author has used in the story to the rhyme scheme that hangs a poem together, to the placement of an adjective in front of a noun as part of the shape of the sentence, to the underlying rhythmical structure in a line of prose or poetry, to the "ed" ending as part of the shape of a word.

Exposure to a wide range of literature and other printed material provides the storehouse from which children can draw as they write. We share many ideas for using children's literature in Chapter 9.

Demonstrating Writing

Recall the discussion in Chapter 2 of Brian Cambourne's conditions for literacy learning. One of those conditions was demonstrations. We mentioned there that teachers seem to come easily to demonstrations of reading, but have far greater difficulty providing children with demonstrations of writing.

But writing demonstrations, across genre, across time, are critical to the development of lifelong writers in our classrooms. Consider a demonstration you could offer.

You have received a money clip from your cousin Dixie Lee for your birthday. As you approach the overhead projector, the chalkboard, or the large-screen computer monitor you say, "I got a money clip from my cousin for my birthday and I need to write her a thank you note. Let's see, what goes in a thank you note?

Well, I need to be sure and thank her for the clip and to tell her I will enjoy using it. Here is what I'll write."

> Dear Dixie Lee, *No, I don't like that. I don't call her Dixie Lee, I call her Dix. I'd better call her Dix in this note.*
> Dear Dix, *Yes, I like that better.*
> Thank you so much for the beautiful money clip. *Wait, I don't really think the money clip is beautiful. I can't honestly say that.*
> Thank you so much for the money clip. *Ya, that's better. Now what do I say? Well, I want to tell her I will enjoy using it.*
> I will enjoy using it because I don't have a wallet. My money is always crumpled up in my pocket. *That sounds pretty good. Is there anything else I should put in this thank you note? I'll just tell her thanks again. No, I'll tell her I do appreciate the gift and then say thanks again.*
> I really do appreciate the gift. Thanks, again, so much.
> Sincerely, *No, "sincerely" sounds silly. She is one of my best friends and favorite relatives. I tell her I love her on the phone, so I had better say "love" here.*
> Love, *That's good, now I'll just sign my name.*

During this demonstration students would see you struggle with the demands of the genre, tentatively trying out language and then changing it because of your audience. They would see you selecting the appropriate form and revising as you go. This recursiveness in writing must be demonstrated frequently if children are to be willing to risk trying it themselves.

Appreciating and Recognizing Children's Work

Children view their teachers as wonderfully important persons. What you say about a child's work will have a tremendous impact on the child and on future work. It is very important that children perceive you as someone who values the work of children and the other children as allies who value the work of their classmates.

Teachers Who Value the Child's Work

The classroom environment is often a direct reflection of the teacher's attitude about what is important work for children and what accomplishments

"Basic skills" such as using the dictionary become important in a program that encourages real writing.

© 1994 George White

are valuable. Teachers who expect children to write well will demonstrate that they value the products of writing efforts. They will, for example, encourage children to publish frequently—to contribute to class books and write their own books. They will display children's writing and find a way to highlight outstanding passages, pointing out a word that carries exactly the right connotation to communicate a feeling, a unique phrase, or an especially evocative line of poetry. Perhaps they will also ask children to explain how they achieved a particularly outstanding line or composition.

Teachers also use children's writing products for instruction. The children read writing produced by their classmates in order to gain skill as writers and readers. They use the work of other children as models for their own stories or poems. In 1978 the poet David Greenburg observed that children writing poetry respond best to samples written by other children. In our classroom observations we frequently see children responding in enthusiastic and caring ways to the writing of their classmates. Alert teachers will be aware of opportunities to display, to publish, and to share the work of their writers.

Children Who Value Each Other's Work

You may have heard parents or other adults remark, "Children say the meanest things!" It's true that children can be very open—even blunt—with their comments. They need an adult to help them learn tact. However, children can also be very supportive of the writing efforts of their classmates, given the opportunity and some guidance from the teacher with respect to appropriate responses. Visiting classrooms where writing was taught with enthusiasm and respect, we have seen children eagerly reading their work to their peers, with truly positive results. There is something special in children's discovery that their writing pleases their friends.

Providing Libraries of Children's Work

A classroom library is essential to an environment that supports reading and writing. The library corner should be stocked with materials drawn periodically from the school library, the city library, and the teacher's and children's home libraries. Perhaps the most valuable additions to a classroom library are the works of the authors who occupy that classroom. Each publication by an author in the classroom should be honored just as much as the works of professionally published authors.

A nice plus would be the establishment in the school library of a system for cataloging the edited publications of the children and circulating them throughout the school. Two of our former students, teachers at an elementary school, created what their students called the "Do Your Own Thing Library." These teachers' fifth-grade classes obtained permission from the school media teacher to take over a corner of the library. A section of the library was partitioned off using portable bookcases and refrigerator cartons. The children created various kinds of display units. When the physical space was finally ready, all the classes in the school were notified that the "Do Your Own Thing Library" was about to open and was accepting donations of written work and artwork by authors and artists in the school. Each donated piece would be cataloged into the "Do Your Own Thing Library" for a three-week period, during which time it could be checked out by anyone in the school. Open before and after school, the library was completely managed by students in the two fifth-grade classrooms. The project was a tremendous success, and certainly communicated the message that the work of children was important.

When Does the Writing Get Done?

Writing is not a school "subject." It is an art and a craft we must struggle throughout the school years to master as we use writing to communicate across the curriculum. Writing should be happening throughout the school day—as part of reading activities, as part of living together in the classroom and school—as part of exploration in science, social studies, math, and art. We believe that there should not be a single time set aside in the daily schedule for writing. The notion of "writers' workshop" has become popular in many American schools. This is usually a 45-minute period during which a variety of writing activities occur. Some children draft and compose, some children select and order information, some children edit and publish, some children conference with the teacher, engage in small-group instruction, or work with an editing group or committee. Although all of these are wonderful activities that promote growth as writers, they should not be restricted to a single 45-minute period of the day. In a very real sense the entire school day should be a "writers' workshop." The schedule for each day should be unique in order to meet the needs of the children. We envision one daily schedule that looks like the following (times are approximate):

▼   *Morning Meeting* (20 minutes): Here the plans are made for the day, news is shared, a story is read. The teacher briefly checks with each child to confirm what that child will be doing during part of the morning.

▼   *Integrated Instructional Period* (45 minutes): During this large block of time many literacy activities are engaged: spelling, handwriting, reading, writing, content area study. Children might be busy in revision or editing groups, teacher conferences, small-group instruction, buddy reading, researching and organizing information, preparing publications, and so forth. The teacher could be modeling writing or perhaps engaging in guided reading activities or mini-lessons with small groups. During this time the teacher spends at least one, maybe two, 10-minute periods moving among the children to be sure all are on task ("What are you doing? What will you be doing next?") and perhaps to do a careful observation of one child, making notes in the anecdotal record book.

▼   *Morning Break* (15 minutes)

▼   *Math* (45 minutes): In addition to instruction in math, children might be writing their own story problems or writing explanations of problem solutions or the instructions for working through a math operation.

▼   *Integrated Instructional Period* (60 minutes): During this time the teacher would take one or two groups for guided reading activities, perhaps a group for writing instruction regarding punctuation of dialogue, and a small group for handwriting instruction. Importantly, he or she would also spend at least 20 minutes making careful observation of selected children and/or doing a running record (a form of miscue analysis) with a couple of children. The children not engaged with the teacher are continuing activities begun earlier in the morning: selecting topics, determining audience, selecting forms, composing and drafting, publishing, using writing models available to them, working in groups, doing research, enjoying the listening center, and so forth.

▼ *Lunch and Midday Recess* (60 minutes)

▼ *Physical Education, Art, Music, Science or Social Studies, Literature Studies* (90 minutes): During much of this time children are still engaged in reading and writing activities. Science could well be a time for conducting experiments or collecting data on existing/ongoing experiments that will be written up during this time or in the morning. If the time is spent on literature studies, children could be reading the work of a single author, writing responses in journals, composing a letter to be sent to the author, or researching questions that extend from their reading.

We trust from this example that you can see how writing and reading are connected throughout the day, not in just a select period of the day. This typical daily schedule invites children to take responsibility for their learning and affords the teacher time to make the critical observations of the children's work. Consider this simply as one example and not a model or blueprint to transfer to your classroom.

Major Ideas in This Chapter

▼ Writing is a developmental process that can be observed and encouraged. It takes time for children to achieve competence as they move through characteristic stages from scribbling to conventional spelling.

▼ Children explore written language much as they explore the spoken language. By observation and experimentation they discover the principles and conventions that govern writing.

▼ Writing success can be achieved when writing is viewed as a recursive process that includes forming intentions, composing and drafting, and publication and response. Writing daily and working recursively through the stages of writing will increase children's skills as writers and as readers.

▼ Selection of writing to be carried through the writing process to publication and sharing should be a joint decision between teacher and student. There is a wide choice of forms for presentation.

▼ Instruction in writing and editing skills requires careful organization and planning by the teacher.

▼   Spelling instruction is a highly debated topic. Spelling competence increases with reading and writing. Spelling instruction should focus on the words children have nearly approximated in their writing and the mastery of high-frequency words in writing.

▼   The daily schedule should provide authentic opportunities for children to write (and read) throughout the day across curriculum areas. Writing should not be restricted to one "writers' workshop" period of the day.

Discussion Questions: Focusing on the Teacher You Are Becoming

1. A parent complains that her child talks all the time about the writing she is doing in reading class. The parent is concerned her child isn't learning to read. What responses can you make?

2. The father of the 6-year-old who wrote "wusr apon a time. Ther was a robot thet dint aint have a oonere" expresses concern at the open house that his son is not learning to spell properly. How will you explain the concept that spelling ability is developmental, and what will you say to make the father feel better about his son's progress?

3. Having children read and write as much as we have suggested will take up a lot of the time usually spent filling in blanks in workbooks. What are the issues involved here, and how will you resolve them?

4. If you have 35 children in a small classroom, you may not have room for all the centers we have suggested. What are ways to achieve the goals of the centers in a limited space?

5. Who should serve on editing committees? Should only the most talented writers have such positions, or are there ways for virtually all children to have a turn?

6. We have recommended a move away from a published spelling program toward individualized work in spelling. What work will you have to do with parents and colleagues to gain support for this approach?

Field-Based Applications

1. Ask the children to select one of their favorite authors and write a letter to him or her asking how the author wrote a particular story or section

of a story. Encourage the students to ask specific questions about revisions and rewriting.

2. Write something yourself and share it with your students. Elicit their feedback for revisions or changes that would make the writing better.

3. Collect wonderful phrases or words from the literature that you and the children are sharing. Discuss how the author might have decided to use that phrase or word.

4. Make a bulletin board from the children's writings on a particular topic or theme, and bind them into a book when the display is taken down.

5. Set aside a time each week for children to share the writing they have done during that week. Give children the option of reading their own work or having you read it for them. Not every child will have something to share every week.

6. Ask children to submit some of their work to the local newspaper or one of the children's magazines.

7. Survey children's writing portfolios and make a list of skills that you could teach over the next few weeks.

Chapter 4
Emergent Literacy

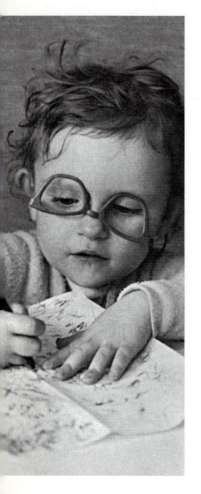

Chapter Overview

▼ *Emergent literacy* is a term used to describe the young child's developing knowledge of printed language. It implies there is no identifiable starting point for children's literacy learning.

▼ Classroom environments can contribute to the child's use and understanding of the world of print. Environmental factors include both the physical environment and psychological support for the child.

▼ Planned literacy instruction for emergent readers includes reading to children and reading with them as they learn important concepts about words, directionality, and sound–symbol relationships.

▼ Literacy instruction for young children includes planning for experiences with literature, music, and writing. Such instruction must focus on what children know about print.

▼ Emergent writers need specific support as they learn about the written language system. The classroom environment, writing materials, and a knowledge of the stages of development in children's writing make this support possible.

▼ Play is important in helping children become aware of print in the real world and its use in society. Teachers can plan and encourage the use of authentic literacy materials in various play areas.

▼ Communicating with parents about their children's abilities as literacy users is an important part of the teacher's role. Helping parents understand the importance of their role in the child's literacy development and helping them understand how literacy is treated in the classroom setting are vital skills.

Emergent Literacy

A relatively new concept in education, **emergent literacy** is defined as the child's development of knowledge about printed language that takes place before formal instruction. Generally, children from about age 2 to about age 6 are considered to be emergent readers, although older children who have not had successful reading instruction could be also. Goodman (1990) writes,

> All children have some knowledge about literacy as a cultural form, and they have attitudes and beliefs about literacy as a result of their developing concepts about literacy. They know the functions that written language serves, and they know who may participate in its use. Children know what reading is and in what kinds of materials reading can occur. They know who reads, where people read, what different people use reading for, and who can and cannot read. Children know what writing is and what kinds of forms writing takes. They know who writes, what people write with, and what people use writing for. (p. 116)

For years educators ignored literacy behaviors that preceded formal instruction in reading and writing and assumed the child came to the instructional context as a blank slate. Emergent literacy as a concept recognizes the child's learning about print and how it works before any kind of formal instruction in how to read and write. In essence, we appreciate what children know about reading and writing before they come to school and we build on this important knowledge.

The question in today's world is not whether children in kindergarten or younger should be given literacy instruction, but what do they know already and how can the teacher guide their progress on the continuum of acquiring literacy? In Chapter 1 we described the acquisition of literacy as a continuum that begins at birth and goes through the life of the individual. No person ever reaches the point where there would be no more to learn—one could always read more or write more or read or write in a genre new to the individual. Several years ago Smith (1973) wrote some tongue-in-cheek "rules" for reading instruction. His last rule (not tongue in cheek) was to find out what the child is trying to do and help him do it. That's the rule for teachers of young children. It takes both knowledge and skill, but it can make acquiring literacy a rewarding process for both teachers and learners.

The knowledge that teachers need is two pronged. First, teachers have to understand the usual developmental stages exhibited by children as they gain an understanding of language in its written form, both reading it and writing it. Second, teachers must also know how to plan and present instruction to young children, either individually or in groups that will aid them in developing literacy abilities. The chart in Figure 4.1 will help you review the stages of oral language, reading, and writing development.

You might observe some similarities in the stages of development. For example, babbling and scribbling have some common elements. You will also note that children take several years to become mature speakers, writers, and

Stages in Oral Language Development	Stages in Writing	Stages in Reading
Babbling	Scribbling stage	Magical stage
Expressive jargon	Linear repetitive stage (with	Self-concept as a reader
One-word expressions	some scribbling)	Bridging stage
Multiple-word expressions,	Random-letter spelling	Takeoff stage
questions, negatives	Letter name writing, or	Independent reading
Mature patterns mixed with	phonetic writing	Skilled stage
immature forms	Transitional spelling	Advanced skilled stage
Mature speech	Conventional spelling	

Figure 4.1—Stages of Different Aspects of Literacy

Source: From Brewer, J. A., *Introduction to Early Childhood Education.* Copyright ©1992 by Allyn and Bacon. Reprinted by permission.

readers. They do not complete all of the oral language stages before beginning to understand print.

In summarizing a number of studies of early literacy, Mason and Sinha (1993) listed the following points:

▼　Literacy emerges before children are formally taught to read.

▼　Literacy is defined to encompass the whole act of reading, not merely decoding.

▼　The child's point of view and active involvement with emerging literacy constructs is featured.

▼　The social setting for literacy learning is not ignored. (p. 141)

The studies cited by these authors and many more have changed the view of literacy and what it means for a child to become literate.

Looking at the growth of literacy abilities as an emerging process is very different from the traditional view of literacy. In the past, children were described as being "ready" to learn to read at a given point in time. Readiness was an important term in planning instruction.

Reading Readiness

The traditional view of reading readiness assumed that children needed to possess a discrete set of skills in order to be successful at learning to read. These skills usually included knowing the names of letters of the alphabet, visual discrimination skills such as finding the picture of a pig with a different tail in a row of four pictures of pigs, auditory discrimination skills such as recognizing rhyming words, and the ability to follow directions such as "put your finger on the star at the top of page 6." In order to teach these skills, teachers in preschools and kindergartens and sometimes first grade assumed that children knew nothing at all about print and reading when they entered school. They began instruction by selecting letters in a sequence, and teaching children to recognize those letters in upper- and lowercase forms. This instruction was often in the form of worksheets with a letter on each page and directions to the child to circle all the "*bs.*"

While learning letter names, children often were required to learn the letter–sound correspondences as well. For example, children would be asked to bring objects from home that were spelled with the initial sound being studied, such as *jar* for /j/. At school, worksheets were presented on which the children circled all the pictures beginning with a given sound or sorted small plastic toys into cartons labeled with a letter of the alphabet. Other activities included learning alphabetical order. Many games, worksheets, and puzzles were designed to teach children to put the letters in order. Examine the sample readiness worksheet in Figure 4.2. Try to determine what the child would need to know in order to complete it and what might be learned about reading from being asked to complete this task.

Some of the vestiges of this kind of thinking can still be found in classrooms where teachers organize the curriculum around a "letter of the week" and all the activities for a week revolve around learning a letter and its associated sounds.

Organizing a program around a letter of the week presents several problems for the most effective reading instruction.

1. A letter alone is decontextualized and has no meaning. Letters appear in words and texts, but by themselves have little value.

2. Focusing on a letter is concentrating on the most meaningless piece of information that is useful for real reading. No one would argue that children do not need to know letters and the sounds they often represent, but the first instruction children receive should focus on the functions of print, the thinking strategies of the reader, and so on. Focusing on letter–sound relationships leads children to believe that other strategies for reading are less important. For mature readers, letter–sound relationships are used much less frequently than other cues for reading.

3. Focusing on letter–sound relationships encourages parents to believe that mastery of this one aspect of reading is tantamount to mastery of reading.

4. A focus on letter–sound relationships ignores what children already know about such relationships and attempts to teach children what

Figure 4.2—Traditional Reading Readiness Worksheet

Source: Reprinted by permission of McClanahan Book Company.

many already know. Such instruction fails to distinguish between children who have already learned the letters before school, those who will learn the letters when immersed in a print-rich environment, and those who will need instructional support for learning them.

5. A focus on a letter of the week violates the principle of good skills instruction, which says such instruction should always be presented when it is needed by the learner.

Children practice what they know about how print works in a variety of settings.

© 1994 Steven Lunetta/StockUp

The assumption of a letter-of-the-week curriculum is that when children complete it, they will be able to read or be ready for reading instruction. Absolutely no evidence supports this assumption. We have already discussed the fallacy of thinking that a child suddenly reaches a point where he or she is "ready" to read. Even if the children bring objects from home and write in their journals about the letter to be learned, the focus is still on the letter, not on the reading process.

Citing the flaws of a letter-of-the-week curriculum does not imply that children should not be helped to learn more about letter–sound relationships, but it means that such activities should be developmentally appropriate and designed for individual children. Alternatives to a letter of the week include focusing on a given letter in stories, charts, chants, poems, song lyrics, or other print for children who do not yet understand that particular relationship. Reutzel (1992) recommends creating alphabet books from environmental print, creating an alphabet center in the classroom with wooden, magnetic, and sandpaper letters; using stencils, chalkboards, and other writing materials; and providing alphabet cookies and cereals especially for pairs or small groups so children can sort them and eat them while talking to others about the letters they have. He goes on to suggest that art experiences such as compiling a collage of objects that begin with a given letter are enjoyable and meaningful. Finally, he recommends the frequent use of alphabet books in the classroom. After repeated readings, children can create their own alphabet books.

Writing Readiness

Children's so-called readiness for writing programs resembled those for reading readiness. Children were asked to draw straight lines or circles on large sheets of paper folded into lines. When they had the fine motor ability to control the crayon or pencil well enough to make the line begin and end where they were instructed to make it, the spaces were reduced in size until they were writing on regular lined paper. Then the children were taught to make letters in a particular sequence, usually beginning with the simpler letters such as *l*, *t*, and *h* and continuing until all the letters had been introduced. Examine the writing of a first grader in the first, second, and third month of school (Figures 4.3, 4.4, and 4.5). Think about emerging literacy in interpreting this work. What are some important changes in the progression from September to November?

The concepts of reading readiness and writing readiness completely ignored what children had learned about printed language before they came to school and their understanding of what it means to read and write. Readiness, at least as it was once conceptualized, means very little in determining what children actually know about reading and writing and how it is used in the real world.

What is important is that the teacher understands the normal stages of development in reading and writing and provides the classroom environment and individualized instruction that will aid the child in moving along the continuum of literacy. Such instruction requires skilled observation and careful planning.

Supporting the Development of Literacy

The development of children's emerging literacy abilities can be enhanced by a classroom environment that encourages interesting activities, a print-rich environment, play in the classroom, and a well-stocked writing center. Teachers must support the development of literacy with careful thought about each of these strategies.

Classroom Environment

In a classroom setting that encourages the emergence of literacy abilities, the teacher thinks sensitively about both the psychological and the physical environment. The children must feel free from threat and from pressure to know certain information on a schedule or at the same time other children might know it. It must be individually appropriate for each child. A second element

Figure 4.3—September in First-Grade Writing Sample

of psychological safety is a teacher who understands the developmental nature of learning to read and write, who expects all children to be successful at learning, and who accepts approximations in form as signs of growth, rather than a cause for remediation. Approximations are not difficult to accept when children are learning language. No caretaker would demand that an infant produce the adult form of the word *water* before giving a child a drink. In reading and writing, approximations may be in the form of reading what the child thinks the text says or writing in scribbles or invented spellings.

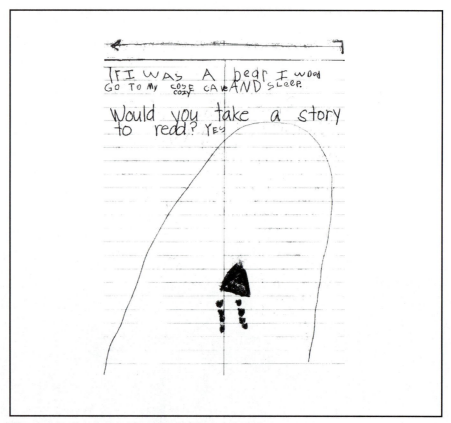

Figure 4.4—October in First-Grade Writing Sample

Physically, the classroom must be arranged so children have access to materials and time to use them. Materials for writing—paper, writing instruments, and so on—should be stored so children can get them and put them away with as little adult help as possible. Books should be stored on open-faced shelves so children are attracted to them and can use them when they wish. The furnishings should be comfortable for both writing and reading activities. Place tables and chairs close to the writing materials for children who prefer to write at a table. Other materials, such as slates, pieces of hard-surfaced board, or clipboards, should also be available so children can write in any area of the classroom or on the floor. A mailbox for each child may encourage the writing of notes. Children should know where to write what is needed for their work, such as adding "glue" to the list when more is needed.

A Print-Rich Environment

One of the most important factors in emerging literacy is a print-rich environment. We do not simply mean hanging charts of songs and chants, displaying books, or making available other print materials. It means arranging an environment that is print rich in the sense of meaningful print the children actually use. For example, a teacher might have notices and announcements the children need to read, or involve the children in keeping the attendance and milk money records so print is not only useful, but necessary. Print-rich environments require children to actually interact with the print, not just look at it.

Print rich does not mean the teacher has put labels on all the objects in the classroom; rather it means there are ample opportunities for engaging in the literacy process—books to read, announcements, invitations, schedules, task assignments, and so on. There are signs that children are using print in their play such as a sign delineating the space for the veterinarian's office and a clipboard with pads for recording information about the "patients," a sign-up sheet for who gets the next turn to have the new game, and so on. There are also indications that children are writing for many purposes (from pieces of writing in the classroom) and signs that children are solving problems using print (a note to another class inviting them to attend a class reading). There are also books everywhere—the hamster cage sits on a table where there are also several books about hamsters, the art area contains several books about art, and the library corner is filled with good books.

Play in the Emergent Literacy Classroom

Play in the classroom has intrinsic value; in other words, it is valuable in ways other than what children can learn about literacy through play experiences.

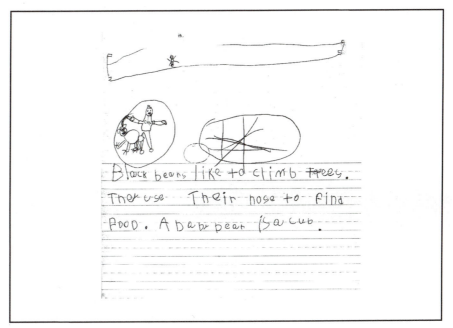

Figure 4.5—November in First-Grade Writing Sample

Children sometimes use signs to establish their roles in dramatic play.

© 1995 Robin Sachs

Do not make the mistake of thinking that if young children are not engaged in play that involves literacy in some obvious way the play has no value. Children playing develop many social/emotional, intellectual, and physical abilities. They learn to attend to a task, take turns, solve problems, and express themselves—all valuable abilities in literacy even though the link might not be obvious to the uninformed observer.

Play, especially sociodramatic play in which children role-play, is also very valuable in terms of literacy development. A child who plays the role of the checker at the supermarket is learning to put himself or herself in the role of another. Children involved in such play also learn to pay attention to the topic at hand for longer periods of time. Children who have a broad range of experience also bring the necessary background knowledge to their reading so it is possible to construct meaning.

Engaging in play experiences certainly contributes to children's ability to write. Writing a message requires a child to select from a repertoire of symbols the ones most useful for the purpose and arrange them in a given order. Children playing are selecting and arranging in many situations. A child at the easel may select the colors of paint needed and then arrange them to achieve the desired pattern. A child playing with blocks has to gauge the distance a given block will span when bridging from one part of a structure to another. Such play contributes to the child's ability to place letters on a page and gauge the space needed for writing tasks.

More direct connections to the development of literacy can be achieved through intervention by the teacher in the children's play activity. Several studies (Christie, 1990; Morrow & Rand, 1991; Neuman & Roskos, 1992) have found that the engagement of children in literacy activities during play increases when teachers intervene by deliberately adding literacy materials to play environments and encouraging the use of such materials. For example, Christie (1990) believes dramatic play can support the development of literacy in young children if they are provided with literacy materials to use in their play. He notes that giving children time to play is not enough; teachers must also intervene to promote the literacy activities. Such intervention may take the form of thinking about what literacy materials could be added to the play areas, encouraging children to play in theme centers where literacy is a natural response to the theme, or modeling literacy behaviors in the play areas. For example, a teacher might offer ticket books to children who are playing "riding on the train," set up an office or a grocery store area where literacy would be encouraged by the nature of the theme, or invite a child to write a label for his or her block construction.

Other theme areas that involve many literacy experiences include a doctor's office, a shoe store, a restaurant, a home (making lists, checking the TV listings, reading the newspaper, reading to babies, and so on), and a post office. Neuman and Roskos (1992) suggest real literacy objects rather than pretend objects. For example, they used real file folders and forms to encourage children's use of literacy. They also evaluate literacy props in terms of whether children would have knowledge of the use of the props from their real-world experience. For example, if children were familiar with the forms and clipboards used in many doctor's offices, those would be good choices for props in an office play area.

Morrow and Rand (1991) make these suggestions: Keep literacy materials in clearly marked places and change them frequently to keep interest high, model the uses of the materials as needed or suggest possible uses when appropriate, and accept all levels of development for the most positive results.

Connections between sustained play and literacy were noted in two ways by Roskos (1988). Her observations revealed that links to literacy were found in both the "story making" and "literacy stance" of young children. Each dramatic episode was found to contain story-making elements such as setting, characters, and a goal, concern, or conflict. Literacy stance was observed in more than 450 distinct reading and writing acts displayed during play. These acts were categorized into activities (such as reading books), skills (such as printing letters and words), and knowledge (of ways to use literacy in social settings).

Roskos suggests that teachers in day care centers, preschools, and kindergarten do three things to help link dramatic play and literacy:

1. Create play centers that encourage symbolic play, including experimentation with literacy.

2. Convert children's pretend-play stories into language-experience charts.

3. Observe children's play carefully for indications of literacy understanding.

Writing Centers

A writing center can be furnished with the materials that make writing attractive and accessible to young children. Establishing such a center does not imply that the only writing in the classroom is done at the center, but it is better conceptualized as a storage area for writing materials. Some writing materials should also be kept at all the other centers in the classroom to demonstrate that writing takes place everywhere. Many kinds of paper and writing instruments should be stored in a writing center along with such items as a typewriter or computer if one is available, and pictures, books, simple picture dictionaries, and anything else that will aid the children in achieving their writing goals. Emergent writers, like any other writers, need a purpose for writing and an audience so that they get a response to their writing. They do not need story starters or topics they must write about.

One teacher who had been teaching in a multiage classroom for many years did an annual project in which the children hatched and cared for silkworms. She admitted she had once required all the children to write about the silkworms. After a while, she realized that if they were interested enough in the project, they would write about it without the requirement. That principle is true in most other situations. If the children are interested enough in what is going on in the classroom, they will write about it. Otherwise, there is little gain in assigning children to write about given topics. Remember the old story of the little boy on a field trip who has his eyes covered? When asked why, he responded that if he looked, he would have to write about it when he got back to school. Try to encourage your students to keep their eyes open.

Planned Literacy Instruction

Our responsibility as teachers is to teach; therefore, we do not leave the development of children's literacy abilities to chance. In addition to setting up an environment that is as supportive as we can make it, planned instruction is also very important. Clay (1991) states that children learn many skills in their first few months in school. The following list will give you an idea of how many skills they learn, but it is not comprehensive:

▼ Directional control appropriate for print

▼ How to draw on and use background experience

▼ Using pictures as an aid to reading print

▼ Using some conventions of print

▼ Searching for meaning

▼ Taking risks (on the basis of available information)

▼ Word-by-word reading

▼ Rerunning for various purposes

▼ Cross-checking two types of cues

▼ Self-correcting following recognition of errors

▼ Confirming attempts in an alternative way

▼ Using some letter–sound relationships

▼ Using first letters

▼ Using word endings

▼ Correcting medial sounds

▼ Using letter clusters

▼ Getting to new words by analogy with known words

▼ Building a vocabulary of high-frequency reading words

▼ Building a vocabulary of high-frequency writing words. (Clay, 1991, p. 226)

Children learn all these skills through a variety of strategies including hearing stories read, participating in shared reading, becoming involved in experiences based on songs, language experience, and, of course, writing and reading.

Reading to Children

Reading aloud to children is such a pleasurable activity, it seems unnecessary to remind teachers to do it frequently, but some teachers feel they have so many curriculum goals to meet that they have no time for reading aloud. Reading aloud contributes more than just pleasure, although certainly the bonding and pleasure are important to a child's learning to read (Fox, 1993). Reading aloud allows children to hear fluent reading, sparks children's interests in reading independently, broadens the vocabulary of the listeners, and helps develop listening skills. Mem Fox (1993) describes an experience she and a colleague had in working with a group of less-successful readers. They intended to teach "lessons" but found the children were learning so much from being read to, that they spent the entire time reading aloud to the group. The children learned how reading was supposed to sound, learned to appreciate the content of books, learned the pleasures that books can provide, and learned how language in books differs from spoken language. The books, if carefully chosen and well-read, do their own teaching.

Bill Martin (1988) says we must have "book language" in our ears long before we are expected to read print, just as we have spoken language in our ears long before we are expected to produce it. Reading aloud gives children that store of book language to use. Mem Fox (1993) tells about her daughter Chloe who wanted to eat dessert before she ate the rest of her lunch and excused herself by saying "one must sustain oneself," a phrase she had learned from Winnie the Pooh. One of our granddaughters, when just 2, responded she was "rather hungry" like Goldilocks. Enthusiasm for reading and books is contagious, and reading aloud is one of the best ways to kindle that enthusiasm.

Mooney (1990) describes the stages of reading to, reading with, and independent reading. In Figure 4.6, the diagonal line illustrates the support needed by children over time. In the beginning stages, reading to children is the responsibility of the teacher and the learner needs only to enjoy the experience, but takes no responsibility for the print features. In shared reading, the reading is still primarily the responsibility of the teacher, and the learner's responses are usually motivated by the structure of the story. The learner takes little responsibility for the mechanical process of reading. In the following sections on Big Books, predictable books, and music for emerging readers, you will notice that some of the activities are reading to children, where the learners are involved aurally but are not responsible for reading alone, and some are shared reading so that more of the responsibility is placed on the learner.

Reading aloud provides children with many opportunities to become more literate:

1. The teacher can demonstrate the nature, pleasures, and rewards of reading, which increase children's interest in books and their motivation to read for themselves.

2. Children become familiar with the ways in which language can be recorded.

3. Children realize that some of their experiences and thoughts are similar to those that have been recorded by authors.

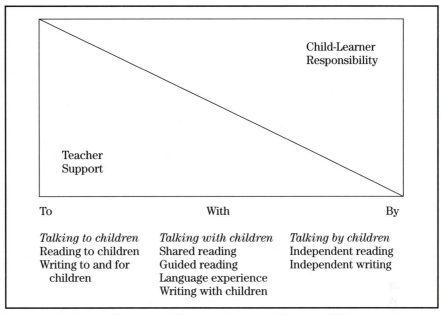

Figure 4.6—Teacher Support and Learner Responsibility in *To, With,* and *By*

Source: Mooney, Margaret E. (1990). *Reading to, with, and by Children.* Richard C. Owen Publishers, Inc. Katonah, NY. Reprinted with permission.

4. Children who listen to stories make narratives in their own heads and want to create and record their own texts.

5. They refine their understandings about patterns, sounds, rhythms, and styles of language.

6. Listening to known stories allows children to confirm their predictions about how the episodes are arranged to make the story work. Known stories also allow for the discovery of new levels of meaning in a story.

7. Children with extensive experience in listening to stories are more able to edit their own stories in their heads.

8. Children need to be challenged by reading material beyond their independent reading level.

9. Reading aloud a variety of different texts throughout the day can help children understand that reading goes well beyond any lesson or school day. (Adapted from Mooney, 1990, pp. 21–24)

Reading aloud needs to be a time when books are shared in a comfortable setting with a positive attitude on the part of all participants. One way of achieving these goals is to make sure children are seated comfortably and close to the reader. They should feel like you are reading to them and that they are involved in the reading experience. The following guidelines will help you create a good experience.

Once the children are settled, introduce the book. Try to call attention to print features that will be relevant to the group and perhaps get some predictions about the story from looking at the cover or thinking about the title. Do not reveal too much about the book or tell the listeners what to think. For example, you might want to say something like "This is a story about a little bear" but not "This is the funniest story you have ever heard."

Read the story with enthusiasm. Reading in a deadly monotone is worse than not reading at all. Create some drama in your voice and perhaps with your hands and body. This is a *story*, not the reading of a will. If you are successful, be prepared to read it again (and again and again, even if it has to be on other days!). The very best response may be the sigh of satisfaction when the story is finished.

Try not to interrupt the story to enforce discipline or to explain parts of the narrative. If you think explanation is needed or the children will not understand the story, then do it before reading. Usually, a look or a touch can keep children tuned in to the story without a verbal reaction from the teacher. Comments like "Sit down on your bottom" or "Don't pull her hair" really distract from the reading.

After the story is read, teachers have a variety of choices about what to do next. The best choice is sometimes nothing—to just let the story shimmer in the air. If follow-up activities are desirable, then children should have as much choice in those as possible. Usually follow-up activities need to come after a second or third reading, rather than immediately after the first wonderful reading. Follow-up activities might include drama, art, construction, writing, or other language activities. For example, if children had heard *The Very Hungry Caterpillar* (Carle, 1969) several times, some children might want to make pictures of caterpillars or butterflies, some might want to write about things they would like to eat, some might want to build a habitat for a caterpillar they had found. Not all children will want to do any of these things. Some may just want to read the book again by themselves or with a partner. Some may want to do nothing related to the story.

In thinking about follow-up activities, be sure the activities are as authentic and meaningful as possible. Mooney (1990) stated that many follow-up activities are not authentic. She said no adult reader she had ever known had made a papier-mâché puppet after reading a book. We would agree that activities need to be meaningful, but these are children in school and art is part of the curriculum. So if children want to create art that is related to a book, it would be meaningful. If the teacher assigns every child to make an egg carton caterpillar, it is not authentic. Activities such as worksheets or other such tasks should be avoided. We want children to love reading and stories, not dread what comes after.

An enlarged text facilitates demonstration of the reading process.

© Susan Lapides

When children ask for the same story over and over, some people describe that as "choosing their own curriculum." Usually, they are in the process of learning the words, learning a certain phrase, or thinking more about the illustrations. If children choose a story repeatedly, they need its repetition. Children hearing a story for the second or third time (and parents know that children often request the same book over and over until parents think they cannot read that story again under any circumstance and have even been known to hide a book to avoid reading it again) have a chance to learn more about the vocabulary, learn more about how stories are structured in their culture, learn more language in discussion, and learn more about the ability to follow the plot and the causal sequences in the story (Clay, 1991; Department of Education, 1985; Holdaway, 1980). Many teachers plan story time so they introduce and read a new story and then repeat a story from another day on request. Familiarity in this case does not breed contempt; it breeds knowledge and skill.

Many children come to school without having the experience of being read to and sharing stories with a caring adult. These children may need some special care before they are able to benefit from the typical story reading times in a classroom. First, they may need to be read to often individually or with one or two other children. Paraprofessionals, volunteers, and older children may be recruited for this reading. In group times, they may need the teacher to begin with storytelling rather than story reading. Storytelling allows the teacher to maintain constant eye contact, shorten the story if needed, add more drama if needed, and so on. Once the children are accustomed to participating in the group and behaving as an "audience" for the story, the teacher may move to telling stories from books so the book is there to be shown, but the teacher tells the story so eye contact is not broken and nothing is between the listener and the speaker. Finally, the teacher moves to a more typical story-reading structure when the children are ready to respond.

Reading with Children (Shared Reading)

As children gain experience with listening to stories and understanding the reading process, teachers will want to spend some time each day in shared reading. *Shared reading* means that both the teacher and the listener take some responsibility for the success of the reading experience. The teacher may introduce the story using the strategies just described but with more focus on the print features and on prediction and bringing what the children know about the topic to a conscious level. If the book were *Greedy Cat* (Cowley, 1988), for example, the teacher might read the title and then ask the children what they know about cats and the meaning of the word *greedy*. Then she might ask for predictions about what the cat is going to do in the story. On the title page, she might make sure the children know what the title page is and what information is found on it. As the story is read, the teacher might ask children to confirm or reject their original predictions and make new ones two or three times. On the second or third reading, the teacher would expect the children to join in the reading of the repetitive phrase, "and that was the end of that." On further reading, the teacher might ask some children to read other repetitive phrases in the book. Obviously, pieces chosen for such reading experiences must be interesting enough so they can be reread a number of times without causing boredom, but they must also have enough repetition so children can participate in the reading.

Sulzby (1991) found that children who had experience with "reading" storybooks moved through predictable stages in their responses to books. These stages are described in Figure 4.7 in a simplified version. Teachers who are trying to engage emerging readers in reading experiences will want to use these stages as observation guides and as a guide for planning literacy experiences. For example, Sulzby notes that the teacher's manuals that often accompany Big Books recommend calling children's attention to print in an explicit manner. She believes that until a child is attending to print, such strategies are not very useful to the learner.

As children gain ability in reading, you might want to use the developmental reading checklist in Figure 4.8 to record their progress. Please note that this is not a sequential checklist—children are not expected to achieve these abilities in the order they appear on this checklist.

Broad Categories	Brief Explanation of Categories
1. Attending to Pictures; Not Forming Stories	The child is "reading" by looking at the storybook's pictures. The child's speech is *just* about the picture in view; the child is not "weaving a story" across the pages. (Subcategories are "labeling and commenting" and "following the action.")
2. Attending to Pictures; Forming *ORAL* Stories	The child is "reading" by looking at the storybook's pictures. The child's speech weaves a story across the pages but the wording and the intonation are like that of someone telling a story, either like a conversation about the pictures or like a fully recited story, in which the listener can see the pictures (and often *must* see them to understand the child's story). (Subcategories are "dialogic storytelling" and "monologic storytelling.")
3. Attending to Pictures; Reading and Storytelling Mixed	This category for the simplified version was originally the first subcategory of (4). It fits between (2) and (4) and is easier to understand if it is treated separately. The child is "reading" by looking at the storybook's pictures. The child's speech fluctuates between sounding like a storyteller, with oral intonation, and sounding like a reader, with reading intonation. To fit this category, the majority of the reading attempt must show fluctuations between storytelling and reading.
4. Attending to Pictures; Forming *WRITTEN* Stories	The child is "reading" by looking at the storybook's pictures. The child's speech sounds as if the child is reading, both in the wording and intonation. The listener does not need to look at the pictures (or rarely does) in order to understand the story. If the listener closes his or her eyes, most of the time he or she would think the child is reading from print. (Subcategories are "reading similar-to-original story" and "reading verbatim-like story.")
5. Attending to Print	There are four subcategories of attending to print. Only the *final* one is what is typically called "real reading." In the others the child is exploring the print by such strategies as refusing to read based on print-related reasons, or using only some of the aspects of print. (Subcategories are "refusing to read based on print awareness," "reading aspectually," "reading with strategies imbalanced," and "reading independently" or "conventional reading.")

Figure 4.7—Levels of Child Engagement in Storybook Reading

Source: Figure 1 from "Assessment of emergent literacy: Storybook reading," Elizabeth Sulzby, *The Reading Teacher*, March 1991, p. 499. Reprinted with permission of Elizabeth Sulzby and the International Reading Association.

Repetitive-Language Books

Books containing words, phrases, or sentence patterns that repeat throughout the story are described as repetitive-language books or patterned books. The repetition is particularly helpful to young children in recognizing sight words and gaining fluency. Children can also model their own stories after the original story. Several authors (Downhower & Brown, 1992; Heald-Taylor, 1987; May, 1986; Rhodes, 1981; Wuertenberg, 1983) point out the value of using patterned books in reading instruction. Books that contain predictable patterns or words help children build familiarity with "book" language, an

READING DEVELOPMENT CHECKLIST

Name _____

STAGE 1—THE BEGINNING READER	Date				
• Enjoys listening to literature					
• Voluntarily chooses to look at books					
• Uses literature as a basis for dramatic play or painting					
• Has favourite stories and wants to hear them repeatedly					
• Can retell past experiences					
• Can relate a sequence of events					
• Understands some environmental print and common words					
• Shows a desire to see his/her words written down					
• Role-plays reading by attempting to match his/her memory of the selection with the actual words on the page					
• Reads back short-experience stories written by the teacher					
• Can follow a line of print in enlarged text					
• Realizes that print has constant or fixed meaning (it always says the same thing)					
• Understands directionality of print (left-to-right, top-to-bottom)					
• Can identify and name most letters					
• Can make meaningful predictions using context and syntax clues					
• Attempts to write using some consonant sounds					
STAGE 2—THE DEVELOPING READER	Date				
• Understands the concept of a word					
• Recognizes some phonic generalizations (rhyming words, words that start or end the same, blends)					
• Sometimes finger points while reading					
• While writing, he/she represents all syllables using invented spelling					
• Uses some conventions of print in writing					
• Reads some things independently					
• Has a store of sight words in reading and writing					
• Uses all the cueing systems					
• Makes meaningful substitutions when reading					
• Comprehends what has been read; can retell a story					

Figure 4.8—Reading Development Checklist

Source: From *Impressions: Teacher Resource Book: East of the Sun* by Jack Booth et al. Copyright ©1985 by Holt, Rinehart & Winston of Canada. Reprinted by permission. Pp. 273–274.

understanding that is especially useful to those children who are not accustomed to having books read to them. Children who have been read to frequently know to expect words and sentence patterns in books that they do not normally hear in spoken language.

Strategies for using predictable books usually include the following:

1. Select a book that is appropriate for the group in terms of concept and interest.

READING DEVELOPMENT CHECKLIST

Name _____

STAGE 3—THE INDEPENDENT READER	Date				
• Reads silently but sometimes subvocalizes when the text is difficult					
• Makes predictions about a word (is likely to be using all three cueing systems)					
• Self-corrects when reading does not make sense					
• Comprehends at different levels (literal, interpretive, critical)					
• Adjusts silent reading rate to material and purpose					
• Invented spellings are closer to standard spelling					

Notes: _____

Figure 4.8 (*continued*)

2. Discuss the book cover. Ask questions about the cover illustration, the title, and the author. Ask what children think the book will be about and why. If the author or illustrator is a familiar one, ask if they remember other books by that person.

3. Begin reading the text (passing your hand under the lines of text for beginners).

4. Encourage the children to participate in the reading as soon as they can. They can make sounds for the characters or join in on the repetitive parts.

5. After reading a few pages, stop and ask for predictions about the outcome of the story.

6. After the story is finished, ask one or two questions such as "Did the story end the way you thought it would?" "What did you think of the story?" "What did you like best about this story?"

7. Give children as many choices as possible of extension activities: rereading the story, listening to the story on tape, making an illustration for the story, making a game from the story, writing another story based on the pattern in the book, and so on. (Adapted from Heald-Taylor, 1987)

Of course, not every patterned book will lend itself to precisely this treatment. Some will need to be read repeatedly, and some may be read by the group from Big Books. Some invite imitation and innovation by having the children substitute their words for words in the text. For example, children might listen to the poem "Alligator Pie" (Lee, 1974) and then substitute other words for *pie* or *alligator*. One class wrote "Crocodile Pie" and another wrote "Alligator Stew" (without hearing the second verse of Lee's poem).

Children can be encouraged to create their own variation based on the original repetitive book (Lawrence & Harris, 1986; Wuertenberg, 1983), just as they might write new lyrics to songs they have learned. For example, *Brown Bear, Brown Bear* (Martin, 1970) can be used at the beginning of kindergarten as the model for very simple stories. The children might write, "Ricardo, Ricardo, what do you see? I see Jennifer looking at me. Jennifer, Jennifer, what do you see? I see Noah looking at me," and so on, until all the children in the group have their names in the book. Another class might write a Halloween version following the same pattern: "Witch, witch, what do you see? I see a goblin looking at me. Goblin, goblin, what do you see?" One teacher used the pattern to help students remember the order of the planets when they were studying the solar system: "Flaming Sun, Flaming Sun, What do you see? I see Tiny Mercury looking at me. Tiny Mercury, Tiny Mercury, what do you see?"

Research by Bridge, Winograd, and Haley (1983) found that children who were taught a sight-word vocabulary in a program that employed predictable books learned significantly more words than children in a preprimer program. These children also had more flexible strategies for decoding unfamiliar words and more positive feelings about reading aloud. Teaching with predictable books is not only interesting but also effective!

Big Books

Holdaway (1979) found that children who learned to read early often did so because they were sitting on the lap of a parent or caregiver and could see the print as it was being read. When Holdaway (1979) realized what was happening with these children, he developed Big Books so a group of children could

Singing song lyrics can provide successful reading experiences.

© George White Location Photography

see the print while the teacher read the book. Today, there are many titles available to teachers in a Big Book format. The Big Book allows the teacher to engage in strategies with a large group that would have been possible with only one or two children with a regular book. For example, he or she can point out print features and discuss details of the illustrations.

The first step in using a Big Book is to read the book aloud following the guidelines for introducing a book and reading it well. In this first reading, demonstrate directionality by using your hand or a pointer to sweep under the lines as they are read. You might also invite predictions about the story based on the cover illustrations and help children think about what they know about the topic of the story or the genre. For example, if the story is about caterpillars, get them to tell what they know about caterpillars. If it is a folk story, get them to tell what they know about such stories (animals can talk, there are adventures, and so on).

On the second (and other subsequent readings), the teacher can empha-size the vocabulary of texts such as word, sentence, and page. Depending on the group and their knowledge, other conventions of print or punctuation could be the focus, as could building a sight vocabulary, drawing attention to letter–sound relationships, or the purposes for reading. After the book has been read several times, the children might be encouraged to explore the book on their own. Some Big Books have regular-sized versions of the book or a set of small books for independent use. These books are useful for allowing children to read the book by themselves or take it home to share with their families.

Children can become involved in making their own Big Books using tagboard or heavy paper. Their topics can be the themes being studied in the classroom (All About Birds), categories of things (What Is Blue?), or a text created to follow the pattern of a known Big Book (Little Bug, Little Bug, What Do You See?). Often these big books are laminated so they will withstand the heavy use given them in the classroom.

Other activities with Big Books include choral reading, comparing and analyzing the illustrations, sequencing or retelling the stories, and opportunities for children to create books of their own. Big Books do not guarantee good teaching, nor are they all worth the time to read and reread. The teacher must be as thoughtful and selective when choosing a Big Book as any other book, and the activities must be carefully tailored to fit the literacy needs of the individual children in the group. There is nothing magic about a book simply because it is large.

Music and Emergent Literacy

Music is a natural part of children's play. The next time you visit a playground or park, pause and listen to the things children are saying. There and in the backyard and on the street, you will hear children making up songs, chanting rhymes, and caroling tunes that are a part of their lives. Music belongs in the classroom, too—not as a frill but as a serious educational tool.

Music is so natural for children that it can be described in the same terms applied in current literature on emergent literacy to the act of reading: It's a natural extension of children's language and experience. Children learn to use written language in much the same way they learn to use oral language—through constructing their own rules and relationships (Goodman & Goodman, 1983; Graves, 1983). The more language, especially "book" language, children can hear, the more opportunities they have for constructing the rules.

Teaching reading holistically requires that the materials used be meaningful to the child, that the language be treated as a meaningful message from an author to a reader, and that the teacher's role be one of assisting the child in the endeavor, much as a parent assists a child in learning to talk. In holistic instruction in reading and writing, the units of language are sentences and story units (Hall, 1981). Music and singing readily fit the needs of such instruction. The songs can come from the child's environment, experience, or imagination and can have very personal meaning. Even the nonsense songs of childhood can be meaningful to a child, as well as fun to play with. The teacher's role is that of helping children learn at their own pace and fitting the songs to the needs of the individual.

Activities Using Music

Activities that use music to teach reading and writing fall into four categories: learning favorite songs, meeting the lyrics in print, reading song charts and booklets, and engaging in comprehension extension activities, including writing. Even if you don't think of yourself as especially musical, you can find suggestions here that will work for you.

Learning Favorite Songs

The first step in using singing to help children develop their ability to read and write is filling the classroom with songs that will quickly become favorites. Bringing favorite songs to the classroom requires only that the teacher be willing to spend some time selecting the songs and to employ records, tapes, or an instrument in teaching the songs to children. Because of the ready availability of recorded music, one need not be an accomplished musician to use singing to teach reading. Teachers can also seek the music teacher's help or use songs the children are learning in music class. Folksongs, raps, rhymes, nursery songs, and other simple songs are all suitable for teaching young children. For now, the important point is that children should have repeated exposure to songs so rote learning occurs.

The songs should be sung over and over again so the language becomes as familiar to the children as if it were their own. A total of 15 exposures to the words and music of a song over a two- or three-day period is not excessive. Learning to read by singing will be successful only if the children are totally familiar with the lyrics they will eventually meet in print.

Meeting the Lyrics in Print

When children have sung a song enough times to be comfortable with the tune and lyrics, they are ready to meet the lyrics in print. The easiest language for children to read is language with which they are very familiar. They delight in seeing the songs they know in print, and the teacher is truly rewarded when the children shout, "I can *read* this!" Their pleasure in their own success is an essential ingredient in any beginning or remedial reading experience.

Prepare for this activity by printing the song lyrics on large lined chart paper with a dark marker. The chart stand can hold your growing library of songs. Or print the lyrics on large pieces of tagboard that can be filed in a box and placed on an easel or chalk tray for presentation.

Introduce the song charts by explaining to the children that they are now going to read the words to the song they have been singing. Show them the chart, and invite them to sing along as you move your hand or a pointer under each line of print. After singing the song once or twice using the chart, stop and encourage the children to celebrate the fact they can *read* the words. Recognizing the words in this given context is an important step in learning to read.

Reading Song Charts and Booklets

These are some word-identification activities you can do with the song chart:

1. Invite individual children to come up to the chart to point to words pronounced by the teacher.

2. Invite individual children to come to the chart and identify words they recognize.

3. Encourage children to locate words that appear in more than one place on the chart.

4. Write individual words of the song on separate pieces of tagboard, using the same size print as on the chart. Have children match the words on the cards with the words on the chart.

Once children have learned to sing the songs with confidence from the song charts, and the teacher is comfortable that a concept of word has been developed, the children may be introduced to individual song booklets. Make the booklets by duplicating the lyrics on sheets of 8 ½ x 11-inch paper, cut in half, folded, and stapled along the fold. Print only a few lines of lyrics on each page, leaving plenty of space for the children's illustrations.

When they use their own song booklets, the children know they are reading. And they are! The teacher can be confident that the children are developing a sight vocabulary when they point to words or phrases accurately as they sing along in their booklets. The booklets lend themselves to many activities that reinforce the learning of the words. These are some we recommend:

1. Sing (read) the song lyrics while sharing the song booklet with a friend.

2. Sing (read) the lyrics to a friend who does not know the song.

3. Follow the lyrics in the booklet while listening to the recorded song at the listening center.

4. Use the song booklet to locate the words of the songs in other books and magazines.

This last activity helps the children understand that the same letters, same sounds, and same words they now can read occur over and over again, in many places. It is fun to listen to the excitement of the children as they make this important discovery.

Engaging in Comprehension Extension Activities

Reading has not really occurred until the reader interacts with the ideas represented by the words. Remembering the meanings of words read is one of the most valuable contributors to comprehension. It is appropriate to ask children about the meaning of words or phrases in the songs they have learned to sing and read. After the children have read and sung a song, select key words or phrases that are essential to understanding the ideas in the song, and ask children to tell what the words mean. When the children are unsure of meanings, explain the words or phrases to them. Be certain they can explain the word meanings in their own words and are not simply parroting back the definition that you gave them. Given the importance of memory of word meanings to overall comprehension, it is essential to spend time ensuring that children understand the songs they learn to sing and read.

Comprehension can be extended through drawing illustrations for songs, dramatizing phrases in songs, creating puppets of characters in songs, and creating motions to accompany a song.

Writing Activities

After children have read and sung a song, invite them to draw, color, or paint a picture to illustrate the song. Some children will want to write on the pictures themselves. These beginning writing efforts will soon lead to the writing of stories about the songs and the characters in songs and the composing of additional song lyrics. We can suggest some writing activities that grow out of singing and reading:

1. Write invitations to parents to come hear the children sing their favorite songs.

2. Write books about a song or the characters in a song.

3. Write letters to the composer of a song.

4. Create new lyrics to a familiar tune.

5. Write a script for a play based on a favorite song.

6. Illustrate a songbook made by the class.

The Language-Experience Approach

When we view printed language as an extension or another form of oral language, then teaching children to read by using their own experiences and language makes sense. Over the last few years, language experience has given way to the broader concept of whole language, but teachers of emerging readers may find some of the work with language experience valuable.

Definition of Language Experience

In simplified terms, using the **language-experience approach** in reading instruction means presenting children with some sort of stimulus to which they write a response, or they write about something they choose to write about. The writing they produce is used for teaching the various skills of reading.

Some of us used the language-experience approach long before we had a name for this strategy. We learned it when faced with children who did not respond well to basal reader instruction and who had had many failures reading. Language experience offered a way to tap into these children's interests and vocabulary and to make reading something meaningful and relevant to their lives. Many teachers choose language experience for readers who are not progressing as well as they might in the basal program. Other teachers turn to language experience for those readers who need a challenge and whose interests do not conform to the selections in the basal. For gifted children, language experience offers the opportunity to move along the reading continuum as quickly as they can while writing and reading about topics they find personally interesting.

Advantages of Language-Experience Reading

As a method of reading instruction, language experience has many advantages. In Chapter 2, we described reading as a developmental process, one that is closely related to the child's understanding of language. In Chapter 3, we further described writing as a developmental process related to the child's understanding of language and how it works. The language-experience approach to reading brings together the child's experiences and the child's expressions about experiences through the processes of speaking, reading, and writing. This connection between experience and language is the greatest advantage of using language experience. Materials for reading instruction in language experience are always relevant, current, and meaningful—characteristics not always found in other types of material. The following story was dictated by a first grader who was not succeeding in reading in the reading program at his school, but he loved anything about science:

I like science. I'll tell you about science. If you want to know
about making sparklers. You need aluminum filings and you need

charcoal powder. You need sulfur and potassium nitrate. You buy these things at a pharmacy. You mix all these chemicals together to make sparklers. You put the stuff on wires like those in plant holders. You wait a night and a day.

Language experience builds on the child's knowledge of language and how it works. For example, as children write their own reading material, they reveal their understanding of the conventions of word spacing, capitalization, punctuation, and paragraphing. A teacher helping children become more skillful readers will not spend instructional time on teaching capitalization to children who have demonstrated they understand it; for them, that instruction is redundant. (As new instances of need for capitalization arise, such as words in a title, instruction will be given.) For children who do not yet write sentences at all, however, instruction in capitalization is useless because they cannot yet apply it. The children who need such instruction—those just beginning to write sentences—can be easily identified using a language-experience approach.

Another advantage of the language-experience approach is that it treats language as a whole, not as bits and pieces. Children learning through language experience do not practice language skills outside the act of communication. Practice of a "proper" form, such as the old drills on *can* and *may* when the form is not needed for communication, is not useful in helping children speak or write more effectively. A teacher can insist a young child repeat the form "My brother and I," but until the child can hear the difference between "Me and my brother" and "My brother and I" and has a need to use the more mature form, practicing the skill will not change the child's oral or written language. Children have learned a great deal about language before they ever have any formal instruction in it; language experience allows the teacher to build on that knowledge.

Language experience has some psychological advantages, too, as a method of reading instruction. One of them is the feeling of success that is possible for every child. Children are compared only with themselves, not with other children, and success is measured in terms of individual growth rather than ranking in the class. Research has found that success is necessary for more success (Berliner, 1984). Too often teachers, striving to challenge students, have given them tasks that result in failure. What is needed for maximum achievement is the opportunity to be successful over and over. In many classrooms, all the children know is who reads the most difficult material and who does not. In language-experience classrooms, such comparisons are not easily made.

Language experience is also highly motivating. No words are quite as precious to us as our own words. One group of low-achieving readers in first grade wrote their own stories. When the stories were returned to them typed and bound, their response was a joyous "These are *our* words!" Children need to feel their own words are important.

Using language experience as a method for teaching reading will not necessarily raise children's reading scores on standardized tests, but studies have shown that children participating in language experience have better concepts of themselves as readers and a more positive attitude toward reading (Harris, 1969; Wilson & Parkey, 1970). Children who feel more capable as readers are much more likely to choose reading when given a choice of activities. Just as adults do not like to participate in activities in which they do not do well, children prefer those activities in which they perceive their performance to be positive. Lillian Katz (1986) has said that one of our jobs in education is to help children develop the disposition to continue an activity when they are not required to do so. We want readers who can read and who choose to read outside of school. Language experience, because of its close connection to real experience, tends to help children view reading and writing as responses to events in their lives, not as something one does for a short period of time in school. One young man of about 6 must have had a teacher who used language experience in his classroom. Exploring the tide pools at the coast with his father one July, he was overheard to exclaim, "We can make a book about this when we get home!" He had the idea about reading and writing.

Teachers who choose language experience must have respect for the children and their language and thinking. One way to demonstrate that respect is to share children's own written materials with other class members and use them for instruction. Children who come to school from different cultural or linguistic backgrounds may be required to read in the basal a language far removed from their home language. Teachers must accept the child's language as a vital part of the child and then help the child gain competence in using more standard English.

Research on Language Experience

There is not much current research on language experience as an approach to reading instruction, primarily because research for the past few years has focused on whole-language instruction. Researchers who compared groups using language experience and basal readers reported that children in language-experience programs made gains in oral language (Cox, 1971; Stauffer & Pikulski, 1974). When they used language experience with a low-achieving reading group, Bridge, Winograd, and Haley (1983) found that it spurred children in their acquisition of sight vocabulary, encouraged the use of contextual clues, and created more positive feelings about reading aloud. As one would expect, children's writing abilities increase when they write their own material (Oehlkers, 1971; Stauffer, M., 1973). Children who do more writing also tend to be better spellers (Cramer, 1970). Children do develop a satisfactory reading vocabulary when they are engaged in language-experience instruction (Hall, 1965; Kelly, 1975).

In a study that found most independent skill-practice exercises to be ineffective in fostering beginning reading, Evans and Carr (1985) identified writing

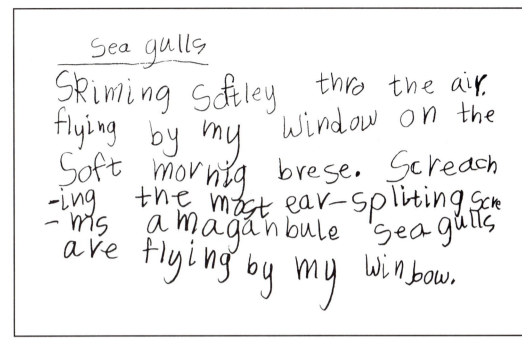

Sea gulls

Skiming softley thro the air.
flying by my window on the
soft mornig brese. Screach
-ing the most ear-spliting scre
-ms a maganbule sea gulls
are flying by my winbow.

Figure 4.9—Story by a First Grader

as an exception to that pattern. They recorded a positive relationship between reading achievement and activities that involved writing, which helps children gain insight into letter–sound correspondences and therefore serves to reinforce practice in word analysis. These and many other studies have confirmed that the language-experience approach can help children develop as competent readers and better writers with more positive feelings about reading.

The authors of *Becoming a Nation of Readers* (Anderson, Hiebert, Scott, & Wilkinson, 1985, p. 79) speak in support of writing in the reading program:

> Opportunities to write have been found to contribute to knowledge of how written and oral language are related, and to growth in phonics, spelling, vocabulary development, and reading comprehension. Students who write frequently and discuss their writing with others approach reading with what has been termed the "eye of the writer."

The first grader who wrote "Seagulls" (Figure 4.9) demonstrates both knowledge of how language works and a wonderful sense of the poetic. Not all the spelling is conventional, and neither is the placement of words on the page, but surely every teacher would value the child's abilities.

Taking dictation provides another opportunity for demonstrating how reading and writing work.

© Elizabeth Crews/Stock Boston

Both Calkins (1986) and Graves (1983), in their work with children's writing, have observed that when children write they also read. They read to get started writing again, they read to enjoy what they have written, they read to edit, and they read to share their writing. Reading contributes to growth in writing, and writing contributes to success in reading. Children develop strategies in their writing that transfer to their reading. Boutwell (1983) described the strategy used by one child when she met a confusing passage in her reading (p. 725): "When Marta encountered confusing parts, she reread them. This strategy sprang from the same question she asked in reading her own writing: Does this make sense?"

Experience and Language: Bringing Them Together

This section is a brief how-to guide offering some ideas on how to manage language experience. However, each teacher must work out his or her own system; following a set pattern is not what language experience is about. It is about making professional decisions concerning reading instruction and being accountable for those decisions. These are the basic steps in language experience for young children:

1. Selection of purpose for instruction

2. Presentation of stimuli

3. Discussion

4. Writing

5. Reading

6. Skills instruction as needed

7. Extension to the work of other authors.

Selection of Purpose

The first step in language-experience instruction is to determine the focus of instruction. Suppose a child has brought a frog to school and the children are excited and want to write about it. You would consider the age, experience, and previous writing of the children in establishing the most important goals of this specific writing experience. If the children were just beginning to read and write, you might want to emphasize the /fr/ blend; if they were beginning independent readers, you might want to concentrate on the sight words they recognize; if they have a little more experience, you might focus on the different story structures of reports about frogs and toads, narratives about frogs, and personal observations about frogs. The purpose for instruction serves as a guide in determining how the other steps are implemented.

Presentation of Stimuli

Finding something for children to write about should not become a problem for a teacher when interesting things are going on all the time. In a classroom where there are animals, visitors, and activities evolving out of the teacher's and children's interests, the stimuli for language experience are just daily activities. In response to the children's interest in frogs and toads, the teacher finds books and poems about frogs. The children take a walk to a nearby pond and collect some tadpoles, which they put into an aquarium in the classroom. The tadpoles, frogs, and books about toads and frogs all become the stimuli for writing. While taking advantage of an expressed interest of the children, the teacher has arranged for the stimuli within the realm of usual classroom activities.

Depending on their needs, the teacher might help the children think of and record on the chalkboard some words they could use in writing about frogs. The words would simply be available to them, but not required in their writings.

Discussion

After a common experience, the teacher will want to engage the children in discussing it, so the group has a common direction. Usually the discussion is short, sometimes to help the children focus on the experience, sometimes to share ideas about format or audience for their writing, sometimes to explore pertinent words. If in the class with the new frog the teacher wanted to focus on the structure of reports about frogs, the discussion would include reminders about the scope, content, and presentation of reports.

Writing

Let's say the children are obviously interested in the frogs, toads, and tadpoles. Some want to write about the trip to collect the tadpoles. The teacher might help them think about adventure stories and use one as a model for their accounts. Others might keep a pictorial and written record of the changes they observe in the tadpoles. The teacher will help these children think about scientific reports, including the information necessary to enable other scientists to replicate their findings. Some children will decide to record the facts they have learned about frogs and toads. The teacher will help them think about reference materials and how they are written and arranged, suggesting they compile a class encyclopedia about amphibians. Others might want to model their writing on stories such as *Frog and Toad Together* (Lobel, 1972). The teacher would give group instruction to children working on each kind of writing and encourage them to help one another as they worked through their writing problems.

The choice of taking dictation from the students or asking them to write independently depends on the goals of instruction and/or the age and ability of the students. Dictation would be preferred if the goal were to help younger children record their words quickly so instruction could focus on learning to recognize given words on sight. Dictation might also be the choice if the teacher wanted to help the children create a group story or to assist a child whose motor disabilities make writing a struggle. However, most of the time the children, even the younger ones, should write independently.

Taking dictation for a specific purpose does not mean children cannot do their own writing on the same topic. After the teacher had taken dictation about the tadpole-collecting expedition, for example, the children could be encouraged to do their own writing as they painted frog pictures or prepared the aquarium. The main use of dictation should be to record group responses rather than individual responses.

Teachers taking dictation have an obligation to record children's words as they are dictated. If the child's language forms are not standard English constructions, the teacher may help the child (over a period of time) think about alternate ways of expressing a thought in more standard English. If the point of taking dictation is to help children see that thoughts can be recorded in print and that print can serve as a way of storing those thoughts for later reading, then the words must be exact. The words of a child who speaks a dialect should be spelled in conventional spelling. When the child reads the passage aloud, the teacher must expect dialectal pronunciation. Making changes in the children's words gives children the message that their words are not good enough and they cannot communicate successfully. This to not to say that teachers should not help children move toward competence in standard English; but for a beginning reader, it is important to remember the purpose of taking dictation, which is to let children see their own ideas in print.

Reading

The children would be involved in reading as the process of writing continued. They would listen as a response group to a piece read by the author and they would read their own compositions to the class. Some pieces would be bound into books, to become a part of the class library for any child to check out and read. The children would also read many of the reference books and trade books that the teacher had helped them locate.

In the language-experience approach, both oral reading by the teacher and choral reading are important. The teacher would read aloud to the children frequently. Read-aloud sessions would include reading the children's work and reading narrative or information books related to the topic. Children can be involved in choral reading as they read a chart that has been dictated or as they read a book that has been composed by one child or by the class. Both listening to the teacher read and choral reading aid the development of fluent, efficient reading.

Skills Instruction

Skills instruction in language experience is a natural outgrowth of the reading, not an overlay. Skills might be as simple as letter–sound relationships or directionality of print or as complex as examining the development of fictional characters or analyzing the language used to achieve a particular mood. In between those extremes, instruction can focus on phonics, sight words, clarity, coherence of text, story structure, assumptions of prior knowledge by the author, changes needed to adapt the text for different audiences, and so on. Instruction can also focus on the mechanics of writing, such as capitalization, punctuation, and paragraphing. Children's vocabularies certainly present as many opportunities for teaching skills as does professionally prepared reading material. The difference is that their vocabularies are not controlled, nor is there the planned redundancy found in basal readers. Children who learn to read through the language-experience approach may read a selection over many times before they finish with it, so repeated exposure to the same words is very likely even though the words themselves are not repeated.

Large-group instruction in skills is appropriate when a new topic is introduced to the class. For example, the teacher might determine that the entire class needs instruction in recognizing the characteristics of poetry. If some, but not all, children need instruction in letter–sound relationships, it would make sense to use small-group instruction in skills. Individual instruction in skills would also take place on a regular basis as teachers talk with individual children about the content of their reading or listen to the child read orally.

The products of language experience may include any type of material, from directions for making things to poetry. The outcomes may include books, dictionaries, encyclopedias, journals, pamphlets, and posters.

Extension to the Work of Other Authors

Whatever the theme or topic of study, books can be found that will extend the children's work to the work of other authors. If the children were writing humorous stories, they might enjoy some humorous stories about pigs such as *Pig Tale* (Oxenbury, 1973), *The Amazing Bone* (Steig, 1976), *Roland, the Minstrel Pig* (Steig, 1968), and *Hamilton* (Peck, 1976). The children could keep a chart of the different genres, the audiences for different pieces, and the purposes of different pieces. Teachers could emphasize the words or phrases used by the authors so children could incorporate those into their own writing. Children need to know that other people write about topics they themselves write about and find interesting.

Key Words and Word Banks

One approach to language experience was developed in New Zealand by Sylvia Ashton-Warner (1963), who was working with Maori children whose first language was not English. She began recording their words of the day, each child's daily choice of an important word he or she wanted to learn. She felt these words were of real interest and meaning to the children. Every few days she would have the children read back their collections of words. The words a child could not remember were discarded. She felt the words they remembered were especially significant to the individual child. Over a period of a few weeks, the children would build their own collections of words they could read on sight. This strategy has been called the **key word technique.** The collection of words that become part of the child's sight vocabulary is called a **word bank.**

Teachers use the key word technique in several ways. Children may be asked to dictate their word of the day as they enter the classroom each day. The teacher writes the word on a card, involving the child by asking him or her to tell the teacher what letters to write or to identify the sounds in the word. After recording the word, some teachers ask the child to copy the word into a booklet with a title like "My Important Word Book" or "My Beautiful Word Book." The child may then draw an illustration or write a sentence about the word. Over a period of time, the children can read and reread their books and recall their words. This technique works especially well with children whose first language is not English; these words they know in English have a special significance.

Figure 4.10 is a sample page of a child's "important word book." The key word is *tide pool.* Note that the important word was taken from a classroom activity, the creation of a tide pool in the classroom.

Word banks—the words children collect as sight words—can inspire a variety of activities. Teachers will be able to think of many meaningful ways for the children to use their word banks. The following are just examples:

▼   Use the word bank as a dictionary when writing.

▼   Choose your favorite word and write about it.

▼   Tell a friend why you chose one or two of the words.

▼   Look for one or two of the words in a newspaper.

▼   Draw a picture to illustrate a word.

▼   Build a model with clay or blocks to illustrate a word.

▼   Find three objects in the classroom whose names rhyme with one of the words.

▼   Group words that are related and explain how they are related.

Figure 4.10—Key Word Entry in a Student's Booklet

Relationship to Whole-Language Instruction

We have talked about whole-language instruction as instruction that begins with meaningful material and then helps children with the skills of reading as they are needed in order to achieve meaning. This progression from whole to part to whole is, by definition, required in the language-experience approach. Points at which language-experience advocates and whole-language advocates diverge are the follow-up activities planned for the children's writing and the strong emphasis of whole language on genre restrictions on writing. In whole-language instruction, writing would most typically follow reading instruction. For example, children might read a story and then write a review of that story or use the story as a model for their writing. In language experience, the writing usually comes first, and reading instruction is based on the children's writing.

Advocates of whole language believe all writing is bound by the rules of the genre. In other words, all narratives have certain structures in common, an essay has certain structures that define it as an essay, and textbooks or reference books have certain structures. Some teachers using language experience have not been especially aware of the restraints on writing that are imposed by the genre and have therefore failed to help children learn about the genre and the audience for their writing. Language experience at its best always extends the children's work to the work of other authors who have written on the same or similar topics and uses the literature as a model for future writing. For example, if children have written about their experience in making soup, the teacher might then read *Stone Soup* (Brown, 1947) and encourage some children to write in narrative style rather than report style. Others might find a soup cookbook and write an introduction to their own collection of favorite family soup recipes. There are numerous opportunities for connecting children's experiences, their writing, their reading, and the worlds of literature and expository writing.

In other respects, the language-experience approach and whole-language instruction are very much alike. They both honor language and believe reading is for meaning. Both treat skills instruction in a meaningful context and want children actively involved in learning to read. They both believe language, reading, and writing are learned through children's involvement in using them, not through activities that are separated from real communication.

Emergent Writing

Teachers of young children must be knowledgeable about the stages of development in children's writing (composition) and spelling. Yetta Goodman (1987) found that children make discoveries about the principles of print and how it is used depending on their experiences. They learn that print can control the behavior of others, that it can help extend one's memory, how English is spelled and how it looks, and about different kinds of text and the rules for

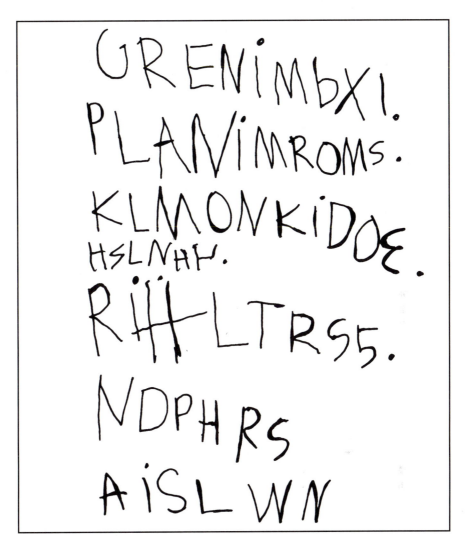

Figure 4.11—Writing of a 4-Year-Old

writing each one. The example in Figure 4.11 was written by a 4-year-old. Read it before you read the explanation here.

Did you discover the writing sample was a list? What does the writer know about the text structure of lists? What does she know about the functions of print? What does she know about the orthographic system of English? The translation reads: Jewelry in my box. 1. Play in my room 2. Climb on Quadro. 3. Have lunch. 4. Write letters and draw pictures 5. This piece is a good illustration of Jensen's (1990) findings that young children use different organizational patterns for different writing tasks.

Often children begin writing by labeling or writing on their drawings. Drawing is an important organizational strategy for young children, and there is no reason why they should not be encouraged to draw first and then write. Some teachers want children to write first and then illustrate their writing, which is a much more difficult task, especially for younger children. Wuertenberg (1993) says three things can be done with children's writing: post it, produce it, or publish it. *Posting* refers to simply displaying the work to share with others—on a bulletin board, in the hall, on a wall, for example. *Producing* a piece means it can be acted out in a skit, a play, a puppet play, a video, or some other medium. *Publishing* means the work is refined and perfected and published in some form—a book or a collection of stories, poems, or expository pieces. For emergent writers, the most frequent choice may be to post it. Posting does not have to be at school; some children are really anxious to take their writing home to share with their families. If the piece is important for illustrating new growth steps, you can make a photocopy and still send the original piece home. Some teachers like to choose a piece of the child's writing and ask if they would like to turn it into a book for others to read, but this is done infrequently with emergent writers.

Emergent writers need a classroom environment that encourages writing as well as reading; they need authentic reasons to write (invitations, announcements, letters, lists, and so on); and they need a response to their writing (dialogue journals in which the teacher answers questions or responds to statements), a teacher who listens to the child's piece and makes appropriate comments, or a chance to read the piece to a group or to the class.

Teachers of emergent writers do not need to worry about the writing process except the planning or prewriting stages and the opportunity to write. Emergent writers do not have to revise or edit their writing.

Writing is the most appropriate time for helping children develop the letter–sound relationships. Skilled teachers know which letter–sound relationships the child already knows by observing the child's writing. When children are writing, they often ask how to spell a word or how to write a word. This is a perfect opportunity for asking the child what he or she hears as the word is pronounced slowly. Even if the teacher has to name the letters to be recorded, the child must listen and associate the sounds and letters. As children attend to what they hear and how those sounds can be represented in writing, they are learning phonics. Learning phonics in the context of writing gives the child a reason to learn the sounds and letters, is meaningful to the child at the time, and is individually appropriate.

Phonemic Awareness and Phonics Instruction

Phonemic awareness, defined by Cunningham (1988) as the ability to examine language independent of meaning and to manipulate its component sounds, is an important predictor of children's reading success. Phonemic

awareness is not equivalent to phonics instruction because it is not necessarily a child's ability to spell the sounds, but to be aware of them. Several
studies have indicated the importance of such awareness (Juell, 1988; Juell,
Griffith, & Gough, 1986; Lomax & McGee, 1987). An assessment of phonemic
awareness can be made through various tasks, such as asking the child to
identify the sound at the beginning or end of a given word or to segment the
sounds in a given word. Experts argue about whether phonemic awareness
comes before reading or is a result of reading instruction (Yopp, 1992). Yopp
(1992) contends it is both: Some amount of phonemic awareness is necessary
for reading, and that reading increases the child's awareness of sounds.

For children who need to become aware of sounds, books with rhyming
words or alliterative patterns can be read and the sounds highlighted. Writing
experiences provide excellent opportunities for teachers to assess children's
awareness of sounds and to help them become more aware of sounds. When
a child can invent spellings the teacher can be assured that phonemic awareness is developing. Whatever activities are selected, the teacher must make
sure the instruction is individualized and appropriate for the child.

Phonics instruction is probably the most controversial area of reading
instruction. Some would argue that good phonics instruction is the answer to
all reading problems; others would say that phonics robs reading of meaning
(Stahl, 1992). Traditionally, phonics lessons were usually presented to children in groups. In a typical group of 25 children, several will know the material and find the instruction useless, several will not have any need for the information and find the instruction useless, and only a few children will be able to
make the desired connection between the instruction and what they are trying
to do as learners of reading and writing. Phonics instruction is certainly important because the graphophonic system, the use of the alphabet to record
sounds, is one of the cueing systems we use to create meaning, but it should
be considered in context and as it is meaningful to individual children. Stahl
(1992) recommends that instruction in phonics build on what children know
about language, be integrated into real reading experiences, and not require
memorizing rules. He goes on to say that good phonics instruction should be
over quickly—it does not go on all through elementary school. Our most
important rule for phonics instruction is that children who do not need the
instruction do not get it. The best way we know to do that is to engage in phonics instruction as we work with individual children as they write.

Figure 4.12 is another example of a first grader's writing. This sample was
collected in November. What does this emerging writer know about the conventions of print? What would be appropriate instructional goals? How would
you relate this writing to reading instruction?

The Social Context of Literacy

Not all children are socialized into literacy in exactly the same ways.
Teachers must learn to look at the experiences of children in various settings

Figure 4.12—Writing of a First Grader

as different experiences, but not as obstacles to the child's learning. We have already discussed the work of Heath (1983) as she looked at language learning and use in different communities. In the same study, she explored how the different communities used reading and writing. Heath studied two communities that were actually composites of several small communities in the region. The population of Roadville was primarily white, the population of Trackton, black. These communities have much in common with each other, but not much in common with the mainstream city communities. Heath's point is not that some groups are more literate or some experiences are better, but that the social and cultural uses of literacy are different in different cultures. Teachers need to be sensitive to these differences in order to plan the best instruction for their children and to think of literacy as possible for every child, regardless of cultural or language differences from those of the school.

Figures 4.13 through 4.16 will help you think about the focus of instruction in your classroom and how much experience the children may have had with a particular literacy activity. They may also help you plan for some literacy experiences that will match the children's home activities.

In encouraging teachers to think about cultural differences in literacy, Au (1993) suggests that "teachers may explore with their classes the ways in which students and their families use literacy at home and in the community. Students and their families may use literacy in sophisticated ways which are not necessarily familiar to teachers from a mainstream background" (p. 32). Au goes on to say that teachers might engage children with the forms and documents that are part of their home literacy experiences. Pellegrini (1991) reminds teachers that many homes are supportive of literacy with materials other than narrative stories. He believes many more children would be successful in school if teachers made a point of teaching the "rules" of different literacy experiences. For example, if children do not know the rules for interacting around a story, then the teacher has to call attention to the specific behaviors expected, such as listening, responding when asked a question, and pointing to items in the illustrations.

INSTRUMENTAL:	Reading to accomplish practical goals of daily life (price tags, checks, bills, telephone dials, clocks, street signs, house numbers).
SOCIAL-INTERACTIONAL/ RECREATIONAL:	Reading to maintain social relationships, make plans, and introduce topics for discussion and storytelling (greeting cards, cartoons, letters, newspaper features, political flyers, announcements of community meetings).
NEWS RELATED:	Reading to learn about third parties or distant events (local news items, circulars from the community center or school).
CONFIRMATIONAL:	Reading to gain support for attitudes or beliefs already held (Bible, brochures on cars, loan notes, bills).

Figure 4.13—Heath's Results: Types of Uses of Reading in Trackton

Note. Listed in relative order of frequency of occasions when time on these types of tasks exceeded 5 minutes per day.

Source: From Shirley Brice Heath, *Ways with Words: Language, Life and Work in Communities and Classrooms.* Copyright ©1983 by Cambridge University Press. Reprinted with the permission of Cambridge University Press.

MEMORY AIDS: (primarily used by women)	Writing to serve as a reminder for the writer and, only occasionally, others (telephone numbers, notes on calendars).
SUBSTITUTES FOR ORAL MESSAGES: (primarily used by women)	Writing used when direct oral communication was not possible or would prove embarrassing (notes for tardiness or absence from school, greeting cards, letters).
FINANCIAL:	Writing to record numerals and to write out amounts and accompanying notes (signatures on checks and public forms, figures and notes for income tax preparation).
PUBLIC RECORDS: (church only)	Writing to announce the order of the church services and forthcoming events and to record financial and policy decisions (church bulletins, reports of the church building fund committee).

Figure 4.14—Heath's Results: Types of Uses of Writing in Trackton

Note. Listed in relative order of frequency of occasions when time on these types of tasks exceeded 5 minutes per day.

Source: From Shirley Brice Heath, *Ways with Words: Language, Life and Work in Communities and Classrooms.* Copyright ©1983 by Cambridge University Press. Reprinted with the permission of Cambridge University Press.

Communicating with Parents

One of the challenges of teaching young children is communicating success-fully with the parents about their child's literacy growth. Remember that noth-ing about school is more important to most parents than their child's perfor-mance in reading and writing. Parents are generally less concerned with the art curriculum or the science curriculum. They are very much aware that their child's success in school may be largely determined by the child's ability as a reader and writer; therefore, it is very important that parents be kept informed about their children and feel positive about the progress their child is making.

The following are suggestions for helping parents understand and sup-port their child's literacy growth. Some of these activities could be the pro-gram for parent meetings, others could be shared with individual parents, and some can be accomplished through writing or newsletters.

1. Collect writing samples from children at a variety of stages (from scrib-bling to transitional spelling) and make overhead transparencies to be presented at a parent meeting. Focus on what children know about the conventions of print. Invite parents to "read" several other examples and make a list of what the children who wrote them know.

MEMORY AIDS:	Writing to serve as a memory aid for both the writer and others (grocery lists, labels in baby books, outlines of sequence and content of circle meetings, frequently called telephone numbers jotted in front of phone book).
SUBSTITUTES FOR OR REAFFIRMATION OF ORAL MESSAGES:	Writing used when direct oral communication was not possible or to follow up on oral exchanges (notes for tardiness and absence from school, assignments following class discussions, messages left by adults for children coming home before parent).
FINANCIAL:	Writing to record numerals and to write out amounts and purposes of expenditures and for signatures (checks; signing forms; filling out church, school, and mail-order forms).
SOCIAL-INTERACTIONAL:	Writing to give information and extend courtesies and greetings pertinent for maintaining social linkages (letters, notes on commercial greeting cards, thank you notes).

Figure 4.15—Heath's Results: Types of Uses of Writing in Roadville

Note. Listed in relative order of frequency of occasions when time on these types of tasks exceeded 5 minutes per day.

Source: From Shirley Brice Heath, *Ways with Words: Language, Life and Work in Communities and Classrooms.* Copyright ©1983 by Cambridge University Press. Reprinted with the permission of Cambridge University Press.

2. Demonstrate how you would introduce a story in a Big Book and how you would provide some needed skill instruction based on the story selected.

3. Write a note to parents when their child has made a change in writing. If the child is learning to leave spaces around individual words or is using more conventional spelling, for example, be prepared to highlight these changes for the parent.

4. Reinforce the importance of parents as literacy teachers by explaining how much the child knew before school and how much they continue to learn at home. Use the list of literacy activities suggested by Spiegel, Fitzgerald, and Cunningham (1993) to help parents select activities that are useful even when they cannot read to their child every night. Their list is featured in Figure 4.17.

5. Help parents make a list of things they do at home that are related to literacy, even if they cannot read—storytelling, talking about the plot of a television program, listening to tape recordings of books with their child, talking about family events in sequence, and so on.

INSTRUMENTAL:	Reading to gain information for practical needs of daily life (telephone dials, clocks, bills and checks, labels on products, reminder notes, school messages, patterns for dressmaking).
NEWS RELATED:	Reading to gain information about third parties or distant events (newspaper items; church denominational magazines; memos from the mill on the union, health and safety, etc.).
CONFIRMATIONAL:	Reading to check, confirm, or announce facts or beliefs (the Bible, Sunday School materials, camper or sports magazines, newspaper stories, appliance warranties and directions).
SOCIAL-INTERACTIONAL: (primarily used by women and children)	Reading to gain information pertinent to social linkages and forthcoming activities (church newsletters, greeting cards, letters, newspaper features—especially on sports page).
RECREATIONAL/EDUCATIONAL:	Reading for temporary entertainment or planning a recreational event ("funny papers" or comics in newspapers; brochures on campgrounds; advertisements for home shows, movies, or musical programs; ball game schedules, scores, and lineups; bedtime stories to preschoolers).

Figure 4.16—Heath's Results: Types of Uses of Reading in Roadville

Note. Listed in relative order of frequency of occasions when time on these types of tasks exceeded 5 minutes per day.

Source: From Shirley Brice Heath, *Ways with Words: Language, Life and Work in Communities and Classrooms.* Copyright ©1983 by Cambridge University Press. Reprinted with the permission of Cambridge University Press.

6. Distribute the brochure "Literacy Instruction and Pre-First Grade: A Joint Statement About Present Practices in Pre-First Grade Reading Instruction and Recommendations for Improvement." This brochure is available from International Reading Association, 800 Barksdale Rd., P.O. Box 8139, Newark, DE 19714. The cost is very reasonable for a bulk order of 100 brochures.

7. Demonstrate responding to a child's independent reading efforts (for example, how to focus on meaning, how to respond to questions about unknown words, and how to respond to errors).

8. Invite parents to observe in the classroom and provide them with a guide to help them observe the literacy events in the classroom. For example, you might ask them to look for any use of reading/writing in play, to note the books and writing materials available to children throughout the classroom, to observe the children's reading behaviors, to observe the use of print to carry out simple classroom routines, and to observe planned instruction.

Each week try to do at least three activities from List A, two from List B, and one from List C. You may choose to do the same activity more than one time, or you may do one activity several times.

List A: Casual Holistic Activities Requiring No Preparation

Read to your child for 10 minutes.

Let your child see you reading something, either for fun (such as a magazine or a book) or to get a job done (reading a recipe or *TV Guide*).

Give your child paper and something to write with.

Encourage your child to read a book or magazine, pretend-read, or look at the pictures in a book or magazine for five minutes.

Talk with your child about something you have read together.

Let your child listen to books on tapes or records.

List B: Interactive Activities Dealing with Literacy Skills or Strategies

Encourage your child to point to words or letters (on signs or labels in your home) that she or he knows.

Talk to your child about words or letters.

Encourage your child to tell you a story, either one that is already familiar or one the child has made up.

Let your child help you make a shopping list.

Play sound games with your child, such as "I am thinking of something in this room that rhymes with *fat* or that begins like *Dan*."

Play word games with your child, such as "Let's see how many animals (or colors or vegetables) we can name."

List C: Extended Activities Requiring a Substantial Time Investment

Take your child to the library to check out books.

Help your child write a letter to a friend or relative.

Have your child tell you a short story while you write it down; then your child can draw a picture to go with the story.

Take your child to the zoo, a museum, a farm, the airport, or someplace she or he has never been before; talk about what you see.

Figure 4.17—A Weekly Menu for Home Literacy Activities

Source: From "Parental Perceptions of Preschoolers' Literacy Development: Implications for Home-School Partnerships" by D. L. Spiegel, J. Fitzgerald, and J. W. Cunningham, 1993, *Young Children*, 48(5), p. 76. Copyright ©1993 by the National Association for the Education of Young Children. Reprinted by permission.

Knowledgeable parents and teachers can help emergent readers and writers move along the literacy continuum while maintaining learners' confidence in their own abilities as users of print. There is much to do and it helps if both parents and teachers are working together.

Major Ideas in This Chapter

▼ The concept of literacy and what it takes to achieve effective instruction in literacy has undergone a radical change over the last 20 years.

▼ The concept of readiness as a specific point at which a child could benefit from reading instruction has been replaced by the idea that children know a great deal about print when they come to school and that what they know is the basis for further instruction.

▼ A print-rich classroom environment, play that offers literacy experiences, the use of predictable books and music in planned literacy instruction, and teachers who involve children as participants in reading and writing activities help children gain success as readers and writers.

▼ Language experience is an approach to reading instruction in which the teacher uses the child's own language to help the child learn to read and to improve as a writer.

▼ Emergent writers need supportive and sensitive teachers as they gain control of the various forms of writing and learn the conventions of print.

▼ Classroom activities must reflect the cultural backgrounds of the children and their literacy experiences in the social context of their homes.

▼ Keeping parents informed about what their children know and how they are learning is vital to the success of an emergent literacy program.

Discussion Questions: Focusing on the Teacher You Are Becoming

1. How would you explain to a parent the difference between a readiness concept and the concept of emergent literacy?

2. In a small group, discuss your literacy history. How did your family use reading and writing? Which types of experiences were most common? Are there some classroom activities that reflect your own literacy community?

3. Discuss the importance of reading aloud to children as a teacher and as a parent.

4. Discuss the importance of parental support for an emergent literacy program. Make a list of ways to communicate successfully with parents about their children's literacy abilities.

Field-Based Applications

1. Plan a reading experience based on a Big Book. Think about what questions you might ask and what print features you might emphasize.

2. Select a piece of writing from a kindergartener and write a letter to the parents explaining what the child knows about written language.

3. Plan a play theme for a classroom that would involve the children in literacy experiences. Make a list of the materials that could enhance the literacy play.

4. Read a book aloud to a small group. Plan how you will involve the children in terms of prediction, print features, supplying text, and so on.

Chapter 5
Assessing Children's Reading and Writing Progress

Chapter Overview

▼ *Assessment* is the collection of data on a learner's performance. *Evaluation* is the interpretation of that data to identify progress and the next learning steps. We should evaluate what we *value* in readers and writers.

▼ A distinction must be made between traditional forms of assessment and responsive assessment. Traditional forms of assessment involve testing. Responsive assessment requires a knowledgeable teacher to carefully record observations of students' work, synthesize the information, and then plan instruction.

▼ Teachers gain insight into children's understanding of the reading process by analyzing running records and asking children to retell everything they can remember about a selection. Creating meaning is more important than correctly decoding graphophonic cues; knowing how a child processes reading is more helpful than knowing the grade level at which a child reads.

▼ Evaluating a child's writing using specific models and making suggestions for improvement teaches children more about writing than does assigning a grade.

▼ When we administer tests of children's knowledge or skill, we are measuring the product of teaching and learning. When we observe their use of reading and writing, we are assessing the process of teaching and learning, which is of equal importance to the product.

▼ Teachers must frequently place children in groups for instructional purposes. The traditional method, ability grouping, is not as effective as flexible grouping or cooperative learning groups.

▼ Activity centers facilitate student self-direction in learning. Centers permit students access to instructional materials without the direct assistance of the teacher.

▼ Managing the classroom so children are productive and happy is aided by planning instructional activities that are challenging and meaningful and by following certain guidelines.

Making Assessment Decisions

Teachers do not make decisions randomly. They make careful instructional decisions by using a variety of data available to them. In this section we examine the various sources of decision-making data used by teachers. Collecting the data is known as *assessment*. Interpreting that data in terms of the learner's progress and next learning steps is called *evaluation*. Deciding what to evaluate is critical in bringing children to literacy.

Evaluating What We Value

As we noted in Chapter 3, when you examine the word *evaluate* you see that *value* is the heart of the word. Teachers, parents, and children should evaluate efforts toward literacy in terms of what we value in readers and writers. We have often asked groups of teachers in workshops to list the things they value most in a reader or writer. The lists never begin with "correctly sounding out short vowel sounds" or "accurate spelling in rough drafts." High on the lists are more likely to be statements such as "enjoys reading, reads for recreation, writes creatively and thoughtfully."

Consider the weekly spelling test often given on Fridays in many classrooms. When carefully examined, this practice suggests that what we value most in spellers is correct spelling of words in isolation on a test one day a week. Is that really what we value in spellers? We suspect not. What we really value in spellers is correct spelling daily in the context of edited and polished writing. Therefore, we should be evaluating spelling performance in the context of writing across the curriculum daily rather than once a week on a spelling test. In deciding what to evaluate in literacy, it is imperative to first determine what we value in emergent, developing, and fluent readers and writers.

We believe teachers, parents, administrators (and maybe even children) should come together within a school and list what is valued in readers and writers at each stage of development. Assessment tools would then be selected or designed to collect data on what is valued and appropriate evaluation would occur. We further believe that data should be collected on children's learning using as wide a variety of strategies as possible. These include teacher observation, child self-assessment, parental assessment, testing, and careful examination of the products of the child's reading and writing.

Regardless of how evaluation decisions are made, two critically different kinds of assessment are in use in schools today: traditional assessment and responsive assessment.

Traditional Assessment

Traditionally data collection has been done by testing. Here we discuss two kinds of tests: criterion-referenced tests and norm-referenced tests.

Criterion-Referenced Tests

Criterion-referenced tests are so named because the criterion for passing them is determined in advance and the student's performance is measured against it. Criterion-referenced tests measure performance against specified objectives (such as reading skills) with predetermined criteria ranging from unsatisfactory to outstanding performance. The examinations you take in a college course are probably criterion referenced. If so, the professor establishes in advance that in order to get an A you must earn a certain percentage of the possible points on the exam.

Teachers are commonly the designers of criterion-referenced tests. For example, a teacher might design a criterion-referenced test to be given at the end of a unit of study. The test would be written to assess performance on the instructional objectives for the unit, administered and scored by the teacher. Performance would be evaluated against predetermined criteria the teacher had established. In some instances school districts design criterion-referenced tests to assess mastery of the district's instructional objectives in reading. Such tests are frequently administered to fourth, eighth, and twelfth graders to evaluate the district's performance in teaching reading. Now some states have statewide criterion-referenced tests to measure reading achievement. Some of these tests, such as the Informal Reading Inventory (IRI), are used primarily by reading specialists or by classroom teachers when the progress of an individual student is particularly puzzling.

Informal Reading Inventory

The Informal Reading Inventory may be purchased or made by a teacher. Sometimes it accompanies basal readers. In short, an IRI consists of graded word lists, graded reading selections, and comprehension questions. The IRI is individually administered as the child reads aloud to the teacher. Oral reading errors are coded and scored; then comprehension questions are asked and scored. Typically the percentage of words read correctly is calculated, and then the percentage of comprehension questions answered correctly is determined. These percentages are used to determine whether a particular selection is at a reader's independent reading level (can be read alone), instructional reading level (best for instructional purposes), or frustration level (too difficult at this time).

The percentages used to determine these levels are not consistent from one IRI to another. Typically they are as follows:

Independent	Oral reading = 99%	Comprehension = 90% +
Instructional	Oral reading = 95%	Comprehension = 75% to 89%
Frustration	Oral reading = 90% or less	Comprehension = 50% or less

We have included this discussion of IRIs because they are used in many schools and you need to know about them. However, we do not recommend them. We suggest taking running records and doing miscue analysis as we discuss later in this chapter. Here are our reasons for recommending against IRIs:

1. All oral reading errors are counted with equal weight without regard to whether or not meaning was maintained. We know that even fluent readers make mistakes when they read. The issue is not the number of mistakes per se, but the number of mistakes that damage the creation of meaning and go uncorrected.

2. Comprehension is measured in the IRI by asking comprehension questions. We believe, as you learned in Chapter 2, that each reader creates meaning based on the interaction between the text and the reader's background knowledge and experience. Often multiple interpretations of a text may be made. Asking comprehension questions to assess the creation of meaning assumes that only one (the question writer's) interpretation of the text is possible and accurate.

3. Whether a given test is too easy or too challenging rests more with the reader's purpose for reading and background knowledge than with the length of sentences or number of syllables. Texts may be assigned a grade level using a readability formula. All such formulas are based on the notion that shorter words and shorter sentences are easier to read than long words and long sentences. We reject this notion in favor of considering the reader's purpose for reading and background knowledge in deciding what text to place in a child's hands. Furthermore, a child may engage with an interesting text several times, the first time finding it very challenging followed by easier encounters with it.

Another common form of criterion-referenced tests are those that accompany basal reading programs. They may accompany basal reader materials or other textbooks, or they may be purchased separately as additional instructional supplies.

Basal Reader Tests

Basal readers are sequentially graded pupil texts, workbooks, teacher's guides, and supplementary materials for grades K through 8. The tests that accompany the basal readers are undoubtedly some of the most widely used criterion-referenced tests in the educational system. Although there are variations among publishers, essentially these tests consist of placement tests, end-of-unit tests, and end-of-book tests. The testing program that accompanies a basal reader is intended to help you place children in the reading series and to move them through the series as they master various skills.

Basal placement tests are administered to a group of children at one time. They typically test reading comprehension following the reading of short selections from the basal. The intent of the tests is to help you decide which level of difficulty within the reading program is most appropriate for a given child. The greatest limitation of using these tests is that you cannot learn much about a child's view of the reading process. Their greatest advantage is that they are quick to administer and interpret.

End-of-unit tests that accompany the basal are administered at points throughout the use of a given book to check mastery of various skills. Basal publishers claim that end-of-unit tests can help prevent reading failures by enabling you to ascertain that "critical skills" are mastered before a child moves on in a book. The assumption is that you will reteach skills students have not mastered before moving further into the text.

In the same way, end-of-book tests give you information about a child's skill attainment within a book or level of the basal program. The intention is that you will not place a child in a more advanced level until the child has mastered the skills at a given level.

We believe the most serious limitation of basal tests is that they are essentially quantitative rather than qualitative. They tend to count all errors with equal weight without really examining the *processes* the child uses in reading. No one error in reading is important. Patterns of errors can be important. But how the child views the reading process is of utmost importance. Procedures that allow you to examine the child's view of the reading process and his or her reading behaviors are more useful than the typical basal test.

However, basal publishers are making serious efforts to respond to the changes in educational philosophy, and thus assessment, happening in many schools. For example, the Harcourt Brace *Treasury of Literature* series recommends to the teacher the following seven different kinds of criterion-referenced assessment and evaluation:

1. *Portfolio assessment.* Recommended for use throughout the year, both children's use of reading and writing processes as well as products are collected in portfolios. The teacher is offered suggestions and strategies for initiating, maintaining, and evaluating the collection.

2. *Reading-writing performance.* At the end of each unit of instruction students are given reading tasks and then asked to write in response to the reading. Teachers are provided with model papers to help them determine a score.

3. *Reading comprehension.* To be used at the end of each unit of instruction, fiction and nonfiction passages are followed by multiple-choice questions that focus on literal, inferential, and critical thinking. In an effort to improve on the traditional multiple-choice questions that

permit only one interpretation of the text, these tests permit the students to respond to some free-response questions.

4. *Reading skills assessment.* Multiple-choice tests to assess progress in the skills of decoding, vocabulary, comprehension, literary appreciation, and study skills. These are provided for use at the end of each unit of instruction.

5. *Language skills and writing assessment.* Multiple-choice and open-ended questions to assess mastery of language skills and writing ability at the end of each unit of instruction.

6. *Individual and group placement tests.* Group tests and running records to help the teacher decide where best to place a child in the basal series.

7. *Informal assessment.* Suggestions are woven throughout the instructional program to help teachers evaluate anecdotal records, work samples, and teacher/student conferences. This also includes suggestions to help students in self-evaluation.

All of the assessment strategies listed here may be far more than a teacher would want to use. Although the basal publishers are working diligently to respond to the demands of the market, teachers must still be critical consumers and make careful selections among the testing and evaluation options.

We recommend you use procedures that are process oriented in making decisions about moving children through a text. Such procedures are discussed in the section on responsive evaluation.

Norm-Referenced Tests

Norm-referenced tests are so named because performance on such tests is judged in comparison with a norm ("normal performance") established in the past. When a norm-referenced test is developed, it is administered to a group that is representative of the people for whom the test was designed called the *norming sample.* Their performance on the test becomes the yardstick against which all future performance is judged. The statistics that describe the performance of the norming sample are the norms for the test. For example, if in the norming sample the average score of the fourth graders was 87 correct responses, the norm becomes 87 as the average fourth-grade standard. When your fourth graders take the same test, they are then compared with the fourth graders (and others) in the norming sample. A school district's announcement that its sixth graders are scoring "above the national average in mathematics" means its average sixth-grade scores were higher than the average sixth-grade scores in the norming sample.

Observation of pupils' work is a critical assessment tool.

© Jeff M. Dunn/Stock Boston

Performance on a norm-referenced test is described in terms of the bell curve over which some statisticians tell us all human traits distribute. At the center of the bell curve (see Figure 5.1) is the mean or average, where scores cluster. The middle 68.26% of the spread of the scores is the bracket marked by one standard deviation above and one standard deviation below the mean. The performance of a child who scored one standard deviation below the mean could be of concern if the test were appropriate for that child. As a professional educator, you should be concerned about the validity and reliability of any test you administer to your students.

Validity Issues

Suppose your professor came into class and announced, "I have decided to stop using the quizzes I create in this class to measure your performance.

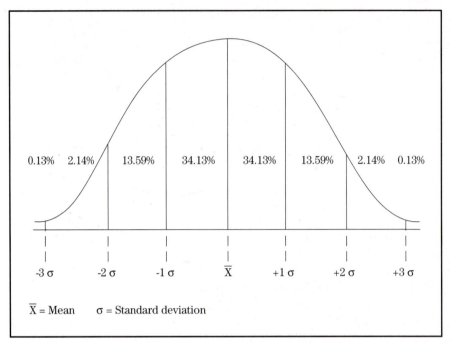

0.13%   2.14%   13.59%   34.13%   34.13%   13.59%   2.14%   0.13%

-3 σ   -2 σ   -1 σ $\overline{X}$ +1 σ   +2 σ   +3 σ

$\overline{X}$ = Mean   σ = Standard deviation

Figure 5.1—Bell Curve

Instead, I will use a new norm-referenced test on the teaching of reading and writing. After I created the test items, I used the doctoral students in reading as the norming sample." How would you feel? Would this norm-referenced test fairly assess your performance in the course?

Probably you would feel very worried. Such a norm-referenced test would not fairly assess your performance. It would not be fair because you and your classmates were not represented in the norming sample. The nature of the norming sample is only one of the questions you should ask about a norm-referenced test. When we ask if a test is valid, we are asking whether it is appropriate to use with our students and whether it tests what it purports to test. There are several validity concerns you should address:

1. Are your students represented fairly in the norming sample? If the ethnic, socioeconomic, and geographic characteristics of your students are not represented in the norming sample, the yardstick by which their performance is to be measured is an unfair one.

2. Do the test items seem to test adequately the curriculum area(s) for which the test is intended? Do the authors of the text define reading as you do? Does there appear to be sufficient breadth in the test items? It is in these respects that norm-referenced tests have a serious

limitation. An examination of test items permits you to infer the test makers' definition of reading—namely, that reading is a process of transforming the print symbols into language, with no interaction between the ideas of the author and the schema of the reader. The typical norm-referenced test is presented in a multiple-choice format. Multiple-choice questions offer the child no opportunity for retelling the story, which is one of the more powerful sources of insight into comprehension.

3. Is there a match between what the test measures and what you teach? Students cannot be expected to do well on a test if they have not been taught the material the test covers. A test that is valid for your students matches your curriculum. Some states are now writing their own norm-referenced tests, thereby achieving a closer match between the goals of the curriculum and the scope of the test.

Reliability Issues

A test is reliable if it yields the same results over time or across equivalent forms of the test. For example, if your students take Form A of a test of reading comprehension the first of the week and then take Form B of the test at the end of the week, their performance on the two forms should be about the same if the test is reliable. Reliability is usually described by a statistic called a coefficient of correlation. A perfect correlation coefficient would be +1.0. This means that when a test was given twice (or two forms were used), the student who scored the highest on the first test also scored the highest on the second test. The student who scored second highest on the first test also scored second highest on the second test, and so on. Rarely do we find a perfect, +1.0 correlation. We could be comfortable about the test's reliability if the correlation coefficient was +0.85 or better.

Being a Critical Test Consumer

Classroom teachers rarely have a choice about whether to use norm-referenced tests or what particular test to use. You are likely to be instructed to administer a certain achievement test to your students (third grade and above) in October and/or again in May. Refusal to do so could be considered insubordination. But the fact that you have to give the test does not excuse you from being a careful and thoughtful test consumer. You are the one who has to interpret the test, both to children and to parents, and be able to explain the various scores obtained. You also must decide whether to implement any instructional changes on the basis of the results. This responsibility obligates you to raise questions about validity and reliability.

Reputable test publishers supply validity and reliability data in the examiner's manual or in a technical supplement to the examiner's manual. Critical test consumers carefully examine this information to assess the validity of the test for their students and the reliability of the test. If the test you use fails to satisfy any one of the conditions of validity or reliability you should deem it inappropriate for your students. It is professionally sound practice to say so to your building principal and to explain your reasons. You might also communicate your concerns in a letter to the district's testing coordinator or the official or committee that selects the tests.

There is some hope that changes will be made in standardized tests. Currently Michigan and Illinois are undertaking ambitious efforts to develop new standardized tests that are congruent with newer classroom practices. We, as a profession, must deal with this challenging issue.

Achievement Tests

Perhaps the most commonly used norm-referenced tests in elementary schools, achievement tests span a broad range of curriculum or skill areas, with a limited sampling within each area. In other words, test items may cover a wide array of subjects, but each is tested to no great depth. Norm-referenced achievement tests have essentially two purposes:

1. They measure overall achievement of students within a school or school district so district administrators and school board members can make a comparison against a "national" norm.

2. They provide a gross screening assessment to alert you to students who may be experiencing achievement losses in certain areas of the curriculum. When a student scores well below average on an achievement test (one standard deviation below the mean or more), that finding should alert you to increase your observation of that child, to use some criterion-referenced measures to examine performance more carefully, and possibly to confer with the child and the parents. Poor performance on an achievement test may indicate a need to refer a child to specialists within your building or district who can do additional in-depth diagnosis. Poor performance, however, is not always a sign of limited achievement on the part of the child. A child who is not motivated to do well on the test may perform very poorly. Sometimes the test content or test items are clearly inappropriate for the age and development of the child. Conversely, a child who is highly motivated may work at frustration level, effectively inflating scores above typical daily performance in reading.

Diagnostic Tests

Norm-referenced diagnostic tests sample a single curriculum or skill area in considerable depth. It is possible to determine a student's strengths and weaknesses in reading comprehension or word recognition, for example, from a diagnostic test. Typically, norm-referenced diagnostic tests are used by specialists in reading or learning disabilities rather than by classroom teachers. These tests are frequently used after you have referred a child in your classroom for further diagnosis.

Scores Used on Norm-Referenced Tests

Typically, three scores are obtained from administering a norm-referenced test: the raw score, the percentile score, and the grade score.

Raw Score

The first score obtained on a norm-referenced test is a **raw score,** which represents the number of test items correctly marked. The raw score alone is relatively meaningless, telling you nothing about how the student performed in comparison with the norming sample. Suppose the teacher in the grade following the one you teach reports to you that one of your former pupils scored 48 on a reading achievement test. You wouldn't know whether to offer praise or to worry about the child's achievement! To evaluate performance on an achievement test, you have to know more than the raw score.

Percentile Score

One of the scores most commonly used to interpret normed test performance is the **percentile score,** which tells you the proportion of the norming sample your student outperformed, that is, the percentage of the norming sample that scored below your student's score. A percentile score of 89 means the student scored as well as or better than 89 percent of the norming sample. Percentile scores should not be confused with percentage scores. Percentage scores tell you the percentage of total test items marked correctly. Percentile scores give you a comparison between your student's performance and that of the norming sample.

Stanine Score

Perhaps the easiest norm-referenced test score to explain is the **stanine score,** which shows you where your student stands in relation to the norming sample by placing his or her score along the baseline of the bell-shaped curve. Stanine scores range from 1 to 9, each score representing a percentage of the distribution from the lowest to the highest scores along the baseline. For example, a stanine score of 5 places your student in the middle stanine—the one bracketing the mean (average) score in the norming sample. Both percentile and stanine scores permit you to compare a student's performance across subtests and years. They are more stable and reliable than grade scores, which are, in fact, the most confusing and most difficult to explain.

Grade Score

The **grade score** is intended to tell you how your student performed in comparison with the norming sample. A grade score of 4.3 means your student performed as well as the average fourth grader in the third month of fourth grade. That is all the grade score means. Here comes the confusion. People often assume a grade score is equivalent to an instructional-level score. We have observed that a grade score often overestimates an instructional-level score if a test taker is highly motivated. The confusion becomes deeper when a grade score is statistically extrapolated. For example, you may have a student who receives a grade score of 10.4 on a norm-referenced reading test. To many, it might suggest this student can read tenth-grade material. In fact, there may have been no tenth-grade material on the test. Arrived at by statistical calculations, the grade score of 10.4 means only that the student performed as well on the test as the average tenth grader in the fourth month of tenth grade.

The International Reading Association passed a resolution in 1981 calling for test publishers to cease using grade scores because of the confusion they create. Many of the publishers have acceded to this request. We suggest that if you are asked to interpret grade scores to parents, you point out the limitations we have discussed here.

Understanding scores derived from norm-referenced tests becomes even more critical when you realize that in many school districts the scores are published in the newspaper comparing school to school. Some advocate the publication of state scores so states can be compared one to the other. The International Reading Association, at its annual meeting in May 1991, took a position against the use of tests that define reading as a sequence of discrete skills and the use of test data to make comparisons of performance school by school, district by district, state by state, and province by province. Despite these efforts, such comparisons proliferate. The 1981 and 1991 IRA Resolutions are in Appendixes E and F. We believe the most sensible approach to assessment and evaluation places us closest to the child and his or her work; it is not derived from test scores. This kind of assessment is known as *responsive* assessment.

Responsive Assessment

Cambourne and Turbill (1990) realized that parents and other caregivers engage in a very natural kind of data collection and analysis of children's growth and development. They noted that parents and others were constantly assessing children's development. The basic processes parents employed to do this were observing, reacting, intervening, and participating in many of the activities their children undertake every day.

Parents and others are able to do this naturalistic assessment and evaluation (known as responsive evaluation) because they spend a great deal of time observing and interacting with their children. They also have indicators or criteria by which they evaluate the data they gather on their children. Cambourne and Turbill (1990) noticed that parents and others have "broad

A teacher unobtrusively records a child's miscues for later analysis.

© Michael Hagan

markers" such as learning to walk, learning to talk, or getting a first or second tooth by which growth of the child is evaluated.

This same kind of naturalistic, responsive evaluation may be applied in the reading/writing classroom. Here teachers are keen observers of children, interact with them constantly across a wide range of literacy events, observe children in action, and collect artifacts that provide markers of growth.

For more than 40 years, we have thought of assessment in reading (and to some extent in writing) as test based. The proliferation of psychological tests during and after World War II set the stage for educational assessment for years to come. This test-driven view of assessment is now undergoing serious questioning and debate. Two issues central to the move toward responsive assessment are the role of the teacher and the assessment of process versus product.

Role of the Teacher

The role of the teacher as observer is crucial to good assessment and decision making. The teacher's elevation to this role assumes truly professional, even expert, behavior on his or her part. A novice at classroom evaluation looks at a sample of writing and sees scribbles. The expert sees evidence of a developing writer. The novice listens to a child read and hears mistakes. The expert hears a child using increasingly more semantic, syntactic, and schematic cues (Johnston, 1987). The teacher who is an expert observer has little, if any, need for traditional tests as assessment tools. Observations of and interactions with children are far more significant.

In making the same argument, Johnston (1987, p. 747) stated, "This view of evaluation implies the need to liberate teachers and students from the disempowering and isolating burden of centralized, accountability testing. The cost of the liberty is increased responsibility on the part of the classroom teacher, some of which is passed on to the student." In fact, if teachers and students are to be freed of the burden of accountability testing, teachers will have to accept the responsibility for ever more expert observation, analysis, and recording of student behavior. Paradoxically, as teachers trade in the tests born of the accountability movement for their own expert observation of children's progress, they are in effect becoming *more* accountable for the learning of their students.

Teachers are responsible for having their students meet the instructional objectives specified in the curriculum. The ultimate objectives of whole-language instruction are the same as objectives in reading instruction have nearly always been: Children read and write effectively and with enjoyment. But many of the interim objectives have changed. For example, along the road to proficient literacy we are much more concerned about the child's ability to create meaning in reading and to write a variety of clear sentence structures than we are about drilling on decoding initial consonant *d* or punctuating someone else's sentences on a worksheet. What has changed is not the product of our instruction but the processes for generating that product.

Assessment of Process Versus Product

When we give a test to determine what a child knows or can do, we are look-ing at the product of teaching and learning. When we assess the child's under-standing of literacy through observing his or her use of reading and writing, we are looking at the processes of teaching and learning. Products are impor-tant, but the processes are more important still. Likewise, an examination of the processes is far more instructive to the teacher than is looking only at the product.

Professional organizations are recognizing the importance of a process-oriented assessment model. The International Reading Association's Early Childhood and Literacy Development Committee has endorsed a process-oriented view and offered six principles of assessment (Teale, Hiebert, & Chittenden, 1987, pp. 772–774):

> With insights from research, we are formulating views of early childhood literacy development, with conclusions like the following: (a) Listening, speaking, reading and writing abilities develop concurrently and interrelatedly in early childhood, not sequentially. (b) The functions of reading and writing are as much a part of literacy learning as are the formal skills. (c) Children's early behaviors are a legitimate phase of, rather than a precursor to, literacy. (d) These behaviors and conceptualizations develop in predictable ways toward conventional literacy.
>
> The principles presented here are grounded in the perspective just described, which implies the need for a comprehensive assessment program, not a one-shot test of a child's general knowledge of reading and writing. These principles also reflect the new concept of emergent literacy.
>
> In the best beginning literacy programs, assessment facilitates the goals of the curriculum and shows the following characteristics:
> (1) Assessment is a part of instruction. Assessment and teaching go hand in hand. Assessment enhances teachers' powers of observation and understanding of learning. . . .
> (2) Assessment methods and instruments are varied. Conventional assessment (e.g., standardized readiness tests or screening inventories) is only one approach. Analyses of performance samples (tapes of children's reading, compositions they wrote) and systematic teacher observation of everyday behaviors (looking at or reading books, listening to stories, using environmental print, using print in dramatic play) are integral parts of the assessment program.
> (3) Assessment focuses on a broad range of skills and knowledge reflecting the various dimensions of literacy. The cognitive and linguistic resources that children bring to reading and writing tasks

are identified. Programs capture a complete view of emerging literacy.

(4) Assessment occurs continuously. The teacher constantly assesses the children's behavior informally in order to arrange appropriate activities. Regular systematic assessments (e.g., analysis of performance samples) are scheduled to ensure that each child's progress is documented over the year. . . .

(5) Literacy is assessed in a variety of contexts. Because reading or writing requires integration of processes, children may perform differently on tasks that presumably measure the same skill (e.g., not recognize a letter on a test sheet but readily identify it in a familiar book). Assessment of a particular skill should assume several forms.

(6) Measures are appropriate for children's development levels and cultural background. Good measurement strategies permit the child some choice in how and when to respond and are appropriate to a variety of cultural backgrounds. . . . Especially important: informal assessments that resemble regular classroom activities.

The National Association for the Education of Young Children (NAEYC) in 1987 adopted a similar statement on standardized testing of young children. See Appendix C for the complete text of the NAEYC statement. The statements on assessment presented by these two very large and important professional organizations clearly indicate that assessment in literacy is changing. We hope soon to see process assessment as the norm, with far less reliance on test scores derived from fragmenting the processes of literacy. The focus on process, the movement toward responsive assessment, and the revaluing of teacher observation have all lent credibility to the intuition of the teacher. For many years our culture has placed emphasis on test scores as the measure of student achievement at the cost of ignoring teacher intuition.

Intuition

One of the most important decision-making data sources you have is your intuition as a teacher. The things you know intuitively are things you just know, without rational, logical explanation of how you know them. It is acceptable to know things intuitively. We do not always have to explain *how* and *why* we know everything we know. How does this apply to teaching?

We live in an age of accountability in education. Our critics demand that we document student learning gain in a variety of ways, virtually all of which involve testing. We agree that teachers must be accountable for student learning. But we disagree that accountability invariably requires testing. If you are sure a student knows certain things or possesses certain skills, the intuitive basis of that information is sufficient. You do not need to test that student to prove what you know about him or her.

Some principals have been known to advise teachers to record the date on which they intuitively knew a child had mastered a skill or grasped a concept, rather than testing for that skill or concept. Such advice will shock some teachers who have been encouraged to believe the *only* way they can know a child possesses a skill, trait, or knowledge is to test. To deny teacher intuition is to ignore half of the teacher's brain. The left hemisphere of the cerebral cortex knows things in logical, linear, rational ways. The right hemisphere is intuitive, divergent, and holistic. We want teachers to use their whole brains in the teaching/learning act. Not only is it acceptable for teachers to be intuitive but in fact the longer you teach, the more intuitive you will become as a teacher (if you are a good teacher).

Observation

Like intuition, observation is one of the most important and helpful sources of data available to you in making important instructional decisions. You may have heard that teachers have eyes in the backs of their heads. It would be wonderful, although unsettling to our hair stylists, if that were true. But experienced teachers behave as if they did have eyes in the backs of their heads. Developing your observational skills is one of the most helpful things you can do as a beginning teacher. Every encounter you have with children should, in a sense, be diagnostic. For example, you may observe that a child never chooses to go to the library corner, so you introduce the child to a new book. You note that a child usually writes very short sentences, so you propose sentence expansion activities.

You need to search continually for signs that point to what the child knows and needs to learn next, how the child learns and feels, what challenges the child and what fails to capture the child's interest. Much of the time the observations will become the basis for your instructional decisions.

Some teachers who respect their own observations and thoughts record them in notebooks. Called *anecdotal records*, these notes can then be referred to later during planning time or during parent conferences. We suggest you carry a supply of gummed blank labels in your pockets. As you are moving about observing your students at work, you can pull a label out and record your observations. Later you can transfer the label to the child's designated page in a loose-leaf binder. Figure 5.2 lists the anecdotal notes taken by a first-grade teacher over a short period of time.

Miscue Analysis

We said in Chapter 2 that readers select from the myriad of cues on the printed page to process the reading. When a reader misuses the cues, makes an error in using the cueing system, this is called a miscue. By analyzing the miscues a child makes, we can draw some valuable inferences about the cueing systems upon which the child relies as a reader. For example, if the text word is *house* and the child reads "horse" without noticing the loss of meaning, we can infer that this reader relies much more heavily on graphophonic cues than on semantic cues. If, on the other hand, the miscue makes sense because the word *home* was substituted for *house*, we can infer that the reader relies

▼ Jim balked at writing time. After I typed his story he settled down and illustrated it. Jim scribbled on his desk and refused to wipe it off. In some ways he is acting apprehensive and afraid of writing. (A later time) He was the first to finish his book. He seemed proud to read it to the class.

▼ Christina's illustrations on her book about her brother are beautiful. She does not know how to count by 5s—ESL teacher was helping her—she will practice with her dad.

▼ Mack is able to read the menu and write it on the board for the kids to see—Mack has stepped up a level in his journal. Now he is able to ask me questions and draw little puzzles for me to figure out.

▼ For the first time today, Shelley miscued and noticed it did not make sense. She reread and corrected her mistake. Hooray!

▼ Byron is finally taking risks and attempting to decode words he is not sure of. He approximated the decoding of *happiness* several times and finally got it correct. I must be sure and reinforce this over the next several stories.

Figure 5.2—First-Grade Anecdotal Records

most heavily on semantic and syntactic cues and places less reliance on graphophonic cues.

Miscue analysis helps us understand whether a reader is attempting to construct meaning when reading or simply decoding letter–sound relationships. This information will help us build on the reader's strengths while improving reading weaknesses. We can learn a great deal about how a reader views the reading process through miscue analysis. Miscue analysis is done in American schools in essentially two ways. Some teachers use running records, which is a form of miscue analysis developed by Marie Clay in New Zealand. Others teachers use the Reading Miscue Inventory (RMI) developed by Yetta Goodman, Carolyn Burke, and Dorothy Watson in the United States.

The Nature of Running Records

Running records are a system for recording all that we can observe about a child's behavior as a reader. Invented by Marie Clay (1972), they are used extensively in New Zealand and are gaining ground in the United States. Because running records reflect what really occurs while a child reads, they assist in our accurate observation and interpretation of the child's use of the reading process. Running records do not require a typed script. They may be done on any piece of paper. With practice teachers can take a running record at any time, anywhere, on any text because the opportunity arises or because what the child as a reader is doing at the moment is critically important.

Some of the most important teaching is done as a child is developing a piece of writing.

© Joel Gordon

Taking a Running Record

Clay acknowledges that learning to take a running record can "unsettle teachers" because the process is so simple. All you have to learn before you begin to take running records is the set of marks (conventions) that are used to record reading behavior. Educators in New Zealand argue that all teachers observing reading behavior through running records should use the same conventions. This way a teacher in another school or in another school year can look at a past running record and interpret it. We agree with this position. It is best if all teachers use the same conventions in marking running records.

Step 1. Learn the conventions so you can mark easily. (Hint: It will be helpful to you, although not necessary, to tape-record the reading in the first running records you do. You can't ask a child to go back and make the same miscue again.)

Step 2. Give yourself permission to make mistakes and move slowly. You can't expect perfection in early attempts at running records. You will get better with practice.

Step 3. Identify a child about whom you would like to know more as a reader. We suggest that in kindergarten through grade 2, you do a running record on each student so no record is older than three weeks. Establish a schedule so you can rotate through the class doing running records on this three-week cycle. Beyond second grade, you need do running records only on children whose behavior as readers is troubling or puzzling to you.

Step 4. Select a text for the running record. This text may be one the child has never read before or it may be familiar. Taking a running record on a familiar text will help you determine whether or not the text is of appropriate difficulty and how well the child is using reading strategies that have been taught before.

Whole short stories or expository pieces are best. If not a whole piece, the selection should be between 100 and 200 running words and take about 10 minutes to read (Clay, 1993). Of course, the text has to provide enough challenge to cause the reader to miscue, or the running records will be essentially useless. (Hint: When we think of difficulty of text we think in terms of percentage of running words read correctly. Not all professionals agree on the percentages. Commonly, we think of 95% to 100% accuracy as easy or independent; 90% to 94% as instructional level; and 80% to 89% as hard or frustrating.) Taking a running record on an unfamiliar text helps us see how the reader uses strategies independently and how willing the reader is to take risks.

Step 5. Ask the child to read the title, or read it yourself. Explain that you are going to make some marks on paper as the child reads aloud to you so you can know him or her better as a reader. Record all reading behaviors that you can, using the conventions.

There are only three things you should say during the running record; (1) the title, (2) "try that again" when you think a rerun over a piece of text would be helpful, and (3) a word when the reader asks you for it. Resist the temptation to teach while you are taking the running record. At this point you are simply recording all of the reading behaviors you can for further analysis and teaching later. All that is necessary is to have visual access to the text the child is reading. You can sit beside or behind the child and see the text as you mark the reading behavior. It may be helpful in inital running records to do the making on a copy of the text. Eventually, you want to be able to do a running record on any piece of paper you have handy. For a detailed discussion on taking and analyzing a running record, refer to Clay's (1985) *The Early Detection of Reading Difficulties* (3rd ed.) or *An Observation Survey: Of Early Literacy Achievement* (1993).

Step 6. Ask the reader to retell everything he or she can remember about what was read. Record your impressions of this retelling. If the retelling is not as rich as you would like, assist the reader in thinking of more details.

Use questions such as, "Remember when . . . ? What more can you tell me about that?"

Analyzing a Running Record

Analysis of a running record can provide invaluable insight into a child's reading behavior. Here we have an accurate and objective description of reading behavior we can analyze in terms of the nature and number of miscues. Analyzing the miscues helps us see which of the cueing systems the reader is using, the degree to which the reader is willing to take risks, the reader's strengths in processing text, and the next learning goals for each reader. Analysis of running records is a skill that develops over time. Give yourself permission to make mistakes, take small steps, and keep trying. Hint: Begin taking running records on the children who puzzle you most as readers. Increase the number of children as your ability and confidence increase.

The Nature of the Reading Miscue Inventory (RMI)

In the RMI the reader is asked to read aloud as the teacher records the miscues; then the reader is asked to retell what he or she recalls, discussing important aspects of the selection with the teacher. During the retelling the teacher also asks the reader to reflect upon the reading experience much as we recommend in the Guided Metacomprehension Strategy in Chapter 8.

It is recommended that you select a text challenging enough that you will have 25 consecutive miscues to analyze. The passage should be complete in itself and typically be more than 500 words long. The reader is told that he or she is to read the entire selection aloud, working to understand the text. The reader is also told that he or she will be asked to tell you all about it afterward. If the reader stops at a challenging point in the text he or she is asked to work it out for himself or herself as if reading alone. The teacher records the miscues on a copy of the text the child is reading.

Analyzing the RMI

The retelling of the selection is often scored on a 100-point scale, allocating a possible 40 points to retelling of characterization and 60 points for retelling of events. It is important to ask questions during the retelling so you can get to the reader's true understanding of the text. Consider the responses to these questions in analyzing the retellings.

In analyzing the miscues several questions are asked. They are:

▼ Was the miscue dialect-related or ESL-related?

▼ Did the miscue go with the preceding text?

▼ Did the miscue go with the following text?

▼ Was the essential meaning of the sentence intact?

▼   Was the essential meaning of the selection intact?

▼   Was the miscue corrected?

▼   Was the miscue either meaning-preserving or corrected?

For a detailed discussion of taking and analyzing Reading Miscue Inventories refer to Goodman, Watson, and Burke's *Reading Miscue Inventory: Alternative Procedures* (1987), published by Owen Publishing Company, or Weaver's *Reading Process and Practice* (1994), published by Heinemann.

Differing Views on Meaning

As described above, when running records are being analyzed, the New Zealand model has the teacher analyze the child's use of meaning by asking, "Does the child use meaning (M) in making the oral reading error?" If what Jack, for example, says as he reads makes sense, even though it is inaccurate, the child is thought to be applying his knowledge of the world to his reading. He is making meaning.

American teachers often take a different view of how the creation of meaning is to be handled in analyzing a child's miscues. Many teachers look at the miscue and ask, "Does the miscue mean relatively the same thing as the text word" ("home" for *house*, for example)? Only if the *meaning of the text* has been relatively well maintained would the reader be credited with creating meaning. We recommend taking the New Zealand position with very young readers. With them it is important to discover that they know reading is a meaning-making process. With more experienced readers, we would credit the reader with making meaning only if the meaning of the text has been reasonably well maintained.

Holistic Writing Analysis

As we move away from a view of literacy development as a compilation of discrete skills building one upon the other until a child can finally read or write, we have increasing need for ways to assess the processes of developing literacy. What running records do for our assessment of a child's understanding of the reading process, the Analytical Trait Writing Assessment (ATWA) does for our measurement of a child's understanding of the writing process. The ATWA is an example of what is known as *holistic grading* of writing. When we grade a writing sample holistically, we do not assign a letter grade to the piece; instead, we rate it overall against a model or specified criteria.

The ATWA was developed by the Beaverton School District in Oregon. Using the prescribed set of writing traits or characteristics, the young author is trained to analyze his or her own writing, with the goal of bringing each new piece closer to the criteria or model. The selection is read and an overall rating is assigned to the piece. The manuscript is judged as a whole (hence the term *holistic writing assessment*). It is not dissected. Comments are not written on the paper. Instead, an overall rating is assigned for each of six categories: ideas and content, organization, voice, word choice, sentence structure, and writing conventions. Within each category the paper is assigned a rating of 1, 3, or 5, with 5 representing the best effort.

To understand better how each paper is judged, examine Figure 5.3, which lists the criteria for the "ideas and content" rating. As you read the criteria for each higher level, notice the increase in writing sophistication it demands. The complete Analytical Trait Writing Assessment is reprinted in Appendix B.

The use of holistic assessment in writing allows you to track the writing growth of your students as well as to involve them in the assessment. Over time you will see the proof of your literacy program as your students' papers earn increasingly higher ratings. The rating system also permits you to see where a student's progress is arrested. When a student seems to be stuck at a certain rating in one or more categories, you can use the scale as a decision-making tool and then focus your instruction in writing on the troublesome traits within those categories.

Perhaps the most compelling argument for using a rating scale in writing is that such scales are meaningful. Not only do they offer specific feedback to the young writer but they provide clear criteria for ways to improve writing. When an author's work is rated 3 in "word choice," one need only look at the scale to see ways to improve (use fewer general or ordinary words, eliminate new words that do not fit, eliminate "big" words that were used to impress, reduce the use of slang). Such assessment of writing is much more to the point for the writer than getting a paper back from the teacher with the notation "B+, Good Job," which does not tell the author what was good about the piece or how to improve it.

Using Portfolios in Assessment and Evaluation

A portfolio is a collection of student work that exhibits the student's efforts, progress, and achievement in one or more areas of the curriculum (Paulson, Paulson, & Meyer, 1991). When you hear a teacher refer to a reading portfolio or a writing portfolio, determine the purposes for the portfolio. Some teachers have children keep their current writing pieces, pieces under development, in a folder and call that a "writing portfolio." In some classrooms children keep reading logs and other reading-related materials in a folder called a "reading portfolio."

We suggest making a distinction between *writing portfolio, reading portfolio*, and *assessment portfolio*. The reading and writing portfolios would be as just described, folders in which current reading- and writing-related materials are kept. The assessment portfolio is a collection of work samples and

I. Ideas and Content

5 Paper

The paper is clear and holds the reader's attention all the way through.

▼ The writer seems to know the topic well, and chooses details that help make the subject clear and interesting.

▼ The writer is in control of the topic and has focused the topic well.

▼ Important ideas stand out. The writer uses the right amount of detail (not too much or too little) to make the important ideas clear.

3 Paper

The reader can figure out what the writer is trying to say, but the paper may not hold the reader's attention all the way through.

▼ The writer has some things to say, but doesn't seem to know quite enough about the main idea(s).

▼ Some ideas may be clear, while others may be fuzzy or may not seem to fit.

▼ The writer may spend too much time on minor details and/or not enough time on main ideas.

1 Paper

The paper is unclear and seems to have no purpose.

▼ The writer has not thoughtfully explored or presented ideas; he or she may not seem to know the topic very well.

▼ Ideas seem very limited or seem to go off in several directions. It seems as if the writer wrote just to get something down on paper.

▼ Ideas are not developed. The paper may just restate the assignment.

Figure 5.3—Analytical Trait Ratings for Ideas and Content

Source: © 1986, Interwest Applied Research. This document may be used and reproduced without permission for instruction and assessment by state and local educational agencies, colleges and universitities. However, the document (or portion thereof) may not be sold, included in a document to be sold, used for commercial purposes, nor attributed to another source without written permission. Revised 11/12/86.

various evaluation materials. The assessment portfolio could be a dynamic, ongoing collection created by both teacher and child—either can contribute or remove items (Graves, 1990). There are two critical decisions to be made about assessment portfolios: their purpose and what will they contain.

Purposes of Assessment Portfolios

Assessment portfolios typically contain work samples and evaluations that are collected over time, across subject areas. In deciding the purpose of the portfolios, the following questions need to be answered: Who will see the portfolio? Is it just for the child and the teacher to see? Will it be seen by parents? Will it be used as a tool in conferences between the teacher and child, or between the teacher, child, and parents?

Questions concerning content also must be answered: Is the "life" of the portfolio to be just one school year or several? If several school years' growth is to be documented in the portfolio, how many years' collections of work samples and evaluations are reasonable to keep in one portfolio? Will all curriculum areas be covered, or only reading and writing?

Other critical questions concern who will be responsible for management of the portfolios, where they will be housed, who will have access to them, and how they will be transported.

Potential Portfolio Contents

The specific contents of an assessment portfolio would depend on the answers to the questions we have posed. Let's assume you are planning a literacy assessment portfolio that is going to be used as a tool in conferencing between you, the teacher, and the child and parents. The contents might include the following:

▼ *Writing samples with your evaluation attached as illustrated in Chapter 3.* Student self-evaluations could also be an important part of the portfolio. If you have children keep a list on the inside of their writing portfolio that records important achievements and next steps as a writer, this list might go into the assessment portfolio. Perhaps a summary of "My Accomplishments as a Writer" would be included. The same thing could be done with reading.

▼ *Running records as "work samples" of reading.* The running records could include evaluations of progress by both the teacher and the child. A first-grade teacher in Maine does running records with her children regularly. In the latter part of the year it is common for children doing buddy reading to take running records on each other and analyze them together (Giard, 1993).

▼ *Developmental checklists.* The checklist illustrated in Chapter 4 could be marked across the year and included in the portfolio.

▼ *Conference notes.* You could examine your notes on reading and writing conferences monthly with individual children. Write a summary of the highlights of such conferences and include it in the portfolio.

▼ *Anecdotal note summaries.* Periodically comb through the anecdotal notes you have taken on each of your students. Develop a chronological summary of the highlights.

If you keep assessment portfolios they must not just be a collection of work samples. Portfolios are only really useful if *evaluations* of the content are also included: evaluations by both the teacher and the learner. This way portfolios can effectively be used to document growth over time and to determine the next learning steps.

Major Ideas in This Chapter

▼ Collecting the data with which teachers make decisions is called *assessment.* Interpreting the data is called *evaluation.* Traditionally data collection has been done by testing.

▼ Criterion-referenced tests are largely teacher made. Performance is judged against a predetermined criterion. Frequently used published criterion-referenced tests are those accompanying basal readers.

▼ Norm-referenced tests, although regularly used, are not necessarily valid for a given group of students with a given curriculum. The child's abilities to use effectively all four cueing systems in reading and to write clearly and creatively are rarely assessed by norm-referenced measures.

▼ Responsive evaluation is based on the teacher carefully, knowledgeably observing the work of children, their use of reading and writing processes, and their literacy products.

▼ Observation of children at work—a skill that strengthens with time—is an indispensable source of decision-making data. One form of observation, running records, permits examination of a child's use of the reading process. The taking of a running record is a quick, easy way to do miscue analysis. Holistic writing analysis is an effective way to evaluate progress in writing.

▼ Assessment portfolios can be a useful way to document progress and to identify next learning steps. Important questions must be answered about using portfolios. Assessment portfolios are only truly useful when they contain evaluations by both teachers and learners.

Discussion Questions: Focusing on the Teacher You Are Becoming

1. Some schools release achievement test scores, sometimes even broken down by classroom, for publication in the local newspaper. How do you think these schools view the processes of reading and writing?

2. Are the miscue analysis and analytical trait evaluations of writing worth the time and effort they require in terms of useful information they give the teacher?

3. Some schools report pupil progress by indicating the grade-level material the child is reading. Others use running record data to document progress. Compare and contrast the information from these two sources.

Field-Based Applications

1. Interview five classroom teachers about their opinions of norm-referenced tests. Ask them what use they have made of norm-referenced test data. Begin to formulate your own position regarding norm-referenced testing in the elementary school.

2. Take a running record on three children: a kindergartener, a first grader, and a second grader. Complete the analyses and share your findings with the classroom teacher or a classmate.

3. First with a group of second-grade children and then with a group of fifth-grade children, use the Analytic Trait Writing Assessment (Appendix B). What differences do you see in the writing of the two groups? For each child, what writing improvement goals would you set?

Chapter 6
Working with Children with Special Needs

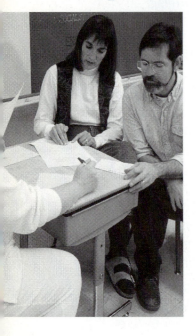

Chapter Overview

▼ Good teaching is good teaching for all children. We try always to identify a child's strengths and next learning steps. But no matter how hard you try, some children in your classroom will present needs you cannot meet by yourself. You will have to collaborate with specialists to meet these needs.

▼ You will need to make special accommodations to meet the needs of children who are gifted and talented, learning disabled, or non-English speakers.

▼ Public Law (PL) 94-142 changed the face of special education in the United States. The Regular Education Initiative (REI) has created a partnership between regular education and special education.

▼ Cambourne's conditions for literacy learning apply equally to children with special needs and all other learners.

▼ Children may be gifted and talented in a variety of ways, some difficult to detect. These children need a very challenging curriculum and opportunities to work and learn with other gifted children.

▼ By the year 2000 less than 50% of American's school population will be Anglo. Regular classroom teachers must learn to work with children with limited English proficiency.

Many Children, Many Needs

It would be wonderful if we could personally meet every need of every child in each of our classes. But that would not be a realistic expectation. You will have some children in your classroom who are gifted and you may need assistance in meeting their needs. You will encounter other children who, because of certain disabling conditions, cannot progress as you would like in your classroom. Some children will have very limited proficiency with English. What do you do then?

Help is usually available, although the amount of help may vary dramatically from school to school or district to district. Here we look at the special needs of children who are learning disabled, the special needs of gifted children, and the special needs of children with limited English proficiency. Our focus is twofold: one, what challenges do these children present; and two, how to accommodate their needs in your classroom.

The Student Services Team

In most large schools a group of professionals called the student services team (sometimes called the student assistance team, pre-referral team, or child study team) is charged with collaborative decision making about children with special needs. This group typically consists of a learning disabilities teacher, a counselor, a reading specialist, the principal, the classroom teacher, and other consultants called into service on special occasions. The student services team is charged with handling referrals, screening, diagnosis, planning, and instruction of children with special needs. You are a vital member of this team. Because you know your students better than anyone else, you are often the person responsible for bringing children with special needs to the attention of the student services team, which brings us to the important matter of referral.

We have heard beginning teachers say they are reluctant to refer a child for special help because they fear it will make them look like failures. But it is no failure to recognize that a child needs more than you personally can provide. The true failure is the failure to take the steps necessary to get special help for children who need it. Another failure is to stigmatize children with labels they have to bear throughout their school years. Determining the child's next learning steps is better than labeling the child. However, it is acceptable, as a classroom teacher, to recognize you cannot meet every child's special needs. After careful observation and consideration, it is good to seek the help of other professionals.

Under Public Law 94-142, known since 1975 as the Handicapped Children Act, the federal government has made funds available to the states to serve the needs of children with disabilities. This law was reauthorized in 1990 as Public Law 101-476, the Individuals with Disabilities Education Act (IDEA). It requires children with disabling conditions to be educated in the "least restrictive environment," meaning they are to be taught in the regular classroom if possible. Now you see why you are such an important part of the student services team. In cooperation with specialists, you will be helping design and carry out the instruction of the child with disabilities. Under federal law, an individualized education program (IEP) must be written for each child who is identified as disabled. You will probably have an important role in creating as well as executing the IEP for your own students.

Getting special help for a child typically proceeds by the following steps:

REQUEST FOR STUDENT SERVICES

Copy for student's Behavioral File

____________________ today's date

(This form must be completed and a copy sent to the referring party within ten school days of the date of referral)

Student's Full Legal Name ____________________ last first middle nickname

BIRTHDATE ____________________ month day year M F circle

____________________ referring person

SCHOOL ____________________ GRADE ________

____________________ phone

____________________ parent's name

____________________ relationship to student (teacher, parent, etc.)

____________________ parent's address ________ zip code

PHONE ____________________ home ____________________ other

CHECK ALL AREAS OF CONCERN:

___ Academic (Subject: __________)	___ Clothing	___ Health	___ Speech/Language
___ Attendance	___ Educationally Advance	___ Hearing	___ Vision
___ Behavior	___ Family	___ Motor Skills	___ Other ________

DESCRIBE BEHAVIOR OR PROBLEMS: ____________________

WHAT EVALUATIONS HAVE ALREADY BEEN DONE? ____________________

WHAT ACTION WOULD YOU LIKE TAKEN? ____________________

This form should be given to the in-building Student Services Team Coordinator

____________________ signature of person completing form

FEEDBACK REPORT

(This form is for surveying information already on file, *NOT* for requesting an assessment)

Information to be gathered:	Task assigned to:	Date of informaton	Initialed when task completed

Recommendation:
- ☐ No action to be taken.
- ☐ Action plan to be developed.
- ☐ Assessment plan to be developed (Form SS-2).
- ☐ Other ____________________

Explanation: ____________________

Date referring person given feedback report ____________________

Signed ____________________ Student Services Team Coordinator

CONFIDENTIAL INFORMATION – REVIEW AND RETURN TO STUDENT SERVICES TEAM COORDINATOR

DISTRIBUTION:
white — Student's Behavioral File
canary — Special Education Teacher
pink — Student Services Team Coordinator
white — Referring Party

Lift page for directions on completing form

Figure 6.1—Student Referral Form

1. You realize the child is not learning as well as he or she should. Or the child arouses your concern in some other way, such as having emotional outbursts, appearing to have difficulty hearing, squinting when looking at the board, or being ill a great deal.

2. You make a decision to refer this child to your building's student services team. If there is none, you refer the child to your principal, who

then brings the case to the attention of the appropriate specialists. Figure 6.1 is an example of a referral form.

3. The student services team examines your referral and may ask you for additional data. The team makes a decision to assess the child, to refer the child to outside specialists, or not to assess at all.

4. The child's parents are informed by the leader of the student services team of the suspected problems and the plan for assessment. The approval of the parents is granted, or the process stops here. You may be

---

PARENTS RIGHTS IN IDENTIFICATION, EVALUATION AND PLACEMENT

The following is an explanation of your rights according to federal and state rules and regulations (45CFR 121a.500, ORS 343.163, ORS 343.173 and OAR 581-15-075). The intent of these rules and regulations is to keep you fully informed concerning the decision about your child, as well as your rights should you disagree with the decision.

EVALUATION
Right to refuse consent for preplacement evaluation.
You can deny permission for your child to be tested for intial placement in special education.

Right to obtain an independent evaluation
If you disagree with the identification, evaluation, individualized education plan, placement or the provision of a free appropriate education to your child, you may request that an independent educational evaluation be made pursuant to OAR 581-15-094. **You** can also have the right to request from the school district information about where an independent educational evaluation may be obtained.

PLACEMENT
Right to refuse consent for initial placement of your child in a program providing special education and related services.

RECORDS
Right to request a list of the types and locations of educational records collected, maintained or used by the **school district.**

Right to inspect and review your child's records
You have the right to inspect and review all educational records with respect to the identification, evaluation, individualized education plan, and educational placement of your child, and the provision of a free appropriate public education to your child. **You** also have a right to a response from the school district to reasonable requests for explanations and interpretations of your child's records. **You** have a right to request that the school district provide copies of records at a reasonable cost unless the fee would effectively prevent you from exercising the right to inspect and review the records in which case the copies shall be provided without cost to you. **You** have the right to have your representative inspect and review your child's records.

Right to request that your child's records be changed.
You have the right to request amendment of your child's educational records if there is reasonable cause to believe that they are inaccurate, misleading, or otherwise in violation of the privacy or other rights of your child. If the school district refuses this request for amendment, it shall notify you within a reasonable time, not to exceed 30 days, and advise you of your right to a hearing to challenge information in the records.

Right to refuse consent for the use of your child's records.
You have the right to refuse consent for the disclosure of personally identifiable information related to your child to anyone other than school officials or persons acting in an official capacity for the school district collecting or using the information. **You** also have the right to refuse consent for the use of personally identifiable information related to your child for any purpose other than the identification, evaluation, individualized education plan or educational placement of your child, or the provision of a free appropriate public education to your child.

Right to request the destruction of your child's records.
You have the right to request the destruction of personally identifiable information collected, maintained, or used by the school district for special education when it is determined by the school district to be no longer needed to provide educational services to your child. However, the required contents of the permanent record must be retained in accordance with the provisions of OAR 581-22-717.

HEARING RIGHTS
Right to ask for an impartial due process hearing.
If you disagree with the schools' actions at any point concerning the identification, evaluation, individualized education plan, or educational placement of your child, or the provision of a free appropriate public education to your child, you have the right to request a hearing. If you desire a hearing, you must notify the school district in writing within 20 days of the date the prior notice was mailed to you. The school district will inform you of any free or low cost legal and other relevant services available in the area if you request it or if either you or the school district initiates a hearing.

Figure 6.2—Statement of Parents' Rights

asked to join in the meeting with the parents. At this point the parents are presented with the parents' rights statement. Figure 6.2 is a statement of parental rights under Public Law 94-142.

5. The necessary assessment is carried out. This may involve testing by specialists in your building, by specialists brought in from the school district or elsewhere as consultants on this referral, or by medical professionals.

6. Those involved in the assessment process meet to share their data and make recommendations for fulfilling the needs of the student with disabilities. The student services team, including the classroom teacher, participates in this meeting. By law, the parents are also included. If the child is found to have special needs, the IEP (see sample in Figure 6.3) is presented and modified as necessary. Once the parties have agreed on the plan and the parents have indicated approval, the plan is put into effect.

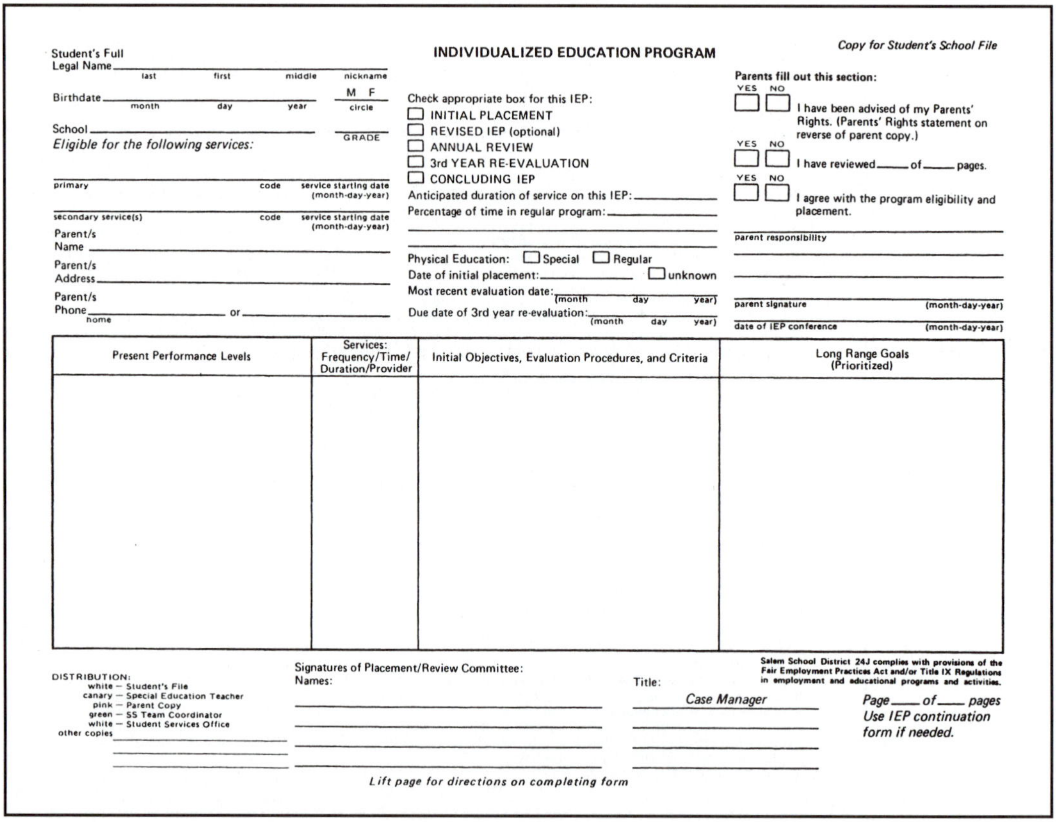

INDIVIDUALIZED EDUCATION PROGRAM

Copy for Student's School File

Student's Full Legal Name ____ (last, first, middle, nickname)

Birthdate ____ (month, day, year) M F (circle)

School ____ GRADE ____

Eligible for the following services:

____ primary — code — service starting date (month-day-year)

____ secondary service(s) — code — service starting date (month-day-year)

Parent/s Name ____

Parent/s Address ____

Parent/s Phone ____ (home) or ____

Check appropriate box for this IEP:
- ☐ INITIAL PLACEMENT
- ☐ REVISED IEP (optional)
- ☐ ANNUAL REVIEW
- ☐ 3rd YEAR RE-EVALUATION
- ☐ CONCLUDING IEP

Anticipated duration of service on this IEP: ____

Percentage of time in regular program: ____

Physical Education: ☐ Special ☐ Regular

Date of initial placement: ____ ☐ unknown

Most recent evaluation date: ____ (month day year)

Due date of 3rd year re-evaluation: ____ (month day year)

Parents fill out this section:

YES ☐ NO ☐ I have been advised of my Parents' Rights. (Parents' Rights statement on reverse of parent copy.)

YES ☐ NO ☐ I have reviewed ____ of ____ pages.

YES ☐ NO ☐ I agree with the program eligibility and placement.

____ parent responsibility

____ parent signature (month-day-year)

____ date of IEP conference (month-day-year)

Present Performance Levels	Services: Frequency/Time/ Duration/Provider	Initial Objectives, Evaluation Procedures, and Criteria	Long Range Goals (Prioritized)

DISTRIBUTION:
white – Student's File
canary – Special Education Teacher
pink – Parent Copy
green – SS Team Coordinator
white – Student Services Office
other copies ____

Signatures of Placement/Review Committee:
Names: ____ Title: *Case Manager*

Salem School District 24J complies with provisions of the Fair Employment Practices Act and/or Title IX Regulations in employment and educational programs and activities.

Page ____ of ____ pages
Use IEP continuation form if needed.

Lift page for directions on completing form

Figure 6.3—Individualized Education Program

The Changing Face of Special Education

PL 94-142 dramatically changed the face of special education in the United States. Enacted on November 29, 1975, the Education for All Handicapped Children Act stated,

> In order to receive funds under the Act every school system in the nation must make provision for a free, appropriate public education for every child between the ages of 3 and 21 (unless state law does not provide free public education to children 3 to 5 or 18 to 21 years of age): regardless of how, or how seriously, he may be handicapped.

About this act, Haring (1990, p. 13) has said it is the "most sweeping statement this nation has ever made about rights of handicapped children to full educational opportunity." The immediate effect of the act was to make it unlawful to exclude exceptional children, because of their differences, from normal learners. Further, the act requires that an individually planned education must be offered to meet the unique needs of each disabled child. Consider terminology carefully here. Some teachers use the terms *handicapped* and *disabled* interchangeably. We see a real difference. A child, for example, who uses a wheelchair is disabled and may be "handicapped" when it comes to some physical activities, but may be able to learn to read and write perfectly normally. In that case, the wheelchair is not a handicap.

The provision of the Handicapped Children Act that had the most profound effect on classroom practice was the stipulation that children and youth with disabilities must be educated in the "least restrictive," or most normal environment feasible. As a result, the following conditions are now operative:

▼ School districts offer a continuum of placement options. These options range from the most restrictive care, such as residential institutional care, to the least restrictive care, which is full-time placement in a regular classroom.

▼ School districts cannot assign children to a more restrictive setting unless it can be proven this assignment is better than a less restrictive placement.

▼ Students must be placed in schools as close to home as possible.

▼ Students must be placed in the company of nondisabled peers as much as possible.

▼ When children must be restricted from the regular classroom, disabled and nondisabled children must be together as much as possible, for physical education, lunch, and assemblies (Haring, 1990). The entire

Classroom teachers may have to make minor instructional adaptations for some children.

© Susan Lapides

special education profession has taken a turn away from special classes for special needs children. More and more, children with special needs are included in the regular classroom.

The Inclusion Model in Special Education: The Regular Education Initiative

Madeleine Will, then assistant secretary of education, wrote a 1986 report to the secretary of education that began a true revolution in special education. The stage for meeting the special needs of children had clearly been set by the Handicapped Children Act, but Will outlined her view that "problems have emerged which create obstacles to effective education of students with learning problems" (p. 4). She did not call for radical reforms but argued that "the creation of special programs has produced unintended effects, some of which make it unnecessarily cumbersome for educators to teach—as effectively as they desire—and children to learn—as much and as well as they can" (p. 4).

Will (1986) called for a new partnership between regular education and special education. She hoped this new partnership would end the segregation and labeling of special needs children, end the lowering of expectations for these children, and end the adversarial relationship that sometimes exists between parents and teachers.

This new partnership has become known as the Regular Education Initiative (REI). In short, it says that except in the most extreme circumstances, all disabled children will be educated in the regular classroom. The REI is based on a set of assumptions (Ralabate, 1989) that include the following:

▼ Students are more alike than different.

▼ All good teachers use the same basic techniques and strategies.

▼ Pull-out programs, where special needs learners are segregated by need, should be eliminated.

▼ The separation of special education and regular education programs results in inefficiency, duplication, and fragmentation.

▼ Labeling is unnecessary and stigmatizes students.

▼ Physically separate education is discriminatory and unequal.

The Regular Education Initiative simply moves most special needs students from resource rooms and other special education settings into the regular classroom. No educational shift has caused more debate. During a summer session graduate seminar, one of the authors of this text invited a special education professor to discuss REI with a class studying issues in reading. It brought highly emotional reactions from the teachers taking the course.

The heated debate ranged from complete acceptance of the Regular Education Initiative to complete rejection of it. Advocates of REI said it is about time we stopped treating children at risk of failing to meet their full potential as though they are defective, and time to recognize their potential, which could best be done in the regular classroom. Opponents of REI argued that the movement is simply a way to save money on special education without regard to the needs of learners.

One thing seems very clear to us. You, as a classroom teacher, are going to be challenged to meet the needs of a wide range of children, some of them with very challenging disabilities and very special needs.

Making the Special Ed./Regular Ed. Partnership Work

Those teachers just described who were taking the greatest exception to REI were the ones in difficult teaching situations. Many of them had been assigned children with special learning needs and left alone to deal with the challenge. This is, undoubtedly, REI at its worst. Teachers who had positive reactions to the initiative had experienced significant amounts of assistance from special educators in planning for and working with children with exceptionalities newly assigned to their regular classrooms. REI was conceived as a partnership between the regular classroom teacher and those trained to work with learners with special needs. REI appears to work best when the special education teacher and classroom teacher work side by side in a highly collaborative arrangement.

Many regular classroom teachers do not feel trained or equipped to work with children with special needs. Phillips (1990) surveyed 314 teachers to examine their attitudes and perceived ability to work with students with disabilities. Findings showed that, as a group, respondents were willing to teach students who were gifted and students with physical disabilities, but were not willing to teach students with mental disabilities. The teachers reported a lack of skills in teaching students labeled severely/profoundly handicapped, severely emotionally disturbed, and visually impaired. They felt confident in their abilities to work with parents, provide individual assistance, adapt materials, participate in IEP conferences, adapt curriculum, and manage behaviors. The teachers felt they lacked confidence in or ability to write behavioral objectives, interpret assessment results, and write IEPs. To the extent these 314 teachers are representative of teachers in the United States, the Regular Education Initiative will require training, collaboration, and assistance for regular classroom teachers.

Myers and Bounds (1991) described a model program for mainstreaming children who were primarily learning disabled or severely language impaired. Some students had emotional problems or mild mental retardation. Their program incorporated four components: placement in regular classes, development of integration plans, implementation of integration plans, and evaluation of integration plans. After a pilot program, the model was implemented throughout the elementary and middle school programs of a large urban school district. An evaluation of the program found support for the model in terms of the majority of staff attitudes and opinions. In terms of student academic self-concept and academic achievement, findings were mixed. Findings in opposition to the model occurred in staff attitudes and opinions about adequacy of resources and mainstreaming time. Planning for integration and evaluation of integration plans are critical to the success of REI.

In another study, Allington (1990) found improvement in at-risk children's acquisition of reading ability when a coherent curriculum plan exists that provides learners with sets of activities that link together and foster learning. He concluded that remedial and special education programs should build on, extend, reinforce, and balance the classroom lessons. Allington asserted that coherent curriculum plans should identify the reading/language-arts curriculum from which all children will work, create opportunities for the development of "shared knowledge" among all professional staff, and foster a collaborative planning and teaching environment.

The regular education initiative will only work when there is cooperation and collaboration between the regular classroom teacher and the educational specialists who can help support the effort for at-risk learners. Cooperative planning needs to look at more than just the curriculum and evaluation. Roles of participants should be clearly defined, schedules should incorporate flexibility and time for planning/collaboration, steps should be taken to assure program ownership among participants, and the program should be modified in terms of ongoing feedback from all involved (Harris, 1990).

With varying degrees of support, with varying degrees of disabilities, and with varying degrees of training, you will find yourself challenged to work with children with special needs. One such group are children who are learning disabled.

Working with Learning-Disabled Children in the Reading/Writing Program

The term *learning disability* has many connotations. The estimate of numbers of definitions of learning disabilities ranges from 12 (Lavoie, 1990) to approximately 40 (Beattie, 1994).

Learning disability has been defined by the federal government in PL 94-142 and by several professional organizations. Across this set of definitions of learning disabilities there appear to be some commonalities. Learning-disabled students are characterized as having the following characteristics:

1. Some type of academic disorder

2. Some types of learning strengths

3. Average or above average intelligence

4. Learning problems that are not due to environmental disadvantage

5. Learning problems that are not due to mental retardation or emotional disturbance

6. No modality impairments such as blindness or deafness

7. The opportunity to learn (no evidence of poor teaching, excessive absences, or frequent moves).

The PL 94-142 definition is used by over half the states and a slightly modified version of it is used by the rest (Hresko, 1992). PL 94-142 defines learning disability as follows:

> *Specific learning disability* means a disorder in one or more of the basic psychological processes involved in understanding or in using language, spoken, or written which may manifest itself in an imperfect ability to listen, think, speak, read, write, spell, or do mathematical calculations. The term includes such conditions as perceptual handicaps, brain injury, minimal brain dysfunction, dyslexia, and developmental aphasia. The term does not include children who have learning problems which are primarily the result of visual, hearing, or motor handicaps, of mental retardation, of emotional disturbance, or of environmental, cultural, or economic disadvantage.

Learning-disabled children present certain identifiable characteristics. Gearheart, Mullen, and Gearheart (1993) have identified the 11 general characteristics listed here. No learning-disabled children present all of these characteristics, but most of them exhibit more than one:

1. *Underdeveloped or unevenly developed learning strategies.* Manifests in a lack of learning behaviors usually exhibited by age peers. Examples include inability to take notes, to locate key words or phrases in readings, to schedule time and assignments, to learn from outlining or summarizing.

2. *Disorders of attention.* Manifests in distractibility, which is the inability to sort out what to pay attention to—everything is interesting. Disorders of attention can present perseveration, which is the inability to draw attention away from an attraction, as well as hyperactivity, the inability to modify activity to demands or expectations of the immediate situation.

   Hyperactivity often manifests itself in a condition known as attention deficit hyperactivity disorder (ADHD). ADHD has been defined by the American Psychiatric Association (1987) as follows:

> The essential features of this disorder are developmentally inappropriate degrees of inattention, impulsiveness, and hyperactivity. People with the disorder generally display some disturbance in each of these areas, but to varying degrees. Manifestations of the disorder usually appear in most situations, including at home, in school, at work, and in social situations, but to varying degrees. Some people, however, show signs of the disorder

in only one setting such as at home or at school. Symptoms typically worsen in situations requiring sustained attention, such as listening to a teacher in a classroom, attending meetings, or doing class assignments or chores at home. Signs of the disorder may be minimal or absent when the person is receiving frequent reinforcement or very strict control, or is in a novel setting or a one-to-one situation (e.g., being examined in the clinician's office, or interacting with a videogame). (p. 50)

Not all experts agree that children with ADHD should be classified as learning disabled.

3. *Poor spatial orientation.* Manifests in inability to deal with new surroundings where age peers would have no difficulty.

4. *Underdeveloped, inadequate-for-age time concepts.* May manifest in the inability to keep track of time, to be on time, or to normally conceive of time.

5. *Difficulty in judging relationships.* Results in confusion over the differences between backward and forward, in and out, big versus little, near versus far.

6. *Poor general motor coordination.* Manifests in poor balance, general clumsiness, and the tendency to fall.

7. *Poor manual dexterity.* May be present in the inability to handle a pencil, to open small objects, handle a doorknob, or open latches.

8. *Inability (not unwillingness) to follow directions.* Commonly results in confusion in following even the simplest directions. Adults often mistake this characteristic for stubbornness or disobeying.

9. *Perceptual disorders.* Includes disorders of visual, auditory, tactual, or kinesthetic perception. Visual perceptual disorders can result in the inability to accurately copy letters or to discriminate between letters and shapes. Auditory perceptual problems may result in inability to recognize the difference between sounds and to use the graphophonic cueing system. Perceptual disorders in tactual or kinesthetic modalities may mean the student receives faulty feedback when engaging with the environment.

10. *Memory disorders.* Visual memory of words and letter sequences may be absent, and some students may not be able to repeat simple

sentences immediately after hearing them. Visualization of familiar scenes when not there may be difficult and visualization of scenes in stories may be virtually impossible.

11. *Social imperception.* May manifest in the inability to tell when others are irritated by the student's behavior, which then, unchecked, results in conflict that could normally have been avoided.

Although learning-disabled children can have problems affecting spoken language, written language, arithmetic computation, reasoning, and memory, we only address the classroom adaptations to be made in written language (reading and writing) in this text.

Adaptations for Learners with Learning Disabilities

When we review the research on instruction and learning for learning-disabled students one thought is inescapable. What is good teaching for one child is good teaching for all children. All of the instructional strategies we have recommended in this text for regular students may apply to students with learning disabilities. Pace may need to be slowed, explanations repeated more often, strategies reinforced more frequently, or expectations more frequently stated.

There are some clear indications for instructional adaptations that can be made for learning-disabled children in the reading/writing classroom. For example, Ellen Brandoff Matter (1989) is a remedial reading teacher who has discovered a way to help children visualize. This may be helpful with the learning-disabled students who have perception disabilities or memory disorders. Matter says that whole lessons on visualizing or spare minutes here and there can have great impact on reading comprehension. She tells the children to close their eyes and picture what is being said. The students may be asked to decide where they are, who is talking, or what object is being described. After the visualization is described, students are asked to give an answer as well as their supporting reasons. She warns not to be surprised if students are completely wrong or have no ideas at first. They get better with practice.

We can see that this visualization practice could be further applied to reading by reading a piece of text to students, asking them to listen with their eyes closed, and then to verbally describe the pictures they made in their minds as they listened to the text.

Two Success Stories

Learning-disabled students need help in learning to be responsible for their own learning and to see the relationship between what they do in school and their own learning. Jane Hansen (1992b) interviewed children in an elementary school to find out what they had learned recently in writing, what they would like to learn next to become better writers, and how they intended to go about learning what they decided to learn. Interestingly, she discovered that children could easily answer the questions. However, when she asked the same three questions about reading, the children could not answer the second and third questions. They saw themselves as in control of their learning as writers, but felt no control over their learning as readers. Changes were made in the reading curriculum. Hallmarks of the new reading program were lots of time for reading from books of the children's choice, opportunities for them to talk about books with classmates, no basals, no ability groups, and sessions within which children could plan their growth as readers.

Hansen shares the poignant story of a learning-disabled child's progress under this system of learners identifying their own next learning goals and planning how to take the steps. About Jessica, Hansen says,

> Jessica, a fourth grader who had been retained twice, had left her regular classroom for reading and writing for 6 years. She walked around with hunched shoulders and kept her eyes down when you talked to her. Her body language showed that she placed very little value on herself.
>
> Over a period of several months Jessica's teacher, the resource room teacher, and Professor Wansart taught Jessica the skills she needed in order to participate in the classroom reading/writing workshop. As a result, Jessica's head started to rise. Eventually she stayed in the regular classroom instead of going to the resource room. When she chose an Amelia Bedelia book to learn to read, two other girls brought Amelia Bedelia books and joined Jessica in a corner to help her learn.
>
> When the class received a computer, the resource room teacher taught Jessica how to use it, and she became the class expert. Children sought her expertise. Her head rose higher.
>
> When the class formed a circle, she placed her chair within it instead of 3 feet back as she had always done. She joined the group. Finally one day in the spring she raised her hand for the first time and asked another student a question after he'd read a piece of his writing to the class.

There are several important lessons for us in the Jessica story. She was highly capable of learning many things. Her teachers capitalized on her learning strengths while accommodating her weaknesses. In working with learning-disabled students, always find their strengths first and focus attention on those. Jessica was able to learn how to examine her own learning and set her own learning goals. Learning-disabled students need help in learning to take responsibility for their learning. The pace of Jessica's learning was slower than her age peers, but the expectations were the same. We know that disabled

Children need to take responsibility for their own learning.

© Susan Lapides

learners approach learning passively and often fail to see the link between their own effort and their own learning (Thomas & Pashley, 1982). This weakness is overcome when we get children actively engaged in their own learning as Jessica's teachers did.

We once had a learning-disabled child named Keith in a fourth-grade class. Keith, like so many learning-disabled children, was bright and highly capable in many ways, but had failed miserably at learning to read and write. To make matters worse, his brother was starting first grade that fall—as a reader. Keith was so devastated by his failure that he shrugged his shoulders and said "I can't," no matter what we asked him to do. How did we accommodate our instruction for Keith's needs? First, we discovered his strengths and capitalized on those. Keith was bright and articulate and good at math. We started sending him to a first-grade classroom (not his brother's) to help with math manipulatives. When Keith returned to his own classroom we took his dictation about his work with the first graders and put together books about his experiences. We then used those books for shared reading and independent reading. We also used them to teach the graphophonic cueing system (Keith's greatest challenge) and reinforced this knowledge with Keith's own writing. He was reading as well as most fifth graders when the school year ended and was proud of himself as a learner.

Classroom Applications

The stories of instructional adaptation for Jessica and Keith illustrate the nature of classroom practice required for the success of at-risk learners. Linda and William Blanton (1994) have offered an extensive list of classroom practices appropriate for learning-disabled children. Consider the number of items on the Blanton's list that are illustrated in the stories of Jessica and Keith.

▼   Help students understand they are active learners and will gradually accept responsibility for their own reading performance.

▼   Help students establish realistic goals for their reading performance and achievement.

▼   Expect students, including students with learning problems, to become independent readers by using instructional strategies that are matched to particular reading goals.

▼   Ensure that students achieve success in reading performance on a regular basis.

▼   Provide opportunities for free reading.

▼   Teach students how important it is to monitor, check, and evaluate the use of learning strategies during reading.

As you read the list here you might well have thought, "These things just sound like good teaching!" We agree. As we said earlier, good teaching is good teaching for all learners. In Chapter 2 we talked about the importance of Cambourne's conditions for literacy learning. These conditions are important for all children, but even more so for children with learning disabilities. Smith-Burke, Deegan, and Jaggar (1991) have considered Cambourne's conditions in terms of children with special needs. They have adapted the conditions to what they called "conference settings" (working with at-risk children) and have described the teacher's role in that setting. Figure 6.4 illustrates their thinking.

At the Munsey Park School in Manhasset, New York, teachers decided to move from a traditional philosophy to a whole-language philosophy. In an inspiring article in *The Reading Teacher*, Scala (1993) describes how she

Condition	Adaptation	Teacher Role
Immersion	Every session proceeds from and returns to a whole text.	Enabler
Demonstration	Teacher models strategies used to solve literacy problems; teacher uses language to talk about language.	Model
Expectation	Teacher provides support for learning; child, with support, can work beyond actual level; no learner is seen as deficient.	Mentor
Responsibility	Learner attends to conference session; learner brings new knowledge to class setting.	Trustee
Approximation	Learners are encouraged to be risk takers; teacher understands role of error in learning.	Coach
Use	Teacher lets the learner do the work; teacher follows learner's lead.	Facilitator
Response	Teacher engages in ongoing decision making; teacher responds to students' needs/concerns.	Collaborator

Figure 6.4—Cambourne's Conditions with Learners with Special Needs

Source: Reprinted From Smith-Burke, M. T., Deegan, D., and Jaggar, A. M., "Whole Language: A viable alternative for special and remedial education?" in *Topics in Language Disorders*, Vol. 11:3, pp. 58–68, with permission of Aspen Publishers, Inc., ©1991.

moved her children with learning disabilities into mainstream classrooms and worked in partnership with regular classroom teachers. The learning situations she describes are hallmarks of Cambourne's conditions applied to all learners. The Scala article chronicles her learning and the changes in the children across the school year. She concludes the piece,

My students suddenly imitate prolific writers, ending the year with some four-page responses. . . . The reading specialist distributes surveys in the spring; the children answer honestly, showing an awareness of their own learning. . . . Tom announces he will be in Utah with his dad; he has asked to go to some Indian reservations, a new interest. Could I give him a journal to take? Mike, the former career skateboarder, asks if I think he can get into Harvard. . . . Why did this program work? We have blurred the lines between abled and disabled, teacher and specialist, and right and wrong. (pp. 227–228)

In another report of successfully applying whole-language philosophy and strategies to working with children with learning disabilities, Zucker (1993, p. 669) said, "The lasting impact of incorporating a literature-based whole language teaching/learning philosophy in the education of students with language and learning disabilities was that it changes their attitudes and literacy enactments so that they came to see themselves as readers and writers, rather than as failures."

Peer-Mediated Instruction and Other Strategies

In working with children with learning disabilities, it is important to remember they are capable learners who need special assistance in overcoming some specific difficulties. Cooperation and collaboration between student and teacher and between regular classroom teacher and the special education teacher are critical to the success of students with learning disabilities. Peer-mediated instructional strategies provide a way to build student-to-student cooperation into the classroom with considerable benefit to the students with learning disabilities (Maheady, Mallette, Harper, Sacca, & Pomerantz, 1994).

One form of peer-mediated instruction is **cooperative learning.** Cooperative learning can take several forms. Typically, the operational features of cooperative learning include the following:

1. *Teacher instruction.* Lessons often begin with a presentation by the teacher.

2. *Team practice.* Students work in mixed ability groups of four or five to practice the material and master the lesson presented by the teacher. During this time, student activities may include completing appropriate written assignments, drilling one another on information, teaching a lesson to team members, formulating and discussing common answers, and assessing each other's learning. The goal is to have each member of the group succeed at learning so the team will be cooperatively successful.

3. *Individual assessments.* Each student's learning is individually assessed by the teacher.

4. *Team recognition.* Each individual student's score or performance is averaged with the rest of the team to produce team scores. Special recognition is given to teams that reach a certain predetermined criterion of performance. The basic idea underlying all cooperative learning models is to motivate each student to do a good job of helping fellow group members learn.

Slavin (1990) has noted that cooperative learning strategies may differ along six dimensions: (1) group goals, (2) individual accountability, (3) equal opportunities for success, (4) team competition, (5) task specialization, and (6) adaptation to individual needs. The careful setting of group goals inspires cooperation within the group. Carefully attending to individual accountability permits the learning-disabled student to have a manageable piece of the work to do.

Another form of peer-mediated instruction is peer tutoring, which can be of assistance in mainstreaming efforts. Cross-age tutoring involves older students with mild disabilities instructing younger, similarly labeled pupils. The review of research on cross-age tutoring with disabled students indicates that such instruction benefits the younger learner and the older tutor academically and helps the tutor learn important instructional procedures (Osguthorpe & Scruggs, 1986).

A second form of peer tutoring has been shown to be effective with both disabled and nondisabled learners (Top & Osguthorpe, 1987). In this design called "reverse-role tutoring" older disabled students tutor younger nondisabled students. Results indicate that both tutors and tutees make significant academic progress, and tutors improve their perceptions of their own academic performance.

We suggest you use peer-mediated instruction in place of workbook or seatwork activities. Peer-mediated instruction will be facilitated by your careful observation of the processes and debriefing the activities with the students. Have them evaluate their performance and set goals for the next session.

In addition to peer-mediated instruction, there are other "smaller" things you can do to accommodate the needs of learning-disabled children in your classroom. Consider the following possibilities:

1. Become clear in your thinking about what *fairness* means to you. We have known teachers who have not made accommodations for learning-disabled children because "it wouldn't be fair to the other children." Think about this. Does fairness mean every child is treated the same way? Or does it mean each child's needs are being met? A fourth-grade teacher we know was told by a special education teacher that it would be helpful to a learning-disabled child in her room if the child could hear a story read well before trying to read it herself. The specialist suggested the use of a grandparent volunteer who was in the room daily or the use of several fluent readers in the classroom or a neighboring classroom. The regular classroom teacher rejected the idea because it "wouldn't be fair to the rest of the kids."

    The rest of the kids didn't need to hear a story well read before they were able to read it. Only the learning-disabled child needed that. In our view, it was unfair not to make this accommodation.

2. If a child has difficulty writing, let him or her dictate a composition into a tape recorder for transmittal to others. Or have a volunteer transcribe the taped composition using the word processor.

3. If a child has difficulty completing as many tasks as others in the same amount of time, evaluate on the basis of the number correct of the number attempted rather than the total completed by others.

4. In group discussions, let the learning-disabled child know in advance that you will be calling on him or her at a certain time or in a certain order so the child can anticipate and be ready.

5. If a child has difficulty working in a group, create "buddy" situations.

6. Give directions or instructions in small steps and demonstrate what you mean whenever possible. Use simple, clear vocabulary.

7. When making presentations to your class, always use visuals to outline your main points. Emphasize important points by highlighting with color or a special shape. Provide outlines that the learning-disabled student fills in as he or she listens to a lecture. Tape-record your presentations so the child can listen to them later at his or her own pace.

8. Remember that just because you said something to a child does not mean it was comprehended. Have the child repeat the instructions or points made by you. Ask for clarification if you think the understanding is vague.

9. Accentuate the positive. Every week (or more often with some children) have them draw a picture, make a collage, or write a list of "things I am doing well." Share this with others and take it home.

10. Remember that you are not alone. Do not be reluctant to call on the help of the special education teacher, the counselor, the physical therapist, the speech therapist, the principal, or whoever can assist you in meeting the needs of learning-disabled children in your room.

This discussion of working with learning-disabled children should help you in your mainstreaming efforts. We know that the discussion is not exhaustive.

More and more schools in the United States are using Reading Recovery, a New Zealand program for working with young children who are not making developmental progress in learning to read. Although we are not suggesting these children are learning disabled, they are children with special needs. In some schools these special needs are being met by trained Reading Recovery teachers.

Reading Recovery

Reading Recovery was developed by Marie Clay (1979) to meet the special needs of a small percentage of children who were not succeeding as readers in their first year of reading instruction. It is a one-to-one program where a teacher trained in Reading Recovery methods works with one student for 30 minutes each day for a limited number of weeks and when the child is reading on the level of the average child in his or her age group, the child is returned to the regular classroom. No child stays in Reading Recovery for an indefinite period of time. The success rate for Reading Recovery has been incredibly good (Clay, 1979; Pinnell, Fried, & Estice, 1990).

The lessons in Reading Recovery are opportunities for the child and teacher to work together on reading and writing in an intimate setting. No set sequence of lessons is followed in Reading Recovery. Each lesson has a basic format, but beyond that, the teacher must decide what the individual child is doing and what he or she can be helped to do next. The following components are usually included in a Reading Recovery lesson:

1. *Reading of familiar stories.* Some of the books are selected by the teacher for the teaching opportunities they present; others are selected by the child. The books are placed in a box for the child, and lessons usually begin by having the child reread several familiar books.

2. *Taking a running record of text reading.* A running record is a technique for marking each miscue as the child reads aloud. The teacher analyzes the information from the running record to make predictions about the strategies children are using. This process was described in detail in Chapter 5.

3. *Working with letters.* The teacher may work with plastic letters and a magnetic board if the child needs work on letters or features of print. These letters may be used as children construct words or analyze print.

4. *Writing a message or story.* Each day the child writes a short message or story, usually one or two sentences in his or her writing book. Writing books are blank books with a top page for working out the words needed and a bottom page for recording the message. The teacher records the message on sentence strips and cuts the words apart to be reassembled by the child.

5. *Reading a new book.* The manner in which the book is introduced depends on the child's needs, but the book is not read to the child. The teacher and child may look at the book and talk about it, clarifying ideas about the plot and the concepts that are needed in order to understand the story. If the child is more experienced, the child may look at and read the book independently, asking for help if it is needed (Pinnell, Fried, & Estice, 1990).

Those who are using Reading Recovery in some form (Pinnell, Fried, & Estice, 1990) remind us that it is no panacea. No single program will solve all the problems in education or all the problems of some individual children. However, with the positive results that have been achieved, Reading Recovery seems to be the most effective strategy for helping those children who need special help in learning to read.

Working with Gifted and Talented Children in the Reading/Writing Program

We now turn our attention to a group of learners who have special instructional needs just as great as those of the learning-disabled children. These children are exceptional too, but in very different ways. Consider the following:

John Torres was a strong, energetic, 12-year-old sixth-grader who had never learned to read. He was known as the school vandal. Although no one could ever prove that he and the boys he led made a shambles of the school each weekend, he had been a problem for teachers almost from the first day of his schooling. No one thought he could learn.

His sixth-grade teacher thought he was gifted. He was a veritable mechanical genius and could repair any kind of audiovisual equipment or anything else mechanical. He was also a genius in leadership. He could attract other boys, organize them, and lead them in doing almost anything. His artwork was also superior.

John's sixth-grade teacher influenced the student council to appoint John the chairperson of the lunchroom committee, which was responsible for the arrangement and functioning of the school cafeteria. John recruited several of his friends to help in this effort, and became involved in other school leadership activities. Almost magically, school vandalism ceased, and John made rapid improvement in reading, soon catching up with many other sixth-graders in reading ability. He decided he liked going to school. (Torrance, 1985, pp. 2–3)

Jessica Williams learned to read when she was about 3 years old. She had favorite books that she had her mother, father, and grandmother read to her over and over again. Gradually, her caregivers began to notice that they couldn't skip parts of the story or make up segments because Jessica would call them on it and pointing to the text say, "That isn't what that says." From the time she was 3 until she started school, her parents worried about her because when given the choice, she would almost always choose to read to herself rather than do anything else.

When she began school she was often in trouble because she didn't like the typical activities in reading and she had difficulty

Children can read surprisingly challenging material when interest is high.

© Jerry Berndt/Stock Boston

making friends. She developed an incredible array of avoidance procedures in reading class, and the teacher thought she was just lazy or quarrelsome. Most of the other children excluded her from their activities.

Jessica further drew the attention of her teacher because of her writing ability. She would often write lengthy poetry expressing her feelings of "being left out" or of "my aloneness." In first grade! Her writing was clearly superior to even the most talented sixth grader.

Is John a gifted child? Is Jessica a gifted child? Are they both gifted? One of the difficulties with gifted children is that sometimes their talent is hidden or very difficult to detect. Some might be potentially gifted, talented, or creative and yet those abilities could go underdeveloped. In some cases the teacher would readily suspect that a child is exceptional in one or more ways.

We would say they are both probably gifted and/or talented. John's giftedness would be difficult to detect because he was in trouble much of the time. He was considered a problem at school. His teachers saw him as a child who could not learn. Yet look at his gift in organizing the children to run the lunchroom.

In contrast to John, Jessica was easily spotted by her teacher as gifted because of her talents in reading and writing that so clearly set her apart from other children. Her behavior was also a key to her frustrations.

Clearly, some children in our schools are exceptional in that they are gifted. Others are exceptional because they are talented. Yet others are exceptional because they are creative. One individual may be all three, although it is more common to find only one or two of the traits in any individual. The services a district provides to these exceptional children depends on whether it defines them as gifted; gifted and talented; or gifted, talented, and creative.

When U.S. educators first became interested in gifted education, *giftedness* was defined only as intellectual exceptionality. Terman's 1925 definition of giftedness required an IQ of 140 or above. More recently our thinking, as a profession, about intelligence has been broadened by the work of two theorists. J. P. Guilford (1967) offered a model that describes domains of intelligence that are not tested in the typical intelligence test. His three-dimensional model, called "the structure of the intellect," defines 120 distinct types of intellectual ability. Gardner (1984) described seven basic intelligences: linguistic, logical-mathematical, musical, spatial, body-kinesthetic, interpersonal, and intrapersonal.

The education profession now recognizes that gifted and talented learners may present their exceptionalities in ways other than intellectual giftedness. This realization is reflected in definitions used by the federal government.

The Marland Definition

Although you, as a classroom teacher, would not be the person to determine that a child is legally described as gifted and deserving of special educational services, it is instructive to consider the federal government's definition. In 1972 the commissioner of education, Sidney Marland, offered the following definition that is now known as the Marland definition:

> Gifted and talented are those identified by professionally qualified persons, who, by virtue of outstanding abilities, are capable of high performance. These are children who require differentiated educational programs and/or services beyond those normally provided by the regular school program in order to realize their contribution to self and society.
>
> Children capable of high performance include those with demonstrated achievement and/or potential ability in any of the following areas, singly or in combination:
>
> 1. general intellectual ability
>
> 2. specific academic aptitude
>
> 3. creative or productive thinking
>
> 4. leadership ability

5. visual and performing arts

6. psychomotor ability. (p. 2)

In 1976 the federal definition of gifted and talented changed as part of PL 93-380. The only real difference between the 1976 definition and the Marland definition is that the 1976 statement deleted psychomotor giftedness. Regardless of how states or school systems define gifted and talented, these children do have certain characteristics that set them apart from their age peers.

Characteristics of Gifted and Talented Children

A classic way of considering the characteristics of gifted children is to turn to the work of Lewis Terman. This remarkable longitudinal study looked at the characteristics of 1,528 subjects who had been identified as intellectually gifted 35 years earlier (Terman & Oden, 1959). The findings reported when these subjects were studied the second time included the following:

1. The gifted men were far more likely to hold professional and higher level business positions than were a group of randomly selected men of the same age.

2. Their mortality rate was lower than that of the general population.

3. Their incidence of crime and delinquency was very low compared with the general population's.

4. The gifted group had nearly double the income of others in the same job categories.

5. The divorce rate was significantly lower than their age peers in the general population.

6. The children of these gifted persons had an average intelligence quotient of 132.7 (the average in the population is 100), and 33% of the children had an IQ of 140 or above.

Whereas Terman's description of these subjects looked only at intellectual ability, others have defined characteristics of the gifted in broader terms. The Association for the Gifted, a division of the Council for Exceptional Children, has described behavioral characteristics, learning characteristics, and creative characteristics. Although few children display all of the characteristics, the lists may be helpful to you in identifying potentially gifted children in your classroom. The association's list is found in Figure 6.5.

As with learning-disabled children, it will take you and a team of specialists to identify those children who are truly gifted and talented and who need specialized programs. The critical issue for you is how to accommodate these children once they are identified.

Accommodating the Needs of Gifted and Talented Children

Considerable controversy surrounds the question of how best to meet the needs of gifted and talented children. A study that asked 1,200 teachers,

General Behavioral Characteristics

- Many typically learn to read earlier with a better comprehension of the nuances of the language. As many as half of the gifted and talented population have learned to read before entering school. They often read widely, quickly, and intensely and have large vocabularies.
- They commonly learn basic skills better, more quickly, and with less practice.
- They are better able to construct and handle abstractions than their age mates.
- They are frequently able to pick up and interpret nonverbal cues and can draw influences which other children have to have spelled out for them.
- They take less for granted, seeking the how and whys.
- They display a better ability to work independently at an earlier age and for longer periods of time than other children.
- They can sustain longer periods of concentration and attention.
- Their interests are often both wildly eclectic and intensely focused.
- They frequently have seemingly boundless energy, which sometimes leads to misdiagnosis of "hyperactive."
- They are usually able to respond and relate well to parents, teachers, and other adults. They may prefer the company of older children and adults to that of their peers.
- They are willing to examine the unusual and are highly inquisitive.
- Their behavior is often well organized, goal directed, and efficient with respect to tasks and problems.
- They exhibit an intrinsic motivation to learn, find out, or explore and are often very persistent. "I'd rather do it myself" is a common attitude.
- They enjoy learning new things and new ways of doing things.
- They have a longer attention and concentration span than their peers.

Learning Characteristics

- They may show keen powers of observation, exhibit a sense of the significant, and have an eye for important details.
- They may read a great deal on their own, preferring books and magazines written for youngsters older than themselves.
- They often take great pleasure in intellectual activity.
- They have well-developed powers of abstraction, conceptualization, and synthesizing abilities.
- They generally have rapid insight into cause–effect relationships.
- They often display a questioning attitude and seek information for the sake of having it as much as for its instrumental value.
- They are often skeptical, critical, and evaluative. They are quick to spot inconsistencies.
- They often have a large storehouse of information regarding a variety of topics which they can recall quickly.
- They show a ready grasp of underlying principles and can often make valid generalizations about events, people, or objects.
- They readily perceive similarities, differences, and anomalies.
- They often attack complicated material by separating it into its components and analyzing it systematically.

Figure 6.5—Behavioral, Learning, and Creative Characteristics of Gifted and Talented Children

Source: Reprinted by permission of the Council for Exceptional Children.

Creative Characteristics

- They are fluent thinkers, able to produce a large quantity of possibilities, consequences, or related ideas.
- They are flexible thinkers, able to use many different alternatives and approaches to problem solving.
- They are original thinkers, seeking new, unusual, or unconventional associations and combinations among items of information. They also have an ability to see relationships among seemingly unrelated objects, ideas, or facts.
- They are elaborative thinkers, producing new steps, ideas, responses, or other embellishments to a basic idea, situation, or problem.
- They show a willingness to entertain complexity and seem to thrive in problem situations.
- They are good guessers and can construct hypotheses or "what if" questions readily.
- They often are aware of their own impulsiveness and the irrationality within themselves and show emotional sensitivity.
- They have a high level of curiosity about objects, ideas, situations, or events.
- They often display intellectual playfulness, fantasize, and imagine readily.
- They can be less intellectually inhibited than their peers in expressing opinions and ideas and often exhibit spirited disagreement.
- They have a sensitivity to beauty and are attracted to aesthetic dimensions.

Figure 6.5 (*continued*)

administrators, and parents their preferences for the best strategies for meeting the needs of gifted and talented children in elementary schools showed that 42% favored pulling children out of regular classes into a resource room for a few hours a day. Approximately 24% favored the creation of a special class; about 18% wanted a consultant teacher. Favored by 10% or less were such strategies as special schools, independent study, or community mentors (Gallagher, Weiss, Oglesby, & Thomas, 1983).

In the study just described, only 10% favored enrichment within the regular classroom. It seems that most parents, teachers, and administrators do not believe the regular classroom teacher knows how or has the time to adequately challenge the gifted and talented student. We believe gifted children need to be with other gifted children at least part of each day. Hopefully, you will teach in a situation where some kind of special program is offered to gifted and talented children. Nevertheless, the question of what you as a classroom teacher can do must be addressed.

Wolf (1990) has offered these ten tips for helping gifted and talented children:

1. Make special arrangements for high-achieving students to take selected subjects in higher grades.

2. Introduce elementary-age students to research methods.

3. Teach debating skills and encourage students to sponsor and participate in debates on topics of their choice.

4. Provide access to computers and allow students to do their own programming.

5. Let students express themselves in art forms such as drawings, creative writing, and acting.

6. Make public services available and try to guide students to the resources they need: develop a catalog of resources, such as agencies providing free and inexpensive materials, local community services and programs, and people in the community with specific expertise.

7. Provide learning experiences that address both cognitive and affective domains.

8. Use a questioning technique to help students arrive at information or concepts, for example, hypothetical "what if" questions.

9. Provide learning experiences that go beyond the basic curriculum, drawing on mentors in the community.

10. Emphasize concepts, theories, ideas, relationships, and generalizations.

Another strategy you can invoke in your classroom is independent study contracts. Because the gifted and talented child will be working at levels far above the rest of the class, you and the child's parents can negotiate contracts with the child that spell out the parameters of special independent study. The contract would probably include a statement of the problem or research questions or a statement of the goals of the project. Next, the contract would specify the procedures to be used in conducting the study and the possible resources. The resources section would include print and people resources within and outside of the school. Electronic data bases may be included as well. The contract would also specify how the student will present the knowledge gained or the goals accomplished. Finally there would be a section on how the project will be evaluated, both through self-evaluation and peer and/or teacher evaluation. The parents might play a role in the evaluation as well.

Even with the tips for helping listed here and the independent study contract in place, you may well be left wondering how better to challenge the gifted learner in your room. As a final suggestion, we draw on the work of Maker (1982). Maker offers guidelines for curriculum modification in terms of content modifications, process modifications, product modifications, and learning environment modifications.

Content Modifications

▼   Abstractness: Emphasis is on studying abstract concepts, moving the memorization of facts to a supportive position.

▼   Complexity: Make the topics of study as complex as possible.

▼   Variety: Topics not usually included in the regular curriculum are studied.

▼   Organization and economy: A few key concepts serve as organizers for the variety of topics studied.

▼   Study of people: Leaders in science, industry, and the arts are studied, often with a special focus on how they solve problems.

▼   Study of methods: The tools of the scientists, artists, and craftspersons are studied within each discipline.

Process Modifications

▼   Higher level thinking: Using knowledge is emphasized over acquiring knowledge.

▼   Open-endedness: Create situations where study leads to more questions for more study.

▼   Discovery: When the stage is set for discovery, the gifted child's natural curiosity is enhanced.

▼   Evidence of reasoning: Engage children in self-evaluation of their reasoning ability and the products that result.

▼   Freedom of choice: The gifted learner should often be permitted to choose the course of study and the process.

▼   Group interaction activities and simulations: Caution must be exercised that the gifted learner is not always operating alone. Cooperative learning group work in problem solving is helpful.

▼   Pacing and variety: Set the pace so the gifted child is challenged.

Product Modifications

▼   Real problems: Challenge the gifted child to work on real-life problem solutions.

▼   Real audiences: The products produced by the gifted learner should reach real audiences through newspaper, television, personal presentation, and computer networks.

▼   Transformation: The focus should be on transforming existing knowledge into new views and applications rather than just summarizing existing knowledge.

▼ Evaluation: The products created should be evaluated by authentic consumers or experts in the field.

Learning Environment Modifications

▼ Independence: Learners should be responsible for their own learning.

▼ Openness: Flexibility should be designed into learning so new ideas, problems, materials, and persons can be introduced.

▼ Acceptance: Care must be taken to assure acceptance of the gifted child and his or her work with age peers and others.

▼ Mobility: High mobility should be assured within the learning environment. The gifted learner needs the freedom to move to the library, computer center, or resource center as needed.

Fundamental changes must be made in the curriculum, your expectations, and even the learning environment in order to meet the needs of gifted and talented children in your classroom. Once again, when we look at these suggestions for modifying the curriculum for gifted children, we note that good teaching is good teaching. Although not every child can cope with all these suggestions, *all* children need challenging and interesting work to do in school. To some extent these same considerations need to be made in working with limited-English-proficient children, but here the greatest need is for you to understand the cultures of the children with whom you work.

Working with Limited-English-Proficient Children in the Reading/Writing Program

Reading and writing—everyone wants every child to learn them! The children least likely to do so in our population are linguistically diverse children. Many of these children do not speak English as their first language. We know that many linguistically diverse children are classified by their schools as "at risk," meaning simply that they have not been as successful in traditional school settings as children from mainstream groups. We also know that our society is rapidly becoming ethnically diverse, and this presents new and important challenges.

The population of the United States is becoming older and less white. By the year 2000 one in every three Americans will be an African American, Hispanic, or Asian American (Yates, 1988). By the year 2000 whites will compose less than 50% of America's school population. With this changing cultural scene, you will have to meet the challenge of LEP (limited-English-proficiency) students in your classroom. These are children for whom English is a second language and who are limited in their ability to benefit from English-language instruction. We use the descriptor LEP here because it is the most widely used in schools, although some have suggested it promotes negative attitudes toward learners and that other descriptors should be used (Freeman & Freeman, 1992). Alternative terms that have been suggested included PEP, Potentially English Proficient (Hamayan, 1989), and REAL, Readers and Writers of English as Another Language (Rigg & Allen, 1989). Whatever the descriptor, it is reasonable for you to predict that your classroom will house a culturally diverse group of learners.

Characteristics of Linguistically Diverse Students

It would be folly for us to try to describe in any detail the characteristics of students from widely differing cultural backgrounds. The critical point here is that you will find this diversity in your classroom, and you must do all you can to learn about the cultures represented there. Gearheart, Mullen, and Gearheart (1993) have described five major sociocultural factors (originally defined by Collier, 1988) you should consider in coming to know children with diverse cultural and linguistic backgrounds in your classroom.

Cultural and Linguistic Background

You need to study the culture and learn how education is viewed, what the dynamic is between children and adults, how the culture handles discipline, the nature of the work ethic, and so on. Learn all you can about how the language works so you can better appreciate the challenges posed by learning English. Determine which members of the family take leadership roles and what the role is of extended family members. Try also to determine family attitudes toward professionals and toward accepting assistance.

Experiential Background

Learn all you can about the life experiences of the child. A Native American child who has learned the family history orally will have a different view than the Anglo child who reads to gain information. Our experiences working with Native American children in the Southwest quickly showed us that the Anglo notion of having a child look into the adult's eyes when spoken to were very much at odds with the children's experiences.

Acculturation

Try to discover how fully the child has adapted to a new cultural environment. Adaption to the mainstream culture ranges from families who truly struggle against losing their own culture to families to adapt to the new culture readily. Try to learn the desires of the family here. We know one first grader whose family speaks only Chinese at home and are dismayed their daughter is not behaving at school as her Chinese heritage would dictate. The teacher here must try to understand the clash between school and home, and be prepared to assist the child.

Sociolinguistic Development

Carefully examine the degree to which the child has learned English and can benefit from instruction in English. Can the child use English to communicate within the social context? Seek support such as a translator or see if the school can hire an instructional assistant who speaks the language.

Cognitive Learning Styles

Knowing the learning style typical of the culture can help you understand the child. Many Asian children, for example, may have a very passive learning style as will many Native Americans. Some cultures do not prize the individual ahead of the group as our mainstream culture seems to do. Competition is not encouraged in some cultures, or only if it's for the common good. Try to understand the degree to which the cultural learning style may be reflective as compared to quick and impulsive. Is the child expected in the native culture to learn globally or to take a very analytical approach to learning?

Accommodating the Needs of LEP Students

Children who are native speakers of English read before they have complete control of the form. Many young children who are still using constructions such as "gots" and "goed" read. Therefore, second-language speakers can also begin reading before they have mastered all the oral forms. If reading is defined as the construction of meaning through the interaction of what the child knows and print symbols, then children who are not native speakers can be encouraged to use their own experiential knowledge and their knowledge of how language works to begin predicting texts. Teachers should concentrate on the child's ability to demonstrate comprehension through retelling, drawing, or drama rather than on correct pronunciation. If possible, children should be able to discuss their reading in their native language (with an adult or other children). Often children understand much more than they can say in English.

Ideally, children for whom English is a second language would learn to read, initially, in their native language. Once they know *reading*, they could more easily learn to read in English. In practical terms this may not be possible, but it should be the first preference.

Reading for second-language learners is as dependent on background information as it is for first-language learners. Teachers should try to match reading material to the child's cultural background and to provide real experiences, rather than a study of vocabulary words, before reading activities. In our own teaching experience, our second-language learners had not had experience with birthday parties, eating in a restaurant, riding an escalator or in an elevator, or attending a circus. Rather than teaching them vocabulary words, we participated in these experiences, reading about them (oral reading by the teacher and reading books on their own) and writing about them. Some of the writing was in the form of labels for drawings or models, some in reports, and some in narratives. Some was dictated and some was written independently. Talking, reading, and writing all supported the child's growth in literacy.

We recommend using the techniques of the language-experience approach (Chapter 4) as one means of providing reading material that is relevant to the second-language learner's experience. Language experience gives the teacher opportunities to learn about the child's language, practice forms that are needed, and build on what the child knows rather than what is not known.

In observing a structured English as a second language (ESL) lesson one day, we found the language used outside the lesson to be much more interesting and complex than the language used during the lesson. In the lesson, children were practicing the forms "I wash my face. He washes his face. She washes her face. We wash our faces" and other sentences related to self-care such as combing hair, brushing teeth, and so on. Before the lesson began, the children were chatting with each other. One child had a very large pencil with a fuzzy ball on the end. Another child asked, "Do they have those in another color?" At the front of the room, a large chart had been constructed entitled "Foods We Eat." There were four columns on the chart, one labeled breakfast, one lunch, one dinner, and one snack. In the column labeled snack, someone had stuck drawings of houses made by the children. One child said to the child

School becomes a comfortable place when the cultures of all children are valued.

© Gail Meese/Meese Photo Research

next to him, "Look what we have for snack—our houses!" If the teacher had been using language experience, she or he would be aware of the forms the child needed in order to communicate his or her ideas. Instruction could be focused on what the child needed, not what was already known (Brewer, 1990).

In order to take advantage of the child's oral and print knowledge, some teachers of young children begin the school year by asking children to sign in as they come to school. Whether they can write their names in a conventional way or not, the teacher learns quickly how much the child knows about writing. Do they make a scribble, produce some random letters, produce letters in their names, or write their names conventionally? Such a simple activity provides many opportunities for conversing and a purposeful reason for writing. Some children recognize words and logos in print that can be used to help them learn spoken English. It is important that literacy activities be as meaningful as possible and they be kept as whole as possible. Children whose first language is not English do not need more drill on isolated elements of language; they need more meaningful reasons to use English in speaking.

Literacy programs for children whose first language is not English must be planned so the child has real, functional needs for learning the language and for using it. Language learning, as you saw in Chapter 1, is not a linear activity. One cannot control the individual components of language (listening, speaking, reading, and writing) so that children are taught only one component at a time. Teachers who want to help children move toward literacy in English will respect the child's ability to learn and will respect the child's cultural heritage. Lim and Watson (1993) described how they applied the principles of whole-language instruction with students who were learning English as a second language. They took a strong and successful position that they could best help youngsters reach their potential English proficiency by shifting the focus of instruction from direct teaching of language to using classroom strategies in which language was naturally and functionally learned.

We close this discussion on the LEP student with McCormick's (1990) list of ten tips for helping children in your classroom who are not native English speakers:

1. As you identify the different ethnic groups in your classroom, become informed about their characteristics and learning styles.

2. Encourage and assist students in sharing their culture in the classroom; you can start the process by sharing your own cultural values and traditions.

3. Avoid textbooks and materials that present cultural stereotypes.

4. Learn as much as possible about the students' home and community, interests, talents, skills, and potentials and develop an instructional program accordingly.

5. Find out how the students in your class wish you to refer to their ethnic group; for example, some Mexican Americans prefer to be called Chicanos whereas others may take offense at the term.

6. Include ethnic studies in the curriculum to help minority students gain a more positive self-image.

7. Make parents your partners.

8. Treat all students equally; do not fall into the trap of reverse racism.

9. Make sure assessment techniques used are appropriate and take into account cultural and linguistic differences.

10. Avoid imitating speech patterns of linguistically diverse students; rather than an aid in education, this may be viewed as mockery.

Major Ideas in This Chapter

▼ PL 94-142 requires that an individualized education program (IEP) be written in collaboration with parents, the classroom teacher, and specialists to meet the special needs of children with disabilities. As a classroom teacher you play a crucial role in the identification and support of such children.

▼ Special education and regular education have formed a powerful (although controversial) relationship of cooperation and collaboration as a result of the regular education initiative.

▼ Many classroom teachers do not feel trained or equipped to work with children with special needs. REI will require training and assistance for regular classroom teachers if the initiative is to succeed.

▼ The concept of fairness is a critical consideration in working with learning-disabled children. *Fairness* means each child getting what he or she needs, not all children getting the same thing.

▼ In modifying the curriculum for gifted and talented children we need to carefully consider content modifications, process modifications, product modifications, and modifications in the learning environment.

▼ We need to examine the cultural and linguistic background, experiential background, acculturation, sociolinguistic development, and cognitive learning styles of linguistically diverse children in our classrooms.

▼ Literacy programs for children whose first language is not English must be planned so the child has real, functional reasons for learning the language and using it.

Discussion Questions: Focusing on the Teacher You Are Becoming

1. As beginning teachers, what do you and your classmates see as *essential* support you will need to be successful in mainstreaming exceptional learners in your classroom?

2. Some argue that REI is simply a way for the government to cut spending for special needs learners. Others argue that it is finally a way to meet the needs of these children. Discuss the merits and shortcomings of these two opposing positions.

3. Smith-Burke, Deegan, and Jaggar showed how Cambourne's conditions apply to learners with special needs. They also defined various roles of the teacher. Revisit Figure 6.4 and discuss what the teacher roles of enabler, model, mentor, trustee, coach, facilitator, and collaborator mean to you.

4. Programs for the gifted and talented range all the way from a few special assignments in the regular classroom to special schools. What is the school's responsibility to meet the needs of these learners, and how should it be done?

5. Discuss the things you could *realistically* do the first year you teach to get to know the cultural diversity represented in your classroom.

Field-Based Applications

1. Ask to see an individualized education program written for a child in the classroom in which you are working. Collect as much information as you can from the classroom teacher about the *process* of writing that IEP. Ask especially about the role of the classroom teacher in the process. If IEPs are confidential in the school district where you work, ask the teacher to tell you how they are written.

2. Make arrangements to interview a classroom teacher, a special education teacher, a parent, and a building administrator about the REI and their reaction to it.

3. Make arrangements to view the Public Broadcasting System videotape entitled "How Difficult Can This Be" (F.A.T. CITY Workshop). PBS Video can be reached by dialing 1-800-424-7963. This tape provides powerful examples of what it is like to be learning disabled.

4. Visit two or three schools (urban, suburban, elementary, middle) to observe the programs for the gifted. Share your observations with classmates and discuss them in light of the information in this chapter.

5. In the school where you are working, spend time getting to know a child whose native language is not English. Try to find information about the conflicts between English and the child's language. See what you can learn about the child's experiential background and acculturation.

Chapter 7
Using the Cueing Systems

Chapter Overview

▼ Moving from printed language to oral language (decoding) in reading is a very complicated process. It relies on a variety of cues found on the printed page. Readers use only a small portion of the available cues.

▼ Word identification requires the use of several cueing systems: grapho-phonic, semantic, and syntactic. These cues are in the text. Another cueing system, schematic cues, the reader brings to the text. Good readers use all four cueing systems as needed to create meaning.

▼ A teacher's view of the reading process determines the kinds of curricular decisions the teacher makes. In one view, reading should be taught beginning with sounds, then words, then sentences and stories. In another, reading instruction should begin with whole stories.

▼ Decoding instruction should be guided by a set of principles to ensure that in the course of skills instruction the teacher never loses sight of the reading process.

▼ Skills lessons (regardless of the skill being taught) should consist of activities to develop knowledge, promote practice, provide application, and permit reinforcement.

▼ Learning the strategies of the reading process is more valuable than learning individual subskills. Instruction in reading strategies should be an important part of the reading program.

How do we get from print to language to creating meaning when we read? We accomplish this complicated task by the simultaneous use of a variety of *cueing systems*, all the data we use to "cue" us as to the meaning of the text. Some of the cues (syntactic, semantic, and graphophonic) are resident in the text. Others (reader-based) are the schematic cues the reader brings to the text as a result of experience. All the strategies readers use to move from print to language are grouped under the global term *word identification*, also known as *decoding* (signifying "breaking the print code"—moving from the print symbol to its language equivalent) and *word recognition* (containing the sense of word identification and decoding, and including the idea that a word is in one's listening vocabulary; that is, its meaning is understood when it is heard).

The Cueing Systems

A page of print is rich in cues to help the reader decode the print (get from print to language) and construct meaning—far more, in fact, than readers usually need. Mature readers rely on the various cues as needs and purposes for reading dictate.

Text-Based Cues

Text-based cues are those resident in the text that we are able to use because of our knowledge about how language works. To understand text-based cues, think about what you do while reading when you come to a word that is not in your sight vocabulary. Chances are you skip it and go on, in the hope (or on the assumption) the word is not important. When you realize you are not creating meaning, you finally stop and go back to deal with the unknown word. Maybe you even feel as if you'd been caught in the act of trying to evade the unfamiliar word. At this point, you usually rely on (1) the structure of the sentence in which the word occurs (syntactic cues), (2) the meanings of other words in the sentence and nearby sentences (semantic cues), and (3) the sound–symbol relationships within words (graphophonic cues).

Consider each of these text-based cueing systems in turn.

Syntactic Cues

The structure of the sentence in which the word occurs can sometimes cue us to the identification of the unfamiliar word. The term for the arrangement of words in a sentence and the relationship among the words is *syntax*. The principles that describe how words may be arranged make up the syntax of our language, and the cues they provide are called *syntactic cues*. Consider this sentence:

The rambunctious boys broke the lamp.

Suppose the word *rambunctious* was not in your sight vocabulary. How could the structure of the sentence cue you to identify the word? The first word in the sentence provides some help. *The* is a noun marker, indicating a noun follows. Other examples of noun markers are *those, this, that, some, his, her,* and *their*. When you see a noun marker, you know a noun will follow it next or very soon. In the sample sentence, you realize that *boys* is a noun. That means the unknown word has to be an adjective, a word that describes or modifies a noun. Now you ask yourself what words you know that can describe boys. At this point you probably would jump to the use of another cueing system and consider the beginning sounds in the unknown word to limit the possible *boy* descriptors you will consider. As a start in identifying the unknown word, syntactic cues are helpful because of what you know about how the language works.

Semantic Cues

The meanings of words around the unknown word, in the same or nearby sentences, often provide cues called *semantic cues* to help identify the word. Known meanings of other words can help you predict the identity of an unfamiliar word. Semantic cues could help you identify *rambunctious* in the sample sentence if you considered what breaking the lamp suggests about the boys' behavior and the nature and level of their activity. Cues to the identity of *rambunctious* exist in the meaning of *broke the lamp.*

Words within a sentence often cue other words semantically. In the following examples, semantic cues occur in the same sentence as the unknown word:

> His sock was worn through; the /// was growing larger with each
>   step he took.
> He put the milk in the /// to keep it cool.
> It was an easy book, and reading it was not at all ///.

Those sentences have such clear semantic cues that you probably correctly predicted the missing words to be *hole, refrigerator,* and *difficult.* Semantic cues are not always that clear, but they are still helpful in identifying an unknown word. Consider these examples:

> His favorite dessert was ///.
> The girls' favorite team sport was ///.

Here, semantic cues occur in a sentence that follows the unknown word:

> The student who was the team's best center was supercilious. Some
> of the fans called him a supercilious jerk. In fact, he was the most
> haughty member of the team.

If you did not know the meaning of *supercilious,* how would the surrounding sentences help you identify the word? The idea that the player is supercilious is in essence repeated two sentences later with the word *haughty.* This would cue you that *supercilious* must have a meaning like *haughty.*

Graphophonic Cues

When a word is not in your sight vocabulary and the use of syntactic and semantic cues fails to help you identify it, the next step is to use your knowledge of the graphophonic cueing system. Our language is an alphabetic one.

Sounds are represented by letters of the alphabet. This set of phoneme (sound) and grapheme (letters) correspondences constitutes the graphophonic cueing system. The difficulty here is there are approximately 44 sounds in American English and only 26 letters with which to represent them. This lack of phoneme/grapheme correspondence is challenging to persons learning to use the graphophonic cueing system.

There are interesting links between writing and reading in terms of learning to use the graphophonic cueing system. Since the early 1970s there has been a growing awareness that children's invented spellings (incorrect attempts at writing words correctly) are powerful indicators of both their developing phonemic awareness and knowledge of sound–letter relationships (Cunningham & Cunningham, 1992). Some research has even indicated that second-grade students' abilities to spell words correctly is a high predictor of their ability to read those same words (Hall, 1991). Clearly, the ability to use the graphophonic cueing system is beneficial in both reading and writing.

Reader-Based Cues: The Schematic Cues

Schematic cues are all the information, assumptions, and theories (schemata) about the world the reader brings to the act of reading. The reader creates meaning through the interaction of the ideas of the writer and the background experiences and knowledge of the reader, in light of the reader's purposes for reading. Consider a typical example of the way in which the schemata two readers bring to the text dramatically affect the interpretation of that text.

Suppose Chris and Sean have both been to dog shows. Chris's experience at the dog show was wonderful. She enjoyed seeing all the different breeds, even got to pet a few dogs, and loved trying to predict which dog would be the winner in each event. Sean, who had been seriously bitten by a large dog a year earlier, saw the dog show with very different eyes. The barking reminded him of the dog that bit him. He was uncomfortable the whole time he was at the show.

Chris and Sean would read stories about dogs and dog shows very differently because of the background experiences and mental images (schemata) they have for dogs. They could each begin with the same printed text, but they would individually create very different meanings. The reader's schemata have a tremendous impact on the meaning that is created while reading. Consequently, it is unlikely that the meaning the reader creates and the meaning with which the author began are ever *exactly* the same.

Orchestrating the Use of the Cueing Systems

The process of using the cueing systems can be very rapid. Although we have taken it apart in order to discuss the components, the reader may in fact combine them so speedily that the separations are not apparent. If the separations of the components are not apparent in use, then why separate them in teaching them? This question has generated heated debate within the reading profession. Where do readers look first? Do they move from the whole of a written piece to sentences, words, and then sounds, or do they begin with the smallest units—sounds—and build to words, sentences, and paragraphs? Do they begin from the top and work down or from the bottom and build up?

If you were to ask children what they do when coming to a word they don't know (cannot read), the response would be very informative. If a child said, "I sound the word out" this would indicate that the first line of attack is to use the graphophonic cueing system. If, however, the child responded, "I skip it and read on to see if I can figure the word out. All words aren't real important." This response would tell you that the child has more than a sound-it-out strategy. This child is using the other cueing systems as well.

Our goal in reading instruction is to have all children create meaning when they read by using all of the cueing systems in concert with one another. The child who always sounds out first is as crippled in the use of the systems as the child who never sounds out words.

It is crucial to help children see how the systems work together to help us create meaning. Young readers must become comfortable and very accustomed to asking themselves three critical questions as they are using the cueing systems and predicting what unknown words may be: "Does my prediction look right? Does my prediction sound right? Does it make sense?" The use of these questions will advance the goal of becoming an independent, self-monitoring reader (Clay, 1991).

Children learn to orchestrate the use of the cueing systems on their own, through adult modeling, and through instruction. The kind of instruction in the cueing systems children receive in the primary grades, particularly, depends very much on the beliefs of the teacher (recall top-down and bottom-up views from Chapter 2).

Teachers' Beliefs Drive Instructional Decisions

How teachers see the reading process very much determines the kinds of curriculum decisions they make and the goals they set for students. For the past 65 years a behavioristic view of learning has dominated the teaching of reading (May, 1986): Learning has been seen as a response to a stimulus, which, when reinforced, is finally remembered. The stimulus/response approach to learning sought to break the learning act down into its smallest pieces and then reinforce the student's learning of each piece. In reading, the smallest pieces are the sound–symbol relationships. Therefore, the behaviorist teacher of reading would begin by teaching letters, then sounds represented by those letters, then words, and finally sentences and longer discourse.

Typically, the vocabulary in beginning materials was carefully controlled so that once students learned a sound–symbol relationship they did not encounter variations in that relationship in textual materials. This part-to-whole approach to the teaching of reading has been challenged in the past ten years by those who believe the reading process works from the top down. In their view, the most significant element within the reading process is not sound–symbol relationships but sentences, which represent meaning.

What has now come to be known as the whole-language movement originated in the view of learning suggested by Gestalt psychology: Learning moves from wholes to parts. The learner is seen as looking for wholes— complete forms—called gestalts. Our perceptions are dominated by our schemata. When we witness an event, look at a picture, or pick up a book, we do so with expectations of what we will see, hear, find. Expectations created by our background experiences color our perceptions. As we read, we continually make predictions about what the author is saying to us. We use the fewest possible cues on the printed page to confirm our predictions. Mature readers do not even decode all the words in a sentence. In attempting to proofread a paper, you have probably had to fight the urge to skim. Only when we become aware that the reading process has broken down do we begin to use more of the cues, ultimately resorting to a careful examination of the sound–symbol relationships. Since the early 1980s this whole-language, top-down, whole-to-part view of the reading process has gained wider and wider acceptance.

The question of whether to engage in part-to-whole or whole-to-part instruction in word identification is best answered by considering what you want children to believe about the reading process. Answer each of the following questions to determine where you stand on the issue:

1. Do you want young readers to believe that reading is constructing meaning or unlocking sounds?

2. Do you believe children should first read their own language or first read a controlled vocabulary so that sound–symbol relationships are consistent?

3. Do you believe that before children read a selection they should hear it well read by another, or should children always decode a selection on their own?

4. Do you believe children learn to read by reading and writing, or do you believe they must master word-identification skills before they can read?

5. Do you believe the information children bring to the printed page affects their understanding, or do you believe all the meaning resides in the words?

6. Do you believe children understand an author's ideas without reading every word, or must they understand every word in order to comprehend a selection?

7. Do you believe that when children read aloud they may substitute meaningful alternatives to the printed words, or must they read every word accurately?

8. Do you believe that when a child reads incorrectly and loses the meaning, you should say, "Here is what you read, does that make sense?" or should you simply correct the child's errors?

9. In reading, are the basic units of instruction sentences and paragraphs, or are the basic units of instruction sounds, letters, and words?

10. Do you believe the structure of a sentence often determines the meanings of words, or are word meanings independently stable?

If you answered yes to the first part of each question you have sided with the whole-to-part advocates. Agreement with the second half of each question puts you in the part-to-whole camp. When you examine the five principles we state here, you will see we advocate whole-to-part instruction. One of our goals is to convince the part-to-whole advocates of the benefits of a whole-to-part approach in teaching the use of the cueing systems.

Instruction in Using the Cueing Systems

Our instruction in the use of the cueing systems is guided by the following set of principles:

Principle 1. Instruction in the use of the cueing systems should be seen as an aid to constructing meaning, not as an end in itself. We do not teach children the sound(s) represented by a certain letter because that knowledge is important as such. We teach the sound–letter correspondence so the process of constructing meaning may go on as effortlessly as possible.

Principle 2. What we do in skills instruction should be as much like the reading act as possible. In skills instruction we should use examples taken from meaningful texts, preferably texts written by children.

Principle 3. Before instruction of young children in the graphophonic cueing system can begin, three conditions must be met: The children must have (1) auditory discrimination (the ability to hear differences in sounds), (2) visual discrimination (the ability to see differences in letters and between words), and (3) the understanding that reading is a process of constructing or reconstructing meaning.

Principle 4. While engaging in instruction in the components of the reading process we must respect the reading process. Having broken down the process in order to examine individual steps, we should put it back together before ending the instruction, so children can see the relationships between the parts and the whole.

Principle 5. Cueing system instruction is useful only when the words identified are in the reader's listening or speaking vocabulary. The use of word-identification cues will not be effective if children cannot recognize miscues when they make them and self-correct. Word identification is useless if readers do not know the words they have identified.

Teaching the Use of the Syntactic Cueing System

The importance of syntactic cues was made clear by Durkin (1978–1979), who stressed that English is a *positional language* in which meaning very often depends on word order. She pointed out the importance of word order in sentences such as these:

> The boy fed the kitten.
> The kitten fed the boy.

and in such expressions as *day off* and *off day*. Because meaning is so dependent on word order, the structure of sentences signals meaning. However, the importance of syntactic cues must not be overestimated. The context assists readers in understanding the meaning of words that are primarily redundant. Frequently, words whose meaning is signaled by context are words that contribute little new meaning to the text (Hittleman, 1988). The effectiveness of context cues depends on readers' ability to see connections, to solve problems, and to recognize a word as being in their listening vocabulary once they have decoded it. We suggest activities like these to develop children's use of the syntactic cueing system:

1. Play word games in which the order of words is changed to illustrate the positional nature of our language. Show that word order sometimes changes the meaning and other times renders the sentence meaningless.

2. Teach the concept of noun markers. Have children brainstorm and later predict the words that can occupy a slot following a noun marker. For example, which words could go in this empty slot?

    The /// were sweet and juicy and made wonderful juice.

3. Teach the concept of the preposition as a noun marker and do activities similar to the ones suggested in activity 2.

4. Teach the concept that some words signal the nature of other nearby words. Have children predict possible words signaled by syntactic cues in sentences such as this:

The /// did not cover the sides of the window.

Special Note: It is very difficult to talk about any one of the cueing systems in isolation from the others. As we said before, the cueing systems are used in conjunction with each other. Activity 4 is a good example of a time when after helping children see the cues in the syntax (*the* is a noun marker; a noun will follow), next help them see how they can use schematic cues to identify the unknown word. What they know about things that could cover the side of windows will limit their predictions to a few words. *Elephant* certainly is not a likely prediction. *Curtain, shade, drape,* or *blind* are much more likely. Once they understand this, you can further extend the orchestration of the systems by asking, "If the first letter of the unknown word was *B*, how would that help us decide which of our predictions might be true?" Pointing out that the unknown word begins with /b/ would then demonstrate how the graphophonic cues can further help us identify the unknown word.

5. Develop modified cloze activities using text from which words have been omitted not randomly but systematically: Those words that are syntactically cued are removed. This activity may be simplified by indicating the initial letter of each omitted word. Figure 7.1 is an example of a modified cloze activity. As you predict the words that might fit in the blanks, consider all the contextual and other language information you are using. It is interesting to do this activity with a partner and discuss the reasons for your predictions.

Teaching the Use of the Semantic Cueing System

The semantic cueing system includes the ways in which meanings of words are signaled. This involves knowing the meanings of words themselves, using prefixes and suffixes to unlock meanings, and using the meanings of words found elsewhere in the text to create meaning. The following techniques will help children understand the power of the semantic cueing system:

1. Demonstrate that in some sentences words are simply defined; for example,

A carpenter's square is a device to measure or create 90-degree angles.

2. Demonstrate that in some sentences the meaning of words is explained by examples introduced by words such as *such, like, such as,* and *for example:*

THE CIRCUS

For a week the circus posters had been displayed on the Stanfield signboards. Billy had stood by while the men _____ them on, and he and Larry almost knew the different _____ by heart.

"It ain't as _____ as Barnum's," said Robert. "I saw that at Madison Square Garden. I tell you it was _____!"

The Brandenberg children were not _____ to argue on this subject. It was to be their first _____, and if it proved as good as the posters represented, it would be _____.

"How do you suppose he can _____ on such a thin wire way up in the _____?" asked Billy.

"She's a star if she can _____ on a _____ when he is on the gallop. Look there, she's going to _____ through _____ and land on _____ on the other side!" exclaimed Tom.

Figure 7.1—Modified Cloze

Many cities are altering their skylines with towers such as Toronto's CN tower and the Space Needle in Seattle.

3. Offer a meaningful introduction of vocabulary. After the children have read a selection, present important words to them using a sentence from the selection. Have someone read aloud the sentence containing the word, and invite volunteers to tell what the word means. This permits them to use the context of the selection to come to understandings of the word's meanings. Ask the children to use the word in their own sentences to show they understand it. If the children cannot respond, then you define the word and use it in a sentence. Always end this activity by having children use the words in sentences of their own that illustrate *meaningful* understanding of the word rather than just the ability to parrot it back. This activity is especially important when dealing with words of multiple meanings.

4. Provide special word lists. During the teaching of a unit or theme, keep an ongoing list of important words (in sentences) on a large sheet of paper hanging in the classroom. Take time periodically to examine the growing list and talk about the words added recently. Older children can keep their own lists.

5. Introduce "important word" books. Children maintain their own books of words that have become important to them in some way. The words may then be used in writing activities.

6. Provide a structured overview. Present vocabulary to children in a way that shows the interrelationships between and among terms.

words, we cannot read something about which we have no knowledge at all and expect to comprehend it. We call this same idea the *Velcro theory:* If we do not have at least some prior knowledge to bring to the reading experience, the new words and ideas do not stick. (Our term itself illustrates the idea!)

So comprehension is much more than just thinking when we read. It is the application of our schemata to the act of reading. We comprehend when we are able to combine the words (ideas) of the author with our own schemata (mini-theories about the world). Interaction is central to the process. Thus we define *comprehension* as the interaction of the author's ideas and the reader's schemata that results in the creation of meaning.

The Process of Creating Meaning

In order to understand how readers create meaning with texts, we need to focus on three areas. The first is the *reader's purpose* for engaging with the text. Our purpose for reading a text very much determines how we use the reading process. The second consideration is the *reader's monitoring of the process*. This includes consideration of how the reader self-monitors and adjusts the use of the reading process. Finally, we need to focus on the *reader's response to the text*. This includes the reader's emotional response to the text as well as what the reader does after engaging with the text.

We now consider each of these three key areas in turn, helping you understand the concepts and how to develop each area with children.

Reader's Purpose

In Chapter 2 we discussed the reading process as an interaction between the language and thought of the author and the language and background knowledge of the reader. In years past teachers tended to view readers as "blank slates, empty vessels" onto or into which the ideas of the author were to be placed. It was thought that when a reader engaged with a text, *only one meaning could be made*. That meaning, the one intended by the author, was considered the "correct" meaning.

As we have come to a better understanding of the reading process we have realized that whenever a reader reads there are always three texts operating. The first text is in the head of the author, the second text is on the printed page, and the third text is in the head of the reader. You know from your own writing that the text in the head of the writer is never exactly the same as the text on the printed page. You know from your own reading that the text you render when you read is never exactly the same as the one on the printed page. Even very fluent readers make miscues when they read, thus changing the surface structure of the text. We all make our own interpretations of the meaning thus changing, however slightly, the deep structure—the meaning—of the text.

Louise Rosenblatt (1978, p. 12) described this process as follows:

The reader brings to the text his past experience and present personality. Under the magnetism of the ordered symbols of the text, he marshals his resources and crystallizes out from the stuff of memory, thought, and feeling a new order, a new experience, which he sees as the poem [not necessarily what we think of as a poem, but any literary work created by a reader in the process of reading a text]. This becomes part of the ongoing stream of his life experience, to be reflected on from any angle important to him as a human being.

You may recall from Chapter 2 that in Rosenblatt's terms the *reader* is the person seeking to make meaning by transacting with (this means actively reading) a text. The *text* is the set of word symbols and language patterns on the paper, the thing you hold in your hands when you read. The *poem* is the literary work created as the reader transacts with the text. *Poem* in this sense is a metaphor for any literary work you read. Rosenblatt's central message is that the meaning is not *in the text* as we once thought, but in the mind of the reader as he or she transacts with the thought and language of the author. The poem is that third text we just described.

How does purpose relate to all of this? One's purpose for engaging with a text very much determines the degree of latitude one has as a reader to create a meaning different from that intended by the author. For example, when reading a Russian novel for pleasure the reader may take great liberties with changing difficult names to easier ones with almost no change in meaning. In the case of studying a text for an exam, the reader's meaning had better be very close to the meaning intended by the author. When preparing a cheese soufflé, the meaning created by the reader had better match the author's nearly perfectly or a real disaster may occur. The important point here is that how we read a text is very much determined by our purpose or purposes for reading that text.

Developing Students' Understanding of Purpose

We suggest that you make a routine part of your repertoire as a teacher the practice of focusing students' attention on their purposes for reading a text whenever you engage them with text. Talking about *why* they are reading a text and thus *how* they will read it will help reinforce this kind of thinking in them, and hopefully, make it a "natural" part of their own engagement with text. When you assign the reading of a text you might ask questions such as "Are you going to read this simply for pleasure? Will you be reading this text to find out the causes and effects of certain historical events? Are you reading this text to appreciate the style and talent of the author? Are you reading to gain background knowledge or do you want to be able to do something with the information after you read? Are you reading to take something away with you or are you reading mainly for the experience: what you are thinking and feeling during the reading" (Rosenblatt, 1991).

Responses to these questions would then be followed with questions such as "Will you therefore skim the text looking for key words? What key words will you be seeking? Will you be memorizing certain facts or sequences of information? How will you go about this? Do you want to remember key points? Would taking notes be useful here?"

Another factor affecting purpose for reading is the amount of background knowledge the reader brings to the text. Reading a text about which one already knows a great deal would imply a different approach to the reading than if the information was new to the reader. It is important to have readers consider what they know about a topic before they read. It can be helpful to have students write down everything they know about a topic before they read, and then to write questions they want to answer in the reading.

A classic strategy for helping readers set purposes for reading is SQ3R, which was developed by Robinson (1962). Students are taught this strategy when their purpose is to take information away from the text. In this strategy the name stands for *survey, question, read, recite,* and *review.* The *survey* piece invites the reader to examine the text looking at headings, highlighted items, illustrations, charts and graphs, questions posed by the author, and the first and last paragraphs. The *question* piece involves turning the headings and subheadings into questions the reader wants to answer while reading. These strategies help establish purpose for reading. Following the reading, the reader recites answers to the questions to himself or herself, and then reviews the material for mastery.

Stauffer (1975) and Smith (1978) long ago helped us see the importance of prediction as purpose setting. When the reader engages with a text through predicting what the author has said, the reader has set purposes for reading. The purpose for reading is to see if predictions can be confirmed. Helping readers predict what they will find in a text is a valuable way to help them establish a purpose for reading.

Meaning is created first by establishing a purpose for engaging with the text. Then the reader must monitor his or her use of the reading process.

Reader's Monitoring of the Process

When a reader monitors his or her own creation of meaning, it is called *metacomprehension,* which means "along with" and "after" comprehension. It signifies thinking while reading (or just afterward) about how we are comprehending what we read. Lowenthal (1986) has called this process "private, silent speech." Metacomprehension is our own personal monitoring of comprehension (May, 1986). Good readers seem to engage in the process of metacomprehension rather effortlessly. However, the skill is slow to develop. Baker and Brown (1984) have discovered it is very hard for children in primary grades to explain why they are having trouble understanding something they have read. Intermediate-grade children who are good readers can usually tell you they don't know a word or know what the word means. All children, and especially poor readers, would benefit from instructional strategies that improve metacomprehension ability.

Monitoring One's Comprehension

As you proceed through this text you are probably reading quite easily. In fact, you are likely to be using very few of the many graphophonic, semantic, and syntactic cues that are on this printed page. As a mature reader, you are probably relying most heavily on the semantic cues, followed by a combination of syntactic cues and your own schematic cues; you are paying little attention to individual words and almost none to the sounds in the words. In fact, in addition to using few of the cues on this page, you are probably making ongoing predictions about what we are going to say _____ .

Did you predict the word in the blank would be *next?* That is because as you read or listen to a speaker you are continually making predictions about what will follow. Ken Goodman (1967) has called reading a "psycholinguistic guessing game." This term refers to the prediction-making aspect of reading. As long as your reading confirms your predictions, you have comprehended. Frank Smith (1978) has said that evidence of comprehension is the state of having no unanswered questions. When we ask ourselves what the author is going to say next, make the prediction, and then confirm that prediction by reading, comprehension has occurred.

What does all this have to do with metacomprehension? When your predictions have not been confirmed—and you know it—you are engaged in metacomprehension. To say to yourself, "Hey, this isn't making any sense. I'd better go back and read more carefully" or you say, "I'm following this author's arguments every step of the way" is to engage in a personal comprehension-monitoring task known as *metacomprehension*. Realizing you are in trouble as a comprehender, you then begin to use more of the cues on the printed page. Whereas you might have been relying heavily on semantic and syntactic cues as long as your reading flowed smoothly and logically, you must now slow down and make careful use of graphophonic cues to get you out of comprehension difficulty. Good readers do this kind of comprehension monitoring. Poor readers do not.

Here is another example of how metacomprehension works. Suppose you were reading this text:

The boy ran to the house. It was yellow with white shutters.

If you read, "The boy ran to the horse. It was yellow with white shutters," and did not notice you had made a major mistake, you would be reading much as poor readers often do. In this case you would have been relying on the graphophonic cues without regard to meaning. A poor reader who makes this kind of error is not engaged in metacomprehension probably because he or she does not know that, first and foremost, reading is supposed to make sense.

Now suppose when you misread *horse* for *house* you very quickly noticed the sentence was not making sense. Your background experiences have taught you that horses are not yellow (except on merry-go-rounds) and they never have shutters. You say to yourself, "Hey, this is not making sense." You then reread more carefully and understand the author's message. You have engaged in metacomprehension. You thought about how you were comprehending while you were comprehending. It is important to help readers do this kind of self-monitoring and to correct breakdowns in comprehension when they occur.

Good readers tend to use the four cueing systems with considerable facility, relying here on one, there on another, and often integrating all four. The good reader's ability to use the cueing systems goes hand in hand with the ability to engage in metacomprehension. It is comprehension monitoring that signals the failure of one system and the need to shift to another. When the reader who has been relying primarily on schematic and syntactic cues suddenly realizes that comprehension has failed, making the switch to more intense use of semantic or graphophonic cues is a clear indication of good metacomprehension skill. This is why running records and their analysis are so important. Miscue analysis, as you saw in Chapter 5, helps us track this use of the cueing systems and the development of metacomprehension ability.

Making Inferences to Aid Comprehension

Lapp and Flood (1984) have identified several ways in which good readers differ from poor readers. One of those ways is that good readers are adept at drawing inferences, and they know when they have failed to do so. Most of the time, we rely heavily on our ability to draw inferences in order to make sense of what we read. The following example will provide some insight into the importance of inference in reading comprehension.

Susan and Michael have taken their allowance money to the local mall, where they are shopping for a sweater to give their mother for her birthday.

"Look at that one," said Susan. "It's perfect."
"No, it's not," said Michael. "It's not right at all."

To understand these two lines, you must make several inferences. You might infer, for example, that Susan is pointing to some kind of sweater in a shop window or a store display when she says, "Look at that one." From "It's perfect" you might infer that it appears to be the right size, the right color, and a style she thinks their mother would like. When Michael says, "No, it's not," he may mean it is not the right size, color, or style or it costs too much or he doesn't like the store or he doesn't want Susan to be the one to make the selection. You would certainly make numerous inferences just in understanding those two simple statements.

In their 1984 research, Lapp and Flood also concluded that good readers are adept at predicting what authors are going to say next (Goodman's psycholinguistic guessing game). In both cases of inference drawing—reading between the lines of the text and predicting what comes next—metacomprehension is at the heart of the matter.

To summarize, it is very important that the teacher help children become interactive readers who monitor their own comprehension. In other words, they need to know they don't know, to know why they might try certain strategies, and to know how well they are doing. Let's consider how to help children develop this ability to monitor their use of the reading process.

Helping Children Monitor Their Use of the Reading Process

In Chapter 4 we introduced the concept of *reading with* children. There we described shared reading. Another kind of *reading with* activity is guided reading. In the context of *reading to*, *reading with*, and *reading by* (Mooney, 1990), guided reading is a strategy for reading with the teacher in which the teacher has examined the challenges presented by a text and has decided a particular text at a particular time is too challenging for a reader or readers to read by themselves. Yet the text does not present such great challenges that it should not be used as a shared reading text or a *read to* text with these children at this point. This means the text can be used as a guided reading text. Guided reading is a strategy in which the teacher works with an individual or small group (usually a group) and guides them through segments of a text focusing on the use of background knowledge, the reading process, and other skills or strategies the children may need.

We have examined what is known about the reading process and helping children monitor their use of the process and have devised a form of guided reading we call the *Guided Metacomprehension Strategy (GMS)*.

The Guided Metacomprehension Strategy

I.   *Schemata awareness*. Focus: drawing on the reader's schemata to assist in relating the text to his or her background experiences.
   A.   Tell readers the topic or theme of the selection. Probe their background experiences and knowledge about the topic or theme.
   B.   Ask them to think about three questions: (1) What do I know about the topic? (2) What experiences have I had with the topic? (3) What will I need to remember from my experience as I read?
   C.   Engage them in thought about the purposes for reading the text—for information, for entertainment, to be persuaded, for example. Purpose depends on the nature of the text; for example, the purpose of reading an expository piece on Egypt would be very different from the purpose of reading a poem.

Comprehension often relies on previous experience.

© Michael Hagan

II. *Prediction making.* Focus: drawing on available clues, the reader makes predictions about the story.
   A. Give readers clues: the title, a picture, a sample sentence or paragraph, an incident.
   B. Get predictions. Ask, "What do you think will happen in this story?" Be sure to get a prediction, or at least concurrence with another child's prediction, from each child in the group. (Note: Do not try this prediction strategy with children who have already read the story. It will not work!) As children are making predictions, point out to them the ways in which they are drawing on their background knowledge in the process. Underscore this important schemata–reading link.

III. *Silent reading.* Focus: Silently reading pages assigned by the teacher. You decide the most interesting way to segment the selection.

IV. *Discussion and oral rereading.* Focus: proving or disproving predictions.
   A. Ask, "Which of our predictions can we prove? Which ones were not proven?" Ask, "Can you read aloud the part that proves or makes us change our predictions?"

    B. This is a good time for questions about story structure ("Where are we in the plot? Who are the central characters? What is the conflict? Where does the story take place?").

V. *Prediction making.* Focus: Making predictions about the next section of the selection.
    A. Invite reflection on the story so far; it is now a clue to what will follow.
    B. Ask, "What do you think will happen next?" We suggest you note students' predictions on a pad of paper or the chalkboard so you do not accidentally overlook a prediction.

VI. *Silent reading.* Assign further specified pages.

VII. *Continuing to conclusion.* Recycle through steps IV, V, and VI as many times as necessary to complete the story.

VIII. *Bringing reading to a conscious level.* Focus 1: helping readers think about how they used the reading process. This step could be used at various points of discussion throughout the selection as well as at the end of the reading.
    A. Ask readers to retell as much as they can remember about the story.
    B. Ask readers questions about how they dealt with the reading process:
        1. How did you learn from the story?
        2. What parts of the story were easy to read? Why? Difficult? Why?
        3. How did you overcome difficulties you had with the text?
        4. What did you do when you came to a part that was not making sense?
        5. What did you do when you came to words you did not know?
    Focus 2: helping readers think about their response to the text. This is done by asking questions that focus readers' attention on their personal response to the text: "Did anything particularly interest you? Frighten you? Surprise you? Make you think? What information do you want to be sure to remember from this text? Have you ever felt like the characters in the story felt? How has your thinking changed as a result of reading this text (or this section of the text)?"

IX. *Concept development.* Focus: broadening understandings of important concepts.
    A. Evaluate the retellings and discussion in terms of students' understandings of important concepts.
    B. Students' understandings can be broadened and deepened by

modeling, drawing, explaining, demonstrating, examining, and acting.

Here is how a guided reading of *Ira Sleeps Over* (Waber, 1972) might sound using the GMS:

YOU: Today we are going to read a story about a boy who is invited to stay overnight at a neighbor's house. How many of you have ever stayed overnight at a friend's house? Who can tell us about it?

KATIE: One time when my mom and dad were going to a convention I got to stay with Rochelle. She is my best friend.

YOU: Katie, can you tell us some of the things you and Rochelle did?

KATIE: We played with her dolls, we went for long bike rides, and we raked up leaf piles to jump in.

YOU: That sounds as if it was lots of fun. Can someone else tell us about a time you stayed overnight at a friend's?

RANDY: I stayed at my cousin Jim's place for two nights. We played computer games and helped his mother bake cookies, and we played army in his fort. We got to sleep in the fort, but Jim got scared.

YOU: What happened after Jim got scared?

RANDY: We had to go sleep in his room. That was okay, though.

YOU: Today we are going to read a story called *Ira Sleeps Over.* (Show children the picture on the cover of the book.) What do you think might happen in this story?

MARIKO: I think it will be about boys who get bored watching TV and get into trouble.

YOU: That is an interesting idea, Mariko. Who else has a prediction?

Explain to students that predictions are "educated guesses," and discourage wild guessing. Invite children to draw on their background experiences in formulating predictions.

JOEL: It looks like this story is going to be about friends.

YOU: Joel, do you have any ideas about what these friends are going to do or what is going to happen?

JOEL: I guess they are going to have a big secret.

At this point you would gather any other predictions and then get everyone to make a commitment to one or more predictions, that is, to signal their agreement with the predictions they favor as you review the list. Even if each child did not offer a prediction, it is important that each child commit to at least one. Insist if necessary; do not let children "sit behind their eyes." The commitment to a prediction creates what we have called a "cognitive itch," a desire to know if one's predictions are right. Thinking, "I know what this story will be about. It will be about . . ." is exactly how the interactive reader establishes purposes for reading.

YOU: Let's read the first 4 pages to see which of our predictions we can prove. Count up 4 pages in the book, put your bookmark there, and then close the book when you come to the bookmark.

Insist that none of your students read ahead. Competition to make "perfect" predictions by reading ahead is harmful to the interactive process.

YOU: Which of our predictions can we prove?

MARIKO: Joel said it was going to be about friends, and he was right. But I don't think they will have a big secret.

YOU: Mariko, can you read us the part of the story that proves what you think?

After Mariko reads, take this opportunity to have children draw on their schemata to relate to the story. Discuss times children in the group have stayed overnight at a friend's home. Then take each of the original predictions in turn, discussing which can be proven and which cannot. Invite oral reading to prove or disprove the predictions.

YOU: Well, what do you think is going to happen next in the story?

CARLOS: I think Ira is not going to take his bear.

YOU: Carlos, have you ever had to decide whether or not to take a stuffed animal to a friend's house? Tell us about it.

CARLOS: One time my mom told me not to take my elephant to my cousin's house. She thought my cousin would wreck it.

YOU: Well, what did you decide? Did you take the elephant or leave it at home?

CARLOS: I took it, but I should have left it at home 'cause my cousin did pull one of his ears off. I think Ira will leave his bear at home. He'd better.

YOU: Are there any other predictions?

JOEL: I think Ira will take his bear with him.

YOU: How many of you think Ira will leave his bear at home? How many think he will take it with him? Let's read the next 3 pages to find out what happens.

Remember that it is important to get a commitment to a prediction from each child in the group whether or not that child made a prediction.

You continue to cycle through the GMS in this fashion until the children have finished the story. At some of the story breaks and at the end of the selection you use steps VIII and IX of the GMS outline, you bring the use of the reading process to a conscious level, discuss response to the text, and do concept development, if indicated.

Endorsing the practice of asking children to read carefully to prove their predictions, Nessel (1987) states that requiring students to use information from the text to make logical predictions about outcomes actively engages the readers in problem solving and surmises that their arguments over the merits of various predictions may be the most compelling type of motivation to read further. Good reading instruction must include this schemata–reading link.

Prediction Mapping

Another way of guiding metacomprehension is prediction mapping, a strategy in which you record children's predictions on a diagram. Walker (1985) found prediction mapping was useful in helping children follow the internal thought processes that good readers use automatically. This technique is very similar to the GMS, except that as the predictions are made they are written on an overhead projector or chalkboard and then revised as the children read the sections of the story. For *Ira Sleeps Over*, the map might look like the one in Figure 8.1.

Selection of Material

Selecting material for use in teaching children to make predictions requires thought and care. Obviously the materials must be sensible and be written so the outcomes are at least probable from the information given. Leu, De Groff, and Simons (1986, p. 352) have recommended patterned books as a good source of material for primary grades because

> When reading predictable text, attention for both good and poor readers is available for comprehension processing but for different reasons. Good readers are able to attend to the meaning of a story because of their automatic, context-free word-recognition skills. Poor readers are able to attend to the meaning of a story because of their automatic use of repetitive sentence context. Thus, some thought should be given to using predictable texts in helping poor readers develop important comprehension skills. Predictable texts may give poor readers important early opportunities to make inferences, draw conclusions, predict outcomes, and engage in other processes traditionally associated with comprehension instruction, opportunities that they seldom have because their attention is often occupied by word-recognition demands.

Figure 8.1—Prediction Map for *Ira Sleeps Over*
Source: Waber (1972).

One good source of such material for intermediate-grade children is well-constructed mystery stories. Children can make predictions about the outcomes at various points in the story and then read on to verify their predictions. And sometimes when the solution is revealed they will have to backtrack, just as adult mystery fans often have to do, to find the clues they might have missed or misinterpreted.

Comprehension is facilitated when teachers help children understand text structures.

© Susan Lapides

Recognizing Story Structure

An awareness of the development of story structure (Fitzgerald & Spiegel, 1983) is an aid to metacomprehension. Knowledge of story structure involves an understanding of plot, character development, setting, theme, and time. It can help children make predictions and apply previous experience as they read. Folktales are excellent examples from which to teach story structure. Mandler and Johnson (1977) have demonstrated that young children have some knowledge of story structure, which varies with developmental level, and that children's abilities to recall stories differ qualitatively. In other words, as children gain ability to analyze stories they can begin to organize information from new stories into familiar story structures. Knowing that children already possess a basic grasp of story structure, Fitzgerald, Spiegel, and Webb (1985) found that the only new skill fifth and sixth graders exhibited after instruction in story structure was recognition of more complex structures such as subplots and embedded episodes.

Smith and Bean (1983) have suggested that teachers help children recognize the patterns in stories, sketching a diagram of the sequence of events to enable the children to visualize them. Figure 8.2 illustrates simple depictions of structure in two stories: *The Turnip* (Tolstoi, no date) and *Millions of Cats* (Gag, 1928). *The Turnip* can be illustrated in a vertical sequence, showing only one character in the first box, two in the second, and so on, until the conclusion of the story. *Millions of Cats* follows a circular pattern. In a circular story, the character comes back after various adventures to the place where he or she began. *The Runaway Bunny* (Brown, 1942) and *Journey Cake, Ho* (Sawyer, 1953) are circular stories. Once children can recognize these patterns, they can base predictions on them and also apply them in their own writing.

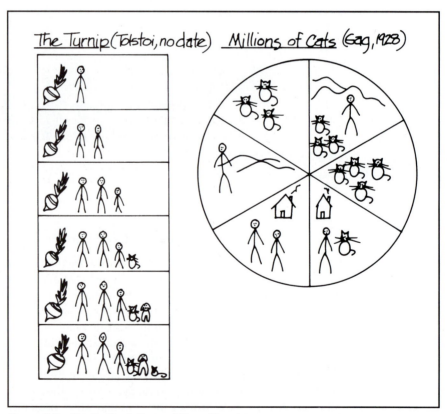

Figure 8.2—Simple Depictions of Story Structure

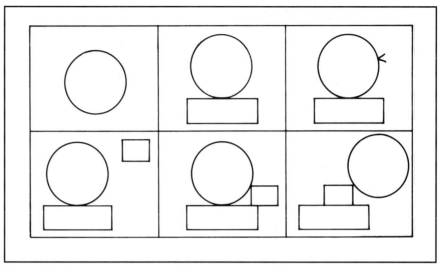

Figure 8.3—Simplified Drawing of "Little Miss Muffet"

Source: Gatheral (1984).

One good device for helping youngsters analyze stories is a simplified drawing of a nursery rhyme, such as Figure 8.3, "Little Miss Muffet" (Gatheral, 1984). Each box represents a story element—the main character, the setting, exposition, the introduction of the antagonist, the conflict or problem, and the resolution of the story. In the first box, the circle represents Miss Muffet, the main character. In the second box, the tuffet represents the setting. The exposition tells us what is going on. The spider is the antagonist, and sitting down beside her is the problem. Resolution comes when Miss Muffet runs away. We prefer to draw these pictures on separate 8 × 10-inch cards to match each story because not every story begins with the introduction of the main character. Even young children, we find, can begin to recognize the parts of the story and relate them to story structure in general. This skill is important for both reading and writing. As children read, they form expectations about what will happen next; as they write, they need to think about story elements and the arrangement of those elements.

Modeling the Comprehension Process

To help students develop better comprehension, teachers have successfully used the technique of thinking through the comprehension process aloud and training the children to ask themselves questions as they read. Nolte and Singer (1985) reported that children trained to question themselves about their own comprehension were able to improve their scores on comprehension tests and that the improvement had some transfer to materials not included in the training. First the teacher reviewed with the students their knowledge of story structure. Then, as the students read the material, she modeled appropriate questions such as, "Is this what I expected to happen?" After a limited number of modeling experiences, the teacher grouped the children and had one child lead the questioning in each group. The children worked next in pairs, and finally independently. The training was completed in 15 days.

Nist and Kirby (1986) used a similar technique, suggesting that the teacher first introduce any new terms in the reading material and then explain the purpose for the reading. The next step is probably the most important: The teacher thinks aloud for the students, showing them how a mature reader/thinker solves reading problems and constantly monitors comprehension. Next, the students go through the process themselves, find out where their techniques are ineffectual, and, with help from the teacher, adopt a more effective method. Most students will require more than one demonstration before they can effectively carry out the thinking processes independently.

Guided Imagery

Another strategy for helping students achieve the metacomprehension abilities used so unconsciously by mature readers is that of guided imagery or mental imagery. Children learn to visualize the people, events, places, or things they encounter in their reading. Of course, the usefulness of the technique is related to the purposes of the reading and the reader's experience. Gambrell and Koskinen (1982) found that helping children form mental images produced better literal comprehension when done prior to the reading experiences than when done afterward. Fredericks (1986) encourages teachers to follow a progression: Children first create images of concrete objects, then images of objects or experiences from recall, then images of their predictions on the next events while listening to stories. Finally, they think about the relationship between the images in their minds and the words on the page when they read. Teachers can invent a series of activities that will help children move through these stages of imagery. Walker (1985) suggests that creating guided imagery before the reading may help some readers access their previous experiences more easily than they would with direct questioning. For example, the teacher develops guided imagery in which the children are asked to visualize the main points in a reading selection. The children are encouraged to visualize the resolution of the story before they read and to write how they solved the problem. They are then eager to read the story to compare the author's version with their own.

Fredericks (1986, p. 81) lists the following guidelines for imaging:

1. Children need to understand that everyone's images are different and are affected by their own experience.

2. There are no right or wrong images. Teachers should not attempt to change individual images, but they can help children reformulate images through rereading or relistening to a story.

3. Provide sufficient opportunities for children to create their images prior to discussion. Children who need a long time to create or embellish their mind pictures should be encouraged to draw illustrations of their images, which can then be shared with the teacher or the class.

4. Provide adequate time for students to discuss their images—not to arrive at a "correct" image but to encourage sharing of ideas in a supportive atmosphere.

5. Stimulate image development through a series of open-ended questions. The questions provide structure to the child's image formation by soliciting details.

Following strategies that help children monitor their own creation of meaning, we need to be concerned about children responding to the texts they have read.

Reader's Response to the Text

There is an endless variety of ways in which we can think about children's responses to the texts they have read. Rosenblatt (1982) has asserted (and we agree) there are two responses a reader makes to a text. She has suggested that in engaging with any text, the reader adopts one of two stances: the efferent stance or the aesthetic stance.

When a reader adopts an *efferent stance* to a text, he or she is focused on what can be taken from the text. Here reading is done to obtain information: to learn the steps in a process, to learn facts for a test, to seek a conclusion to a debate. In an efferent stance the reader is *using the text* to meet specifically identified needs. When a reader adopts an *aesthetic stance*, the focus is on what was being created as the reading occurred. Here reading is appreciated for the emotional impact it has on the reader. The reader is attending to the personal, private feelings, perceptions, and attitudes that the text creates *in the reader.* Rather than using the text, the reader is attuned to the affective response to the piece.

We understand the difference between these two responses by thinking about our reading of an article in the daily paper or a research report we have reviewed in preparation for writing this text compared to the stance taken when reading *The Bridges of Madison County* (Waller, 1993).

Rosenblatt (1982, p. 270) has described the aesthetic stance as follows:

In aesthetic reading, we respond to the very story or poem that we are evoking during the transaction with the text. In order to shape the work, we draw on our reservoir of past experiences with people and the world, our past inner linkage of words and things, our past encounters with spoken or written tests. We listen to the sound of the words in the inner ear; we lend our sensations, our emotions, our sense of being alive, to the new experience which, we feel, corresponds to the text. We participate in the story, we identify with the characters, we share their conflicts and their feelings.

Helping readers get in touch with their feelings about a text was described earlier as part of the Guided Metacomprehension Strategy. There are, however, other considerations to be made about helping children respond to texts.

Teachers often invite children to respond to texts through what are called *enrichment activities*, which build bridges between reading and other curricular areas—and offer students opportunities to enrich and extend their comprehension of story content. For example, the child who dons an old police officer's hat in the dramatic play center and pretends to hand out parking tickets or help children cross the street will have a much better understanding of the roles and relationships of police officers when he or she meets the helpful policeman in *Make Way for Ducklings* (McCloskey, 1941). Making finger puppets of two dogs and acting out their quarrel over a bone helps a child comprehend the story in *Finders Keepers* (Lipkind, 1951). Comprehension of *Where the Wild Things Are* (Sendak, 1963) is enhanced when the reader writes a sequel telling of another (perhaps personal) dream experience. Meeting a challenge to write a story about his or her own fears equips a child to relate to Mafatu's struggle to overcome his fears in *Call It Courage* (Sperry, 1940).

A word of caution seems appropriate here. When teachers determine the activities through which children will respond to a text those activities are often inauthentic responses. Take the example of the children reading *The Very Hungry Caterpillar* (Carle, 1969) and then being assigned to make a caterpillar out of the leg of pantyhose, tissues, string, and construction paper. This activity, if assigned by the teacher, cannot be an authentic response for all of the children who read the text. Authenticity of response is characterized by two things: the honest choice of the reader and an activity that a real lifelong reader would select as a response to a text. We have never been motivated to make a pantyhose caterpillar despite the countless times we have read *The Very Hungry Caterpillar*. This is not to say an art activity cannot be an authentic response to a text. It simply must be the honest response of the reader.

Our experience suggests that we can gain much more authentic responses to texts when we give children the choice of how they wish to respond. Texts "speak" to each of us in different ways. Individual response may vary greatly. The greater range of response we encourage, the more personal the responses are likely to be.

Responding to Texts by Writing

Writing improves reading comprehension. When children write, they gain awareness of style, thematic elements, and authors' development of the parts of story structure. A review of the research on the relationship between reading and writing shows that almost all studies supported the use of writing activities to improve reading comprehension (Stephens, 1991). These are just a few examples of useful writing activities, provided that children choose them as a way to respond:

1. Write a help-wanted advertisement for a job that a character in a book might apply for.

2. Write what might happen if characters from two different books met each other.

3. Write an adventure a character might have if moved forward or backward in time.

4. Write an obituary for a character in a book.

5. Write riddles whose answers are book characters.

6. Develop scripts for skits, plays, or puppet plays.

Responding to Texts with Drama

Dramatic activities not only increase comprehension and retention but provide a means to assess them. The way children act out a portion of their reading material makes obvious their understanding or lack of it. For example, if the bird in the story is supposed to glide, but the children are flapping their arms as they act the part, then they probably do not understand *glide*. Drama allows children to take the part of another person, assuming character traits and perhaps even a language register different from their own. This experience aids comprehension by helping the child learn to identify with a character. Children also remember episodes that they have acted out much longer than comparable ones they have only read. Both planned and spontaneous dramatic activities are good for extending comprehension. Here we suggest merely a few ways of using drama:

1. One child or a small group pantomimes a character or event from a story, and the rest of the class tries to guess who or what it is.

2. Children can adapt a story or an excerpt from a story and present it as a puppet play for the other children. Young children can make simple stick puppets; older ones can handle even very elaborate papier-mâché figures.

3. Using a "talk show" format, the "host" interviews the "guest" as if he or she were a character in a book.

4. Children stage a "talk show" where characters from two different books meet and discuss a topic. For example, a girl from *A Gathering of Days* (Blos, 1979) might meet Margaret from *Are You There, God? It's Me, Margaret* (Blume, 1970) to discuss what is expected of them in their daily lives.

Drama is another way of demonstrating comprehension.

© Elizabeth Crews/Stock Boston

5. Children dramatize what might have happened next if the story had gone on to another episode.

6. Children choose an exciting excerpt to present to the class in the format of a movie preview to arouse the others' interest in reading the book.

Responding to Texts with Art

Another strategy for enriching reading and enhancing comprehension is the use of art to extend understanding. Arts and crafts activities can encourage others to read the books on which the activities are based, as well as clarifying the reader's images of the words portrayed in the writing. We suggest activities like these:

1. Design a book jacket or an advertising poster to "sell" the book or story.

2. Draw a map that illustrates the travels of a character in a book or story.

3. Make murals that depict events in a book or story as the murals in the Capitol building depict American history.

4. Make a collage of images that represent characters or events in reading materials.

5. Make a puppet to represent a character in a story.

6. Make a mobile of figures representing the major characters from a story.

7. Construct a diorama or shadow box representing a scene from a book.

8. Dress dolls in costumes to represent characters in books or stories.

9. Stitch a quilt or wall hanging with each square representing a scene from a book or from different books.

10. Design props for a theme for the reading center; for example, a spaceship for books about space, a covered wagon for the Laura Ingalls Wilder books, a castle for fairy tales, a closet for the *Chronicles of Narnia*, a safe or a Sherlock Holmes hat for detective stories.

11. Draw the dress you would design for Cinderella if you were her fairy godmother.

12. Make a mask for a character in a book.

13. Design a home for a character in a book; for example, a miniature house for *The Borrowers* (Norton, 1953) or a mouse house for *Whose Mouse Are You?* (Kraus, 1970).

Writing, drama, and art are all avenues for children to make authentic responses to text so long as they are not assigned as a specific way to respond, but are sincerely a choice of response by the child.

Developing Comprehension Ability

In this section we describe several activities or strategies you can use to develop comprehension ability in your students. We examine the goals of comprehension instruction and areas of direct instruction in comprehension including vocabulary development, using multiple levels of comprehension, understanding question-answer relationships, and discussing texts by responding to questions.

Goals of Comprehension Instruction

Metacomprehension is an ongoing process occurring simultaneously with reading. It is the interaction between the words of the author and the schemata of the reader. Comprehension is not an accomplishment to *test* after the child has read; it is a process that the reader *monitors* during the act of reading.

Our primary task in teaching comprehension is to ensure that our students can monitor their own reading comprehension. We want readers to know when they understand what they are reading, to know when they are not understanding what they are reading, and to be able to do something about the problem. "Comprehension monitoring entails keeping track of the success with which one's comprehension is proceeding, ensuring that the process continues smoothly, and taking remedial action if necessary" (Baker & Brown, 1984, p. 22). Langer (1982) has described the metacomprehension monitoring system as having two components: (1) awareness of the goal of the reading assignment, what is known about the topic, what needs to be known, and the strategies that can facilitate comprehension; and (2) self-regulatory actions that readers engage in as a response to their self-monitoring—what they do when the process breaks down.

What, then, are the goals of comprehension instruction? The major ones are these:

1. Readers will be able to monitor their creation of meaning during the reading act and take necessary corrective action.

2. Readers will be able to establish their own purposes for reading a selection and then choose the most appropriate reading strategies.

3. Readers will be able to adjust their reading rate to fit their purposes for reading the selection.

4. Readers will draw on their schemata to interact with the ideas of the writer. They will construct meaning from this interaction.

5. Readers will recognize when comprehension has failed, will then read on, reread, or consult an expert source (book or person), and will apply the most efficient corrective strategy.

6. Readers will ask for help when the comprehension process has faltered.

With respect to goal 4, the research of Baker and Brown (1984) suggests that many readers do not even know they are supposed to interact with the text.

Direct Instruction in Comprehension

Can comprehension be taught? Some would argue we can only teach children to use the four cueing systems and that comprehension will follow. Others contend that comprehension can be taught only by breaking the reading process down into its irreducible components and teaching those pieces (subskills). We take the position that comprehension can be taught by continually bringing the reading process to a conscious level, by modeling interaction with print for children, and by arranging instructional strategies that help them develop metacomprehension abilities. Pearson and Johnson (1978, p. 4) list the following things we can do to *teach* comprehension:

1. Model comprehension processes for students.

2. Provide cues to help them understand what they are reading.

3. Guide discussion to help children know what they know.

4. Ask pointed, penetrating, or directional questions; offer feedback.

5. Generate useful independent practice activities.

6. Help expand and clarify children's vocabularies.

7. Teach children how to handle various formats (charts, graphs, tables).

8. Offer guidance about how to study a text.

Although comprehension can be taught, it may be useful to consider the amount of time allocated to teaching "comprehension skills" as time robbed from real reading. Reutzel and Hollingsworth (1991) conducted a study to see if instruction in specific comprehension skills would lead to better comprehension. The skills in which the experimental group was trained were locating details, drawing conclusions, finding the sequence, and determining the main idea. A control group engaged in sustained reading of self-selected trade books. No differences were found between the two groups. This study argues for a holistic view of reading comprehension in which students read a great deal.

A SPECIAL NOTE ON SOMETHING NOT TO DO

Many teachers persist in the practice of round-robin reading, which you probably remember from your childhood. The teacher brings a group of children together to read a selection. Each child, without benefit of silently reading the selection first, is invited in turn to read aloud a segment of the text. Such practice is detrimental to comprehension and to the development of metacomprehension ability (Lynch, 1988). Please don't do this to children. Use the Guided Metacomprehension Strategy or one of the many instructional strategies described here.

Development of Vocabulary

To address the issue of vocabulary development, we discuss the strategies used by teachers to help children understand word meanings when they read. The fact that the knowledge of word meanings is the single most powerful contributor to overall comprehension (Davis, 1968) gives teachers permission to spend considerable time working to develop children's understanding of words. In fact, teachers must become word advocates.

Oral Language Activities

As a teacher you need to be excited about words. Your focus on and excitement about words should begin with oral language and continue on a daily basis throughout the year. "That's an interesting word. What does it mean?" should be heard frequently in your classroom, as well as questions like this: "Can anyone think of another word to describe that color? Who knows what *russet* means? How can we talk about the shape or the texture, the feel, of the bark? What are some words we can use?" When you are engaged in class discussions, one of your jobs as a teacher is to focus on language and build interest and excitement in your students about words and their meanings. You must take time to listen carefully to children and respond to both their ideas and their language. Hang a long strip of paper at the front of the room for children to add interesting words to as they encounter them. Use another strip to display words related to a unit of study in social studies or science. Refer to these words frequently in class discussion. Be excited about them! Recognize, too, that silent reading contributes to vocabulary growth, and be sure to build time for silent reading into the daily schedule.

Words in Reading Selections

At times it will be important to deal with the meanings of words in a particular selection before or after children read the selection. These words may either be new to the children or be so important to comprehending the selection that they warrant special attention. How do you develop vocabulary knowledge when children are dealing with a reading selection, as opposed to a class discussion? The steps we follow are fairly common across reading programs:

1. Show the children a sentence containing the word, printed on a card or the chalkboard. It is helpful to underline the word. Presenting the word in a sentence permits children to make use of multiple cues.

2. Ask, "Who can read this sentence?" If no one responds, read the sentence to the children.

3. Ask, "Who can tell us what this underlined word means?" If no one responds, tell the children the meaning of the word.

4. Say, "Listen, and I will use the word in another sentence." Note that the definition given in step 3 and the sentence used in step 4 should be consistent with the meaning of the word as used in the reading selection.

5. Ask, "Who can use this word in a sentence of your own?" Listen to several volunteers.

6. Discuss the meaning of the word with the group. Discussions of word meanings are important because through the discussion children begin to "own" the word.

As you develop knowledge of word meanings with children, encourage them to use the new words in their writing. You should always be looking for ways to link the words children are learning to read with the words they *may* choose to use as they write. The links must come from the children, however, and *never* from an assignment to "use all your new words in your story," a practice that denies the essence of the writing process. Writers always begin with ideas and then select the language (words) to express those ideas. It is a violation of that principle to tell children they *must* use given words in their writing.

Structured Overviews

A structured overview is a way of presenting vocabulary terms that shows the interrelationships among the terms. It is best used when presenting information to students as a part of a unit of instruction in one of the content areas (such as social studies, science, or health). Using an overhead projector or the chalkboard, you place the terms on a diagram as you present them in order to show their relationship to each other. Suppose you were introducing a unit on westward expansion. Your structured overview might look like that in Figure 8.4.

Not just as you begin the unit but as you proceed through it, you can use the structured overview to introduce new topics of study, expanding the original diagram as needed. The main idea is for students to see the relationships among terms that are new to them and important in their study. We suggest you put the structured overview on paper so it can be displayed throughout the unit of study. You will find students referring to it as they come across the terms in their reading.

Multiple Levels of Comprehension

Comprehension occurs on more than one level at a time. For example, literal comprehension of the laundry-sorting description yields specific information you might be able to recall if questioned. At another level is inferential comprehension, a more creative process in which we use our own prior knowledge to supply missing information or information that might have been assumed by the author (as in the sweater shopping example). Rumelhart (1984, p. 3) suggests that a reader is "constantly evaluating hypotheses about the most plausible interpretation of the text. Readers are said to have understood the text when they are able to find a configuration of hypotheses which offer a coherent account for the various aspects of the text."

Critical comprehension is the level at which the reader evaluates the author's ideas in terms of the reader's prior experience, the author's authority in writing about the subject, and the quality of expression in comparison with a standard (you might be doing this right now). All these levels of comprehension are directly related to the purpose(s) the reader brings to the reading task. How you read *this* text will differ greatly depending on whether you expect to take a test on it or you just happen to be skimming it casually. You may also read it differently if you are a veteran classroom teacher applying your own experience to the teaching of reading. Comprehension is clearly an interactive process that occurs when a reader with an unique set of purposes and experiences meets a given text.

For many years teachers have believed they could determine the degree to which a child has comprehended a text or the level of comprehension by asking comprehension questions. Teacher's guides have lengthy sets of questions for teachers to ask children during and after reading a selection.

We have recommended retelling what students remember from their reading as a part of the guided reading process in the GMS. We endorse the use of retellings as an alternative to asking comprehension questions. Retellings with no teacher intervention are known as free or unaided retellings. When the teacher intervenes to help children recall more of their reading these are known as aided retellings. We embrace retelling as a more powerful measure

As you introduce the unit ("Today we are going to begin our study of westward expansion"), the diagram looks like this:

As you tell students about Manifest Destiny, the diagram begins to look like this:

As you discuss the incentive to westward expansion created by the offer of free land, your structured overview looks like this:

Figure 8.4—Structured Overview for "Westward Expansion"

As you speak about the modes of travel used by the pioneers, your structured overview looks like this:

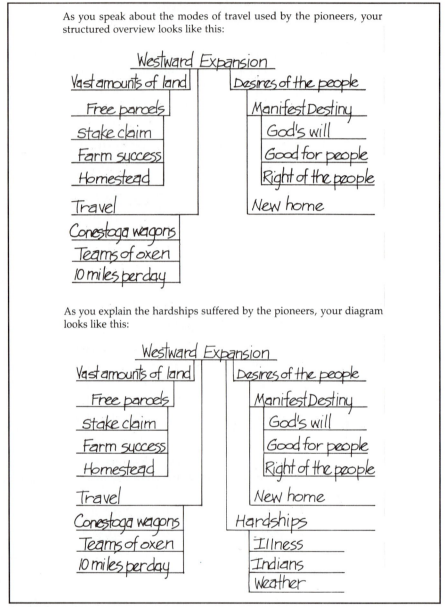

As you explain the hardships suffered by the pioneers, your diagram looks like this:

Figure 8.4 (*continued*)

of comprehension than the traditional asking of comprehension questions. The work of Gambrell, Miller, King, and Thompson (1989) established the superiority of retellings over teacher questioning as a measure of comprehension. The work of Gambrell, Pfeiffer, and Wilson (1985) established the power of retellings over illustrating as a measure of comprehension.

Retellings rather than answering questions make sense on another level as well. If we subscribe to the notion that three texts exist when one reads (in the head of the author, on the printed page, and in the head of the reader), then we would have to question the validity of asking comprehension questions to see if comprehension has occurred. When a teacher asks a comprehension question, the "correct" response has been determined by the poem (Rosenblatt's term) created when the *teacher read the text*. In retellings we are hearing the poem created in the mind of the reader. That is the true measure of comprehension.

Although we believe retellings are a more powerful measure of comprehension than asking comprehension questions, the fact remains that basal teacher's guides encourage teachers to ask questions, and many teachers believe answering comprehension questions is a good way to learn. When students have difficulty answering comprehension questions, teachers often assume they have not read the text carefully. We suspect that this failure may often be attributable to the fact that children have not been taught how to analyze a question in order to find the correct answers. Instruction in the relationships between questions and answers improves readers' abilities to answer comprehension questions.

Understanding Question-Answer Relationships

Of greater importance than readers being able to answer questions about a text is the ability to analyze the *sources of information available* for answering questions about a text. Raphael (1982, 1986) proposed the study of QARs: question-answer relationships. She argued that helping readers understand the mental operations involved in answering questions would promote a deeper understanding of the relationships between the question, the text, and the background knowledge of the reader. QARs improve readers' ability to answer questions about text by teaching them how to find information they need.

In studying question-answer relationships, readers come to understand that one source of question-answering information is the text itself. Recall kinds of questions are right there in the text. The answer is easy to find. Other questions can be answered by searching the text carefully for cues to the answer, which Raphael called a think-and-search strategy. The answer is in the story, but a little harder to find. You would never find the words in the questions and words in the answer in the same sentence. Readers have to search the text and think about relationships among pieces of information found there. Let's use *Ira Sleeps Over* here as an aid to understanding these two kinds of information sources. *Right there* answers are explicitly in the text. "What was the name of Ira's next-door neighbor?" *Think-and-search* answers are implicitly in the text, but they have to be thought about and searched out. "How did Ira feel as he was trying to decide whether or not to take his bear to Reggie's house?" In studying QARs readers come to understand that a second source of information for answering questions about texts is in the head of the reader. Questions that are very broad, not text implicit or explicit, signal to the reader that "I am on my own." The answer won't be told by words in the story. You must find the answer in your head. Understanding that a question is an on-my-own question guides the reader in tapping the appropriate information source. "Was it right or fair for Ira's sister to treat him the way she did?" is an example of an *on-my-own* kind of question.

We believe that teaching children the relationship that exists between questions about text and the text and the reader is critically important, far more important than the ability of the reader to answer the questions themselves.

Discussing Texts by Responding to Questions

You can deepen and refine children's comprehension of text by carefully planned discussions following the reading of a selection. Sometimes it makes sense to ask questions at junctures in the guided reading activity. Usually the QAR should be examined in answering questions. Vacca, Vacca, and Gove (1991, p. 196) have identified three types of questions that should be asked at key points in the discussion to keep children actively engaged in the discussion: (1) a preliminary question to identify a problem or issue; (2) a question or two to clarify or redirect the discussion; and (3) a final question or two that tie together loose ends or establish a premise for further discussion.

Where do the teachers' discussion questions come from? One source is the research that has attempted to define the components of comprehension. One of the most significant pieces of such research was done by Frederick Davis in 1968. Davis used a very complicated procedure called *factor analysis* to isolate those factors that make up this thing called comprehension and discover the extent to which each of them contributes to the whole. Of the five comprehension components Davis identified, the most powerful contributor was knowledge of word meanings and the least powerful was the ability to answer recall questions. This is the order in which they contribute to comprehension:

1. Recalling word meanings; knowledge of word meanings

2. Drawing inferences from the text

3. Following the structure of the passage

4. Recognizing an author's purpose, attitude, tone, and/or mood

5. Answering recall questions—questions whose answers are found in the text.

Teachers could use these five components of reading to formulate discussion questions.

Dialogue about a text can be enhanced by asking carefully constructed questions. The dialogue can be even further enhanced by attending to the nature of the dialogue when a group discusses a selection. Remember that dialogue is both difficult and enjoyable. It is difficult because it requires initiative, inquiry, critical thinking, and invention from all involved. It is enjoyable because we can see ideas come to life (Peterson & Eeds, 1990).

In their informative book *Grand Conversations: Literature Groups in Action*, Peterson and Eeds (1990, pp. 23–24) offer suggestions for thinking about the dialogue in which your students engage:

▼ *Approximation:* Accepting approximations is fundamental. Children's ability to articulate their responses to text grow over time. Children are encouraged to share, and responses are not judged as right or wrong.

▼ *Demonstration:* Teachers need to demonstrate the power of books in their own lives. Children need to see these responses by the teacher. Teachers frequently have to win children over to the beauty and power of literature, to demonstrate the joys and rewards that exist in the world of story.

▼ *Practice and feedback:* It takes time, practice, and feedback to develop the attitudes, knowledge, and habits required for re-creating meaning from texts and sharing our insights with others. Teachers as well as students are learners in the dialogue. Keep it simple.

Guided reading is a critical component of a balanced reading program.

© Elizabeth Crews/Stock Boston

Major Ideas in This Chapter

▼ Comprehension—resulting from the interaction of our schemata with the ideas of the author—is a personal creation of meaning. Our creation of meaning with text is influenced by our purpose(s) for reading, our monitoring of the reading process, and our response(s) to text.

▼ Three texts are in existence when we read: (1) in the head of the author, (2) on the printed page, and (3) in the head of the reader. Our purpose(s) for reading determine how similar the second and third text must be.

▼ We can teach children to monitor their use of the reading process using a form of guided reading called the Guided Metacomprehension Strategy. Here we focus on background knowledge, prediction, and bringing the reading process to a conscious level and response.

▼ We develop metacomprehension ability through guided reading, prediction mapping, careful selection of materials, recognizing story structure, modeling the comprehension process, and guided imagery.

▼ We must invite authentic responses by readers to texts. Authenticity of response is marked by the honest choice of response by the reader and an activity in which a real lifelong reader would engage. Response may include writing, drama, art, and other forms.

▼ The goals of comprehension instruction can be met through direct instruction in the development of vocabulary, the use of multiple levels of comprehension, understanding question-answer relationships, and responding to discussion questions.

Discussion Questions: Focusing on the Teacher You Are Becoming

1. How do you think you would respond to a colleague who asserted that comprehension can be taught by teaching a series of subskill lessons such as recalling details, identifying main idea, or seeing cause and effect?

2. Set up a debate within your class: "Metacomprehension strategies are of utmost importance in teaching comprehension" versus "Asking comprehension questions is of utmost importance in teaching comprehension."

3. Describe the differences (if any) you see between the recommendations made in this chapter and what you remember about learning to read. How do you account for the changes?

4. Have a discussion with a small group of your classmates on what you think will be your greatest challenges in learning to teach children metacomprehension strategies and comprehension skills.

Field-Based Applications

1. Select a trade book to read to a small group of children. Prepare plans for introduction of vocabulary as outlined in this chapter.

2. Plan a Guided Metacomprehension Strategy for a selection from a basal reader. Repeat the GMS with another story, adding the use of prediction mapping. Repeat these two steps using favorite trade books.

3. Either read a story to children or plan a guided reading activity and then follow it with an enrichment activity in art. Select two other stories and follow them with activities in writing and drama. Be sure to give children choices of response avenues.

4. Select a text to have a group of children read and plan for studying QARs during and after the reading. Share your experiences with classmates.

Chapter 9

Basal Readers in the Reading/Writing Program

Chapter Overview

▼ Basal reading series are sequentially graded student texts, workbooks, teacher's guides, and supplementary materials designed for reading instruction in grades K through 8.

▼ The currently popular basal reading series share some common elements in their approaches to reading instruction: Most suggest activities involving recognition of words by sight, phonic analysis, pattern recognition, some reading strategies, and writing skills. Most series include selections (or excerpts) from a wide range of children's literature.

▼ Teachers use basal readers in various ways: as the primary reading material, as supplementary material, and as the source of materials selected to fit thematic units.

▼ Teacher's guides that accompany basal reading texts contain suggestions for activities before, during, and after reading. Teacher's guides have become more and more detailed over the years.

▼ Skillful teachers never turn over their responsibility to teach reading to a basal series, but use basal material if it can help meet the needs of individual children. Teachers choose selections that will meet their reading objectives and choose activities that will help children read the selections successfully.

Introducing Basal Readers

If you were asked to predict the equipment and supplies one might find in the elementary classrooms of the United States, you would be very safe in guessing there would be a basal reading series of some kind. Most of the reading instruction in today's schools is either conducted directly from a set of basal readers or built around a basal. There are numerous choices to be made when a school or district adopts a basal reading series. Various publishers' basal series differ in philosophy, sequencing of skills taught, and content presented. They may also vary in the amount and type of material that accompany the books the children will use. This chapter will help you recognize the strengths and weaknesses of basal readers and present some suggestions for using the texts in reading instruction.

Definition

Basal means forming the base, or fundamental; in an educational context, it refers to something used for teaching beginners. Basal readers are textbooks designed specifically for reading instruction. Most basal reading series begin with readiness material and include graded material that is planned for each of the grades through grade 6 or grade 8. Readiness material typically consists of tasks that help children learn to recognize letters of the alphabet and perhaps match them with the sounds they represent. First-grade material often comes in several books: preprimers, primers, and a first reader. Sometimes the material for higher grades is divided into two books, the second more advanced than the first. The students' texts contain stories, poetry, expository material, and perhaps selections or excerpts from literature. Most modern basal reading series include teacher's guides, assessment systems, workbooks, skill practice sheets, and other materials to be used in reading instruction, such as tape recordings and word cards. If you learned to read with Dick and Jane or Tom and Janet, then your teacher used a basal reader for your instruction. Even if you do not remember Dick and Jane, you probably had a basal text if groups of children in your class were all reading the same book.

History of Basals

In colonial America, the earliest books used for reading instruction were hornbooks, consisting of a single page mounted on a piece of wood and covered with a translucent piece of horn to protect it from wear. The hornbook contained the alphabet, a syllabarium, and the Lord's Prayer (Goodman, Shannon, Freeman, & Murphy, 1988). At the beginning of the 18th century, the *New England Primer* was probably the most popular text for reading instruction. The primer contained religious sayings for each letter of the alphabet. By midcentury, reading was usually introduced from a spelling book. Venezky (1987) reports that Webster's spelling book was the most popular reading text from about 1790 to about 1840.

Around the turn of the 19th century, as more children attended school and the school year was extended, some reading books began to appear in a series. Elementary schools were first organized into grades in about the middle of the 19th century, and by the end of the century reading books were also graded. The most popular of the instructional books published in the 19th century were the *McGuffey Eclectic Readers*. From their first publication in 1836 until 1920, about 120 million copies of the readers were sold. Figure 9.1 is a copy of a page from *The New McGuffey Fourth Reader*, published in 1901. You might want to compare it to a modern fourth-grade basal. After the Civil War, reading series that resemble today's readers began to appear. Most had

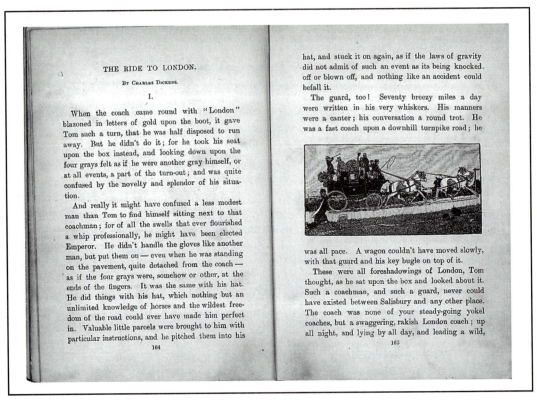

THE RIDE TO LONDON.

By CHARLES DICKENS.

I.

When the coach came round with "London" blazoned in letters of gold upon the boot, it gave Tom such a turn, that he was half disposed to run away. But he didn't do it; for he took his seat upon the box instead, and looking down upon the four grays felt as if he were another gray himself, or at all events, a part of the turn-out; and was quite confused by the novelty and splendor of his situation.

And really it might have confused a less modest man than Tom to find himself sitting next to that coachman; for of all the swells that ever flourished a whip professionally, he might have been elected Emperor. He didn't handle the gloves like another man, but put them on — even when he was standing on the pavement, quite detached from the coach — as if the four grays were, somehow or other, at the ends of the fingers. It was the same with his hat. He did things with his hat, which nothing but an unlimited knowledge of horses and the wildest freedom of the road could ever have made him perfect in. Valuable little parcels were brought to him with particular instructions, and he pitched them into his 164

hat, and stuck it on again, as if the laws of gravity did not admit of such an event as its being knocked off or blown off, and nothing like an accident could befall it.

The guard, too! Seventy breezy miles a day were written in his very whiskers. His manners were a canter; his conversation a round trot. He was a fast coach upon a downhill turnpike road; he was all pace. A wagon couldn't have moved slowly, with that guard and his key bugle on top of it.

These were all foreshadowings of London, Tom thought, as he sat upon the box and looked about it. Such a coachman, and such a guard, never could have existed between Salisbury and any other place. The coach was none of your steady-going yokel coaches, but a swaggering, rakish London coach; up all night, and lying by all day, and leading a wild, 165

Figure 9.1—Two Pages from *The New McGuffey Fourth Reader* (1901)

a primer and five or six graded readers. In the early part of the 20th century, a preprimer was added to help children learn the vocabulary of the primer. After World War II, readiness materials were added; the series then looked very much like modern reading series. Books designed for teaching reading were not commonly labeled *basal* until the early 1960s, although the term was first used by a publisher in the 1930s (Venezky, 1987).

Books used to teach reading changed over the years, and so did the reasons for encouraging reading. For early American settlers, reading was important chiefly for the sake of Bible study. Reading instruction for many years continued to rely heavily on religious or moralistic stories that also taught children how to behave and what to value while they learned to read. The purposes for reading instruction have broadened greatly since the days of the colonists.

Suggested methodologies for reading instruction—that is, techniques that teachers use to help children learn—have also evolved. The reading methodology most popular in colonial times was to teach children to recognize the letters, then to spell words, and finally to read the words, so early reading books were really spelling books. Rote learning of entire texts was common in early schools. Teachers often asked students to recite what they had learned or led children in choral readings of texts. These methods were probably necessary to some extent because of the lack of books and paper. Most schools did not even have chalkboards or slates, so the reading/writing program of today would hardly have been possible. The emphasis in reading instruction gradually moved from the names of the letters to the sounds of the letters to words and finally to meaning.

Among other changes in reading instruction is the treatment of oral reading. The early Americans considered reading to be primarily an oral activity. The reading books published for older students in the 19th century were elocution texts, and reading instruction was focused on oral presentation of material. In the "Elocutionary Introduction" to *The New McGuffey Fourth Reader*, there are several pages of instructions for reading aloud that include directions for how one is to stand while reading. Later in this chapter we discuss the current instructional purposes of oral and silent reading.

Instructions to teachers included with the reading materials have undergone drastic alterations. One author (Venezky, 1987) noted with some irony that the more knowledgeable teachers become, the more detailed are the teacher's guides that accompany reading material. Teachers in early schools had little or no training as teachers; many had not even graduated from high school. Yet no instructions to teachers accompanied most early reading materials. In the early 1800s, materials for teaching reading began to include some instructions for teachers. Compared with the teacher's guides of today, these instructions were minimal. For example, a reader copyrighted in 1886 devoted two pages to instructions to the teacher, consisting of vague suggestions like this: "An occasional drill on these sounds, or a part of them, is advised for the sake of clear articulation" (Campbell, 1886, p. iii).

Instructions to the teacher became slightly more detailed in the early 1900s. In 1926 Lippincott published *Silent Reading for Beginners* (Watkins, 1926) and included in the teacher's edition "full notes" consisting of about a page of instructions to the teacher for each story: lists of vocabulary words and sections called "How to Teach the Lesson," "Check-Up," and "Follow-Up." The instructions are not very specific. In "How to Teach the Lesson" (p. 18), the notes say, "You can not start too early to train little children in the duties of citizenship, which include the care of school property, buildings, books, sidewalks; their relation to each other and the rights of others." The "Check-Up" section on the same page says, "Can the child read page 30 orally and do it well?" Compare these instructions with those in modern teacher's guides, which typically contain as many as 100 pages of instructions for a small paperback preprimer.

Instructional Approaches Incorporated in Basal Readers

Over the years several approaches to reading instruction have emerged. Early reading methodology required children to spell words before reading them. Gradually, spelling was separated from reading, and the word method was introduced, which required students to read whole words and then talk about their meaning. The average person on the street, if asked how reading is taught, would probably answer either "by phonics" or "by sight." Both these approaches have grown out of the historical roots of teaching spelling, sounds, or words. Chall (1967) classified approaches to reading as having code emphasis or meaning emphasis. In her scheme, phonics and linguistic (patterns in words) approaches are code-emphasis approaches; sight-word and language-experience approaches are meaning-emphasis approaches.

What the authors of basal reading series believe about learning to read usually has to be inferred from statements concerning goals of the program and from the exercises and materials presented for reading instruction. Authors of reading materials rarely state in direct terms their philosophy of how children learn to read. But the basal reader itself reveals the authors' intent to concentrate either on a skills-driven approach or on a more holistic view of the reading process. If the book contains stories in which the vocabulary is highly controlled by phonic regularity, and skills exercises that are drills in letter–sound relationships, then the authors lean in the direction of phonics as the basic tool for unlocking the meaning in print. If, however, the basal contains selections of literature for children and suggests that children read pieces orally together or that they learn a piece by rote before they are introduced to the words in print, and the "skills" exercises involve comparing the forms of several pieces and thinking about different points of view, then the authors lean more in the direction of whole-language instruction. All the basal readers today have an eclectic approach, which means they include activities from all the approaches and are not usually identifiable as being sight, phonics, or linguistic readers.

Several current basal series label themselves as "whole language" readers. Most of these readers have content selected from the body of children's literature rather than written for that series, and their suggestions to teachers reflect a focus on language and writing conventions. Some of the materials labeled "whole language" are not whole language in philosophy at all, but it is now very popular to call materials whole language whether they are or not. If the basal program asks students to fill out worksheets as follow-up activities after having read stories, it is not a whole-language approach, even if the stories are well-known pieces of children's literature. Teachers must examine all materials carefully and not be fooled by the term *whole language*.

The Teacher's Role in Reading Programs

In addition to differing in their approaches to reading, basal series also demand different levels of involvement from teachers. Some programs, such as DISTAR (Englemann & Bereiter, 1983), which are tightly controlled and highly prescribed, specify all the teacher behaviors and responses needed to teach the program. Teachers do not have to decide what to teach, or in what order, or what activities to assign. Language-experience and whole-language approaches, which are heavily teacher dependent, require significant teaching decisions. Teachers must choose the content to be taught, the order in which to teach it, and the activities that will help the children achieve reading goals. Most basal programs fall somewhere in the middle, requiring teachers to make some decisions but prescribing others, such as sequence of presentation.

Teacher's Guide

The typical basal reading series is accompanied by a teacher's guide containing several sections. One section, the scope and sequence chart, provides the teacher with an overview of the skills to be covered in the reading program and the order of their introduction. Figure 9.2 is a sample scope and sequence chart from the Harcourt Brace *Treasury of Literature* (1995). It includes scope and sequence sections for each of the following topics: strategic reading, comprehension, vocabulary, decoding (phonics and structural analysis), study skills, literary appreciation (literary elements, author's craft, literary forms/genre), multiculturalism, and language (composition, listening, speaking, integrated spelling). Note that this program calls for introducing each skill at a certain grade level, and testing the skill within the grade levels

Children benefit from reviewing what they know about a topic before reading.

© George White

Treasury of Literature
Scope and Sequence

Grade/Level	K/1	1–1	1–2	1–3	1–4	1–5	2	3	4	5	6	7	8
Observing													
Brainstorming													
Classifying and Categorizing													
Comparing and Contrasting													
Visualizing													
Evaluating													
Synthesizing													
Analyzing													
EMERGENT LITERACY													
Phonemic Awareness													
Print Awareness													
STRATEGIC READING													
Active Reading Strategies													
Read Fiction (Narrative Text)													
Read Nonfiction (Expository Text)													
Analyze Details													
Synthesize Ideas/Information													
Make Inferences													
Decoding Strategy: Use phonetic/structural analysis plus context to unlock pronunciation													
Vocabulary Strategy: Use phonetic/structural/contextual clues to determine meanings													
Use Self-Assessment Strategies													
Cause-Effect							♦	♦	♦	♦	♦	♦	♦
Classify/Categorize	♦						♦						
Compare and Contrast							♦	♦	♦	♦	♦	♦	♦
Draw Conclusions						♦	♦	♦	♦	♦	♦	♦	♦
Fact-Fantasy/Nonfact					♦		♦						
Author's Purpose									♦	♦	♦	♦	♦
Author's Viewpoint													
Fact-Opinion								♦	♦	♦	♦	♦	♦
Main Idea (Global Meaning)/Details						♦	♦	♦	♦	♦	♦	♦	♦
Make Generalizations											♦	♦	♦
Make Judgments											♦	♦	♦
Paraphrase									♦	♦	♦		
Make Predictions				♦			♦	♦	♦	♦	♦	♦	♦
Referents													
Sequence	♦						♦	♦	♦	♦	♦	♦	♦
Summarize							♦	♦	♦	♦	♦	♦	♦
Key Words/Selection Vocabulary	♦	♦	♦	♦	♦	♦	♦	♦	♦	♦	♦	♦	♦
Synonyms/Antonyms													
Multiple-Meaning Words											♦	♦	♦
Homophones/Homographs													
Context Clues				♦			♦	♦	♦	♦	♦	♦	♦
Vocabulary Strategy: Use phonetic/structural/contextual clues to determine meanings													
Analogies													
Connotation/Denotation													
Glossary													
Dictionary (for Word Meaning)												♦	♦
DECODING													
Phonics													
Initial/Medial/Final Consonants		♦	♦	♦	♦								
Phonograms			♦	♦	♦	♦							
Short Vowels/Long Vowels			♦	♦	♦	♦							
Consonant Clusters/Digraphs (Initial/Final)			♦	♦	♦	♦							
R-Controlled Vowels						♦							

■ Modeling Instruction/Application   ♦ Tested
Testing options include Unit Reading Skills Assessment, Unit Holistic Reading Assessment, Unit Language and Writing Assessment, and Unit Integrated Performance Assessment.
For a complete scope and sequence of the kindergarten program, see the Teacher's Edition for that level.

R117

Figure 9.2—Scope and Sequence Chart

Source: Excerpts from *Treasury of Literature*, Teacher's Edition Grade 5, Out of This World, copyright ©1995 by Harcourt Brace & Company, reprinted by permis-

marked with a diamond. For example, for the skill of decoding phonics, the program introduces initial consonants in level 1 and tests them in levels 1, 2, 3, and 4, even though it is expected that children will continue to use the skill of decoding initial consonants throughout the program. In the literary appreciation section, notice that setting is introduced in level 1 and tested in levels 1 through 8.

The teacher's guide suggests activities for students to carry out before reading a selection. In almost every basal, the first activity is an exercise to introduce the "key words" for the selection. After all the word activities, the teacher is directed to ask the children to turn to the beginning of the story. After the new words are presented, many basal guides suggest that students make predictions about the story. Some manuals suggest that the teacher

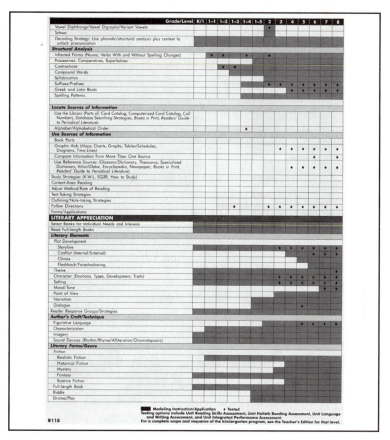

Figure 9.2 (*continued*)

record these predictions; others ask the children to record their own predictions. Having completed all the introductory activities, the children read the story independently, a page or a specified number of pages at a time. (The teacher's guide nearly always includes a reproduction of the text as given to the students.) Most manuals provide questions to ask during the reading.

The teacher's guide offers suggestions for follow-up activities after reading the selection: questions to ask, guidelines for rereading the selection, and activities for extending the reading experience. Some basal series include spelling exercises, suggestions for art, science, math connections, and writing suggestions.

Basal guides also include work in skills that may range from reviewing letter–sound relationships to classifying words in the story or creating charts of how inferences can be gained from the story. In one basal, children were asked to study possessives after they had read the story in which possessives appeared. They were also to be instructed in compound words when not a single compound word was used in the story to which the skills lesson was attached. In making instructional decisions about using the skills activities, teachers must decide what their learners need and what they will learn from completing the suggested tasks.

Figure 9.3 is a copy of a page in the Harcourt Brace *Treasury of Literature* Teacher's Edition (1995), which reprints an excerpt from *Sarah, Plain and Tall* (MacLachlan, 1985). On this page, the teacher is directed to ask questions to monitor the children's comprehension as they read the pages of their text and to set purposes for reading the next four pages. Contrast the differences in a group reading this excerpt with a group reading the entire book in a literature study group. What would be the differences in terms of student choice? Purposes for reading? Monitoring of comprehension? Leader of the discussion? Possible follow-up activities?

Some News About Basals

Most teachers in the United States use a basal reading series, whether it constitutes their entire reading program or is one of several resources they use to complement their reading program. In a recent survey of fourth-grade teachers, about half reported that they used a combination of basals and trade books for reading instruction. Thirty-six percent used basals as their sole reading material and 15% said that they did not use basals at all ("New NAEP Report," 1994). These teachers reported that 33% of the fourth graders used worksheets and workbooks daily and 48% said they used them at least weekly. More than half (51%) of the fourth graders themselves reported they did worksheets daily. With the pressure that some teachers feel to say what someone wants them to say, the results of surveys must be taken with a grain of salt, but they do give us an idea that basals are still very important in the majority of classrooms. In a recent survey of elementary principals, 77% reported that basals were used in their schools (Jacobson, Reutzel, & Hollingsworth, 1992).

There are many reasons why teachers rely so heavily on basal readers. They believe they are covering all the skills if they follow a basal, they feel they do not have time to organize and run individualized reading programs, and they believe more children will learn to read successfully through a structured program. They may also believe the district administration expects them to complete the basal program. Some districts do put pressure on teachers to complete the basal work and rely on basal test results to group children within and across classes. Shannon (1982) believes teachers rely on basal readers because, being excluded from making instructional decisions for reading, they see themselves as technicians whose task is to apply the materials. This view is particularly likely to hold in districts where decisions are made at the district level and teachers are not fully involved in making them.

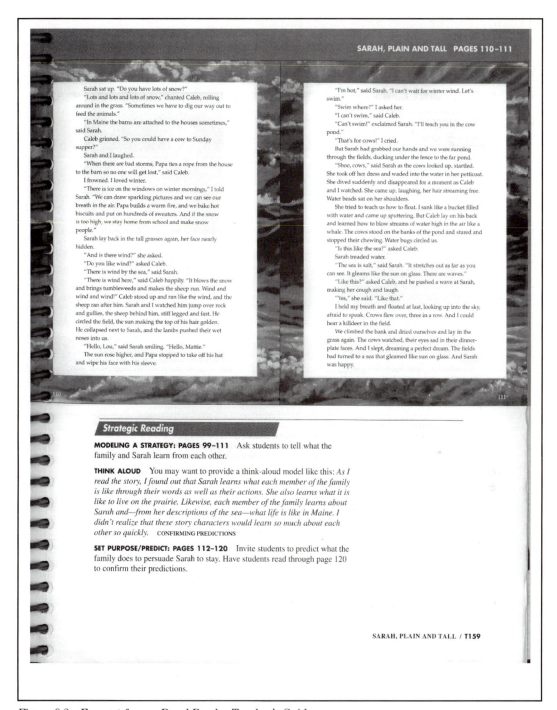

SARAH, PLAIN AND TALL   PAGES 110-111

Sarah sat up. "Do you have lots of snow?"

"Lots and lots and lots of snow," chanted Caleb, rolling around in the grass. "Sometimes we have to dig our way out to feed the animals."

"In Maine the barns are attached to the houses sometimes," said Sarah.

Caleb grinned. "So you could have a cow to Sunday supper?"

Sarah and I laughed.

"When there are bad storms, Papa ties a rope from the house to the barn so no one will get lost," said Caleb.

I frowned. I loved winter.

"There is ice on the windows on winter mornings," I told Sarah. "We can draw sparkling pictures and we can see our breath in the air. Papa builds a warm fire, and we bake hot biscuits and put on hundreds of sweaters. And if the snow is too high, we stay home from school and make snow people."

Sarah lay back in the tall grasses again, her face nearly hidden.

"And is there wind?" she asked.

"Do you like wind?" asked Caleb.

"There is wind by the sea," said Sarah.

"There is wind here," said Caleb happily. "It blows the snow and brings tumbleweeds and makes the sheep run. Wind and wind and wind!" Caleb stood up and ran like the wind, and the sheep ran after him. Sarah and I watched him jump over rock and gullies, the sheep behind him, stiff legged and fast. He circled the field, the sun making the top of his hair golden. He collapsed next to Sarah, and the lambs pushed their wet noses into us.

"Hello, Lou," said Sarah smiling. "Hello, Mattie."

The sun rose higher, and Papa stopped to take off his hat and wipe his face with his sleeve.

"I'm hot," said Sarah. "I can't wait for winter wind. Let's swim."

"Swim where?" I asked her.

"I can't swim," said Caleb.

"Can't swim!" exclaimed Sarah. "I'll teach you in the cow pond."

"That's for cows!" I cried.

But Sarah had grabbed our hands and we were running through the fields, ducking under the fence to the far pond.

"Shoo, cows," said Sarah as the cows looked up, startled. She took off her dress and waded into the water in her petticoat. She dived suddenly and disappeared for a moment as Caleb and I watched. She came up, laughing, her hair streaming free. Water beads sat on her shoulders.

She tried to teach us how to float. I sank like a bucket filled with water and came up sputtering. But Caleb lay on his back and learned how to blow streams of water high in the air like a whale. The cows stood on the banks of the pond and stared and stopped their chewing. Water bugs circled us.

"Is this like the sea?" asked Caleb.

Sarah treaded water.

"The sea is salt," said Sarah. "It stretches out as far as you can see. It gleams like the sun on glass. There are waves."

"Like this?" asked Caleb, and he pushed a wave at Sarah, making her cough and laugh.

"Yes," she said. "Like that."

I held my breath and floated at last, looking up into the sky, afraid to speak. Crows flew over, three in a row. And I could hear a killdeer in the field.

We climbed the bank and dried ourselves and lay in the grass again. The cows watched, their eyes sad in their dinner-plate faces. And I slept, dreaming a perfect dream. The fields had turned to a sea that gleamed like sun on glass. And Sarah was happy.

Strategic Reading

MODELING A STRATEGY: PAGES 99-111 Ask students to tell what the family and Sarah learn from each other.

THINK ALOUD You may want to provide a think-aloud model like this: *As I read the story, I found out that Sarah learns what each member of the family is like through their words as well as their actions. She also learns what it is like to live on the prairie. Likewise, each member of the family learns about Sarah and—from her descriptions of the sea—what life is like in Maine. I didn't realize that these story characters would learn so much about each other so quickly.* CONFIRMING PREDICTIONS

SET PURPOSE/PREDICT: PAGES 112-120 Invite students to predict what the family does to persuade Sarah to stay. Have students read through page 120 to confirm their predictions.

SARAH, PLAIN AND TALL / T159

Figure 9.3—Excerpt from a Basal Reader Teacher's Guide

The Good News About Basals

Basals can sometimes serve as instructional tools for helping teachers achieve their reading goals. Their content is much improved over the content of just a few years ago. Many basal series now include literature such as the texts of picture books, excerpts from books, adapted versions of popular books, children's poetry, and nonfictional material. However, teachers must think about the quality of the literature selected. Some of the basals have been criticized for changing the language in children's stories when they are included in reading texts, but others are faithful to the original. Some literature selections include only a portion of the original. Teachers have to evaluate the effect of using only a part of a book as opposed to using the entire selection.

The vocabulary used in basals has also been improved. For many years the content of basals was controlled by readability formulas, which count the number of words in a sentence and the number of syllables in words to yield a grade-level score of difficulty. Cassidy (1987) believes most publishers now consider the content and writing style as well as the readability scores when making decisions about placing material in a given basal. Cassidy also reports that teacher's guides were criticized for containing instructions to teachers that helped them test comprehension, not teach it. Today's guides are more likely to contain specific suggestions for teaching comprehension. Suggested questioning strategies have also been improved in recent years.

The teacher's guides that accompany basal readers can be helpful, especially to beginning teachers who might not feel comfortable about which reading skills are possibilities for instruction or what is commonly taught at a specific grade level. Once teachers have determined the objectives to be met in reading, the basal guide can provide much useful information for reading passages and planning activities that will help children meet those objectives. Suppose these were among the objectives defined for your students:

Building Background

1. Reads silently daily

2. Is read to daily

3. States what is already known about content (prior knowledge)

4. Predicts content

5. States purpose or goal for reading

Comprehending

6. Uses word identification strategies to read fluently

7. Summarizes, clarifies, questions, and predicts while reading

8. Monitors own comprehension and self-corrects when necessary

Presenting

9. Reads and demonstrates comprehension of a personal experience narrative

10. Reads and demonstrates comprehension of a story

11. Reads and demonstrates comprehension of an informational report

12. Reads and demonstrates comprehension of a form of communication

13. Reads and demonstrates comprehension of a poem

14. Reads and demonstrates comprehension of a summary

15. Reads and demonstrates comprehension of an essay. (Arizona Department of Education, 1989)

You might look through the basal reader and select a story or stories that would be appropriate for meeting these objectives. For example, you might choose a poem that children could read and discuss in a small group. Or you might have them compare a story in the basal to a story from another source, such as a children's magazine, emphasizing the structure of a story and how the author achieved his or her goals in writing a story.

The skills lists in the basal series can be helpful to teachers in planning instruction. For example, if contractions are introduced in the basal series at second grade, then second-grade teachers can emphasize contractions in children's writing and call attention to them in reading even if they are not using the basal reader.

Teachers have listed the following as the strengths of basals: (1) the logical sequence of skills presented, (2) easily identifiable story lines, (3) increasing difficulty of stories, (4) controlled vocabulary, (5) convenience of having the same book for every child at a given level, and (6) the comprehension and word analysis strategies that are suggested in the teacher's guides (Russavage, Lorton, & Millham, 1985). But many teachers view some of these same features as weaknesses. A teacher who believes there is no best sequence for teaching skills does not regard a skills sequence as a positive feature. Many teachers object to the controlled vocabulary, feeling that language in texts should be as much like real language as possible.

The Not-So-Good News About Basals

Students' perceptions of the reading process are influenced by the kinds of activities that are presented to them as "reading." When teachers rely heavily on basals for instruction, children are likely to believe reading is mostly a matter of decoding and/or word recognition skills (Cairney, 1988). They also believe success in reading depends on their behavior, completion of tasks, neatness, and written answers.

Teachers who want children to believe reading is constructing meaning from print in a variety of forms and for a variety of functions are careful not to present skill exercises as reading. Whenever schools or districts place too much emphasis on test scores in reading, they run the risk that teachers will spend disproportional amounts of time on skills instruction rather than on reading. When basal programs are used, only 10% to 15% of reading time is spent in silent reading of cohesive texts (Goodman, Shannon, Freeman, & Murphy, 1988). Many children spend as little as two or three minutes a day of their "reading" time actually reading; the rest of the time is spent completing worksheets or practicing skills.

Some basal readers ignore what children already know about print and how it works before they come to school. (Recall the description in Chapter 2 of reading as a developmental process.) Children know about many of the functions of print, may recognize words and logos that are meaningful to them (their names, "love," "the end"), and have a good sense of the alphabetic nature of our language before they come to school. Basals tend to begin reading instruction with studies of letters or letter–sound relationships that are out of context and not connected to children's experiences. Some children beginning school will know the letters and be able to write them, whereas others will have too little experience with print to make sense of the instruction. Bloome and Nieto (1989) believe basal readers mask the cultural and linguistic biases of such instruction and, therefore, more minority children are assigned to inferior status (low reading groups), which further limits their instructional opportunities.

Teachers' perceptions of children may also be influenced by the use of a basal program. A very thoughtful teacher recently reported she had begun to think differently about the children as learners and readers after they were grouped by reading level for instruction in the basal program. She had started the year using whole-language reading activities, primarily with whole-group instruction. After experiencing some pressure to identify individual children's reading levels, she assessed the children with basal tests and placed them in ability groups. Soon she realized she was beginning to think of children in the lower group as less capable learners and readers. Knowing the research (Purkey, 1970) clearly indicates that teacher perceptions of student abilities greatly influence student achievement, she returned to whole-language instruction so the work of each individual could be valued without comparison to the work of others.

Teachers who identified some of the strengths of basal reader programs were asked in the same study to name the weaknesses. They cited (1) quality of story content, (2) lack of opportunities to apply word analysis and comprehension skills, (3) controlled vocabulary, (4) lack of stories on current topics, and (5) inability to meet individual needs (Russavage, Lorton, & Millham, 1985). It is obvious that what is to some teachers a strength is to others a weakness. These differences of opinion occur because teachers have different views on how children learn to read and what activities are most useful in helping them along in the process.

What teachers actually do in the course of instruction may not be very good news either. Durkin (1984) has done several studies of what teachers actually do in reading instruction, in comparison to what teacher's guides suggest they do. Most teacher's guides recommend about the same sequence for lesson presentation: first some prereading activities, then silent reading of the stories, with questions by the teacher at intervals, next oral reading of parts of the story, and finally skill development. What Durkin found was that, contrary to suggestions in the guides, most teachers introduced the new vocabulary without context. None of the teachers she observed spent any time in developing background information for the selection to be read, and very little use was made of prereading questions. Most of the silent reading was done at the students' desks, without observation by the teacher.

As they continued the lessons, teachers often asked the suggested comprehension questions *after* the reading, but not during. They often required written answers, justified by the need to see which students could actually answer the questions—a check they said was not possible with oral answers. The teachers' expressed goals in having the children read the selections orally, round-robin fashion (with each child reading a passage in turn), were (1) to check on the child's ability to read the new words (although none made note of which children missed words), (2) to check on comprehension (even though the children had previously demonstrated understanding), and (3) to ascertain that the children were able to read with expression. All the teachers skipped some of the skills lessons but assigned all the worksheets. All the teachers did isolated phonics work, whereas the manuals always recommended phonics instruction within the context of words. None of the teachers told the children why an assignment was being given or how it related to learning to read. The teachers were most concerned with monitoring students' ability to finish the assignments and get the right answers (Durkin, 1984). From listening to teachers and parents, there is little reason to believe these practices have changed very much since the 1984 study.

Some teachers find it difficult to alter their use of the basal even when evidence demonstrates that some adaptation increases their effectiveness. For example, researchers helped a group of teachers to analyze the basal material and reorganize their instruction (Duffy, Roehler, & Putnam, 1987). Their collective analysis of the skills lessons showed that many were not reading lessons but spelling lessons, such as exercises in changing the y to i and adding -*ed*, and that many had no applications in the stories they accompanied. The researchers guided teachers in recasting some of the skills lessons as strategies and helped them place skills with stories to which they could be applied. At the end of the study, the children demonstrated increased knowledge not just of subskills but of strategy usage and achievement. However, the teachers found it difficult to continue making such decisions in the face of pressures to follow the basal recommendations. This is one of the reasons that Harste (1989) says improving the basals is not the answer; teachers must take responsibility for teaching.

Even the best of the new basals with selections from literature, more expository pieces, and more writing suggestions to accompany the pieces read can result in very poor reading instruction. For example, if skills lessons are presented without regard for the needs of the learners, it does not matter if the basal is improved or not. If children are given no choice in their writing, but assigned to write a letter to a character in the story, it is still not the best instruction in the writing process, where writing should be authentic and the writer should make decisions about audience and form. Some of the newer basals are arranged in themes so several pieces on a topic such as friendship are put together. These themes violate the principle of building a theme on the interests of children and with input from the children about what they want to learn.

The Basal Reader and the Reading/Writing Connection

Helping children become literate does not mean the teacher cannot use the basal reader. It does mean that, while choosing instructional materials and activities, the teacher must think carefully about the goals of instruction, the outcomes likely to result from various activities, and what is known about the process of becoming literate. The following suggestions for using the basal reader are merely suggestions and nothing more. Professional teachers have to evaluate basal reader activities and assume responsibility for selecting those that best meet the needs of the individual children in their classes.

Teachers read to children when the book is too challenging for the children to read by themselves.

© Susan Lapides

Selecting Basal Reader Activities

Classroom teachers must make decisions about which, if any, of the basal reader selections they can use to meet their instructional objectives. They must make decisions about what they will do before, during, and after a reading experience.

Before Reading

One of the tasks of the reading teacher is to build background information before reading a selection. Recall the example in Chapter 2 of the passage from a biology journal that was difficult to read without background information about the topic. Children are often presented with stories or expository writing that are made unnecessarily difficult by lack of background information. In the Harcourt Brace *Treasury of Literature*, the story "In Rare Form" is about swimming and a swimming competition. The teacher is urged to ask the students what they know about swimming and how competition might make them feel or their previous experiences with competitions. Because skilled readers are constantly matching the text they are reading with their own experience, the more the reader's schemata can be activated, the easier the material will be to comprehend.

Another strategy for helping children connect what they know with information presented in a reading selection is to use guided imagery, a technique for encouraging children to think about how an incident would feel, how a setting might look, and how characters might respond. Guided imagery is helping children create mental pictures and does take some practice. The following steps may help you get started with this technique:

Stage 1. Give readers opportunities to create images of concrete objects. Talk about how our images differ from those of others. Reinforce the concept that there are no right or wrong images.

Stage 2. Have readers visualize and describe familiar objects, scenes, or past experiences outside the classroom. Don't hurry them. Images don't form quickly as they do on TV. You might have them visualize their grandparents' kitchen and then have them describe it. Use it in preparation for reading a story and key the images to important scenes in the story.

Stage 3. Read stories to your students that have easy to visualize scenes. Stop from time to time to have students describe their images. Ask questions that focus their attention on the details of their images.

Stage 4. Finally, children will be able to fairly easily create their own images as they read (Harp, 1988, p. 590).

Harp (1988) believes guided imagery improves comprehension because it increases the children's visualization of settings, characters, and actions. They can then relate their previous experience to the new information presented.

Children reading *I Have a Sister, My Sister Is Deaf* (*HBJ Treasury of Literature*, 1993) would be asked to think about how it might feel to be deaf and how they might communicate if they could not hear. Guided imagery before reading increases comprehension more than do questions after reading.

Reutzel (1985) looked at the sequence of instruction suggested in the teacher's guides and recommended rearranging the elements of instruction to reflect more of what is known about learning to read. For example, he found that many of the enrichment activities following the lesson would make good prereading activities, building background information that could aid comprehension.

During Reading

When children begin to read a selection, the teacher can use the Directed Reading Activity and the Guided Metacomprehension Strategy described in Chapter 8. Making predictions, reading to confirm or deny the accuracy of those predictions, and then making new predictions are techniques that assure active involvement on the part of the reader. Any time readers are thinking about what they are reading, comprehension will increase.

Silent Reading

Most of the children's reading time should be spent in silent reading. For beginning readers, comprehension remains about equal whether the children are reading silently or orally. For children past the beginning stages of reading, comprehension is greater during silent reading. The reason is obvious: Oral reading is a performance. When the reader attends to the pronunciation, speed, tone of voice, and other elements of performing a piece, it is difficult to attend to the content of it too (Spache, 1981).

Oral Reading

Perhaps you may remember sitting in a small group with your elementary teacher and taking turns reading a selection aloud. Such reading is called round-robin reading. It is difficult to trace the beginnings of the round-robin method of oral reading (Hoffman, 1987). Teacher education programs do not teach the use of round-robin reading, nor is it suggested by the authors of the teacher's guides for basal readers. It seems to be learned primarily from tradition. What actually happens during round-robin reading is that the child due to read next is practicing his or her portion of the text, and the children who have already read are thinking about other things. Even if children really did what their teachers often admonish them to do—"Keep your eyes on the words that Nicole is reading"—they would be developing inappropriate reading habits. An efficient reader (past the very early stages of reading) can read much faster silently than anyone can read orally. Following text as it is read orally can force a reader into the habit of reading too slowly. Comprehension is reduced when attention is directed to following the words being read aloud, rather than to the meaning of the print.

When Durkin (1984) asked teachers why they had children read entire selections aloud in round-robin style, they said it was to check knowledge of new words, monitor comprehension, and check ability to read with expression. Teachers choosing oral reading need to think carefully about the purposes of the experience. For example, children may know the meaning of words they cannot pronounce. Reading aloud requires the reader to know the pronunciation of each word, but comprehending a selection does not. There are more effective means of demonstrating comprehension than oral reading, such as retelling the story, answering questions, modifying predictions, drawing pictures, performing a skit, and writing a story following the same model.

The reading that most adults do is silent. Very few occupations—for example, broadcasting, teaching, and the ministry—require oral reading. Oral reading can certainly contribute to the reading program if the activities are thoughtfully selected and their purposes are clear. Some basic guidelines will help make oral reading more productive as a means of gaining reading skill. First, children should not read aloud material they have not had a chance to read silently. Ideally they will also have had a chance to practice reading the material aloud before they are asked to perform it for an audience. One way of organizing this kind of reading experience is to set aside a certain time when children are encouraged to share some material with their classmates through reading orally. Children might select an excerpt from a book they are reading, a poem, a riddle, a newspaper clipping, or some interesting fact they have discovered in a reference book. They choose their own material, have a chance to practice their presentation, and then share it with an audience. "Audience" implies that only the performer has the text!

Another guideline is that children should read material orally that has been modeled by a fluent reader. The teacher should read a passage aloud and after practice time help the child read the same passage. This technique has been particularly helpful with readers who are not achieving as well as they might (Hoffman, 1987).

Conducting Skills Instruction

Skills instruction in most basal reader programs is poorly placed, coming after rather than before the stories and depriving children of the chance to apply the skills in real reading. No instruction in skills should take place without letting the children know how those skills will make them more efficient and knowledgeable readers. Skills instruction should also be determined by the needs of the children. Nothing kills interest in reading more quickly than having to sit through unneeded skills instruction. Skills can be approached through many different activities and should not be isolated from the child's real experience with reading.

One way of approaching skills is through writing experiences. Many of the skills listed in the basal are encoding skills that children need for putting together discourse, not interpreting it. For example, the guides often include what are spelling skills or language arts skills. The teacher might focus a mini-lesson on sequence as children are writing personal narratives. They could talk about why an author needs to put events into a sequence for the reader. Children could use alphabetizing skills in order to keep a personal dictionary or to use the class dictionaries. Skills should always be related to real tasks that are meaningful to the learners.

Teachers who decide to use workbook pages to help children develop control of some skills should make careful selection of the pages. Teachers must think about the most important aspects of what is being taught before assigning workbook pages and use only those pages relevant to the instruction. Workbook tasks should involve reading and writing; avoid cute non-functional tasks. Teachers should make sure there is enough content in workbook tasks to enable children to learn something from completing them. Workbook assignments should be made only when the assignment is the best way to achieve reading objectives.

Writing is an appropriate response to reading.

© Susan Lapides

Integrating the Basal with Reading and Writing Experiences

The basal reader can be one resource when teachers think about reading and writing activities in the classroom. For example, if the children had read "Is There Anybody Listening?" (*HBJ Treasury of Literature*, 1993) then the following reading and writing experiences might be appropriate. ("Is There Anybody Listening?" is an excerpt from Gary Paulsen's [1987] book, *Hatchet*, about a young boy lost in the Canadian wilderness and his survival.)

▼   Read the entire book of *Hatchet*. What is significant about the excerpt? Why do you think it was selected for the reading book?

▼   Read other survival books, such as *My Side of the Mountain* (George, 1959) and *Island of the Blue Dolphins* (O'Dell, 1960). Write a comparison of the survival of the main characters to Brian's story in *Hatchet*.

▼   Discuss what the authors of these books would need to know before they could be written. Make a list of the major ideas.

▼   Read one of the descriptive passages that describe the environment or setting of the book. Draw a picture or produce a diorama that illustrates the description. Talk about what words the author used to evoke images of the setting. If you have a clear picture of the setting in your head as you read, was the author successful?

▼   Discuss survival as a concept. Can survival stories be set in the city as well as in the wilderness? What are some common elements of survival in the city and in the wilderness? Create a chart to illustrate these elements.

▼   Read *The River* (Paulsen, 1991), which is a sequel to *Hatchet*. What is a sequel? Discuss the dangers in writing a sequel to a book or making a sequel to a movie. Discuss the plot of *The River*.

▼   Read other books by Gary Paulsen. Discuss their common themes and characteristics.

Activities like these can help children see that reading in the basal is not an isolated experience but one that can be connected to "real" reading and writing that interests them.

Integrating the Basal into a Thematic Curriculum

Using a basal reader as the core of a reading program does not exclude the possibility of a thematic approach to curriculum. Teachers who have chosen to organize their curriculum around a particular theme or topic can use the basal as a resource or, as in our examples, a beginning point for organizing other curricular experiences. We also illustrate the use of the basal in planning themes.

In planning a theme, one can choose any of several organizers. One of these could be an author and the works of that author. For example, if the teacher felt the children were interested, they could choose to organize a theme around the works of Chris Van Allsburg. Children could be encouraged to read one or more of Van Allsburg's books. After becoming acquainted with his work, children could participate in some of the following experiences.

Reading

▼   Compare one of Van Allsburg's stories with those of another author you enjoy. How do they differ in style? What are the elements of each that make them enjoyable reading?

▼   Read "The Garden of Abdul Gasazi" in the basal *Cross the Golden River* (1986). Why did the author of the textbook choose this story to include in the collection? Prepare a commercial for this story in oral, written, or videotaped form. How would you persuade someone who had not heard of it to read the story?

▼   Read or ask an adult to help you read the author profile of Chris Van Allsburg in *Language Arts* (Kiefer, 1987). What do you think are the most important influences on his writing?

▼   Read or ask an adult to help you read Van Allsburg's (1986) speech when he accepted the Caldecott award. Did you learn something new about his writing and/or illustrating?

Writing

▼   Write a story for one of the illustrations in *The Mysteries of Harris Burdick*.

▼   Write a critical review of one of the books for the school newspaper. Be sure to read several book reviews in your local newspaper first so you will know what to include in your review.

▼   Write a sequel to *Jumanji*.

▼   Write your answer to the riddle of the identity of the visitor in *The Stranger*. List your evidence. Seal your answer in an envelope. When all envelopes have been collected, open them and compare the answers. Get your principal to help all of you think about how well you looked for clues.

▼   Van Allsburg uses a ship's log to tell the story in *The Wretched Stone*. Compare the style of the writing with one of his other books. Do you agree with the message in this book?

▼ In *Just a Dream*, Van Allsburg makes a strong environmental statement. What statement would you make if you were a well-known author?

▼ In *The Sweetest Fig*, Van Allsburg writes a fantasy that has an unusual twist. If you could dream and make that dream come true, what would you dream?

Social Studies

▼ Find the landmarks that are included in *Ben's Dream*. Locate them on a map. Are there other landmarks you would have included in the book? Find information about one of the landmarks in a reference book. Be sure you can tell where it is, when it was built, and why it is important.

▼ Why is it important to the farmers in *The Stranger* that the seasons change? Compile a list of occupations that depend on the weather for success.

Science

▼ Find information about the animals included in *Jumanji*. Where do they live, and what do they eat?

▼ In *The Wreck of the Zephyr* a sailboat can sail on air. Find information about how airplanes are able to fly. Tell or write why you think a sailboat can or cannot fly; if not, what adaptations would make flying possible?

Art

▼ Find information about the art techniques that Van Allsburg uses in his illustrations. You may need to visit a local art museum or have an art teacher come in to talk about the various techniques.

▼ Choose one of the techniques that Van Allsburg uses in his illustrations and try it in illustrating one of your own stories.

▼ How are the illustrations in *The Widow's Broom* similar to the illustrations in some of the other books? How are they different?

▼ One of the interesting aspects of Van Allsburg's art is his use of perspective. Find other artists who have used perspective in unusual ways.

This is certainly not an exhaustive list of what could be done with an author theme built on a basal reader story. You could also choose other themes, such as the environment, and include the basal reader material. Some of the newer basals have arranged the contents by themes; however, these themes are usually brief and most teachers would want to expand them.

Final Comments on the Basal Reader

The basal reader offers many possibilities for good instruction when used thoughtfully by the teacher. A teacher thinking about individual needs of children would never believe every child should "read" every page of a given basal and complete every workbook exercise. Thoughtful teachers treat the basal as one resource that can be used to achieve curriculum goals when appropriate. The danger in using a basal may be that a teacher often believes the authors of the basal know more than he or she knows and, therefore, teachers should do what the basal recommends. Today's teachers are well educated and knowledgeable about the process of reading. They know how to select materials from many sources that meet the needs of the children, including the basal. Teachers may take advantage of the skills ideas in doing their own planning for instruction, but they do not mindlessly put children through skills exercises without reference to larger goals. Just as in using any other instructional tool, the teacher is responsible for helping children see how learning in school relates to real experience and how reading and writing are invaluable in life—not just exercises to be completed at school.

Major Ideas in This Chapter

▼ The basal reader has been in existence for many years and continues to be utilized by a large number of teachers for classroom reading instruction.

▼ Basal reading series differ in their philosophies and their approaches to skills instruction. Current basal reading series include activities that reflect a broad range of ideas about reading instruction.

▼ Basal readers are just materials; inherently they are neither good nor bad. What can make a difference in the quality of reading instruction in a classroom where basals are used is *how* they are used.

▼ Teachers who use a basal are still responsible for making good decisions about what children need to do in order to become more capable readers and writers. They are still responsible for selecting and sequencing instructional activities that help children move along the literacy continuum.

Discussion Questions: Focusing on the Teacher You Are Becoming

1. What do you personally consider the strengths and weaknesses of basal readers?

2. Discuss reasons for choosing not to order the workbooks that accompany the basal. How might you convince a principal that this action is appropriate?

3. Recall your own experiences in learning to read. How did you feel about reading orally to the class? Do you think most students shared your feelings?

4. How will you plan instruction in literacy if the district where you are employed has an adopted basal reader and expects teachers to use it?

Field-Based Applications

1. Examine the teacher's guide to one or more basal series. Do the following: (a) determine what the philosophy of the authors is in terms of top-down or bottom-up views of reading instruction; (b) walk through a guided reading lesson and determine the extent to which you would have to supplement the guide from the Guided Metacomprehension Strategy; (c) walk through a skill lesson and then determine the degree of match between the skill lessons in the basal and the format for a skills lesson described in Chapter 5. Would you want to use this basal with children? Why or why not?

2. Choose one selection from a basal for a grade you want to teach and develop two or three ideas for building background information before the children read the story. Check the teacher's guide and compare your ideas with the ones it suggests.

3. Choose one selection from a basal and think about writing activities that would be appropriate to accompany that selection.

4. Choose one selection from a basal and think about how it could be integrated into a thematic approach to curriculum.

5. Plan an oral reading experience using one selection in the basal. Possibilities include having two children read the dialogue in a story and another read the narration, having one child read the story (or an excerpt from it) to the class, and setting up partner reading, in which two children read aloud to each other.

6. Compare the original version of a book with the version printed in a basal reader. What changes, if any, were made in the language? Why do you think they were made?

Chapter 10
Literature in the Reading/Writing Program

Chapter Overview

▼ Learning the skills of reading and becoming a reader for life are not necessarily the same. Literature can help children feel the power of being a reader—not just able to read, but a lover of reading. Only real books that invite the reader to enter the story and become a part of it can lead children to become readers.

▼ Literature can be used as the base for reading and writing instruction in the classroom. Children's literature offers source material for instruction in literacy abilities, including recognizing the structures of various genres and learning more about the craft of writing.

▼ Picture books, available for all ages, can serve a variety of functions in the elementary curriculum.

▼ Reading aloud is an important component of reading instruction. It can contribute to vocabulary development, increase interest in reading, and serve as a model of reading.

▼ A variety of curricular experiences can be organized around literature, which can enhance activities in social studies, science, art, music, and mathematics.

▼ Reading and writing instruction based on literature can be organized using specific strategies for individuals and groups.

Literature-Based Reading Instruction

We must bring children and books together in ways that encourage children to read, to love reading, and to become better readers and writers through their experiences with literature.

California is one state that has taken a stand on the importance of literature in the reading program. The California Reading Initiative is a comprehensive plan for including the reading of literature in the elementary curriculum. It includes a book list, a language arts framework based on literature, and a testing program matched to the reading program. State Superintendent Bill Honig stated (Cullinan, 1986, p. 766),

Reading is one of the most effective ways of learning. I want to encourage students to read and I want them to enjoy reading. Good reading skills are critical to success in all academic areas. We are launching the California Reading Initiative to address serious concerns about student's reading abilities and practices. Recent figures indicate that we are experiencing an alarming increase in illiteracy in this nation. Many of our students who can read are having difficulty understanding what they read. Further, many of our students who can read and who can understand what they read simply don't read.

The California Reading Initiative has been developed to address these concerns. An important part of our strategy is to improve reading instruction and to provide students access to good books. A love of reading and books is one of the most important gifts that teachers and parents can give our young people.

The California Reading Initiative is a statewide effort to recognize the importance of literature in the curriculum and the importance of books in achieving the goal of lifelong readership. Cullinan (1985) reported that statewide literature/literacy initiatives exist in seven states and programs that depend on literature in 16 other states. Many other states reported they do not have state curricula and therefore do not have a state literature initiative, but that many local districts in their states have such initiatives.

Support for Literature-Based Reading Instruction

Teachers in places other than California are also more interested in literature-based reading instruction than ever before. Teaching reading with literature as the material for instruction is certainly not a new idea, but the renewed interest seems to be from both the "disenchantment with traditional reading practices and the abundant selection of quality literature being published today" (Thompkins & McGee, 1993, p. 9).

The research supports literature-based reading instruction. Several studies (Cohen, 1968; Cullinan, Jaggar, & Strickland, 1974; Eldredge & Butterfield, 1986) found that "the use of children's literature to teach children to read had a positive effect upon students' achievement and attitudes toward reading—much greater than the traditional methods used" (Eldredge & Butterfield, 1986, p. 35). Of special interest are the studies on literature as reading material for children with limited English abilities. Larrick (1987) found that of children with limited English abilities who had been taught with a literature and language-experience approach, all except 3 of 350 children passed the district comprehension tests by the end of first grade. Those three had been in the United States less than six months. Other researchers have looked at the effects of literature-based reading instruction on failed or stalled readers.

Chomsky (1978), Tunnell (1986), and Reutzel and Fawson (1988) all found that strong gains were made with readers who had not been successful in reading programs before when they were involved in literature-based programs.

Teachers who choose to base their reading programs on literature also understand literature is no longer taught so there is one "right" answer found in the text. One of the differences in using a basal reading program where children are asked to read a selection and then answer given questions about the selection and using literature is that the reader and the text interact in ways that are under the control of the reader. Several theorists have studied the interaction of readers and texts, but the best known of these is Rosenblatt (1978, 1991). She described the reading process as circular or reciprocal. Readers make a choice about their purpose for reading the material and then draw on all their past experience in order to create meaning from the written text. No two readers would get exactly the same message from a text because each would create their own meaning based on individual experiences and knowledge. A reader reading to get specific information reads in what Rosenblatt describes as an "efferent" stance. A reader who responds to the text more from the point of the feelings evoked than the facts presented is taking what Rosenblatt describes as an "aesthetic" stance to the reading. These stances are not mutually exclusive. Sometimes the reader moves back and forth between these stances in reading the same material. For example, if you were reading a scientific piece on the life of cockroaches, you might take an efferent stance in learning the information while your aesthetic stance would evoke unpleasant feelings about cockroaches. Children might read the same piece without the aesthetic response because they have not had experience being revolted by cockroaches.

Teachers who believe in the developmental nature of learning language and becoming literate want to avoid the one-answer response to reading materials and to help students go beyond simply decoding, answering questions, and analyzing only what is asked of them by the teacher. The book needs a reader to be complete because only the reader can add all that is missing from a book (Paulsen, 1989).

Literature offers meaningful texts for reading, which can come from all genres and take the form of fiction, nonfiction, or poetry. The appeal of literature lies not only in its variety but in its intrinsic interest, which motivates reading. Literature of the very highest quality should be offered to children. It has something for every individual, from those who want to know about asteroids to those who are zoo lovers. Whether a child likes hot rods, motorcycles, or dolls, books and poetry can be found to fit that interest. Very few children actually got personally involved with the tales of Dick and Jane, but many have eagerly read all the books in *The Chronicles of Narnia* (Lewis, 1950–1956). Interest and motivation are critical in any reading program.

Literature can add zest and interest to the classroom. It can enliven topics in the traditional subject matter, motivate further reading, and broaden children's reading interests. Helping children analyze their reading in ways meaningful to them will deepen their understanding of literature. Writing experiences can be encouraged through an introduction of some of the models of writing found in literature. The authors of the best in children's literature use literary techniques that children can learn to apply in their own writing efforts. Noticing the words and phrases chosen by outstanding authors will help children become more knowledgeable and thoughtful about the words and phrases they use.

One other very important benefit of a literature-based reading program is that literature can be selected to enhance the multicultural goals in the classroom.

Selecting and Using Literature

Thousands of books are published each year. Selecting the best of these for use in the classroom is sometimes difficult. Obviously, no teacher can read every available book. Help can come from your school's media specialist and from book reviews in professional journals. Your school library probably subscribes to *Horn Book*, the premier journal in children's literature. Very useful book reviews are also found in *Language Arts*, *The Reading Teacher*, *Childhood Education*, *Young Children*, and *The New Advocate*. Each year the October issue of *The Reading Teacher* publishes "Children's Choices," a list of new books that are selected by children as their favorites. In addition to book reviews, *Language Arts* features biographical articles on authors and illustrators of children's books. A newer publication, *Book Links*, offers themes and classroom ideas as well as reviews. Some newspapers also have book review sections for new children's books. Even though these sources cannot review every new book published, they will certainly help you know the best of the new work in the field of children's literature.

When choosing books for the classroom, the teacher must think about intended use: Will the book be read aloud to the class or made available for free reading? Will it add interest and depth to particular topics of study, help children solve problems, or aid in reading and writing instruction? In each case, there are some general and specific guidelines to follow when selecting books.

In general, the theme, setting, plot, characterization, and style must be considered when choosing a book of fiction for classroom use. The theme must be worthwhile. For example, many books have themes that help children better understand relationships, perseverance, honesty, or courage. Settings are important if they make the book more or less difficult to understand. A book set in another time or place, such as historical fiction, may require explanations or background knowledge in order to be comprehensible. The plot of the story must be lively. Most children enjoy action and a plot that moves along. The characterization must be such that children can relate to the characters in the book. Children need to be able to relate to the emotions of the characters and feel their actions are plausible. Style is basically the quality of writing. It means the author has interesting sentence patterns, chooses words and phrases carefully, paces the story appropriately, and writes so as not to distract the reader. Books should contain a quality of language and writing that will serve as models for children's writing. Good books also serve to increase children's vocabularies and understanding of figures of speech such as similes and metaphors.

As children move into the intermediate grades, their individual reading interests vary widely. Many children become avid readers during this time, reading everything they can find on a given subject, such as horses or space travel, some pursuing a particular genre, such as mystery or biography. It is very important that teachers continue to select literature for a broad range of interests and reading abilities. Teachers selecting books for the classroom must also consider multicultural books.

Multicultural Literature

Teachers who believe children learn to read best if they find themselves in stories will be active in selecting literature that will help every child find himself or herself. Teachers will also select literature that will increase the understanding and sensitivity of the class to the cultural and ethnic differences in

Reading aloud is important for children of all ages.

© Gail Meese/Meese Photo Research

our society. The first standard for selection of books that are multicultural is literary quality. Harris (1992) comments,

> . . . mindful of the underlying rationale for including multicultural literature in the curriculum—the creation of a more equitable society—some teachers select fiction with the intention of using it to teach lessons about tolerance or to provide specific information about various cultural groups. Some children's fiction is written with didactic intent, but often the writer of such a book neglects important aspects of literary quality. (p. 48)

She goes on to say that books of fiction are not social studies texts and should not be used as if they were.

In addition to literary quality, multicultural books must be authentic. The teacher must also be sure the literature reflects the diversity within and across human cultures. For example, not all African Americans are living in poverty, not all Asians are the top students in their schools, Native Americans exist in today's world, not just in the past. Teachers must also learn to recognize the cultural traditions from which stories arise and not to judge the stories only by Euro-American standards. The Council for Interracial Books for Children (1974) has an excellent list of criteria for evaluating books. Other resources for selection are Slapin and Seale (1992), Norton (1987), and Harris (1992).

Read-Aloud Books

Reading aloud is a valuable element in any program of reading instruction. Reading aloud is championed so much it has been compared to the cure-all of taking two aspirins and bed rest that was so common years ago (Hoffman, Roser, & Battle, 1993). Research and testimony both support the value of reading aloud (Cochran-Smith, 1984; McCormick, 1977; Teale, 1984). Reading aloud can provide a model for fluent reading, spark interest in new genres or authors to be read independently, help develop vocabulary, and increase comprehension.

A book that is to be read aloud by the teacher should meet several criteria:

1. It should be a book the teacher enjoys personally. There are too many wonderful books available to choose a book that is not appealing to the reader.

2. It should be suitable for reading aloud: short enough to fit into a reading period or divisible into chapters or segments that can be read separately.

3. Its content and subject matter must be appropriate to the audience.

4. If the book has illustrations, their size and clarity should be considered with respect to visibility at a distance from the reader.

5. The book should contain action or dialogue that makes listening interesting.

6. The book should contain language that is slightly above the reading level of most members of the group. Books that are written to be "easy to read" are not usually good choices for reading aloud because the level of the language is not interesting to the listener and the stories are rarely very interesting to the reader. Children deserve the very best in terms of language use and writing style.

Reading aloud to intermediate-grade children introduces them to many different genres and exposes them to books they might never have chosen on their own. It provides a common reading experience and can be the stimulus for other reading and writing activities. Teachers can provide lead-ins to stories that children might find difficult to read on their own. For example, because the names of many mythological figures are difficult to pronounce, many children find myths overwhelming to read without an introduction by the teacher. Once the teacher has read some myths aloud and given the children a chance to relate them to their own experience (references in other literature, references in advertising, terms used in sports, and so on) then they are much more likely to be successful in reading myths independently. Usually the most popular book in the classroom for individual reading is the book the teacher has just finished reading aloud.

In addition to choosing quality literature for reading aloud and setting aside time in the school day for reading aloud, teachers can choose literature that is related to other literature, provide for discussions that are thought provoking and encourage personal responses, offer a wide range of follow-up activities, and reread selected pieces (Hoffman, Roser, & Battle, 1993). Reading aloud is not only pleasurable for both children and teachers, it is also important in the development of literacy abilities.

Picture Books

Picture books are books in which the illustrations are of equal importance with the text. In fact, the text of a picture book is rarely sufficient to carry the story. Imagine reading Sendak's *Where the Wild Things Are* (Sendak, 1963) without the illustrations. There are only about 300 words in the text, and there wouldn't be much left of the story if the illustrations were missing.

Picture books have changed rather drastically since Comenius published the first picture book—*Orbis Pictus: The World Illustrated*—in 1657. We would describe this book more as an illustrated dictionary than as a picture book. Technological advances in printing have made possible the reproduction of various art techniques and print/picture layouts that would not have been possible a few years ago. Picture books deal with family life, school experiences, friends, animals, and adaptations of folktales. Today's picture books also treat topics once considered taboo for children, such as death. Another relatively new idea is the wordless picture book, of which *Tuesday* (Wiesner, 1991) and *Free Fall* (Wiesner, 1988) are good examples. There has also been renewed interest in pop-up books and books that have movable parts. Jan Pienkowski's books, such as *Dinnertime* (1981), are examples.

Picture books appeal to a vast audience; they are certainly not meant to be restricted to the youngest children. Picture books for older children include *Sundiatia: Lion King of Mali* (Wisniewski, 1992) and *An Angel for Solomon Singer* (Rylant, 1992). These books have sophisticated material and require background knowledge that young children do not usually possess. *The Geranium on the Window Sill Just Died But Teacher You Went Right On* (Cullum, 1971) is a picture book written for an adult audience. If the media center in your school or public library labels the picture book section "Easy," perhaps you could lobby for a change in designation to "Everybody's Books."

In addition to considering the plot, theme, characterization, setting, and style of the text, the illustrations must be considered carefully when selecting a picture book for classroom use. The following questions will aid you in choosing the best of the picture books:

1. Are the illustrations and text synchronized?

2. Does the mood conveyed by the artwork (humorous/serious, rollicking/quiet) complement the story?

3. Are the illustrative details consistent with the text?

4. Could a child get a sense of the basic concepts or story sequence by looking at the pictures?

5. Are the illustrations or photographs aesthetically pleasing?

6. Is the printing (clarity, form, line, color) of good quality?

7. Can children view and review the illustrations, each time getting more from them?

8. Are the illustrative style and complexity suited to the age level of the intended audience?

9. If the book is a hardcover edition, how have the endpapers been treated? Do they add to the aesthetic balance of the book? (Questions adapted from Jalongo, 1988)

Picture books can be used to introduce new topics of study, explore topics in science and social studies, explore issues of concern such as homelessness and war, introduce genres such as biography or fantasy, and serve as models for children's writing experiences.

Alphabet Books

Alphabet books provide an excellent format for children's reading and writing experiences. Many alphabet books are most appropriate for older children; the alphabet format certainly does not imply simple content. Some alphabet books are arranged by theme, with each entry related to the topic, and some are focused on the letters themselves rather than on a topic. Creating an ABC book can be a fine activity to culminate various classroom studies. After studying their own state, children could write an ABC book of their state. The project would require careful reading of background material and decision making about the most suitable entry for each letter.

Alphabet books can serve as writing models for older children as well. *Ashanti to Zulu* (Musgrove, 1976) describes African people and traditions; it can serve as a model for putting together information on almost any topic. Other alphabet books that might challenge older children to create a book of their own are *Antics* (Hepworth, 1992) and *Eye Spy: A Mysterious Alphabet* (Bourke, 1991). In *Antics*, each letter is represented by a word containing the letters "ant." For example, the entry for B is "brilliant." In *Eye Spy*, each letter is represented by a pair of homophones and each set has a connection to the next set. The entry for U, for example, are three depictions of uniforms and the fourth panel is a set of weather vanes that are all exactly alike. The entry for V is a weather vane, and so on.

For intermediate-grade readers, alphabet books can serve as an introduction to topics such as a study of geography or the ocean; a stimulus for research if children want to find out more about trees or plants mentioned in alphabet books; and a way to promote oral and written language development as they learn the names of the many objects presented in some books or value the word play presented in others. They may also use the alphabet as an organizer for presenting information on personal topics of study (Chaney, 1993).

There are hundreds of good alphabet books on the market and many more are being published each year by commercial publishing houses and in elementary classrooms across the country. Many ideas for using alphabet books in the classroom are presented in *Alphabet: A Handbook of ABC Books and Activities for the Elementary Classroom* (Roberts, 1984).

Poetry

When selecting poetry for use in the reading and writing program, teachers should be aware of the difference between poetry written about childhood and poetry written for children. Many poems about childhood are sentimental recollections from an adult point of view and rarely appeal to children. Interesting poetry is available for any topic that would be part of an elementary curriculum and any interest a child might have. Children respond well to a variety of types of poetry. They like humorous poems, narrative poetry, and descriptive poetry.

There are many collections of poetry for children. Shel Silverstein, Jack Prelutsky, and Lee Bennett Hopkins all have interesting collections. Poems about poetry have been collected in *Inner Chimes: Poems on Poetry* (Goldstein, 1992). Poetry can be included as part of a theme or as enrichment for topics of study in the classroom. For example, if the topic of study were seasons, then *In for Winter, Out for Spring* (Adoff, 1991), *Ring of Earth* (Yolen, 1986), and *Summer Is . . .* (Zolotow, 1967) would be good choices for enrichment.

Poetry is written to be read aloud, and teachers should do so often. It is also important to encourage children to share poems they like with their classmates. Perhaps a period each week could be set aside for sharing favorite poems.

Writing poetry can encourage children to select words carefully, appreciate the use of figurative language, discover more colorful adjectives, and value the skill of talented poets. Before they begin to write, children should have many opportunities to listen to poetry. Teaching children to write specific forms of poetry such as haiku, limericks, or cinquains give children more options and choices for their own writing efforts. When teaching a form, the first step is to share many examples. Then the teacher might lead a class discussion of the characteristics of the form. Once they understand the form, the class could write a piece as a group, then as a small group, and then as individuals. Writing in a group provides a chance for each student to feel safe and nonthreatened, which is very important in attempting poetry. It also gives children a chance to review the form once again with support from peers before they attempt to write on their own.

Greenberg (1978) suggests to teachers that they never offer negative criticism of children's efforts and they not allow children to write rhyming poetry in the beginning. He believes children will not continue to attempt to write poetry if teachers are negative about their efforts and that children get so caught up in trying to produce words that rhyme they lose meaning. He also suggests that, as in any writing, content should always be valued over form. Form can be polished later if the content is worthy of more work.

Literature for Independent Reading

As teachers think about the abilities, needs, and interests of their classes, they will be able to select the best books for independent reading in the classroom. Books selected need to span a wide variety of topics, genres, and reading levels.

Fiction

Literature available for children to choose in their free reading time should cover a wide range of reading levels, treat a variety of topics, and employ

In an individualized reading program children select their own reading material.

© Elizabeth Crews/Stock Boston

various formats. The range of reading abilities in a classroom of younger children can easily span five years; among older children, it may be even wider. Children's interests vary as much as those of adults, and changing themes of study throughout the year also mean changes in the class library. Teachers may choose to provide multiple copies of class favorites, but a single copy of most books is probably adequate.

For younger readers, include a wide variety of picture books, wordless picture books, books with repetitive language, and easy-to-read books. Many beginning readers will want to look at books they know, so books the teacher has read aloud and books of familiar stories, such as folktales, are good choices. As children become concerned with text, they will often choose the beginning reading books. With children's progress in reading ability comes increasing sophistication in the class library. Children will read more books written in chapters and look for a wider variety of genres. By the end of elementary school, class libraries should contain books from all genres, on a broad diversity of topics and covering a wide span of reading difficulty.

Because the interests of older children vary widely, teachers will want to include mystery stories, sports stories, survival stories, and stories about growing up. It is difficult to draw the line between literature for children and literature for young adults. By the end of elementary school, some children are beginning to read young adult literature. Classroom libraries should include the works of such authors as Scott O'Dell, Cynthia Voight, Mildred Taylor, Ann Nolan Clark, and Joseph Krumgold. Some classes may be ready for the work of S. E. Hinton or Robert Cormier. The teacher must be very knowledgeable about the literature available and the needs of the class.

Children can keep a record of books read in free time by writing personal responses to books in a reading log, by simply writing the titles on a record sheet, by preparing some sort of book report, or by entering their books into a computer cataloging program. Such records help teachers monitor students' interests, provide information about reading ability, and give clues to what to suggest for further reading—for example, another book by the same author or a book that broadens the child's interests. Whatever the teacher chooses to do, one caution is to emphasize the quality of reading rather than the number of books read. When success is measured in quantity, children have reason to favor books that are short and easy to read and have little incentive to reread a book.

Nonfiction

In addition to fiction, teachers will want to provide expository books as choices for independent reading. Books selected to enhance specific subject matter themes must be evaluated in terms of accuracy of information, format, and style. The author must be careful to signal the inclusion of opinion in a factual format. Teachers will want to choose the most up-to-date books and to help children learn to check the facts with several sources. For example, children studying their state's history could read accounts of the same incidents in more than one textbook or reference book and compare them. Questions of format concern whether the material is organized logically and presented in segments that aid the children's comprehension. Like format, style may vary a great deal. How the author chooses to present facts can determine how palatable the facts are. Tomie dePaola's *The Cloud Book* (1975), *The Quicksand Book* (1977), and *The Popcorn Book* (1978) present the facts in the context of a story.

Libraries in most primary-grade classrooms need many books about animals, plants, machines, the earth, insects, and space. The topics children study in science and social studies should be complemented by books that are available for free reading.

Organizing for Literature-Based Reading Instruction

Reading instruction based on children's literature can be organized in several different ways. One way is individualized reading in which each child reads a book of his or her own choice, another is literature sets in which the class is organized into small groups so each group reads a given book; another is organizing around a theme so each student reads a book related to a given theme; another is reading based on the work of a single author; and another is organizing around genres in which each child reads a book categorized in a given genre.

In each of the following scenarios, we assume the language arts period is 1½ hours each day. We know children will be reading and writing throughout the day, but specific instruction in literacy is also a part of the planned curriculum. We also assume children will read expository materials during other parts of the school day and that teachers introduce a wide variety of literary forms such as poetry during read-alouds or mini-lessons. How these teachers choose to organize that time period varies and the emphasis varies, but all know teaching reading and writing is not accomplished without planning.

Individualized Reading

Welcome to the fourth-grade classroom of Mr. Curt Wolf. In this classroom, children are engaged in an individualized reading program. Curt has explained to the parents that an individualized program has the following advantages for the children: (1) wide exposure to genres, (2) development of reading ability at an individual rate, and (3) individual attention for the child through a conference with the teacher. He shares his belief that when children choose their own reading material and progress at their own pace they make better progress and have better attitudes about reading. Individualized programs also get children actively involved in reading more than some other approaches to reading instruction. He shares the research studies that substantiate his own experience.

Curt is well aware that individualized reading does not mean he is not responsible for reading instruction. He also knows individualized reading is not simply sustained silent reading, but a program requiring good organizational skills and careful planning. He keeps a loose-leaf notebook with a page (and eventually pages) for each child. Here he records the books that each child has read, his conference notes about instruction and progress, and any other comments. Because these children are older, he usually conferences with each child whenever a book is completed. With younger children he would probably conference on a schedule of four or five children each day.

Curt begins the language-arts period with a short 10- to 15-minute group lesson on whatever the class needs. He may present a lesson on story structure, a needed writing skill, a discussion of the characteristics of a genre, a read-aloud time, or whatever other skills the whole group needs. He spends the major part of the period conferencing with students. In his room, students sign up for a conference when they have completed a book. During the conferences he may ask children questions about the book they have read or ask the child to read a passage aloud. The questions focus on some element of the author's craft, some personal response, some connections with other literature, or some challenges for the reader in the book. In other words, the questions do not ask the reader to simply recall information about the details of the plot or characters. Sometimes he roves among his students as they read silently, stopping to discuss a point with a child or to suggest another book or topic. If a child is having difficulty with the reading, Mr. Wolf may offer individual skills instruction. At the end of the period, he asks students to spend about ten minutes writing in their response logs and then spends a few minutes as children discuss what they are reading, share books they think others would enjoy, or read a passage that is exceptional to the class. The skills instruction is provided for each individual during the conference.

Curt realizes that an individualized reading program has some possible disadvantages. He knows, for example, that there is a risk a child would choose material that is not challenging, but he monitors each child's work through conferences and reading their response logs daily. He also knows that making sure each child makes progress in reading skills requires careful attention on his part. He manages his time well so he can provide small-group, whole-group, and individual instruction.

Figure 10.1 outlines some possible roles for teachers and students in an individualized reading program. Figure 10.2 provides some possible questions for individual conferences with children about their reading. Curt tries to select one or two questions from each category at each conference. Figure 10.3 is a record-keeping format for use with the ring binder he finds most successful in recording the work of each child.

In the response logs the children write how they feel about their reading and their thoughts and impressions about the individual book they are reading at the time. Curt modeled response logs in the group instruction period several times at the beginning of the year and he occasionally does another mini-lesson on response logs. He wants the children to avoid writing a summary or the typical book report, but to delve into how the author treats characters, settings, plots, and themes and a personal response to the writing. Figure 10.4 is a page from a response log of a child reading *Shiloh* (Naylor, 1991).

One of the problems with individualized reading programs is finding enough books. In this classroom, children borrow from the school library, the public library, and sometimes bring books from their own personal libraries. Parents and volunteers are encouraged to donate books to the classroom. Books used meet the criteria for good children's literature, and both children and parents are becoming skilled in recognizing quality in literature.

> **A Plan for Individualized Reading**
>
> **I.** Teacher and student planning
>   **A.** Book selection
>   **B.** Self-directed activities
>   **C.** Selection of students for conference
>   **D.** Selection of students for group work
>
> **II.** Activities
>
> | *Students* | *Teacher* |
> |---|---|
> | **A.** Read themselves out (i.e., to the point of satiation) | **A.** Conferences
  1. Questions, etc.
  2. Records
  3. Closure |
> | **B.** Preparation for teacher | |
> | **C.** Self-selected activities
  1. Book center
  2. Writing center
  3. Art center
  4. Science center
  5. Manipulative materials center
  6. Supply center | **B.** Group work
  1. Special-needs groups
  2. Friendship groups
  3. Interest groups
  4. Novel: creative reading |
>
> **III.** Sharing of individual activities
>
> **IV.** Cleanup

Figure 10.1—Sample Individualized Reading Plan

Literature Studies

In Mrs. Pamela Murphy's third-grade class, the children are learning to read with literature, but she chooses to organize her instruction around literature studies. In her room, she presents five or six books to the class giving a short book talk on each. Children then select the book they want to read. If more than six or seven children choose the same book, she will have two groups reading it (if she has enough copies) or some children will have to read their second choice this period and will get to read their first choice next reading period. Pamela has found from experience that groups of about six or seven work best; groups that are too small do not have as many differences of opinion or discussions that are as lively. In contrast, groups that are too large afford too few opportunities for individual members to participate actively.

Pamela has explained to the parents of the children in her class that she agrees with the research on literature-based reading instruction, but she chooses to organize literature study groups rather than an individualized reading program. She believes the advantages of the literature studies approach include allowing the child to select his or her reading material, enabling children to share reading experiences with others, creating opportunities for

Conference

I. Comprehension skills
  A. Central thought
     1. What kind of story is this?
     2. What is it mainly about?
     3. Does its setting make a difference?
     4. Does its time affect the story?
     5. Does this book remind you of any other book?
     6. Did you think it is a _____ story? (happy, funny, exciting, scary, etc.)
     7. Could you describe this in a couple of words?
  B. Inferences and critical reading
     1. Do you think the story is really about _____?
     2. Is there something here that isn't actually said?
     3. Is there a lesson to be learned in this book?
     4. Was there anything in the story that was not the same as you've heard somewhere else?
     5. Do you think you can believe what it said?
     6. What is the problem of the character in the story?
  C. Value judgments
     1. Do you agree or disagree with this story?
     2. What is your own opinion about _____ in the story?
     3. Is this something everyone should read?
     4. If only a few people should read it, who would you choose?
     5. Is the story making fun of us all?
     6. If you could pass a law, or have your own wish, would this book influence you?
     7. Do you trust what you read?
     8. Do you believe everything you read?
     9. Can you trust what this author says?
  D. Author's purpose
     1. Who is the author?
     2. What do you know about the author's family, etc.?
     3. What other books of this author's do you know about?
     4. What do you feel the author is trying to tell people in his or her stories?
     5. If you could talk to the author, what would you tell him or her?
     6. Do you think the author has children of his or her own?
     7. Does the author like animals?
     8. What ideas are you sure about when you read this author's stories?
  E. Necessary plot sequence
     1. Tell me the story.
     2. After _____ , what happened next?
     3. Tell me what happened first, then _____.
     4. If such-and-such happened before so-and-so, does it make any difference in the story?
     5. If you could, would you change the story around at all?
     6. What was the best part of the story to you? Beginning, middle, end?

Figure 10.2—Sample Guide for Individual Reading Conference

II. Personality adjustment and reading selections
    A. Insight into personal interest in story
        1. Was this a good story?
        2. Why did you choose this book?
        3. Did you ever have an experience like this?
        4. Would you like to be just like the person in the story?
        5. What about this story made you angry?
        6. If you could become one of the characters in this story, which one would suit you?
        7. If you could, would you wave a magic wand and live in this time?
    B. Awareness of group reaction
        1. Who do you know that likes this type of book?
        2. Would he or she like this one?
        3. Are you going to tell him or her about it?
    C. Insight into possible personality behavior change
        1. Did you have a problem like this person in the story?
        2. Does this story make you feel like doing something?
        3. Did you see something about yourself after you finished this story that you didn't know before?
        4. Is there something here you didn't like and never would do?
III. The mechanical skills
    A. Word definitions
        1. Here is an unusual word. Can you tell me what it means?
        2. Here is another: _____.
        3. Can you tell me another word that means the same thing?
        4. If I said _____ (homonym or antonym), would you say this word was the same or the opposite of it?
        5. Did you find any words that meant something different when you read them somewhere else?
    B. Study skills
        1. Show me the index.
        2. Find the page where such-and-such is described.
        3. How do you find things in the index?
        4. Did the pictures help you read this book?
        5. Can you find the place on the map where the story was set?
        6. Can you find the general topic of this story in another book?
    C. Ability to analyze unknown words
        1. Show me a word that you didn't know. How did you figure it out?
        2. What is in this word that you know (digraph, initial letter)?
        3. Let me cover up part of it. Now what do you see? Say it. Now here's the whole word. Can you say it?
IV. Ability to hold audience attention
    A. Oral reading of selection
        1. What part of the story did you choose to read to me?
        2. Tell me what happened up to this point.
        3. (After the reading) Now tell me what happened next.
    B. Retelling of long story briefly

Figure 10.2 (*continued*)

Name			
Date	Book	Problems, concerns	Notes and Interests

Figure 10.3—Sample Reading Conference Record-Keeping Form

small-group instruction, and facilitating the development of speaking, listening, reading, and writing around common interests. Use of literature sets requires the teacher to make important instructional decisions, including which books to offer and what activities should accompany each book.

She sits as a member of each discussion group, but is not the leader. She may ask questions or guide the discussion as would any other member, but her job is not to ask comprehension questions in the group setting. She wants the children to take charge of the discussions and respond to issues and questions that are their own. Her role in the groups is to model and coach.

After the groups are organized, they meet together to decide how far they will read before the next group meeting. In this classroom, they meet every other day, so they may decide one or two chapters will be finished before the meeting. They have to finish the book in a two-week period in this room, although other teachers may determine that one or three weeks works better for them. As they read, they write in their response journals. Pamela has modeled the sorts of entries that will help them examine more than the details of a plot as they respond, and she reads their journals daily. Sometimes the other members of their group also read their journals. When the book is finished, the group decides on a way of sharing the book with the class; sometimes it is a bulletin board, videotape of each group member sharing their favorite part, a song, a skit, a poem, or whatever seems most appropriate.

When they were in first grade, these children often participated in literature studies that began with the teacher reading a Big Book. After several rereadings, they often read the book independently or with a partner and then discussed the author's choice of words, the story structure, special words that signal to the reader what is to follow, or why they thought the author chose one word as opposed to another. They also talked about the meaning of the story and how it made sense to them personally.

Now that they are in third grade, the children read independently the books they select and are encouraged to evaluate their reading strategies. For example, they are often asked to think about whether their reading speed was appropriate for the material, how the author's organization helped them read

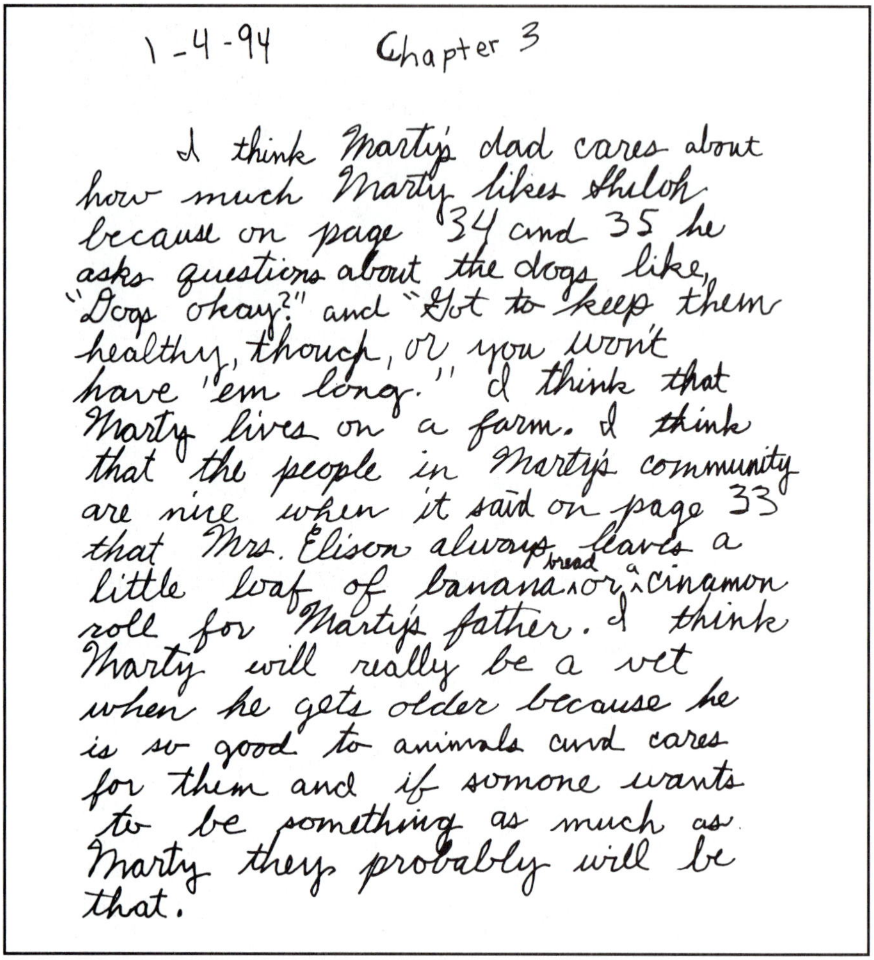

> 1 -4 -94   Chapter 3
>
> I think Marty's dad cares about how much Marty likes Shiloh because on page 34 and 35 he asks questions about the dogs, like, "Dogs okay?" and "Got to keep them healthy, though, or you won't have 'em long." I think that Marty lives on a farm. I think that the people in Marty's community are nice when it said on page 33 that Mrs. Elison always leaves a little loaf of banana or cinamon bread roll for Marty's father. I think Marty will really be a vet when he gets older because he is so good to animals and cares for them and if somone wants to be something as much as Marty they probably will be that.

Figure 10.4—Fourth Grader's Written Response to *Shiloh*

Source: Naylor (1991).

more easily (or lack of it hindered their reading), whether the author was qualified to write the material (especially expository material), what the author needed to know to write the piece, and so on.

Pamela asks some of the following questions when meeting with her groups:

1. What makes it easy for you to read this book?

2. What helps you deal with vocabulary you do not already know?

3. How does using the context make it easier for you when you come to ideas and words you may not know?

A diorama of a favorite scene extends comprehension of a book.

© Howard Dratch/The Image Works

4. What do you know about the topic of this book that may help you as you read?

5. Have you had any experiences related to the topic of your book?

6. How do you use those experiences to make reading the book easier?

7. How can you deal with changes in setting in the book and still understand what is happening?

8. How do prologues and epilogues help you as you read? Do they help you predict or better understand the book you have read?

9. How does the author's use of tension and conflict affect you as a reader, pulling you through the book? (Porterfield, 1993, p. 26)

Pamela has worked out her own system for literature studies, but knows that teachers and children have to determine what works best in each classroom. Figure 10.5 is an outline of possibilities for literature studies, but it is not a prescribed program.

In their book *Grand Conversations* (1990), Peterson and Eeds developed a checklist for evaluating student's response to the literature studies and a form for recording the student's preparation and participation in the studies

LITERATURE STUDY GROUPS

Primary Grades	Older Readers
Teacher presents a choice of books	Teacher selects and presents books
Children select book to read	Children select book to read
Teacher leads reading	Children read book independently
Reading from a Big Book (if possible)	Children keep a log of reading responses
Children and teacher discuss book	Children participate in group discussions of reading
Children draw or write a response to book	Extension activities
Children participate in group discussions of reading	Children create posters, bookmarks, bulletin board
Rereading experiences	based on book
Assisted reading	Children participate in written conversations (serial
Echo reading	comments on paper, ultimately returned to originator)
Teacher reads, children join in when possible	about book
Children read in pairs	Children create songs, dances, drama based on book
Children read individually	Children share poetry or special passages from book
Extension activities	Evaluation
Children write or dictate a story based on model of book	Evidence of reflective thinking in discussion/writing
Children draw/paint illustrations, murals, posters	Children's evaluation of reading/writing
Children create puppet plays, mime activities, drama	Children's increasing ability in literacy
based on book	Critical reading
Children review other books on same theme, by same	Writing techniques modeled in individual writing
author, and so on	Comprehension
Evaluation	Other reading goals
Participation in selecting, reading books	
Increasing ability in literacy skills	
Motivation/interest in reading	

Figure 10.5—Literature Study Group Activities

Source: Based on Watson (1988, December).

(Figures 10.6 and 10.7). Both of these forms should prove useful in helping teachers evaluate and plan for further literature studies.

Skills instruction is handled in the small groups, and often one child will teach another what is needed to read and understand a passage in the book. Whole-group instruction is offered in mini-lessons that reflect the needs of the group. These lessons focus on decoding skills, writing skills, or whatever the class needs at the time.

At Pamela's school, she is allowed to order book sets of eight copies of each title that she selects rather than spending the money on basal readers. She trades titles with some of the other teachers and the library now owns several hundred book sets, so finding books is not a problem, although it was more difficult when she started her program.

Reading Based on a Theme

Mr. Fred Camden has been teaching for several years. He believes in the value of literature-based reading instruction, but chooses to organize his classroom instruction around themes. He has a different theme every two or three weeks during the school year. So far this year the children have read on the environment, homelessness, justice, survival, and other big issues that Fred believes are important. He also puts in a reader's choice theme at least twice a year, so that children choose their own topic and develop their own interests. He chooses core books for each theme and everyone must read at least one of the core books. He also supplies a list of other books from which children must choose one or two other books to read (depending on the length of the theme). He tries

---

Response to Literature Checklist

	Often	Occasionally	Rarely
I. Enjoyment/Involvement			
• Is aware of a variety of reading materials and can select those he or she enjoys reading.	——	——	——
• Enjoys looking at pictures in picture storybooks.	——	——	——
• Responds with emotion to text: laughs, cries, smiles.	——	——	——
• Can get "lost" in a book.	——	——	——
• Chooses to read during free time.	——	——	——
• Wants to go on reading when time is up.	——	——	——
• Shares reading experiences with classmates.	——	——	——
• Has books on hand to read.	——	——	——
• Chooses books in different genres.	——	——	——
II. Making Personal Connections			
• Seeks meaning in both pictures and the text in picture storybooks.	——	——	——
• Can identify the work of authors that he or she enjoys.	——	——	——
• Sees literature as a way of knowing about the world.	——	——	——
• Draws on personal experiences in constructing meaning.	——	——	——
• Draws on earlier reading experiences in making meaning from a text.	——	——	——
III. Interpretation/Making Meaning			
• Gets beyond "I like" in talking about story.	——	——	——
• Makes comparisons between the works of individual authors and compares the work of different authors.	——	——	——
• Appreciates the value of pictures in picture storybooks and uses them to interpret story meaning.	——	——	——
• Asks questions and seeks out the help of others to clarify meaning.	——	——	——
• Makes reasonable predictions about what will happen in story.	——	——	——
• Can disagree without disrupting the dialogue.	——	——	——
• Can follow information important to getting the meaning of the story.	——	——	——
• Attends to multiple levels of meaning.	——	——	——
• Is willing to think and search out alternative points of view.	——	——	——
• Values other perspectives as a means for increasing interpretative possibilities.	——	——	——
• Turns to text to verify and clarify ideas.	——	——	——
• Can modify interpretations in light of "new evidence."	——	——	——
• Can make implied relationships not stated in the text.	——	——	——
• Can make statements about author's intent drawn from the total work.	——	——	——
• Is secure enough to put forward new ideas to benefit from others' responses.	——	——	——

Figure 10.6—Checklist of Responses to Literature

Source: From *Grand Conversations: Literature Groups in Action* by Ralph Peterson and Maryann Eeds, p. 71. Copyright by Scholastic, Inc. Reprinted by permission of Scholastic, Inc.

IV. **Insight into Elements Authors Control in Making Story**
- Is growing in awareness of how elements
  function in story.   _____   _____   _____
- Can talk meaningfully about:
  - characters   _____   _____   _____
  - setting   _____   _____   _____
  - mood   _____   _____   _____
  - incident   _____   _____   _____
  - structure   _____   _____   _____
  - symbol   _____   _____   _____
  - time   _____   _____   _____
  - tensions   _____   _____   _____
- Draws on elements when interpreting text/constructing
  meaning with others.   _____   _____   _____
- Uses elements of literature in working to improve
  upon stories written.   _____   _____   _____
- Is intrigued by how authors work.   _____   _____   _____
- Makes use of elements in making comparisons.   _____   _____   _____

Figure 10.6 (*continued*)

to allow students as much choice as possible in their reading and in the activities they choose to do.

Some activities to accompany each theme are designed to be completed by the class; others are individual. The current theme in Fred's class is on World War II and is organized in the following way:

World War II

Theme: Ordinary People Do Extraordinary Things

Reading Goals

▼ Evaluates plot structures, character development, and settings

▼ Compares the work of several authors on the same topics

▼ States purpose or goal for reading

▼ Uses word identification strategies to read fluently

▼ Summarizes, clarifies, questions, and predicts while reading

Writing Goals

▼ Identifies purpose for writing

▼ Identifies audience for writing

Record of Preparation for and Participation in Literature Study*

Name_____ Date_____

Author_____ Title_____

Preparation for Literature Study

Brought book to group.   Yes _____   No _____

Contributed to developing a group reading plan.   Yes _____   No _____

Worked according to group plan.   Yes _____   No _____

Read the book.   Yes _____   No _____

Took note of places to share
(ones of interest, ones that were puzzling, etc.)   Yes _____   No _____

Did nightly assignments as they arose from the day's discussion.   Yes _____   No _____

Participation in Literature Study

Overall participation in the dialogue.   Weak _____   Good _____   Excellent _____

Overall quality of responses.   Weak _____   Good _____   Excellent _____

Referred to text to support
ideas and to clarify.**   Weak _____   Good _____   Excellent _____

Listened to others and modified responses
where there was reason to do so.**   Weak _____   Good _____   Excellent _____

_____**

_____**

* We suggest using this form at the end of a literature study to evaluate each literature study participant.
** The rest of the items are intended to tailor this evaluation for your individual students. Choose appropriate items to finish the evaluation from those listed in the Response to Literature Checklist, or add those you think are most appropriate.

Figure 10.7—Checklist for Preparation for Participation in Literature Study

Source: From *Grand Conversations: Literature Groups in Action* by Ralph Peterson and Maryann Eeds, p. 73. Copyright by Scholastic, Inc. Reprinted by permission of Scholastic, Inc.

▼   Decides organization for writing task

▼   Revises and edits as appropriate

Social Studies Goals

▼   Describes and explains significant events in world history

▼   Researchs and identifies people and issues that are important in American history

Art Goals

▼   Arranges different media using processes of joining into either a two- or three-dimensional composition

▼   Demonstrates ability to work with craft processes

▼   Recognizes media and techniques observed in adult art

Activities

1. Read at least one of the core books. Be prepared for group discussions and other activities.

2. Read at least two other books on World War II, fiction or nonfiction. Keep a response log. The log should have a minimum of three entries for each book.

3. Contribute at least two pieces of information to be included in a time line from 1938 to 1946. This information will include information about the war, about inventions, about science, and so on.

4. Create a "museum" for one of the books you read. Displays in the museum can be gathered, made, drawn, or sculpted. Each piece should be accompanied by an information card that explains its significance in the book.

5. Make a puppet of the character you selected for Who's Who.

6. Select an individual who played a significant role in World War II. Write a one-page biography of that person. These biographies will be collected and displayed as a Who's Who on a World War II bulletin board.

7. Research and write a two-page paper on a topic related to World War II. These topics include causes of World War II; effects on daily life of World War II (in the United States or in Europe); major battles in Europe, Africa, or the Pacific; the French resistance movement; Pearl Harbor; fascism; Nazism; concentration camps; Japanese internment camps; or other topics if you discuss them with your teacher.

8. Interview someone in your community about his or her experiences in World War II as a civilian or as a part of the military forces. Contribute to the development of an interview guide sheet.

9. Take notes on the presentation of a guest speaker(s).

10. Use a large wall map of Europe drawn at the time of World War II. Compare that map with a current map. How have the political boundaries changed? Which boundaries are still the same?

Organizational Suggestions

1. Introduce the unit with a KWL organizer—what we know, what we want to know, and what we learned. Begin by drawing three columns on a very large piece of paper. Label the first, *Know;* the second, What We *Want* to Know; and the third, What We *Learned.* As you discuss the topic with the class, record what they know and their questions. Keep the chart in the room for the duration of the study. Add to it daily (Ogle, 1986).

2. Agree on a time line for the study. When will the core book be completed? The other two books? When will the museum displays and puppets be completed? When will the research papers and biographies be completed?

3. Agree on how the reading logs or response logs will be kept. How many entries per book? Any other requirements?

4. After completing the first section of the organizer (what we know), discuss and agree on some questions to be answered in the unit of study. Read aloud (one each day) *Rose Blanche, Faithful Elephants, Let the Celebrations Begin!, The Lily Cupboard,* and *Hiroshima No Pika.* Take time to discuss each after reading.

5. As the study progresses, answer the questions posed on the first day. Make sure that students note the sources where they found the answers. Each student can keep an inquiry chart to answer questions from his or her reading or research. These answers can then be transferred to the whole-class chart.

Who's Who

Omar Bradley

Neville Chamberlain

Chiang Kai-shek

Winston Churchill

Charles de Gaulle

Dwight Eisenhower

Joseph Goebbels

Herman Goering

Heinrich Himmler

Hirohito

Adolf Hitler

Douglas MacArthur

Bernard Montgomery

Benito Mussolini

Chester Nimitz

Robert Oppenheimer

George Patton

Henri Pétain

Erwin Rommel

Franklin Roosevelt

Albert Speer

Joseph Stalin

Harry Truman

Bibliography

Carrie's War (Bawden, 1973)

Twenty and Ten (Bishop, 1964)

The House of Sixty Fathers (DeJong, 1956)

Rose Blanche (Innocenti, 1985)

When Hitler Stole Pink Rabbit (Kerr, 1971)

Journey to America (Levitin, 1970)

Number the Stars (Lowry, 1989)

Hiroshima No Pika (Maruki, 1980)

Snow Treasure (McSwigan, 1942)

Waiting for Anya (Morpurgo, 1990)

The Lily Cupboard (Oppenheim, 1992)

The Island on Bird Street (Orlev, 1981)

The Upstairs Room (Reiss, 1972)

Faithful Elephants (Tsuchiya, 1988)

Journey to Topaz (Uchida, 1985)

Hide and Seek (Vos, 1991)

Let the Celebrations Begin! (Wild and Vivas, 1991)

The Devil's Arithmetic (Yolen, 1988)

As you can see, this theme incorporates reading, language-arts, and social studies instruction. It also provides for individual work and instruction in both small and large groups. Children work on their theme activities for a large part of each day. Some teachers alternate themes that have an emphasis on science with themes that emphasize social studies and do not otherwise provide instruction in either science or social studies. The advantages of this approach include letting children make choices about their reading, permitting flexibility and choice in when to do the reading, being able to meet individual needs through packet materials, and allowing the opportunity to provide both group and individual instruction. The concerns include the amount of time the teacher must spend in developing the packets and the limitation that individual reading selections places on the children's chances to interact with others who are sharing their reading experience.

Organizing Around Author Studies

Miss Leslie Franklin is a first-grade teacher who is in her second year of teaching. She is organizing her reading instruction around the works of different authors. This year she and her class have studied Ezra Jack Keats, Pat Hutchins, Bill Martin Jr, Elizabeth Howard, and now Eric Carle. Her plans for a study of Eric Carle are as follows:

Bibliography

Animals Animals. Philomel, 1989

Do You Want to Be My Friend? Crowell, 1987

Dragons, Dragons, Philomel, 1991

Draw Me a Star, Philomel, 1992

The Grouchy Ladybug. Scholastic, 1977

Have You Seen My Cat? Scholastic, 1987

A House for Hermit Crab. Picture Book Studio, 1987

The Mixed-Up Chameleon. Harper & Row, 1975

1, 2, 3 to the Zoo: A Counting Book. Philomel, 1968

Pancakes, Pancakes! Picture Book Studio, 1990

Papa, Please Get the Moon for Me. Picture Book Studio, 1986

Rooster's Off to See the World. Picture Book Studio, 1972

The Secret Birthday Message. Harper & Row, 1972

Today Is Monday, Philomel, 1993

The Very Busy Spider. Philomel, 1984

The Very Hungry Caterpillar. Philomel, 1969

The Very Quiet Cricket. Philomel, 1990

Writing and Reading

▼ Choose another animal and write a very _____ _____ story

▼ Write a secret message

in code

with disappearing ink

▼ Write a text for *Do You Want to Be My Friend?*

▼ Write a story about the mouse in *1, 2, 3 to the Zoo.*

▼ Find all the words to describe greetings in *The Very Quiet Cricket* and make a collection of other categories of words—words for saying good-bye, words for describing walking, etc.

▼ For Carle's first book, the editor helped him with the concept of the book. What is the editor's job as he or she works with an author?

▼ Compare the stories of Eric Carle. Find any similarities of style. How many have predictable language patterns?

▼ In the collections of poetry, would you have selected the same poems? Find other animal poems or dragon poems and evaluate Carle's decision.

▼ What did the author have to know to write each of the books?

▼ On some of the book jackets, Carle discusses how he got the idea for the story. How do authors get ideas about writing?

▼ How does Carle make his books interesting for the reader? Is there a surprise or a problem to be solved?

▼ Compare Carle's *A House for Hermit Crab* to McDonald's *Is This a House for Hermit Crab?* (1990). She wrote the book because a hermit crab got loose in her house and her family helped her look in various places for it. In the book, the crab tries on different things that might really be found at the beach.

▼ Compare Carle's *Pancakes, Pancakes!* to dePaola's *Pancakes for Breakfast* (1978). Do they include the same ingredients? What similarities/differences are there in the stories? Create the text for *Pancakes for Breakfast.*

▼ Compare Carle's *Papa, Please Get the Moon for Me* to Thurber's *Many Moons* (1990). How did the author's use the changing phases of the moon as a basis for a story? What is similar and what is different about the stories?

▼ The subtitle of Carle's *Dragons, Dragons* is *& Other Creatures That Never Were.* Find other dragon stories in the library such as Grahame's *The Reluctant Dragon* (1938) or Nash's *Custard & Company* (1980). Write descriptions of dragons.

▼ Try writing some poetry about animals or other creatures.

Children exhibit interest in a wide variety of reading material.

© Joel Gordon

Art

▼ Try illustrating with tissue collage. Explore how Carle creates shades and depth with tissue.

▼ Look at the end papers in the books. How do they relate to the content of the book? How do you think the decision was made about the end papers?

▼ Some of the collages are enhanced with pencil lines. Can an artist use more than one media to create an impression?

▼ Several of the books have cut and/or folded pages. This costs more than plain pages. Why do you think they are included?

▼ Try making a book with either cutouts or foldouts on the pages.

▼ Read Irvine's book, *How to Make Pop-Ups* (1987). Learn to make one kind of pop-up art in a book of your own.

▼ Create caterpillars or dragons from other materials such as clay.

Science

▼ Look at the life cycle of the caterpillar in *The Very Hungry Caterpillar.* Observe a real caterpillar life cycle. Keep records of the changes in the caterpillar.

▼ Order some ladybugs for the classroom. Learn about the life cycle of the ladybug and about their usefulness in insect control. Invite an organic gardener to speak to the class about using insects to control pests rather than pesticides. Learn the traditional rhyme about ladybugs.

▼ Learn about the life cycle of the hermit crab. Keep a hermit crab in an aquarium. Observe its behavior. Provide different materials that could possibly provide shelter for a hermit crab and observe the one it chooses. Compare the behavior of hermit crabs to other species of crabs. Read the entry in the encyclopedia about hermit crabs. Were the authors of the two books about hermit crabs accurate in their descriptions?

▼ Compare all the different cats in *Have You Seen My Cat?* What characteristics do they share? Where might you find these cats? Locate the habitats on a map.

▼ Keep a spider (or several spiders of different varieties) in the classroom. If you put a small tree branch with several twigs or limbs on it upright in a deep dishpan, the spider will spin its web on the branches and will not leave the pan. Observe the web. Observe the life cycle of spiders. Discuss the classification of spiders and learn why they are arachnids rather than insects. What purpose do spiders serve in insect pest control?

▼ Study the phases of the moon in *Papa, Please Get the Moon for Me.* Does the moon change or does its appearance change? How does a mask or costume change the person wearing it? Read about the phases of the moon in a reference book. Was Carle accurate in describing the changes?

▼ Observe a chameleon for several days. What changes can a chameleon really make? Why does it make these changes? Read reference material to learn how to care for a chameleon.

▼ Learn about the insects that the cricket meets in *The Very Quiet Cricket.* Keep a cricket in the classroom and learn how to care for it. Write a manual for caring for a cricket.

Basic Knowledge

▼ In *The Very Hungry Caterpillar*, review numbers and days of the week.

▼ In *1, 2, 3 to the Zoo*, review numbers. Create your own counting book with animals of the desert (or your own region).

▼ In *A House for Hermit Crab*, review the months of the year.

▼ In *The Grouchy Ladybug*, review the concept of time passing. Note the clocks and the position of the sun.

▼ In *Rooster's Off to See the World*, review number concepts.

▼ Review seriation by size in *The Grouchy Ladybug*.

Enrichment Experiences

▼ Cook some pancakes. Look at several recipes for pancakes. Select one and make it. Talk about the sequence of ingredients and procedures. Eat the pancakes, of course.

▼ Construct appropriate habitats for classroom pets (crabs, crickets, spiders, etc.). Learn to follow the directions given in reference material.

Leslie has been able to provide skills instruction as needed by individual children as they read the book or books they have selected and in small or whole groups in mini skills lessons. Children who need more help in decoding are grouped for instruction using one of Carle's repetitive books. She believes the children benefit from repeated oral readings of the stories, uses Big Books when she has them for instruction, and provides shared and guided reading for individuals and small groups. Organizing instruction around the work of one author does not mean simply collecting the books and making a comparison chart, but it does provide children with authentic reasons to be learning to read and write.

Reading by Genre

Finally we visit the classroom of Mrs. Diana Garcia. She teaches sixth grade and enjoys organizing the reading her class does around different genres of children's literature. These genres generally include the broad categories of biography, historical fiction, realistic fiction, poetry, traditional literature, and modern fantasy. Within these categories one might also distinguish science fiction, mysteries, sports stories, and so on.

Diana explained to the parents that she believes in children having as many choices as she can arrange, so she selects most of the books but will accept a child's choice if it fits the genre being studied. Sometimes she has weeks when the children are engaged in individualized reading of their own choice and sometimes she handles the books in a genre by organizing literature study groups. The fantasy unit that follows is one example of what she does in preparing for a genre study:

Reading Goals

▼ Evaluates plot structures, character development, and settings

▼ Compares the work of several authors on the same topics

▼ States purpose or goal for reading

▼ Uses word identification strategies to read fluently

▼ Summarizes, clarifies, questions, and predicts while reading

Writing Goals

▼ Identifies purpose for writing

▼ Identifies audience for writing

▼ Decides organization for writing task

▼ Revises and edits as appropriate

Art Goals

▼ Arranges different media using processes of joining into either a two- or three-dimensional composition

▼ Demonstrates ability to work with craft processes

▼ Recognizes media and techniques observed in adult art

Bibliography

The Book of Three (Alexander, 1964)

The Black Cauldron (Alexander, 1965)

The Castle of Llyr (Alexander, 1966)

Taran Wanderer (Alexander, 1967)

The High King (Alexander, 1968)

The Search for Delicious (Babbitt, 1969)

Knee-Knock Rise (Babbitt, 1970)

Tuck Everlasting (Babbitt, 1975)

The Eyes of the Amaryllis (Babbitt, 1977)

Nellie: A Cat on Her Own (Babbitt, 1989)

The Dark Is Rising (Cooper, 1973)

The Grey King (Cooper, 1975)

The Selkie Girl (Cooper, 1986)

James and the Giant Peach (Dahl, 1961)

Charlie and the Chocolate Factory (Dahl, 1964)

Charlie and the Great Glass Elevator (Dahl, 1972)

The BFG (Dahl, 1982)

The Witches (Dahl, 1983)

The 21 Balloons (duBois, 1947)

The Halfmen of O (Gee, 1982)

The Haunted Mountain (Hunter, 1972)

A Stranger Came Ashore (Hunter, 1975)

The Mermaid Summer (Hunter, 1988)

A Wrinkle in Time (L'Engle, 1962)

A Wind in the Door (L'Engle, 1973)

Dragons in the Waters (L'Engle, 1976)

A Swiftly Tilting Planet (L'Engle, 1978)

Many Waters (L'Engle, 1986)

A Wizard of Earthsea (Le Guin, 1968)

The Tombs of Atuan (Le Guin, 1971)

The Farthest Shore (Le Guin, 1972)

Tehanu (Le Guin, 1990)

A Ride on the Red Mare's Back (Le Guin, 1992)

The Chronicles of Narnia (Lewis, 1950–1956)

The Blue Sword (McKinley, 1982)

The Hero and the Crown (McKinley, 1984)

Mrs. Frisby and the Rats of NIMH (O'Brien, 1971)

The Hobbit (Tolkien, 1966 [1938])

Dragon's Blood (Yolen, 1982)

Heart's Blood (Yolen, 1984)

A Sending of Dragons (Yolen, 1987)

Class or Small-Group Activities (Led by Teacher)

1. After students select the book of fantasy they are going to read, ask them to pay especially careful attention to the descriptions of the characters. They can make illustrations of one or more of the characters. Provide them with a list of physical attributes and have them write a physical description of a character they invent. The next day, give them a list of psychological attributes and have them write a psychological description of their character. They can exchange descriptions and create an illustration from someone's descriptions.

2. Teach a mini-lesson on writing leads. How do authors of fantasy get the reader hooked?

3. Collect a set of common objects and discuss how they are used and what they reveal about our culture. Collect a set of strange objects. Tell the students they are from planet X and repeat the exercise. (They do not have to be real objects. Make some objects from aluminum foil, funnels, and so on.)

4. Discuss the techniques used by the various authors to transport their characters to another planet or time. If the story begins on a planet, is there an explanation about how the characters got there originally?

5. Demonstrate how to use a graphic organizer for cause and effect.

6. Spend some time each day imagining. Brainstorm in whole or small groups about characters, settings, plots, and so on.

Activity Suggestions

1. Write character descriptions including both physical and psychological characteristics.

2. Create maps of the lands described and/or maps of the travels of the characters.

3. Develop a code that would be used in the land where their fantasy is set.

4. Develop a chart that lists what is real and what is not (or scientifically possible or not, at this time).

5. Create a museum for their book, objects that are important to the story and descriptions of the objects. After they arrange their display, they can act as docents giving tours of their display.

6. Use a graphic organizer to keep track of the cause and effects in the various stories.

7. Write descriptions of how to get their characters from this planet to the fantasy land in three different ways.

8. Stage an "invention convention." Have students think about and list needs for the world, the school, the family, and themselves. Invent something that would fulfill one of the identified needs.

9. Write a newspaper story about the major events in the book. One story could be a news story format that answers the five questions—where, when, what, who, how. Another might be a feature story, a cartoon, an editorial, and so on. If enough students are interested, a complete newspaper could be produced.

10. Design the costumes in case your book is made into a movie.

11. Write poetry (a choice of forms) about the characters, settings, or events in your book.

12. Create an economy for the land of your setting that includes money or a bartering system.

13. Find some articles in newsmagazines about new technologies in science or medicine, for example, and add these or a variation of them to a story of your own.

14. Create a magic object and describe what it does.

15. Create posters for your book when it is made into a movie.

Organizational Suggestions

1. Introduce the study by reading *A Ride on the Red Mare's Back* (Le Guin, 1992) and the next day *Nellie: A Cat on Her Own* (Babbitt, 1989). Discuss the elements that would make these books fantasy.

2. Agree on a time line for the study. When will the museum displays and puppets be completed? When will the inventions be completed? When will the character descriptions and other writing assignments be completed?

3. Agree on how the reading logs or response logs will be kept. How many entries per book? Any other requirements?

4. Make a bulletin board caption with space for displaying projects. Decide how other writing projects will be handled. Bound in a class book? Posted on the bulletin board? Traded with another class studying fantasy?

5. Make table space available for their book museum displays.

Mrs. Garcia keeps portfolios of the work of the children and uses those to plan the next steps in instruction. She uses the language-arts period each day for the children to read, to provide mini-lessons as needed, to read aloud, and to provide individual skill instruction as needed. Reading instruction, no matter how it is organized, takes planning and dedicated work on the part of the teacher.

Major Ideas in This Chapter

▼ Children's literature is important in providing motivation and interest in the reading/writing program.

▼   Children will be more likely to want to read real books than portions of
a book designed for reading instruction. Teachers must select good-
quality literature for use in the classroom.

▼   Criteria for selection include plot, theme, setting, characters, and style.
In selecting picture books, the illustrations must also be considered.

▼   Literature can serve as a core for many curriculum experiences that will
contribute to the goals of the teacher and many reading and writing
experiences that are authentic and interesting. Classroom libraries need
to reflect the interests of the children and the varied abilities of the
readers.

▼   Teachers can organize their literature programs around a topic, an
author, a genre of literature, or children can read individually. Each of
these organizational patterns offers children many choices in reading
material and in activities that will interest them.

Discussion Questions: Focusing on the Teacher You Are Becoming

1.   How do you select books for your own reading? Can you use any of
the same techniques to help children select books in a classroom?

2.   Compare and contrast the various approaches to organizing reading
instruction around literature presented in this chapter.

3.   Discuss the place of literature in the reading program: Should it be the
basic source of reading material or should literature activities be for
enrichment?

4.   How can teachers avoid inauthentic follow-up activities to accompany
literature in the classroom?

Field-Based Applications

1.   Choose a picture book and develop plans for extended reading and
writing activities based on the book.

2.   Develop a unit based on a folktale, a topic of study in science or social
studies, an author, an illustrator, or a genre of literature.

3.   Plan a writing experience (not a narrative) based on children's
literature.

4. Choose a book for reading aloud and practice reading it well. List as many possibilities as you can for children's growth from the reading experience (vocabulary, listening, language patterns, and so on).

5. Participate with some of your peers in a literature study group. Keep a log of your responses to your own reading and to the group's discussions. Many teachers are arranging such studies with their colleagues because it is so difficult to find time to read for pleasure in a busy professional life. Try it, you'll like it!

Chapter 11
Assisting Children with Content-Area Reading

Chapter Overview

▼ Content-area reading—the reading of expository texts—presents challenges to the reader not found in narrative texts. Our job has been done well when students can draw on their background experiences and create meaning while interacting with expository texts.

▼ Content-area texts challenge readers with special text structures, a heavy concept load and thus a difficult vocabulary, and special text features such as graphs and charts, calling for a variety of instructional strategies.

▼ Content-area instruction presents special writing challenges to children. Writing activities need to be linked to content-area instruction so the content texts become models for expository writing.

Content-Area Reading

Reading in the content areas has become a common topic in reading instruction. What does the term *content areas* mean? The concept of content areas is confusing because *all* reading has content. Mystery stories have content. Poetry has content. A grocery list has content! Without content, we cannot read. So why call certain reading selections "content-area reading"? We do not have a really good answer. Traditionally, those subjects that involve factual, expository writing, such as science, social studies, and health, have come to be known as content areas. This usage is not intended to imply that other kinds of writing, such as fictional prose or poetry, lack content.

Let's reexamine our definition of reading comprehension. In Chapter 8 we said, "Thus we define *comprehension* as the interaction of the author's ideas and the reader's schemata that results in the creation of meaning." It is crucial, as students read in the content areas, that we keep this definition of comprehension—and therefore of reading, because reading is comprehension—in mind. Because comprehension is the primary objective in content-area reading, we need to help the student draw on his or her background experiences to create meaning in interacting with the text. Three important conditions support comprehension of content texts: motivation, authentic activities, and extensive reading.

Supporting Conditions

1. Readers' comprehension of content texts is enhanced by strong motivation to read the material. This condition assumes that teachers create background experiences—and ways to draw on students' background experiences—so readers approach text with heightened interest and motivation. Field trips, television, film, trade books, magazines, speakers, news media, and artifacts all work to build interest in, and schemata for, reading content texts. Therefore, exposure to them increases students' likelihood of success.

2. Comprehension is heightened by authentic classroom activities that draw on content-area knowledge, among them activities that provide real reasons to write. The guiding of content reading will be effective when children see real reasons to read and real, authentic activities that grow out of that reading. An assignment to "read and answer the questions" is not enough. Content materials should be read as resource materials in instructional units and thematic units and as part of real problem-solving situations.

3. Just as we cannot teach children to ride a tricycle by giving pedaling lessons first, then steering lessons, so we cannot teach children to read content texts by teaching them first to read isolated, specialized vocabulary, then to read headings and subheadings, and then to read the text. Content-area reading skills are learned by reading content-area texts. Helping students deal with the challenges of content texts *as they read them* will help them learn to read content material effectively.

Reading Challenges in Content-Area Materials

Reading and writing about content-area subjects present challenges to students far greater than those posed by the reading and writing of fiction texts. In 1987 Flood and Lapp reported that the content of basal readers was almost exclusively literary. Sixty-five percent of the selections and 72% of the pages in eight basal programs studied were either narratives or poems. Although the authors of the new basal series have made efforts to change the amount of expository reading, the majority of reading in basals is still narrative; expository selections are rarely included. A look at the table of contents of any of the new basals reveals about five to six times more literary pieces than expository pieces. The expository reading that is required in science, social studies, mathematics, and health presents text structures, sentence structures, and specialized vocabulary that are foreign to narrative reading. Writing about content subjects requires the use of new formats, sentence structures, and vocabulary. The schemata that children bring to content-area reading may not accommodate the new concepts presented. In fact, children may have no background, very limited background, or inaccurate information about topics covered in content-area texts. In these cases teachers have to plan activities that provide the experiences children need to build the images required to make sense of expository writing. Teachers must be aware that reading instruction should begin with developmental, recreational, and functional reading and that reading instruction of all these types must continue throughout the grades. The old saying that children learn to read in primary grades and read to learn in intermediate grades is not true.

The reading of content-area texts presents special challenges to the reader. Three major reading challenges posed by content-area texts are text structure, specialized vocabulary occasioned by heavy concept load, and special text features.

First Challenge: Text Structure

The overall organization of an expository text, as well as its sentence and paragraph structures, differs from the features of narrative writing, with which children have typically had more experience. Compare the excerpts from a fifth-grade story about a boy who is trying to photograph cranes and an expository piece about cranes in Figures 11.1 and 11.2. What differences do you see in the structures of the two passages? The story selection has a plot, setting, and characters. Dialogue helps the reader create meaning. In the

---

IN SEARCH OF A SANDHILL CRANE

Link cooked an early dinner at his campsite and then, with his sleeping bag and enough food for breakfast, he hiked back through the woods to a spot not far from the "blind" he had made—a hiding place of cut bushes from which he could watch the birds without being seen. He slept well and got up a short while before dawn and ate a cold breakfast of a banana, two pieces of bread, and a slice of cold ham. He would have liked a cup of hot coffee and an egg, but he did not want any smoke rising from a campfire to alarm the cranes. When he had finished he carried his sleeping bag out to his blind and made a comfortable spot where he could sit or lie while he waited. He had scarcely settled himself when Olson appeared. The wildlife expert had come up quietly and Link had no idea he was around until he was within a few feet of the blind. . . .

Olson inspected and loaded his gun—not with bullets, but with tranquilizing darts. Link checked his camera as the field grew lighter.

"Cranes eat seeds, berries, roots, worms, bugs, almost anything," Olson said. "My guess is that at this time of the year it's grasshoppers and bugs that they're after in a place like this. You'll want to wait until the sun gets up a ways so you will have good light for your pictures. They'll hang around for several hours if they come, so there's plenty of time."

Figure 11.1—Sample Narrative Text

Source: From *In Search of a Sandhill Crane* by Keith Robertson. Copyright ©1973 by Keith Robertson. Used by permission of Viking Penguin, a division of Penguin Books USA, Inc.

> **SANDHILL CRANES**
>
> Each year, sandhill cranes migrate from their nesting grounds in the North to wintering grounds in the Southwest. They sometimes fly at altitudes of 10,000 feet or more.
>
> After the eggs—usually two—are laid, the mother and father crane take turns sitting on the nest. The eggs, three to four inches long, hatch in about 32 days. The crane chick can walk and swim when it is a few hours old.
>
> The crane's long toes keep it from sinking into mud at the bottom of the marsh. Its long legs, long neck, and long bill help it to walk about in marshlands and catch fish. Cranes eat a great variety of foods, including worms, frogs, small snakes, and grasshoppers, as well as grain and other vegetation. A sandhill crane will sometimes eat 500 grasshoppers and worms a day.

Figure 11.2—Sample Expository Text

Source: Excerpt from "Sandhill Cranes" in *HBJ Reading Program, Level 11, Reader 5, Landmarks* by Margaret Early, Bernice E. Cullinan, Roger C. Farr, W. Dorsey Hammond, Nancy Santeusenio, and Dorothy S. Strickland, copyright ©1987 by Harcourt Brace & Company, reprinted by permission of the publisher.

expository piece there is no plot, setting, or story characters. Instead, each sentence presents one or more facts. In the narrative piece, the facts about cranes are woven into the story. In the expository piece the facts are simply presented, to be remembered by the reader. The mental images that are built by the reader in the story selection are very different from those that must be built in the expository selection. The reading challenge is to move from dealing with story structure to dealing with processing facts in such a way that they make sense to the reader.

Second Challenge: Specialized Vocabulary

Comprehending a text heavily laden with concepts, which are labeled by a specialized vocabulary, presents a challenge to the reader. It is impossible to write about content subjects without using specialized vocabularies. Despite authors' attempts to write in simple language, the expository selection must inevitably present the reader with vocabulary challenges. It would be ridiculous, for example, to write a piece about the Constitution and avoid the multisyllabic word *Constitution* by referring to it as "the big paper."

Figure 11.3 is an excerpt from a third-grade science selection. Consider the specialized vocabulary the author must use in order to write accurately about precipitation and the reader must relate to his or her schemata in order to create meaning.

Reexamine the selection in Figure 11.3, asking the question, "Can this selection be made any easier?" Our answer is no. When authors attempt to write expository material without using the necessary technical vocabulary, they have simplified the selection—often to the point of rendering it meaningless. An editorial in the *San Francisco Chronicle* on September 13, 1988,

---

PRECIPITATION

Both the waterdrops or ice crystals in clouds are very small. They are so small they hang in the air. Sometimes the drops or crystals grow too large. When they grow large enough, they are too heavy to stay in the air. The drops or crystals fall to the ground. Water that falls from clouds is called precipitation (prih sihp uh TAY shun).

Rain and snow are two kinds of precipitation. Rain is liquid water that falls when the air is warmer than 0 degrees C. Snow is made of ice crystals that fall when the air is colder.

Sleet and hail are two other kinds of precipitation. Sleet is frozen rain. Some hail is formed from many layers of ice. The picture shows hailstones. Why might it be dangerous to be out in a hailstorm?

Figure 11.3—Vocabulary Challenge

Source: *Accent on Science*, Grade 5 (Columbus, Ohio: Charles E. Merrill, 1983), p. 123. Reprinted by permission of Macmillan Publishing, Inc.

decried the practice of "dumbing down" books, calling it "insulting." Reporting an example in which Goldilocks ate fish when she entered the three bears' house, the editors suggested that the book's publishers had apparently decided children could not understand—or learn—what porridge is. Such violations of the original language of a story occur when publishers rely too heavily on readability formulas to simplify the text. They also occur in nonfiction texts.

Readability formulas are based on a shaky hypothesis that language complexity can be assessed by measuring sentence length and by counting syllables (Brewer, Jenkins, & Harp, 1984). The hypothesis is that longer sentences and multisyllabic words are more difficult to read than shorter sentences and one-syllable words. Yet experienced teachers readily acknowledge that children can read words like *airplane, transformer, Tyrannosaurus Rex*, and *birthday* much more easily than shorter words such as *these, this, there*, and *their*. When we try to write nonfiction without using the essential vocabulary, we have dumbed down the text past all usefulness. Instead of counting syllables and words per sentence, we should be asking whether the children for whom a piece is written can understand it. Perhaps even more important is the question of whether or not children will find their expectations about how language works confirmed by the text. Dumbed-down texts do not meet children's expectations about how language works.

Teachers may need to plan special instruction to help children clarify the meanings of vocabulary words or develop the concepts needed so the reading material can be understood. If the material is about caterpillars, then perhaps observing and discussing a caterpillar prior to the reading would provide enough information for the child to develop adequate concepts. Films, videos, filmstrips, photographs, and other media may help fill the gap when real experiences are impossible.

DERMIS

The dermis is much thicker than the epidermis. It may be three or more millimeters thick. The dermis is made of living cells. Nerves and blood vessels are in this layer of skin. Blood supplies food and oxygen to the skin cells. The blood also takes away cell wastes.

The dermis contains hair roots and some glands. **Glands** are special groups of cells which produce and store substances. Some glands are oil glands. They release an oily liquid which keeps the skin soft and smooth.

The oil rises to the skin's surface through pores. **Pores** are small openings in the skin. The pores let the oil travel from the glands in the dermis to the skin's surface.

Figure 11.4—Sample Text: Dermis

Source: *Accent on Science*, Grade 5 (Columbus, Ohio: Charles E. Merrill, 1983), pp. 138–139. Reprinted by permission of Macmillan Publishing, Inc.

Third Challenge: Special Text Features

Content-area reading assignments require students to attend to features of the text that are unique to expository writing. Charts, graphs, tables, and maps, as well as subheadings and special ways of highlighting information, are all challenges to readers of expository material. Often the reader must learn to rely on the special text features to make up for a lack of background experience and thus of schemata with which to relate to the text. Read the fifth-grade science selection in Figure 11.4 and then examine the illustration in Figure 11.5. It is easy to imagine that a child would be able to create much

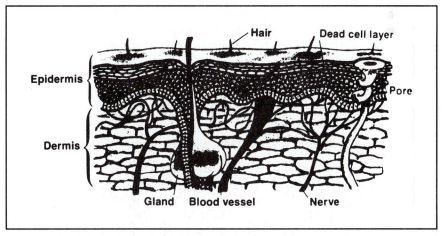

Figure 11.5—Sample Illustration: Dermis

Source: *Accent on Science*, Grade 5 (Columbus, Ohio: Charles E. Merrill, 1983), p. 138. Reprinted by permission of Macmillan Publishing, Inc.

more meaning with the aid of the illustration than without it. However, children have to be taught how to make use of special text features. Otherwise they tend to ignore them!

By teaching we mean pointing out the features to young readers and explaining how they may make use of them to better understand the text. For example, with the illustration of the skin in Figure 11.5, the teacher would help children recognize that this is a cross section of the skin perhaps by demonstrating a cross section of a vegetable. Then the teacher needs to explain how this illustration is magnified so the details are clear. If children had not had experience with magnifying glasses or microscopes, then they would need that experience now. If they were experienced in using magnification and understood that concept then it might only need to be brought to their attention. Illustrations should say how many times a figure is magnified. Only if children understand *how* charts, graphs, tables, and maps improve their understanding will they use them independently. Your reference to them in class discussions (including displaying some special text features with the overhead projector) will illustrate their importance.

Meeting Content-Area Reading Challenges

The activities used to meet content-area reading challenges are either teacher directed or independent. Teacher-directed activities are those the teacher does with children to assist their reading of content texts. Independent activities are things children can learn to do on their own to increase their understanding and use of content texts.

Teacher-Directed Activities

As teachers plan for instruction in content-area reading, they will want to know how difficult a given text is for the children in their class, provide opportunities for children to gain needed background knowledge, teach about text structures, use graphic organizers, provide a wide variety of materials and resources, and teach children vocabulary and concepts needed for comprehension of expository material.

Gauging Children's Ability to Comprehend the Text

The teacher must know for whom the text is too difficult. Not every child in a class can read the social studies or science text with ease and understanding. For example, the fact that a child is in fourth grade does not mean he or she can read the fourth-grade social studies text. The fourth-grade text will contain a considerable range of difficulty, perhaps from third to eighth or ninth grade. The range of reading achievement levels in a typical fourth-grade class stretches from first to sixth or higher. As we move up through the grades, the ranges become even broader.

Science texts provide unusual challenges to the reader.

© Jean-Claude Lejeune/Stock Boston

An effective and efficient way to determine which children will be unable to read a text with good comprehension is the cloze procedure. Studied extensively by John Bormuth (1968), the procedure is based on the assumption that reading is interactive. As readers predict words to fill in blanks, they are calling on their knowledge of syntax as well as their relevant schemata to demonstrate their understanding of the syntactic and semantic relationships within the text.

To construct a cloze test, select a passage of about 250 words in length from each of several places within a textbook. Type the selections, leaving the first and last sentences intact but omitting every fifth or seventh word in the rest of the text. Type a blank line of about 15 spaces where each word is removed. Do not omit proper names. For the process to be reliable, you need a passage incorporating 50 blanks. Have students fill in the blanks.

To score a cloze exercise, count the number of blanks in which the student replaced the *exact* word that had been omitted. If the student exactly replaces 45% to 59% of the words, the selection is probably at the student's instructional level; if 60% or more, at the independent level. If the correct replacements amount to less than 45%, the book is at the reader's frustration level and should not be assigned as independent reading material.

Try filling in the blanks in the following example before you continue reading:

> . . . This shape becomes the body of the clay figure my grandmother teaches me to make. It is the figure of a Pueblo Storyteller.
>
>   Since the early days (1)_____ pueblo life, our people (2)_____ learned about the past (3)_____ listening to storytellers. Until (4)_____, we have never had (5)_____ written language, so many (6)_____ our stories cannot be (7)_____ in books. This is (8)_____ the storyteller is an (9)_____ person in our culture. (10)_____ is also why so many (11)_____ in Cochiti Pueblo make (12)_____ figures of the storyteller.
>
>   (13)_____ my grandmother makes a (14)_____, she always thinks about (15)_____ own grandfather. When she (16)_____ a young girl, she (17)_____ many happy hours in (18)_____ company. In those days, (19)_____ didn't have a television (20)_____ a gas heater. She (21)_____ sit on her grandfather's (22)_____ near a little fireplace (23)_____ the corner of the room (24)_____ listen to him tell stories (25)_____ his life.
>
>   Working on (26)_____ clay figure, my grandmother (27)_____ a face that looks (28)_____ her grandfather's. She gives (29)_____ the traditional hairstyle of (30)_____ pueblo man from the (31)_____ days. She models the clay to show his long hair pulled back in a loop behind his head with a colorful band to hold it in place. (From *Pueblo Storyteller* by Diane Hoyt-Goldsmith [1991], pp. 10–11)

The exact replacements are used because that is the way the original formulas were calculated. You may want to consider synonyms or words that do not change the meaning, because exact words matter much less frequently (directions, recipes, legal agreements, and so on) than words that maintain the meaning.

You might also want to think about how you knew which word went in the blank as you completed the cloze exercise. Think about the various cues and how you employed them and how children might use the cues or how they might have failed to use them. Cloze procedures are often used for reasons other than to determine if a specific text is appropriate for a reader. For such purposes, the cloze procedure can be modified in various ways such as omitting the function words. [The exact replacements are (1) of, (2) have,

(3) by, (4) now, (5) a, (6) of, (7) found, (8) why, (9) important, (10) This, (11) potters, (12) clay, (13) When, (14) Storyteller, (15) her, (16) was, (17) enjoyed, (18) his, (19) they, (20) or, (21) would, (22) lap, (23) in, (24) and, (25) about, (26) the, (27) creates, (28) like, (29) him, (30) a, (31) old.]

Once you know for which of your students the adopted text is too difficult, you can make arrangements for them to read easier material or get the necessary information in another way. Having identified material your students can read, you should engage in important schemata-enhancement activities to assist them in bringing what they know about a topic to a conscious level and to relate their knowledge to their reading.

Providing Schemata-Enhancement Opportunities

Because comprehension depends on the reader's ability to integrate his or her past experiences (schemata) with the author's ideas, it is essential we attend to schemata before children read content texts. Schemata can be enhanced by providing children with experiences by which they may build new schemata or refine existing schemata. Edgar Dale (1969) proposed a Cone of Experience (Figure 11.6, as modified by Rodgers [1975]) that may be helpful to teachers in designing schemata-enhancement activities. Clearly the best schemata-enhancement activities are "direct, purposeful experiences." For example, working in a lumber mill before reading about the role the lumber industry plays in the economy of Pacific Rim countries would be the best form of schemata enhancement. But barring that possibility, a computer simulation of the lumber milling process might be the next best option, followed next by dramatization of working in the lumber mill or of the importance of lumber to economic development. As the teacher's planned activities move up Dale's cone, the likelihood of truly enhancing schemata diminishes. Each step up the cone moves the experience to a more abstract level. The most abstract experience, of course, will be reading the text. The further down the cone the teacher can design schemata-enhancement activities, the more effective they are likely to be.

Focusing on Text Structure

Techniques that help children focus on the organization of content texts assists their understanding. Expository texts are very different from narrative texts. Comparing and contrasting these two kinds of texts and looking at patterns of organization not only increases comprehension of expository texts but improves the writing of expository material.

Comparing and Contrasting Narrative and Exposition

Just as we illustrated in Figures 11.1 and 11.2, share with children both narrative and expository texts and compare their distinguishing characteristics. After reading examples of both types of writing, children can analyze the major differences, such as presence of plot, setting, and characterization versus organization around facts, and look for similarities. Children's understanding of

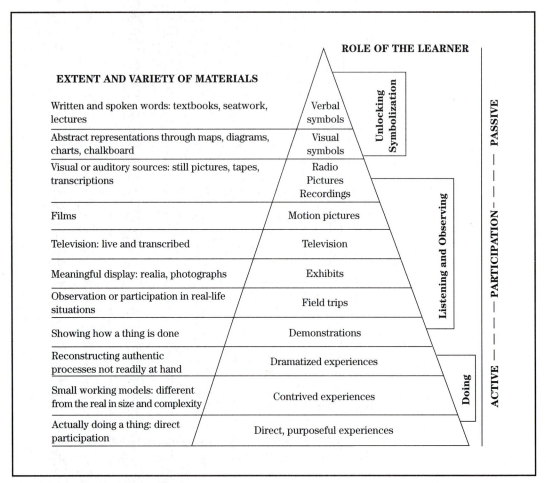

Figure 11.6—Dale's Cone of Experience

Source: From *Curriculum and Instruction in the Elementary School* by Frederick A. Rodgers. Macmillan Publishing Company. Copyright ©1975 by the author. Reprinted by permission.

expository writing will be aided by exposure to many models of it, as well as by opportunities to write expository material.

Hartman and Hartman (1993) suggest that teachers help their students read across texts by providing both narrative and expository texts and expanding the resources to include nonlinguistic sources as well. One strategy is to have children read a text, compare it to other texts, and then reread the original text. Another is to read a text and then enhance the reading with related paintings, film, or music. For example, we observed a display focused on tigers that included poetry, photographs, paintings, reference material, and narratives. Films, videos, and music could also be added to give students a chance to experience a wide variety of texts.

Studying Patterns of Text Organization

Authors of expository materials choose from a variety of organizational patterns, each of which may be a topic of study and a focus of writing experiences as examples arise in content-area books. Comprehension of texts is enhanced by a reader's recognition of the text's organization (Weaver, 1994). After learning about organizational patterns, a group of ninth graders remembered two times as much from their reading as they could before (Meyer, 1982). Authors rarely confine themselves to a single organizational pattern; a text normally reveals several. The following list describes some common patterns of text organization:

1. *Major idea/supporting details:* Author states the major idea or conclusion and then offers the evidence to support it.

2. *Details/conclusion:* Author offers the data first, then draws conclusions.

3. *Time order:* Author relates events in the sequence in which they occurred, using chronological order or ordinal markers such as "first, second, third" or "then, then, and finally."

4. *Cause/effect:* Author explains events or phenomena in terms of conditions that create them and follow from them.

5. *Comparison/contrast:* Author examines similarities and differences between things.

6. *Flashback:* Author sequences information by beginning in the present and then moving to an exposition of past events that led up to the present events.

7. *Question/answer:* Author asks a question and then answers it, perhaps repeating the device throughout the text.

Children understand these patterns best if they use them in their own writing after studying them. When do they study them? We suggest that as you are assigning an expository selection, you point out the organizational patterns the author uses. For example, discuss the pattern of organization based on cause and effect before the students read a text arranged that way. Then have the students perform a science experiment that demonstrates a cause-effect relationship and write about it using the model you have provided. Practicing the use of various patterns in class discussions of topics important to the children is another helpful strategy. When a class discussion exhibits a particular pattern, be sure to point that out to your students.

Believing that classifying is very important in helping children understand expository material, Hess (1991) asked children to generate questions they wanted to answer as part of developing a purpose for reading and then asked them to record the facts they learned on specially lined paper so they could be cut apart and grouped into categories for the writing that was to follow. Figure 11.7 illustrates how two children worked together to put their facts into categories about parrots. When children are able to categorize, they begin to understand how the authors of nonfiction material have grouped the facts or categorized the information.

Another teacher has learned that her class understands cause-effect structures in expository material after some whole-group instruction in noting cause and effect on a chart. She read a piece of nonfiction, then modeled the thinking process for what were the effects and what caused them in the piece. Next she read another piece and the class worked together to fill in the chart. Then the children filled in their own charts and discussed them in small groups and finally did their individual charts on an expository piece. She

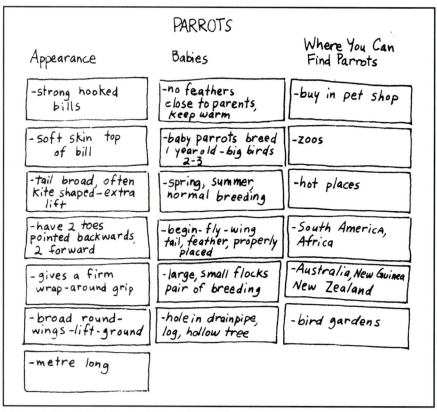

Figure 11.7—Children's Categorization of Information About Parrots

Source: Figure 3, page 230 of "Understanding nonfiction: Purpose, classification, response." Mary Lou Hess, *Language Arts, 68* (3), March 1991. Copyright ©1991 by the National Council of Teachers of English. Reprinted with permission.

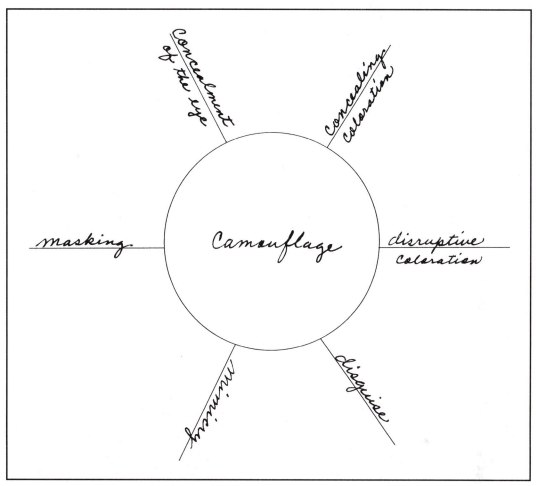

Figure 11.8—Descriptive Graphic Organizer

found that thinking about the effects first and then what caused them was much easier for the children than thinking about the causes first (Conrad, 1989). In addition to classifying and cause and effect, graphic organizers are also useful for helping children understand text structure.

Using Graphic Organizers

Figure 11.8 is a graphic organizer useful for helping children see how authors use a major idea and supporting details as a text organizer. You can model its use by reading aloud a short passage, having the children fill in the major idea in the circle, and then adding supporting details on the lines. You may have to read the same piece more than once in order for them to remember the

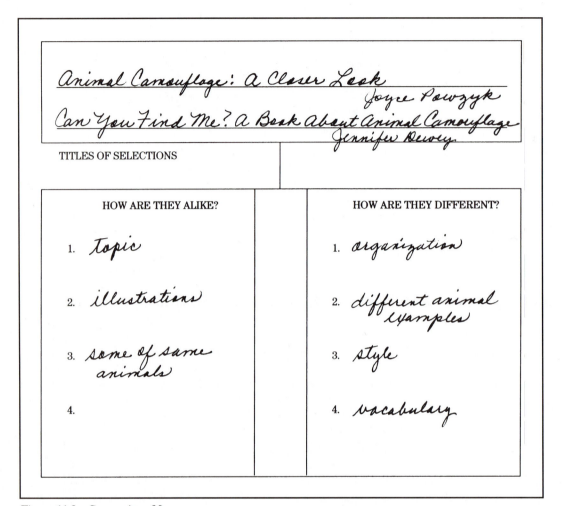

Animal Camouflage: A Closer Look
Joyce Powzyk
Can You Find Me? A Book About Animal Camouflage
Jennifer Dewey

TITLES OF SELECTIONS

HOW ARE THEY ALIKE?

1. *topic*

2. *illustrations*

3. *some of same animals*

4.

HOW ARE THEY DIFFERENT?

1. *organization*

2. *different animal examples*

3. *style*

4. *vocabulary*

Figure 11.9—Comparison Map

details. After you use it, encourage children to make such a diagram when they want to write an expository piece of their own using that text structure.

Figure 11.9 illustrates a comparison map that could be used to compare two different books on the same topic. In our example, the two books are about animal camouflage. Children can use such a chart in increasingly more sophisticated ways. They might, for example, compare text structures, vocabulary, additional information outside the main text, and so on.

You can invent graphic organizers to meet your needs in teaching text structure. For example, you could invent a chart for the question-answer format, a sequence chart to illustrate the flashback structure, or a time line to illustrate chronological sequence.

Providing a Variety of Materials and Resources

In order to meet the challenges of expository structure and specialized vocabulary, teachers have to locate a variety of materials for children to read in the content areas. This task can be difficult, but it is not impossible. Here are some suggestions for meeting the materials challenge.

Use Child-Authored Texts

Each time you teach a unit, duplicate a selection of the books that the children have published and keep them in the classroom library for next year's class to read during the study of the unit. Our experience has been that child authors produce some of the clearest, most readable content-area materials. Individually written or group-authored books produced to culminate a unit of study not only will be informative but will provide writing models for the next group of students.

Use Trade Books

The media specialist can be an invaluable partner in the search for materials that supplement the content-area texts. A few weeks before you begin a social studies or science unit, talk with the media specialist about the kinds of trade books (books published for noninstructional purposes) you would like to have in your classroom during the study. He or she will probably be able to pull together an assortment of books ranging from picture books to reference materials that relate to your topic. When the library corner or learning center is filled with trade books related to the current topic of study, children of varying reading abilities will be able to find information that is pertinent and interesting to them. You can read trade books to your students as a way of building background that makes it easier for them to read other texts.

One of the helpful resources in planning for trade book use is Freeman and Person's book, *Using Nonfiction Trade Books in the Elementary Classroom: From Ants to Zeppelins* (1992). The Children's Book Council also prints a bibliography of outstanding trade books that are related to science and to social studies each year. The science bibliography is printed in *Science and Children* every April and the social studies bibliography is printed in *Social Education* every May/June issue. They can also be ordered from the Children's Book Council and are free with a stamped, self-addressed envelope. The address is 568 Broadway, New York, NY 10012.

Use Periodicals

In addition to the popular weekly magazines, which often have pictures that can be used in content areas, many periodicals are published for children. Many of their articles on content topics are written at levels more easily read than textbooks. Here is a list of children's periodicals that teachers have found useful:

Calliope (Cobblestone Publishing)

Cobblestone (Cobblestone Publishing)

Faces (Cobblestone Publishing)

International Wildlife (National Wildlife Federation)

National Geographic World (National Geographic Society)

National Wildlife (National Wildlife Federation)

Odyssey (Cobblestone Publishing)

Owl (The Young Naturalist Foundation)

Ranger Rick (National Wildlife Federation)

Scienceland (Sekai Bunka Publishing)

3-2-1 Contact (The Children's Television Workshop)

Your Big Back Yard (National Wildlife Federation)

Zoo Books (Wildlife Education Ltd.)

Use Recorded Texts

Some expository materials are so well written or distinctive that a teacher wants the children to experience them just the way they are, not simplified or recast as a series of illustrations. It is effective (and efficient) to ask a volunteer who enjoys oral reading to tape-record those selections. The tapes can be played for the whole class or placed in the listening center for small groups of children to hear, with or without copies of the text in which to follow along.

Use Other Media

Ask the media specialist to identify filmstrips, films, and videotapes that can be used to supplement the written material in the content areas. Computer software is even available to simulate certain real-life situations, letting children experience the flavor of a given time and place. Using other media in conjunction with written material can help children develop concepts in the content areas. However, the teacher must carefully prepare for the use of audiovisual media by previewing them and planning strategies for children to respond to them. Showing a film without careful planning is of no more value than simply turning on the television!

Use Guest Speakers and Field Trips

Make a study of the resources available in your community, such as businesspeople who are willing to make free presentations to schools. Recognize that taking children on a trip to actually see what they are studying will make the study much more relevant to them. Resourceful teachers often find worthwhile destinations within easy walking distance of their schools so field trips are not costly.

Use the Guided Metacomprehension Strategy

The Guided Metacomprehension Strategy, introduced in Chapter 8, is a way to help children become interactive readers, assisting them in the vital metacomprehension functions that set good readers apart from poor ones. Stauffer (1975, p. 33) argues that when children are not engaged in reading strategies

Children enjoy sharing what they have learned in science with others.

© Joel Gordon

that develop self-generated learning about the reading process, "reading and thinking deteriorate into a waste of energy through an idle recital of facts and a round-the-robin oral reading that incline pupils toward dogma and cant and a mindless disregard for thoughtful reading."

We illustrated the GMS strategy with the reading of *Ira Sleeps Over* in Chapter 8. The key questions asked by the teacher were, "What do you think this story will be about?" and "What do you think will happen next?" These questions lend themselves to narrative text but not to expository text. Asking children, "What will this story be about?" before they read a social studies selection on the transcontinental railroad would be silly, given that the selection is not a story and the title tells what the selection will be about. However, we can still use the GMS before children read an expository selection by asking questions that direct their thinking to certain key facts or concepts it contains. Like the GMS for narrative material, the expository GMS engages the readers in schemata enhancement, predicting, reading, and proving their predictions. The teacher asks what the readers think and why they think so, and invites them to read aloud to prove their answers. The important steps in bringing reading to a conscious level are still included when reading expository texts.

The following application of the GMS with fifth-grade students involves expository material:

TEACHER: What can you tell me about what causes us to have seasons such as fall and winter?

JESSICA: The earth tilts on its axis, so sometimes one part of the world is having summer when another part is having winter.

ETHAN: The earth goes around the sun. That's what makes seasons.

TEACHER: Today we are going to read a selection about how the position of the earth affects the seasons on the earth. What answers do you think you will find to these questions? What determines a day?

ROBERT: 24 hours.

PATTI: One daytime and one nighttime.

DAMON: When the Earth turns away from the sun.

TEACHER: Why are the days hotter and longer in the summer?

ANDREA: Because the Earth is closer to the sun.

JOANNE: The days are hotter because they are longer.

TEACHER: What is meant by "summer solstice"?

SONJA: It's a party in the summer.

ROBERT: It's the beginning of summer.

DAMON: It has something to do with where the Earth is to the sun.

TEACHER: Let's read from page 202 through page 205 to see which of your predictions you can prove and which ones you will want to change.

Now the children read the selection from which Figure 11.10 is excerpted.

TEACHER: One of your predictions was that a day was determined when the Earth turns away from the sun. Can anyone read a part of the selection that proves or disproves that prediction?

PATTI: It says, "Earth makes one complete rotation in 24 hours. This amount of time is called a day."

TEACHER: Does that prove or disprove the prediction?

ETHAN: It sort of proves it because we said the Earth turns away from the sun, and that is what it does when it rotates. One part of the earth turns away from the sun. All of our first predictions were partly right. We just didn't explain enough.

TEACHER: You said that days are hotter and longer in the summer because the earth is closer to the sun. Can someone read us the part of the text that proves or disproves that prediction?

(*Discussion continues.*)

TEACHER: Who can tell me what you learned from reading this selection?

JOANNE: We learned we were right about what makes a day.

LUPE: We learned about the four seasons and the revolution of the Earth around the sun.

VINH: We learned that summer solstice is not a party. (Laughter.)

TEACHER: How did you make use of the illustrations in the selection?

ANDREA: That one picture helped me see how one side of the Earth is dark when the other side is sunny.

(*Discussion continues.*)

Teaching Words and Concepts

The vocabulary of content-area texts may offer many challenges to readers. Every area of study has its own vocabulary and much of it may be unfamiliar to elementary children. Armbruster and Nagy (1992) remind us that there is a distinction between target vocabulary (concepts that are introduced and explained in the text) and prerequisite vocabulary (words and concepts that

CHAPTER

THE EARTH
AND
THE MOON

1 DAYTIME, NIGHTTIME, AND SEASONS

What time of the day is it now? Is the sky bright or dark? How will the sky look twelve hours from now? Why do you think a change occurs?

When you finish this lesson, you should be able to:

○ Tell how Earth moves in space.

○ Explain how Earth's movements cause daytime, nighttime, and seasons.

Figure 11.10—Passage from a Fifth-Grade Science Text

Source: Excerpt from *Holt Elementary Science*, Grade 5, by Joseph Abruscato, Jack Hassard, Joan Wade Fossaceca, and Donald Peck, copyright ©1980 by Holt, Rinehart and Winston, Inc., reprinted by permission of the publisher.

may be needed for understanding the text). They recommend teaching prerequisite vocabulary before the reading, but not the target vocabulary. They also remind us that "teachers should repeatedly model *how* to derive the meaning of words from text" (p. 551) (italics in original).

Earth is a **planet**. A *planet* is a solid body in space that does not give off its own light. Earth gets its light from the sun.

Planet: A solid body in space that does not give off its own light.

Earth is shaped like a ball. Therefore, only the half of Earth that faces the sun gets light. Places on the half that is lit have daytime. Places on the other half are dark and have nighttime.

Earth moves in space. It spins, or **rotates (row-tates)**. Do you feel the movement? Earth makes one complete *rotation* in 24 hours. This amount of time is called a day. Within 24 hours, or one day, most places on Earth have a daytime and a nighttime.

Rotate: To spin.

Earth rotates from west to east. That is why the sun seems to rise in the east and set in the west.

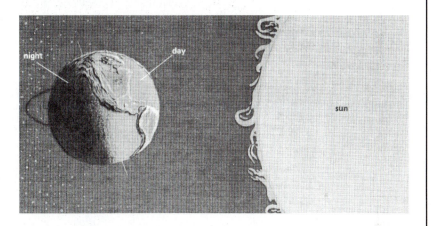

Earth also **revolves (ree-volvs)**, or moves around, the sun. Earth makes one complete *revolution* around the sun every 365¼ days. This amount of time is called a year. Within one year, most places on Earth have four seasons. Can you name them?

Revolve: To move around something.

Earth tilts toward or away from the sun at different times of the year.

Figure 11.10 (*continued*)

Although teachers are aware that all children may need specific help with content vocabulary, they should be especially sensitive to the difficulties faced by second-language learners or those with limited English proficiency in comprehending content material. For these learners, the more technical and concept-laden vocabulary may pose special problems (McKenna & Robinson, 1993).

Summer soltice: The first day of summer in the Northern Hemisphere.

Winter solstice: The first day of winter in the Northern Hemisphere.

Vernal equinox: The first day of spring in the Northern Hemisphere.

Autumnal equinox: The first day of fall in the Northern Hemisphere.

On June 21, Earth's North Pole is tilted toward the sun. In the Northern Hemisphere, this is the first day of summer. June 21 is called the **summer solstice** (sole-stis).

On December 22, Earth's North Pole is tilted away from the sun. In the Northern Hemisphere, this is the first day of winter. December 22 is called the **winter solstice** (sole-stis). Look at the diagram below. Can you find the position of Earth at the *summer solstice* and *winter solstice?*

In the spring and fall, Earth is not tilted toward or away from the sun. In the Northern Hemisphere, March 21 is the first day of spring, or the **vernal equinox** (vernal ee-kwi-noks). The first day of fall in the Northern Hemisphere, September 23, is called the **autumnal equinox** (awe-tum-nal ee-kwi-noks). Look at the diagram again. What is the position of Earth at the *vernal equinox* and *autumnal equinox?*

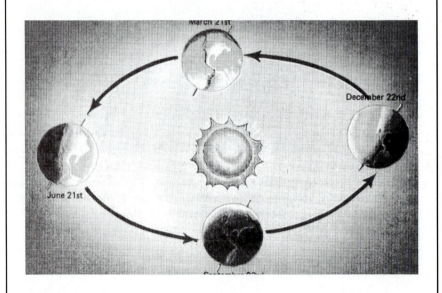

Figure 11.10 (*continued*)

Word Study

For the duration of a unit, keep a large sheet of paper hanging in the classroom where children may record interesting words and their meanings. Take time during class discussions to zero in on words—to point out uncommon uses of words and alternate ways of expressing something. It is important to

How is a summer's day different from a winter's day? Why do you think the days are hotter and longer in the summer than in the winter? This activity may help you find out.

A. Place one sheet of paper on your desk. Hold the lit flashlight over the paper as shown in the first picture below.

B. With the chalk draw a line around the lit area.

C. Place the other sheet of paper on your desk. Hold the lit flashlight over the paper as shown in the second picture. Then draw a line around the lit area.

1. How are the lines you drew different from each other?

Materials
chalk
flashlight
2 sheets of black
   construction paper

Figure 11.10 (*continued*)

help children see the multimeaning vocabulary in content areas. Vocabulary knowledge needs to grow vertically by adding new words and horizontally by adding new meanings to known words (for example, *cabinet*, *act*, and *apron*). To explore the true extent of multiple meanings, look up *run* in your dictionary. Ours devotes nearly a whole page to the meanings of *run!*

Koskinen and colleagues (1993) suggest videos with captions as one more strategy for helping children with difficult vocabulary. Captioned video has the advantage of showing the content and supplying the words at the same time and is not expensive or complicated to use. Hadaway and Young (1994) suggest a card sort strategy in which the teacher selects important terms and concepts and randomly arranges them on a sheet. The students then arrange the words/concepts in a hierarchy from general to specific and glue down the cards.

Structured Overviews and Semantic Maps

Both structured overviews and semantic maps can help children with complex concepts and the language labels attached to them. Refer again to our discussion of structured overviews in Chapter 10. Semantic maps, less complex than structured overviews, are likewise intended to show the interrelationships among ideas. Introduced as a note-taking and study technique by Hanf (1971), the semantic map can provide a way for children to organize what they know about a topic before the reading, can be developed during the reading of a selection, or can follow it as a part of a group discussion. Figure 11.11 is a semantic map based on the excerpt from "Sandhill Cranes" presented in Figure 11.2.

Olson and Gee (1991) surveyed primary teachers and asked them about the usefulness of content-area reading strategies. The six strategies that were considered to "provide outstanding help" or "provide very good support" were identified as previewing concepts and vocabulary, using concrete manipulatives to develop concepts, requiring retellings, developing summaries, visualizing information, and brainstorming.

Combining Many Strategies

Much of content instruction can be supported by literature and reading and writing experiences. Casteel and Isom (1994) recognized the importance of relating the content and processes of content studies to the development of abilities in literacy. For example, they see relationships between the questioning, hypothesizing, organizing data, analyzing, drawing conclusions, and reporting of good science lessons and literacy-based activities. In Figure 11.12 they illustrate these connections clearly.

Social studies content offers teachers many of the same opportunities to think about how the processes in the social sciences and the literacy activities are related and how they can complement each other.

Independent Activities

Independent activities are those things children can do on their own to make content-area reading more meaningful. We have labeled them "independent" because once you have taught them to do these things, they can do them with-

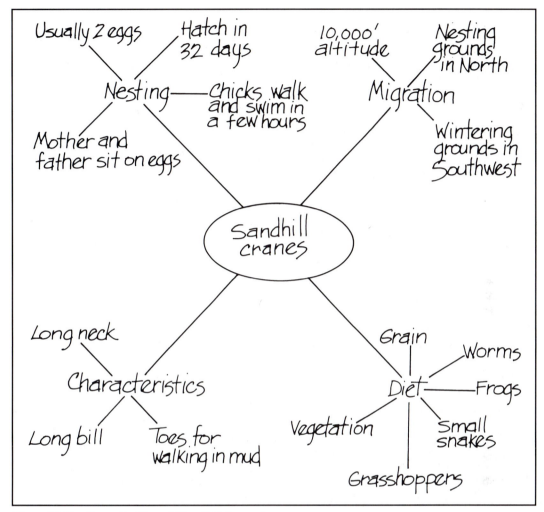

Figure 11.11—Semantic Map of "Sandhill Cranes"

out further instruction from you. For the most part, the activities described in this section are the traditional "study skills."

Identify Purposes for Reading

Children need to understand that we read texts for a variety of purposes. If the aim is to find specific pieces of information, we approach the reading process very differently from the way we would when reading to understand a difficult concept. We read about Egyptian history one way if it is for a hobby and another if it is for a school assignment and we know we will be tested on

Science Activities	Literacy-Based Activities
Questioning Ask questions about conditions leading to different types of weather. Example: What is weather? What conditions contribute to changes in the weather?	**Purpose setting** Set purposes for reading a trade book about weather by having students write information they hope to find in response journals. Read to find out what conditions contribute to weather changes.
Hypothesizing Form hypotheses about what will happen when air temperatures and pressures change. Example: Conditions of the air contribute to changes in weather. Temperature contributes to rain, sleet, snow, and hail conditions.	**Predicting** Predict how weather conditions might influence plot and affect characters, setting, and mood in various stories.
Gathering/organizing data Record and categorize daily pressure/temperature changes and weather conditions. Also, record results of experiments on air temperature such as making a hygrometer to measure moisture. Participate in computer simulations of weather experiments. Research methods for collecting weather data such as the use of weather balloons.	**Organizing ideas** Create cognitive maps to organize information learned from reading trade books about weather. Also, complete word webs or semantic feature analyses relating to technical vocabulary words.
Analyzing results Analyze all collected data and identify factors that affected results. Use charts, tables, and diagrams to illustrate analysis.	**Constructing/composing** Discuss personal experiences relating to different types of weather conditions and participate in language-experience activities to write comparisons between weather conditions and effects on human behavior.
Drawing conclusions Meet in cooperative groups to review data and draw conclusions relative to the hypotheses.	**Evaluating/revising** Make judgments about and edit written compositions about weather. Example: Evaluate accuracy of facts, clarity of ideas, and use of mechanics in writing.
Reporting Prepare a written report summarizing information learned. Make oral presentations to another class.	**Comprehending/communicating** Publish a classroom book about weather. Share individual entries through the use of the author's chair.

Figure 11.12—Parallels in Science and Literacy Processes

Source: Figure 3 from "Reciprocal processes in science and literacy learning," Carolyn P. Casteel and Bess A. Isom, *The Reading Teacher*, April 1994. Reprinted by permission of Carolyn P. Casteel and the International Reading Association.

the information. Clearly, children will be more highly motivated to read a piece if they have a purpose or purposes for doing so. We know comprehension is increased when readers have a purpose for reading.

The best purposes often grow out of the student's own questions. The teacher also asks leading questions: "Why would reading this be helpful? What do you expect to learn from reading this selection? What kinds of information do you expect to find here? How will you approach this reading—will you skim or will you read very carefully?" By asking questions like these each time you assign expository reading, you model the kind of "purpose for reading" thinking that children need to learn to do on their own.

Recognize Prior Knowledge and Knowledge Desired

The schemata-enhancement activities you do as part of the GMS are intended to help children focus on what they know before they read. You can combine this activity with writing by having pairs or small groups of children write down what they know about a topic before they read the text (Hammond, 1986). This step leads naturally to identifying the things they are not sure about and the things they want to find out when they read. After reading the selection they can determine the accuracy of their prior knowledge and note which of their questions have been answered. Confirming what children know and finding answers to their questions are two very compelling purposes for reading. Ogle (1986) proposes that students make a chart with the reading topic and purpose for reading written at the top. Three columns are then headed "Know," "Want to Know," and "Learned" (or the equivalent in question form). The columns are completed before and after reading, and finally the answer to the purpose question is written at the bottom of the chart.

Figure 11.13 is an example of part of a KWL chart from a primary class involved with a study of wolves.

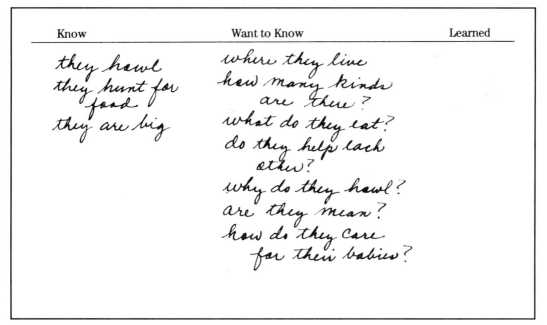

Know	Want to Know	Learned
they hawl they hunt for food they are big	where they live how many kinds are there? what do they eat? do they help each other? why do they hawl? are they mean? how do they care for their babies?	

Figure 11.13—KWL Chart

We can invoke the power of prediction by having children predict answers to their questions in the third column of the chart, or by getting their predictions to questions at the start of a unit of study. Suppose the next unit of study is the space shuttle and related concepts. Instead of *telling* children what they are going to learn about the space shuttle and space travel during the next two weeks, you might begin the unit by letting them help plan it: "We are going to spend the next two weeks studying space travel and the space shuttle. What would you like to know?"

Organize children's questions into categories and ask them to predict what the answers will be. This example might yield categories like these: eating on the shuttle, steering the shuttle, takeoffs and landings, daily life on the shuttle, and miscellaneous. Record the questions and predicted answers for reference throughout the study. This record could be kept on the chalkboard or on a large piece of paper. Have the children form groups to research the answers to questions in a given category. As the children discover the answers, they write them into the group record below the question. Finally, the group selects a way to present its findings to the whole class.

Help Children Locate and Select Information

The instructional strategies that help children deal with charts, graphs, indexes, glossaries, illustrations, maps, and so on, are often played out as self-contained "skills" lessons. A worksheet on the card catalog or on the use of a glossary assumes the study skills can be effectively taught in isolation and then transferred to real reading and study situations.

The purpose of instructional strategies in the area of study skills is to help children engage in independent study in which they make maximum use of the available resources. They have to learn to locate information, select the information that is most useful, organize the information they select, and then retain that information in some practical, meaningful way. These skills should not be taught in isolation. They should be taught and practiced while students engage in *real* units of study with *real* reasons for reading and writing and *real* needs to know.

Table of Contents

A table of contents is useful in locating and selecting information. Figure 11.14 illustrates a table of contents from a fifth-grade social studies text.

Appropriate instructional strategies include large- or whole-group instruction on the nature of the table of contents and its use. Children should be helped to understand that the table of contents demonstrates how the book is organized and the kind of information it contains. Essential questions in using the table of contents are "Does this book contain the information I need?" and "Where is it?" Large-group instruction should then be followed by the actual use of tables of contents as students engage in research during a thematic unit or as the teacher instructs children to locate selections in

Contents

Figure 11.14—Sample Table of Contents

Source: From *Heath Social Studies: The United States Past and Present, Grade 5.*Copyright ©1985 by D.C. Heath & Co. Reprinted by permission.

books. Giving children a worksheet on which a table of contents is reproduced and having children answer questions about the table is not an effective strategy. Transfer of the knowledge about tables of contents to practice will occur only when children are given many opportunities to actually use tables of contents in real study situations.

Content area studies provide authentic reasons to use the resources in the media center.

© Gail Meese/Meese Photo Research

Index

The index is another tool for locating and selecting information. Children should recognize that the index provides more detailed information about the contents of a book than does the table of contents. Index entries show the page locations of specific topics, as well as the breakdown of entries by subtopic. By consulting the index, a student can often determine quickly the relevance of a book to the current study. To use indexes effectively and efficiently, children must be able to deal with alphabetical order, carefully predict key words in a domain of study, and see relationships among topics. These skills can be developed through specific instruction by the teacher, but they must be applied frequently in actual research use. The best instructional strategy is to guide the children's reference to indexes as they use them in their research, reminding them frequently of their potential value. Figure 11.15 is a portion of an index from a fifth-grade social studies text.

Figure 11.15—Sample Index

Source: From *Heath Social Studies: The United States Past and Present, Grade 5.* Copyright ©1985 by D.C. Heath & Co. Reprinted by permission.

Card Catalog

Although the card catalog in many libraries is now computerized, elementary school libraries still have card catalogs. The card catalog is an indispensable aid in content-area reading and research. Instructional strategies must include familiarization with the nature and use of the three kinds of cards found in the library's card catalog: author, subject, and title. Students will need instruction in reading the text of each kind of card. Practicing using the card catalog in real research situations will be far more effective than isolated drill with worksheets. Figure 11.16 illustrates a subject card from a card catalog.

Other Resources

Other research tools that will be helpful to students as they study in the content areas include glossaries, charts, graphs, maps, encyclopedias, atlases, dictionaries, and the *Readers' Guide to Periodical Literature.* Their use is taught over years of school as students' need for them increases. For example, the concept of table of contents may be taught in first grade as an aid to locating favorite stories in books. Later, as the learning is reinforced, it will have wider application. Instruction in the use of tools for locating and selecting information begins in kindergarten and culminates in high school with much more sophisticated use of computerized information systems. Along this continuum, teachers should instruct and guide children in the use of the tools while challenging them to ask more and more questions—and to seek the answers.

```
J
973.3           The American Revolution
L425a           Lawson, Don
                    The American Revolution; America's
                first war of independence. Illustrated
                by Robert F. McCullough. Abelard-Schuman,
                c1974.
                    176p.   illus   maps
```

Figure 11.16—Sample Card Catalog Entry (Subject Card)

Help Children Organize Information

The organization of information involves posing questions and research hypotheses, taking notes, outlining, and planning the presentation of the information. We suggest that as part of the introduction to any unit of study, children be asked to *pose their own questions*, which they hope the study will answer. Certainly the teacher has the right and responsibility to add questions to the list, but the initial questions should come from the children. Drawing on the schemata the children bring to the study, this approach makes the study their own. It suggests that children are responsible for their learning, not just the teacher.

Once the questions for a unit of study have been organized, the strategies for locating and selecting information come into play. Then the information gathered must be organized in a way that is helpful to the learner. Techniques of retaining and organizing information should be taught together. The way in which information is retained should be related to the purpose of collecting the information. For a report, notes and an outline may be most useful. For a mural or diorama, sketches might be the best way. A science experiment would require notes and diagrams produced in a carefully timed sequence. Data collected for a report on an historical event could be organized by cause and effect. We believe it is as important and beneficial to children to present the information gained in content-area study as it is to do the research. Children should know before beginning the unit of study that they will be responsible for presenting information to others. They should have a major say in how to do it.

Having decided on the form of presentation, they should identify the best ways to retain important information. This is where both note-taking and outlining skills are helpful. We recommend these instructional strategies:

1. Help children discriminate between information related to their questions and information that is irrelevant.

2. Help children identify the patterns of text organization described earlier in this chapter. Discuss the ways in which text organization may affect the kinds of notes they take.

3. Show children how to take notes on 5×8-inch cards, one topic per card.

4. Show children how to outline information. First, use a two-stage outline like this:

    Care of a dog
      I. Feeding
        A. Kinds of food
        B. Water

II. Living conditions
  A. Kennel
  B. Dog house

5. Follow this simple outlining with much more complex three- and four-stage outlines. Underscore the relationship between the pattern of text organization and the outline.

6. Help children decide on the level of detail necessary in notes and outlines depending on the nature of the research questions.

7. Help children see the relationships among semantic maps, structured overviews, and outlining. Whole-group lessons can be built around turning a semantic map into an outline.

Note taking seems to follow a developmental sequence. From kindergarten through grade 2, the teacher makes class notes. Children can make notes in groups in grades 3 and 4 and finally can work individually in grades 5 and 6.

Writing Challenges in Content-Area Texts

In the preface to her book, *Coming to Know: Writing to Learn in the Intermediate Grades*, Atwell (1990) tells a story of an experience that many of us share. She confesses that she was assigned to do a report on Great Britain and although she was good at plagiarizing *The World Book* and tracing maps, she did not do the report. Her teacher did not know she had not done the report until the last day of school, a full three months later. She explains that the reason she did not write the report and her teacher did not read the reports was the same: sheer boredom. That is what we want to avoid in writing in the content areas.

The "integration of reading and writing" and "writing across the curriculum" are increasingly popular topics in educational circles. In some classrooms, however, writing is used for very limited purposes (Langer, 1986). Writing can be used in the content areas for important purposes beyond determining what children have learned: It can make students aware of what they know, what they do not know, and what they need to learn. Content-area writing presents challenges to the young author that are just as great as the reading challenges. In the primary grades, most of the children's writing is narrative. From third grade on, children are asked to do increasingly more writing in the content areas, so they must learn to deal with new writing formats and new sentence and paragraph structures.

Teachers who carefully guide the reading of expository material are preparing children to use it as a model for their writing. Writing activities should be planned in terms of both content and format. While establishing reasons for children to write expository material, teachers must be sure the children understand both the content and the format they are to use.

Establishing a purpose for writing about expository topics is a challenge to the teacher. Getting a grade is not a legitimate purpose. In planning instructional units, teachers need to think of purposes for expository writing, such as presenting reports to an interested audience, doing write-ups for the class newspaper, dramatizing scripts based on real-life experiences, and creating captions for items in a display. Writing about content topics can involve the use of note taking, outlining, report writing, and the creation of charts and graphs. Each of these formats needs to be taught and used in situations in which real communication occurs. Children should practice note taking, for example, during the preparation of a report, not as an isolated workbook exercise. They should exercise their outlining skills during the process of taking real notes rather than during a contrived drill on a worksheet. Children will see the value of writing in these formats when that writing is purposeful.

Meeting Content-Area Writing Challenges

In this section we present three strategies to help children meet the challenges of content-area writing: learning logs, a repertoire of writing formats, and use of paragraph frames. Each of these strategies must be modeled by the teacher more than once before children can use them comfortably. You may want to schedule a mini-lesson on one of these strategies periodically.

Learning Logs

Learning logs are journals or logs of what children are learning in various subject matter areas such as science, social studies, or math. Learning logs can also be arranged by topic such as a study of oceans or animals or ancient Greece. Learning logs kept by students as they work on projects can take several forms. Some teachers have students do summaries of what they have learned; some have them do what they call a double-entry journal, where they record what they learned through charts, drawings, and narratives on one side and how they felt about their work on the other side of the page. Some teachers have found that using prompts (questions) will help keep the logs from becoming so predictable. A prompt must be engaging and help children think about the subject. It must also be open ended and ask children their own opinions or draw on their prior experience. Prompts might ask children to "list, brainstorm, chart, map, sketch, pose questions, set goals, guess, predict, express opinions, note observations, summarize, role-play, envision, correspond, and shift to a new mode, such as poetry or fiction" (Atwell, 1990, p. 167). For example, the following prompts might be used for a study of geography and maps. Remember these are just ideas, not a prescription.

▼   What is geography?

▼   What would you like to know about maps and making them?

▼   What do we use maps for? List as many reasons as you can think of.

▼   We'll be taking an imaginary trip to Yellowstone National Park. List at least five questions you'd need to have answered before our trip.

▼   Choose any two cities on the U.S. map. Figure out the distance between the two and write about how you did it.

▼   List or draw any land forms you can remember from our reading.

▼   How does a legend help you?

▼   Draw a simple map with a key.

▼   List all the water bodies/land forms that you can think of. (Atwell, 1990, p. 172)

These prompts might not be needed in your class, but if they are perhaps they will help you avoid the "Today we learned how to make a battery light a bulb" learning log with nothing more than a summary with no detail of what happened in the class.

Writing Formats

Teachers need to plan activities that teach writing formats and invite children to use those formats in purposeful ways. Consider each of the writing formats listed here in terms of the unique characteristics—and challenges—it presents to the author.

Children learning to write in various formats should see examples from content texts, trade books, and periodicals. With exposure to many good models, time, ownership, and response, and real communicative purpose, children will be able to write expository material as well as they write narratives. Direct instruction and feedback on the use of each format will be necessary.

Note taking, outlining, and captions all require particular writing skills and result in different products. You must take the time to teach children how to do each of these formats and how to select the most useful format for what they need at the time.

The table in Figure 11.17 lists possibilities for reports that will help children avoid the boredom of copying a report from the encyclopedia and will encourage them to find their own voices as writers of nonfiction material.

Paragraph Frames

The challenges of expository reading and writing can be reduced with the use of paragraph frames (Cudd & Roberts, 1989). An adaptation of the cloze procedure, the paragraph frame begins with a sentence written by the teacher that includes specified signal words or phrases. Students then proceed on their own, following one of the text organization patterns discussed in the section on text structure earlier in the chapter. A paragraph frame used by Cudd and Roberts (1989, p. 393) began with "Before a frog is grown, it goes through many changes." This was followed by the key words used in organizing a paragraph through sequential ordering: "First, the mother frog . . . Next, . . . Then, . . . Finally, . . . Now they . . ." A second grader named Elena wrote,

> Before a frog is grown, it goes through many stages. First, the mother frog lays the eggs. Next, the eggs hatch and turn into tadpoles. Then, slowly the tadpoles legs begin to grow. Finally, the tadpole turns into a frog. Now and then they have to go into the water to keep their skin moist.

The paragraph frame strategy is a demonstrably successful way to guide children's writing of expository material.

1. Individual bound books for the classroom library.
2. Picture books that introduce younger children to a topic and are based on student's knowledge of good content-area literature for children (e.g., illustrated books about electricity, black bears, local architecture, the human skeleton).
3. Textbooks for which each student in the class writes a chapter (e.g., the results of statistical surveys conducted by students in a math class; an anthology about life in ancient Greece; an examination of the effects of World War II on the local community).
4. Correspondence between two real or imagined historical personages (e.g., a woman from ancient Sparta and one from Athens; Thomas Paine and a 20th-century fifth grader; Harriet Tubman and a young slave).
5. Journals or diaries of real or imagined historical personages (e.g., the diary of a serf; the journal of a young survivor of the flu epidemic of 1918).
6. Oral histories and interviews, transcribed and supplemented by background information, photographs, drawings, poetry, etc.
7. Scripts: radio and television plays to be tape recorded or videotaped; speeches, plays, and skits to be performed; interviews; and filmstrips.
8. Historical fiction: short stories about historical personages or about imagined people taking part in important historical events (e.g., a day in a child's life during a plague or on a wagon train; a fictional account of Anne Hutchinson's trial).
9. Autobiographical sketches of real or imagined historical personages or living things (e.g., a first-person account of the boyhood of Alexander the Great; a deciduous tree describes a year in its life).
10. Poetry: collections of poems about a topic-free verse, rhymed, counted syllable, and/or acrostic formats—in which information about a topic is embedded.
11. Science fiction: short stories or novellas set in the future or on another planet in which contemporary issues are explored.
12. Animal stories: a favorite genre of third through fifth graders; the stories must strike a balance between presenting the animal as a character and giving an accurate account of its existence without anthropomorphizing it.
13. How-to books in which students pass on specialized knowledge related to a unit of study (e.g., blacksmithing, trapping, tapestry weaving, stargazing, reducing fractions).
14. Field guides that describe characteristics of a particular species or community.
15. Class or individual newspapers in which each article, column, advertisement, editorial, interview, want ad, and cartoon is related to a time and place in history (e.g., a Boston newspaper from 1776; a Gettysburg paper from 1863).

Figure 11.17—Genres for Report Writing

Source: Reprinted by permission of Nancie Atwell: *Coming to Know: Writing to Learn in the Intermediate Grades* (Heinemann, a division of Reed Elsevier, Inc., Portsmouth NH, 1990).

16. Columns or feature articles published in the local newspaper (e.g., an interview with a local artist; a story about the nesting habits of the osprey; Christmas in Maine in colonial times).

17. Math concept books: short stories or picture books in which mathematical information is embedded.

18. Recipes of a period or people: foods eaten in ancient Rome, during medieval times, by Native Americans, etc.

19. Games and puzzles that demonstrate and require a knowledge of a time, place, or unit of study (e.g., a trivia game about Portland; a crossword puzzle with the solar system as its theme).

20. Annotated catalogs of artifacts (e.g., the dress of men and women of ancient Greece; cooking implements found in the kitchen at Sturbridge Village).

21. Annotated family trees of real or imagined historical personages (e.g., Greek gods and goddesses; a passenger on the *Mayflower*).

22. Friendly letters to individuals outside the classroom in which students describe their new knowledge and what it means to them (e.g., letters to pen pals from another school, grandparents, cousins, and other relatives).

23. Bulletin boards of drawings or photos with accompanying text (e.g., plants that grow in the desert; Portland then and now).

24. Choose-your-own-adventure stories in which success in proceeding through the stories is based on specific knowledge of math or science concepts.

25. Posters, murals, time lines, and mobiles that include text (e.g., a dinosaur mobile; a mural depicting the destruction of Pompeii; a poster showing a plant's life cycle).

26. Coloring books with accompanying text, to be photocopied for classmates and/or younger children (e.g., scenes from New England states; the Underground Railroad; the life of a hermit crab).

27. Calendars, each page annotated with a drawing and text related to the topic (e.g., a medieval knight's calendar; a calendar for stargazers; a puffin calendar).

28. Alphabet books in which each letter supplies relevant information about the topic (e.g., a Beverly Cleary ABC; an astronaut's ABC; a geologist's ABC).

29. Pop-up books in which the format replicates a natural phenomenon (e.g., the solar system; the earth's layers).

30. Shadow boxes or dioramas with accompanying text (e.g., the habitat of the eastern panther; Anne Frank's secret annex; the parts of a stem).

Figure 11.17 (*continued*)

How does this all work in a real classroom? Perhaps the following scenario will help you understand how content-area reading occurs in real classrooms.

A Classroom Example

Mr. Bob Klein's fourth-grade class is very interested in squirrels because one got into their classroom. They decide that although they all had seen squirrels before and some of them knew a few facts about squirrels, they would all like to know more. Bob began the study by completing the K and W columns of a KWL chart with the class, including having them predict the answers to their questions. The class also decided they would make books about squirrels to share with their first-grade reading buddies. Next, Bob modeled a three-stage outline form and the children filled in the title "squirrels" and predicted some categories such as food, nests, and so on. He then showed a wildlife film about squirrels that followed a baby squirrel from its birth to its adulthood and discussed what it ate, where it lived, and so on. After the film, he asked the children to complete some of the L column with information they had learned about squirrels and note that the answers came from the film. Next, with the help of the librarian, Bob provided books and magazine articles he had found about squirrels. The children reviewed the questions they had and began searching the books for the answers. They took notes and then worked in groups to categorize the facts they learned about squirrels.

Each day began with a discussion period so Bob could help the children stay focused on their purpose and the audience for their products. He used the information books that had been collected to teach mini-lessons on text features such as table of contents, indexes, and glossaries, and the patterns of text structure. In the process of using these books, the children became critical consumers as they found books in which it was difficult to find the information they wanted or in which an index was missing or not useful to them. They also discussed the role of illustrations in information books and the benefits and drawbacks of photographs as compared to drawings. Now the children began planning their own books by making a list of the things they were going to include and then rewriting the list to indicate the order in which the topics would be included.

Reading *with* is an appropriate strategy for content-area texts.

©Joel Gordon

As the work on their books progressed, the children devoted much time to talking about the books—what should or should not be included, what would make the first graders like the books, how many illustrations they should have and what kind of illustrations would be best, should a glossary be included, and so on. They also shared their writing frequently and helped each other write a text that was as clear and readable as they could make it.

Major Ideas in This Chapter

▼   Our major objective in content reading is to help the student draw on personal background experiences to create meaning in interaction with the text. Content-area reading presents special challenges to the reader.

▼   Challenges to the content-area reader are presented by text structure, specialized vocabulary and concept load, and special text features.

▼   A variety of instructional strategies may be employed to meet the challenges of content-area reading. In any case, comprehension of content texts is enhanced by motivation to read, authentic classroom activities that draw on content-area knowledge, and real quests for information.

▼   Content-area study presents writing challenges to students. Writing activities should be planned in terms of both content and format. Writers need time, ownership, and response when writing in the content areas.

Discussion Questions: Focusing on the Teacher You Are Becoming

1.   Should primary-grade children (beginning readers) have experiences with expository writing? Build your most convincing arguments.

2.   What are the most common text features of the textbooks you are using in your other college classes? If you were asked to tutor a college freshman who was having difficulty comprehending a science text, what are the three steps you would take?

3.   Were you surprised to discover that some of the strategies for helping children comprehend content materials were ones you use in your own studying? Which strategies did you rediscover?

4.   Discuss the content-area reading strategies you think would be most helpful in adult life outside of school.

Field-Based Applications

1. Develop and use a cloze procedure to determine the children for whom a social studies or science text is too difficult. When scoring the procedure, analyze the extent to which readers relied on semantic and syntactic cues.

2. Select a chapter from a social studies, science, or health text and plan instructional strategies to help learners meet the reading challenges.

3. Plan lessons that help students locate information, select information, organize the information, and present the information to others.

4. Plan authentic content-area writing activities that provide time, ownership, and response for the writer. Include the use of paragraph frames to guide expository writing.

Chapter 12

Planning for Literacy Instruction Throughout the Day

Chapter Overview

▼ Planning for literacy instruction throughout the day means thinking about how children can learn literacy skills while they are involved in learning the content of social studies, science, mathematics, and the arts.

▼ Teachers must make decisions about how to organize the curriculum. Two common strategies for organizing activities in the classroom are units and themes.

▼ Units of instruction focus on one subject matter area over a period of days or weeks. Themes integrate all subject matter areas and last longer than single-subject units.

▼ Social studies, science, and mathematics have often been viewed as separate subjects that are unrelated to literacy development. These subjects can provide interesting content for the children's reading and writing experiences.

▼ Although the arts are often not taught by the classroom teacher as subjects, they can be very useful to the classroom teacher in motivating children to become more skilled in their literacy abilities.

Literacy Instruction Throughout the Day

The purpose of this chapter is to help teachers plan for literacy instruction throughout the entire school day. We know the best literacy instruction is not confined to a period of the day for reading and another for writing or even a period called language arts. Certainly teachers want to schedule periods of instruction in which they have time to focus on the literacy needs of the group, but they also know that even during specific language-arts periods children have to read and write and talk about *something*. It's that something this chapter is about: the science, social studies, mathematics, and the arts that fill up the elementary school day and how they can be related to literacy. Having children involved in literacy activities related to topics in which they are interested meets two goals: (1) the reading and writing experiences are authentic, not just meaningless tasks; and (2) children see that reading and writing serve real purposes in life, that they are not merely subjects for study in school. So how does the planning and organizing get done for the most effective instruction? The first step is selecting instructional activities.

Selecting Instructional Activities

1. *Activities should help connect new information to the knowledge children already have.* For example, having selected the solar system as a topic for a unit or theme, the teacher might use a variety of means to ascertain what the children know: asking direct questions, having children dictate what they know about the solar system, asking children to write individually about the solar system, or having children pool their knowledge in small groups and report to the class. As we mentioned previously, KWL charts, semantic webs, and discussion webs can be useful here. The teacher can then select activities to help children gain new knowledge and make connections with what they originally knew by revising dictated charts, rewriting reports, or resuming discussions.

2. *Activities should be of interest to the children.* When Dewey (1938) suggested children would more easily learn what they were interested in, he was putting forward a relatively novel idea for his time. Students' interest can be the result of some happening in the school or world, or it can be generated by the teacher. For example, as reports from the Voyager spacecraft first hit the news, they would surely awaken interest in the solar system. If the teacher had selected rocks as a theme, bringing in rocks of many types would probably generate considerable interest.

3. *Activities should involve the children in as many direct hands-on experiences as possible.* Children can't go fight in the American Revolution, but they can make candles, quilts, and posters appropriate to the period, and they can read from as many original documents as possible. Some schools are located within field-trip distance of Revolutionary War sites.

4. *As much as possible, children should be allowed to select individual activities that interest them most.* For example, if the teacher had chosen amphibians as a suitable topic of study, then the children might pick a specific amphibian for intense study. In small study groups, children might divide up the task according to personal interests, such as reading reference material, recording careful observations of the animal subject, making scientific drawings, and studying the animal in a broader context, such as its place in the ecosystem or food chain. The extensive list of possible genres for reports in Figure 11.17 is a reflection of teachers attempting to allow children choices in how they report what they learn.

5. *Activities should have multiple outcomes.* An activity such as reading information in a textbook and answering review questions at the end of the selection may have a limited outcome, primarily the recall of factual information. But if the children are learning to use headings and subheadings to locate specific information in the text, practice skimming the text for selected information, compare the structure of the text with the structure of another genre of writing, and use the review questions to guide their reading for information, then reading the text and answering the questions will have multiple outcomes. Most hands-on activities, such as making candles, have multiple outcomes. For example, children will learn some scientific concepts, such as how wax changes when subjected to heat and how different wax and wick materials affect the quality of the product. At the same time they will find out that producing goods and services to meet daily needs in colonial times required a large investment of time and that most goods were made at home. Of course, the activity will also reinforce the importance of reading and following directions.

6. *Activities should involve a genuine need for literacy skills.* For example, if the instructional goal is to teach children to take notes from written material for use in writing a report, then the children should actually be involved in writing a report that will be presented to an audience and provide a communicative experience in sharing information.

7. *Activities should give children opportunities to learn and to share what they have learned through various modes of presentation.* For example, children should be encouraged to construct (models, maps), create (puppets, posters, paintings, collages), and dramatize (role plays, puppet plays), as well as write.

After you have given some thought to selecting instructional activities, then you must decide how to organize the activities so they can be presented to the children in a sensible way. Two ways of organizing activities are most common: units and themes.

Planning Units or Themes of Instruction

Preparing content-area instruction typically means developing plans for classroom activities that help children build concepts and learn facts about a given topic. Whether units or themes are selected as organizational strategies, both extend over longer periods of time than single class periods and usually include a variety of activities, such as reading from a textbook, viewing media, listening to guest speakers, creating art projects, using the computer to access information or to take part in a simulation exercise, and participating in drama or role playing.

A unit of instruction is usually defined as a topic that extends over several days or weeks of instruction in a given subject. For example, in social studies one might have a unit on transportation or communities. In literature, one might plan a unit on survival stories or the depiction of the elderly in literature. In science one might plan a unit on electricity or the solar system. Typically, a unit is planned for a given period of instruction each day although teachers may combine periods to create longer time frames for working on the unit. If you had planned a unit on plants for science, you might also use the time scheduled for language arts as well as the time scheduled for science instruction as time to work on the unit.

A theme of instruction is usually defined as an organizational strategy that makes it possible to relate all the subject matter areas to one major topic of instruction. A theme might last for several weeks, several months, or an entire year.

Units and themes cannot be planned without considering the goals and objectives to be met by the activities in the unit or theme and how those relate to the school or district goals and objectives. The following steps will help you think about how a unit or theme fits into the overall curriculum plan:

Step 1. Review state and district guides for the literacy skills appropriate to the grade level.

Step 2. In planning a unit of instruction, review the curriculum guides for social studies, science, literature, or math; in planning a theme, review the guides for goals from multiple subject matter areas.

Step 3. Identify major literacy and content goals of the unit or theme.

Step 4. Specify important objectives, recognizing children will determine some of them as they choose areas of personal interest to study in depth.

Step 5. Collaborate with the media teacher to review library and media resources available in the school or district. Select appropriate resources.

Step 6. Consult with local resource people, such as Chamber of Commerce, historical society, local speaker's bureau, educational director of museum, and so on.

Step 7. Develop a time line for the unit or theme.

Step 8. Plan specific activities for each lesson.

Step 9. Develop a scheme for monitoring students' progress.

Step 10. Plan evaluation strategies for each lesson, activity, and unit or theme.

Units can be planned for any subject matter area. The following unit is an example of a unit planned for social studies.

A Social Studies Unit

Suppose you have reviewed the district and state goals in social studies and found that a unit on the American Revolution would be appropriate at your grade level. You follow the planning steps we recommended and decide that the resources are available for a unit of study focused on the American Revolution.

The broad goals of the unit could include content goals such as the learning of facts about the Revolution (participants, battles, military strategies, chronology of events) and the development of concepts about the causes of the Revolution. Literacy goals might include making and using maps, conducting library research, and taking notes. The goal of all the instruction would be for the learners to be able to evaluate the importance of the Revolution in the development of our democratic form of government and to apply their knowledge of the American Revolution to current world situations.

Once the broad goals and time frame of the unit are established, then for each instructional period short-term goals are set that will help the students meet the unit goals. For example, during one instructional period the students could write a newspaper article describing the Boston Massacre from the point of view of a colonial or a British reporter. The goals for the instructional period would include learning factual information about the Boston Massacre, placing the event in a chronology, reviewing the structure of writing in newspapers, and recognizing a given point of view.

Let's assume a six-week schedule of instruction for the unit. The following plan illustrates the range of possibilities for teaching the unit and highlights the literacy goals that can be achieved.

Semantic webs are useful in units and themes.

© Steven Lunetta/StockUp

Introduction of the Unit

Introduce the unit with a poster of a Minuteman. Discuss the poster, and as a group list on a large chart things the students know about the American Revolution. Separate students into smaller groups to develop questions they have about the Revolution. Categorize the questions into broad areas, such as life in revolutionary times, information about battles, causes of the Revolution. The charts will be reviewed and revised as children gain new information from films, filmstrips, videotapes, reading materials, and reports.

Presentation of Information

Show films, filmstrips, or videotapes that present information about the American Revolution. Assign selected portions of the social studies textbook. Have children read facsimiles of original documents from the revolutionary period, such as the Declaration of Independence, records kept by the colonial army, and diaries and letters. Let individuals or small groups make reports to the class.

Individual or Small-Group Activities

1. After viewing films and reading for background information, select an event from the Revolution to learn more about. The children conduct library research on the event and prepare to make an oral presentation, such as a report or newscast, to the class. They would have to write an outline or script for the presentation and might also make maps or other supporting visuals.

2. Participate in hands-on activities such as making quill pens, candles, a square for a quilt, a puppet of a participant in the Revolution, or a toy typical of the period. Each of these activities would require reading for information and directions, and each would encourage other literacy experiences. With the quill pen, for example, the children could write a letter to a friend describing some aspect of life in colonial times; with the puppet of an historical character, they could create a play.

3. Participate in choral readings and in dramatizing events of the Revolution. For example, the teacher could read some poetry from or about the colonial period and encourage the children to participate in choral readings of other selections. Small groups could dramatize events such as the Boston Tea Party or could role-play a conversation between a loyal British colonist and a supporter of the Revolution as they discuss an event of the war.

4. Write a newspaper account of an event in the Revolution. Write summaries of films or oral presentations. Write scripts for plays or reports. Write reports of research findings. Write journals.

5. Read texts, newspapers, diaries, journals, government documents, biographies, reports, and reference materials.

Instructional Opportunities

The unit creates a variety of instructional opportunities. Some of the instruction would be presented to small groups, some to the whole group, and some individually. Instructional opportunities include helping students recognize the structure and organizational patterns of the text material, comparing readings in several genres, and skimming the text for specific information. The teacher might present techniques for taking notes on written and oral material and locating information in the library or in different reference books. Lessons might focus on making and reading maps, developing abilities in outlining and summarizing, and recognizing the special structure of newspaper writing and biographies. Another reading experience not likely to arise in the basal is the interpretation of charts and graphs that have real meaning to the readers. The difference in children's reading a graph that they have been involved in developing and a graph that is presented to teach how to read a graph is significant. Structured this way, the unit would make a number of literacy experiences possible.

Literacy Experiences

▼ Skimming material to find relevant information

▼ Predicting content of text material from headings/questions; confirming or rejecting predictions

▼ Reading text material

▼ Locating information in library

▼ Reading newspaper reports

▼ Taking notes on reference materials

▼ Writing scripts for presentation

▼ Summarizing material presented in oral form

▼ Reading charts

▼ Reading maps

▼ Writing letters

▼ Participating in choral reading

▼ Reading and following directions

▼ Writing journal entries

▼ Writing an ABC book

A study of the American Revolution can be enhanced by using children's literature. Books of historical fiction such as *Johnny Tremain* (Forbes, 1943) and *My Brother Sam Is Dead* (Collier & Collier, 1974) offer children a chance to personalize the events of any historical period. Teachers must select historical fiction carefully and be prepared to discuss the books in terms of what is factual and what is fictional in the stories. Other books offer children a view of such issues as slavery, women's rights, and other topics that are important in the social studies curriculum.

A Thematic Example

Organizing curriculum experiences around a theme offers many advantages to the learner and the teacher. When the teacher understands how the activities are related to the theme and long-range goals, he or she will be much more able to help children see the connections between and among their daily activities. Theme studies provide opportunities for the following:

1. In-depth exploration of a topic and learning that is more than just superficial coverage

2. More choice and therefore more motivation to learn and satisfaction with the results

3. Reduced student stress and a more brain-compatible learning environment

4. More active learning

5. An opportunity for the teacher to learn along with the children and model lifelong learning

6. A more effective use of student and teacher time.

Thematic organization does not mean the teacher is not responsible for teaching, but less of the teacher's time may be spent in lecture or direct instruction. More of the teacher's time will be spent in helping children achieve their own learning goals (individual instruction), securing resources, and arranging learning experiences.

A thematic approach to curriculum means a theme is selected that will allow the teacher to meet long-range goals as well as content and skill objectives. Long-range goals are the broad goals of a school year such as learning to communicate more effectively, learning to use skills to meet individual needs and personal desires, and learning to retrieve and organize data. Content and skill objectives must be related to the long-range goals. Content objectives might include learning to write three forms of poetry, learning to classify animals, learning to use the calculator and computer to solve mathematical problems, and learning to recognize the patterns of family organization. Skills objectives might include learning to select the best reference source to achieve a goal, learning how to use the dictionary effectively, learning how to use a database program to record the growth of the classroom hamster, and learning how to read and interpret graphs. Content and skill objectives are taken from the curriculum guides of the school or the state curriculum.

In selecting a theme, teachers must consider their goals and objectives, the interests of the children, and the interests of the teacher. Some examples of themes that could unify the curriculum are communication, change, patterns, pathways, energy, cycles, and survival. Once the theme has been chosen, then a number of topics related to the theme can be selected. Depending on the age of the class and the resources, two, three, or four topics might be selected. Topics for the theme of pathways for fifth grade might include the westward movement, the human body, and the solar system. Topics for cycles for second grade might include life cycles, water cycles, and the seasons. Topics are selected that will allow for the achievement of content and skills objectives, are interesting to both children and teachers, are age appropriate, for which resources are obtainable, and whose content is worthy of teaching. Brophy and Alleman (1991) say content should be that which would be taught regardless of whether the curriculum is integrated or not. None of these criteria would support the selection of such "superficial units or themes" as circus, dragons, kites, bears, cars, animals, and so on (Routman, 1991). It is easy to fall into the trap of cute or "decorator" themes that have no real content.

Figure 12.1 is a sample unit planner for a theme of environmental change. It illustrates that the teacher must plan for activities that meet curriculum goals as well as evaluation.

After the selection of the theme and the topics, teachers must plan activities. As we previously stated, the topic must be one in which real and concrete activities are possible. The first stage in these activities is the gathering of information. In this stage everyone can be successful and the activities are concrete, not abstract. For example, in a study of the human body, the class might take a field trip to a museum where human skeletons are on display, have a doctor visit the class to talk about the human body, draw outlines of their own bodies, dissect the lungs or heart of a cow, or dissect a pig or frog, and so on. In the second stage, the activities would be more abstract such as finding

UNIT Our local park	**CLASS** 3/4 **4 WEEKS** (_____/_____/_____)

Understandings: (i) The natural environment is constantly changing. (ii) There are a range of factors that influence this change. (iii) Humans have had an adverse impact on the natural environment.

CONTENT Social studies, science and technology, personal development

TUNING IN

Engaging children
Outdoor activity: Children listen to and describe outdoor sounds.
Read a page from *Storm Boy* that describes the environment; imagine that you are there; describe what you see and hear. Children share descriptive passages from other texts.

Preparing to find out
Focus questions: Why do we have local parks? What do you know about our local park? Groups paint murals to show the park in the four seasons. Interview parents about their use of the park. List questions for the ranger. Decide on personal issue for study. What animals do you think live in the park? How do you think they affect the park?

INVESTIGATING

Shared experiences—at the local park
1. Session with the ranger
2. Look at leaf and bark samples, make rubbings
3. List types of litter
4. Write information found on any signs
5. List play equipment and facilities
6. Record evidence of animal habitation
7. Record evidence of effects of people
8. Interview people about their use of the park

Gathering, sorting, and presenting
Return to work done before the excursion. What do you need to change or add? Take leaf and bark rubbings, sort and label display. What have you found out about people in the park? Animals in the park? Uses and abuses of the park? Proposal to build a skateboarding ramp in the park—children take roles of various people involved and act out meeting. Writing of argument presenting different points of view and stating conclusion. Writing of draft statements of generalization in groups—groups meet and whole class statements are prepared. Share future literature, collect newspaper articles. Revising generalizations.

OUTCOMES

Drawing conclusions, reflection, and action
Revising generalizations: What do we know now? Review statements, photographs, artwork, graphs. Complete a fact sheet (for others) with important, amazing new information. Planting of seedlings, making a new garden bed, constructions of flower boxes or preparing pot plants. Produce a pamphlet to advertise local park facilities—could involve local council or local newspaper. Design a board game using uses and abuses of the park as "positives" and "negatives."

Figure 12.1—Sample Unit Planner
Source: Reprinted by permission of Eleanor Curtain Publishing.

and reading reference materials of various kinds that detailed the systems (pathways) of the human body, interviewing a physician, nurse, or dietician, and learning to calculate the calories needed to maintain one's body weight.

The last stage of activities is the time for solidifying and organizing information. Activities would include making a report, creating diagrams, charts, and other writing activities.

Finally, teachers must think about assessment, both of the children's progress and of the topic itself. Assessment of the individual may take many

(iv) Animals and people depend on the natural environment for their survival. (v) There are many things that we can do as individuals that will help reduce the stresses on the environment. (vi) People respond to the changing environment in different ways, but change ultimately affects us all.

PROCESSING INFORMATION	RELATING SKILLS AND STRATEGIES	EVALUATION
Language/drama/art/math/music	**Activities that emanate from work-in-progress**	**Student assessment**

Oral reading: sharing of passages from narratives that describe different environments →	skimming and scanning to locate appropriate passages	• Unit booklet: 2 entries per week
		  1. Content—what have I learned?
		  2. Process—how did I learn it?

Storytelling: sharing stories about experiences in parks		• Each student to keep a log (or to document in some way) ways in which they gather information
Painting: visual representation of knowledge about parks →	use of appropriate colors and textures to represent the different seasons	(e.g. , sketch book, journal, photograph, album)
Interviewing/brainstorming: to collect information. Listening to and questioning the ranger. Investigating and recording. →	writing and asking effective questions	• Reading—a negotiated response to a text by Colin Thiele
Photography		• Writing—a written (and published) report on some aspect of the unit
Art: leaf and bark rubbings →	image reproduction—a form of printing	• Math—a completed graph (which is "published"—shared/explained)
Maths: pattern work—symmetry, tessellations		**Unit evaluation**
Writing: labelling →	adjectives (describing)	Revisit unit understandings. Were these achieved? Any new (or unplanned) understandings?
Drama: clarification of roles through discussion, role play through meeting. Groups write argumentative piece together. →	summarizing skills; debating skills in argument presentation; statement of position with accompanying evidence; summary of position	Compare children's generalizations with stated understandings.

Math: What are the major uses of the park to (a) people (b) animals? How many types of animals have the park as a habitat? Design a "key" that indicates habitat (e.g., type, location). →	graphing: bar
	          column
	          pie	

Writing/reading: to clarify meaning, to find out about procedures →	synthesizing information from many sources	

Figure 12.1 (*continued*)

forms, including developing a portfolio of work that demonstrates growth toward the content and skill objectives. Assessment of the topic itself may include asking questions about the opportunities for meeting curriculum goals, the worth of the content to the students, and the contributions of the topic to the long-range goals. Some schools with many years of teaching with a thematically organized curriculum find it is difficult to integrate mathematics in an authentic manner, so they schedule a mathematics period in which mathematics is taught as a separate subject (Gamberg, Kwak, Hutchings, Altheim, & Edwards, 1988). Of course, there are theme topics in which math could be authentic and integral. In these cases mathematics would not need a separate period. Figure 12.2 is a sample schedule of how theme studies are handled in one school.

The following is a sample topic of life cycles under the theme of cycles for third or fourth grade. (This is only one part of the topic. Most teachers

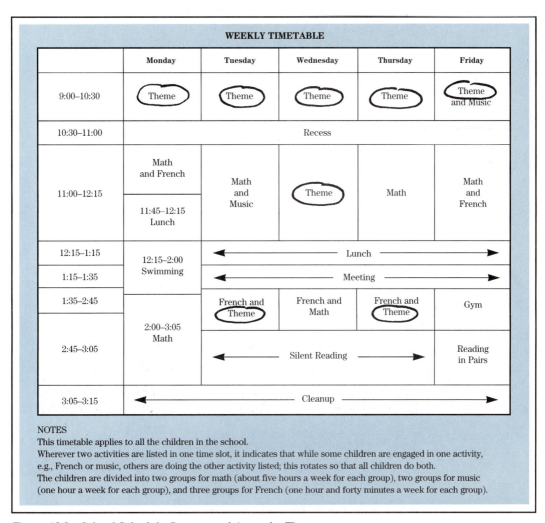

WEEKLY TIMETABLE

	Monday	Tuesday	Wednesday	Thursday	Friday
9:00–10:30	Theme	Theme	Theme	Theme	Theme and Music
10:30–11:00	Recess				
11:00–12:15	Math and French / 11:45–12:15 Lunch	Math and Music	Theme	Math	Math and French
12:15–1:15	12:15–2:00 Swimming	← Lunch →			
1:15–1:35		← Meeting →			
1:35–2:45	2:00–3:05 Math	French and Theme	French and Math	French and Theme	Gym
2:45–3:05		← Silent Reading →			Reading in Pairs
3:05–3:15	← Cleanup →				

NOTES
This timetable applies to all the children in the school.
Wherever two activities are listed in one time slot, it indicates that while some children are engaged in one activity, e.g., French or music, others are doing the other activity listed; this rotates so that all children do both.
The children are divided into two groups for math (about five hours a week for each group), two groups for music (one hour a week for each group), and three groups for French (one hour and forty minutes a week for each group).

Figure 12.2—School Schedule Constructed Around a Theme

Source: Reprinted by permission of Ruth Gamberg, Winniefred Kwak, Meredith Hutchings, Judy Altheim: *Learning and Loving It: Theme Studies in the Classroom* (Heinemann, a division of Reed Elsevier, Inc., Portsmouth, NH, 1988).

would probably include the life cycles of plants and perhaps human beings in this life cycle study.) As teachers plan the activities, they develop a tentative time line for the stages. The first-stage activities may take a few days or in some cases, a few weeks to allow children to gather enough basic information with which to work. The second-stage activities depend on the experience and needs of the class, but may last for a few weeks. The final stage where children summarize and record may take less time than the other stages.

Content: Children will be able to:

1. Describe the life cycles of given insects, amphibians, reptiles, and mammals.

2. Describe the life cycle of given plants.

3. Use the vocabulary of life cycles appropriately.

   Skill: Children will be able to:

1. Write a report.

2. Make an oral presentation (informational).

3. Use various forms of poetry to express knowledge and feelings.

4. Read various reference materials such as a dictionary and encyclopedia.

5. Use a CD-ROM computer program to search for given information.

6. Read narrative materials more effectively.

Stage I Activities

▼ Collect various insects, amphibians, reptiles, and mammals for the classroom.

▼ Invite an entomologist to speak to the class.

▼ Invite a zoologist to speak to the class.

▼ Visit a zoo, looking for evidence of life cycles.

▼ Visit a pet shop focusing on life cycles.

▼ Write invitations and thank you notes to speakers.

▼ Learn note-taking skills.

▼ Invite the zoo mobile or the fish and wildlife officers to bring animals to share with the class.

Stage II *Activities*

▼ Read the descriptions of the life cycle of a given creature in the encyclopedia.

▼ Find information on the life cycle of a given creature using the CD-ROM.

▼ Read narratives about given creatures that focus on the life changes of that creature.

▼ Create habitats for the classroom animals, following the directions in books.

▼ View films or videos that detail the life cycles of given creatures.

▼ Learn how to write given forms of poetry such as haiku or cinquains.

▼ Learn how to write a report.

▼ Learn to use reference materials.

▼ Record the changes in the classroom animals.

Stage III *Activities*

▼ Choose a form of poetry and write about facts or feelings about insects or a selected insect.

▼ Write a report on the life cycle of a selected animal.

▼ Present an oral report of the life cycle of a given animal.

▼ Prepare a chart comparing/contrasting the life cycle of two or more animals.

▼ Create costumes and present poems from *Joyful Noise* (Fleischman, 1988).

▼ Write and illustrate the "life history" of a selected animal.

▼ Create a puzzle or a game that illustrates the life cycle of a selected animal.

▼ Create the lyrics to a song that describe the life cycle of a selected animal.

▼ Create a collage that illustrates the life cycle.

▼ Create movements or a dance to illustrate the life cycle.

At the completion of this part of the theme, the teacher evaluates the work of each student and the value of the topic in terms of meeting the instructional goals for both content and literacy and introduces the next topic related to the theme.

Now that we have looked at organizational strategies, we examine the subject matter areas in terms of their importance to literacy instruction, the research that has been done on the relationships between the subject and literacy, and the benefits to the literacy learner of including the subjects in planning for the growth of children's literacy abilities. First, we look at social studies and science, then mathematics, then the arts including music, art, and drama.

Social Studies, Science, and Literacy

Having been given examples of a unit in social studies and a theme that is science based, you are certainly aware that both social studies and science contribute most to literacy instruction in terms of interesting content. Once we kept a record of the words children requested when using some key word activities. Of the words requested, by far the largest category was science words. That probably does not surprise you because children are very interested in animals and plants and other science topics. What might surprise you is that the next largest category of words was social studies words. Children are also interested in social studies topics—the world of work, people, and communities are all fascinating to them. Content is very important, but so are the styles and formats of social studies and science materials.

Both social studies and science offer children opportunities to learn to read expository material that presents facts and generalizations and they offer graphs, charts, maps, diagrams, and other materials unique to these content areas.

Some have speculated that the first writing was probably to keep records of farm products and sales, certainly related to social studies. Copies of original documents, journal entries, newspapers, magazines, maps, and other materials help children understand how the history presented in the history books is constructed. More recent history is also recorded on film and video.

Interesting content motivates children to share their learning.

© Susan Lapides/Design Conceptions

Gaining skill in reading and analyzing social studies materials is necessary if we expect children to become participating members of a democratic society.

Social studies can provide the topics for themes of study around which the curriculum can be designed. For example, change, conflict, tradition, and interdependence are social studies themes that would lend themselves to study in the elementary classroom.

Social studies materials can help children recognize point of view and evaluate accuracy in the materials they read. For example, in reading about Custer's Last Stand in the history books, one gets a white Euro-American point of view. If children read Goble's *Red Hawk's Account of Custer's Last Battle* (1969/1992) at the same time, they can compare points of view. If they read the encyclopedia's account of Paul Revere's life and read Longfellow's poem at the same time, they can determine what is accurate and not accurate in the poem. Social studies material is also excellent for teaching children to recognize cause and effect. If they read about the Civil War, they cannot avoid the issues of cause and effect.

Writing activities related to social studies topics come naturally in most classrooms. In addition to the types of writing listed in the units, think of the class, school, and community surveys that could be done, newspaper articles, records of field trips or visitors, scrapbooks of artifacts, books (in a variety of formats from ABC to historical fiction), poems, and songs that can be related easily to topics in social studies. Remember that writing needs to be as authentic as possible and children need to be involved in choosing the format and the audience for their writing. The temptation is to assign everyone to write a letter or a poem, but the best instruction allows students to choose.

Science as a subject also has much to offer children in terms of literacy experiences. In the theme on animal life cycles, many different kinds of reading, writing, and speaking experiences were suggested as possibilities. Topics in science do create many opportunities for growth in literacy because the materials for science come in many forms: encyclopedias, textbooks, magazine articles, trade books, dictionaries, and so on. All these forms of print provide the teacher with authentic reasons to help children learn to read the materials. Writing is also inherently important in science. The idea of writing across the curriculum was not that math or science teachers would teach English in the traditional way along with teaching their content, but that they would help students learn how to use literacy as a professional in the field would use it. Therefore, in science students need to learn to write reports, to write results of lab projects, and to write articles explaining their findings to different audiences (such as technical reports and reports for a lay audience to be published in the newspaper or in popular magazines). They might also share scientific information through trade books (as Mr. Klein's class shared their books with younger readers), through reference material, and through poetry (as Byrd Baylor shares information about desert creatures in *Desert Voices*, 1981).

Of course, before children can learn to write in these formats they must learn to read and interpret the formats. Teachers must supply many models of the different kinds of materials that real scientists use in their investigations and help children learn to read the different formats. Then children will be able to learn to choose the most appropriate form for sharing their own work with their classmates and with others.

Do you recall the story about science in Chapter 4 written by a first grader who was not doing well at all in the school's reading program? He would struggle to read anything that had to do with science, and that year we read about how to make disappearing ink (and then wrote messages with the ink), about how to make a pinhole camera and then made one, and other science topics. At home he also read about science and one day dictated the directions for making sparklers. For some children, science provides the motivation they need to learn to read and write.

As with social studies materials, science materials provide opportunities for children to learn to read charts, graphs, and diagrams. As children are involved in science they can create their own charts, graphs, and diagrams to use in explaining their findings. Real classrooms where children observe, talk about, read about, and write about things that interest them will be classrooms alive with science projects.

In recent years, teachers have begun to look at the possibilities of connections between children's literature and the concepts taught in the science curriculum. Butzow and Butzow (1989) have suggested many possibilities for such connections in their publication, *Science Through Children's Literature: An Integrated Approach*. A more recent publication of the Lawrence Hall of Science (1993), *Once Upon a GEMS Guide: Connecting Young People's Literature to Great Expectations in Math and Science*, offers literature suggestions to accompany the GEMS projects. The wide choices of good trade books makes it possible to enhance the study of almost any topic with literature. For example, a few of the books suitable for use when studying the environment include *Just a Dream* (Van Allsburg, 1990), *The Great Kapok Tree* (Cherry, 1990), *The Window* (Baker, 1991), and *Someday a Tree* (Bunting, 1993).

Mathematics and Literacy Instruction

Mathematics offers possibilities for literacy instruction that many teachers fail to recognize. Mathematics is a language in the sense that it is certainly a way of recording and communicating ideas. Just as children must learn to interpret the graphophonic symbols in reading, they must learn to interpret the mathematical symbols in mathematics. There are common strategies for learning to interpret these symbol systems. One of these is an emphasis on meaning. We read to get meaning from print and we use mathematical symbols to describe our world or solve our problems. We also know that children involved in applying the strategies of the reading process realize that more than one strategy may be needed to achieve the goal of making meaning. In the same sense, more than one strategy may be needed to solve mathematical problems.

Several strategies that are successful in helping children learn to read also are effective in helping children learn mathematics. Winograd (1992) found that children could write their own problems, which was a meaningful writing experience in which children not only learned to create math problems, but also learned language-arts skills. Children learning mathematics can keep learning logs in which they record in words the strategies and algorithms they are learning.

Figure 12.3 is an example of writing algorithms. This child wrote about the strategies she used in solving subtraction problems.

Silverman, Winograd, and Strohauer (1992) suggest that teachers begin a story-problem writing experience by sharing a personal story and helping children generate the math problems that could logically be connected to the story. Next, they recommend that teachers lead a brainstorming session in which children identify topics that would be suitable for story-problem generation. Third,

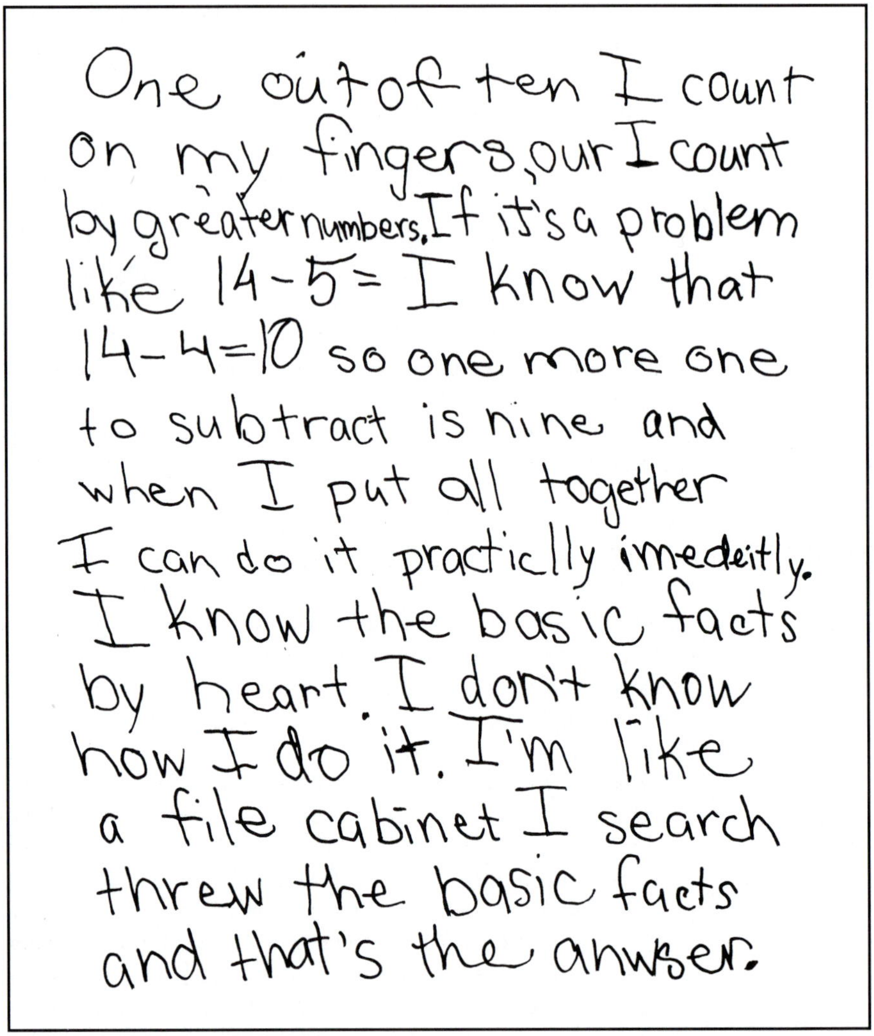

> One out of ten I count on my fingers, our I count by greater numbers. If it's a problem like 14-5= I know that 14-4=10 so one more one to subtract is nine and when I put all together I can do it practiclly imedeitly. I know the basic facts by heart. I don't know how I do it. I'm like a file cabinet I search threw the basic facts and that's the anwser.

Figure 12.3—Fourth Grader's Explanation of Subtraction Strategies

the students write their own stories. Fourth, the students share (and explain if needed) their problems in small groups. The creation of a "mathematics chair" modeled after the author's chair of Graves and Hansen (1983) gives students a chance to share their problems. They observed that the mathematics chair provided opportunities for

▼ posing new questions from the problem

▼ teaching or reviewing a heuristic that is pertinent to the problem

▼ generating new topics for problems similar to the one on the chalkboard

▼ sharing and weighing diverse solution strategies

▼ assessing the coherence of, and recommending revisions to, the problem (Silverman, Winograd, & Strohauer, 1992, p. 9).

Finally, the problems of the students are published at least once every two weeks.

For example, the teacher might tell a story about a recent vacation trip he had taken. The children would then help to develop problems that could be generated from the story such as miles traveled, cost per mile, distance between points, time elapsed between points, costs per day for food and lodging, costs per person for entertainment, comparison of costs when traveling by car, by train, or by air, and so on. Next the students would brainstorm ideas for appropriate stories from which problems could be generated such as care of a pet, hobbies, and families. Then the students would write stories and generate problems to be shared in small groups.

Richards (1990) summarizes the types of writing that children do when writing about mathematics as follows:

▼ Summaries: of findings, processes used; learning done

▼ Translations: of definitions, information; concepts and how they are applied

▼ Definitions: of terms used; mathematics areas

▼ Reports: on an area of mathematics; their work and what they've done

▼ Personal writing: feelings; conversational reports and responses; letters of response

▼ Labels: for diagrams accompanying explanations; numerical representations

▼ Instructions: for solving a problem (steps involved)

▼ Notes: from books; from other children's books; from peers' tutor sessions; from teacher/tutor sessions; ideas to follow through

▼ Lists: of findings, knowledge; words; symbols/terminology; ideas; questions; goals, content

▼   Evaluations: feedback sheets; comments about work

▼   Descriptions: of procedures; conversations

▼   Predictions: for outcomes; strategies; meanings of terms; results; methods

▼   Arguments: to persuade others and give their point of view

▼   Explanations: of learning processes; findings; terms; strategies; answers; where challenges come from; applications; procedures; how they came to beliefs/interpretations; rules or patterns. (p. 18)

Literature offers many possibilities for introducing, connecting, and strengthening concepts in mathematics. In *Books You Can Count On*, Griffiths and Clyne (1988) suggest books for use in introducing, exploring, or defining the concepts of counting; computation; pattern and order; classification; spatial relations; measurement; time, money, and recording. A similar publication, *Strengthening Math Achievement in K–2 Classrooms: Using Integrated, Whole Language Strategies* (Wrightman, 1992), offers many suggestions for developing the math concepts presented in children's trade books. In *Math and Literature* (Burns, 1992), the author offers a collection of sample math lessons based on books. In *Read Any Good Math Lately? Children's Books for Mathematical Learning K–6* (Whitin & Wilde, 1992), the authors provide many examples of books and writing activities arranged by mathematical topics. Most of the books recommended by these authors are narrative stories that happen to include mathematical ideas or problems. Other trade books provide specific information about mathematics.

The Arts and Literacy

In addition to social studies, science, and mathematics, the arts are very important in literacy instruction. The arts include music, art, and drama, and each has something to offer the teacher who wants to help children become successful readers and writers. In support of the arts in literacy instruction Hoyt (1992) says, "We must find ways to engage the learner's affective as well as cognitive self through a wide variety of interactions and experiences in many kinds of literacies" (p. 584).

Music and the Literacy Connection

Singing is a celebration of language. Language naturally has rhythm and melody; one need only listen to the language of children to hear it. Children bring this natural music of language with them to the task of learning to read, and so using singing to teach reading draws on the native understanding of language that all children share although they may not be able to verbalize their knowledge. It makes sense to integrate music and reading in the elementary school classroom: Language and music go together like walking and dancing.

Spontaneous Expression

Using singing to teach reading may sound like a simplistic approach to what some see as a very complex task. Holdaway (1980) has said that too often we become confused by the complexities of teaching reading and find it hard to see the "wood for the trees." In teaching reading, he says, we must provide for the most "sensible and obvious things first." Holdaway continues,

> What are the simple and obvious things? What *is* common sense in teaching reading? Perhaps we could agree as a starting point that reading is a language activity and that *anything we do in the teaching of reading should be consistent with the nature and purposes of language.* Most importantly, reading is the accomplishment of full, accurate, and satisfying meanings. (p. 13, italics in original)

We believe using songs to teach reading is consistent with the nature and purposes of language. Songs puts readers in touch with satisfying meanings.

Aid to Learning

The most compelling reasons to use music in reading instruction are it increases the likelihood that children will experience success, and it represents another way of allowing children to experience language as a whole. Although the research studies that would support the actual benefits are mixed in their results (Groff, 1977), many teachers have written about their experiences in using music in the classroom. Zinar (1976) found the following beneficial effects of music instruction on reading:

1. Slow readers learn to read music well.

2. Better music readers are better language readers.

3. High interest in music increases attention span.

4. Sensory activity is increased through music.

5. Self-concept is improved through successes in music.

6. Common connections exist between eye and ear understanding in both music and reading.

Expression through art is another way of communicating meaning.

© Jerry Speier/Design Concepts

McCarthy (1985) suggests that the elements of music—rhythm, melody, harmony, dynamics, form, and mood—are qualities that promote the development of language. Suggestions for the classroom include using action songs that are highly repetitive and simple to sing. Murphy (1987) discusses his success in teaching second-language learners using music and songs. He believes music is a meaningful language learning activity.

Baechtold and Algier (1986) used limericks and rhymes set to the melody of well-known songs to help students learn vocabulary. They found that students did remember the vocabulary better and were more motivated to learn. Think how easy it is for children to remember the jingles they hear on television; advertisers are well aware of the value of rhymes and songs in remembering. Collett (1991) describes a program called Learning to Read Through the Arts in which the music teachers and classroom teachers develop themes and integrate curriculum experiences. This program has helped children improve their reading and writing abilities. She says the teachers in the program "realize that the visual and performing arts provide children with the concrete, hands-on experiences that are essential to developing each child's ability to reason, think, solve problems, analyze, and evaluate, and to enhancing his or her creativity" (p. 45). Even though more research needs to be done to establish direct links between learning music and literacy skills, music certainly has the potential to be effective in helping elementary students achieve literacy goals.

Writing experiences that are authentic can be based on music. For example, children can design and administer a survey to determine the musical preferences of their classmates or of children in the school. They can write reviews of new music for the class newspaper (after reading model music reviews from the local paper or from magazines). They can write a play and then choose the music that would best accompany the action. And, of course, they can write new lyrics to familiar melodies or new songs.

Art and the Literacy Connection

At first glance it might seem that doing art activities during reading time would rob the reading program; however, closer examination reveals another picture. If reading is defined as the act of bringing individual experience to a printed text in order to construct ideas, then reading and art share some common characteristics. A reader must take in information and evaluate it in terms of his or her own experience. In doing art, too, the child is taking in information, evaluating it against personal experience, and constructing symbol systems for representing what he or she sees and knows. Therefore, the mental processes required in art and reading have some elements in common (Van Buren, 1986).

A review of the literature reveals only a handful of articles that deal with the relationship between art and reading. Most authors, such as Bookbinder (1975) and Macey (1978), describe ways to use art to motivate reading. Others, such as Jansson and Schillereff (1980), have reported using art activities with remedial readers. In most cases art is used as a subject of study leading to reading or as a way to add interest to the reading act. A very limited number of authors report relationships between art activities and specific reading skills. McGuire (1984) presented strong evidence for the position that whereas the visual arts and music may diverge from the cognitive/perceptual process of language and reading in some aspects, they overlap in others. McGuire reported on others' work that shows interactions between language and drawing, between making associations in the arts and making associations in reading, between imagery in the arts and imagery in reading, and between arts-centered curricula and reading achievement.

Art may also help children clarify their experience in order to be able to write about it. Lucy Calkins (1986, p. 47) reports sitting down with a first-grade child and asking what he was going to write about that day. He responded, "I don't know. I haven't drawed it yet." Some experiences become focused enough for children to begin to describe them through language after they have selected the elements of the experience and drawn them.

Art as Motivation

On a more practical level, the heart of the relationship between art and literacy seems to be motivation. Criscuolo (1985, p. 13) reports, "Most kids like art, and that's something you can capitalize on when it comes to the teaching of reading. Reading and art have one very important thing in common: both offer pleasure to the child." Criscuolo asserts that art can mean a welcome break from drill in reading because it lends itself to a whole host of activities. Four of the 15 art activities he proposes to integrate with reading are drawing costumes for a favorite book character, making a collage to illustrate a favorite story, decorating a container such as a coffee can to reflect the theme of a book and putting into the container five or six objects mentioned in the book, and making shadow puppets with which to present a story.

A good example of art used to motivate reading was described by Cunningham (1982), who found a series of how-to-draw books that included interesting descriptive material in the text. In addition to furnishing the directions for the drawings, the books offered multiple opportunities for teaching vocabulary. *How to Draw Cats* (Rancan, 1981) includes the following informational passage about cats:

> Persian cats originally came from Asia. Their luxurious coats can grow up to 5" (12 centimeters) long. These cats require a lot of brushing and special care to keep them looking well-groomed. Persians have short legs and stocky bodies. They are bred in a variety of colors.

In the directions for drawing cats, the instructions specify drawing "slanted eyes" and making fur that looks "soft, not hard and stiff." Reading these directions, children learn vocabulary terms in a meaningful and interesting context.

Another series, the thumbprint books of Ed Emberley (1977), have also proved to be very useful in reading and writing instruction. Children have created thumbprint characters and then written narratives about them, as well as using the thumbprint characters to illustrate stories they had already written. Children practice the reading skills of sequencing and following directions when they read and follow Emberley's instructions. They can also write their own directions for characters they invent.

Classroom teachers can combine art and literacy instruction without the use of a set of books. Working with the district art specialist to plan thematic instruction, the classroom teacher chooses the content to be introduced to the children. The art teacher helps plan related art experiences, such as sculpting and painting models of birds while the children are reading and writing about birds. As the children carry out the art activities, they review and expand their concepts and their ability to relate printed information to their own understandings.

Integration of Art and Literacy Activities

Some school programs combine art and reading. For example, art, reading, and writing experiences can be planned around a theme. Each student can keep a journal in which original stories, vocabulary lists, and detailed directions for art projects are recorded. It is logical that involvement in describing experiences both visually and verbally will help children think and communicate more effectively (Rabson, 1982).

Another strategy for integrating art with literacy is described by Thoms (1985). Children are encouraged to express through poetry their feelings about a selected painting. In writing poetry, the children are using one art form to express the complexities of human response to objects in another art form.

Writing about art and one's response to art could take other forms too. For example, children might write a factual report on the history of a painting or perhaps compose a letter explaining their response to a painting or a newspaper article critiquing the painting. Each of these writing experiences would require reading models of similar writing and gaining enough knowledge about the art object to write about it.

Illustration is an effective way to relate art and literacy. Many of the techniques of illustration can be introduced through picture books. Picture books provide examples of illustrations in many media. For instance, the artist of *Once a Mouse* (Brown, 1961) illustrates the fable with woodcuts. Although woodcuts are too difficult for elementary children, they could explore a similar medium such as linoleum prints. Geometric shapes and bright colors characterize Gerald McDermott's (1974) *Arrow to the Sun*. Children could try making figures on graph paper or using pattern blocks to create shapes and figures. In *The Snowy Day*, Ezra Jack Keats (1962) works with collage and paint. Children might try sponge painting the background for their own illustrations and then adding paper cutouts. Denise Fleming illustrates her books *Lunch* (1992), *In the Tall, Tall Grass* (1991), and *In the Small, Small Pond* (1993) with handmade paper. Children as young as first graders could be assisted in making paper with colorful images. For older children, the cut paper illustrations of Wisniewski's books, *Sundiata: Lion King of Mali* (1992), *The Warrior and the Wise Man* (1989), and *Rain Player* (1991), could challenge students to produce cut paper designs of their own.

Preparing special paper on which to write poetry or to mount a page of poetry can add a dimension to children's writing experiences. Doing a watercolor wash or preparing marbleized paper helps children feel their work is valuable and increases the ways in which they can experience ownership of it. The poetry of *In a Spring Garden* (Lewis, 1965) is printed over beautiful washes and illustrations created by Ezra Jack Keats.

If art is often employed as a motivational tool in teaching reading and writing, art can also be the subject itself. Children can be encouraged to read about artists and about art techniques and styles. They could write a dictionary of art terminology. Catalogs from art galleries might serve as models for descriptions of pieces of art. Perhaps the students could prepare a catalog of works of public art to be used by the local chamber of commerce.

An art-related writing experience of another sort would be a how-to manual for art techniques. For example, children could write all the directions for creating a crayon resist, a tie-dye piece, or a batik painting. The manual could be placed in the art center for use by children doing actual projects. Reading of various sources and then taking notes while observing the process during execution would be necessary before doing the writing. The skills of organization, thoroughness, and accuracy involved in writing how-to directions are of enormous practical value in both scholastic and professional careers.

Clearly, art and reading can be instructional teammates. Art can be the motivating element in encouraging reading and writing experiences. Art can embellish the pieces of writing the child chooses to publish and encourage pride in the presentation of ideas. Art can help children clarify and represent experiences about which they can then talk and write. Art can serve as the subject of reading and writing experiences that are interesting and meaningful.

Drama and the Literacy Connection

Literacy development and drama are natural partners. Booth (1985, p. 193) eloquently states the case for combining reading and drama:

> As an act of learning, reading is basically a private experience and drama generally a shared one. When children read, they understand what the words say to them, translate the experience being read about into their own context, and conjure up feelings, attitudes, and ideas concerning everything from the author's values to their own life situations. They react and respond personally, free from outside intervention, to enter as deeply as they decide into this new world of meaning.
>
> The interactive, participating model of the drama experience helps children grow in a different way, moving them forward toward new, collective understanding. This does not mean, however, that drama is just an activity to be used after reading a story, as a check of comprehension, or as a means of motivating children to read a particular selection. It may assist in these goals, but it is, on its own, a powerful medium for helping children make learning happen.

In a description of some of the drama activities at a school for gifted children, Pigott (1990) writes, "Drama helps in almost every step of children's learning and understanding" (p. 5).

Dramatic Activities

Drama and reading have in common the creation of meaning from words, the use of language to express meanings, and the requirement that the participant bring his or her own experience to the material in order to interpret it. Several forms of drama are useful in literacy instruction: improvised drama or role play, story dramatization, readers' theater, and dramatic play. These forms of drama also provide a meaningful context in which children can apply and extend their abilities in reading and writing.

Improvised Drama

Drama that is performed without benefit of script, costumes, or staging and with little or no rehearsal is improvised drama. This sort of drama takes place when children act out something they have read, either in a story or in content-area materials. Improvised drama may be very spontaneous. Just a quick

Readers' theater encourages in-depth comprehension of the material.

© Steven Lunetta/StockUp

enactment of something they are reading can help fix its meaning in children's minds. For example, if children are reading about magnets and two children demonstrate the actions of repelling and attracting, that is improvised drama. So is the role playing of a person's actions in a given situation, which can help children understand that person's responses or behaviors.

Older children can role-play various social situations to help them clarify their understandings of language use and the interactions of characters. For example, they could role-play a town hall meeting to decide where a new road should go through the city, taking the roles of citizens who would lose their homes, business owners who would reap financial gains, environmentalists who believe the new road would destroy some animal habitats, and others. Each of these situations helps children see things from someone else's perspective and think about how others use language to express themselves.

Drama can add new dimensions to a study of history as children dramatize scenes from the past or political debates of the present. Certainly drama is important when children are studying biography as well as narratives. McGruder (1993) encourages her students to write a story, then dramatize it, and with the help of the group, rewrite and revise. She finds children are willing to revise if the piece is to be dramatized.

When used with intermediate-grade children in two economically disadvantaged regions of a large eastern city, improvisational dramatics resulted in improved reading achievement and in more positive attitudes, specifically those regarding self-expression, trust, acceptance of others, self-awareness, and awareness of others (Gourgey, Bosseau, & Delgado, 1984).

Story Dramatization

Dramatizing stories can help motivate children to read. When children know they are going to dramatize a story, they tend to read it with increased attention to detail and to think about the characters so they will be able to bring life to them in the dramatization. Story dramatization also leads to improved comprehension. Miccinati and Phelps (1980) suggest that drama provides a way for teachers to assess comprehension beyond the usual asking of questions. Martin, Cramond, and Safter (1982) theorize that dramatizing a story causes children to view the story in its entirety, whereas answering comprehension questions draws attention to only small parts of the reading. A landmark study, frequently referred to in the literature, was reported by Henderson and Shanker (1978). In this study both high and low achievers in reading who dramatized basal stories performed better on comprehension questions than did students who only read the stories. This study is often cited as evidence that dramatization is more powerful as an indicator of comprehension than is answering comprehension questions.

Other researchers have also found positive results on measures of comprehension when dramatization of stories was added to reading instruction. Yawkey (1980) and Pellegrini and Galda (1982) report improved comprehension as a result of role playing and fantasy. Kindergartners and first graders demonstrated better story comprehension through fantasy play than through the typical discussion and drawing of pictures.

Other ways of dramatizing stories include pantomime and puppet shows. Pantomime experiences offer children an opportunity to express nonverbally the meanings they have taken in verbally, whether from literature or from a box of cards prepared for the purpose. For example, a child might pantomime the actions of Little Red Riding Hood as she wanders through the woods picking flowers, meets the wolf, knocks on her grandmother's door, and is surprised by the wolf. Or the child might select a card that describes an activity, read it, and present the pantomime for the class. Cards could call for such actions as eating a very long strand of spaghetti, walking a dog, lifting a very heavy box, and getting dressed to go out to a party.

Readers' Theater

McCaslin (1990) defines readers' theater as "the oral presentation of drama, prose, or poetry by two or more readers" (p. 263). Readers' theater has been found useful in the reading programs for many readers including struggling readers.

Larson (1976, p. 359) describes the characteristics of readers' theater:

1. The use of scenery and costumes is slight. Perhaps only a hat or held prop is used to identify a character.

2. There is not much physical movement or action. Instead, vocal inflections, gestures, and facial expressions suggest action and mood.

3. A narrator fills in much of the setting and action beyond what is carried by the dialogue.

4. A script is used, and the participants read the parts rather than memorizing them.

5. The readers communicate directly with the audience rather than with each other. As they read their parts they make eye contact with the audience.

Readers' theater requires in-depth comprehension of material, careful selection of pieces to be presented, thoughtful adaptations of stories not written for this kind of production, and, of course, much practice in reading as the material is rehearsed and presented. Sloyer (1982) outlines the benefits of readers' theater in the classroom. Included are literary comprehension and enjoyment, good listening habits, oral skills, and creative writing. She explains that children must often write the introductions and transitions that are necessary when material is adapted for a performance.

Johnson (1987) suggests that the sequence of instruction in helping children make adaptations of material for readers' theater includes having an experienced person prepare an adaptation of a familiar story and then having the children compare the original story with the adaptation, noting and discussing the changes and reasons for them. He also suggests that children be taught to recognize the characteristics of stories that would be suitable for readers' theater, characteristics such as these (p. 147):

▼   It must be a good story.

▼   It needs plenty of conversation.

▼   It should have several characters.

▼   It can have a narrator but the narrator's part should not be too long.

Johnson concludes (p. 148), "To say that dramatization helps to develop comprehension is a colossal understatement. . . . Dramatic role-playing is the final word in comprehension."

Wolf (1993) describes a readers' theater program in which at-risk readers were successful in many literacy tasks. These learners had been labeled and placed in special reading instruction. "Through the analytical talk of Readers Theatre—the negotiation, decisions, gestures, set design, reading, drawing, and writing—the boys created and enacted an interpretation of text that demonstrated what they knew and understood about text and the world around them" (p. 545). Many learners can benefit from experiences with readers' theater.

Readers' theater can be done with a variety of genres. For example, one might put together a program of poetry, narrative pieces, or expository pieces. Young and Vardell (1993) recommend the use of nonfiction in the content areas as a good source for readers' theater. They have found that children who participate in the experience of selecting and adapting a nonfiction piece for a theater production not only learn the content, but also gain reading and writing skills. They used science, social studies, health, and math books for successful theater productions.

Expository pieces such as Baylor and Parnall's *Desert Voices* (1981) could be adapted easily to readers' theater. Fleischman has collected poems on birds (*I Am Phoenix*, 1985) and insects (*Joyful Noise*, 1988) which could serve as a basis for readers' theater on those topics. Lee Bennett Hopkins has collected baseball poems in a volume entitled *Extra Innings* (1993). Several of these selections would make an interesting production (and props—gloves and hats—are readily available). An introduction would have to be written by the group and then different characters could read the poems with a transition by the narrator where it was needed. You could begin with Isabel Joshlin Glaser's poem, "Prediction: School P.E."

Someday
When the baseball's
   hurtling
like some UFO
   blazing
like some mad thing
   toward me
   in outfield
I *won't* gasp
and dodge. Oh, no!
Instead, I'll be
calmer than calm
   —so la-de-da!—
I'll just reach out
   like a *pro*
and catch it and—quick!—
   throw it to second.
And everyone will say, "Hooray!
Natalie made a double-play!"
Some day. (p. 12)

Other poems about baseball could round out the presentation. You might also want to include Ernest Thayer's well-known narrative poem, "Casey at the Bat." There are many ways to organize and present readers' theater that will appeal to an audience and help the participants gain skill.

Benefits of the Drama Connection

Creative drama involves many forms of improvisation, each of which brings excitement to learning. Whether as story dramatization, pantomime, puppet shows, or dramatic play, drama is one of the best ways to integrate curriculum. Language skills become an important part of reading, social studies, and science when children dramatize what they are learning.

Drama makes the use of language purposeful and meaningful. Children have valid reasons to read, speak, and listen when they are preparing for and presenting dramatizations. They see real reasons for reading when they know they are going to dramatize a story.

Drama is a natural companion to reading. When children dramatize they are drawing on the same language and thinking skills they use in reading. They must comprehend and express the details of story sequences, word meanings, plot, and character. Maybe the most important link is that in dramatizing a story they truly draw on their own background to bring meaning to the reading. As children struggle with how to make characters come alive and how to make situations real, they are working to find matches between the ideas in the story and their own experience. They learn that the meanings of words may be personal as they negotiate differing views of how a scene should be played. Dwyer (1990) writes, "Creative dramatics in the reading classroom encourages children to become emotionally as well as academically involved in stories and content oriented reading. Such involvement encourages comprehension through multi-sensory experiences" (p. 2).

McGruder (1993) summarizes the benefits of drama in the classroom:

> The strength of drama in the curriculum is social and personal, academic, and imaginative. Drama allows children to take risks in a safe environment. It provides a socially acceptable way for children to get attention. Drama builds self-confidence. It allows children and teachers to find and appreciate the uniqueness in others, and perhaps more importantly, in themselves. Drama requires cooperation and group effort. It requires a balance between freedom and self-discipline. It helps children develop the ability to relax, to concentrate, to remember, to focus, and to imagine. Drama provides children with a broader means of creative expression. And finally, because children are encouraged to use all the tools of language, body, voice, and mind, they become better, happier learners within an academic setting. (p. 158)

Drama and Writing

Children have many opportunities to write when they are involved with drama activities. They can write scripts for skits, plays, or puppet plays. Readers' theater usually requires that a piece be adapted or the narration written to connect pieces together into a coherent whole for presentation. Other drama such as story dramatization might encourage children to write their own stories for others to dramatize. Writing for production is certainly highly motivating and provides purpose for the children's writing. Drama is also a good reason for children to learn to write dialogue with its unique features. Reviews of dramatic productions for the school newspaper can also be a good writing experience for children.

Major Ideas in This Chapter

▼   Activities selected for instructional purposes should help children connect what they already know to new information, have multiple outcomes, be interesting to children, involve children in hands-on experiences, include genuine needs for literacy, and allow children as much choice as possible.

▼   Strategies for organizing curriculum include planning units and themes. Units usually last several days or several weeks and are focused primarily on one subject matter. Themes may last from several months to a year and integrate all the subject matter areas into instruction.

▼ Social studies and science offer the teacher opportunities to involve children in reading that interests them and has unique features such as graphs, maps, charts, and tables. The goal in social studies and science is to involve children in literacy experiences that social scientists, historians, and scientists use in the real world.

▼ Children can read and write and discuss mathematics as well as other subject matter areas. There are many ways of helping children become more literate based on the content of mathematics.

▼ The arts—music, art, and drama—offer support and motivation for mastering literacy skills. The arts, as well as other subject matter areas, provide children with real reasons for reading and writing.

Discussion Questions: Focusing on the Teacher You Are Becoming

1. More puzzled than critical, a parent inquires why his son is drawing at school when he should be learning the basic skills. How will you respond?

2. A debate is going on around the lunch table in the staff room. The kindergarten teacher is trying to convince the fifth-grade teacher that dress-up boxes would be as appropriate in fifth grade as in kindergarten. What position would you take and how would you defend it?

3. This chapter argues the case for developing some literacy abilities through social studies and the sciences. Discuss the differences between materials included in basal readers and materials found in social studies and science texts.

4. Discuss the advantages of organizing social studies and science instruction so you can help children gain abilities in literacy while they learn content.

5. Some curriculum planners are worried the content of social studies and the sciences will be neglected if they are included in thematic approaches. Discuss ways in which you could make sure children learned content material well.

6. On the surface, mathematics seems to be the least promising of the subject matter areas for helping children become more literate. With a group, make a list of as many ways as you can think of that connect math and literacy.

Field-Based Applications

1. Encourage children to draw illustrations for a story before they write it so you can see what the child meant when he said he couldn't say what he would write because he hadn't "drawed it yet."

2. Assemble a collection of picture books that use a variety of media in their illustrations. Explore the various media with children and invite them to use them in their own illustrations.

3. Experiment with the power of story dramatization. Have one group of children read a story without making any mention of dramatization before they read. Have another, similar group of students read the same story, but first talk with them about plans to dramatize the story later on. See how differently the two groups approach the reading activity.

4. Borrow a social studies or science curriculum guide from a school district. Choose a topic that is recommended and develop a list of possible activities around that topic. Highlight the activities that would help achieve goals in literacy.

5. Examine the topics in an intermediate-grade mathematics text. Plan a literacy experience around one of the topics.

6. Interview several intermediate-grade students about their interests in social studies and science topics. Relate what you find to the topics in the textbooks for their grade.

Chapter 13

Reading, Writing, and Technology: Making the Connection

Cathy Gunn, Ph.D.
Assistant Professor, Educational Computing and Technology
Center for Excellence in Education, Northern Arizona University,
Flagstaff, Arizona

Chapter Overview

▼ Technology should support the curriculum, not direct it.

▼ Using technology with children requires careful decision making; a question that should be foremost in a teacher's mind: "Is this developmentally appropriate?"

▼ One of the most effective uses of a computer is word processing. With a word processor, children can revise and edit their writing. Suddenly there is no such thing as a first draft.

▼ A frequently asked question by teachers is, "How can I use one computer in my classroom effectively?" Answer: Connect the computer to a large screen monitor or use an LCD projection panel to model the writing process.

▼ One of the biggest issues facing educators today in technology is the issue of equity, especially with female students. Modeling the reading and writing process with one computer in the early grades may be one of the best solutions to decrease inequality of computer usage.

▼ Children's perceptions of computer use may determine their own choices in using a computer. Teachers must be aware of perceptions and help build appropriate schema when necessary. This can be done by modeling, by using a computer for writing and communication.

Introduction

Technology in the 1990s means much more than overhead projectors, VCR players, and computers. To embrace the full range of technology available to

443

a literacy environment, the term *technology*, rather than *computers*, is used often throughout this chapter. Technology in a classroom today might include one or more computers; a computer lab; a multimedia workstation consisting of CD-ROM, interactive laser disc, a scanner, movie cameras, video digitizers, bar code readers, still cameras; telecommunications through modem and phone lines; and a TV studio. Technology is one computer connected to a VCR/television monitor for group instruction. Technology is also an overhead projector coupled with a liquid crystal display (LCD) projection panel to project computer images on a screen for large-group display. Children in today's classrooms may receive instruction through distance learning—various content instruction via satellite with the teacher in a studio classroom thousands of miles away and with interaction through a telephone. Although most classrooms have libraries of trade books, student-published books, and reference materials, many will also house books and dictionaries on CD-ROM discs and might include a telecommunications link to national reference databases. A technology-enriched classroom can support a literacy environment, but if not properly used can also interfere with learning.

A computer, a laser disc player, a CD-ROM player, a modem: All offer *alternative* ways of problem solving and developing ways of thinking. Technology should not take the place of books and other sources of text, but instead is one more medium to support literacy development. Making technology work for us in the literacy classroom means selecting and using technology and related materials within a framework of how literacy is learned and taught.

Writing is a complementary aspect of the reading curriculum in a literacy classroom, particularly when meaning is emphasized. Reading and writing are similar in many ways. They are both fostered by the learner's natural desire to communicate, and they both involve the construction of meaning in order to communicate. Whether students are writing their own stories or reading stories written by others, they are actively engaged in a search for meaning using written language. In this chapter, reading and writing activities supported by technology are described.

This chapter is organized into two main sections. The first part presents grades K–3 and 4–8 classroom scenarios with technology definitions and discussions. The second part introduces the topic of teacher decision making in the areas of software selection, gender and economic equity, placement of computers, and children's perceptions of technology.

Technology Supporting Literacy: A View of One School

Stonier and Conlin (1985) discuss education for an information society centering on three C's, children, computers, and communication, rather than the traditional three R's of an industrial society. We know that literacy develops best when children have real reasons to read and write, when reading and writing are used for communication. Books, paper, and pencil are traditional technologies we use to transmit information about ourselves and our culture. Howie (1989) writes that the importance of a book is not in its publication, but in the human activities of reading and writing it. The importance of newer technologies such as computers lies in the human activities involved with its use.

Technology is becoming more available for education and more appropriate. Computers and other technologies are moving into schools, both because they're seen as a part of modern life that students should know about and because educators are finding ways to use them to enhance learning. Teachers are learning how to integrate computer use with classroom learning, rather than simply teaching about computers (Koltnow, 1992). The goal is not to have more teachers and children using computers, but rather to have teachers use wise decision making when choosing when and how to use technology for instruction. You would not construct a lesson plan by sitting down and thinking, "What can I do with the chalkboard today?" Educational technologies are tools to be employed toward educational goals (Dockterman, 1991). In schools everywhere, teachers are learning that using technology in the teaching of reading and writing can offer many instructional advantages.

Following is a description of seven different classrooms in a fictitious, but based on real-life, school. Each classroom may have varying uses of technology to support the reading and writing process. The descriptions of technology use, equipment, software, and terms are given to provide description and a context for each classroom but are not peculiar to a specific grade level (i.e., a word processor is a universal tool used in eighth grade as well as first grade). Teachers and students using technology in reading- and writing-related tasks are described as a way of building background knowledge for the text on technology that follows.

Classroom Scenarios, Grades K–3

Mary's kindergarten class is standing around a large, clear, plastic computer keyboard lying on the floor. The keyboard is approximately 3 feet by 9 feet, and has been made with large markers (because the plastic is clear, Mary was able to trace over a model used in a workshop she had taken without needing letter templates or measuring). A red marker line is drawn from top to bottom midway on the keyboard, dividing the keyboard into left and right sides. Keys that are found on "home row" (asdfjkl;) are shaded blue, indicating where hands are placed to begin typing. Each child has a tagboard sign with a lowercase letter written on it and hung around the neck with yarn. As a word is written on the board, each child looks around to find who has the matching letters. The word is "April" and Monica shouts she has the letter "A." She hops on and then hops off of the keyboard letter "A" (the students have seen what happens when one key is held down too long on the computer keyboard and know to hop on and off to keep the letter from repeating). Jimmy has the letter "p" and can match the lowercase to uppercase easily. Eric has help finding the capital "R" on the keyboard to match with his tagboard "r," but now the majority of the class begin discussing the next step. The next two letters, "i" and "l" have confused the owners of those letters and several others. Jeff explains that the "L" is on home row, and the "i" is on the row above. When Mary asks him how he knows that, he tells her, "I know a capital "l" looks like this: "L" so the stick (I) must be an "i." This activity supports the other letter recognition activities that have been provided in Mary's classroom: reading alphabet books, finding pictures in magazines for a letter dictionary, finding letters in text, and so on. The keyboard is hung on the classroom wall after this lesson for other identification activities that will follow.

On another occasion, Mary's class has been working on left and right and the plastic computer keyboard is used again, but this time there are two children with signs—one with "left" and one with "right." The children tell who is to hop on and off the keyboard to spell the word "yellow." The child with the "right" tag hops on the letters "Y," "L," "L," and "O,"; the child with the "left" tag hops on the letters "E" and "W."

An identical plastic keyboard hung on a hallway wall is used by a number of children each morning as they come into the school building, and anytime they are walking through the hallway. Children can be heard as they walk down the hallway: "I see the letter 'C'—my name starts with that." Or a child can be seen pounding out her name as she calls out each letter as her hand slaps the picture of that letter.

An alternative keyboard, *Muppet Learning Keys*, is used for Mary's early writers. On this keyboard, letters of the alphabet are in ABC order rather than modeled after the traditional keyboard. This allows her young students to find letters easily, but Mary does not use this keyboard with writers for long. She wants them experiencing a keyboard and learning to use two hands as part of her keyboarding instruction. She has found a good mix, by encouraging writing with the *Muppet Learning Keys* and informal play and writing on the traditional keyboard.

▼▼▼▼▼▼▼▼▼▼▼▼▼

Manny's first-grade classroom has one computer, which is placed prominently in the front of the classroom. Connected to the computer is a large-screen monitor that doubles as a VCR monitor. *FrEdWriter*, a public domain word processor, is seen both on the computer monitor and on the large-screen monitor. Children are sitting on the floor, gathered around the monitor, and are writing a group journal about a book by Audrey Wood (1982) they just read together, *Quick as a Cricket*. Parts of the journal (using a "template") were written ahead of this class and saved to disk by Manny. Using a language-experience approach, after reading the book together, the children tell Manny what to include in their journal as he types: today's date, the name of the book, the author, the illustrator, facts about the illustrations, and their favorite parts.

A discussion takes place on the similes read in the book *Quick as a Cricket*, and why authors might use similes in their writing. Manny has typed ahead of

time a simile pattern with the words " 'I'm as _____ as a _____,' said _____."
25 times—once for each child. Each child is given a moment to think of a simile of their own, and Manny types their responses in the simile format. Andy tells him to type " 'I'm as hot as fire,' said Andy."

While Manny has been typing, he has been modeling his typing process as well. As he makes a typing error that does not change the meaning, he tells his students that this is a first draft and he is typing for ideas right now. Later he will go back through and edit, correcting spelling as needed. But as he makes a typing error that might be unreadable for meaning later, he tells his students orally what he is doing: "I can arrow to the word I need to change with the arrow keys . . . I need to be on the right side of the 'ing' so I can use the Delete key to get rid of those letters . . . Delete, Delete, Delete . . . now I will arrow down to where I was typing." Through hearing Manny's verbalization of his writing/typing process, his students see Manny's writing process in action.

When it is John's turn, he tells Manny his simile: "'I'm as cold as ice cream,' said John." Manny types, filling in the blanks, and asks John what kind of ice cream he likes. John tells him "strawberry" and Manny asks if he should insert the word "strawberry" into his sentence. As he begins typing that word, Manny verbalizes the process for inserting text. John interrupts him and asks if he can change his mind. Manny tells John that of course he can change because they are using a word processor, which makes it easy to revise. John wants to change the word "cold" to "red" and now his sentence reads, "'I'm as red as strawberry ice cream,' said John."

When all children have given their simile, the file is edited, saved, and printed out for duplication. Each child takes their group simile writing home to read to three people. Because each child's name is with their simile, developing readers have context (student names, memories of discussion, etc.) to use as they practice reading similes.

After printing the collective simile writing activity, Manny prints each students' individual simile with one simile at the top of each page. These are illustrated by students and published as a class book, with the journal writing included at the beginning of the book. The covers are laminated and the book is put on the shelves of the classroom library for checkout. Soon the book's pages are tattered as it is read over and over again by interested readers.

Manny is able to see the results of this lesson as several students begin to use similes in their writing to provide more description. He also notices that John is using more revision skills as he tries different words, but he is also asking to use the computer instead of paper and pencil for writing more often. Jason, who has wonderful descriptive writing in his "chapter" books, is adding quotation marks around his dialogue. Dialogue has been modeled for him in the simile journal and he refers back to his copy as he writes. No longer is Manny's computer in the back corner of the classroom, used only for drill and practice as children finish their work. Instead, it has become a focal point for group writing activities and for modeling writing processes.

▼▼▼▼▼▼▼▼▼▼▼▼▼

Jan has a computer in her combination second- and third-grade classroom that is used almost every minute of the school day by writers. A colleague asks her how she can schedule all of her students to be at the computer with access to only one. What is Jan's secret? She tells her colleague that it is creative scheduling, but in reality, it is also an awareness of "the haves and the have-nots."

Until recently, Jan's computer was placed in a quiet corner of the room and was used by students who had completed their work early. The software usually found next to the computer was drill and practice math or phonics drill. But Jan attended a "One Computer in the Classroom" workshop recently sponsored by her school district. By reflecting on her own classroom computer practices, she realized she had been promoting inequity of computer use by the male and female students in her classroom. Jan was made aware of research that suggested boys, rather than girls, are encouraged to use the computer when it is used as a reward for completing work early. She also realized that the first students finished with work in her classroom were always the same two or three boys, and that usually their work was not complete. Jan spent the next several weeks observing the use of the classroom computer when it was used as a reward. She noticed Patty was usually the first student finished with her work, but she also was aware now that Patty was spending time checking over her work, and in one case, was actually *pretending* to work. Patty kept an eye on Chris, a student who loved spending time at the computer and had a computer available at home. When Chris and his friend Kirk were settled at the computer as the first students done with their math practice, Patty then, with obvious relief, took out a book to read. Jan remembered that one of the strategies suggested by the "One Computer in the Classroom" workshop facilitator to help eliminate inequity by gender or economics was to use the computer in early grades for language-arts activities, especially writing. Jan became an earnest promoter of providing equal access to computers in her classroom through her choice of activities available and by classroom computer management. One conscious choice was to eliminate any game playing, drill, and practice software that did not support classroom instruction, and to no longer use the computer as a reward.

Jan knows that Kirk, Ellen, and Chris have computers at home. She is also aware that five of her students are in the talented and gifted program (TAG), which is using a computer for writing. Because these eight children have opportunities to use a computer outside of the classroom, Jan assigns writing time at the computer for them and the rest of her students who don't have frequent access.

She asks the three students who have computers at home to help her with special classroom projects—typing a list of books for a learning center, writing a report or article for the class newsletter, an alternative writing assignment, or a list of student names with matching information. For these projects, writing at home on the computer is necessary. All three children enjoy the chance to work on a class project at home and don't see it as extra work. In some cases, Jan substitutes a homework assignment with a special project that requires word processing at home for these three children. Not only do the children with the assignment benefit, but Jan and the rest of the class have a use for the projects in class.

The TAG teacher works closely with Jan, so the writing these gifted students are doing is not a duplication of what they would be doing in class, but an extension. The rest of the students, the "have-nots," the students without regular access to computers, are now scheduled for the computer for writing. A shoebox contains a data disk for each student, and the computer is loaded with a word processor at the beginning of each day. Jan has scheduled the time so students who are good at math can miss an occasional math session; students who enjoy reading and take advantage of any free time to read are scheduled during an occasional reading session. A chart is posted with each child's name and spaces for checking off computer use.

In some cases, Jan takes advantage of a special opportunity for writing by assigning one child to use the word processor while the rest use paper and pencil. For example, during a science report planning time, Jan assigns Bruce to write his report on the computer. It is not necessary for everyone to use the computer for writing the same report. In fact, it is impossible to arrange for every student to access the computer for the same assignments. Bruce has been given the opportunity to use the computer for writing whenever possible during the next couple of days.

A week later, after a discussion on the state capital, Cedric is assigned to write about his trip to the capital for a bulletin board display. He is encouraged to use whatever time he needs to work on this writing, and is excused from several other assignments to allow time for writing. Jan is aware that missing a few assignments or lessons is not a tragedy, and she encourages her students to take advantage of every opportunity for writing. In fact, an observer will see Jan use these same strategies for paper and pencil writing also.

Jan has found other ways to use technology in her classroom using one computer. She checks out a computer and a laser disc player that are moved from room to room as needed on rolling carts. This class is studying about mammals, and Jan remembers from her preview of a laser disc, *Rain Forest* (National Geographic Society), several video clips of animals. She locates the video clips of several insects and mammals from the index and records the frame beginning and ending numbers in her lesson plans. During a lesson on mammal characteristics, Jan uses the laser disc player remote, and the first video clip of a snake shedding its skin is displayed on a monitor. As the narrator talks about what is happening on screen, the students in Jan's class write down their prediction of whether the snake is a mammal. At the conclusion of the lesson, the students divide into small groups to compare their predictions. They are directed to their text and any other resources available in the classroom to write a rationale for their predictions. Cedric and Bruce ask to check their predictions on a CD-ROM disc in the Media Center they remember seeing, a CD-ROM encyclopedia disc on mammals.

Students in Jan's classroom see demonstrations of technology used for real reading and writing activities. Jan models her own use of technology as an instructional and productivity tool. Her students are encouraged to use the technology available to them for the same.

Definitions and Discussion

Plastic Floor Keyboard

A plastic floor keyboard can be ordered through school supply catalogs, but is easily made. Consider a group "Make-It-and-Take-It" workshop where several teachers work together. Purchase clear plastic from a fabric store in lengths of 3 yards (36-inch wide is standard). Use large black markers and 3-inch stencils to draw squares for keys and to fill in letters, numbers, and key function words. Draw a line down the middle of the keyboard with a large red marker to mark the division of left-hand and right-hand letters. Outline the letters of the home row (asdfjkl;) with a blue marker. Once one keyboard is made, others can be traced by placing the original keyboard under the clear plastic lengths.

Keyboarding

Computer keyboarding skills are primarily typing skills, that is, striking desired keys accurately and quickly, including the skills needed to correctly use special keys such as ESC and CTRL.

For a teacher to begin using a word processor for writing with a class of students, several factors must be taken into consideration. Students need time and guidance to become efficient at using a word processor. The process of writing has to be emphasized in a meaningful context, and a teacher has to plan for adequate access to the computer. An issue that must be addressed before using any word processor with children is prior keyboarding instruction. Wheeler (1985) states, "Current research indicates that without proper teaching, inexperienced writers do not improve their writing by using a word processor" (p. 58). This includes keyboarding. Students who type better are more enthusiastic about using the computer for writing. Students who have adequate keyboarding skills use their time at the computer efficiently. That is, they can concentrate on problem solving or composing, rather than on the mechanics of typing (Wetzel, 1985). A rule of thumb is to introduce keyboarding to students immediately before they begin using a computer for writing. Educators anxious to integrate a word processor into their literacy curriculum should not let fears of teaching keyboarding keep their students from writing at the computer.

Although lack of typing ability does not prevent writers from using word processors, the more typing ability they have, the faster they will be able to get things done. There are a number of typing practice programs available, many of which take the form of games that make learning to type interesting and fun. Many elementary teachers use introduction to the keyboard as an opportunity to provide practice with the alphabet and numbers. Keyboarding can be taught as an integral part of learning to write. Students as young as kindergarten can learn about the computer keyboard. Keyboarding in this case does not mean correct finger placement, although this age student can learn to use both hands. Think about the literacy acts students are already involved in at this age.

> Jonathon is learning how to keyboard in a new way. He thinks about the sounds in the word he wants to write and associates each sound with a finger stroke on the keyboard. He has actually learned a difficult cognitive task—the whole process of encoding—as part of learning to keyboard and word process. (Herron, 1992, p. 31)

Word processing provides another opportunity for using the writing process.

© Spencer Grant/Stock Boston

Recognition of letters and numbers, spelling of names and color words, words used in story writing—all of these literacy events can be supported with the keyboard. Primary students can be taught the position of the home row keys and the correct finger for touching each key. This requires little additional instruction time; when a reading lesson introduces a new letter, students can practice the letter on paper keyboards at their desks.

It is suggested that students have access to keyboarding instruction daily for a specific length of time, such as 4 to 6 weeks for concentrated instruction and practice, rather than one time a week all year. This method assumes, however, that students will continue using the computer for writing and other keyboarding throughout the year to maintain their keyboarding proficiency. Providing keyboarding instruction and practice for 20 minutes a day, 3 to 4 days a week, for 4 to 6 weeks, allows children to concentrate on keyboarding specifically (especially correct fingering and posture) in preparation for the year's word processing activities. Keyboarding once a week for 15 to 20 minutes only strings the instruction out, and in many cases is the main computer use for many children. If a school has one computer in each classroom or several computers shared among classrooms in a department, keyboarding is probably a waste of effort. There are strategies that schools with limited computers can engage in that does make keyboarding effective.

Let's look at how one school effectively taught keyboarding skills to their writers using the above method just described. This school had a total of seven computers that were shared by sixteen classes, grades 1 through 8. The teachers were aware of the need to introduce keyboarding before their students began writing with word processing, but how could they do this effectively with seven shared computers? It was important at this stage in their planning to decide as a group that keyboarding was to be an initiative, because the plan was to move all computers to one location. For this plan to work, all teachers involved needed to understand the benefits to keyboarding because they would not have access to "their" computer for four weeks. A keyboarding blitz began at the beginning of the school year. Parent volunteers were organized by one teacher, and the seven computers were used every minute before school, during the day, and after school. Students from third through eighth grade cycled through the computer lab for four weeks of keyboarding instruction. The success of this particular keyboarding program was due to the support of the teachers (giving up their computer for four weeks, allowing students to leave during their assigned times), the support of parent volunteers, and a concerted effort to make keyboarding a schoolwide priority to prepare students for word processing activities throughout the year. At the end of the four weeks, beginning students were starting with their fingers on "home row" (asdfjkl;) using both hands, and in many cases, using correct fingers. Project that plan through several years when each class goes through a first four weeks of keyboarding training or a refresher course again and again, and you can imagine how proficient students will become. But keyboarding does not have to wait until third and fourth grade.

Teachers interested in children writing at a computer need to determine what keyboarding means to them. In the past, keyboarding was taught in high school typing classes, with the end goal of speed and no errors. Keyboarding with children in kindergarten must obviously have a different definition. Teachers have been encouraged in the past to allow students to use a word processor once they have reached approximately 25 words per minute. Wetzel (1985) suggests that with varying degrees of skill, students need to type quickly and accurately enough to make relatively efficient use of the computer and to accomplish the purposes of the academic program and concludes that students who achieve 10 wpm can make adequate use of the computer for tasks which require a significant amount of keyboard entry. Before adopting this philosophy, first ask this question: "How fast must a child write with a pencil?" This isn't a question usually asked in a primary classroom (or any other classroom, for that matter!). But let's suppose for our purpose here that we do ask that question. Should first graders write 20 words per minute? Fifteen wpm? Five wpm? Does it matter? If we celebrate a child's attempt at communicating with the written word, does it really matter if they laboriously write one word per minute or 50 words per minute? Does it matter, then, if a child types 1, 10, 15, or 20 words per minute? Try timing a pencil and paper writer for one minute. Should our goal be any different for a writer using a word processor?

When a new topic such as keyboarding is included into the already full curriculum, it is imperative we integrate these new objectives into the existing curriculum. Keyboarding integrates beautifully into language-arts activities. Remember, however, that keyboarding does not by itself teach students to write.

Computer/VCR Monitor Connection

The use of a large monitor or TV with the appropriate connectors is crucial to effective utilization of one computer in a classroom. Without these items, the computer is usually only used by one student at a time or a very small group at most. For group activities using a computer, an Apple IIe computer can be connected to a VCR or television monitor with inexpensive parts from an electronics store such as Radio Shack: a 6- to 12-foot monitor cable and a Y-connect plug for splitting the signal from the computer (the program can be seen on both the computer monitor and on the VCR monitor at the same time). For older monitors (sound is not necessary), it is necessary to purchase an RF modulator, also available at Radio Shack. Now that students can see the VCR monitor or the computer screen, an effective teaching tool is ready. For those teachers who are unsure of this process, contacting a district computer coordinator, an electronic store clerk, or an interested parent may provide a more detailed explanation of the actual hookup required.

Word Processor

A computer program that allows text to be typed and stored in computer memory where it can be changed, deleted, added to, saved to disk, or retrieved is called a word processor. Many teachers are finding the use of word processing to be one of the most important means of extending literacy via the computer in the classroom (Strickland, Feeley, & Wepner, 1987, p. 9). Word processing programs come in many forms. Some are designed for professional writers and include many sophisticated features. Others are designed for children or letter writers and have minimal capabilities. As a general rule, the more features a program has, the longer it takes to learn how to use.

All word processing programs contain a basic set of capabilities. Probably the most important feature of word processing is the ability to make unlimited changes to a document before printing. This includes adding and erasing characters, sentences, and paragraphs. Another important feature is the capability to copy or move text from one place to another, often called cut and paste. Graphics can also be pasted into text in many word processors. Other important features of word processing programs include pagination, margin and tab settings, line spacing, and search/replace. Some word processing programs today also have advanced functions of automatic footnoting, page headers and footers, hyphenation, and indexing. Many also include desktop publishing capabilities (e.g., column layout, page previews).

FrEdWriter

FrEdWriter (Rogers, 1987) is a public domain, or freeware, word processor that can be copied but not sold. Al Rogers, a teacher in California, developed *FrEdWriter* so teachers and students would have access to a writing medium that was inexpensive (in this case, free), could support the writing process, and could be seen on a television monitor for group writing with its 40-column display. *FrEdWriter* contains many of the word processing features available in more sophisticated word processors, including prompted writing.

Prompted Writing

Prompted writing is a technique writers can use as an aid to structure and organization during the composing process. Prompted writing has been compared to the use of training wheels for young bicycle users (Simonson & Thompson, 1990). After a few prompted writing exercises, students no longer need the prompts because the responses to the questions become an automatic part of the writing process. Prompts help young writers include more explicit detail in their writing. Prompted writing offers numerous possibilities for teachers attempting to help students structure their writing during the composing phase of the writing process. Simple prompts can be used to encourage students to write topic sentences, include supporting details, and write summary statements in paragraphs. Several programs, including *FrEdWriter*, allow students to print out their writing without the teacher prompts. In short, prompted writing is a scaffold for writers.

The following is a prompted writing example:

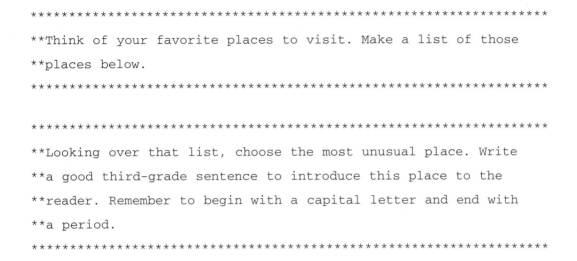

```
* * * * * * * * * * * * * * * * * * * * * * * * * * * * * * * * * * * * * * * * * * * * * * * * * * * * * * * * * * * * * *
**Think of your favorite places to visit. Make a list of those
**places below.
* * * * * * * * * * * * * * * * * * * * * * * * * * * * * * * * * * * * * * * * * * * * * * * * * * * * * * * * * * * * * * *


* * * * * * * * * * * * * * * * * * * * * * * * * * * * * * * * * * * * * * * * * * * * * * * * * * * * * * * * * * * * * * *
**Looking over that list, choose the most unusual place. Write
**a good third-grade sentence to introduce this place to the
**reader. Remember to begin with a capital letter and end with
**a period.
* * * * * * * * * * * * * * * * * * * * * * * * * * * * * * * * * * * * * * * * * * * * * * * * * * * * * * * * * * * * * * *
```

40-Column Display

In 40-column display, 40 characters and spaces of text are seen on a computer monitor, and in certain programs, on printed copy (e.g., word processors such as *Bank Street Writer* [Scholastic], *Magic Slate* [WINGS for learning]). Forty-column print is twice as large as the usual 80-column print found in most word processing programs used by adults. When using a TV or VCR monitor for group writing, 40-column print is necessary.

Process Writing

Process writing is a view of writing that includes the recursive subprocesses of prewriting, composing, sharing, revising, editing, and publishing. It can be supported by using a word processor because of the editing features available, where text can be changed, deleted, added to, saved, or retrieved.

Template

A template can be thought of as a model for a document that one uses repeatedly. It already has the type styles and layout in place, allowing the user to change names and content into a new document. For example, teachers might have templates of parent letters, lesson plans, classroom forms, and writing activities saved to a disk to be used each year. As a template is needed, it is accessed with the word processor, information is changed or added, and the revised document is ready for either printing or for use on-line with the computer. The following is an example of a group reading journal template:

* *

Today is *(date)*. We read the book *(title)*, by *(author)*. The illustrator of *(title)* was *(illustrator's name)*. The book was published by: *(publishing company)*. The end papers were: *(description)*. The medium used by the illustrator was: *(description)*. Our favorite parts were "____," said ____; "____," said ____; and "____," said ____.

* *

Drill and Practice Software

Programs that present a skill and elicit a student response, provide immediate feedback, and then proceed to another problem are called drill and practice software. Many such programs allow students to move to more difficult problems and/or problems of a different nature.

One-Computer Classroom

The typical classroom today has one computer for 30 or more children. Some teachers store the computer in a corner where it is used infrequently or is often found gathering dust. Several strategies are useful for capitalizing on the computer's capabilities. Included is connecting the computer to a VCR monitor or to an LCD projection panel for group activities. The classroom teacher with access to one computer and a VCR monitor has a valuable teaching tool that supports both reading and writing in a language-rich environment and complements and reinforces comprehension strategies. Another one-computer-classroom teaching strategy is to integrate the computer across all curricular areas. Probably most crucial for successful integration is organization of computer activities and management of student use.

A temporary solution to one computer at a time in a classroom is to cluster computers. DeGroff (1990) suggests that teachers bargain for computers and time. Many schools use a "roving computer" model: Several computers on movable carts are checked out to each teacher for a period of time, usually one day. If a teacher or a group of teachers within a school would normally get a computer for the classroom one day a week, the teachers each would have the computer for one fifth of the school year. The teachers bargain to have the computer for 8 weeks in a row rather than 40 Fridays throughout the year. But clustering is only a temporary solution. The goal, according to DeGroff, should be a level of access that assures all students of time for learning throughout the year.

LCD Projection Panel

A liquid crystal display (LCD) projection panel is a portable device placed on an overhead projector and connected to a computer. The LCD panel links to a computer, digitally translating computer video-out signals into images on a wall screen via light from an overhead projector. This enables a teacher or student to present software to a large group.

Laser Disc Technology

Physically, a laser disc (sometimes referred to as a videodisc) is a large cousin of the audio CD. These disc formats are examples of optical storage technology, where microscopic pits embedded within the disc surface carry digital data that can be reconstructed into video, music, or other information when the disc is read in a player. One side of a laser disc can hold 54,000 still pictures or a mixture of still photographs and motion video sequences, along with a half hour of CD-quality stereo sound. On the most commonly used laser disc in interactive video applications, each frame of video is given a unique identifying number (from 1 to 54,000), and those numbers are used by the computer to tell the laser disc player where to start and stop video sequences, or which frame number to display as a still image.

The key advantage laser discs have over videotape is free random access to any video sequence or still frame on the laser disc nonsequentially, with search time almost instantaneous. Images are read from disc by a laser beam. Unlike a videotape, a laser disc player never needs to be rewound—and even the most inexpensive laser disc players can jump from information at one end of a disc to information at the other end of a disc in about two seconds.

Most instructional uses of laser disc technology are basically as a vehicle for the delivery of instruction. A typical interactive laser disc workstation consists of a personal computer, a laser disc player, and a video monitor or television set. The laser disc player is attached to the computer and receives instruction by way of a single cable connection to the modem port on the back of the computer.

CD-ROM

A CD-ROM is a small disc, similar in size and appearance to the common household variety of musical CDs found in many homes and cars, that holds text, graphics, and stereo sound. The initials that make up the CD-ROM name stand for "Compact Disc-Read Only Memory." "Read Only Memory" means the disc is commercially prepared and the information on the disc when purchased is all that will ever be on that disc. The common configuration for a CD-ROM player in schools is a CD player connected to a computer with a cable attached in a speaker port on the back of the computer. Small audio speakers can also be attached to the CD player to amplify the music, sounds, or voices found on the disc.

Technological advances such as CD-ROM continue to expand the array of options for using computers in reading and writing. The number and diversity of CD-ROM titles have grown dramatically in recent years. CD-ROM content varies from interactive stories, to compact libraries (e.g., the works of Shakespeare), to graphics and sounds, to full-volume encyclopedias. One CD-ROM is equal to 1,500 floppy disks, or the equivalent of a typist typing 90 words per minute, 8 hours a day, for 8 years (Neilsen, 1991).

Interactive stories and compact libraries are probably the most common CD-ROMs that might be found in reading classrooms. *Just Grandma and Me* (Broderbund) is an example of an interactive story on CD-ROM disc with cartoon animation. Children can choose to have the computer read the story aloud, or they can play within each screen, using the computer's mouse to evoke actions, sounds, and dialogue from characters and objects. The program is multilingual, supporting English, Spanish, and Japanese, and is just one volume of a Living Books series. CD-ROM interactive books and their effectiveness for supporting the reading process have not been tested thoroughly, but teachers have definite reactions when they see this technology demonstrated. They seem to love the idea of children reading via CD-ROM, or they hate the idea. A common reaction has been that the children are no longer holding and reading a real book. A CD-ROM disk is a book that does not smell or feel like a book. Children are viewing the "book" on a screen, which is a much different way of seeing a book than looking at paper pages of a book on one's lap or desktop.

However, outstanding teachers are always on the lookout for one more way to reach the student who is not motivated, who has not been reached by our repertoire of teaching methods. Picture the student who has not found the spark for reading. Perhaps the attention span in front of a book, either listened to or read personally, is short enough to interfere with the reading process. Picture also the student who has been reading from a book silently, but is an auditory learner.

Consider the student who *tries* to listen to the teacher reading a book, but just can't sit still or concentrate on the text. An interactive book on CD-ROM *requires* interactivity. For the book to progress, the reader or listener must use the computer mouse to turn pages. As each word or phrase is read, the text is highlighted so the reader can follow the oral progression of words. The book is laid out linearly, but a student may choose to move a bookmark and enter any page. The mouse can be used to click on any word to be read again singly, and in another language. Pictures on each page are interactive and the characters are animated if the child chooses to click on a picture. Labels are available for most pictures and are pronounced in English, or another language. As for motivation, children may not read better using CD-ROM, but the technology supporting the reading process seems to attract many children.

Research-based CD-ROM discs contain text and graphic references that can be searched. *New Grolier Multimedia Encyclopedia* (Grolier), for example, contain 33,000 articles and the entire text and pictures from the 21

Liquid crystal displays allow everyone in the class to "use" the computer.

SmartView™ 1600 Courtesy of In Focus Systems

volumes of Grolier's *Academic American Encyclopedia*. The 1992 edition introduced multimedia elements such as digitized video segments of historical events, famous people, NASA missions, and animation sequences. Text and graphics can be printed out and included in student written reports. Audio excerpts are included from famous speeches, musical compositions, animals sounds, bird calls, and musical instruments.

Classroom Scenarios, Grades 4–8

Esther's fourth grade is studying text as found in newspapers. To operationalize what they have been learning about writing for the typical newspaper reader, the class has formed a newspaper publishing center. Esther has established some criteria for the newspaper, such as all content areas must be addressed in each edition, but the students are responsible for planning, writing, and printing the bimonthly newspaper. The first edition was published for parents, but Esther's principal and parents of students encouraged her to make the newspaper available for a wider audience—the other students in this K–8 school. Her students chose to change positions once each month so they could become familiar with all roles, and because each job looked like more fun than the last!

First, Esther's students analyze actual newspapers and become familiar with the various sections and the composition. They are introduced to the various staff roles involved in publishing a newspaper and visit the local newspaper office to see how a real newspaper is produced.

Students select the roles they want to take (e.g., reporter, writer, editor, photographer, production supervisor, advertising director, scanner operator, keyboarder, etc.). Mini-workshops are held on interviewing techniques, and reporters and writers are encouraged to conduct personal interviews with persons relevant to their beat. Writers can choose to either write their copy with paper and pencil or by typing into a word processor. Copy is submitted to the editors for reviewing or rewriting. Writers plan with photographers to find photos to illustrate the stories. Students in charge of advertising compose and develop ads from the student body, teachers, staff, and parents.

Photos are scanned using a scanner connected to a computer, which prepares the graphics as a file that can be used in a desktop publishing software program.

The editor-in-chief position is shared each period by two students who are responsible for the arrangement or organization of the newspaper. They work together with the production supervisor to determine the exact layout and assembly of the paper. Students in these roles are given instruction on leaving plenty of white space, breaking pages into several columns, using headings and titles, using lines and boxes to organize, and avoiding the use of too many different typefaces or type sizes. Once the paper is completed using desktop-publishing software, it is printed, duplicated, and distributed to the school/community.

Esther uses this organization for writing across the curriculum and to practice news reporting and reading. The students in her class are aware that the readers of their newspaper have varied reading abilities, and they work hard at preparing text that can be read by most people. They began including a section for young readers when the newspaper expanded readership to primary grades. Esther uses the newspaper project throughout the school year as a way to tie curricular units together and to assess her students and their learning. She knows a concisely written report about content will give her important information about a student's comprehension of material studied. Esther's students leave her class with an interest in reading other newspapers and an appreciation for reporting and writing news text.

▼▼▼▼▼▼▼▼▼▼▼▼▼▼

Roberto teaches fifth grade and looks for software that will support reading comprehension strategies for large-group demonstration and practice. One program he uses in his classroom is *Where in the USA is Carmen Sandiego?* (Broderbund), a social studies software simulation package. This program comes with a written "dossier," an information source on suspects who might have stolen a national treasure in the simulation program, and a copy of *Fodor's USA* (Fodor's Travel Guides) travel guide. Roberto adds additional reference documents for his students to use as they work toward solving a mystery by following written clues and by "flying" to cities around the United States to apprehend the suspect. The class is divided into groups: a Fodor's USA group, a dossier group, an almanac/atlas group, a note-taking group, and a trivia group. Roberto uses one computer connected to a VCR monitor to display the program for full group participation.

Roberto has chosen this particular software to demonstrate questioning strategies for reading comprehension *because* it is not a reading program. He has found his students enjoy the gamelike format of the *Carmen* programs, they are gaining information on the states they are studying in geography, and they are learning and practicing reading strategies in a content area. Because this program is a simulation, the episodes are always different and the students must read to gain clues to continue their travel. Students can use information sources to search for the location of a wanted person. The *Carmen Sandiego* programs demonstrate that the data-handling, graphics, and sound capabilities of the computer make it a very effective means for creating realistic educational environments in which students can actively participate. Using the social studies-oriented simulation for reading comprehension extends the active participation into an enjoyable project that his students ask for often.

As the class begins using *Where in the USA is Carmen Sandiego?* in their designated groups, Roberto introduces background for questioning strategies as written by Raphael (1986): "Right There," "Think and Search," and "On Your Own." As the students begin searching for clues to follow the wanted person from one state to another, they first must decide what kind of question they are asking themselves ("Right There," "Think and Search," or "On Your Own"). Because of varying background knowledge, the students soon become aware that what is a "Think and Search" question for some may be an "On Your Own" question for others. Roberto models the questioning strategy aloud frequently and reminds the students occasionally of the need for questioning.

While some students investigate a clue in *Fodor's USA*, others look in available sources, such as a text, encyclopedia, atlas, or maps. As clues are collected, one group records the data that becomes a much asked for resource as clues accumulate. As the students travel to each new state, a brief description appears of that state, including historical and geographical information.

The "trivia group" take the responsibility of recording some bit of information on which they will try to stump their classmates at the end of the session. After the first couple of sessions, all students now read this state description and many take notes. Although they know the information is not critical for their clues, they have begun a competition by groups for trivia recall.

When one group of students mentioned to Roberto they were accumulating state information that could be used again in this program and in their own studies, Roberto introduced a sixth group. The new group became responsible for creating a database of states. The students of this group first recorded the information by hand until they were introduced to an electronic database. Once they began inputting information into their database on the computer, they were able to quickly search for data that could help in searching for clues. Students requested a second computer in the class so searching could be conducted as the data was needed, or to add new information. This is an example of students taking responsibility for their own learning. Roberto is also facilitating the development of metacognitive processes in his students' literacy acts. Now when these students are involved with finding information from varied sources in any context, questioning strategies are a part of their process.

In another classroom project, Roberto's fifth-grade class sees the causes and effects of acid rain by visiting a cemetery to observe the eroding effects of acid rain on tombstones and to a local power plant to see what causes acid rain. They are studying the environmental problems of acid rain as a National Geographic Kids Network (National Geographic Society) team. This international telecommunications-based science and geography curriculum allows the students to share information about acid rain with other fourth through sixth graders in 48 states and 18 foreign countries.

Roberto's students begin the eight-week program by defining acid rain, locating the other schools in their research group on a map, and building their own acid rain collectors. They use pH paper to measure and record the acidity of local rainfall. With the help of a scientist at the National Oceanic and Atmospheric Administration, the students compare data with other schools in their research group via a computer linked by a modem and phone line. They keep a weekly log of readings from their family cars to determine how much nitrogen oxide they themselves have introduced into the atmosphere. These fifth graders are empowered by communicating with other kids. Throughout the unit, the students write letters to their research teammates discussing the local significance of acid rain. When the information yielded by the nationwide data is returned, Roberto's students begin to compare their own findings with those of other research team classes. They write to each other for clarification, to share ideas, and to pursue the questions or theories their studies have engendered. They take the information collected and write group research reports on activist topics. They write their own newspaper article for the local newspaper, and write editorials about the use of Styrofoam in local restaurants and the school cafeteria, and the effects of car pooling. Technology is not what motivates these students to read and write about world environmental issues; it is the issues themselves, and a teacher who provides the kind of environment that supports their literacy efforts.

▼▼▼▼▼▼▼▼▼▼▼▼▼▼

Marty's sixth-grade students are working on an environmental project with five other sixth grades around the world. Students are gathering information on recycling projects in other cities located not just in their own state or country, but in other countries as well. The class, in teams, researches their own community, types their data into a database, and then distributes that data to other schools involved in the project. The data are sent and received electronically via phone lines. Several students sit in front of their classroom computer, which has a small rectangular box, a modem, attached. A telephone cable runs from the modem to a phone jack in the wall. Using telecommunications software that translates the phone number to phone pulses, the modem dials to a nearby university mainframe and gives the students access to Internet (a worldwide "roadway" of computers, on-line resources, and people). There, they log on to Marty's electronic mail (E-mail) account and find messages waiting for their class from their partners in Japan, Texas, Virginia, Germany, and Mexico. They are in their final stages of data collection and each class is sending their data to be shared with all of the other classes. The data will be compiled into the class database, using the criteria all six classes chose together. The data will be used this week to compare and contrast recycling efforts in these six places, as all students use their class databases to sort information, answering the collective questions they shared at the beginning of the project.

Marty has integrated language arts and math into this science project. Reading activities have involved reading fiction relating to the environment, practicing research strategies, reading for information through scientific resources, and writing for audiences where English is a second language. Drew has read information received from the class in Japan with interest and wants to incorporate the facts about land reclamation with garbage into the report he is finishing on Japan. He writes a message to a Japanese student, asking for more details. He discusses with Marty referencing etiquette when the source is an electronic mail message and makes arrangements to use the computer lab to finish his written report.

Marty makes multiple copies of the database to be used in tomorrow's session in the computer lab so each group of students can sort and search for information, according to the large-group consensus. Each small group in Marty's class is responsible for presenting a report using one piece of technology. One group has chosen to videotape footage of the need for more recycling in their city. Another group has used Internet resources to research outside references in a written report. A third group has chosen to use *FrEdWriter* to make a prompted writing activity—a personal survey for others in their school to complete concerning individual efforts for recycling. A final group has interviewed a panel of community members, and, using parts of their tape-recorded interviews, has put together a *HyperCard* (Claris) presentation on the computer of environmental topics complete with recorded statements.

As students became more involved with their data collection, Marty and the teachers from the participating classrooms discuss other collaborative projects and settle on a peer conferencing/sharing activity for writing short stories, letters, and news items. Students begin sharing work with writing partners for feedback and peer editing. One team of students begin a round-robin story, where one student begins the story, sends it on to the next writer, who writes a new section and sends the story on to a new participant.

At the completion of the environmental and writing projects, several students have exchanged both E-mail and what they call "snail mail" addresses with students from other locations to continue correspondence. Marty has made arrangements with the teachers from each of the other five schools to stay in touch and collaborate on future projects. The success of these projects has made telecommunications an indispensable tool in Marty's classroom writing program. This student network provides Marty's students with a purpose for writing, a real-world use for word processing, and a real audience to read their writing. With an audience beyond the classroom, students become authors who care about the quality and effectiveness of their writing.

▼▼▼▼▼▼▼▼▼▼▼▼▼▼

Cecilia's junior high students have a number of multimedia projects in place. Many of these activities have not been designed with reading or writing as their primary objective, but each project illustrates the literacy support that multimedia provides this age student.

In their music appreciation class, seventh- and eighth-grade students are discovering the inner workings of a symphony using The Voyager Company's *Beethoven's Ninth Symphony* CD and accompanying software. Students listen to the symphony while a narrative displayed on the computer screen describes what is being played. They learn about instrumentation by selecting a family of instruments, then hearing a portion of the symphony that highlights those instruments. They are also able to read about Beethoven's life by choosing that option on a screen menu. Because this is a music class, Cecilia has planned this unit with the music teacher. The students are also reading selections of fiction, biographies of Beethoven and other musicians, and historical references that were written about the time Beethoven composed the Ninth Symphony.

The students in Cecilia's class are also involved in writing a group literary magazine with six other classes, called a "learning network." The project was created by the seven teachers via a subscription telecommunications program supported by a long-distance phone company. The seven classes are located in the United States, Germany, and Israel, and students have been sharing information about their schools and communities via the computer and a telephone modem. Each class exchanged a packet of memorabilia that would help explain their culture. Included in the packet sent from Cecilia's class was a photocopy of a license plate, the school handbook, a class photo, brochures of surrounding points of interest, a state map, and an introduction of each student written by a partner. The teachers, through early collaboration before beginning the literary project, have developed a writing unit and have delegated responsibilities for the literary magazine to each class. As students collect the writing from the participating classes, they are aware of their audiences and have gone through extensive revision with their peers. Each class from the participating schools/countries prepare their portion of the literary magazine using a word processor. Occasionally a team of students sends a message to a student writer at another school, asking for clarification. When Cecilia's class has finished their portion of the magazine, it is saved to disk and sent electronically to the long-distance phone company that will compile all seven sections for printing.

During the semester Cecilia's class was involved in this learning network, the Berlin Wall came tumbling down, and her students received eyewitness reports from their electronic partners in West Germany. One student from Germany wrote Cecilia's class frequently, answering other students' questions and providing a valuable perspective of the historic events unfolding in his city. Through such exchanges of information, students helped each other investigate various global issues and prepared reports that described their findings and insights.

Cecilia has more computers in her classroom than the average teacher, and she shares that wealth of hardware with other classes. For example, her students are paired with Lee's special education students for writing projects. Cecilia's students sit at a computer with their special education partner throughout most of the writing process: for brainstorming, help in locating resources, advice on word processing procedures, peer editing, and enjoyment in the sharing of the finished product.

Using a computer and an LCD projection panel, Cecilia uses student writing to teach skill lessons in writing. With each student's permission and no names, student-written material is displayed on the computer screen and on a wall screen for large-group instruction. A lesson might center on verb tense, on paragraph construction, or comparing a student's descriptive essay with a descriptive passage by a well-known author. Cecilia uses this method to model good writing, to discuss revision procedures, for brainstorming, and to model word processing procedures.

Electronic dialogue journals is another way Cecilia combines writing and technology. With one of her seventh-grade classes, Cecilia and her students use technology to create journals, with the students submitting their writing on disk. In journaling via computer, Cecilia finds her response time shorter than when she writes by hand in margins and whatever space is left for her on student journals. It is just easier for her to type her responses, and convenient to place her responses in the context of the student writing. She finds that her students seem more motivated to write via computer. Many of her students experiment with different size and styles of fonts, and a number of students add graphics to their entries. She has begun using computer symbols with her students to illustrate her mood as well, such as :<) for a smile face, and <grin> to show humor. Cecilia has found that some students don't enjoy journaling in this form, and she has encouraged them to go back to paper and pencil journals. Although the process of writing journals is not really changed with the medium of computers versus paper and pencil, Cecilia has found she can write in more detail and that many students respond with longer entries.

Definitions and Discussion

Desktop Publishing

Next to writing activities and word processing applications, the second most popular use of computers in schools is probably for desktop publishing. Desktop publishing is closely related to writing and emerges naturally from word processing activities. Whereas word processing focuses attention on the process of writing and content, desktop publishing concerns the way in which information is assembled and distributed.

Desktop publishing refers to the use of computers to produce professional-looking documents. Desktop-publishing software allows the user to use text, graphics, and organizational tools that provide columns. These special-purpose software programs enable students and teachers to produce high-quality, professional-looking bulletins, newsletters, and newspapers right in the classroom.

Software for desktop publishing is available in easy-to-use packages appropriate for the beginning writer, to software used by high school students for the school newspaper, literary magazines, and yearbook. The same program used by some schools for literary magazines is also used by professional journals for camera ready publications. High school students can prepare a yearbook or literary magazine as *camera ready*, which means the student's product is professional looking and the printer does not have to typeset the document but can photocopy instead. Young children can use a desktop-publishing software package to publish their writing in anthologies, or a classroom newsletter with graphics and writing to describe the events taking place in their classroom. Desktop publishing makes it possible for students of any age to have access to their own electronic print shop.

Combined with a word processor, a desktop-publishing system can be used to enhance the young writer's sense of audience. In the scenario described earlier, the students are writing to real audiences and have an opportunity to experience a heightened sense of writing as communicating with a real person. Students are not writing just as an exercise for the teacher; they are writing with a specific communication goal in mind.

Scanner

Scanners digitize text photographs or line art and store the images as a file, one that can be transferred into a paint program, directly into a word processor, or into a desktop-publishing software program. Scanners look like copying machines or laser printers except they work in reverse. Instead of producing printed documents, they produce an electronic version of the document that is scanned. You can save the scanned image (e.g., photograph, illustration, drawing) as a disk file and then load it into a desktop-publishing program. The scanned file can also be loaded into a paint program and modified.

Scanners are available in several forms. There are hand-held scanners that you move across something you want to convert to electronic form. These are relatively inexpensive and useful for desktop publishing projects. Most scanners only scan black and white, although more expensive color scanners are available.

Ethical issues of scanners: A scanner makes it easy to capture illustrations or photos from books and magazines for republishing in new documents. Students must be taught to always credit their sources and to request permission to use other people's work.

Simulation

A simulation is a representation or model of an event, an object, or some phenomenon. A simulation is generally an incomplete model that contains the essential elements of the thing simulated (Simonson & Thompson, 1990, p. 107). The main advantage in using simulations is that they give the student the power to manipulate various aspects of the model. With a computer simulation, students become an active part of their learning environment and can usually see the results of changing different variables in the model. Usually a simulation will require students to perform application-, analysis-, and synthesis-level activities. *Where in the USA is Carmen Sandiego?* is a social studies oriented-simulation available in many classrooms. This program (like *Where in the World . . .* , *Where in Europe . . .* , *Where in Time . . .* , and *Where in America's Past . . .*) allows students to use clues to search for the location of a wanted person. In the program, students need to use knowledge of geography to make use of the clues provided. Students can use information sources that accompany the program and additional almanacs and maps to secure the information they need to locate the missing person. Information is given on the screen for each state (country, time) visited.

The scenario just described demonstrates the use of any of the *Carmen Sandiego* series as a tool to demonstrate and practice reading comprehension. The skills required for both reading and writing are similar and instruction in one context can impact performance in the other. The value of interactive reading and writing experiences is that they break down the distinctions between the reader and writer (Anderson-Inman,

1987). By providing an environment in which the learner moves back and forth between the role of reader and the role of writer (or even plays both roles simultaneously), the computer promotes a recognition that reading and writing are interrelated events (Anderson-Inman, 1990). To comprehend what has been written, the reader must construct meaning from the writer's words, looking for relationships among the different parts of the text. Becoming familiar with different types of text structures, as well as an internalization of stylistic devices and conventions used in any given type of writing, can help students develop strategies in reading and writing (Anderson-Inman, 1986).

National Geographic Society Kids Network (a Subscription Service)

This on-line network offers structured science and geography projects for grades 4 through 6. Teachers subscribe for eight-week study units. Students across the world work as scientists, collecting data, developing hypotheses, drawing conclusions, and sharing.

Database

John Naisbitt in his book *Megatrends* wrote, "We are drowning in information but starved for knowledge" (Naisbitt, 1982, p. 24). Students must learn skills to organize, retrieve, manipulate, and evaluate the facts they have acquired. Whenever there is a large amount of information to be managed, there is a need for software called a data management system that controls the storage and organization of data in a database. A database is a collection of information organized according to some structure or purpose. Examples of non-electronic databases include an address book, student files on index cards, a dictionary, phone book, and recipe files. A user can retrieve and store information in a systematic way; the computerized database lets a student retrieve information using a key word or words. For example, students in the scenario described earlier could search for all the files that contain "mandatory recycling" and display the cities in alphabetical order. Or they could use the key words "plastic recycling" and "glass recycling," ordering the cities shown by population. Although databases are not developed specifically for reading and writing instruction, students must interact with data, first by collecting data through research, then by typing the information into an electronic database, and finally by determining search strategies and analyzing information. All of these steps involve reading and writing strategies using a text structure that is commonly found in their life outside the classroom using real-world databases. Examples of classroom databases include student favorites, mammals, whales, hobbies (i.e., sports cards, music tapes), periodic table, rocks, states, presidents, Olympic games, wars, disasters, explorers, classroom books, storybook characters, and authors.

Telecommunications

Telecommunication involves the transfer of data from one computer to another via communications media such as telephone lines. Computer communication systems allow nearly instantaneous transmission of information and for the storage of that information in the receiving computer until it is ready to be used. A computer, communications software, and a modem are needed to convert the output of a computer into a signal that can be transmitted over regular telephone lines. Often called telecomputing, telecommunications with a computer and modem helps break down barriers to access and interactions with people, information, and other resources—barriers of physical distance, time, organization, and culture. Through telecomputing, interaction with people or information on other computers can be either immediate (sometimes referred to as "real time") or delayed in various ways. With telecomputing, participants in a written conversation can interact at a time convenient to them. This is particularly important in a school setting where both teachers' and students' time is tightly scheduled (or if communicating classrooms are on opposite sides of the world).

Teachers have many different reasons for using telecommunications in the classroom. Some want to provide their students with real and diverse audiences for writing activities, whether those students are in the same building, school district, state, country, or elsewhere in the world. Some want to promote collaborative learning. Others find that they and their students need access to written information or expertise that is not available in their school building or local community.

Another powerful characteristic of telecomputing is that the information sent or received can be manipulated by virtue of being in electronic form and by virtue of the fact that the communication is mediated by the computer. This means the user can store, modify, analyze, reformat, combine, and in all other ways control the information. In the simplest form, children typically compose their electronic mail messages on a word processor and then transmit them via the electronic network to local or remote readers. In turn, the receivers can store the messages for later printing, reading, revising, or responding. The receiver can easily file a particular message with other material related to a topic or project. For writing comments on another person's message, various conventions can be adopted. For example, a student playing the role of a peer editor of another's message might intersperse comments in uppercase to distinguish them from the originator's writing.

Modem

In order for computers to connect to a remote network via telephone lines, a device called a modem is needed. The modem converts the digital information from the computer into analog information that can be sent over the telephone.

Internet

Internet is the world's largest computer network, with instant access to an indescribable wealth of information. Through electronic mail and bulletin boards (called "news groups"), a user can search on-line databases, carry on discussions with colleagues worldwide, participate in discussion groups, subscribe to electronic journals, and collect free software. National libraries can be searched and entire books can be accessed and downloaded, which means the book can be sent to a user's computer and printed.

E-Mail

Electronic mail refers to the transmission of correspondence via computer and phone lines. Electronic mail software is needed to use a computer to send and receive messages. Once a message has been entered at the keyboard, the electronic mail software looks up the telephone number of the recipient's computer, dials the number, and when the call is acknowledged, transmits the message. The receiving computer answers the telephone, accepts the message, and stores it until it is time for it to be read.

Consider this example of a wide-area network E-mail system: Using a computer and modem connected to a phone jack, a teacher can use communications software to dial the number of a nearby university's mainframe computer where she has an "account." Using her account address (usually her name) and a password, a teacher can log on to the mainframe and gain access to the Internet. With access to Internet, she can now send a message to anyone else with Internet access anywhere in the world. She can send a message to a teacher in Sweden, who can reply back to her message and attach a list of Swedish students' names. This opens collaboration opportunities with classrooms anywhere in the world. Students can send messages to students, or messages can be sent from teacher to teacher(s).

AT&T Long Distance Learning Network (a Subscription Service)

Teachers and students participate in a "learning circle" with students around the world through phone lines, modems, and computers, building electronic communities of teachers and learners. Teachers and students collaborate on a series of projects over the semester. Students produce a product that is the result of their collaboration (Kearsley, Hunter, & Furlong, 1992). "When writing became a way to share their ideas across time and distance, teachers reported a surprising enthusiasm among students for writing and revision. Students worried about the accuracy of their information as well as the form of their writing" (Riel, 1990).

The basic idea of an AT&T Learning Circle is to match teachers and students into small, geographically diverse working groups to accomplish shared educational goals. To facilitate the group formation, teachers select a particular type of Learning Circle (Computer Chronicles, Mind Works, Places and Perspectives, Society's Problems, Global Issues, or Energy Works) defined by a curricular focus (journalism, creative writing, geography and history, social science, and science) at a grade-level grouping (elementary, middle school, and high school). The participants in a Learning Circle share a task, the publication of a collective journal or newspaper (e.g., the *Journal of Places and Perspectives, Mind Works: Creative Writing Journal,* or the *Energy Works Newsletter*). Participants agree to a specified time frame that defines the phases from the beginning to the closing of the Learning Circle. They each receive a shared curriculum guide with many ideas drawn from the experiences of past teachers. But the teachers and students in each Learning Circle work together to create the activities. Each class is invited to design a group project drawn from their curriculum. Learning Circles allow students from different cultures, regions, religions, ages, perspectives, and with a range of physical and mental strengths or disabilities to work together in a medium that treats diversity as a resource (Riel, 1990).

Students at all levels write about themselves, their feelings, their school, and their world. They write newspaper articles as well as more expressive pieces. Recipes for success, want ads for teenagers, telephone dramas, and peace messages have all been shared in Learning Circles. Stories that are started in one school are sent to other schools to be continued and concluded by students drawing on very different perspectives and real-life experiences.

HyperCard

HyperCard is a software package that is packaged with all Apple Macintosh computers. What *HyperCard* software has done for education is to bring multimedia into the technological age, by making it somewhat easy to combine text, graphics, sound, and even animation on an Apple Macintosh computer. The result is a unique and interactive environment that lets teachers and students interact with and control the flow of information. For MS-DOS users, *Linkway* (IBM) is available as an authoring program for hypertext.

Multimedia

Along with "new media," "hypermedia," and "integrated media," the term *multimedia* describes virtually any conjunction of media on the computer screen. Multimedia products can be purchased already prepared, prepared by a teacher with content specific to his or her classroom, or prepared by a student as a project (e.g., a multimedia term paper). A multimedia document is much like any other document created: It has text, illustrations, footnotes, annotations, indexes, and bibliographies. Multimedia, however, goes beyond text and graphics and includes sound, video, and animation that are seen on the computer screen. Educational multimedia projects may incorporate interactive

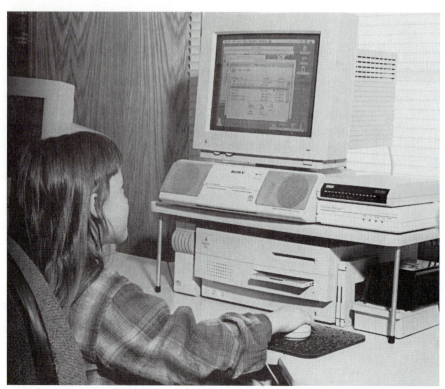

Multimedia give new meaning to the term "hands-on learning."

© Steven Lunetta/StockUp

audio and video from a laser disc player, digital audio or digital video clips stored on a hard disk, or audio playback from a CD player controlled by a computer. Some presentations combine visual media on a single computer screen, but many interactive laser disc projects use two screens, one for the computer and a separate video screen for a laser disc player. Multimedia implies interactivity, where the student is actively engaged in the presentation of information.

Multimedia can be used to motivate and enrich students' reading and writing processes. Using materials such as video, still images, or audio segments, students can make famous speeches come alive to support the printed page. Rather than just reading about a Civil War battle, students can bring the battle to life through the words and images of participants using video and text. Instead of just text and still illustrations, students can create an "electronic book" with text, sound, video clips, animation, or conventional illustrations, or conventional illustrations and photographs scanned into the computer. Students or teachers can include illustrations that are interactive, with pop-up notes or point-and-find tests built into the presentation. A system of links in the software binds text and audiovisual material together into a coherent presentation.

Multimedia can provide a private, nonjudgmental learning environment where the student controls the pace in a hands-on learning experience. A student using a prepared multimedia product can back up, repeat a segment, or ask for further explanations. Interactive learning on an individual basis helps students of all levels. For most learners, multimedia offers the opportunity to explore beyond the basics of the course. For developmentally delayed learners, individualized learning situations using multimedia address all learning styles and increase motivation.

Multimedia can be developed by students, but most often is used through commercially developed programs. For example, many *HyperCard* programs are commercially available for the Macintosh computer that will drive commercially prepared laser discs and CD-ROM discs. Once the computer program is accessed, a menu is available that allows the user to choose one of many topics or menu items that are located on either the laser disc or the CD-ROM disc.

Students at all grade levels can create multimedia reports that require them to decide not only what information to convey, but also which medium best conveys it—a change from the days when text was the only medium both easy and inexpensive enough for them to use. Students can become active consumers of textual information. Educational projects on the computer created by students may have a mysterious air to them, primarily because the technology is often unfamiliar to the teacher. Without a basic understanding of software and hardware, the results can look like magic—interesting, but unusable by the teacher or other students. Multimedia projects can also be seductive, with lots of glitz but with little substance. It is the teacher's role to become familiar with multimedia applications, terms, and the process for creating.

From a few studies that have been done on how multimedia course structure affects student comprehension, researchers found that programs which actively control the student's progress (as opposed to unstructured free exploration) and those that frequently test for comprehension are more effective in raising student test scores (Lynch, 1993).

Scenario Conclusions

This glimpse into representative classrooms using technology is just that, a short look at how a few teachers are using technology to support reading and writing instruction. In several cases, the main objective was not reading and writing, but it is evident that reading and writing were taking place with real audiences and student interaction. Using technology to support instruction and learning does not come without a price. Learning to use today's technology is labor intensive. The skills involved in using the technology just for ourselves, as teachers, require time. As teachers must make professional decisions about reading selections and activities, they must also consider technology as a means to increase reading abilities, and as a support in the literacy environment, with developmentally appropriate software. To integrate technology well into the instructional setting requires patience and time. But the rewards are great. Children in our schools today will need technological expertise to get along in their world tomorrow. Technology is one of many tools available to readers and writers that supports literacy learning and doing. It is in the area of literacy that a teacher can successfully integrate the technology that is already in our schools, and expand on as technology increases.

What kind of decisions must a teacher make to use technology appropriately in literacy development? How can teachers prepare themselves for this decision making? What can a teacher do to be prepared for technology in the classroom, and then to maintain that preparedness? The following sections describe guidelines and strategies for critical decision making when using technology in teaching and learning.

Previewing and Selecting Appropriate Technology

Software Selection Committee

Technology must never drive curriculum; finding an exciting program and looking for a place to use it in the curriculum is working backward. There are several ways teachers can make decisions on appropriate technology for their classroom. First, each school *must* identify a committee of interested individuals who are willing to take time to preview software. This is often easier done in groups where participants are able to share the load of examining software with others with different perspectives. Teaching the same grade level or content is not required, for it is the questions asked by others who aren't sure how a program might be used that require one to look at a program with different eyes. An often asked question is, "How do I get my hands on software to preview?" Organize a software catalog reference area in the school library or computer lab. Contact software companies for a 30-day preview; most companies have 800 phone numbers available. Although a 30-day preview requires packaging software at the end of the loan period and paying for shipping, the money invested in software is precious and only good software should be purchased. Borrowing software from a company for preview gives time for the program to be used with children in a classroom environment.

Children and Previewing

A tip for busy teachers: Loan a piece of software to one of your students who has a computer at home. Have the student use this as an alternative assignment with a required one-page process paper: What problems were encountered?

What made this program fun? Boring? How can one get into it quickly without reading the documentation? Did you use the documentation to learn this program? How would you like to use this program in class? Our students often have the time necessary for learning a new program and they like becoming the experts.

Resources

Another way to find software is to use a network of colleagues, others in the same district teaching your area of content or in nearby districts. Make connections with teachers at professional meetings. Attend reading conferences and browse in the vendor area where reading software is on display. Read software reviews in professional magazines such as *The Reading Teacher* and *The Writing Notebook: Visions for Learning.*

What to Look For: Guidelines for Selecting Reading Software

When the learner's active involvement and control in the process of learning to read and write are considered, several implications for computer-based instruction come to mind. Computer materials are most effective when they allow the learner some degree of decision making and control over the task. Interactive materials, which encourage students not only to respond to stimuli but to influence or control outcomes, are imperative (Strickland, Feeley, & Wepner, 1987). Students should be able to self-check by looking back at previous work or calling up other features. Preference should be given to programs that require the reader to make decisions about progression or direction of the content, because decisions promote active involvement. In all cases, students should be fully informed about the purpose of the computer task and what it requires of them. They should be encouraged to ask questions about the purpose and requirements and to assess their own capability to successfully complete the task.

Guidelines are given by Strickland, Feeley, and Wepner (1987, pp. 9–11) to help teachers of reading match their use of computers with what is known about the reading process. They are presented here with discussion following to provide a framework as teachers make important decisions regarding the use of technology in the teaching of reading.

1. Computer instruction in reading should focus on meaning and stress reading comprehension.

2. Computer instruction in reading should foster active involvement and stimulate thinking.

3. Computer instruction in reading should support and extend students' knowledge of text structures.

4. Computer instruction in reading should make use of content from a wide range of subject areas.

5. Computer instruction in reading should link reading to writing.

1. *Computer instruction in reading should focus on meaning and stress reading comprehension.* Learners should have opportunities to work with whole, meaningful texts to use and extend what they know about reading comprehension. Learners should have opportunities to work with word-recognition programs that stress the use of word meanings in conjunction with phonics and structural analysis. When programs feature the study of individual words and phrases, they should be offered within a contextual framework that helps them make sense to the learner. A program which offers isolated words that learners are to either accept or throw away according to endings may be practicing visual recognition of ending patterns but is not practicing for reading comprehension. Beware of electronic worksheets that provide words in isolation. It is up to teachers to decide whether the computer supports reading instruction and practice in the classroom.

Learners should have opportunities to apply the skills being taught in some meaningful way. Programs that deny the learner an opportunity to make use of what is being taught are merely assessment tools and do little to further the learner's growth. Learners should have opportunities to work with computer materials that use content and language that are within the range of their conceptual development. Tasks should be challenging but not frustrating. Student interests, previous experiences, and purpose play a role in determining whether or not a computer task is comprehensible and worthwhile.

2. *Computer instruction in reading should foster active involvement and stimulate thinking.* Learners should have opportunities to discuss the purpose of the computer task or program. They should be aware not only of what they are supposed to do but also of why doing it is important. Learners should have opportunities to make decisions that control or influence the computer task. Programs that build in opportunities for students to make choices and test predictions help them learn to think and act on their own rather than merely react to someone else's thinking. An exceptional reading program developed with this in mind gives learners an opportunity to use strategies that they are using as readers. Learners should have opportunities to monitor their own learning. Tasks that offer students opportunities to self-check and correct their own errors support the development of independent learners.

3. *Computer instruction in reading should support and extend students' knowledge of text structures.* Learners should have opportunities to encounter a wide variety of text structures upon which to apply and refine their comprehension skills. A variety of narrative and expository structures should be provided. Commercially prepared teacher-authored and student-authored materials also should be included. Reading instruction can take place through all kinds of computer-based materials, not merely those designated specifically

for that purpose. Learners should have opportunities to experiment with text in creative ways to suit their purposes. When students reorganize a story or an informational piece on the computer, they are employing and strengthening what they know about the structure of texts. Software programs designed for content areas outside of reading can be used to provide modeling of comprehension strategies within the text structure provided and can be used to practice those strategies.

4. *Computer instruction in reading should make use of content from a wide range of subject areas.* Learners should have opportunities to use the computer as a means of applying reading strategies to all areas of the curriculum. Programs related to science, social studies, and math require the use of strategies for reading comprehension. Unless students are being helped to use what they know about reading comprehension under these circumstances, they are not progressing as competent readers. Learners should have opportunities to use the computer in conjunction with other modes of instruction. The computer should not operate as a separate and isolated means of learning. Its use should be integrated with that of books and other learning materials. Students need to think of the computer as one additional means of sharing and retrieving information and practicing skills in interesting and meaningful ways.

5. *Computer instruction in reading should link reading to writing.* Learners should have opportunities to create text with the computer for sharing and use by others. When students enter information into the computer for someone else to retrieve and use, they must compose with the reader in mind. This frequently involves making explicit use of what they know about what makes a text comprehensible. For example, decisions might be made about how much information to give, what to stress, whether or not to use topic headings, whether or not the ideas are clearly stated, whether or not spelling, punctuation, and other writing conventions are accurately applied, and so on. Revision and proofreading strategies such as these clearly involve the combined application of reading and writing skills. Learners should have opportunities to use the computer as an information retrieval system. Classroom databases, where several students input information on a particular topic, are excellent opportunities for students to collect, organize, and store information for others to retrieve, reorganize, and use. The information collected may be lists of items or short passages on various topics. In either case students are acting as readers and writers as they peruse information to make decisions about what to collect and store. Later, they search and sample the stored information to make decisions about what to retrieve and how to analyze and then report it.

Design Implications for Literacy Software

There are design implications for computer software supporting literacy development. The following implications are provided by Kelly and O'Kelly

(1993) in a study, "Emergent Literacy: Implications for the Design of Computer Writing Applications for Children."

1. Writing programs should be available to children that encourage and support them in their efforts to make connections to the literature they have encountered. (Children's literature is an excellent medium in which to encourage writing.)

2. A writing application should provide a tool that allows children to easily produce copies of their work for their audiences and for public display. (Children's writing thrives in an atmosphere in which their work is shared and displayed for others to see.)

3. A writing application should be designed in such a way that it permits a child to make decisions about what to write. It should also allow teachers to add features in order to keep apace with the expanding interests of their children. (Children need freedom to write about experiences that excite and enthuse them.)

4. An application designed for emergent writers should provide those users with a means of saving work easily and in a form easily retrieved by the teacher. It should provide a means for a teacher to make notes and document observations about a child's growth. Icon-based (picture-based) applications potentially allow such ease of use. (Assessment of children's growth in writing over extended periods of time is essential.)

5. Writing applications for young students should include devices or prompts that support children's recall of information or stimulate the formation of relevant schemata. In this regard, the use of illustrations is one recommended device. (Children's cognitive processes should be stimulated and supported.) (pp. 7–8)

The emergence of developmental approaches to literacy and classroom use of technology poses challenges to courseware designers who wish to develop and to teachers who wish to purchase tools compatible with the developmental approaches they subscribe to in their classroom. These principles offer guidance to the teacher making software selection decisions.

Software That Enhances the Reading/Writing Connection

Probably the most effective tool for making the connection between reading and writing is a word processor. Word processing with computers is highly linked to reading development (Anderson-Inman, 1986). Although it may be possible to perform many computer activities without thinking about writing, it is virtually impossible to engage in word processing without reading. A great deal of reading occurs during writing, particularly at the revision and proofreading stages, which word processing helps us do more efficiently.

Researchers concerned with computer-based writing have begun to see that the question of whether computers are superior to paper and pencil for developing writers is irrelevant (Hawisher, 1989). Although a word processor does not inherently make the literature/writing connection, teachers can make the connection by modeling the use of a word processor in a context that supports the literary activities children are engaged in. Simon (1986) writes that the most important function of the computer for the English teacher is probably that of word processing because it adds great flexibility to the act of writing. Smith (1985) states that with the word processor, "Students can learn the art of written expression without the fear of having to produce a new copy every time their work is reviewed . . . and allows writers to become more willing to take risks" (p. 557). Observations of young children have shown that risk taking is essential to language learning (Goodman, 1986). Children learn by trying out their developing understandings of how language works. When they stretch to reach new levels of competence, they learn from both their success and errors (DeGroff, 1990).

Writers are constrained by natural physical and cognitive processes, so they have trouble composing and revising simultaneously. They also have trouble being both writer and reader at the same time. "But people are smart, and their minds can form ideas faster than their hands can type. Computers are not so smart, but they are very fast. They have photographic short-term memories and enormous long-term memories that store clearly organized information" (Daiute, 1985, p. 68). Anyone using a word processor for a lot of writing may argue that composing and revising become more simultaneously possible. Much of the drill and practice software available for elementary classrooms is designed to identify children's errors (DeGroff, 1990). But this is not the case with word processors, where the computer accepts a writer's invented spellings or less-than-conventional punctuation. Computers don't make better writing; they facilitate the writing process. The children, not the computer, identify aspects of writing that are within their capacity to change. By watching most writers at a computer, it is clear there may not be such a thing as a printed first draft when using a word processor.

Students and teachers are using computers in many ways both to support their writing process and to expand their portfolio of published materials. Communication skills, including writing, are critical in all subjects. Word processing technology makes it possible for teachers and students to communicate, to find real audiences for their work. At the same time, word processing with computers supports a process model of writing instruction in ways that no other educational tool can (Thomas, 1987). Through the public nature of a large screen, students can see the teacher type on a word processor, revise and edit information as needed, and model the writing process: "Maybe these two ideas could be combined into one sentence—if I take out these words and put in a connector like 'and,' the sentence will make sense." Or "These two ideas are related, maybe I can organize the list if I move this idea up with the other idea." The modeling process used by a teacher can be an effective tool for showing students how we use strategies to help us read and write.

The neat appearance of writing composed on the computer is a wonderful product for young children who have had to turn in smudged, torn, and possibly hard to read copies of their writing. With a word processor, children not only have a neat product, but because of the word processor's capabilities to delete mistakes, they can now correct mistakes without starting over. Word processing makes it easy to get ideas down and revise things. Gone is the tedious erasing and recopying. On-line spelling checkers and thesauruses can be used by students to correct and expand their vocabulary. Typed text is easy to read, which allows students to critique their own and others' writing.

Computer printouts of a student's writing also facilitates sharing. According to Daiute (1985), "Early adolescents work together spontaneously, so writing exercises that build on this penchant have a high likelihood of success. This is a time when feedback on their writing can help children express themselves and reach out to their readers" (p. 174). Papert (1980) writes in his book *Mindstorms* that for most children, "Rewriting a text is so laborious that the first draft is the final copy, and the skill of rereading with a critical eye is never acquired. This changes dramatically when children have access to computers and are capable of moving text. . . . I have seen a child move from total rejection of writing to an intense involvement within a few weeks of beginning to write with a computer" (p. 30).

Many software programs are available to help in the process of writing, such as a dictionary, thesaurus, spell checker, grammar checker, semantic mapper, or idea generator. These programs can be used in traditional fashion to help a writer improve his or her writing. Probably the most important benefit of writing utility software is that young writers can take responsibility for their own writing. No longer does a student need to rely on a teacher to mark incorrectly spelled words or misuse of words. Instead, the computer can mark words that don't follow standard rules and a writer can determine whether to change the text or not. Children learn quickly that the computer will mark words that are correct but unknown to its program, thus requiring decisions, making the editing process truly their own. Teachers can also use these same software applications with students to find patterns in language or to discover a new rule.

The computer and other related technologies, with their ability to prompt and respond to reader interaction, can provide an environment for communication that enhances both reading and writing skills. The following genres of software are available for purchase commercially and can be used to support the literacy environment of a classroom.

Build-a-Book

This software prompts writers through a series of questions, generally about themselves, their family, and friends, with the answers used to personalize a story or poem on disk. The story is printed out and bound into a book. Depending on the software used, books can be printed out as Big Books or as small personal copies. Big books are printed on continuous form-feed paper, where edges can be matched and glued to tagboard to create a Big Book. With some software packages, a class list can be typed and a story or poem is generated with random use of names. The stories found in build-a-book software packages are highly motivational to children and may play a significant role in motivating young and reluctant writers to produce personalized materials.

Electronic Books

Students can combine text and graphics to create books that are meant to be read on the computer. The computer screen becomes the "page" and the writer is provided with electronic tools for writing and illustrating stories, reports, and text materials. Most of the available programs encourage story writing and some are accompanied by familiar cartoon characters. Other electronic books come complete with pictures and stories already written. Many include a point-and-click capability for making characters on the screen animated. Finally, some computer stories are accompanied by synthetic speech, which allows the student to have a story read aloud.

Branching Stories

In branching stories the reader proceeds through an adventure, responding to choices presented and thereby determining the plot and outcome of the story. Usually a reader is given multiple choices for continuing the story. The act of reading the story and making choices in this type of software is also the act of writing the story. A new breed of branching stories is a genre known as "hyperfiction" (Anderson-Inman, 1990). Using the capabilities of hypertext authoring systems such as *HyperCard* (Claris), hyperfiction stories offer the reader multiple links from any given page, often presented as graphic images to be clicked on. Hypertext presents the potential for both reading and writing complex multilinked stories that can be purchased commercially or created by students.

Talking Word Processors

Several word processors also include synthesized speech, usually in a robotic-sounding voice. Although adults seem to have difficulty understanding this robotlike reading of student-produced text, young children delight in the sound and the fact that the computer can read what they wrote. Most talking word processors can be adjusted for "fixing" phonetic sounds. Words, phrases, sentences, and whole pages can be read and reread as often as the reader needs.

The text can be printed. This type of software is often recommended for ESL students, where listening to the text can help in proofreading and can promote interactive participation in the writing and reading process.

Computer Placement: One per Classroom or a Lab?

One Computer (Or More) per Classroom

If computers are to be used as an aid in an elementary writing program, their placement within individual classrooms is strongly recommended. Schools typically outfit a computer lab before placing computers into individual classrooms. If a teacher subscribes to a whole-language philosophy, which includes writing often and related to all curriculum areas, putting everything away to go to the computer lab for writing may inhibit classroom use of computers for writing. This makes writing more contrived. A computer and printer available for classroom use, however, allows for more control of classroom variables by the teacher. Children can use them whenever they wish, or the teacher can schedule their use in an efficient manner. If the writing program is to be an integral part of the school's day, it is helpful for children to be able to use a word processor whenever time permits rather than

Computers enhance learning for all children.

© Gail Meese/Meese Photo Research

on Friday afternoon for 30 minutes. Accessibility to the computer during most of the school day has been shown to be an effective means for increasing the amount of computer use by children (Kurth, 1988).

One computer in a classroom has typically provided a drill and practice tool. If a computer is used primarily for drill and practice, it is probably not supporting curriculum of that classroom. Individual software programs that fit into a drill and practice format do not usually fit what is being studied by students, especially if there is no careful consideration and evaluation by the teacher. Instead, many classroom computers are used as a "reward" for the first student done with a classroom activity.

If school administrators have to choose between a computer lab or one computer in each classroom, it is suggested they opt for one computer in a classroom *if* it is also stipulated that each classroom has a printer and access to a large-screen monitor (such as a VCR monitor). With a printer, writers now have a print shop. All student writing can be printed immediately, rather than waiting for access to a printer after school. Ease of teacher use is one of the components that will make technology a successful curriculum support. Waiting until the end of the day to print out a number of student activities may prohibit future use of the technology.

Mobile Computers

In many schools, computers are shared by several teachers or departments. Usually these computers are on mobile carts that allow the computers to be moved from room to room. Although this arrangement is not ideal, scheduling and careful attention to writing and prewriting activities close to the time computers will be in the room can provide adequate use of computers for writing. This arrangement often provides more than one computer per room as well; several classrooms might share three computers, for example, and all three can be scheduled for a block of time and can remain in the classroom for several days. This works well for writing activities where all children need access to a computer. A department or grouping of teachers might investigate different options for providing computers for writing: one in each classroom, grouping of several computers to be reserved for blocks of time, a computer lab. Rather than a computer lab for elementary schools, one computer in each room with three to five movable computers allows for flexibility and greater support for technology integration.

If computers are located in individual classrooms, the placement of these computers becomes very important. Although room for collaborative efforts or a quiet spot for discussions is important, the computer should also be accessible for teacher use. This is especially important if the computer is used for group writing. Beware of placing the computer in an isolated corner where it becomes difficult for writers to use often as a tool in their writing process.

Children's Perceptions of Computers: Modeling by Teachers

Children need to see their teachers modeling appropriate uses of technology, especially with the writing process. Students today see technology in many forms in their life outside of the classroom: video games, computer games, drill and practice programs at home in game format, and on TV. Children entering classrooms with technology may assume the computer is a game tool, for that is their background. One study conducted with first-grade students (Gunn, 1990) indicates that children's perceptions of computer use may be game oriented, directing classroom use, and suggests that teachers model writing at the computer for real audiences. For example, a teacher can indicate she is writing a note home to parents advertising a school program, a grade report, a memo, or a newsletter. Using one computer with a large group, the teacher might list student responses to a KWL activity (see Chapter 11): "what do we know about . . ." and "what do we want to know about . . ." That list can then be referred to throughout a unit of study and can be finalized with "what did we learn about . . ." One computer can be used for a group writing activity, in which the class members participate in creating an introductory paragraph for individual stories.

Modeling of the writing process using a computer accomplishes several important goals: Students see the writing process in action, they see advantages of using a word processor (e.g., revising, storing, accessing later), and they see a computer used as a writing tool. As a teacher models reading strategies and the writing process in an interactive reading and writing environment, children's understanding of the reading and writing processes will increase, and their writing will reflect increased understanding of text structure, whether the writing is performed with pencil and paper or with a word processor.

Equity

How does modeling the writing process on one computer in primary grades promote equal use of computers later between boys and girls? Remember Jan's second- and third-grade classroom scenario earlier, where the computer had been used for drill and practice until Jan began watching her students? What this scenario tells us in a generalized way is that using the one computer available in a classroom as a reward will promote negatively several issues that educators must deal with: drill and practice, gender inequity, economical inequity, integration, and computers as a gaming tool.

Drill and practice software has a useful place in the classroom, but not when it is the typical software used as a reward. In the scenario here (fictitious but typical), a math drill was used as a reward. Many math drills found in schools are in a game format and often unappealing to girls. What is the likelihood that a math drill will support the curriculum objectives, student need, and support integration? With conscious evaluation and preview, it is possible that math drill and practice *will* support today's lesson, but in many cases, that thoughtful consideration is not typically part of the selection process. Because the math program will probably be in a game format, students continue seeing the computer as a gaming tool. Many girls will not choose to play a game, especially with boys. Although the gender inequity issue is changing as computers are introduced at younger ages and for language-arts activities, females not choosing to use a computer is still an issue that many teachers must deal with.

Children who have a computer at home will often be the first to choose to use a computer at school. It is up to the teacher to be aware of who has technology available to them and incorporate a classroom management system that gives the "have-nots" time at the computer in an equal proportion to those who have access at home.

As for integration, most drill and practice programs, whether math, language arts, or any other content area, may or may not support integration of technology into curriculum. That is up to the teacher who chooses to include drill and practice software in her planning. What happens typically, however, is drill and practice software is available for a student to use when work is completed, and *that* is when the software does not usually support a teacher's curricular objectives. Software should be chosen to support classroom instruction and to help meet educational goals.

So what can teachers do with one computer to help eliminate perceptions of computers as gaming tools, gender and economic inequity, overuse of drill and practice, and technology integration? Connecting a large-screen monitor to the one available classroom computer now provides a means for eliminating some of the former pitfalls of one computer in the back of the room for rewards.

First, introduce the computer as an instructional tool. Rather than using drill and practice software, choose a software program which simulates an environment that might be difficult to create in the classroom. Then practice a reading comprehension strategy, using the software as a medium to practice the strategy. For example, the geography program discussed earlier, *Where in the USA is Carmen Sandiego?* provides opportunities for reading for research (Fodor's USA, suspect dossiers, classroom social studies texts). The use of one computer or other related technologies such as laser disc and CD-ROM players with large groups for instruction, modeling, practice, research, or presentation has a better chance for integrating technology than access to a computer lab.

Next, use the computer as a word processing tool for whole-group or small-group instruction. A word processor may support the integration of technology across all curriculum areas better than any other software application, as well as strengthen literacy development for readers and writers.

With a large-screen monitor or an LCD projection panel, the writing process can be modeled. Voice your own writing process and the steps you are taking as you use the word processor. Let developing writers see how the acts of reading and writing and word processing are connected.

Finally, introduce technology as a literacy support in early primary grades. Let children see the computer used for writing and communicating rather than for gaming. Introduce technology-supported language-arts activities in early grades when girls and boys both are interested in using technology. Encourage girls and boys alike to view technology as a tool that will enhance their writing process and then make sure they have access to the technology.

A Vision: Technology-Supported Reading and Writing

Technology can help in the process of reading and writing and it can aid in beautiful-looking products. It can be used in a classroom to motivate a reluctant reader or to generate new excitement for almost any student. We shouldn't expect technology to relieve us of the responsibility of teaching students how to be readers and writers; rather, we should be seeking ways in which technology can help students to set higher personal goals and then concentrate on helping them develop the competencies necessary to achieve those goals.

Evaluation of literacy development supported by technology must include an understanding of the medium itself. Technology cannot be used in isolation. It is one more delivery system that can support the literacy development of children and its use in a classroom must be supported by thoughtful and informed decision making. It is up to teachers to select the technology and software that support their goals. When teachers use technology in their literacy programs, they begin with their beliefs and understandings of how children learn, keeping foremost in their mind the question, "Why am I doing what I'm doing?"

In a vision of future classrooms where literacy processes are learned through natural, authentic practice in real communicative contexts, there are enough computers so everyone can write every day. Students in kindergarten and first grade learn keyboarding and word processing, which means that eventually all other grades are spending their time writing rather than learning to keyboard. Students are always involved in writing books and reading together, and editing and revising are fun because they don't require laborious recopying when a computer is part of the process. Multimedia technology is available to students to create, to read and write, to share and extend their literacy skills. Classrooms are no longer four walls, but through telecommunications, a global classroom of readers and writers are connecting for real-world communications. Quality software is available and teachers are informed decision makers when it comes to when and how to use technology to support their instruction and their students' learning.

Major Ideas in This Chapter

▼ Technology has many uses in a literacy classroom, but the importance of technology lies in the human activities involved with its use. It takes a teacher to make professional decisions about the support technology will provide.

▼ Word processing software supports the writing process by allowing the writer to take risks; with a word processor, a writer can delete, move, change, save, recall, and print text.

▼ It is the teacher's choices in technology that determine whether technology will support a literacy program.

▼ Keyboarding should be introduced to children as early as they enter school. One computer in the classroom is not enough to provide efficient keyboarding.

▼ Placement and use of one computer in the classroom can help narrow the inequities of computer use.

▼ Demonstration and modeling of computers as a writing tool in primary grades can help clarify a child's perceptions of how a computer can be used and bridge the inequity gaps found in technology.

Discussion Questions: Focusing on the Teacher You Are Becoming

1. Interview five young children (early primary grades), asking them, "Where have you seen computers used outside of school? What do you think computers are used for? How do you use computers at school?" Share the results of your interviews with your classmates and discuss children's perceptions of computer use as they enter school.

2. Teachers are often directed to use technology in their instruction, but are not given time to learn to use the technology for themselves. Investigate the staff development opportunities for the teachers in the school in which you are observing. Are technology workshops provided for teachers? When do teachers practice their technology-related skills? Discuss your findings with your classmates.

3. Discuss your technology background with classmates. What kind of preparation have the members of your class had in preparing for

technology use in the classroom? What opportunities exist for learning more about technology and its integration into the classroom?

4. Visit a school and find out if a computer with either a large monitor or an LCD projection panel is available for use by teachers. If not, discuss with your classmates a plan for creating a display computer for group writing. Get cost estimates, part numbers and location for purchase, and prepare a proposal that might convince a principal to purchase the necessary supplies.

Field-Based Applications

1. Interview a principal and several teachers to find the criteria their school uses for software selection.

2. Preview several reading software programs and compare to the guidelines listed in this chapter.

3. Observe children writing using paper and pencil and children writing with a word processor. Compare the revision strategies used by both.

4. Prepare an integrated lesson plan, where the concept being taught is supported by a software program. Indicate how the software enhances the lesson and provide enough detail for the reader to know what the software does.

5. Help a group of children write a newsletter for their class using desktop publishing software. Observe the literacy events that occur in this process.

6. Making cloze passages, replacing part of a text with blank characters for students to then make back into a whole text, is a popular strategy that is made easier with a word processor. Using text created by students, start a word processing program and type a piece of writing or load a student's writing from disk. Starting at the beginning of the text, use the find/replace function of the word processor and replace parts of the original writing with blanks or keyboard characters (e.g., #$%@). For example, replace all letter "a's" with an "@," all letter "e's" with a "#," and so on. Print and reproduce the cloze activity for use with a student, or work with a student at a computer to replace the symbols with appropriate letters automatically with find/replace. Then have students prepare cloze activities for each other. Students will be learning about word processing as they determine patterns to be replaced (e.g., nouns, verbs, vowels, consonants).

EPILOGUE
PUTTING IT ALL TOGETHER

We have examined in great detail the ways in which literacy develops. We have encouraged, cajoled, and at times even admonished you to think about ways to help children develop reading and writing ability in true communicative contexts. We have repeatedly asserted that children acquire literacy developmentally in settings that encourage the authentic uses of reading and writing. Sometimes we have been very theoretical, and sometimes we have been very practical. The purpose of this epilogue is to integrate theory and practice together in ways that show you how our vision can and does work in real classrooms.

Planning Thematic Units

We will introduce you to four very talented teachers. Each has written an explanation of how he or she uses instruction integrated around a theme to create the kinds of literacy experiences we advocate for children. An understanding of how these teachers do thematic planning and teaching will give you the confidence to do it yourself.

Tying these narratives together are common threads that link them to the major ideas of the text:

1. Children's interests and teachers' interests are accounted for in thematic planning and teaching.

2. Reading and writing are used both to learn and to communicate. Content is important so that there are meaningful things about which to read and write.

3. Students are trusted to want to learn.

4. Students are empowered to make choices and to control much of their time.

5. Curriculum is emerging. When children are involved in making choices about learning, the teacher cannot always predict all of the outcomes.

6. In child-centered, thematic teaching, there are multiple rewards for the teacher, including the joy of watching children grow in ability to use reading and writing for problem solving, communication, and for pleasure.

7. Learning in school is as much like out-of-school learning as possible.

Teachers want to make connections between the outside world and school learning.

8.   The conditions for literacy learning that we presented in Chapter 2 operate in thematic instruction.

9.   Children are grouped for tasks, but not by ability levels.

As you read each teacher's remarks, think about the suggestions that may be most helpful to you in your planning.

Each contributor to this section was asked to write a description of how he or she plans instruction around a theme, using a favorite unit as an example. They plan themes that meet their instructional objectives while allowing for a variety of interesting and meaningful activities.

Climbing the Beanstalk: Kay Stritzel

Kay Stritzel is a kindergarten teacher. As an early childhood educator for more than 25 years, Kay has taught 3-, 4-, 5-, and 6-year-olds in a variety of settings. Currently she is teaching a full-day kindergarten in a primary grade school. This school is a magnet school, meaning that parents from across the school district may elect to enroll their children there. Kay has also taught classes at the college level and is active in the National Association for the Education of Young Children.

Of her educational philosophy, Kay says:

I believe that all children deserve schools that provide for their cognitive, social/emotional, and physical well-being and that are staffed by well-educated individuals. I believe that it is important to work with young children using developmentally appropriate practices.

Here is how Kay told us she plans and teaches thematic units.

When I sit down to begin the planning process, whether it is short-term or long-term planning, I want to use developmentally appropriate themes that will be interesting to the children. I look for themes that will fit an integrated curriculum approach because I do not believe in teaching math, social studies, and language arts as isolated and fragmented skills but as an integrated whole. I want a theme that will cover as many of the curriculum areas as possible; if it does not, I will supplement it with other activities.

I also look for a theme I am interested in. I can remember using a theme I was very interested in one year and having it be quite successful. The following year, it wasn't engaging to the children at all, and it was only when I realized my lack of interest in the theme that I understood why the children were not interested.

When I work up a theme, I try to include many more ideas than I can possibly use. I like to know they are there to use should I want to use the theme again, and if one idea does not work I can quickly substitute another activity. I have a large file cabinet and boxes filled with the themes I have developed over the years. I may not teach a theme the same way in subsequent years, but it is there to visit again.

Many of the themes that I have developed in the last few years have revolved around literature as I have become interested in folktales. It is equally possible to develop an integrated theme starting with any curriculum area. It is easy to emphasize one curriculum area over another by having one area be the cog in the wheel and the other areas be the spokes.

"Jack and the Beanstalk" is a folktale with a long tradition. The story appears to have originated in Celtic traditions and to have been brought to the United States by the Irish, Welsh, and British settlers. With slightly different characters, it appears as a Southern White mountain tale, and it is found in the Black traditions from the Caribbean. Slightly different versions appear throughout Europe.

This and many other folktales appeal to children because they help them work through some important issues, such as:

Independence

Making mistakes

Being afraid of someone large

Outwitting another person

Being a hero.

So I have chosen a theme, and now the specific planning begins. Which activity do I want to do, when do I want to do it, and how long should it last? This theme could be done in one, two, or three weeks. Scheduling decisions depend on what else needs to be done and how much time I have in the year-long schedule. I get busy with my plan book and decide what activities I want to do with the total class and with small groups. This decision is definitely different for each class and depends on how much adult direction the particular group needs and on its ability to work in a large group.

I make sure that I have enough copies of the story on hand. I want the children to be able to listen to the story on their own, so I make a cassette tape of it (if one is not commercially available) to go along with a set of small books or a big book. The tape is often used at a listening center during small-group time, and the children may use it during choosing time. I may even play the story during resting time.

I want some activities that the children can do on their own without adult direction. It is important for them to experience concepts on their own or to repeat an activity as many times as they choose. Following are activities to do with the "Jack and the Beanstalk" theme in language arts, math, science, and the fine arts. Remember that I always plan more activities than I will actually use.

Language Arts

1. Reading the Story

Before I read a book to the children for the first time, I ask them some questions like "What do you know about this book?" and "What do you think happens in this book?" The children will respond with a variety of answers about the characters, the story, the pictures, and other pieces of information. I accept all answers.

When reading it for the first time, I like to read the book all the way through without asking questions. I want them to enjoy the story.

I read the story to the children at the beginning of the unit.

With each subsequent reading of the story or a different version of the story, the following activities can be done. They are not listed sequentially.

2. Predicting and/or Recall

If rereading the story, the children can recall what is going to happen next. If reading a different version of the story, the children can predict what will happen.

3. Sequencing Story Events

Talk about what happened first, second, and third in the story. This can be done in a large group, with the teacher acting as facilitator, not director.

Make a set of picture cards that illustrate the main events of the story. If possible, laminate them or cover them with clear Con-Tact® self-adhesive plastic. Lay them out for the children to work with on the floor, chalkrail, or chart pocket.

4. Creating Their Own Books

Provide each child with a blank booklet made of four to six stapled pages. Have the children paginate their books and draw their own illustrations for the story. They can write down their versions of the narrative themselves or dictate them to an adult. These books are read to the class and can be saved for future reading.

I will often write anecdotal records on the children's versions of stories and put them in the children's folders. Since we do many stories, this helps me see their growth in areas such as story interpretation, sequencing, and use of language.

5. "What if?"

In the large group, ask some questions like these:

What would happen if

—Jack did not plant the beans?

—Jack's mother had gone to market?

—the giant had been a midget?

—the giant had been a woman?

6. Big Book

I use a Big Book version of "Jack and the Beanstalk." If you do not have one, then create your own by having the children draw the different parts of the story on large sheets of paper (18″ × 24″) and write the story at the bottom of the page. Laminate or Con-Tact® this, as it will get a lot of use.

7. Supplying Missing Words

After the story has been read a few times and the children are familiar with it, cover up some of the more predictable words, like *Jack*, *Beanstalk*, and *giant*, and permit the children to call them out.

8. Words, Words, Words

With the total group, brainstorm words that could be used instead of the ones in the story. For example, find synonyms for *giant*, *gigantic*, *ogre*, *angry*, *shouted*, and *screech*.

9. "J" Words

Find words that start like Jack and make a list of them. Or you can make a list of names of people that start with *J*.

10. Refrain

"Fee, fi, fo, fum" is a great refrain that the children love to chant. Have them say it each time the story is read. They do not need much encouragement to do this!

Put the refrain on sentence strips (wide pieces of tagboard about 3″ high) so the children can play with them during free-choice time.

After the sentence strips have become familiar, make a set of word cards for the children to use, alone or in conjunction with the sentence strips.

Transform the refrain using different consonants: *bee, bi, bo, bum; tee, ti, toe, tum; see, si, so, sum.*

11. Refrain

Discuss what "of an Englishman" means. Talk about where England is and ask what else might be substituted.

12. Creating a Class Book

Even if you have the Big Book copy, you might want to create your own version of the story by having the children write and edit the story, and then draw pictures. Save the book for group or individual reading.

13. Comparing Versions

After the many versions of the story have been read once or twice, the children will spontaneously begin to compare the story elements. Take advantage of this "teachable moment" to expand the discussion of the plots, characters, places, events, and names. After the children have engaged in the oral discussion, record the differences and their preferences on a chart that has been made with reproductions from the books.

Math

Many of these activities can easily be adapted for use by large and small groups and by individuals.

1. Story Problems

Make up some situations like these for the children to solve in their heads:

a. Jack was given four beans. He lost one. How many did he have left?

b. Jack planted three beans, but two rotted. How many came up?

2. What Comes Next?

Prepare a set of cards. Each card should show a leaf with a numeral written on it (0–10, 0–20). Shuffle the cards, select one, show it to the children, and ask, "What number comes next?"

3. Estimating

Have the children estimate how many beans are in a glass jar. Draw a large picture of the glass jar. Provide pictures of beans on which the children write their estimates and their names. Paste these "beans" on the paper jar. At the end of the unit, count the beans and see who made the closest estimate.

4. Beanstalk Activities

Construct a large beanstalk somewhere in the room where the children will have easy access to it. I usually use the spot where the large measuring tape is kept on the wall.

a. Count backwards. Children are at the castle and must climb down, counting each leaf as they do so.

b. As a group, count the leaves and mark each with a numeral. I alternate the leaves from one side of the stalk to the other. This reinforces the concept of odd and even numbers, but it is left to the children to discover or talk about it. Once the leaves are labeled, you can begin to count from numbers other than 1 so that the counting exercise is not so rote.

5. Activities with Beans

a. How much is a handful? Each child is given a piece of paper that looks like Figure E.1. Then the child is asked to predict how many beans are in one handful. After picking up a handful of beans, the child will count and record and answer.

b. Compare quantities using a graph. Each child is given a set of four or five different kinds of beans (limas, pintos, white, black, red, garbanzos, and so on). They separate their sets, compare more and less, and talk about who has how many of what bean. Then they glue their sets of beans on their own individual graphs, as in Figure E.2.

6. Calendar

Use the calendar to teach days of the week as the children determine how many days the story takes. The children can vote on which day they wish the story to start so that the days of the week can be added to the storyline. For example, if Jack went to the market on Monday, then he planted the beans on _____ , and the beans grew on _____ , and so on.

7. Time of Day

Using a large clock with movable hands, ask the group to answer questions like these:

What time of the day did Jack leave home?

What time of day did he get to the market?

What time of day did he meet the person who gave him the beans? Was it in the morning, afternoon, or night?

Name ______________		
	P	R
1. 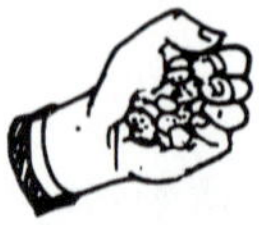		
2. 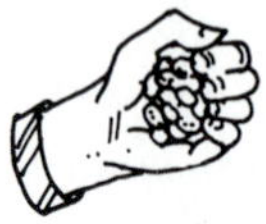		
3. 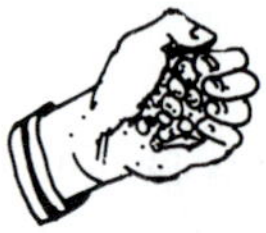		

P=predicted
R=real

Figure E.1—Number of Beans per Handful

Illustrate their answers on the clock.

8. Graphing Story Elements

At large-group time, the children can vote for their favorite versions of the story, their favorite illustrations, or their favorite characters in the story. Create a graph of their responses.

Science

1. Animals

Discussing the cow Jack sold can lead to talking about mammals and milk. The children can name other animals they know that give milk, and the teacher can list them on a chart.

2. Activities with Beans

a. Sort the beans. Put a variety of beans on the science table so the children can sort them into different containers. Label the containers.

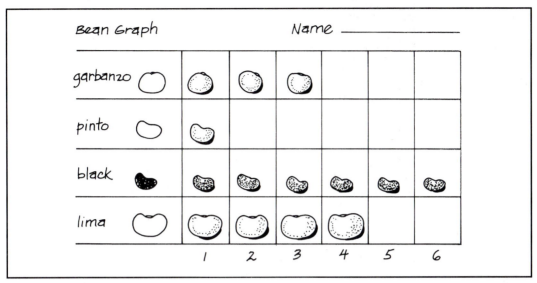

Figure E.2—Bean Graph

b. Talk about what will happen if you put a few beans in water and make a chart of the children's predictions. Soak a few beans of each kind overnight; the next morning, discuss and chart the results.

c. Plant some beans (individual activity). Provide a container for each child so they can plant the beans. I usually use clear plastic ones. Place the beans inside the container, against the side, and stuff the container with wet paper towels. This arrangement allows the children to watch the roots growing. After the roots have grown a bit, we transfer them to another container (styrofoam cups or small pots) and put them near a window so they can grow. Each container is labeled with the child's name. A checklist can be used so children can check when they watered their plants.

d. Plant some beans (group activity). On a different day from the individual planting activity, plant some beans in three different containers as an experiment. Water Plant A and put in the sun. Water Plant B and put it under a box. Put Plant C in the sun and do not water it. Keep a log, chart, or book about what is happening to each plant.

3. Growing Bean Sprouts

Buy some beans that have not been chemically treated and are for sprouting. Mung beans work well. Provide each child with a clear plastic container labeled with their name, ten beans, and a square of cheesecloth. Begin this activity on Monday by soaking the beans in water the first night. Each day the bean sprouts are rinsed through the cheesecloth. Keep them damp and eat them on Friday.

Each child can chart what is happening to the beans by drawing a picture of the beans each day on a chart like the one in Figure E.3.

4. Cooking with Beans

a. Cook a sample of each kind of bean. When the children have tasted them, have them vote for their favorite bean. Tally their responses on a class graph.

b. Create a "Bean Cookbook." Ask the parents to send in a favorite bean recipe from their home. I collect these, along with some of my favorites from many cultures, into a book. I ask the children to illustrate the pages of this book before reproducing it. The Bean Cookbook is distributed to all the families. A copy is also placed in the school library and in the classroom library.

c. Have a "Bean Pot Luck Dinner/Lunch." Invite the families to prepare a bean dish for a meal at school. I provide bread, drinks, and the serving implements. Eating together is a great socializer.

d. Prepare beans throughout the year or on special days ("cowboy beans" during rodeo days, black-eyed peas around the New Year, etc.).

e. Eat some green and yellow beans, cooked and raw, so the children can compare. Create a graph to illustrate their comparisons.

Monday	Tuesday	Wednesday	Thursday	Friday

Figure E.3—Chart of Bean Growth

Fine Arts

1. Dramatizing the Story

"Jack and the Beanstalk" is a great story for children to act out, especially after it has been read several times in different versions so that all the children are familiar with it.

Brainstorm what props are needed and make a list. Brainstorm what characters are needed; if there is a dispute over which characters from different versions to include, take a vote. Choose the players and keep track of who plays what part so that the next time the play is acted out, other children can have a part. Run through the play, with the rest of the children acting as the audience.

Do the play again, and again, until you sense that the children are through with it. For me, the fun of this is acting it out for ourselves. Making it a "production" (rehearsed in fixed form and presented before other spectators) is stressful for both the children and the teacher.

2. Mural or TV Program

The children discuss the parts of the story in a large group. There should be enough segments so that each child can draw a scene from the story. These can be drawn on large craft paper, for a mural to be put up in a spacious hallway, or on a roll of paper, which can be put on a "TV" that has been made from a box with a cutout for the screen.

The children can record the story on tape, or the text can be written (by the children or by an adult) and attached to the drawings.

If the TV format is chosen, the children can "play" it over and over as they wish.

3. A Magic Place

Using any art medium (paints, crayons, collage), the children create a place they would go if they had magic beans. The pictures can be put into a book or displayed on a large bulletin board with their stories.

4. Castles

After being shown some pictures of castles, children can paint or draw a castle or create a castle with clay, blocks, or boxes. Or the carpentry center could provide wood, and the construction could then be painted. Photographs can preserve a record of their constructions.

5. Role Playing

Either before the play or instead of it, children can act out the roles of Jack, the old man, the giant, the wife, the mother, and the cow. They can play with the many ways to present these characters, with the other children offering help.

The children especially like acting out the role of the giant. This can be done outside the context of the story as the children bring their own interpretations of how a giant acts in different situations. An extension to the theme would be to find other giant stories that are favorites of the children.

6. Musical Accompaniment

Children can decide what rhythm instruments would help create the mood of the story. They can play the instruments while the teacher reads the story. Some ideas include using a drum for the giant's steps, a triangle when Jack throws the beans outside, and bells or the xylophone as Jack climbs the beanstalk.

Make a chart listing the story events, the instruments, and who played the instruments.

7. Creative Movement: The Bean

The children pretend to be the bean. This activity can be done with a small group or with the whole group. The children act out the events in the story of the bean: riding in the old man's bag, bouncing in Jack's hand as he carries them home, being thrown out the window, lying in the ground, growing, having Jack climb on the stalk, and being chopped down.

8. Flannel Board Activities

Make a set of the characters and a backdrop from one of the stories. Set it out for the children to use at the flannel board. They are free to choose this activity to tell and retell the story.

9. Puppets

Put out puppets that could be used to represent the giant, the mother, the wife, Jack, and the peddler. The children often create the other props as they act out the story. They are free to choose this activity to tell and retell the story. Sometimes a particular class may wish to put on a performance for the class.

Social Studies/Health Components

1. Gender Switches

Many stories are written with a male lead. When reading stories with my children, I often read the story again and switch the genders. Then we discuss whether or not this works. Some children are very reluctant to "mess" with a story, and this also provides a good discussion.

2. Mapping

When reading the different versions of the story, point out where this story comes from on a world map.

3. Values Discussions

When the children are familiar with the story, gather them in a large or small group to talk about:

Whether Jack was right to steal from the giant

How the story would be different if told from the giant's perspective

Why Jack's mother was mad at him

What it means to be poor

Whether Jack should have gone away from home without telling his mother.

There is a very old version of the story that talks about Jack's father owning the harp and chicken, and how he was killed when the giant was stealing these from him. I sometimes introduce this element into the story. Then we discuss how the children feel about knowing this.

4. Time Travel

Talk about when the children think this story took place. Then create the story as if it were happening today. The children can then discuss the differences.

Integrating Math with Reading and Writing Instruction: Tom Wrightman

Tom Wrightman has been teaching in the primary classroom for 14 years. Of his educational philosophy he says:

> I believe learning occurs through experiences. Experiences that are relevant to development, interests, and needs of children should be used so we can explore and understand concepts. An environment that allows these experiences should encourage risk taking and accept mistakes as part of the learning process. The respect and love of the learner and of learning itself are essential seeds that first must be planted. The love of mathematics has led me to blend that curriculum into the reading and writing processes occurring in the classroom.

In his own words, Tom explains how his thematic planning grew out of sharing a piece of literature after he had built a sense of community in his classroom.

Building Community

At the beginning of the year, (1) the sense of community, (2) cooperation between students, (3) the establishment of classroom rules, and (4) the acceptance of differences all play roles in the building of the classroom environment. Each child comes with different physical, emotional, social, and academic abilities and needs. The acceptance of these differences and the encouragement of recognizing strengths in these areas are critical in building cooperation and respect between the students. It is essential that the teacher models these actions and behaviors to reinforce the importance of them for the children. As the teacher and the children recognize the need for guidelines, this will allow children to operate within the boundaries set and allow the building of a classroom environment that encourages the four goals listed above. This beginning classroom community is built, and explained below, with an integrated study of a pond community.

Using T*he Noisy Counting Book*

The foundation for building this classroom of acceptance and cooperation begins with the introduction of *The Noisy Counting Book* by Jan Buller and Susan Schade. This book is about a boy who goes to a pond to fish. While he prepares himself to fish, a number of pond animals begin making noises. One Frog says, "Ga-dunk!" Two ducks say "Wak, wak!" Three birds say, "Tweet, tweet, tweet!" Four fish say, "Blub, blub, blub, blub!" Five crickets say, "Chirp, chirp, chirp, chirp, chirp!" Six mosquitoes say, "Bzzz, bzzz, bzzz, bzzz, bzzz, bzzz!" In frustration the boy screams "Quiet!" All the animals disappear and he becomes content to begin fishing as one frog says "Ga-dunk!" This book demonstrates the need for cooperation between the animals and the boy so all of them can work and play at their pond community without getting on each other's nerves. The need for the establishment of acceptable noise levels also demonstrates the need for some noise guidelines at the pond. This model is used for initial discussions in the classroom about noise levels, what to do about it, and cooperation among children in our classroom.

The Noisy Counting Book is one of the most recognized and successfully read books in the classroom at the beginning of the year. In our blended classroom, consisting of first and second graders, *The Noisy Counting Book* succeeds in demonstrating that we are all readers. The book can be rewritten on sentence strips and used in a pocket chart. These sentence strips become the text for a Big Book that is created by the class. The book also introduces the oral reading exercise called "Readers Theatre," in which readers have their back to the audience and turn to read or say their part when it is their turn. A number of school staff members can read the text into a tape recorder so children can listen to the story on a tape and be introduced to these important readers at our school.

The children can be introduced to many other books that have similar themes of cooperation and counting connected to them. *The Noisy Counting Book* demonstrates the concept of number and the order of number. There are many books available that can extend and enrich the experiences with number. A few possibilities are *Seven Little Rabbits* by John Becker, *Ten Black Dots* by Donald Crews, *Deep Down Underground* by Olivia Dunrae, *Fish Eyes—A Book You Can Count On* by Lois Ehlert, *Over in the Meadow* by Paul Galdone, *How Many Snails? A Counting Book* by Paul Giganti, Jr., *Just One More* by Michelle Koch, *12 Ways to Get to 11* by Eve Merriam, and *One Woolly Wombat* by Rod Trinca.

The reading activities listed above set the stage for the next two to three weeks as the children begin an integrated journey with *The Noisy Counting Book* as the springboard for many valuable and authentic reading, writing, and mathematical experiences that enrich the classroom environment for all. I have divided the curriculum below only for the purpose of explanation of the components. Many of the activities overlap and occur at the same time.

One of the social studies/health components is the establishment of classroom rules. The animals in the pond community are making too much noise, so the boy can't fish. The same thing can occur in the classroom. When there is too much noise we can't do our best work. The children can discuss and establish rules relating to noise levels and establish positive and negative consequences for following and not following the guidelines. We can also list negative comments that hurt other's feelings.

Prior to Open House the children can do an innovation on *The Noisy Counting Book* called "The Noisy Classroom Counting Book." The children brainstorm comments they use that might interrupt their teacher or others in the classroom. Some examples are "I have to go to the bathroom!" or "She hit me" or "He took cuts!" These comments can be used as situations for role playing and developing positive strategies that accomplish the same results but in a positive manner. The examples are compiled in a list and are referred to during the role-playing situations and times when these comments cause disruptions during class.

Once the list is completed the children compile this into a new book called "The Noisy Classroom Counting Book." The children are assigned roles, and they present this innovation to the parents at Open House. During the presentation three different examples are used. The first is the original text; the second is the original text with musical instruments representing the sounds the animals make (see Figure E.4 under "Music"), finally, the innovation above is presented. After the presentation, the list of those comments that disrupt learning and study time are handed out to the parents and children. They read over them together and discuss how they can solve them without interrupting others. Both children and parents then sign the letter and make a commitment not to use them in the classroom.

Constructing and Studying a Pond Community

In the classroom a pond community can be constructed. A small plastic swimming pool can be used as the pond. As it is being filled with water the children can estimate and then calculate the gallons or liters it will take to fill it up to a designated level. Children can be grouped into committees of three who are assigned to constructing the parts needed to create the pond community. This includes making the correct number of animals, writing their sounds in comic balloons, and making the trees, bushes, and other pond material. Each item is then labeled. The children take a lot of pride in creating this area of the room. It becomes a place for many creative and innovative ideas during the children's center time.

The making and inventing of musical instruments allows children to create noises representing the original animal's sounds. Counting is reinforced because the beats on the musical instrument must match the number of animals. For example, three birds will each tweet once equaling three tweets, or three beats of music. The children can then use the instruments for the animal's voices instead of their own voices during their presentation described above at Open House.

In health and science one of the areas that can be studied is swimming. The children count the number of swimming and nonswimming animals in the pond community and graph the results. The issue of water safety is discussed with the number "two" being important—that is, never go swimming alone. The study of pond water under a microscope can introduce the importance of having a clean water supply and what we can do to keep water clean. It also opens the children's eyes to some things we can't see with our naked eye. The need for clean water for washing and the amount of water our body needs each day can also be discussed.

The population of the pond community contributes to the noise level and cleanliness of the area. More cooperation and respect for each other is needed as populations increase. The class may see the need to decide to limit the number of participants at a center as a result of their experiences with *The Noisy Counting Book*.

Using a Planning Web

The Planning Web shown in Figure E.4 connects all the activities together with the concept of counting and number. This can be used as a planning strategy for the teacher or a record to show children where they are heading.

In each of the areas listed on the web, authentic reasons for using reading, writing, and counting activities have been implemented. The use of these emerging reading, writing, and mathematical processes in purposeful activities reinforce the importance of these areas in acquiring new knowledge and applying it to real situations in the classroom.

Solving a Mystery: Cheri McLain

Cheri McLain has taught for 24 years. She has spent most of her career in a self-contained classroom in a university community, but she has had experi-

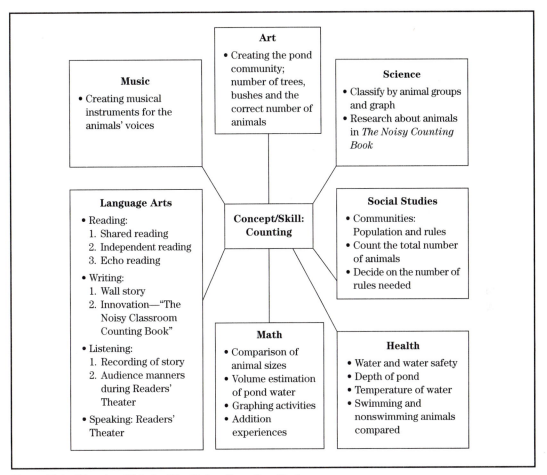

Figure E.4—Planning Web for *The Noisy Counting Book*

ence in special education and teaching university summer workshops. Cheri was chosen Oregon Elementary Teacher of the Year in 1991. She is currently teaching a third/fourth-grade combination.

In describing her philosophy, Cheri states:

Using an integrated approach to curriculum, I work at enhancing self-image through skill building. Having been trained in learning styles, I employ a variety of methods to attempt to meet the learning and emotional needs of all the students. Process curriculum is emphasized—the important thing being the journey. Besides language arts, science is one of the tools I use as a catalyst for thinking skills and literacy.

Cheri shares her blueprint for thematic teaching, which grew out of her interest in science.

I am particularly interested in children being exposed to hands-on science, with an emphasis on using materials found in the children's world. I have found that my student's natural interest in science can serve as a catalyst for teaching reading and writing, as well as the other subjects in the elementary curriculum. One of my favorite themes is that of "Mystery." In the study of this genre, which usually lasts at least six weeks, I integrate lessons in all areas of the curriculum.

We begin by having children pretend to be criminologists. The students solve a crime by identifying a set of fingerprints. This activity serves as motivation for reading and creating their own mysteries. Lessons on the elements of mystery writing, math graphing, and the enjoyment of good literature all contribute to the success of this theme. I use these materials:

▼ *Fingerprinting* and teacher's guide, Great Explorations in Math and Science (GEMS), Lawrence Hall of Science, University of California, Berkeley, CA 94720

▼ Rolls of cellophane tape, paper and pencils, magnifying glasses, overhead transparencies and handouts from *Fingerprinting* teacher's guide, stamp pads, white drawing paper

▼ Mystery books from the school library

▼ Books to read aloud, including *The Mysteries of Harris Burdick* by Chris Van Allsburg, *The Westing Game* by Ellen Raskin, *Solve-Them-Yourself Mysteries* by Alfred Hitchcock, and *Encyclopedia Brown's Book of Wackey Cars* by Donald J. Sobol.

Here are some of the instructional activities I have used in the Mystery theme. You will probably be able to think of others, but this will give you an idea of what we do.

Science (Problem Solving/Critical Thinking)

These activities come from the GEMS *Fingerprinting* materials already mentioned. I usually do these over 4 lessons of about 45 minutes each.

Lesson 1

Discuss fingerprints and criminologists. Tell the children they are going to become scientists called criminologists or forensic scientists. Teach children how to make fingerprints using lead pencil, cellophane tape, and paper. Let them practice. Make a clean set of fingerprints and look at them with a magnifying glass.

Lesson 2

In teams, children classify a set of 10 printed fingerprints using their own systems. Teacher records students' classification systems on the board and discusses with class. Teacher defines the 3 basic fingerprint patterns (overhead transparencies). Students classify 10 printed fingerprints into the 3 basic patterns. Students classify own fingerprints and make own fingerprint formula.

Lesson 3

Teacher tells story of a crime that has been committed and students are given the fingerprint formula found on the safe. Students find fingerprint formulas of suspects and speculate who may have committed the crime. Students given copy of exact prints to match with those of suspects. Hold discussion of reasons this suspect might have had prints on the safe and whether this is conclusive evidence. What other techniques could be used to solve the case?

Lesson 4

Children take notes on teacher's mini-lectures on fingerprinting facts, including why fingerprints are taken, whether fingerprinting has always been used for identification, what other systems of identification are used, and whether there is something like a fingerprint system for animals.

Lesson 5

Another excellent (and easy) science activity to begin this theme is that of chromatography, a process in which the colors of a liquid separate after contacting paper. All you need are cheap coffee filters, colored markers, and water or alcohol. This technique is explained in the book *Gee Wiz!* by Linda Allison and David Katz. "Crime Lab Chemistry," a teacher's guide from GEMS, is set up so the students solve a crime using chromatography.

1. Cut the filter paper into 1-inch strips.

2. Make a mark on the strip 2 inches from the bottom with a colored marker.

3. Either hang the strip from a pencil, or fold the top of the strip over the edge of a clear plastic glass with a little alcohol (if you are not using water-based pens) or water. The end with the colored marker should just be resting a bit above the fluid.

4. Watch as the water "crawls" up the strip and separates into different colors, creating unique chromatograms for each marker.

5. Solve a mystery by matching a chromatogram created by one of three pens used to write a ransom note left by the criminal.

Literature

Chris Van Allsburg's short stories are a splendid way to introduce mysteries. Read *The Mysteries of Harris Burdick* and ask the children to write their own ideas of what happened to Burdick or to explain the mysteries in the stories. Share *The Stranger* and ask them to write their ideas of who the stranger was, where he came from, and why changes happened when he was around.

The short mystery stories of Alfred Hitchcock are also a rich source of material for a "Mystery" theme. Intermediate classes especially like "The Eyeball." Predicting what will happen next and analyzing clues are excellent thinking/reading strategies to practice.

For a complicated mystery to read aloud, especially to fifth- and sixth-graders, an outstanding choice is Ellen Raskin's Newberry Award–winning *The Westing Game.*

Select many different kinds of mysteries from the school library and let the children choose one to read. Have them plan ways to share their books that include analyzing elements of character development, clues, suspense, and satisfactory endings.

Writing

After the first week of science and literature prewriting activities, brainstorm vocabulary words used by forensic scientists. Display them in a structured overview with *Mystery* in the center. Encourage children to use these words in conversation and writing.

Have children write a mystery story. Pay careful attention in the prewriting stage to the creation of clues, character development, and an ending that relates to the clues. Students could write newspaper articles about solving an invented crime using fingerprints and create stories about the suspects in these fictional crimes.

Art

Using Ed Emberley's thumbprint books as a source, do art projects using thumb, full finger, toe, and fist prints. This is a fun way for children to illustrate the stories they have written. Have children use a variety of media to create "Wanted" posters for the suspects in their mysteries.

Using a Curriculum Map

I use such a variety of activities to teach this theme that a map is the most expedient way to graphically demonstrate how I integrate curricula.

In the curriculum map shown in Figure E.5, note the many ways science can be used to begin our study. One of my favorites is to have the children pretend they are criminologists who must solve a crime by identifying a set of fingerprints. I use the GEMS materials, but I also have them use their new detective skills to identify the culprit who removed the M & M's from a candy jar on my desk.

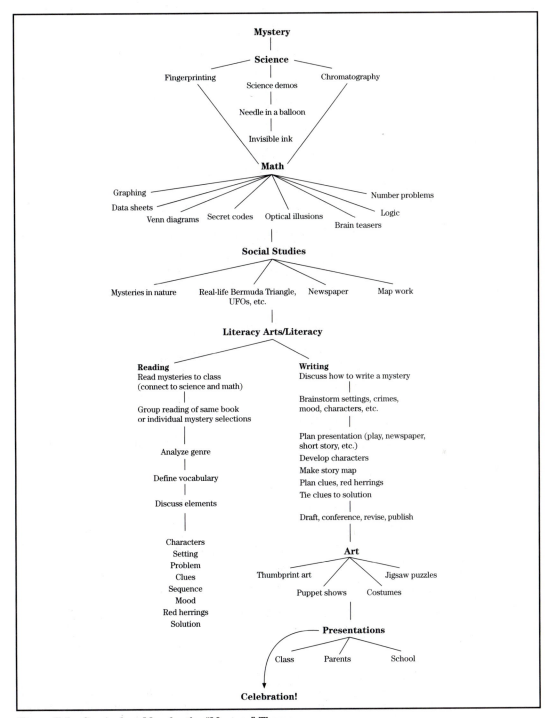

Figure E.5—Curriculum Map for the "Mystery" Theme

Turning Spring Chickens on to Embryology: Hilary Sumner Gahagan

Hilary Sumner Gahagan is a special education teacher who teaches in an elementary school resource program. She works with students identified under IDEA (Individuals with Disabilities Education Act, 1992) as having handicaps that impact their academic development in the regular classroom. These children primarily include those with learning disabilities, attention deficit disorder, and language impairments. These students need specially designed instruction in reading, writing, and/or mathematics (as well as support and modifications in all subjects) to promote their academic success in the classroom.

Her program involves instruction in both a pull-out and inclusion model, depending on the specific needs of each child. Her role as the resource specialist is broad. It involves not only instruction for these special learners, but ongoing assessment, evaluation, staff and parent education, and consultation to help everyone understand the different needs and gifts of these children. Hilary believes that thematic instruction is central to the truly child-centered classroom. This kind of classroom empowers all students, offers them choice, and integrates the curriculum, making learning engaging and relevant.

Hilary describes her educational philosophy:

> Learning is the continual process of constructing meaning between what is new and what has already been experienced. The key is in the learner's reflection of those experiences. My goal and motivation is to orchestrate an environment that invites discovery, risk-taking, and challenge so that my students realize their gifts, advocate for themselves, and feel the comfort and support to keep giving their best effort. The best I can do is to provide a learning environment that inspires, expects them to succeed, and helps them to believe in themselves!

Hilary shares an example of her philosophy through a thematic unit, which started one spring with a couple of eggs and developed into an exciting unit on embryology.

Coordinating the Resource Room with the Regular Classroom

In our resource program, we work with students in a variety of ways. Special Education used to be provided primarily in a pull-out model. In recent years, inclusion of special-needs children in the regular classroom has increased. We try to address the needs of our students by providing instruction in both small group settings and within the classrooms. One of my biggest challenges is to work closely with the classroom teachers to coordinate our instruction, and to help them to modify the regular classroom opportunities so that our children experience success.

Our program is based on a holistic philosophy of learning. Empowering students with their own learning is essential. This engages unmotivated or reluctant learners, fosters independence, and invites their commitment to personal success. Children learn through experience. They interact with their environment and actively seek to construct meaning through the processes of analyzing, hypothesizing, testing, and reorganizing the information from their experiences. They are forming rules about their world and integrating them with previous experiences.

In my classroom we center on the individual child rather than curriculum. We have designed our instructional program to teach the skills and strategies outlined in the students' IEPs (Individualized Education Programs) through thematic units. These themes can include any topic that is interesting and motivating to the students: the culture of our community (and world), the seasons, national issues, holidays, etc. The units are designed in a curriculum web that encompasses reading, writing, speaking, and listening, as well as content subjects and the arts. Thematic instruction is an essential link between school learning and the child's outside world. This approach is especially conducive to a meaningful integration with the regular classroom studies. I believe it is the linchpin of an effective special education program working in concert with regular education to promote student success.

From Eggs to Embryology: The Growth of a Thematic Unit

Each spring for several years, our classroom has enjoyed an in-depth study of chickens and their development. Our curriculum grew in response to the students' interests, fascination, and an incredible school-wide curiosity. We started with a borrowed antiquated incubator and 12 questionable eggs I brought from home. We now have a sophisticated 48-egg incubator purchased by our parent-teacher club, and a full-scale curriculum on embryology. This is an excellent example of how a small, entertaining idea can develop into a complex instructional plan by virtue of student interest.

At first we relied on encyclopedias, a feed store manual on fowl production, and the directions from our borrowed incubator for materials. We now incorporate a wide range of materials, including science books, picture books, student-made books from previous years, videos, models, computer CD encyclopedia research, live chickens, and 21 actual embryos in glass jars from our Science Curriculum Library that show us the day-by-day development during the three-week incubation period.

Each year we coordinate our chicken unit with our spring break. Fertilized chicken eggs can be obtained from a variety of sources, including local farms, feed stores, and the classified ads. We discovered that we could order fertilized eggs from our city Museum of Science and Industry. The eggs must be handled very carefully, and you need to decide what you are going to do with the young chicks when the unit is over. For many years I kept the young hatchlings myself. Then the children were so enthralled with their babies, we started adopting them out to the students' families. With a carefully worded letter to parents, we offered 2 chicks to the first 20 families who wanted them, had appropriate facilities to raise them, and knew how to care for them. Many children have raised these birds for years and will never forget the incredible experience of it all.

Using a Curriculum Web

The curriculum web shown in Figure E.6 illustrates our thematic unit and the integration of possible curricular areas.

The Instructional Plan

The following sample instructional plan shows the format and activities included in our Writing component. Each curricular area (Reading, Art, Writing, Science, Listening, Health, Speaking, and Math) can be extended in this manner. For each, an instructional unit can be designed around the theme. It is important to understand that our primary objective in each area is not the content of embryology, but the specific skills and strategies (in reading, writing, mathematics, etc.) in which the children need assistance and development. The content, however, is the motivation to engage the children in reading, writing, and so on. It is through purposeful activity that learning is natural and relevant.

Because we are a resource program, we work with students in kindergarten through grade 5. Each curricular area and instructional component is adapted to the developmental levels of our students. The beauty of this thematic approach is that we can group across grade and/or developmental levels and incorporate cooperative learning based on interest and intrigue, not deficits and needs.

A. *Project Goals*

1. Understand the basics of the setup and functioning of an incubator.

2. Develop an awareness of the 21-day gestation of a chicken egg.

3. Observe egg candling to evaluate and record embryo growth.

4. Keep a daily journal recording (in writing and/or illustrations) embryological development, days 7–21, and chick behavior, days 1–5.

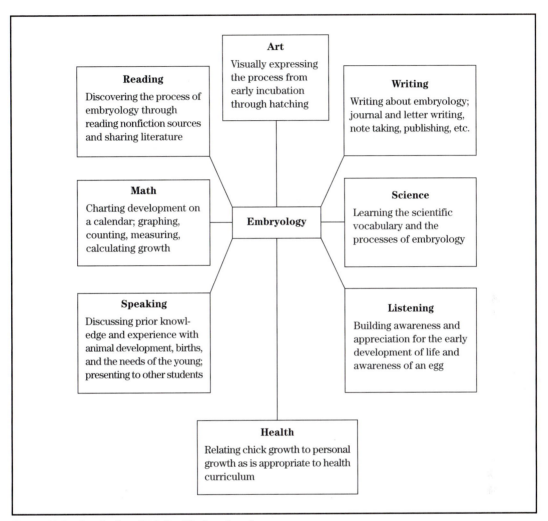

Figure E.6—Curriculum Web for "Embryology"

B. *Writing Goals*

   1. Complete a writing piece reflecting on embryology (journal, story, essay, poem, picture book, report, etc.).

   2. Using the writing process (prewriting, drafting, revising, editing, redrafting/final copy, publishing/presenting), present a piece to an audience and/or reflect on it for a portfolio.

C. *Activities*

   1. Hatching activities can be done with all grade levels.

   2. Writing activities are adjusted for each developmental level accordingly (length, format, criteria for accuracy, invented spelling, mechanics, etc.).

Hatching the Eggs

Incubation: Day 1

1. Student groups observe the eggs newly placed in the incubator. The teacher explains the functioning of the incubator: temperature control, water source for moisture, and egg-turning mechanism. The teacher has numbered the eggs for identification.

2. Each child "adopts" an egg—that is, chooses one egg by number to observe, record notes about, and bond with during the 21-day gestation period. More than one child may choose the same egg. Teacher and children discuss how fragile the embryos are and the fact that many of these will not develop into live chicks. Teacher must be prepared to deal with the disappointment of children whose eggs fail to hatch.

Incubation: Days 2–21

3. Each student beings his or her daily written response journal, including date, time, temperature of the incubator, a description of the growth observed during candling, and any predictions, concerns, and feelings.

4. As the 21st day approaches, study the hatching process (pipping, air sacs, rotational cracking). Each students records observations in a journal. Writing can be shared in small groups, in pairs, with parents, with homeroom classes, with classroom teachers, with the principal.

5. Throughout the incubation period, students can prepare notes for an oral presentation to visiting classes from the rest of the school. Little is more inspiring than to see first- and second-grade learning-disabled children giving embryology lectures to sixth-grade regular education students!

6. If you choose to offer the chicks to the students, an excellent writing activity could be the children's writing letters to their parents or to relatives who live in the country. The letters could be both persuasive and descriptive, explaining the need for good homes with the appropriate environment.

Hatchlings: Days 1–5

7. Once the chicks hatch, each child records observed chick behavior (feeding, socialization, handling).

Writing Activities

There are numerous possibilities for writing projects in this unit. These are some I have done:

▼ Pop-up, shape, flip-up books

▼ Nonfiction writing depicting the hatching process

▼ Research reports on related birds

▼ Student manuals on incubation and chick care

▼ Plays, poems, songs

▼ Fiction stories such as "Chicken Licken," "The Little Red Hen," and "The Ugly Duckling"

Possibilities in this unit are virtually endless, limited only by the students' and teacher's imaginations. Likewise, each of the other curricular areas is expandable. Your librarian and fellow teachers, as well as district resource persons, will undoubtedly help you discover literature, materials, and references to enrich your thematic units.

Teaching children through thematic units incorporates a belief and trust in the process of learning, the process of moving toward understanding rather than the mere mastery of specific skills in isolation. The developmental path is far more important than the final product. Children deserve to have that path be authentic, interactive, and relevant to their real lives.

And Now for the Teacher You Are Becoming

You have had a glimpse into the planning and teaching processes of four remarkable teachers. We hope that they will serve as models for you as you begin to put into practice the things you have learned, not only from this text and course but from your entire teacher education program. Remember that these four teachers have had years of experience. Each year they get better at their work. Take what you can from them at first, and use it, but do not challenge yourself to do everything they do—at least, not in the beginning.

If we have done our work well, you will have students who view literacy as first-grader Kati Field did in this piece:

When I grow up, I'm going to be a writer.

I'm going to write those big fat books like the ones in the library.

People will open those books, and there will be all the words that I wrote for them to read.

I like writing a lot.
It makes me feel like magic.
Sometimes it makes me excited, and
Sometimes it make me peaceful.

I didn't learn my writing.
I came with it.

APPENDIX A
INSTRUCTIONS FOR BOOKBINDING

Instant Minibook

With a few simple folds and a single cut or tear, you can turn a single sheet of paper into an 8-page booklet. If you turn it inside out, you can make a 16-page book. You'll need a rectangular sheet of paper and a pair of scissors.

What to do:

1. Take a rectangular sheet of paper and fold it in half lengthwise.

2. Open it, then fold it in half crosswise.

3. Fold it crosswise again.

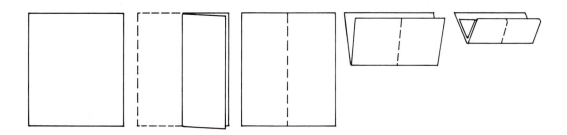

Source: Robinson (1983).

4. Unfold it so that the paper is back as in Step 2. Cut a slit half-way up the middle, like this:

5. Open the paper and fold it lengthwise again as in Step 1, with the slit on the top.

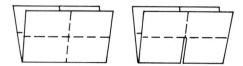

6. Grasp it at either end and push the ends of the slit together like this:

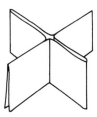

7. Fold it at one edge, like this, to make a book:

8. Punch two holes along the folded edge. Tie string or yarn through the holes to bind the book's pages together.

Hardcover Book

1. Fold two pieces of colored construction paper in half and insert typed or blank page papers within.

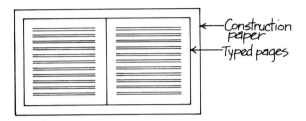

2. Sew page papers together using a bookbinder's stitching pattern down the center fold through the construction paper. Use dental floss or button hole twist (about 20″ long). Beginning at the back of the construction paper at the center, follow the pattern below, leaving 2″ to tie.

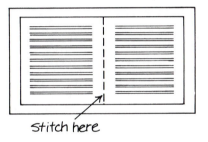

3. Center two pieces of cardboard on wallpaper, fabric, vinyl Con-Tact, or whatever you choose for cover material, leaving about ¼″ in the center between them, and about 1″ of cover material all the way around the cardboard. Draw around the pieces of cardboard so you know where to glue them. Glue them in place with rubber cement.

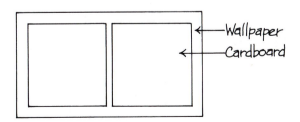

Source: Dr. Lynda Hatch, Northern Arizona University, Flagstaff, AZ.

4. Fold each of the four corners of the cover material diagonally. Glue the cover material under the fold to the cardboard.

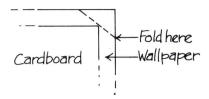

5. Then fold sides of the cover material over the cardboard and glue down. This is your book cover.

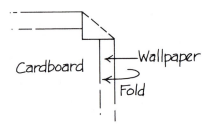

6. Open the book cover so it lies flat, and center the sewn pages inside.

7. Put rubber cement on the back end page (colored construction paper) and press that page onto the cover. Then do the same with the front page.

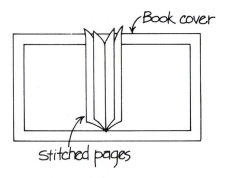

8. Put the book title and your name on the front cover. You might want to add an illustration or design on the end pages. Be sure to put an "About the Author" section on the last page.

9. You have now finished publishing your own book. Hooray!!

Zig-Zag Book

A zig-zag book is one made from a long strip of paper folded in a zig-zag fashion. It requires no sewing, but the folding must be very carefully done if a neat result is to be achieved. Zig-zag books have many uses:

▼ Sequential stories

▼ Autobiographies, showing stages of the person's life

▼ Life cycles of plants and animals

▼ Panels combining picture and description, such as of favorite animals

▼ Cyclical events, like seasons

▼ And many other possibilities.

Books, of course, can be made in any size. The dimensions used in these directions are included just as an example:

> White construction paper: 2 sheets originally $12'' \times 18''$, cut to $6'' \times 18''$ with folded panels to $4\frac{1}{2}'' \times 6''$

> Cardboard covers: 2 pieces $5\frac{1}{2}'' \times 6\frac{1}{2}''$

> Cover paper or fabric: 2 pieces $7\frac{1}{2}'' \times 8\frac{1}{2}''$

1. Cut 2 pieces of cardboard for the book covers. These pieces will need to be $1''$ larger on all four sides than the inside writing paper.

2. Cut 2 pieces of construction paper or fabric (designed with original artwork) at least $1''$ larger on all four sides than the cardboard. Using original artwork as the design on the cover paper or fabric affords the book's creator a much greater sense of pride in authorship.

3. Glue the construction paper or fabric onto the cardboard. Use wallpaper paste for the glue. Wallpaper paste works better than glue because it spreads more easily and smoothly, is less expensive, and is more "forgiving" if a mistake occurs and the paper has to be pulled apart. Spread clean newspaper on a flat work surface. (Plain newsprint is even better, to avoid having black ink come off on the covers.)
   a. Turn construction paper or fabric upside down on a clean piece of newspaper.

b. Use a wide brush to spread the glue evenly. Wide brushes are best because the glue dries so quickly. Spread the glue evenly over all the paper.

c. Place the cardboard in the center of each glued paper or fabric. Do each cover one at a time because the glue dries so quickly.

d. Turn in each corner and glue onto the cardboard. Don't pull too hard or the corners will puncture because they're wet from the glue and are weak.

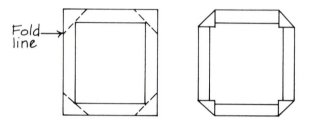

e. Lightly glue each turned-down corner, since there has not yet been any glue on these corners.

f. Turn down each side panel onto the cardboard. Use the clean newspaper underneath to press over the paper that is being glued on the cardboard. This will help keep the paper and fingers clean. Remove the newspaper.

g. Repeat Steps a–f with the second piece of cardboard and the cover paper or fabric.

4. Set the paper- or fabric-covered cardboard pieces aside on a flat surface. Place heavy books on top of them so they don't permanently warp.

5. Fold two pieces of $12'' \times 18''$ white construction paper into four zig-zag accordion-pleat folds. Refold one piece into a stack. Trim down this rectangular stack so that it is $\frac{1}{2}''$ smaller than the three sides of the cardboard. Then trim the other stack of white paper to the same size. The pages, of course, do not have to be white. "White" is used in these directions just to distinguish the writing pages from the other paper of the cover.

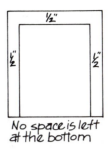

½"

½" ½"

No space is left
at the bottom

6. On a table, stand up the two folded stacks of white pages. Arrange them in an accordian-pleated way. Where the two pieces meet, overlap the two middle panels.

7. Smoothly glue or paste the two middle panels together, being *sure* all the pages are still arranged in an accordion-pleated manner.

8. Cut off and discard *one* end panel. That will leave six panels on each side. This will make the completed book open properly. (The last panel is cut off whenever there is an odd number of writing surfaces so the back opens properly. If 3 sets of folded papers are used, for example, there are 10 writing panels. Since this is an even number, no panel needs to be cut off.)

9. Glue the two end panels of white construction paper onto the insides of the cardboard covers. Place the white pages on the cardboard so the ragged edges of the artwork paper or fabric are neatly covered. However, it is important to have one end *even* with the bottom of the cardboard so the book can stand up open for a display.

10. Place waxed paper or foil between the covers and the dry pages at both ends of the book for the five days the book is drying. If the foil or waxed paper is not placed in the book, the dampness from the glue will go through to the other pages and they will permanently wrinkle.

11. Press beneath books. The weight of the books on top doesn't have to be great but it needs to be consistent and as large as or larger than the zig-zag book. Be sure all corners are even before pressing.

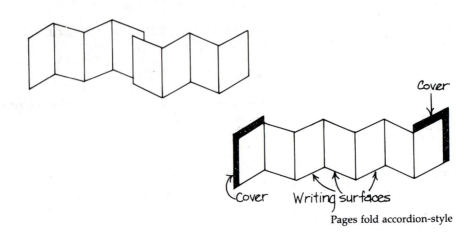

Cover

Cover   Writing surfaces

Pages fold accordion-style

APPENDIX B
ANALYTICAL TRAITS WRITING ASSESSMENT

Ideas and Content

5 This paper is clear in purpose and conveys ideas in an interesting, original manner that holds the reader's attention. Often, the writing develops as a process of discovery for both reader and writer. Clear, relevant examples, anecdotes or details develop and enrich the central idea or ideas.

▼ The writer seems to be writing what he or she knows, often from experience.

▼ The writer shows insight—a good sense of the world, people, situations.

▼ The writing is often enlivened by spontaneity or a fresh, individual perspective.

▼ The writer selects supportive, relevant details that keep the main idea(s) in focus.

▼ Primary and secondary ideas are developed in proportion to their significance; the writing has a sense of balance.

▼ The writer seems in control of the topic and its development throughout.

3 The writer's purpose is reasonably clear; however, the overall result may not be especially captivating. Support is less than adequate to fully develop the main idea(s).

▼ The reader may not be convinced of the writer's knowledge of the topic.

▼ The writer seems to have considered ideas, but not thought things through all the way.

▼ Ideas, though reasonably clear and comprehensible, may tend toward the mundane; the reader is not sorry to see the paper end.

Source: From *Analytical Rating Guide.* Copyright © 1986 by Interwest Applied Research, Inc. Reprinted by permission.

▼ Supporting details tend to be skimpy, general, predictable, or repetitive. Some details seem included by chance, not selected through careful discrimination.

▼ Writing sometimes lacks balance; e.g., too much attention to minor details, insufficient development of main ideas, informational gaps.

▼ The writer's control of the topic seems inconsistent or uncertain.

1 This paper lacks a central idea or purpose—or the central idea can be inferred by the reader only because he or she knows the topic (question asked).

▼ Information is very limited (e.g., restatement of the prompt, heavy reliance on repetition) or simply unclear altogether.

▼ Insight is limited or lacking (e.g., details that do not ring true; dependence on platitudes or stereotypes).

▼ Paper lacks balance; development of ideas is minimal, or there may be a list of random thoughts from which no central theme emerges.

▼ Writing tends to read like a rote response—merely an effort to get something down on paper.

▼ The writer does not seem in control of the topic; shorter papers tend to go nowhere, longer papers to wander aimlessly.

Organization

5 The writer organizes material in a way that enhances the reader's understanding, or that helps to develop a central idea or theme. The order may be conventional or not, but the sequence is effective and moves the reader through the paper.

▼ Details seem to fit where they're placed, and the reader is not left with the sense that "something is missing."

▼ The writer provides a clear sense of beginning and ending, with an inviting introduction and a satisfying conclusion ("satisfying" in the sense that the reader feels the paper has ended at the right spot).

▼ Transitions work well; the writing shows unity and cohesion, both within paragraphs and as a whole.

▼ Organization flows so smoothly that the reader doesn't have to think about it.

3 The writer attempts to organize ideas and details cohesively, but the resulting pattern may be somewhat unclear, ineffective, or awkward. Although the reader can generally follow what's being said, the organizational structure may seem at times to be forced, obvious, incomplete, or ineffective.

▼ The writer seems to have a sense of beginning and ending, but the introduction and/or conclusion tend to be less effective than desired.

▼ The order may not be a graceful fit with the topic (e.g., a forced conventional pattern, or lack of structure).

▼ The writer may miss some opportunities for transitions, requiring the reader to make assumptions or inferences.

▼ Placement or relevance of some details may be questionable (e.g., interruptive information; writer gets to the point in roundabout fashion).

▼ While some portions of the paper may seem unified (e.g., organization within a given paragraph may be acceptable), cohesion of the whole may be weak.

1 Organization is haphazard and disjointed. The writing shows little or no sense of progression or direction. Examples, details, or events seem unrelated to any central idea, or may be strung together helter-skelter with no apparent pattern.

▼ There is no clear sense of a beginning or ending.

▼ Transitions are very weak or absent altogether.

▼ Arrangement of details is confusing or illogical.

▼ There are noticeable information "gaps"; the reader is left dangling, or cannot readily see how the writer got from one point to another.

▼ The paper lacks unity and solidarity.

Voice

5 The paper bears the unmistakable stamp of the individual writer. The writer speaks directly to the reader, and seems sincere, candid, and committed to the topic. The overall effect is individualistic, expressive, and engaging; this paper stands out from the others.

▼ The reader feels interaction with the writer, and through the writing, gains a sense of what the writer is like.

▼ The paper is honest. There is a real effort to communicate, even when it means taking a risk (e.g., an unexpected approach or revealing of self).

▼ The writing is natural and compelling.

▼ Tone is appropriate and consistently controlled.

▼ The writer's own enthusiasm or interest comes through and brings the topic to life.

3 The writer makes an honest effort to deal with the topic, but without a strong sense of personal commitment or involvement. The result is often pleasant or acceptable, yet not striking or compelling in a way that draws the reader in.

▼ The reader has only an occasional or limited sense of interaction with the writer.

▼ Writer may seem self-conscious or unwilling to take a risk—may seem to be writing what he/she thinks the reader wants.

▼ Paper lacks individuality, or the ring of conviction.

▼ The writing communicates, but only in a routine, predictable fashion that tends to make it blend in with the efforts of others.

▼ Voice may be inconsistent; it may emerge strongly on occasion, only to shift or even disappear altogether.

1 The writer may not have understood the assignment, or may simply have felt indifferent toward the topic. As a result, no clear voice emerges. The result is flat, lifeless, very mechanical, and stilted, or possibly inappropriate.

▼   The reader has no sense that this writer was "writing to be read," and experiences virtually no writer–reader interaction.

▼   The writing has virtually no individual personality or character; there is no identifiable voice behind the words.

▼   There is little or no evidence of the writer's involvement in the topic.

Word Choice

5   The writer consistently selects words that convey the intended message in an interesting, precise, and natural way. The result is full and rich, yet not overwhelming; every word carries its own weight.

▼   Words are specific, accurate, and suited to the subject. Imagery is strong.

▼   Lively, powerful verbs give the writing energy, visual appeal, and clarity.

▼   Vocabulary may be striking, colorful, or unusual—but the language isn't overdone.

▼   Expression is fresh and appealing, fun to read. The writer uses cliches or slang sparingly, and only for effect.

▼   The writer may experiment with uncommon words, or use common words in a delightful way.

▼   Figurative language, if used, is effective.

3   The writer's word choice is adequate to convey meaning, but the language tends toward the ordinary. The writer doesn't consistently reach for the "best" way to say something, but instead often settles for the first word or phrase that comes to mind. The result is a sort of "generic paper" that sounds familiar, routine, or commonplace.

▼   Language communicates quite well, but without a sense of satisfying fullness or power; the reader has the feeling it could have been written better.

▼   Imagery may be weakened by overuse of abstract, general language.

▼   Though the reader can interpret the meaning quite readily, some words lack precision or vigor.

▼ Attempts at the unusual, colorful, or difficult are not always success-ful. The language may seem overdone or calculated to impress rather than natural.

▼ Though an occasional phrase may catch the reader's eye, cliches, re-dundancies, and hackneyed phrases pop up with disappointing fre-quency; there are few surprises or enticing twists.

1 The writer is struggling with a limited vocabulary, often groping for words and phrases to convey meaning. Meaning may be difficult to de-termine (e.g., the writer says one thing but seems to mean another), or else the language is so vague and abstract that only the broadest, most general sorts of messages are conveyed.

▼ Writing is often characterized by monotonous repetition, over-whelming reliance on worn, threadbare expressions, or heavy re-liance on the prompt (topic) itself for key words and phrases.

▼ Imagery is very weak or absent; the reader lacks sufficient concrete details to construct any mental picture.

▼ Words tends to be consistently dull, colorless, and trite.

▼ In some instances, word choice may seem careless, imprecise, or just plain wrong.

Sentence Structure

5 The paper is fluid, and reads easily throughout. It has an easy-on-the ear flow and rhythm when read aloud. Sentences have a strong and rhetori-cally effective structure that makes reading enjoyable.

▼ Sentence structure clearly conveys meaning, with no ambiguity.

▼ Writing sounds natural and fluent, with effective phrasing.

▼ Sentences are appropriately concise.

▼ Varied sentence structure and length add interest.

▼ Fragments, if used, are stylistically appropriate. They seem right.

3 Sentences are understandable, but tend to be mechanical rather than fluid. While sentences are usually correct, the paper is not characterized

by a natural fluency and grace. Occasional flaws or awkward constructions may necessitate re-reading.

▼ Sentence structure sometimes clearly conveys meaning—and sometimes not. Structural problems may sometimes create ambiguity.

▼ Some sentences lack energy, character, or effectiveness (e.g., they may be hampered by awkward structure, unnecessary complexity, roundabout expression, wordiness, dangling modifiers, ineffective use of passive voice, or repetitious beginnings—"I did this," "I did that").

▼ Sentence variety (length or structure) tends to be more the exception than the rule.

▼ Fragments, if used, may sometimes be ineffective or confusing.

1 The writing is generally awkward and therefore hard to read aloud. It does not sound natural. Sentences tend to be choppy, incomplete, or so rambling and irregular that it may be difficult to tell where one should end and the next begin.

▼ Because sentence structure frequently does not function to convey meaning, reader may pause several times to question what is meant.

▼ Sentences lack both fluency and correctness. The writer may not write in conventional sentences at all. Or, sentences may seem stiffly constructed, disjointed, endlessly meandering (e.g., many run-ons), or nonsensical.

▼ Short, choppy sentences, relentlessly monotonous rhythms or patterns (e.g., subject–verb or subject–verb–object over and over) that produce a jarring or sing-song effect.

▼ Fragments are confusing or ineffective. Writer seems to have little grasp of how words fit together, or of where one idea logically stops and the next begins.

Writing Conventions

5 The writer's skillful use of standard writing conventions (grammar, capitalization, punctuation, usage, spelling, paragraphing) enhances readability. There are no glaring errors. In fact, while the paper may not be flawless, errors tend to be so minor that the reader can easily overlook

them unless searching for them specifically. (Deliberate, controlled deviations from convention—in dialogue, for instance—are acceptable, provided they enhance the overall effect.)

▼ Grammar (e.g., noun–verb agreement; noun–pronoun agreement; verb tense; forms of nouns, verbs, pronouns and modifiers) is essentially correct.

▼ Punctuation is smooth and enhances meaning. Informalities, such as dashes or contractions, are allowed.

▼ Spelling is generally correct, even on more difficult words.

▼ Usage is generally correct, or acceptable given the purpose of the writing. The writer avoids double negatives (e.g., *couldn't hardly*) and nonstandard usage (e.g., *could of* been, *more better*, she *had ought* to do it, *irregardless*, *leave me* figure this out). Informalities (e.g., *you will find* rather than the more formal *one will find*) are acceptable.

▼ Paragraphing (i.e., indenting) works in harmony with the inherent organization of the paper.

3 Errors in writing conventions are noticeable and begin to impair readability. Reader can follow what is being said overall, but may need to pause or re-read on occasion.

▼ Occasional problems in grammar disrupt the flow of the writing. For example, agreement may be inconsistent; or there may be shifts in tense, improper verb forms (e.g., *lay down* here), improper pronoun forms (*theirselves*, *me and Jim* will go), use of adjectives for adverbs (he did *good*), and so on.

▼ Punctuation, capitalization, and spelling errors may be sufficiently frequent or serious to momentarily distract the reader.

▼ Some usage problems (e.g., double negatives, use of nonstandard expressions such as *irregardless*) may be evident.

▼ Paragraphing is attempted, but paragraphs may not always begin at the right places. As a result, paragraph structure (indenting) does not always complement the paper's inherent organization.

1 Numerous errors in usage and grammar, spelling, capitalization, and/or punctuation consistently distract the reader, taking attention away from the writer's message and severely impairing readability.

▼ The student shows very limited understanding of or ability to apply conventions.

▼ Errors in grammar and usage are frequent and tend to be very noticeable.

▼ Basic punctuation may be omitted, haphazard, or just plain wrong.

▼ Capitalization is often incorrect or highly inconsistent.

▼ Spelling errors tend to be frequent, even on common words.

▼ Paragraphing is illogical or arbitrary (e.g., paragraphs almost never seem to begin in the right places).

APPENDIX C

NAEYC POSITION STATEMENT ON STANDARDIZED TESTING OF YOUNG CHILDREN 3 THROUGH 8 YEARS OF AGE (ADOPTED NOVEMBER 1987)

Statement of the Problem

The practice of administering standardized tests to young children has increased dramatically in recent years. Many school systems now routinely administer some form of standardized developmental screening or readiness test for admittance to kindergarten or standardized achievement test for promotion to first grade. As a result, more and more 5- and 6-year-olds are denied admission to school or are assigned to some form of extra-year tracking such as "developmental kindergarten," retention in kindergarten, or "transitional" first grade (Meisels, 1987; Shepard & Smith, 1988). Such practices (often based on inappropriate uses of readiness or screening tests) disregard the potential, documented long-term negative effects of retention on children's self-esteem and the fact that such practices disproportionately affect low-income and minority children; further, these practices have been implemented in the absence of research documenting that they positively affect children's later academic achievement (Gredler, 1984; Shepard & Smith, 1986, 1987; Smith & Shepard, 1987).

A simultaneous trend that has influenced and been influenced by the use of standardized testing is the increasingly academic emphasis of the curriculum imposed on kindergartners. Many kindergartens are now highly structured, "watered-down" first grades, emphasizing workbooks and other paper-and-pencil activities that are developmentally inappropriate for 5-year-olds (Bredekamp, 1987; Durkin, 1987; Katz, Raths, & Torres, undated). The trend further trickles down to preschool and child care programs that feel their mission is to get children "ready" for kindergarten. Too many school systems, expecting children to conform to an inappropriate curriculum and finding large numbers of "unready" children, react to the problem by raising the entrance age for kindergarten and/or labeling the children as failures (Shepard & Smith, 1986, 1988).

The negative influence of standardized testing on the curriculum is not limited to kindergarten. Throughout the primary grades, schools assess achievement using tests that frequently do not reflect current theory and research about how children learn. For example, current research on reading instruction stresses a whole language/literacy approach that integrates oral language, writing, reading, and spelling in meaningful context, emphasizing comprehension. However, standardized tests of reading achievement still

Source: "NAEYC Position Statement on Standardized Testing of Young Children 3 Through 8 Years of Age, 1988, *Young Children*, 43:3.

define reading exclusively as phonics and word recognition and measure isolated skill acquisition (Farr & Carey, 1986; Teale, Hiebert, & Chittenden, 1987; Valencia & Pearson, 1987). Similarly, current theory of mathematics instruction stresses the child's construction of number concepts through firsthand experiences, while achievement tests continue to define mathematics as knowledge of numerals (Kamii, 1985a, 1985b). As a result, too many school systems teach to the test or continue to use outdated instructional methods so that children will perform adequately on standardized tests.

The widespread use of standardized tests also drains resources of time and funds without clear demonstration that the investment is beneficial for children. Days may be devoted to testing (or preparing for it) that could be better spent in valuable instructional time (National Center for Fair and Open Testing, 1987).

Ironically, the calls for excellence in education that have produced widespread reliance on standardized testing may have had the opposite effect—mediocrity. Children are being taught to provide the one "right" answer on the answer sheet, but are not being challenged to think. Rather than producing excellence, the overuse (and misuse) of standardized testing has led to the adoption of inappropriate teaching practices as well as admission and retention policies that are not in the best interests of individual children or the nation as a whole.

Purpose

The purpose of this position statement is to guide the decisions of educators regarding the use of standardized tests. These administrative decisions include whether to use standardized testing, how to critically evaluate existing tests, how to carefully select appropriate and accurate tests to be used with a population and purpose for which the test was designed, and how to use and interpret the results yielded from standardized tests to parents, school personnel, and the media. Such decisions are usually made by school principals, superintendents, or state school officials. Teachers are responsible for administering tests and, therefore, have a professional responsibility to be knowledgeable about appropriate testing and to influence, or attempt to influence, the selection and use of tests. It is assumed that responsible and educated decisions by administrators and teachers will influence commercial test developers to produce valid, reliable and useful tests.

Standardized tests are instruments that are composed of empirically selected items; have definite instructions for use, data on reliability, and validity; and are norm- or criterion-referenced (see definitions on pages 541–543). This position statement addresses *tests*—the instruments themselves, and *testing*—the administration of tests, scoring, and interpretation of scores. This statement concentrates on standardized tests because such tests are most likely to influence policy. Nonstandardized assessments such as systematic observation, anecdotal records, locally or nationally developed checklists, or mastery tests developed by individual teachers (that do not meet the above criteria for standardization) play a vital role in planning and implementing instruction and in making decisions about placement of children. Decisions made on the basis of nonstandardized assessments should take into consideration the guidelines presented in this position statement.

The field of standardized testing is complex. Various types of standardized tests exist for various purposes. These include: achievement/readiness tests; developmental screening tests; diagnostic assessment tests; and intelligence tests (see definitions). The guidelines in this position statement apply to all forms of standardized testing, but primarily address the uses and abuses of achievement, readiness, and developmental screening tests.

Developmental screening tests are designed to indicate which children should proceed further to a multidisciplinary assessment, only after which a decision regarding special education placement can be made. School readiness tests are designed to assess a child's level of preparedness for a specific academic program (Meisels, 1987). As such, readiness tests should *not* be used to identify children potentially in need of special education services or for placement decisions (Meisels, 1986). Diagnostic assessments are designed to identify children with specific special needs, determine the nature of the problem, suggest the cause of the problem, and propose possible remediation strategies (Meisels, 1985). Intelligence tests are norm- or criterion-referenced measures of cognitive functioning (as defined by a specific criterion or construct) and are often used in diagnostic assessment. No single test can be used for all of these purposes, and rarely will a test be applicable to more than one or two of them. The uses and abuses of diagnostic assessments and intelligence tests have been well documented elsewhere and are beyond the scope of this position statement (Chase, 1977; Goodwin & Driscoll, 1980; Gould, 1981; Hilliard, 1975; Kamin, 1974; Oakland, 1977; Reynolds, 1984).

NAEYC acknowledges and endorses the *Standards for Educational and Psychological Testing* (1985) developed by a joint committee of the American Educational Research Association, American Psychological Association, and National Council on Measurement in Education. Standardized tests used in early childhood programs should comply with the joint committee's technical standards for test construction and evaluation, professional standards for use, and standards for administrative procedures. This means that no standardized test should be used for screening, diagnosis, or assessment unless the test has published statistically acceptable reliability and validity data. Moreover, test producers are strongly encouraged to present data concerning the proportion of at-risk children correctly identified (test sensitivity) and the proportion of those not at-risk who are correctly found to be without major problems (test specificity) (Meisels, 1984). NAEYC's position on standardized testing is intended not to duplicate, but to be used in conjunction with, the *Standards for Educational and Psychological Testing* (1985).

Statement of the Position

NAEYC believes that the most important consideration in evaluating and using standardized tests is the *utility criterion:* The purpose of testing must be to improve services for children and ensure that children benefit from their educational experiences. Decisions about testing and assessment instruments must be based on the usefulness of the assessment procedure for improving services to children and improving outcomes for children. The ritual use even of "good tests" (those that are judged to be valid and reliable measures) is to be discouraged in the absence of documented research showing that children benefit from their use.

Determining the utility of a given testing program is not easy. It requires thorough study of the potential effects, both positive and negative. For example, using a readiness or developmental test to admit children to kindergarten or first grade is often defended by teachers and administrators who point to the fact that the children who are kept back perform better the next year. Such intuitive reports overlook the fact that no comparative information is available about how the individual child would have fared had he or she been permitted to proceed with schooling. In addition, such pronouncements rarely address the possible effects of failure on the admission test on the child's self-esteem, the parents' perceptions, or the educational impact of labeling or mislabeling the child as being behind the peer group (Gredler, 1978; Shepard & Smith, 1986, 1988; Smith & Shepard, 1987).

The following guidelines are intended to enhance the utility of standardized tests and guide early childhood professionals in making decisions about the appropriate use of testing.

1. All standardized tests used in early childhood programs must be reliable and valid according to the technical standards of test development (AERA, APA, & NCME, 1985).

Administrators making decisions about standardized testing must recognize that the younger the child, the more difficult it is to obtain reliable and valid results from standardized tests. For example, no available school readiness test (as contrasted to a developmental screening test) is accurate enough to screen children for placement into special programs without a 50% error rate (Shepard & Smith, 1986). Development in young children occurs rapidly; early childhood educators recognize the existence of general stages and sequence of development but also recognize that enormous individual variation occurs in patterns and timing of growth and development that is quite normal and not indicative of pathology. Therefore, the result obtained on a single administration of a test must be confirmed through periodic screening and assessment and corroborated by other sources of information to be considered reliable (Meisels, 1984).

2. Decisions that have a major impact on children such as enrollment, retention, or assignment to remedial or special classes should be based on multiple sources of information and should never be based on a single test score.

Appropriate sources of information *may* include combinations of the following:

▼   systematic observations, by teachers and other professionals, that are objective, carefully recorded, reliable (produce similar results over time and among different observers), and valid (produce accurate measures of carefully defined, mutually exclusive categories of observable behavior);

▼   samples of children's work such as drawings, paintings, dictated stories, writing samples, projects, and other activities (not limited to worksheets);

▼   observations and anecdotes related by parents and other family members; and

▼   test scores, if and only if appropriate, reliable, and valid tests have been used.

In practice, multiple measures are sometimes used in an attempt to find some supporting evidence for a decision that teachers or administrators are predisposed to make regarding a child's placement. Such practice is an inappropriate application of this guideline. To meet this guideline, the collected set of evidence obtained through multiple sources of information should meet validity standards.

3. It is the professional responsibility of administrators and teachers to critically evaluate, carefully select, and use standardized tests only for the purposes for which they are intended and for which data exists demonstrating the test's validity (the degree to which the test accurately measures what it purports to measure).

Unfortunately, readiness tests (based on age-related normative data) that are designed to measure the skills children have acquired compared to other children in their age range are sometimes used inappropriately. The intended purpose of such instruments is typically to provide teachers with information that will help them improve instruction, by informing them of what children already know and the skills they have acquired. In practice, however, teachers have been found to systematically administer such tests and then proceed to teach all children the same content using the same methods; for example, testing all kindergartners and then instructing the whole group using phonics workbooks (Durkin, 1987). The practice of making placement decisions about children on the basis of the result of readiness tests is becoming more common despite the absence of data that such tests are valid predictors of later achievement (Meisels, 1985, 1987).

4. It is the professional responsibility of administrators and teachers to be knowledgeable about testing and to interpret test results accurately and cautiously to parents, school personnel, and the media.

Accurate interpretation of test results is essential. It is the professional obligation of administrators and teachers to become informed about measurement issues, to use tests responsibly, to exert leadership within early childhood programs and school systems regarding the use of testing, to influence test developers to produce adequate tests and to substantiate claims made in support of tests, and to accurately report and interpret test results without making undue claims about their meaning or implications.

5. Selection of standardized tests to assess achievement and/or evaluate how well a program is meeting its goals should be based on how well a given test matches the locally determined theory, philosophy, and objectives of the specific program.

Standardized tests used in early childhood programs must have content validity; that is, they must accurately measure the content of the curriculum presented to children. If no existing test matches the curriculum, it is better not to use a standardized test or to develop an instrument to measure the program's objectives rather than to change an appropriate program to fit a pre-existing test. Too often the content of a standardized test unduly influences the content of the curriculum. If a test is used, the curriculum should determine its selection; the test should not dictate the content of the curriculum.

Another difficulty related to content validity in measures for young children is that many critically important content areas in early childhood programs such as developing self-esteem, social competence, creativity, or dispositions toward learning (Katz, 1985) are considered "unmeasurable" and are therefore omitted from tests. As a result, tests for young children often address the more easily measured, but no more important, aspects of development and learning.

6. Testing of young children must be conducted by individuals who are knowledgeable about and sensitive to the developmental needs of young children and who are qualified to administer tests.

Young children are not good test takers. The younger the child the more inappropriate paper-and-pencil, large group test administrations become. Standards for the administration of tests require that reasonable comfort be provided to the test taker (AERA, APA, & NCME, 1985). Such a standard must be broadly interpreted when applied to young children. Too often, standardized tests are administered to children in large groups, in unfamiliar environments, by strange people, perhaps during the first few days at a new school or under other stressful conditions. During such test administrations, children are asked to perform unfamiliar tasks, for no reason that they can understand. For test results to be valid, tests are best administered to children individually in familiar, comfortable circumstances by adults whom the child has come to know and trust and who are also qualified to administer the tests.

7. Testing of young children must recognize and be sensitive to individual diversity.

Test developers frequently ignore two important sources of variety in human experiences—cultural variations and variations in the quality of educational experiences provided for different children. It is easier to mass produce tests if one assumes that cultural differences are minimal or meaningless or if one assumes that test subjects are exposed to personal and educational opportunities of equally high quality. These assumptions permit attributing all variances or differences in test scores to differences in individual children's capacities. However, these assumptions are false.

Early childhood educators recognize that children's skills, abilities, and aptitudes are most apparent when they can be demonstrated in familiar cultural contexts. Because standardized tests must use particular cultural material, they may be inappropriate for assessing the skills, abilities, or aptitudes of children whose primary cultures differ from the mainstream. Language is the special feature of culture that creates the greatest problem for test developers. There are many language varieties in the United States, some of which are not apparent to the casual observer or test developer. Although having a common language is definitely desirable, useful, and a major goal of education, testing must be based on reality. For non-native English speakers or speakers of some dialects of English, any test administered in English is primarily a language or literacy test (AERA, APA, & NCME, 1985). Standardized tests should not be used in multicultural/multilingual communities if they are not sensitive to the effects of cultural diversity or bilingualism (Meisels, 1985). If testing is to be done, children should be tested in their native language.

Conclusion

NAEYC's position on standardized testing in early childhood programs restricts the use of tests to situations in which testing provides information that will clearly contribute to improved outcomes for children. Standardized tests have an important role to play in ensuring that children's achievement or special needs are objectively and accurately assessed and that appropriate instructional services are planned and implemented for individual children. However, standardized tests are only one of multiple sources of assessment information that should be used when decisions are made about what is best for young children. Tests may become a burden on the educational system, requiring considerable effort and expense to administer and yielding meager benefits. Given the scarcity of resources, the intrusiveness of testing, and the real potential for measurement error and/or bias, tests should be used only when it is clear that their use represents a meaningful contribution to the improvement of instruction for children and only as one of many sources of information. Rather than to use tests of doubtful validity, it is better not to test, because false labels that come from tests may cause educators or parents to alter inappropriately their treatment of children. The potential for misdiagnosing or mislabeling is particularly great with young children where there is wide variation in what may be considered normal behavior.

Administrators of early childhood programs who consider the use of standardized tests must ask themselves: How will children benefit from testing? Why is testing to be done? Does an appropriate test exist? What other sources of information can be used to make decisions about how best to provide services for an individual child? In answering such questions, administrators should apply the foregoing guidelines.

The burden of proof for the validity and realiability of tests is on the test developers and the advocates for their use. The burden of proof for the utility of tests is on administrators or teachers of early childhood programs who make decisions about the use of tests in individual classrooms. Similarly, the burden of responsibility for choosing, administering, scoring, and interpreting a score from a standardized test rests with the early childhood professional and thus demands that professionals be both skilled and responsible. Ensuring that tests meet scientific standards, reflect the most current scientific knowledge, and are used appropriately requires constant vigilance on the part of educators.

Definitions

Achievement test—a test that measures the extent to which a person has mastery over a certain body of information or possesses a certain skill after instruction has taken place.

Criterion—an indicator of the accepted value of outcome performance of a standard against which a measure is evaluated.

Criterion-referenced—a test for which interpretation of scores is made in relation to a specified performance level, as distinguished from interpretations that compare the test taker's score to the performance of other people (i.e., norm-referenced).

Developmental test—an age-related norm-referenced assessment of skills and behaviors that children have acquired (compared to children of the same chronological age). Sometimes such tests are inaccurately called developmental screening tests.

Diagnostic assessment—identification of a child who has special needs, usually conducted by a multidisciplinary team of professionals; used to identify a child's specific areas of strength and weakness, determine the nature of the problems, and suggest the cause of the problems and possible remediation strategies.

Early childhood—birth through age 8.

Intelligence test—a series of tasks yielding a score indicative of cognitive functioning. Tasks typically require problem solving and/or various intellectual operations such as conceiving, thinking, and reasoning, or they reflect an earlier use of such intellectual functions (e.g., in information questions). Standardized by finding the average performance of individuals who by independent criteria (i.e., other intelligence tests) are of known degrees or levels of intelligence.

Norms—statistics or data that summarize the test performance of specified groups such as test takers of various ages or grades.

Norm-referenced—a test for which interpretation of scores is based on comparing the test taker's performance to the performance of other people in a specified group.

Readiness test—assessment of child's level of preparedness for a specific academic or preacademic program. (See also achievement test and developmental test.)

Reliability—the degree to which test scores are consistent, dependable, or repeatable; that is, the degree to which test scores can be attributed to actual differences in test takers' performance rather than to errors of measurement.

Score—any specific number resulting from the assessment of an individual.

Screening test (also called *developmental screening test*)—a test used to identify children who *may* be in need of special services, as a first step in identifying children in need of further diagnosis; focuses on the child's ability to acquire skills.

Standardized test—an instrument composed of empirically selected items that has definite instructions for use, adequately determined norms, and data on reliability and validity.

Testing—the administration, scoring, and interpretation of scores of a standardized test.

Utility—the relative value or usefulness of an outcome as compared to other possible outcomes.

Validity—the degree to which a test measures what it purports to measure, the degree to which a certain inference from a test is appropriate or meaningful.

> **Content validity**—evidence that shows the extent to which the content of a test is appropriately related to its intended purpose. For achievement tests, *content* refers to the content of the curriculum, the actual instruction, or the objectives of the instruction.
>
> **Criterion-related validity**—evidence that demonstrates that test scores are systematically related to one or more outcome criteria.
>
> **Predictive validity**—evidence of criterion-related validity in which scores on the criterion are observed at a later date; for example, the score on a test with predictive validity will predict future school performance.

APPENDIX D
FORTY-FIVE PHONIC GENERALIZATIONS

	Percentage of Utility		
Generalization (*example*)	Primary (Clymer, 1963)	Grades 1–6 (Bailey, 1967)	Grades 4–6 (Emans, 1967)
1. When there are two vowels side by side, the long sound of the first vowel is heard and the second vowel is usually silent. *(leader)*	45	34	18
2. When a vowel is in the middle of a one-syllable word, the vowel is short. *(bed)*	62	71	73
3. If the only vowel letter is at the end of a word, the letter usually stands for a long sound. *(go)*	100	100	100
4. When there are two vowels, one of which is final *e*, the first vowel is long and the *e* is silent. *(cradle)*	63	57	63
5. The *r* gives the preceding vowel a sound that is neither long nor short. *(part)*	78	86	82
6. The first vowel is usually long and the second silent in the digraphs *ai, ea, oa,* and *ui.* *(claim, bean, roam, suit)*	66	60	58
ai		71	
ea		56	
oa		95	
ee		87	
ui		10	

7. In the phonogram *ie*, the *i* is silent and the *e* is long. *(grieve)*   17   31   23

8. Words having double *e* usually have the long *e* sound. *(meet)*   98   87   100

9. When words end with silent *e*, the preceding *a* or *i* is long. *(amaze)*   60   50   48

10. In *ay*, the *y* is silent and gives its *a* long sound. *(spray)*   78   88   100

11. When the letter *i* is followed by the letters *gh*, the *i* usually stands for its long sound and the *gh* is silent. *(light)*   71   71   100

12. When *a* follows *w* in a word, it usually has the sound *a* as in *was*. *(wand)*   32   22   28

13. When *e* is followed by *w*, the vowel sound is the same as represented by *oo*. *(shrewd)*   35   40   14

14. The two letters *ow* make the long *o* sound. *(row)*   59   55   50

15. *W* is sometimes a vowel and follows the vowel digraph rule. *(arrow)*   40   33   31

16. When *y* is the final letter in a word, it usually has a vowel sound. *(lady)*   84   89   98

17. When *y* is used as a vowel in words, it sometimes has the sound of long *i*. *(ally)*   15   11   4

18. The letter *a* has the same sound (*o*) when followed by *l*, *w*, and *u*. *(raw)*   48   34   24

19. When *a* is followed by *r* and
    final *e*, we expect to hear the
    sound heard in *care*. *(flare)*   90   96   100

20. When *c* and *h* are next to each
    other, they make only one sound.
    (charge)   100   100   100

21. *Ch* is usually pronounced as it
    is in *kitchen*, *catch*, and *chair*.   95   87   67

22. When *c* is followed by *e* or *i*, the
    sound of *s* is likely to be heard.
    (glance)   96   92   90

23. When the letter *c* is followed by
    o or *a*, the sound of *k* is likely to
    be heard. *(canal)*   100   100   100

24. The letter *g* is often sounded
    similar to the *j* in *jump* when it
    precedes the letter *i* or *e*. *(gem)*   100   100   100

25. When *ght* is seen in a word, *gh*
    is silent. *(tight)*   100   100   100

26. When the word begins with *kn*,
    the *k* is silent. *(knit)*   100   100   100

27. When a word begins with *wr*,
    the *w* is silent. *(wrap)*   100   100   100

28. When two of the same
    consonants are side by side,
    only one is heard. *(dollar)*   100   100   100

29. When a word ends in *ck*, it has
    the same last sound as in *look*.
    (neck)   100   100   100

30. In most two-syllable words, the
    first syllable is accented. *(bottom)*   85   81   75

31. If *a*, *in*, *re*, *ex*, *de*, or *be* is the
    first syllable in a word, it is
    usually unaccented. *(reply)*   87   84   83

32. In most two-syllable words that
    end in a consonant followed by
    y, the first syllable is accented
    and the last is unaccented.
    (highly)   96   97   100

33. One vowel letter in an accented
    syllable has a short sound.
    (banish)   61   65   64

34. When *y* or *ey* is seen in the last
    syllable that is not accented, the
    long sound or *e* is heard. *(turkey)*   0   0   1

35. When *ture* is the final syllable in
    a word, it is unaccented. *(future)*   100   100   100

36. When *tion* is the final syllable in
    a word, it is unaccented. *(nation)*   100   100   100

37. In many two- and three-syllable
    words, the final *e* lengthens the
    vowel in the last syllable.
    (costume)   46   46   42

38. If the first vowel sound in a
    word is followed by two
    consonants, the first syllable
    usually ends with the first of the
    two consonants. *(dinner)*   72   78   80

39. If the first vowel sound in a
    word is followed by a single
    consonant, that consonant
    usually begins the second
    syllable. *(china)*   57   48   37

40. If the last syllable of a word
    ends in *le*, the consonant pre-
    ceding the *le* usually begins the
    last syllable. *(gable)*   97   93   78

41. When the first vowel element in a word is followed by *the, ch,* or *sh,* these symbols are not broken when the word is divided into syllables and may go with either the first or second syllable. *(fashion)*   100   100   100

42. In a word of more than one syllable, the letter *v* usually goes with the preceding vowel to form a syllable. *(travel)*   73   65   40

43. When a word has only one vowel letter, the vowel sound is likely to be short. *(crib)*   57   69   70

44. When there is one *e* in a word that ends in a consonant, the *e* usually has a short sound. *(held)*   75   92   83

45. When the last syllable is the sound *r,* it is unaccented. *(ever)*   95   79   96

APPENDIX E

INTERNATIONAL READING ASSOCIATION RESOLUTION ON MISUSE OF GRADE EQUIVALENTS (ADOPTED APRIL 1981)

WHEREAS, standardized, norm-referenced tests can provide information useful to teachers, students, and parents, if the results of such tests are used properly, and

WHEREAS, proper use of any standardized test depends on a thorough understanding of the test's purpose, the way it was developed, and any limitations it has, and

WHEREAS, failure to fully understand these factors can lead to serious misuse of test results, and

WHEREAS, one of the most serious misuses of tests is the reliance on a grade equivalent as an indicator of absolute performance, when a grade equivalent should be interpreted as an indicator of a test-taker's performance in relation to the performance of other test-takers used to norm the test, and

WHEREAS, in reading education, the misuse of grade equivalents has led to such mistaken assumptions as: (1) a grade equivalent of 5.0, on a reading test, means that the test-taker will be able to read fifth-grade material, and (2) a grade equivalent of 10.0 by a fourth-grade student means that student reads like a tenth grader even though the test may include only sixth-grade material as its top level of difficulty, and

WHEREAS, the misuse of grade equivalents promotes misunderstanding of a student's reading ability and leads to underreliance on other norm-referenced scores which are much less susceptible to misinterpretation and misunderstanding, be it

RESOLVED, that the International Reading Association strongly advocates that those who administer standardized reading tests abandon the practice of using grade equivalents to report performance of either individuals or groups of test-takers and be it further

RESOLVED, that the president or executive director of the Association write to test publishers urging them to eliminate grade equivalents from their tests.

APPENDIX F

INTERNATIONAL READING ASSOCIATION RESOLUTION ON LITERACY ASSESSMENT (ADOPTED MAY 1991)

The International Reading Association supports literacy assessment that recognizes and addresses the complex nature of literacy, that is built on goals and standards having broad societal endorsement, and that takes into account background differences among students.

Literacy is a complex process that contributes to people's ability to function in society, to more fully realize their intellectual and psychological potential. Literacy assessment must address this complexity by using a variety of observations, performance measures, and extended response items; it must assess literacy by the use of quality texts of various genre and a range of literacy tasks in a variety of settings. Educational leaders and agencies must explore new forms of assessment, must treat such assessments as tentative and experimental, and must set long range literacy assessment research agendas—thereby avoiding quick, but ineffective, "fixes."

Literacy assessment must build on broad educational goals that have wide societal support and must evaluate students' performance against agreed upon standards. Educators have a professional responsibility to provide leadership in defining the goals and standards. Such formulations should be developed through the active participation of teachers and students and must be reviewed and endorsed by a broad range of citizens.

All assessment must be purposeful. Two major purposes for literacy assessment are: (1) to inform learning and instruction; and (2) to address accountability concerns; that is, evaluating program effectiveness. As educators we have a responsibility to show that our instructional efforts result in expanded literacy among the students and citizens of our nations. Ideally, the same assessment measures and procedures should address both major purposes of assessment. However, given our imperfect understanding of the processes and dynamics underlying literacy and the limitations inherent to assessment procedures, we are often forced to focus on one major purpose or the other. For example, large scale testing is often considered important for addressing program evaluation responsibilities, but large scale test results have been seriously limited in their ability to guide learning and instruction, particularly at the level of the individual and of the class. Likewise, informal teacher observations and portfolio approaches hold great promise for the guidance of learning and instruction, but limitations in funding and in techniques for validly aggregating such data limit their use in addressing large scale program evaluation issues, at least for the present. Because the primary purpose of assessment is to inform learning and instruction, assessment designed to address accountability needs should not be permitted to interfere with or detract from the essential purpose of guiding learning and teaching.

Literacy assessment must respect and acknowledge the intellectual, cognitive, language, social, and cultural differences of students. Literacy responses are constructive and, hence, will reflect individual and cultural differences. Therefore, assessment procedures must be flexible and allow for a variety of legitimate responses, while taking into account the variable contexts of opportunities for learning that confront children in different settings and from differing backgrounds.

An important goal of the Association is to support resolutions that will promote literacy worldwide. However, assessment issues and traditions vary significantly from nation to nation and across cultures. Assessment resolutions with global implications require extensive study and consultation. Since many among the leadership and membership of the Association have the greatest amount of experience with assessment issues in the United States and Canada, these resolutions apply most specifically to these two countries. However, they may well apply to other countries. Units and affiliates of the Association are encouraged to study these resolutions from their own national, regional, and cultural perspectives and to endorse them, comment upon them, expand upon them, and develop positions and applications appropriate to their particular needs and situations. In this manner, guidelines, resolutions, and positions on assessment that are more globally appropriate can and will be forthcoming.

The resolutions that follow reflect the continued commitment of the International Reading Association to provide leadership in improving, revising, and redesigning traditional assessment procedures and measures. They are intended to encourage innovative assessments that incorporate current theory, research, and instructional practice. These resolutions build upon an earlier set of resolutions that were endorsed by the Delegates Assembly of the Association in 1988 and reaffirmed by that group in 1990. Since 1988, however, there has been much discussion, exploration of alternate forms of assessment, and expression of concern for limitations and abuses of testing. Therefore, it is timely to expand the Association's position on literacy assessment. These expanded resolutions focus on the effectiveness of assessments, the assessment development process, the content and form of assessments, and the need for appropriate interpretation of assessment findings.

I. Improving the Effectiveness of Assessment Procedures and Measures

Whereas . . . educators and researchers concerned with literacy assessment are effectively using sampling procedures to increase the usefulness of assessments and reduce the amount of time individual students and teachers must devote to assessments for large scale monitoring purposes, and

Whereas . . . many current reading measures used in the early grades may lead to narrowly focused instruction that insufficiently addresses the language and cognitive skills that become increasingly essential to literacy beyond the early grades, and

Whereas . . . students and educators must strive to attain the highest standards of literacy, and whereas much testing effort has, instead, focused on comparing students, districts, provinces, and states, and

Whereas . . . young children are especially vulnerable to negative experiences with tests, and

Whereas . . . reducing the number of tests administered in school will result in more time for learning and instruction while conserving financial resources, be it therefore

RESOLVED that large scale assessments for the purpose of evaluating program effectiveness, as at the national or state and provincial levels, be implemented on a sampling basis. Sampling approaches are economical and allow the use of more sophisticated, authentic tasks that often require more time for administration and increased resources for scoring and analysis, be it further

RESOLVED that the International Reading Association supports efforts to develop standards for literacy attainment that are applied to authentic texts and call for authentic tasks, be it further

RESOLVED that the International Reading Association opposes the proliferation of school by school, district by district, province by province, and state by state comparison assessments, be it further

RESOLVED that where large scale assessments of outcomes for program evaluation purposes are deemed necessary, such assessments not be imposed on learners before age 9 (grade 4), be it further

RESOLVED that the International Reading Association provide leadership at the national, state, provincial and local educational levels to review current testing patterns and practices to reduce the volume and proliferation of inappropriate or unproductive assessments.

II. The Importance of How Assessments Are Developed

Whereas . . . literacy assessments are often used to make important decisions affecting students, teachers, and schools, be it therefore

RESOLVED that literacy assessments be based upon broad goals and standards developed through consensus of a wide range of involved citizens, teachers, teacher educators, researchers, and representatives of professional organizations such as the International Reading Association, be it further

RESOLVED that literacy assessments be developed on the basis of the best available theory, research, and practice. The International Reading Association, through the professional talents and knowledge of its members and working with related professional organizations, will provide information and assist in creating opportunities to focus discussion, support and encourage research, and promote sound decision making about literacy assessments.

III. The Importance of Assessment Content and Philosophy

Whereas . . . teaching and learning are influenced by the form and content of assessment instruments which often have powerful personal, political, and professional implications, and

Whereas . . . there have been significant advances in our understanding of reading, writing, and language as complex, constructive, and dynamic processes, and in our understanding that definitions of reading as a hierarchical sequence of discrete skills lead to inappropriate assessment and foster inappropriate instruction, and

Whereas . . . students in most educational settings come from varied cultural, social, and ethnic backgrounds and are faced with a diversity of learning opportunities, be it therefore

RESOLVED that literacy assessments must be based in current research and theory, not limited by traditional psychometric concepts, and must reflect the complex and dynamic interrelationship of reading, writing, and language abilities critical to human communications; and therefore, to better inform teaching and learning, be it further

RESOLVED that literacy assessments must incorporate a variety of observations, taking into account the complex nature of reading, writing, and language, and must also include high quality text, a variety of genre, and a range of authentic literacy tasks, be it further

RESOLVED that assessments must reflect a broad based consensus about age appropriate literacy tasks for students, taking into account the learning opportunities that have been provided for children in schools and communities, be it further

RESOLVED that to be of use in the improvement of instruction and learning, literacy assessments need to reveal change over time at the level of the individual child, be it further

RESOLVED that literacy assessments must be designed to eliminate bias toward students whose language, cultural, social, and ethnic backgrounds may be different from those of the majority population.

IV. The Importance of Appropriate Interpretation and Use of Assessment Results

Whereas . . . the International Reading Association recognizes that one valid purpose for assessment is monitoring the outcomes of instruction at the level of the school, the community, the state or province, or the nation, and that a second valid, and distinct, purpose for assessment is to provide input information to the teacher and the pupil for the guidance and improvement of instruction and learning, and

Whereas . . . large scale assessments for the purpose of monitoring outcomes and classroom assessments for the guidance and improvement of instruction and learning presently require different approaches and techniques appropriate to the needs of those who use assessment results, and

Whereas . . . large scale assessments do not address the question of how to improve teaching and learning and because such data are subject to misinterpretation and error when applied to small groups or individuals, be it therefore

RESOLVED that users of assessment results recognize the important of considering a variety of observations, procedures, and instruments, be it further

RESOLVED that users of assessment results take into account the specific purposes for which assessments are made and the settings in which assessments are conducted, be it further

RESOLVED that where large scale assessments are conducted for the purpose of monitoring outcomes results should not be reported for individual pupils, classes, or schools.

RESOURCES

Professional References Cited

Allington, R. (1990). *Curriculum and at-risk learners: Coherence or fragmentation?* King of Prussia, PA: Pennsylvania Resources and Information Center for Special Education. (ED 326 034)

Allison, L., & Katz, D. (1983). *Gee, wiz! How to mix art and science, or the art of thinking scientifically.* Covella, CA: Yolla Bolly.

American Educational Research Association, American Psychological Association, and National Council on Measurement in Education. (1985). *Standards for educational and psychological testing.* Washington, DC: Author.

American Psychiatric Association. (1987). *Diagnostic and statistical manual of mental disorders* (3rd ed., rev.). Washington, DC: Author.

Analyzing the NAEP data: Some key points. (1993/1994). *Reading Today, 11,* 1, 12.

Anderson, R., Hiebert, E., Scott, J., & Wilkinson, I. (1985). *Becoming a nation of readers: The report of the commission on reading.* Washington, DC: National Institute of Education.

Anderson-Inman, L. (1986). The reading-writing connection: Classroom applications for the computer, Part I. *The Computing Teacher, 14*(3), 23–26.

Anderson-Inman, L. (1987). The reading-writing connection: Classroom applications for the computer, Part II. *The Computing Teacher, 14*(6), 15–18.

Anderson-Inman, L. (1990). Enhancing the reading-writing connection: Classroom applications: *The Writing Notebook: Creative Word Processing in the Classroom, 7*(3), 12–15.

Applebee, A. N. (1990a). *Policy and practice in the teaching of literacy: Explorations of the NAEP database. Final report.* Washington, DC: Office of Educational Research and Improvement.

Applebee, A. N. (1990b). *The writing report card, 1984–88: Findings from the nation's report card.* National Assessment of Educational Progress. Princeton, NJ: Educational Testing Service.

Arizona Department of Education. (1989). *Essential skills: Language arts.* Phoenix, AZ: Author.

Armbruster, B. B., & Nagy, W. E. (1992). Vocabulary in content area lessons. *The Reading Teacher, 45,* 550–551.

Ashton-Warner, S. (1963). *Teacher.* New York: Simon & Schuster.

Atkins, C. (1984). Writing: Doing something constructive. *Young Children, 40,* 3–7.

Atwell, N. (Ed.). (1990). *Coming to know: Writing to learn in the intermediate grades.* Portsmouth, NH: Heinemann.

Au, K. H. (1993). *Literacy instruction in multicultural settings*. Ft. Worth, TX: Harcourt Brace Jovanovich.

Aulls, M. W. (1985). Understanding the relationship between reading and writing. *Educational Horizons, 64*, 39–44.

Baechtold, S., & Algier, A. (1986). Teaching college students vocabulary with rhyme, rhythm, and ritzy characters. *Journal of Reading, 30*, 240–253.

Bailey, M. H. (1967). The utility of phonics generalization in grades one through six. *The Reading Teacher, 20*, 413–418.

Baker, L., & Brown, A. L. (1984). Cognitive monitoring in reading. In J. Flood (Ed.), *Understanding reading comprehension* (pp. 21–24). Newark, DE: International Reading Association.

Bearse, C. I. (1992). The fairy tale connection in children's stories: Cinderella meets Sleeping Beauty. *The Reading Teacher, 45*, 688–695.

Beattie, J. (1994). Characteristics of students with disabilities and how teachers can help. In K. D. Wood and B. Algozzine (Eds.), *Teaching reading to high-risk learners: A unified perspective*. Needham Heights, MA: Allyn & Bacon.

Bennett, S. W. (1971). *The key vocabulary in organic reading: An evaluation of some of Ashton-Warner's assumptions of beginning reading*. Unpublished doctoral dissertation, University of Michigan at Ann Arbor.

Berko-Gleason, J. (1985). *The development of language*. Columbus, OH: Merrill.

Berliner, D. (1984). Making the right changes in preservice teacher education. *Phi Delta Kappan, 66*, 94–96.

Blanton L., & Blanton W. (1994). Providing reading instruction to mildly disabled students: Research into practice. In K. D. Wood and B. Algozzine (Eds.), *Teaching reading to high-risk learners: A unified perspective*. Needham Heights, MA: Allyn & Bacon.

Bloome, D., & Nieto, S. (1989). Children's understandings of basal readers. *Theory into Practice, 28*, 258–264.

Bodycott, P. (1993). Personalizing spelling instruction. *Childhood Education, 69*, 216–220.

Bohannon, J. N., & Warren-Leubecker, A. W. (1989). Theoretical approaches to language acquisition. In J. Berko-Gleason (Ed.), *The development of language*. Columbus, OH: Merrill.

Bond, G. L., & Dykstra, R. (1966–1967). The cooperative research program in first-grade reading instruction. *Reading Research Quarterly, 2*, 5–142.

Bookbinder, J. (1975). Art and reading. *Language Arts, 52*, 783–785.

Booth, D. (1985). Imaginary gardens with real toads: Reading and drama in education. *Theory into Practice, 24*, 193–198.

Booth, J. (1985). *Impressions: Teacher resource book: East of the sun*. Toronto: Holt, Rinehart and Winston of Canada.

Bormuth, J. R. (1968). The cloze readability procedure. *Elementary English, 45,* 429–436.

Boutwell, M. (1983). Reading and writing process: A reciprocal agreement. *Language Arts, 60,* 723–730.

Bransford, J. D., & Johnson, M. K. (1973). Considerations of some problems of comprehension. In W. C. Chase (Ed.), *Visual information processing.* New York: Academic Press.

Bredekamp, S. (Ed.). (1987). *Developmentally appropriate practice in early-childhood programs serving children from birth through age 8* (exp. ed.). Washington, DC: NAEYC.

Brewer, J. A. (1990). Literacy development when children's first language is not English. In N. L. Cecil (Ed.), *Literacy in the '90s.* Dubuque, IA: Kendall/Hunt.

Brewer, J., Jenkins, L., & Harp, B. (1984). Ten points you should know about readability formulas. *The School Administrator, 41,* 23–24.

Bridge, C. A., Winograd, N., & Haley, D. (1983). Using predictable materials vs. preprimers to teach beginning sight words. *The Reading Teacher, 36,* 884–891.

Brophy, J., & Alleman, J. (1991). A caveat: Curriculum integration isn't always a good idea. *Educational Leadership, 49,* 66.

Brown, R. (1973). *A first language: The early stages.* Cambridge, MA: Harvard University Press.

Bruner, J. (1983). *Child's talk.* New York: Norton.

Burns, M. (1992). *Math and literature.* Sausalito, CA: Math Solutions Publications.

Butler, A., & Turbill, J. (1984). *Towards a reading-writing classroom.* Rozelle, N.S.W., Australia: Primary English Teaching Association.

Butzow, C. M., & Butzow, J. W. (1989). *Science through children's literature: An integrated approach.* Englewood, CO: Teacher Ideas Press.

Cairney, T. H. (1988). The purpose of basals: What children think. *The Reading Teacher, 41,* 420–428.

Calkins, L. (1983). Making the reading-writing connection. *Learning, 12,* 82–86.

Calkins, L. (1986). *The art of teaching writing.* Portsmouth, NH: Heinemann.

Cambourne, B. (1988). *The whole story: Natural learning and the acquisition of literacy in the classroom.* Auckland, NZ: Ashton Scholastic.

Cambourne, B., & Turbill, J. (1990). Assessment in whole-language classrooms: Theory into practice. *The Elementary School Journal, 90*(3), 337–349.

Campbell, L. J. (1886). *New Franklin second reader.* New York: Sheldon.

Cassidy, J. (1987). Basals are better. *Learning, 16,* 65–66.

Casteel, C. P., & Isom, B. A. (1994). Reciprocal processes in science and literacy learning. *The Reading Teacher, 47,* 538–545.

Cazden, C. B. (1970). The situation: A neglected source of social class differences in language use. *Journal of Social Issues, 26,* 35–59.

Cazden, C. B. (Ed.). (1981). *Language in early childhood education* (rev. ed.). Washington, DC: National Association for the Education of Young Children.

Center for the Study of Writing. (1991). *The quarterly of the national writing project and center for the study of writing & literacy.* Berkeley: University of California.

Chall, J. S. (1967). *Learning to read: The great debate.* New York: McGraw-Hill.

Chaney, J. H. (1993). Alphabet books: Resources for learning. *The Reading Teacher, 47,* 96–104.

Chase, A. (1977). *The legacy of Malthus: The social cost of scientific racism.* New York: Knopf.

Chomsky, C. (1971). Write first, read later. *Childhood Education, 47,* 296–299.

Chomsky, C. (1978). When you still can't read in third grade: After decoding, what? In S. Jay Samuels (Ed.), *What research has to say about reading instruction.* Newark, DE: International Reading Association.

Chomsky, N. (1965). *Aspects of a theory of syntax.* Cambridge, MA: MIT Press.

Christie, J. F. (1990). Dramatic play: A context for meaningful engagements. *The Reading Teacher, 43,* 542–545.

Clay, M. M. (1972). *The early detection of reading difficulties: A diagnostic survey with recovery procedures.* Auckland, NZ: Heinemann.

Clay, M. M. (1979). *Reading: The patterning of complex behaviour.* Auckland, NZ: Heinemann.

Clay, M. M. (1982). *What did I write? Beginning writing behaviour.* Exeter, NH: Heinemann.

Clay, M. M. (1985). *The early detection of reading difficulties* (3rd ed.). Portsmouth, NH: Heinemann.

Clay, M. M. (1991). *Becoming literate: The construction of inner control.* Auckland, NZ: Heinemann.

Clay, M. M. (1993). *An observation survey: Of early literacy achievement.* Portsmouth, NH: Heinemann.

Clymer, T. (1963). The utility of phonic generalizations in the primary grades. *The Reading Teacher, 16,* 252–258.

Cochrane, O., Cochrane, D., Scalena, S., & Buchanan, E. (1984). *Reading writing and caring.* Winnipeg: Whole Language Consultants.

Cochran-Smith, M. (1984). *The making of a reader.* Norwood, NJ: Ablex.

Cohen, D. (1968). The effect of literature on vocabulary and reading achievement. *Elementary English, 45,* 209–213, 217.

Collett, M. J. (1991). Read between the lines: Music as a basis for learning. *Music Educators Journal, 77*, 42–45.

Collier, C. (1988). *Assessing minority students with learning and behavior problems.* Lindale, TX: Hamilton.

Collins, C. (1980). Sustained silent reading periods: Effects of teachers' behaviors and students' achievements. *The Elementary School Journal, 81*, 109–114.

Conrad, L. L. (1989). Charting effect and cause in informational texts. *The Reading Teacher, 42*, 451–452.

Council on Interracial Books for Children. (1974). *10 quick ways to analyze children's books for racism and sexism.* New York: New York Council on Interracial Books for Children.

Cox, V. (1971). *Reciprocal oracy/literacy recognition skills in the language production of language experience students.* Unpublished doctoral dissertation, University of Arizona at Tucson.

Cramer, R. L. (1970). An investigation of first-grade spelling achievement. *Elementary English, 47*, 230–237.

Criscuolo, N. P. (1985). Creative approaches to teaching reading through art. *Art Education, 38*, 13–16.

Cross the golden river. (1986). Toronto: Holt, Rinehart and Winston of Canada.

Crystal, D. (1987). *Child language, learning and linguistics.* London: Edward Arnold.

Cudd, E. T., & Roberts, L. (1989). Using writing to enhance content area learning in the primary grades. *The Reading Teacher, 42*, 392–404.

Cullinan, B. E. (1985). Latching on to literature: Reading initiatives take hold. *School Library Journal, 35*, 27–31.

Cullinan, B. E. (1986). Books in the classroom. *Horn Book, 62*, 766–768.

Cullinan, B. E., Jaggar, A., & Strickland, D. (1974). Language expansion for black children in the primary grades: A research report. *Young Children, 29*, 98–112.

Cunningham, A. E. (1988, April). *A developmental study of instruction in phonemic awareness.* Paper presented at a meeting of the American Educational Research Association, New Orleans, LA.

Cunningham, P. M. (1975–1976). Investigating a synthesized theory of mediated word identification. *Reading Research Quarterly, 11*, 127–143.

Cunningham, P. M. (1982). The clip sheet: Drawing them into reading. *The Reading Teacher, 35*, 960–962.

Cunningham, P. M., & Cunningham, J. (1992). Making words: Enhancing the invented spelling-decoding connection. *The Reading Teacher, 46*(2); 106–113.

Daiute, C. (1985). *Writing and computers*. Reading, MA: Addison-Wesley.

Dale, E. (1969). *Audiovisual methods in teaching* (3rd ed.). New York: Holt, Rinehart and Winston.

Davis, F. B. (1968). Research in comprehension in reading. *Reading Research Quarterly, 3*, 185–197.

DeGroff, L. (1990). Is there a place for computers in whole language classrooms? *The Reading Teacher, 43*(8), 568–572.

Department of Education. (1985). *Reading in junior classes*. Wellington, NZ: Author.

Dewey, J. (1938). *Experience and education*. New York: Macmillan.

Dockterman, D. (1991). *Great teaching in the one computer classroom*. Cambridge, MA: Tom Snyder Productions.

Downhower, S. L., & Brown, K. (1992). The effects of predictable materials on first graders' reading comprehension: A teacher research study. *Ohio Reading Teacher, 26*, 3–10.

Duffy, G., Roehler, L., & Putnam, J. (1987). Putting the teacher in control: Basal reading textbooks and instructional decision making. *The Elementary School Journal, 87*, 357–364.

Dumtschin, J. U. (1988). Recognize language development and delay in early childhood. *Young Children, 43*, 16–24.

Durkin, D. (1966). Children who read before grade one. *The Reading Teacher, 14*, 163–166.

Durkin, D. (1976). *Strategies for identifying words*. Boston: Allyn & Bacon.

Durkin, D. (1978–1979). What classroom observations reveal about reading comprehension instruction. *Reading Research Quarterly, 14*, 481–527.

Durkin, D. (1984). Is there a match between what elementary teachers do and what basal reader manuals recommend? *The Reading Teacher, 37*, 734–744.

Durkin, D. (1987). Testing in the kindergarten. *The Reading Teacher, 40*, 766–770.

Durkin, D. (1993). *Teaching them to read* (6th ed.). Needham Heights, MA: Allyn & Bacon.

Dwyer, E. K. (1990). *Enhancing reading comprehension through creative dramatics*. (ERIC Document Reproduction Service No. ED 316 849)

Edwards, P. (1989). Supporting lower SES mother's attempts to provide scaffolding for book reading. In J. B. Allen & J. Mason (Eds.), *Risk takers, risk makers, and risk breakers*. Portsmouth, NH: Heinemann.

Eldredge, J. L., & Butterfield, D. (1986). Alternatives to traditional reading instruction. *The Reading Teacher, 40*, 32–37.

Emans, R. (1967). The usefulness of phonic generalizations above the primary grades. *The Reading Teacher, 20*, 419–425.

Englemann, S., & Bereiter, C. (1983). *DISTAR reading*. Chicago: Science Research Associates.

Evans, M. A., & Carr, T. (1985). Early development of reading. *Reading Research Quarterly, 20*, 327–347.

Farr, R., & Carey, R. (1986). *Reading: What can be measured?* Newark, DE: International Reading Association.

Farr, R., & Strickland, D. (Eds.). (1993). *HBJ treasury of literature.* Orlando, FL: Harcourt Brace Jovanovich.

Farr, R., & Strickland, D. (Eds.). (1995). *Treasury of literature.* Orlando, FL: Harcourt Brace.

Fitzgerald, J., & Spiegel, D. L. (1983). Enhancing children's reading comprehension through instruction in narrative structure. *Journal of Reading Behavior, 15*, 1–17.

Fitzgerald, J., Spiegel, D. L., & Webb, T. B. (1985). Development of children's knowledge of story structure and content. *Journal of Educational Research, 79*, 101–108.

Flood, J., & Lapp, D. (1987). Forms of discourse in basal readers. *The Elementary School Journal, 87*, 299–306.

Foertsch, M. A. (1992). *Reading in and out of school: Factors influencing the literacy achievement of American students in grades 4, 8, and 12 in 1988 and 1990.* Princeton, NJ: Educational Testing Service.

Fox, M. (1993). *Radical reflections: Passionate opinions on teaching, learning, and living.* San Diego: Harcourt Brace.

Frank, M. (1979). *If you're trying to teach kids how to write, you've gotta have this book.* Nashville: Incentive.

Fredericks, A. D. (1986). Mental imagery activities to improve comprehension. *The Reading Teacher, 40*, 78–81.

Freeman, D. E., & Freeman, Y. S. (1993). Strategies for promoting the primary languages of all students. *The Reading Teacher, 46*, 552–558.

Freeman, E. B., & Person, D. G. (1992). *Using nonfiction trade books in the elementary classroom: From ants to zeppelins.* Urbana, IL: National Council of Teachers of English.

Freeman, Y. S., & Freeman, D. (1992). *Whole language for second language learners.* Portsmouth, NH: Heinemann.

Freeman, Y. S., & Whitesell, L. R. (1985). What preschoolers already know about print. *Educational Horizons, 64*, 22–24.

Gallagher, J., Weiss, P., Oglesby, K., & Thomas, T. (1983). *The status of gifted/talented education: United States survey of needs, practices, and policies.* Los Angeles: National/State Leadership Training Institute on the Gifted and Talented.

Gamberg, R., Kwak, W., Hutchings, M., Altheim, J. & Edwards, G. (1988). *Learning and loving it: Theme studies in the classroom.* Portsmouth, NH: Heinemann.

Gambrell, L. B., & Koskinen, P. S. (1982, February). *Mental imagery and the reading comprehension of below average readers, situational variables and sex differences.* Paper presented at the annual meeting of the American Educational Research Association, New York.

Gambrell, L. B., Miller, D., King, S., & Thompson, J. (1989, February). *Verbal rehearsal and reading comprehension performance.* Paper presented at the National Reading Conference, Austin, TX.

Gambrell, L. B., Pfeiffer, W., & Wilson, R. (1985). The effects of retelling upon reading comprehension and recall of text information. *Journal of Educational Research, 78,* 216–220.

Gardner, H. (1984). Assessing intelligence: A comment on testing intelligence without IQ tests. *Phi Delta Kappan, 65,* 699–700.

Gatheral, M. (1984). *Teaching gifted children in the regular classroom.* Paper presented at a meeting of the Mid-Valley Reading Association, Albany, OR.

Gearheart, B., Mullen, R., & Gearheart, C. (1993). *Exceptional individuals: An introduction.* Pacific Grove, CA: Brooks/Cole.

Gentry, J. R., & Gillet, J. W. (1993). *Teaching kids to spell.* Portsmouth, NH: Heinemann.

Giard, M. (1993). Bringing children to literacy through guided reading. In B. Harp (Ed.), *Bringing children to literacy.* Norwood, MA: Christopher-Gordon.

Gillin, J. G. (1994). *The effect of essay writing strategies on critical thinking in mixed-achievement students.* Unpublished doctoral dissertation, University of Massachusetts at Lowell.

Glass, G. G., & Burton, E. H. (1973). How do they decode? Verbalizations and observed behaviors of successful decoders. *Education, 94,* 58–64.

Goodman, K. (1967). Reading: A psycholinguistic guessing game. *Journal of the Reading Specialist, 4,* 126–135.

Goodman, K. (Ed.). (1968). *The psycholinguistic nature of the reading process.* Detroit: Wayne State University Press.

Goodman, K. (1970). *Reading: Process and program.* Champaign, IL: National Council of Teachers of English.

Goodman, K. (1986). *What's whole in whole language?* Portsmouth, NH: Heinemann.

Goodman, K., & Goodman, Y. (1983). Reading and writing relationships: Pragmatic functions. *Language Arts, 60,* 590–599.

Goodman, K., Shannon, P., Freeman, Y., & Murphy, S. (1988). *Report card on basal readers.* New York: Richard C. Owen.

Goodman, Y. (1980). The roots of literacy. *Claremont Reading Conference Yearbook,* pp. 1–32.

Goodman, Y. (1986). Children coming to know literacy. In W. H. Teale and E. Sulzby (Eds.), *Emergent literacy: Writing and reading.* Norwood, NJ: Ablex.

Goodman, Y. (1987). Reading comprehension: First encounters with written language (video). Instructional Television, Indiana University.

Goodman, Y. (1990). Children's knowledge about literacy development: An after-word. In Y. Goodman (Ed.), *How children construct literacy: Piagetian perspectives* (pp. 115–123). Newark, DE: International Reading Association.

Goodman, Y., Watson, D., & Burke, C. (1987). *Reading miscue inventory: Alternative procedures.* Katonah, NY: Richard C. Owen.

Goodwin, W., & Driscoll, L. (1980). *Handbook for measurement and evaluation in early childhood education.* San Francisco: Jossey-Bass.

Gould, S. (1981). *The mismeasure of man.* New York: Norton.

Gourgey, A., Bosseau, J., & Delgado, J. (1984). *The impact of an improvisational dramatics program on school attitude and achievement.* (ERIC Document Reproduction Service No. ED 244 245)

Graves, D. H. (1983). *Writing: Teachers and children at work.* Exeter, NH: Heinemann.

Graves, D. H. (1990, May). *Portfolios help us rethink assessment.* Paper presented at a meeting of the International Reading Association, Atlanta, GA.

Graves, D. H., & Hansen, J. (1983). The author's chair. *Language Arts, 60,* 176–183.

Gredler, G. (1978). A look at some important factors for assessing readiness for school. *Journal of Learning Disabilities, 11,* 284–290.

Gredler, G. (1984). Transition classes: A viable alternative for the at-risk child? *Psychology in the Schools, 21,* 463–470.

Greenberg, D. (1978). *Teaching poetry to children.* Portland, OR: Continuing Education Publications.

Grieser, D., & Kuhl, P.K. (1989). Categorization of speech by infants: Support for speech-sound prototypes. *Developmental Psychology, 25,* 577–588.

Griffiths, R., & Clyne, M. (1988). *Books you can count on: Linking mathematics and literature.* Portsmouth, NH: Heinemann.

Groff, P. (1977). Reading music affects reading language—says who? *Music Educators Journal, 63,* 38–51.

Guilford, J. P. (1967). *The nature of human intelligence.* New York: McGraw-Hill.

Gunn, C. (1990). *A descriptive study of a developing computer supported writing environment in a first grade whole language classroom.* Unpublished doctoral dissertation, University of Oregon, Eugene, OR.

Hadaway, N. L., & Young, T. A. (1994). Content literacy and language learning: Instructional decisions. *The Reading Teacher, 47,* 522–527.

Hall, D. P. (1991). *Investigating the relationship between word knowledge and cognitive ability.* Unpublished doctoral dissertation, University of North Carolina at Greensboro.

Hall, M. (1965). *The development and evaluation of a language experience approach to reading with first-grade culturally disadvantaged children.* Unpublished doctoral dissertation, University of Maryland.

Hall, M. A. (1981). *Teaching reading as a language experience.* Columbus, OH: Merrill.

Halliday, M. A. K. (1982). Three aspects of children's language development: Learning language, learning through language, learning about language. In Y. Goodman, M. Haussler, & D. Strickland (Eds.), *Oral and written language development research: Impact on the schools.* Urbana, IL.: National Council of Teachers of English.

Hamayan, E. (1989). *Teach your children well.* Plenary address, 12th Annual Illinois Conference for Teachers of Limited English Proficiency Students, Oak Brook, IL.

Hammond, D. (1986). Common questions on reading comprehension. *Learning, 14,* 49–51.

Hanf, M. B. (1971). Mapping: A technique for translating reading into thinking. *Journal of Reading, 30,* 415–422.

Hansen, J. (1992). Students' evaluations bring reading and writing together. *The Reading Teacher, 46,* 100–105.

Haring, N. G. (1990). Overview of special education. In N. G. Haring & L. McCormick (Eds.), *Exceptional children and youth* (5th ed.). Columbus, OH: Merrill.

Harp, B. (1988). When the principal asks: "Why are you doing guided imagery during reading time?" *The Reading Teacher, 41,* 588–590.

Harp, B. (Ed.). (1991). *Assessment and evaluation in whole language programs.* Norwood, MA: Christopher-Gordon.

Harp, B. (Ed.). (1993). *Bringing children to literacy: Classrooms at work.* Norwood, MA: Christopher-Gordon.

Harris, A. (1969). The effective teacher of reading. *The Reading Teacher, 23,* 195–204, 238.

Harris, K. (1990, February). *Collaborative instruction in schools: Key principles.* Paper presented at the Conference of the Learning Disabilities Association of America, Anaheim, CA.

Harris, V. J. (Ed.). (1992). *Teaching multicultural literature in grades K–8.* Norwood, MA: Christopher-Gordon.

Harste, J. C. (1989). The basalization of American reading instruction: One researcher responds. *Theory into Practice, 28,* 265–273.

Hartman, D. K., & Hartman, J. A. (1993). Reading across texts: Expanding the role of the reader. *The Reading Teacher, 47,* 202–211.

Hawisher, G. (1989). Research and recommendations for computers and composition. In G. Hawisher & C. Selfe (Eds.), *Critical perspectives on computers and composition instruction* (pp. 3–9). New York: Teachers College Press.

Heald-Taylor, G. (1987). Predictable literature selections and activities for language arts instruction. *The Reading Teacher, 41,* 6–12.

Heath, S. B. (1983). *Ways with words: Language, life and work in communities and classrooms.* Cambridge: Cambridge University Press.

Henderson, L. C., & Shanker, J. L. (1978). The use of interpretive dramatics versus basal reader workbooks for developing comprehension skills. *Reading World, 17,* 239–243.

Herron, J. (1992). Computer writing labs: A new vision for elementary writing. *The Writing Notebook: Creative Word Processing in the Classroom, 9*(3), 31–33.

Hess, M. L. (1991). Understanding nonfiction: Purpose, classification, response. *Language Arts, 68,* 228–232.

Hiebert, E., & Colt, J. (1989). Patterns of literature-based reading instruction. *The Reading Teacher, 43,* 14–20.

Hill, W. F. (1977). *Learning: A survey of psychological interpretations* (3rd ed.). New York: Crowell.

Hilliard, A. (1975). The strengths and weaknesses of cognitive tests of young children. In J. D. Andrews (Ed.), *One child indivisible.* Washington, DC: NAEYC.

Hittleman, D. R. (1988). *Developmental reading, K-8, teaching from a whole language perspective.* (3rd ed.). Columbus, OH: Merrill.

Hoffman, J. V. (1987). Rethinking the role of oral reading in basal instruction. *The Elementary School Journal, 87,* 367–373.

Hoffman, J. V., Roser, N.L., & Battle, J. (1993). Reading aloud in classrooms: From the modal toward a "model." *The Reading Teacher, 46,* 496–503.

Holdaway, D. (1979). *The foundations of literacy.* Sydney: Ashton Scholastic.

Holdaway, D. (1980). *Independence in reading: A handbook on individualized procedures* (2nd ed.). Distributed in the United States by Heinemann Educational Books, Inc., Exeter, NH.

Howie, S. (1989). *Reading, writing, and computers: Planning for integration.* Needham Heights, MA: Allyn & Bacon.

Hoyt, L. (1992). Many ways of knowing: Using drama, oral interactions, and the visual arts to enhance reading comprehension. *The Reading Teacher, 45,* 580–584.

Hresko, W. (1992). Learning disabilities. In L. Bullock (Ed.), *Exceptionalities in children and youth.* Needham Heights, MA: Allyn & Bacon.

Huey, E. B. (1961). *The psychology and pedagogy of reading.* Cambridge, MA: MIT Press. (Original work published 1908)

Hymes, D. (1974). *Foundations of sociolinguistics: An ethnographic approach.* Philadelphia: University of Pennsylvania Press.

Jacobson, J., Reutzel, D. R., & Hollingsworth, P. M. (1992). Reading instruction: Perceptions of elementary school principals. *Journal of Educational Research, 85,* 370–380.

Jaggar, A. (1980). Allowing for language differences. In G. S. Pinnell (Ed.), *Discovering language with children*. Urbana, IL: National Council of Teachers of English.

Jaggar, A. (1985). On observing the language learner: Introduction and overview. In A. Jaggar & M. T. Smith-Burke (Eds.), *Observing the language learner*. Newark, DE: International Reading Association and National Council of Teachers of English.

Jalongo, M. R. (1988). *Young children and picture books: Literature from infancy to six*. Washington, DC: National Association for the Education of Young Children.

Jansson, D., & Schillereff, T. (1980). Reinforcing remedial readers through art activities. *The Reading Teacher, 33*, 548–551.

Jensen, M. (1985). Story awareness: A critical skill for early reading. *Young Children, 41*, 20–24.

Jensen, M. A. (1990). Functions of writing and signs of organization in young children's written stories, inventories and personal correspondence. *Early Child Development and Care, 56*, 65–79.

Johnson, T. D. (1987). *Language through literature*. Portsmouth, NH: Heinemann.

Johnston, P. (1987). Teachers as evaluation experts. *The Reading Teacher, 40*, 744–748.

Juell, C. (1988). Learning to read and write: A longitudinal study of 54 children from first through fourth grades. *Journal of Educational Psychology, 80*, 437–447.

Juell, C., Griffith, P. L., & Gough, P. B. (1986). Acquisition of literacy: A longitudinal study of children in first and second grade. *Journal of Educational Psychology, 78*, 243–255.

Kamii, C. (1985a). Leading primary education toward excellence: Beyond worksheets and drill. *Young Children, 40*, 3–9.

Kamii, C. (1985b). *Young children reinvent arithmetic*. New York: Teachers College Press, Columbia University.

Kamin, L. (1974). *The science and politics of IQ*. New York: Wiley.

Katz, L. (1985). Dispositions in early childhood education. *ERIC/EECE Bulletin, 18*(2), 1, 3.

Katz, L. (1986, May). *What should children be doing?* Presentation to early childhood teachers and administrators in Salem, OR.

Katz, L., Raths, J., & Torres, R. (undated). *A place called kindergarten*. Urbana, IL: ERIC Clearinghouse on Elementary and Early Childhood Education.

Kearsley, G., Hunter, B., & Furlong, M. (1992). *We teach with technology: New visions for education*. Wilsonville, OR: Franklin, Beedle.

Kelly, A. M. (1975). Sight vocabularies and experience stories. *Elementary English, 52*, 327–328.

Kelly, A., & O'Kelly, J. (1993). Emergent literacy: Implications for the design of computer writing applications for children. *Journal of Computing in Childhood Education, 4*(1), 3–14.

Kiefer, B. (1987). Profile: Chris Van Allsburg in three dimensions. *Language Arts, 64,* 664–673.

Koltnow, J. (1992). A new look at an old issue—planning for educational change. *The Writing Notebook: Creative Word Processing in the Classroom, 9*(3), 5–6.

Koskinen, P. S., Wilson, R. M., Gambrell, L. B., & Neuman, S. B. (1993). Captioned video and vocabulary learning: An innovative practice in literacy instruction. *The Reading Teacher, 47*(1), 36–43.

Krashen, S. (1993). How well do people spell? *Reading Improvement, 30,* 9–20.

Kurth, R. (1988). Preparing the classroom and the children to use computers. In J. Hoot & S. Silvern (Eds.), *Writing with computers in the early grades* (pp. 75–89). New York: Teachers College Press.

Langer, J. A. (1982). The reading process. In A. Berger & H. A. Robinson (Eds.), *Secondary school reading: What research reveals for classroom practice* (pp. 38–51). Urbana, IL: National Conference on Research in English and ERIC Clearinghouse on Reading and Communication Skills.

Langer, J. A. (1986). Learning through writing: Study skills in the content areas. *Journal of Reading, 30,* 400–406.

Lapp, D., & Flood, J. (1984). Promoting reading comprehension: Instruction which insures continuous reader growth. In J. Flood (Ed.), *Promoting reading comprehension* (pp. 273–288). Newark, DE: International Reading Association.

Larrick, N. (1987). Illiteracy starts too soon. *Phi Delta Kappan, 69,* 184–189.

Larson, M. L. (1976). Readers' theatre: New vitality for oral reading. *The Reading Teacher, 29,* 359–360.

Lawrence Hall of Science. (1993). *Once upon a GEMS guide: Connecting young people's literature to great explorations in math and science.* Berkeley, CA: Author.

Lawrence, P., & Harris, V. (1986). A strategy for using predictable books. *Early Years, 16,* 34–35.

Lavoie, R. (1990). *The F.A.T. city discussion guide.* Washington, DC: PBS Video.

Lee, D., & Rubin, J. (1979). *Children and language: Reading and writing, talking and listening.* Belmont, CA: Wadsworth.

Lester, J. (1987). *The tales of Uncle Remus: The adventures of Brer Rabbit.* New York: Dial Books for Young Readers.

Leu, D. J., De Groff, L., & Simons, H. D. (1986). Predictable texts and interactive-compensatory hypotheses: Evaluating individual differences in reading ability, context use, and comprehension. *Journal of Educational Psychology, 78,* 347–352.

Lim, H. L., & Watson, D. J. (1993). Whole language content classes for second-language learners. *The Reading Teacher, 46*(5), 384–393.

Lomax, R. G., & McGee, L. M. (1987). Young children's concepts about print and meaning: Toward a model of word reading acquisition. *Reading Research Quarterly, 22,* 237–256.

Lowenthal, B. (1986). Planning activities to aid metacognition. *Academic Therapy, 22,* 199–203.

Lynch, D. (1988). Reading comprehension under listening, silent, and round robin reading conditions as a function of text difficulty. *Reading Improvement, 25,* 98–104.

Lynch, P. (1993). Interactive media enlivens learning: Teaching with multimedia. *Higher Education Product Companion, 2*(3), 8–11.

Macey, J. M. (1978). Combining word recognition skills and art. *The Reading Teacher, 32,* 64–65.

Maheady, L., Mallette, B., Harper, G., Sacca, K., & Pomerantz, D. (1994). Peer-mediated instruction for high-risk students. In B. Wood & B. Algozzine (Eds.), *Teaching reading to high-risk learners.* Needham Heights, MA: Allyn & Bacon.

Maker, C. J. (1982). *Teaching models in education of the gifted.* Rockville, MD: Aspen.

Mandler, J. M., & Johnson, N. S. (1977). Remembrance of things parsed: Story structure and recall. *Cognitive Psychology, 9,* 111–151.

Marland, S. P. (1972). *Education of the gifted and talented: Report to the Congress of the United States by the U.S. Commissioner of Education.* Washington, DC: U.S. Government Printing Office.

Martin, B., Jr. (1975). *Teaching suggestions for sounds jubilee and sounds freedom ringing.* New York: Holt, Rinehart and Winston.

Martin, B., Jr. (1988, June). *The reading/writing classroom.* Seminar, Oregon State University.

Martin, C. E., Cramond, B., & Safter, T. (1982). Developing creativity through the reading program. *The Reading Teacher, 35,* 568–572.

Mason, J. M., & Sinha, S. (1993). Emerging literacy in the early childhood years: Applying a Vygotskian model of learning and development. In B. Spodek (Ed.), *Handbook of research on the education of young children* (pp. 137–150). New York: Macmillan.

Matter, E. B. (1989). In the classroom: Visualize to improve comprehension. *The Reading Teacher, 42*(4), 338.

May, F. (1986). *Reading as communication: An integrated approach* (2nd ed.). Columbus, OH: Merrill.

McAuliffe, S. (1994). Toward understanding one another: Second graders' use of gendered language and story styles. *The Reading Teacher, 47*(4), 302–310.

McCarthy, W. G. (1985). Promoting language development through music. *Academic Therapy, 21*, 237–242.

McCaslin, N. (1990). *Creative drama in the classroom.* New York: Longman.

McCormick, L. (1990). Cultural diversity and exceptionality. In N. Haring & L. McCormick (Eds.), *Exceptional children and youth.* Columbus, OH: Merrill.

McCormick, S. (1977). Should you read aloud to your children? *Language Arts, 54*, 139–143, 163.

McGruder, S. (1993). Bringing children to literacy through drama. In B. Harp (Ed.), *Bringing children to literacy: Classrooms at work.* Norwood, MA: Christopher-Gordon.

McGuire, G. N. (1984). How arts instruction affects reading and language: Theory and research. *The Reading Teacher, 37*, 835–839.

McKenna, M. C., & Robinson, R. D. (1993). *Teaching through text: A content literacy approach to content area reading.* White Plains, NY: Longman.

Meisels, S. J. (1985). *Developmental screening in early childhood: A guide.* Washington, DC: NAEYC.

Meisels, S. J. (1986). Testing four- and five-year-olds. *Educational Leadership, 44*, 90–92.

Meisels, S. J. (1987). Uses and abuses of developmental screening and school readiness testing. *Young Children, 42*, 4–6, 68–73.

Meyer, B. (1982). Reading research and the composition teacher: The importance of plans. *College Composition and Communication, 33*, 37–49.

Miccinati, J. L., & Phelps, S. (1980). Classroom drama from children's reading: From the page to the stage. *The Reading Teacher, 34*, 269–272.

Mooney, M. E. (1990). *Reading to, with, and by children.* Katonah, NY: Richard C. Owen.

Morrow, L. M., & Rand, M. K. (1991). Promoting literacy during play by designing early childhood classroom environments. *The Reading Teacher, 44*, 396–402.

Murphy, T. (1987, April). *English through music: Singing RPR, walking labs, and music matter.* Paper presented at the Annual Meeting of the International Association of Teachers of English as a Foreign Language, Westende, Belgium.

Myers, C., & Bounds, B. (1991, April). *Evaluation of the cross categorical service delivery model: Is the regular education initiative working?* Paper presented at the Annual Conference of the Council for Exceptional Children, Atlanta, GA.

Naisbitt, J. (1982). *Megatrends.* New York: Warner.

National Center for Fair and Open Testing. (1987, Fall). North Carolina legislature drops exams for 1st, 2nd graders. *Fair Test Examiner*, p. 3.

Neilsen, L. (1991). Writing and research using CD-ROM. *The Writing Notebook: Creative Word Processing in the Classroom, 8*(3), 35–36.

Nessel, D. (1987). Reading comprehension: Asking the right questions. *Phi Delta Kappan, 68*, 442–445.

Neuman, S. B., Roskos, K. A. (1992). *Language and literacy learning in the early years: An integrated approach.* Fort Worth, TX: Harcourt Brace Jovanovich.

New McGuffey Fourth Reader. (1901). New York: American Book Company.

New NAEP report cites need for improved writing skills. (1994). *Reading Today, 12*, 36.

New Zealand Ministry of Education. (1992). *Dancing with the pen.* Katonah, NY: Richard C. Owen.

Newsnotes. (1987). *Phi Delta Kappan, 68*, 484–485.

Nist, S. L., & Kirby, K. (1986). Teaching comprehension and study strategies through modeling and thinking aloud. *Reading Research and Instruction, 25*, 254–264.

Nolte, R. Y., & Singer, H. (1985). Active comprehension: Teaching a process of reading comprehension and its effects on reading achievement. *The Reading Teacher, 39*, 24–31.

Norton, D. (1987). *Through the eyes of a child: An introduction to children's literature* (2nd ed.). Columbus, OH: Merrill.

Oakland, T. (Ed.). (1977). *Psychological and educational assessment of minority children.* New York: Brunner/Mazel.

Oehlkers, W. (1971). *The contribution of creative writing to reading achievement in the language experience approach.* Unpublished doctoral dissertation, University of Delaware.

O'Flahavan, J., & Blassberg, R. (1992). Toward an embedded model of spelling instruction for emergent literates. *Language Arts, 69*, 409–424.

Ogle, D. M. (1986). KWL: A teaching model. *The Reading Teacher, 39*, 564–571.

Olson, M. W., & Gee, T. C. (1991). Content reading instruction in the primary grades: Perceptions and strategies. *The Reading Teacher, 45*, 298–307.

Osguthorpe, R. T., & Scruggs, T. E. (1986). Special education students as tutors: A review and analysis. *Remedial and Special Education, 7*(4), 15–26.

Papert, S. (1980). *Mindstorms: Children, computers and powerful ideas.* New York: Basic Books.

Paulson, F. L., Paulson, P. R., & Meyer, C. A. (1991). What makes a portfolio a portfolio? *Educational Leadership, 48*, 60–63.

Pearson, P. D., & Johnson, D. D. (1978). *Teaching reading comprehension.* New York: Holt, Rinehart and Winston.

Pellegrini, A. D. (1991). A critique of the concept of at risk as applied to emergent literacy. *Language Arts, 68*, 380–385.

Pellegrini, A. D., & Galda, L. (1982). The effect of thematic-fantasy play training on the development of children's story comprehension. *American Educational Research Journal, 19*, 443–452.

Peterson, R., & Eeds, M. (1990). *Grand conversations: Literature groups in action.* New York: Scholastic.

Phillips, W. (1990). *REI: The will and skill of regular educators.* (ERIC Document Reproduction Service No. ED 320 323)

Piaget, J. (1959). *The language and thought of the child* (3rd ed.). London: Routledge and Kegan Paul.

Pigott, I. (1990). Drama in the classroom. *Gifted Child Today, 1,* 2–5.

Pinnell, G. S., Fried, M. D., & Estice, R. M. (1990). Reading recovery: Learning how to make a difference. *The Reading Teacher, 43,* 282–287.

Piper, T. (1993). *Language for all our children.* New York: Macmillan.

Porterfield, K. (1993). Bringing children to literacy through literature studies. In B. Harp (Ed.), *Bringing children to literacy: Classrooms at work.* Norwood, MA: Christopher-Gordon.

Purkey, W. (1970). *Self-concept and school achievement.* Englewood Cliffs, NJ: Prentice-Hall.

Rabson, B. (1982). Reading and writing at Guggenheim. *School Arts, 81,* 13–15.

Ralabate, P. (1989, October). *The regular education initiative (REI): Where do students with learning disabilities fit?* Paper presented at the Annual Conference of the Connecticut Association for Children with Learning Disabilities, South Norwalk, CT.

Raphael, T. E. (1982). Questions-answering strategies for children. *The Reading Teacher, 36,* 186–191.

Raphael, T. E. (1986). Teaching question-answer relationships, revisited. *The Reading Teacher, 39,* 516-522.

Rasinski, T. V. (1988). The role of interest, purpose, and choice in early literacy. *The Reading Teacher, 41,* 396–400.

Reutzel, D. R. (1985). Reconciling schema theory and the basal reading lesson. *The Reading Teacher, 39,* 194–197.

Reutzel, D. R. (1992). Breaking the letter-a-week tradition: Conveying the alphabetic principle to young children. *Childhood Education, 69,* 20–23.

Reutzel, D. R., & Fawson, P. (1988). *A professor returns to the classroom: Implementing whole language.* Unpublished manuscript, Brigham Young University, Provo, UT.

Reutzel, D. R., & Hollingsworth, P. M. (1991). Reading comprehension skills: Testing the distinctiveness hypothesis. *Reading Research and Instruction, 30,* 32–46.

Reynolds, C. (Ed.). (1984). *Perspectives on bias in mental testing.* New York: Plenum.

Richards, L. (1990). Measuring things in words: Language for learning mathematics. *Language Arts, 67,* 14–25.

Riel, M. (1990). Building a new foundation for global communities. *The Writing Notebook: Creative Word Processing in the Classroom, 9*(3), 35–37.

Rigg, P., & Allen, V. G. (Eds.). (1989). *When they don't all speak English: Integrating the ESL student into the regular classroom.* Urbana, IL: National Council of Teachers of English.

Roberts, P. (1984). *Alphabet: A handbook of ABC books and activities for the elementary classroom.* Metuchen, NJ: Scarecrow Press.

Robinson, F. P. (1962). *Effective reading.* New York: Harper and Brothers.

Robinson, J. (1983). *Activities for anyone, anytime, anywhere.* New York: Little, Brown.

Rodgers, F. A. (1975). *Curriculum and instruction in the elementary school.* New York: Macmillan.

Rosenblatt, L. M.(1978). *The reader, the text, the poem: The transactional theory of the literary work.* Carbondale, IL: Southern Illinois University Press.

Rosenblatt, L. M. (1982). The literary transaction: Evocation and response. *Theory into Practice, 21,* 268–277.

Rosenblatt, L. M. (1991). Literature—S.O.S.! *Language Arts, 68*(6), 444–448.

Rosenshine, B., & Stevens, R. (1984). Classroom instruction in reading. In P. D. Pearson (Ed.), *Handbook of reading research* (pp. 754–798). New York: Longman.

Roskos, K. (1988). Literacy at work in play. *The Reading Teacher, 41,* 562–566.

Routman, R. (1991). *Invitations: Changing as teachers and learners K–12.* Portsmouth, NH: Heinemann.

Rumelhart, D. E. (1977). Toward an interactive model of reading. In S. Dornic (Ed.), *Attention and performance VI* (pp. 573–603). Hillsdale, NJ: Erlbaum.

Rumelhart, D. E. (1982). Schemata: The building blocks of cognition. In J. Guthrie (Ed.), *Comprehension and teaching: Research reviews.* Newark, DE: International Reading Association.

Rumelhart, D. E. (1984). Understanding understanding. In J. Flood (Ed.), *Understanding reading comprehension* (pp. 1–20). Newark, DE: International Reading Association.

Russavage, P., Lorton, L., & Millham, R. (1985). Making responsible instructional decisions about reading: What teachers think and do about basals. *The Reading Teacher, 39,* 314–317.

Scala, M. A. (1993). What whole language in the mainstream means for children with learning disabilities. *The Reading Teacher, 47*(3), 222–229.

Schickedanz, J. (1987, May). *Views of literacy development, then and now.* Paper presented at annual conference of the National Association for the Education of Young Children, Anaheim, CA.

Shannon, P. (1982). Some subjective reasons for teachers' reliance on commercial reading materials. *The Reading Teacher, 35,* 884–889.

Shepard, L., & Smith, M. (1986). Synthesis of research on school readiness and kindergarten retention. *Educational Leadership, 44*, 78–86.

Shepard, L., & Smith, M. (1987). Effects of kindergarten retention at the end of first grade. *Psychology in the Schools, 24*, 346–357.

Shepard, L., & Smith, M. (1988). Escalating academic demand in kindergarten: Counter productive. *Elementary School Journal, 89*, 135–145.

Silverman, F. L., Winograd, K., and Strohauer, D. (1992). Student-generated story problems. *Arithmetic Teacher, 39*, 6–12.

Simon, K. (1986). *Using computers to teach English composition classes* (pp. 1–13). (ERIC Document Reproduction Service No. ED 276 056)

Simonson, M., & Thompson, A. (1990). *Educational computing foundations.* New York: Macmillan.

Sitton, R. A. (1990). *Quick-word handbook for everyday writers.* North Billerica, MA: Curriculum Associates.

Slapin, B., & Seale, D. (Eds.). (1992). *Through Indian eyes: The native experience in books for children.* Philadelpha: New Society.

Slavin, R. E. (1990). *Cooperative learning: Theory, research, and practice.* Englewood Cliffs, NJ: Prentice Hall.

Sloyer, S. (1982). *Readers theatre: Story dramatization in the Classroom.* Urbana, IL: National Council of Teachers of English.

Smith, F. (1973). *Psycholinguistics and reading.* New York: Holt, Rinehart and Winston.

Smith, F. (1978). *Reading without nonsense.* New York: Teachers College Press.

Smith, F. (1983). Reading like a writer. *Language Arts, 60*, 558–567.

Smith, M., & Bean, T. W. (1983). Four strategies that develop children's story comprehension and writing. *The Reading Teacher, 36*, 295–300.

Smith, M., & Shepard, L. (1987). What doesn't work: Explaining policies of retention in the early grades. *Educational Leadership, 45*, 129–134.

Smith, N. (1985). The word processing approach to language experience. *The Reading Teacher, 38*(6), 556–559.

Smith-Burke, M. T., Deegan, D., & Jaggar, A. M. (1991). Whole language: A viable alternative for special and remedial education? *Topics in Language Disorders, 11*, 58–68.

Snow, C. (1983). Literacy and language relationships during the preschool years. *Harvard Educational Review, 53*, 165–189.

Snow, C. E., Barnes, W. S., Chandler, J., Goodman, I. F., & Hemphill, L. (1991). *Unfulfilled expectations: Home and school influences on literacy.* Cambridge, MA: Harvard University Press.

Sorenson, N. (1983). *A study of the reliability of phonic generalizations in five primary-level basal reading programs.* Unpublished doctoral dissertation, Arizona State University.

Spache, G. D. (1981). *Diagnosing and correcting reading disabilities* (2nd ed.). Boston: Allyn & Bacon.

Spiegel, D., Fitzgerald, J., & Cunningham, J. W. (1993). Parental perceptions of preschoolers' literacy development: Implications for home-school partnerships. *Young Children, 48,* 74–79.

Stahl, S. A. (1992). Saying the "p" word: Nine guidelines for exemplary phonics instruction. *The Reading Teacher, 45,* 618–625.

Stanley-Samuelson, D. W. (1987). Physiological roles of prostaglandins and other eicosanoids in invertebrates. *The Biological Bulletin, 173,* 92–109.

Stauffer, M. (1973). *Comparative effects of a language arts approach and basal reader approach to first grade reading achievement.* Unpublished doctoral dissertation, University of Delaware at Newark.

Stauffer, R. G. (1969). *Teaching reading as thinking process.* New York: Harper & Row.

Stauffer, R. G. (1975). *Directing the reading-thinking process.* New York: Harper & Row.

Stauffer, R. G., & Pikulski, J. (1974). A comparison and measure of oral language growth. *Elementary English, 51,* 1151–1155.

Stephens, D. (1991). *Research on whole language.* Katonah, NY: Richard C. Owen.

Stonier, T., & Conlin, C. (1985). *The three c's: Children, computers and communication.* Chichester, England: Wiley.

Stotsky, S. (1983). Research on reading/writing relationships: A synthesis and suggested directions. *Language Arts, 60,* 627–642.

Strickland, D., Feeley, J., & Wepner, S. (1987). *Using computers in the teaching of reading.* New York: Teachers College Press.

Sulzby, E. (1991). Assessment of emergent literacy: Storybook reading. *The Reading Teacher, 44,* 498–500.

Teale, W. H. (1984). Reading to young children: Its significance for literacy development. In J. Goelman, A. A. Oberg, & F. Smith (Eds.), *Awakening to literacy* (pp. 110–121). London: Heinemann.

Teale, W. H., Hiebert, E. H., & Chittenden, E. A. (1987). Assessing young children's literacy development. *The Reading Teacher, 40,* 772–777.

Terman, L., & Oden, M. (1959). The gifted group at mid-life: Thirty-five years' follow-up of the superior child. In L. Terman (Ed.), *Genetic studies of genius,* Vol. 5. Stanford, CA: Stanford University Press.

Thomas, A., & Pashley, B. (1982). Effects of classroom training on LD students' task persistence and attributions. *Learning Disability Quarterly, 5,* 133–144.

Thomas, I. (1987). Uses of the computer in teaching the composing process. In S. Franklin (Ed.), *Making the literature, writing, word processing connection: The best of the writing notebook 1983–1987*. Eugene, OR: The Writing Notebook.

Thompkins, G. E., & McGee, L. M. (1993). *Teaching reading with literature*. New York: Macmillan.

Thoms, H. (1985). Creative writing as dialectical interplay: Multiple viewings of a painting. *Art Education, 38*, 10–12.

Top, B. I., & Osguthorpe, R. T. (1987). Reverse-role tutoring: The effects of handicapped students tutoring regular class students. *Elementary School Journal, 87*, 413–423.

Torrance, E. P. (1985). Who is gifted? *Illinois Council for the Gifted Journal, 4*, 1–3.

Tovey, D. R. (1980). Children's grasp of phonics terms vs. sound–symbol relationships. *The Reading Teacher, 33*, 431–437.

Tunnell, M. O. (1986). The natural act of reading: An affective approach. *The Advocate, 5*, 156–164.

Urzua, C. (1980). Doing what comes naturally: Recent research in second language acquisition. In G. S. Pinnell (Ed.), *Discovering language with children*. Urbana, IL: National Council of Teachers of English.

Vacca, J. A., Vacca, R. T., & Gove, M. K. (1991). *Reading and learning to read*. New York: HarperCollins.

Valencia, S. W., Hiebert, E. H., & Kapinus, B. (1992). National assessment of educational progress: What do we know and what lies ahead? *The Reading Teacher, 45*(9), 730–734.

Valencia, S. W., & Pearson, P. (1987). Reading assessment: Time for a change. *The Reading Teacher, 40*, 726–732.

Van Buren, Becky. (1986). Improving reading skills through elementary art experiences. *Art Education, 39*, 56, 59, 61.

Veatch, J., Sawicki, F., Elliott, G., Flake, E., & Blakey, J. (1979). *Key words to reading: The language experience approach begins* (2nd ed.). Columbus, OH: Merrill.

Venezky, R. L. (1987). A history of the American reading textbook. *The Elementary School Journal, 87*, 247–263.

Vygotsky, L. (1986). *Thought and language*. Cambridge, MA: Massachusetts Institute of Technology. (Original work published 1954)

Walker, B. J. (1985). Right-brained strategies for teaching comprehension. *Academic Therapy, 21*, 133–141.

Waller, R. J. (1993). *The bridges of Madison County*. New York: Warner.

Watkins, E. (1926). *Silent reading for beginners*. Chicago: Lippincott.

Watson, D. (1988, December). *Whole language: Where have we been; where are we going?* Paper presented at the Whole Language Umbrella, Tucson, AZ.

Watson, D., & Crowley, P. (1988). How can we implement a whole-language approach? In C. Weaver (Ed.), *Reading process and practice from sociopsycholinguistics to whole language* (pp. 232–279). Portsmouth, NH: Heinemann.

Weaver, C. (1988). *Reading process and practice: From sociolinguistics to whole language.* Portsmouth, NH: Heinemann.

Weaver, C. (1994). *Reading process and practice: From sociopsycholinguistics to whole language.* Portsmouth, NH: Heinemann.

Wells, G. (1986). *The meaning makers: Children learning language and using language to learn.* Portsmouth, NH: Heinemann.

Wepner, S. B., & Feeley, J. T. (1992). Basal selection: What questions should be asked? *Florida Reading Quarterly, 29,* 7–13.

Wetzel, K. (1985). Keyboarding skills: Elementary, my dear teacher? *The Computing Teacher, 12*(9), 15–19.

Wheeler, F. (1985). Can word processing help the writing process? *Learning, 13*(7), 54–62.

Whitin, D. J., & Wilde, S. (1992). *Read any good math lately? Children's books for mathematical learning, K–6.* Portsmouth, NH: Heinemann.

Wilde, S. (1990). A proposal for a new spelling curriculum. *The Elementary School Journal, 90,* 275–289.

Will, M. (1986). *Educating children with learning problems: A shared responsibility.* Washington, DC: U.S. Department of Education, Office of Special Education.

Wilson, R., & Parkey, N. (1970). A modified reading program in a middle school. *Journal of Reading, 13,* 447–452.

Winograd, K. (1992). What fifth graders learn when they write their own math problems. *Educational Leadership, 49,* 64–67.

Wolf, J. (1990). The gifted and talented. In N. Haring, & L. McCormick (Eds.), *Exceptional children and youth.* Columbus, OH: Merrill.

Wolf, S. A. (1993). What's in a name? Labels and literacy in Readers Theatre. *The Reading Teacher, 46,* 540–545.

Wood, A. (1982). *Quick as a cricket.* Singapore: Child's Play (International) Ltd.

Wrightman, T. (1992). *Strengthening math achievement in K–2 classrooms: Using integrated, whole language strategies.* Bellevue, WA: Bureau of Education and Research.

Wuertenberg, J. (1983). *Reading and writing for every child.* Seminar, Oregon State University.

Wuertenburg, J. (1993). *Leading with literature.* Presentation to Northern Arizona Reading Council, Flagstaff, AZ.

Yates, J. R. (1988). Demography as it affects special education. In A. Ortiz & B. Ramires (Eds.), *Schools and the culturally diverse exceptional student: Promising practices and future directions.* Reston, VA: Council for Exceptional Children.

Yawkey, T. D. (1980). Effects of social relationships curricula and sex differences on reading and imaginativeness in young children. *Alberta Journal of Educational Research, 26,* 159–168.

Yopp, H. K. (1992). Developing phonemic awareness in young children. *The Reading Teacher, 45,* 696–703.

Young, T. A., & Vardell, S. (1993). Weaving Readers Theatre and nonfiction into the curriculum. *The Reading Teacher, 46,* 396–406.

Zinar, R. (1976). Reading language and reading music: Is there a connection? *Music Educators Journal, 62,* 71–74.

Zucker, C. (1993). Using whole language with students who have language and learning disabilities. *The Reading Teacher, 46*(8), 660–670.

Zutell, J. (1980). Learning language at home and at school. In G. S. Pinnell (Ed.), *Discovering language with children.* Urbana, IL: National Council of Teachers of English.

Children's Literature Cited

Adoff, A. (1991). *In for winter, out for spring.* New York: Harcourt Brace Jovanovich.

Alexander, L. (1964). *The book of three.* New York: Dell.

Alexander, L. (1965). *The black cauldron.* New York: Dell.

Alexander, L. (1966). *The castle of Llyr.* New York: Dell.

Alexander, L. (1967). *Taran wanderer.* New York: Dell.

Alexander, L. (1968). *The high king.* New York: Dell.

Babbitt, N. (1969). *The search for delicious.* New York: Farrar, Straus and Giroux.

Babbitt, N. (1970). *Knee-knock rise.* New York: Farrar, Straus and Giroux.

Babbitt, N. (1975). *Tuck everlasting.* New York: Farrar, Straus and Giroux.

Babbitt, N. (1977). *The eyes of the amaryllis.* New York: Farrar, Straus and Giroux.

Babbitt, N. (1989). *Nellie: A cat on her own.* New York: Farrar, Straus and Giroux.

Baker, J. (1991). *The window.* New York: Greenwillow.

Bawden, N. (1973). *Carrie's war.* New York: Lippincott.

Baylor, B., & Parnall, P. (1981). *Desert voices.* New York: Scribner's.

Becker, J. (1973). *Seven little rabbits.* New York: Walker.

Bishop, C. (1964). *Twenty and ten* (as told by Janet Jolly). New York: Viking.

Bisset, D. J. (Ed.). (1967). *Poetry and verse for urban children* (3 vols.). New York: Chandler.

Blos, J. (1979). *A gathering of days: A New England girl's journal 1830–32.* New York: Scribner's.

Blume, J. (1970). *Are you there, God? It's me, Margaret.* New York: Bradbury Press.

Bourke, L. (1991). *Eye spy: A mysterious alphabet.* San Francisco: Chronicle.

Brown, M. (1947). *Stone soup.* New York: Scribner's.

Brown, M. (1961). *Once a mouse.* New York: Scribner's.

Brown, M. W. (1942). *The runaway bunny.* New York: Harper & Row.

Bunting, E. (1993). *Someday a tree.* Boston: Clarion.

Carle, E. (1968). *1, 2, 3 to the zoo: A counting book.* New York: Philomel.

Carle, E. (1969). *The very hungry caterpillar.* New York: Philomel.

Carle, E. (1972). *Rooster's off to see the world.* Natick, MA: Picture Book Studio.

Carle, E. (1972). *The secret birthday message.* New York: Harper & Row.

Carle, E. (1975). *The mixed-up chameleon.* New York: Harper & Row.

Carle, E. (1977). *The grouchy ladybug.* New York: Scholastic.

Carle, E. (1984). *The very busy spider.* New York: Philomel.

Carle, E. (1986). *Papa, please get the moon for me.* Natick, MA: Picture Book Studio.

Carle, E. (1987). *Do you want to be my friend?* New York: Crowell.

Carle, E. (1987). *Have you seen my cat?* New York: Scholastic.

Carle, E. (1987). *A house for hermit crab.* Natick, MA: Picture Book Studio.

Carle, E. (1989). *Animals animals.* New York: Philomel.

Carle, E. (1990). *Pancakes, pancakes!* Natick, MA: Picture Book Studio.

Carle, E. (1990). *The very quiet cricket.* New York: Philomel.

Carle, E. (1991). *Dragons, dragons.* New York: Philomel.

Carle, E. (1992). *Draw me a star.* New York: Philomel.

Carle, E. (1993). *Today is Monday.* New York: Philomel.

Cherry, L. (1990). *The great kapok tree.* San Diego: Harcourt Brace Jovanovich.

Clements, A., & Savadier, E. (1992). *Billy and the bad teacher.* Saxonville, MA: Picture Book Studio.

Collier, J. L., & Collier, C. (1974). *My brother Sam is dead.* New York: Scholastic.

Cooper, S. (1973). *The dark is rising.* New York: Atheneum.

Cooper, S. (1975). *The grey king.* New York: Atheneum.

Cooper, S. (1986). *The selkie girl.* New York: Macmillan.

Cowley, J. (1988). *Greedy cat.* Wellington, New Zealand: School Publications Branch, Department of Education.

Crews, D. (1968). *Ten black dots.* New York: Greenwillow.

Cullum, A. (1971). *The geranium on the window sill just died but teacher you went right on.* Belgium: Harlin Quist.

Dahl, R. (1961). *James and the giant peach.* New York: Puffin Books.

Dahl, R. (1964). *Charlie and the chocolate factory.* New York: Knopf.

Dahl, R. (1972). *Charlie and the great glass elevator.* New York: Puffin.

Dahl, R. (1982). *The BFG.* New York: Puffin.

Dahl, R. (1983). *The witches.* New York: Puffin.

DeJong, M. (1956). *The house of sixty fathers.* New York: Harper.

dePaola, T. (1975). *The cloud book.* New York: Holiday House.

dePaola, T. (1977). *The quicksand book.* New York: Holiday House.

dePaola, T. (1978). *Pancakes for breakfast.* San Diego: Harcourt Brace Jovanovich.

dePaola, T. (1978). *The popcorn book.* New York: Scholastic.

Dragonwagon, C. *Alligator arrived with apples: A potluck alphabet feast.* New York: Macmillan.

duBois, W. P. (1947). *The 21 balloons.* New York: Dell.

Dunrae, O. (1989). *Deep down underground.* New York: MacMillan.

Ehlert, L. (1987). *Growing vegetable soup.* San Diego: Harcourt Brace Jovanovich.

Ehlert, L. (1990). *Fish eyes—A book you can count on.* Orlando, FL: Harcourt Brace Jovanovich.

Emberley, E. (1977). *Ed Emberley's great thumbprint drawing book.* Boston: Little, Brown.

Fleischman, P. (1985). *I am Phoenix: Poems for two voices.* New York: Harper & Row.

Fleischman, P. (1988). *Joyful noise: Poems for two voices.* New York: Harper & Row.

Fleming, D. (1991). *In the tall, tall grass.* New York: Henry Holt.

Fleming, D. (1992). *Lunch.* New York: Henry Holt.

Fleming, D. (1993). *In the small, small pond.* New York: Henry Holt.

Forbes, E. (1943). *Johnny Tremain.* New York: Dell.

Gag, W. (1928). *Millions of cats.* New York: Coward, McCann & Geoghegan.

Galdone, P. (1986). *Over in the meadow*. New York: Prentice-Hall.

Gee, M. (1982). *The halfmen of O*. New York: Puffin.

George, J. C. (1959). *My side of the mountain*. New York: Dutton.

Giganti, P., Jr. (1988). *How many snails? A counting book*. New York: Greenwillow Books.

Goble, P. (1992). *Red Hawk's account of Custer's last battle*. Lincoln: University of Nebraska Press. (Original work published 1969)

Goldstein, B. (1992). *Inner chimes: Poems on poetry*. Honesdale, PA: Boyds Mill Press.

Grahame, K. (1938). *The reluctant dragon*. New York: Holiday House.

Gwynne, F. (1970). *The king who rained*. New York: Windmill.

Hepworth, C. (1992). ***Antics***. New York: Putnam's.

Hitchcock, A. (1986). *Alfred Hitchcock's Solve-Them-Yourself Mysteries*. New York: Random House.

Hoberman, M. A. (1982). *A house is a house for me*. New York: Puffin.

Hopkins, L. B. (1993). *Extra innings: Baseball poems*. San Diego: Harcourt Brace Jovanovich.

Hoyt-Goldsmith, D. (1991). *Pueblo storyteller*. New York: Holiday House.

Hunter, M. (1972). *The haunted mountain*. New York: Harper.

Hunter, M. (1975). *A stranger came ashore*. New York: Harper.

Hunter, M. (1988). *The mermaid summer*. New York: Harper.

Innocenti, R. (1985). *Rose Blanche*. New York: Stewart, Tabori and Chang.

Irvine, J. (1987). *How to make pop-ups*. New York: Morrow Junior Books.

Keats, E. J. (1962). *The snowy day*. New York: Viking.

Keats, E. J. (1971). *Over in the meadow*. New York: Four Winds.

Kerr, J. (1971). *When Hitler stole pink rabbit*. New York: Dell.

Koch, M. (1989). *Just one more*. New York: Greenwillow.

Kraus, R. (1970). *Whose mouse are you?* New York: Macmillan.

Lee, D. (1974). *Alligator pie*. Toronto: Macmillan of Canada.

L'Engle, M. (1962). *A wrinkle in time*. New York: Dell.

L'Engle, M. (1973). *A wind in the door*. New York: Dell.

L'Engle, M. (1976). *Dragons in the water*. New York: Dell.

L'Engle, M. (1978). *A swiftly tilting planet*. New York: Dell.

L'Engle, M. (1986). *Many waters*. New York: Dell.

Le Guin, U. (1968). *A wizard of Earthsea.* New York: Atheneum.

Le Guin, U. (1971). *The tombs of Atuan.* New York: Bantam.

Le Guin, U. (1972). *The farthest shore.* New York: Bantam.

Le Guin, U. (1990). *Tehanu.* New York: Bantam.

Le Guin, U. (1992). *A ride on the redmare's back.* New York: Orchard.

Levitin, S. (1970). *Journey to America.* New York: Aladdin.

Lewis, C. S. (1950). *The lion, the witch and the wardrobe.* New York: Collier.

Lewis, C. S. (1951). *Prince Caspian.* New York: Collier.

Lewis, C. S. (1952). *The voyage of the "Dawn Treader."* New York: Collier.

Lewis, C. S. (1953). *The silver chair.* New York: Collier.

Lewis, C. S. (1954). *The horse and his boy.* New York: Collier.

Lewis, C. S. (1955). *The magician's nephew.* New York: Collier.

Lewis, C. S. (1956). *The last battle.* New York: Collier.

Lewis, R. (Ed.). (1965). *In a spring garden.* New York: Dial.

Lipkind, W. (1951). *Finders keepers.* New York: Harcourt Brace.

Lobel, A.(1972). *Frog and toad together.* New York: Harper & Row.

Lowry, L. (1989). *Number the stars.* Boston: Houghton Mifflin.

MacLachlan, P. (1985). *Sarah, plain and tall.* New York: Harper.

Martin, B., Jr. (1970). *Brown bear, brown bear.* New York: Holt, Rinehart and Winston.

Maruki, T. (1980). *Hiroshima no pika.* New York: Lothrop, Lee & Shepard.

McCloskey, R. (1941). *Make way for ducklings.* New York: Puffin.

McDermott, G. (1974). *Arrow to the sun.* New York: Viking.

McDonald, M. (1990) *Is this a house for hermit crab?* New York: Orchard.

McKinley, R. (1982). *The blue sword.* New York: Greenwillow.

McKinley, R. (1984). *The hero and the crown.* New York: Ace.

McKissack, P. C. (1986). *Flossie and the fox.* New York: Dial Books for Young Readers.

McSwigan, M. (1942). *Snow treasure.* New York: Scholastic.

Merriam, E., & Karlin, B. (1993). *12 Ways to get to 11.* New York: Simon & Schuster.

Miller, M. (1991). *You be the detective.* New York: Scholastic.

Morpurgo, M. (1990). *Waiting for Anya.* New York: Viking.

Musgrove, M. (1976). *Ashanti to Zulu: African traditions.* New York: Dial.

Naylor, P. R. (1991). *Shiloh.* New York: Atheneum.

Norton, M. (1953). *The borrowers.* New York: Harcourt Brace.

O'Brien, R. C. (1971). *Mrs. Frisby and the rats of NIMH.* New York: Atheneum.

O'Dell, S. (1960). *Island of the blue dolphins.* Boston: Houghton Mifflin.

Oppenheim, S. L. (1992). *The lily cupboard.* New York: HarperCollins.

Orlev, U. (1981). *The island on Bird Street.* Translated by Hillel Halkin. Boston: Houghton Mifflin.

Oxenbury, H. (1973). *Pig tale.* New York: Morrow.

Paulsen, G. (1987). *Hatchet.* New York: Bradbury.

Paulsen, G. (1989). *The winter room.* New York: Bantam Doubleday.

Paulsen, G. (1991). *The river.* New York: Delacorte.

Peck, R. (1976). *Hamilton.* Boston: Little, Brown.

Pienkowski, J. (1981). *Dinnertime.* Los Angeles: Price Stern Sloan.

Rancan, J. (1981). *How to draw cats.* Mahwah, NJ: Troll.

Raskin, E. (1978). *The westing game.* New York: Dutton.

Reiss, J. (1972). *The upstairs room.* New York: HarperCollins.

Robart, R., & Kovalski, M. (1986). *The cake that Mack ate.* Boston: Little, Brown.

Rylant, C. (1992). *An angel for Solomon Singer.* New York: Orchard Books.

Sawyer, R. (1953). *Journey cake, ho.* New York: Viking.

Schade, S., & Buller, J. (1987). *The noisy counting book.* New York: Random House.

Sendak, M. (1963). *Where the wild things are.* New York: Scholastic.

Sharmat, M. (1980). *Gregory, the terrible eater.* New York: Four Winds.

Sobol, D. (1987). *Encyclopedia Brown's book of wackey cars.* New York: Morrow.

Speare, E. (1983). *The sign of the beaver.* Boston: Houghton Mifflin.

Sperry, A. (1940). *Call it courage.* New York: Collier.

Steig, W. (1968). *Roland, the minstrel pig.* New York: Windmill.

Steig, W. (1976). *The amazing bone.* New York: Farrar, Strauss and Giroux.

Sutherland, Z., & Livingston, M. C. (1984). *The Scott, Foresman anthology of children's literature.* Glenview, IL: Scott, Foresman.

Thurber, J. (1990). *Many moons.* San Diego: Harcourt Brace Jovanovich.

Tolkien, J. R. R. (1938). *The hobbit.* New York: Random House.

Tolstoi, A. (no date). *The turnip.* Moscow: Malysh.

Trinca, R., & Argent, T. (1985). *One woolly wombat.* New York: Kane/Miller.

Tsuchiya, Y. (1988). *Faithful elephants.* Boston: Houghton Mifflin.

Uchida, Y. (1985). *Journey to Topaz.* Berkeley, CA: Creative Arts.

Van Allsburg, C. (1981). *Jumanji.* Boston: Houghton Mifflin.

Van Allsburg, C. (1982). *Ben's dream.* Boston: Houghton Mifflin.

Van Allsburg, C. (1983). *The wreck of the Zephyr.* Boston: Houghton Mifflin.

Van Allsburg, C. (1984). *The mysteries of Harris Burdick.* Boston: Houghton Mifflin.

Van Allsburg, C. (1986). *The stranger.* Boston: Houghton Mifflin.

Van Allsburg, C. (1990). *Just a dream.* Boston: Houghton Mifflin.

Van Allsburg, C. (1991). *The wretched stone.* Boston: Houghton Mifflin.

Van Allsburg, C. (1992). *The widow's broom.* Boston: Houghton Mifflin.

Van Allsburg, C. (1993). *The sweetest fig.* Boston: Houghton Mifflin.

Vos, I. (1991). *Hide and seek.* Boston: Houghton Mifflin.

Waber, B. (1972). *Ira sleeps over.* New York: Scholastic.

Wiesner, D. (1988). *Free fall.* New York: Lothrop, Lee and Shepard.

Wiesner, D. (1991). *Tuesday.* New York: Clarion.

Wild, M., & Vivas, J. (1991). *Let the celebrations begin!* New York: Orchard.

Wisniewski, D. (1989). *The warrior and the wise man.* New York: Lothrop, Lee and Shepard.

Wisniewski, D. (1991). *Rain player.* New York: Clarion.

Wisniewski, D. (1992). *Sundiata: Lion king of Mali.* New York: Clarion.

Yolen, J. (1982). *Dragon's blood.* New York: Dell.

Yolen, J. (1984). *Heart's blood.* New York: Dell.

Yolen, J. (1986). *Ring of Earth.* New York: Harcourt Brace Jovanovich.

Yolen, J. (1987). *A sending of dragons.* New York: Dell.

Yolen, J. (1988). *The devil's arithmetic.* New York: Viking Kestrel.

Zolotow, C. (1967). *Summer is . . .* New York: Crowell.

Recommended Professional Journals

Book Links
American Library Association
50 E. Huron St.
Chicago, IL 60611

Childhood Education
Association for Childhood Education International
11141 Georgia Ave., Suite 200
Wheaton, MD 20902

Horn Book
The Horn Book, Inc.
Park Square Building
31 St. James Ave.
Boston, MA 02116

Language Arts
National Council of Teachers of English
1111 Kenyon Rd.
Urbana, IL 61801

The New Advocate
Christopher-Gordon Publishers
480 Washington Street
Norwood, MA 02062

The Reading Teacher
International Reading Association
800 Barksdale Rd.
P.O. Box 8139
Newark, DE 19714

Young Children
National Association for the Education of Young Children
1834 Connecticut Ave., NW
Washington, DC 20009-5786

Product Information

AT&T Long Distance Learning Network, P.O. Box 716, Basking Ridge, NJ 07920-0716.

Broderbund. (1992). *Just Grandma and Me* [CD-ROM]. Broderbund's Living Books, Broderbund Software, Inc., 500 Redwood Blvd., Novato, CA 94948-6121. (800) 521-6263.

Broderbund. *Where in the USA is Carmen Sandiego?* Broderbund Software, Inc., 500 Redwood Blvd, Novato, CA 94948-6121. (800) 521-6263.

Claris. *HyperCard.* [Computer Program]. 5201 Patrick Henry Drive, PO Box 58168, Santa Clara, CA, 95052-8168. (800) 747-7483 or (408) 727-8227.

IBM. *Linkway.* The IBM Educational Systems Company, 4111 Northside Parkway, Dept. H05B1, Atlanta, GA 30327. (800) IBM-3327.

Fodor's Travel Guides, (1985). *Fodor's USA*. Fodor Travel Publications, 201 East 50th St., New York, NY 10022.

Grolier, *Academic American Encyclopedia*. Grolier Electronic Publishing, Inc., Sherman Turnpike, Danbury, CT 06816. (800) 356-5590.

Grolier, *New Grolier Multimedia Encyclopedia*. Grolier Electronic Publishing, Inc., Sherman Turnpike, Danbury, CT 06816. (800) 356-5590.

Ludwig van Beethoven: Symphony No. 9 CD Companion, The Voyager Company. (800) 446-2001 or (310) 451-1383.

National Geographic Society. *National Geographic Society Kids Network*. National Geographic Society, 17th & M Street NW, Washington, DC 20036. (800) 368-2728.

National Geographic Society. *Rain Forest* [laser disc]. National Geographic Society, Educational Media Division, 17th & M Street NW, Washington, DC 20036.

The Reading Teacher: A Journal of the International Reading Association. 800 Barksdale Road, PO Box 8139, Newark, DE 19714-8139. (302) 731-1600.

Rogers, Al. (1987). *FrEdWriter* [computer program]. San Diego, CA: Computer Using Educator's Softswap.

Scholastic. *Bankstreet Writer* [computer program]. Jefferson City, MO: Scholastic Inc.

The Voyager Company (1991). *The National Gallery of Art* [laser disc and software]. 1351 Pacific Coast Hwy, Santa Monica, CA 90401.

WINGS for learning. *Magic Slate* [computer program]. Scotts Valley, CA: WINGS for learning/Sunburst Communications.

WINGS for learning. *Muppet Learning Keys* [computer software]. Scotts Valley, CA: WINGS for learning/Sunburst Communications.

The Writing Notebook: Visions for Learning. Visions for Learning, PO Box 1268, Eugene, OR 97440-1268. (503) 344-7125.

INDEX

Copyrights and Acknowledgments

Chapter 2: The Reading Process

The description of whole-language classrooms on pages 41–46 is an adaptation of Bill Harp's description of whole-language classrooms in *Assessment and Evaluation in Whole Language Programs*. Copyright ©1993 Christopher-Gordon Publishers. Used with permission of the publisher.

The conditions for literacy learning on pages 46–48 are taken from "The Whole Story" by Brian Combourne. Published by Ashton Scholastic Ltd.

Chapter 3: The Writing Process

Thanks to the New Zealand Ministry of Education and Learning Media Ltd. for permission to use terms and base material on ideas first published in *Dancing with the Pen*, 1992.

Peter Bodycott's description of Mr. D's spelling program on pages 102–103 is reprinted by permission of Peter Bodycott and the Association for Childhood Education International, 11501 Georgia Avenue, Suite 315, Wheaton, MD. Copyright ©1993 by the Association.

Chapter 5: Assessing Children's Reading and Writing Progress

The six principles of assessment on pages 177–78 are from "Assessing Young Children's Literacy Development," William Teale, Elfrieda Hiebert, and Edward Chittenden, *The Reading Teacher*, April 1987, 772–777. Reprinted with permission of William H. Teale and the International Reading Association.

Chapter 6: Working with Children with Special Needs

The characteristics of learning-disabled children on pages 200–202 are from *Exceptional Individuals: An Introduction* (pp. 133–136), by B. R. Gearheart, R. C. Mullen, and C. J. Gearheart. Copyright ©1993 by Wadsworth, Inc. Reprinted by permission of Brooks/Cole Publishing Company, Pacific Grove, CA 93950.

J. Wolf's ten tips for helping gifted and talented children on pages 216–17 are reprinted with the permission of Simon & Schuster from the Macmillan College text *Exceptional Children and Youth* 6/E by Norris Haring and Linda McCormick. Copyright ©1994 by Macmillan College Publishing Company, Inc.

C. J. Maker's guidelines for curriculum modification for gifted children on pages 217–19 are published in *Teaching Models in Education of the Gifted*, copyright ©1982. Reprinted by permission of PRO-ED.

L. McCormick's ten tips for helping ESL children on pages 223–24 are reprinted with the permission of Simon & Schuster from the Macmillan College text *Exceptional Children and Youth* 6/E by Norris Haring and Linda McCormick. Copyright ©1994 by Macmillan College Publishing Company, Inc.

Chapter 12: Planning for Literary Instruction Throughout the Day

"Prediction: School P.E." copyright ©1990 Isabel Joshlin Glaser. This poem first appeared in *Cricket*. Used by permission of Marian Reiner for the author.